NETWORK PRESS®
SYBEX

CCNA: Cisco Certified
Network Associate
Study Guide

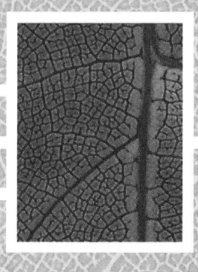

CCNA™: Cisco® Certified Network Associate Study Guide

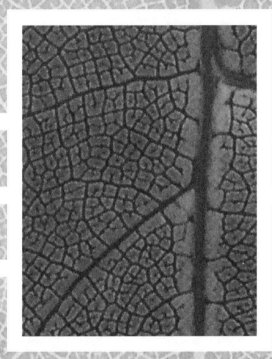

Todd Lammle
Don Porter
with James Chellis

San Francisco • Paris • Düsseldorf • Soest

Associate Publisher: Guy Hart-Davis
Contracts and Licensing Manager: Kristine Plachy
Acquisitions & Developmental Editor: Neil Edde
Editors: Lisa Duran, Mandy Erickson, Brianne Agatep
Project Editor: Diane Lowery
Technical Editors: John Chong, Brian Horakh
Book Designer: Bill Gibson
Graphic Illustrator: Tony Jonick
Electronic Publishing Specialist: Adrian Woolhouse
Production Coordinator: Charles Mathews
Indexer: Matthew Spence
Companion CD: Ginger Warner
Cover Designer: Archer Design
Cover Photographer: The Image Bank

This book is dedicated to all CNEs and MCSEs who refuse to remain content with mediocrity and, instead, seek to continually refine their knowledge and skills.

Acknowledgments

So very many people to thank! It's pretty hard to figure out where to start, so here goes.

Monica Lammle was instrumental in helping the book stay consistent with voicing. She is as brilliant as she is beautiful. Mike Dewey and Dannielle Grubbs from Virtual Networks/Ikon in Irvine, California, were simply vital to the success of this project. Mike provided Don Porter and myself with every piece of equipment and support we needed for this book, and Dannielle is a veritable administrative wizard, who not only helped assemble the materials needed but never failed to provide unerring support whenever we called her. Without Mike and Dannielle's involvement, this project would have been in jeopardy right from the start! And I can't forget to mention the

And, of course, all the astute and tireless editors:

Robert Tripi, MCSE and future CCIE, is a systems engineer for MetaSolv Software in Texas. Robert did a first run edit that helped pinpoint those annoying, irritating, and sometimes frighteningly microscopic errors that most people (except readers, of course)—especially us red-eyed, sleep-deprived authors—seem to miss. Thanks Robert!

Lisa Duran, an editor at Sybex, has a refreshingly great sense of humor and is a complete pleasure to work with. Everyone who reads this book should send her a dollar. We look forward to future projects with Lisa.

Mandy Erickson and Brianne Agatep stepped in last minute and also helped greatly with the editing of this book.

Diane Lowery, the project editor, kept everything going smoothly when deadlines were tight.

Production Coordinator Charles Mathews and Electronic Publishing Specialist Adrian Woolhouse get kudos for their hard work.

John Chong, the technical editor, went tirelessly over the material over 'n' over 'n' over again.

And we especially want to acknowledge Neil Edde, Sybex's acquisitions editor supreme, who is always so calm and patient with us that it's kind of like working with Gandhi.

Last in the editorial chain, but certainly not the least, is Brian Horakh. He did a last editorial review to not only check for technical and grammatical errors but also to ensure that this book meets the CCNA test objectives so that you the reader can pass the exam the first time! Be sure and check out his Web site: www.networkstudyguides.com for the latest in Cisco certification news and updates.

We'd also like to thank the many terrific people that helped put the CD together (the CD material is mentioned in detail later in this introduction):

James Chellis, from EdgeTek Testing Systems, provided the impressive testing engine for all of you readers. Go to www.lammle.com or call 800-800-1NET for Cisco practice tests as well as for more CCNA practice test questions.

Christy Delger, from Visio Corporation—you're a pleasure to work with! Visio provided an awesome product for the CD that can easily help you document your network plus more. Most of the figures in this book were produced in full or in part from Visio.

Janice Spampinato from AGGroup. Thanks to AGGroup, we were able to include network traces throughout this book with one of the best network analyzers on the market: Etherpeek.

Joe Camel, who wrote IPCalc, which is one of the best IP calculator tools I've ever seen. We'd recommend loading IPCalc immediately upon opening this book. Please visit www.progression-inc.com for more information about IPCalc.

Thanks to Ginger Warner at Sybex for pulling the CD together.

And we stand in awe (actually, sit—we're writers), of Jan Johnston-Tyler, who pulled off the truly magnificent art of ensuring that the complete Cisco glossary could be included as an appendix in the book in mere hours! Jan—thank you! Arthur had Merlin; Cisco has you.

Kudos also to Sam Mahood from Cisco for the useful icons and for permission to use the Cisco logos. Thanks for sending all the great CDs chock full of Cisco product photos and the Adobe PageMaker icons that were used throughout this book.

Contents at a Glance

Table of Contents

Introduction

This book is intended to welcome you into the world of Cisco certification and start you out on an exciting new path toward obtaining your CCNA certification. It reaches beyond popular certifications like the MCSE and CNE to provide you with an indispensable factor in understanding today's network—insight into the Cisco world of internetworking.

Cisco—A Brief History

A lot of readers may already be familiar with Cisco and what they do. But those of you new to the field, just coming in fresh from your MCSE, or maybe even those of you with 10 or more years in the field wishing to brush up on the new technology may appreciate a little background on Cisco.

In the early 1980s, a married couple that worked in different computer departments at Stanford University started up cisco Systems (notice the small *c*). Their names are Len and Sandy Bosack. They were having trouble getting their individual systems to communicate (like many married people), so in their living room they created a gateway server to make it easier for their disparate computers in two different departments to achieve this using the IP protocol.

In 1984, cisco Systems was founded with a small commercial gateway server product that changed networking forever. Some people think the name was intended to be San Francisco Systems, but the paper got ripped on the way to the incorporation lawyers. Who knows? but in 1992, the company name was changed to Cisco Systems, Inc.

The first product they marketed was called the Advanced Gateway Server (AGS). Then came the Mid-Range Gateway Server (MGS), the Compact Gateway Server (CGS), the Integrated Gateway Server (IGS), and the AGS+. Cisco calls these "the old alphabet soup products."

Then, in 1993, Cisco came out with the amazing 4000 router, and then the even more amazing 7000, 2000, and 3000 series routers. These are still around and evolving (almost daily it seems!).

Cisco Systems has since become an unrivaled worldwide leader in networking for the Internet. Its networking solutions can easily connect users working from diverse devices on disparate networks. Cisco products make it simple for people to access and transfer information without regard to differences in time, place, or platform.

The Cisco Systems, Inc. big picture is that it provides end-to-end networking solutions that customers can use to build an efficient, unified information infrastructure of their own or to connect to someone else's—an important piece in the Internet/networking-industry puzzle, because a common architecture that delivers consistent network services to all users is now a functional imperative. And because Cisco Systems offers such a broad range of networking and Internet services and capabilities, users needing regular access to their local network or the Internet can do so unhindered, making Cisco's wares indispensable.

Cisco answers this need with a wide range of hardware products used to form information networks using the Cisco Internetworking Operating System software. This software provides network services, paving the way for networked technical support and professional services for maintaining and optimizing all network operations.

Along with the Cisco IOS, one of the services Cisco has created to help support the vast amount of hardware they have engineered is the Cisco Certified Internetworking Expert (CCIE) program, designed specifically to equip people to effectively manage the vast quantity of installed Cisco networks. Their business plan is simple: if you want to sell more Cisco equipment and have more Cisco networks installed, ensure the networks that you've installed run properly. But having a fabulous product line isn't all it takes to guarantee the huge success that Cisco enjoys—lots of companies with great products are now defunct. If you have complicated products designed to solve complicated problems, you need knowledgeable people who are fully capable of installing, managing, and troubleshooting them. That part isn't easy, so Cisco began the CCIE program to equip people in supporting these complicated networks. This program, known colloquially as the Doctorate of Networking, has also been very successful, primarily due to its extreme difficulty. And Cisco continuously monitors the program, changing it as they see fit to make sure it remains pertinent and accurately reflects the demands of today's internetworking business environments.

Building upon the highly successful CCIE program, Cisco Career Certifications permit you to become certified at various levels of technical proficiency, spanning the disciplines of network design and support. So whether you're beginning a career, changing careers, securing your present position, or seeking to refine and promote it, this is the book for you!

Cisco's Network Support Certifications

Cisco has created new certifications that will help you get the coveted CCIE as well as aid prospective employers in measuring skill levels. Before these new certifications, you took only one test and were then faced with the lab making it difficult to succeed. With these new certifications adding a new and better approach to preparing for that almighty lab, Cisco has opened doors few were allowed through before. So what are these new certifications, and how do they help you get your CCIE?

Cisco Certified Network Associate (CCNA)

The CCNA certification is the first certification in the new line of Cisco certifications, and a precursor to all current Cisco certifications. With the new certification programs, Cisco has created a type of stepping-stone approach to CCIE certification. Now you can become a Cisco Certified Network Associate for the meager cost of this book plus $100 for the test. And you don't have to stop there—you can choose to continue with your studies and achieve a higher certification called the Cisco Certified Network Professional (CCNP). Someone with a CCNP has all the skills and knowledge they need to attempt the CCIE lab. However, since no textbook can take the place of practical experience, we'll discuss what else you need to be ready for the CCIE lab shortly.

Why Become a CCNA?

Cisco has created the certification process, not unlike Microsoft or Novell, to give administrators a set of skills, to equip prospective employers with a way to measure skills, or to match a certain criterion. Becoming a CCNA can be the initial step of a successful journey toward a new and highly rewarding and sustainable career.

The CCNA program was created to provide a solid introduction not only to the Cisco Internetworking Operating System (IOS) and to Cisco hardware but to internetworking in general, making it helpful to you in areas not exclusively Cisco's. At this point in the certification process, it's not unrealistic to imagine that future network managers—even those without Cisco equipment—could easily require Cisco certifications of their job applicants.

If you make it through the CCNA still interested in Cisco and internetworking, you're headed down a path to certain success.

To meet the CCNA Certification skill level, you must be able to understand or do the following:

- Install, configure, and operate simple-routed LAN, routed WAN, and switched LAN and LANE networks.

- Understand and be able to configure IP, IGRP, IPX, Serial, AppleTalk, Frame Relay, IP RIP, VLANs, IPX RIP, Ethernet, and Access Lists.

- Install and/or configure a network.

- Optimize WAN through Internet access solutions that reduce bandwidth and reduce WAN costs using features such as filtering with access lists, bandwidth on demand (BOD), and dial-on-demand routing (DDR).

- Provide remote access by integrating dial-up connectivity with traditional, remote LAN-to-LAN access as well as supporting the higher levels of performance required for new applications such as Internet commerce, multimedia, etc.

How Do You Become a CCNA?

Congratulations—you've taken the first step: buying a study guide. The next step is to pass one "little" test and poof! You're a CCNA! (Don't you wish it were that easy?) True, it's just one test, but you still have to possess enough knowledge to understand (and read between the lines—trust us) what the test writers are saying.

And we can't say this enough—it's critical that you have some hands-on experience with Cisco routers. If you can get your hands on some 2500 routers, you're set! But if you can't, we've worked hard to provide hundreds of configuration examples throughout this book to help network administrators (or people who want to become network administrators) learn what they need to know to pass the CCNA exam.

One way to get the hands-on router experience you'll need in the real world is to attend one of the seminars offered by Globalnet System Solutions, Inc. (www.lammle.com) or attend a Cisco certified course. There is also a CCNA study kit available through Virtual Networks/Ikon Technologies. This includes everything you need to gain hands-on experience with Cisco routers. For more information, go to www.virtualnetworks.com/ccnakit.html.

It can also be helpful to take an Introduction to Cisco Router Configuration (ICRC) course at an authorized Cisco Education Center, but you should understand that this class doesn't meet all of the test objectives. If you decide to do that, reading this book in conjunction with the hands-on course will give you the knowledge you need for certification. We've heard that Cisco Authorized Training Centers will offer the CCNA and other certification courses sometime in 1999, but check the Cisco Web page (www.cisco.com) for updated information to be sure. There are hundreds of Cisco Authorized Training Centers around the world—see the Cisco Web page for a location nearest you.

In addition to the Sybex *CCNA: Cisco Certified Network Associate Study Guide*, there are other useful ways to supplement your studies for the CCNA exam. CiscoTests.com (http://www.networkstudyguides.com) offers an online study guide with sample questions and information about the most current release of the CCNA, CCNP, and CCIE exams. CiscoTests also provides a discount for owners of the Sybex *CCNA: Cisco Certified Network Associate Study Guide*. To get instant access and the discount, you should visit the URL http://www.networkstudyguides.com/sybex.html.

Cisco Certified Network Professional (CCNP)

These new Cisco certifications have opened up many opportunities for the individual wishing to become Cisco certified but who is lacking the training, expertise, or the bucks to pass the notorious and often failed 2-day Cisco-torture lab. The new Cisco certifications will truly provide exciting new opportunities for the CNE and MCSE who just didn't know how to advance to a higher level.

So you're thinking "Great, what do I do after I pass the CCNA exam?" Well, if you want to become a CCIE in Routing and Switching (the most popular certification), understand that there's more than one path to that much-coveted CCIE certification. The first way is to continue studying and become a Cisco Certified Network Professional (CCNP). That means four more tests, and the CCNA certification, to you.

The CCNP program will prepare you to understand and comprehensively tackle the internetworking issues of today and beyond—not limited to things

Cisco. You will undergo an immense metamorphosis, vastly increasing your knowledge and skills through the process of obtaining these certifications!

Remember, you don't need to be a CCNP or even a CCNA to take the CCIE lab, but to accomplish that, it's extremely helpful if you already have these certifications.

What Are the CCNP Certification Skills?

Cisco is demanding a certain level of proficiency for their CCNP certification. In addition to those required for the CCNA, these skills include

- Installing, configuring, operating, and troubleshooting complex routed LANs, routed WANs, switched LAN networks, and Dial Access Services.

- Understanding complex networks, such as IP, IGRP, IPX, Async Routing, AppleTalk, Extended Access Lists, IP RIP, Route Redistribution, IPX RIP, Route Summarization, OSPF, VLSM, BGP, Serial, IGRP, Frame Relay, ISDN, ISL, X.25, DDR, PSTN, PPP, VLANs, Ethernet, ATM LAN-emulation, Access Lists, 802.10, FDDI, Transparent and Translational Bridging.

To meet the Cisco Certified Network Professional requirements, you must be able to perform the following:

- Install and/or configure a network to increase bandwidth, quicken network response times, and improve reliability and quality of service.

- Maximize performance through campus LANs, routed WANs, and remote access.

- Improve network security.

- Create a global intranet.

- Provide access security to campus switches and routers.

- Provide increased switching and routing bandwidth, end-to-end resiliency services.

- Provide custom queuing and routed priority services.

How Do You Become a CCNP?

After becoming a CCNA, the four exams you must take to get your CCNP are as follows:

- **Exam 640-403:** Advanced Cisco Router Configuration (ACRC) continues to build on the fundamentals learned in the ICRC course. It focuses on large multiprotocol internetworks and how to manage them with access-lists, queuing, tunneling, route distribution, route summarization, and dial-on-demand.

- **Exam 640-404:** Cisco LAN Switch Configuration (CLSC) tests your understanding of configuring, monitoring, and troubleshooting of Cisco switching products.

- **Exam 640-406:** Cisco Internetwork Troubleshooting (CIT) tests you on the troubleshooting information you learned in the other Cisco courses.

- **Exam 640-405:** Configuring, Monitoring, and Troubleshooting Dialup Services (CMTD) tests your knowledge of installing, configuring, monitoring, and troubleshooting Cisco ISDN and dial-up access products.

If you hate tests, you can take less of them by signing up for the CCNA exam, the CIT exam, and then just one more long exam called the Foundation R/S exam 640-409. Doing this will also give you your CCNP, but beware, it's a really long test that fuses all the material listed above into one exam. Good luck! However, by taking this exam, you get three tests for the price of two, which saves you $100 (if you pass). Some people think it's easier to take the Foundation R/S exam because you can leverage the areas you would score higher in against the areas you wouldn't.

Cisco Certified Internetworking Expert (CCIE)

Okay. You've become a CCNP, and now you've fixed your sights on getting your CCIE in Routing and Switching—what do you do next? For that, Cisco recommends that before you take the lab, you take Exam 640-025 (Cisco Internetwork Design, or CID) and the Cisco authorized course Installing and Maintaining Cisco Routers (IMCR). By the way, no Prometric test for IMCR exists at this writing, and Cisco recommends a *minimum* of two years on-the-job experience before taking the CCIE lab. After jumping those hurdles, you then have to pass the CCIE-R/S Exam Qualification (Exam 350-001) before taking on the actual lab.

To become a CCIE, Cisco recommends the following:

1. Attend all the recommended courses at an authorized Cisco training center and pony up around $15,000–$20,000 depending on your corporate discount.

2. Pass the Drake/Prometric exam. ($200 per exam—so hopefully, you'll pass it the first time.)

3. Pass the two day hands-on lab at Cisco. This costs $1,000 per lab, which many people fail two or more times. (Some never make it through!) Also, because you can only take the exam in San Jose, California; Research Triangle Park, North Carolina; Sydney, Australia; Halifax, Nova Scotia; Tokyo, Japan; and Brussels, Belgium, this means you might just need to add travel costs to those $1,000 big dogs.

The CCIE Skills

The CCIE-Router and Switching will include advanced technical skills required to maintain optimum network performance and reliability as well as advanced skills in supporting diverse networks that use disparate technologies. CCIEs just don't have problems getting a job. These experts are basically inundated with offers to work for six figure salaries! But that's because it isn't easy to attain the level of capability mandatory for Cisco's CCIE level. For example, a CCIE will have the following skills down pat:

- Install, configure, operate, and troubleshoot complex routed LAN, routed WAN, switched LAN and ATM LANE networks, and Dial-Access services.

- Diagnose and resolve network faults.

- Use packet/frame analysis and Cisco debugging tools.

- Document and report the problem-solving processes used.

- General LAN/WAN knowledge, including data encapsulation and layering; windowing, flow control, and relation to delay; error detection and recovery; link-state, distance-vector, and switching algorithms; management, monitoring, and fault isolation.

- Knowledge of a variety of corporate technologies—including major services provided by Desktop, WAN, and Internet groups—as well as the functions, addressing structures, and routing, switching, and bridging implications of each of their protocols. Knowledge of Cisco-specific technologies, including router/switch platforms, architectures, and applications; communication servers; protocol translation and applications; configuration commands and system/network impact; and LAN/WAN interfaces, capabilities, and applications.

Cisco's Network Design Certifications

In addition to the Network Support certifications, Cisco has created another certification track for network designers. The two certifications within this track are the Cisco Certified Design Associate and Cisco Certified Design Professional certifications. If you're reaching for the CCIE stars, we'd highly recommend the CCNP and CCDP certifications before attempting the lab (or attempting to advance your career).

This certification will give you the knowledge to design routed LAN, routed WAN, and switched LAN and ATM LANE networks.

Cisco Certified Design Associate (CCDA)

To become a CCDA, you must pass the CDS (Cisco Design Specialist) Exam 9E0-004. To pass this test you must understand how to do the following:

- Design simple routed LAN, routed WAN, and switched LAN and ATM LANE networks.

- Network-layer addressing.

- Filtering with access lists.

- VLAN use and propagation.

- Network sizing.

Cisco Certified Design Professional (CCDP)

If you're already a CCNP and want to get your CCDP, you can simply take the CID 640-025 test. But if you're not yet a CCNP, you must take the ACRC, CLSC, CIT, and CMTD exams.

CCDP certification skills include

- Design complex routed LAN, routed WAN, and switched LAN and ATM LANE networks, building upon the base level of the CCDA technical knowledge.

CCDP's must also demonstrate proficiency in

- Network-layer addressing in a hierarchical environment

- Traffic management with access lists

- Hierarchical network design

- VLAN use and propagation

- Performance considerations: required hardware and software; switching engine; memory, cost, and minimization

What Does This Book Cover?

This book covers everything you need to become a Cisco Certified CCNA. It will teach you how to perform basic configurations on Cisco routers using multiple protocols. Each chapter begins with a list of the CCNA test objectives covered, so make sure to read over them before working through the chapter.

You'll also learn how to start up and configure a Cisco router as well as attain a clear and detailed understanding of the OSI reference model and how to configure the relevant protocols relative to the OSI model. The book covers how to configure TCP/IP, how to subnet an IP scheme into multiple subnets, and how to apply those abilities to a lab. You'll also learn how to route IPX and create access lists to provide traffic management for your multiprotocol network.

This volume finishes with a WAN chapter that details how to set up and configure Cisco routers with PPP, X.25, Frame Relay, and more.

Each chapter ends with review questions that have been specifically designed to help retain the knowledge presented in it. To really nail down your skills, read each question carefully, and if possible, work through the hands-on labs at the end of Chapter's 5–10.

The CCNA (640-407) exam consists of a combination of the following objectives:

OSI Reference

1. Identify and describe the functions of each of the seven layers of the OSI reference model.

2. Describe connection-oriented network service and connectionless network service, and identify the key differences between them.

3. Describe Data Link addresses and Network addresses, and identify the key differences between them.

4. Identify at least 3 reasons why the industry uses a layered model.

5. Define and explain the 5 conversion steps of data encapsulation.

6. Define flow control and describe the three basic methods used in networking.

7. List the key internetworking functions of the OSI Network layer and how they are performed in a router.

WAN Protocols

8. Differentiate between the following WAN services: Frame Relay, ISDN/LAPD, HDLC, & PPP.

9. Recognize key Frame Relay terms and features.

10. List commands to configure Frame Relay LMIs, maps, and subinterfaces.

11. List commands to monitor Frame Relay operation in the router.

12. Identify PPP operations to encapsulate WAN data on Cisco routers.

13. State a relevant use and context for ISDN networking.

14. Identify ISDN protocols, function groups, reference points, and channels.

15. Describe Cisco's implementation of ISDN BRI.

IOS

16. Log into a router in both user and privileged modes.

17. Use the context-sensitive help facility.

18. Use the command history and editing features.

19. Examine router elements (RAM, ROM, CDP, show).

20. Manage configuration files from the privileged Exec mode.

21. Control router passwords, identification, and banner.

22. Identify the main Cisco IOS commands for router startup.

23. Enter an initial configuration using the setup command.

24. Copy and manipulate configuration files.

25. List the commands to load Cisco IOS software from: flash memory, a TFTP server, or ROM.

26. Prepare to backup, upgrade, and load a backup Cisco IOS software image.

27. Prepare the initial configuration of your router and enable IP.

Network Protocols

28. Monitor Novell IPX operation on the router.

29. Describe the two parts of network addressing, then identify the parts in specific protocol address examples.

30. Create the different classes of IP addresses [and subnetting].

31. Configure IP addresses.

32. Verify IP addresses.

33. List the required IPX address and encapsulation type.

34. Enable the Novell IPX protocol and configure interfaces.

35. Identify the functions of the TCP/IP Transport-layer protocols.

36. Identify the functions of the TCP/IP Network-layer protocols.

37. Identify the functions performed by ICMP.

38. Configure IPX access lists and SAP filters to control basic Novell traffic.

Routing

39. Add the RIP routing protocol to your configuration.

40. Add the IGRP routing protocol to your configuration.

41. Explain the services of separate and integrated multiprotocol routing.

42. List problems that each routing type encounters when dealing with topology changes and describe techniques to reduce the number of these problems.

43. Describe the benefits of network segmentation with routers.

Network Security

44. Configure standard and extended access lists to filter IP traffic.

45. Monitor and verify selected access list operations on the router.

LAN Switching

46. Describe the advantages of LAN segmentation.

47. Describe LAN segmentation using bridges.

48. Describe LAN segmentation using routers.

49. Describe LAN segmentation using switches.

50. Name and describe two switching methods.

51. Describe full- and half-duplex Ethernet operation.

52. Describe network congestion problems in Ethernet networks.

53. Describe the benefits of network segmentation with bridges.

54. Describe the benefits of network segmentation with switches.

55. Describe the features and benefits of FastEthernet.

56. Describe the guidelines and distance limitations of FastEthernet.

57. Distinguish between cut-through and store-and-forward LAN switching.

58. Describe the operation of the Spanning Tree Protocol and its benefits.

59. Describe the benefits of Virtual LANs.

60. Define and describe the function of a MAC address.

We've included an objective map on the inside back cover of this book that will help you find all the information relevant to each objective in this book. Keep in mind that at the beginning of each chapter, we've listed all actual exam objectives covered in that particular chapter.

Where Do You Take the Exam?

You may take the exams at any one of the more than 800 Sylvan Prometric Authorized Testing Centers around the world. For the location of a testing center near you, call (800) 204-3926. Outside the United States and Canada, contact your local Sylvan Prometric Registration Center.

To register for a Cisco Certified Network Associate exam:

1. Determine the number of the exam you want to take. (The CCNA exam number is 640-407.)

2. Register with the Sylvan Prometric Registration Center nearest to you. At this point, you will be asked to pay in advance for the exam. At this writing, the exams are $100 each and must be taken within one year of payment. You can schedule exams up to six weeks in advance or as soon as one working day prior to the day you wish to take it. If something comes up and you need to cancel or reschedule your exam appointment, contact Sylvan Prometric at least 24 hours in advance. Same-day registration isn't available for the Cisco tests.

3. When you schedule the exam, you'll be provided with instructions regarding all appointment and cancellation procedures, the ID requirements, and information about the testing-center location.

Tips for Taking Your CCNA Exam

The CCNA test contains 70 questions to be completed in 90 minutes. You must schedule for a test at least 24 hours in advance (unlike the Novell or Microsoft exams), and you aren't allowed to take more than one Cisco exam per day.

Many questions on the exam will have answer choices that at first glance look identical—especially the syntax questions! Remember, read through the choices carefully because close won't cut it. If you get commands in the wrong order or forget one measly character, you'll get the question wrong. Unlike Microsoft or Novell tests, the exam has answer choices that are really similar in syntax—some syntax will be dead wrong, but more than likely, it will just be very *subtly* wrong. Some other syntax choices may be right, but they're shown in the wrong order. Cisco does split hairs, and they're not at all above giving you classic trick questions. Here's an example: "access-list 101 deny ip any eq 23 denies Telnet access to all systems." This question looks right since most people will refer to the port number (23) and think, "Yes that's the port used for Telnet." The catch is that you can't filter IP on port numbers (only TCP and UDP). So to practice, do the hands-on exercises at the end of the chapters over and over again until they feel natural to you.

Also, never forget that the right answer is the Cisco answer. In many cases, they'll present more than one correct answer, but the *correct* answer is the one Cisco recommends. A good example of this would be a question about which routing protocol is correct for a "small- to medium-sized business"? The correct answer according to Cisco is RIP, even though we would personally be the last people to implement RIP in a medium-sized business! This little idiosyncrasy also comes into play with questions about frame types (for all you CNEs). The most common frame type according to Cisco is 802.2.

Here are some general tips for exam success:

- Arrive early at the exam center so you can relax and review your study materials—particularly IP tables and lists of exam-related information.

- Read the questions *carefully*. Just don't jump to conclusions. Make sure you're clear on *exactly* what the question is asking.

- Don't leave any unanswered questions. They count these against you.

- When answering multiple-choice questions you're not sure about, use a process of elimination to get rid of the obviously incorrect questions first. Doing this will greatly improve your odds should you need to make an "educated guess."

- Because the hard questions will eat up the most time, save them for last. You can move forward and backward through the exam.

- If you are unsure of the answer to a question, choose one of the answers and mark the question so that if you have time, you can go back to it and then go on. Remember an unanswered question is as bad as a wrong one, so answer it because you may run out of time or forget to go back to it.

- Because you're *not* allowed to use the Windows calculator during the test, memorize the table of subnet addresses that appears at the end of Chapter 4, and write it down on the scratch paper supplied by the testing center after entering the testing room but before you start the test. Remember that you must understand IP subnetting to pass this test! Chapter 4 will arm you with all the knowledge you need to understand IP subnetting.

Once you have completed an exam, you'll be given immediate, online notification of your pass or fail status, a printed Examination Score Report indicating your pass or fail status, and your exam results by section. (The test administrator will give you the printed score report.) Test scores are automatically forwarded to Cisco within five working days after you take the test, so you don't need to send your score to them. If you pass the exam, you'll receive confirmation from Cisco, typically within two to four weeks.

One more thing you can do. Go to Brian Horakh's Web site at `www.ciscotests.com`, and go through the exercise and practice test questions he has available. This will really help you keep abreast of any changes made to the test.

How to Use This Book

This book can provide a solid foundation for the serious effort of preparing for the Cisco Certified Network Associate exam. To best benefit from this book, you might want to use the following study method:

1. Study each chapter carefully, making sure you fully understand the information and the test objectives listed at the beginning of each chapter.

2. Complete all hands-on exercises in the chapter, referring to the chapter so that you understand the reason for each step you take. If you do not have Cisco equipment available, make sure and study the examples carefully.

3. Answer the exercise questions related to that chapter. (The answers are in Appendix A.)

4. Note which questions confuse you, and study those sections of the book again.

5. Before taking the exam, try your hand on the practice exams included on the CD that comes with this book. They'll give you a complete overview of what you can expect to see on the real thing.

6. Remember to use the products on the CD included with this book. IPCalc, Etherpeek, and the EdgeTek Learning Systems Edge Test™ exam preparation software have all been specifically hand-picked to help you study for and pass your exam.

To learn all the material covered in this book, you're going to have to apply yourself regularly and with discipline. Try to set aside the same time every day to study, and select a comfortable and quiet place to do so. If you work hard, you will be surprised at how quickly you learn this material. All the best!

What's on the CD?

We've worked hard to provide some really great tools to help you with your certification process. All of these should be loaded on your workstation when studying for the test.

The EdgeTek Learning Systems Edge Test™ Test Preparation Software

EdgeTek Learning Systems Edge Test™ test preparation software prepares you for successfully passing the Cisco Certified Network Associate examination. Questions cover all test objectives on the exam. Go to www.lammle.com. Watch for the entire line of Cisco Certified test simulators.

Visio

Visio Professional, combined with Visio Network Equipment, offers the most complete network documentation solution. Work with over 14,000 exact-replica, manufacturer-specific network hardware and telecom shapes to create proposals, implementation plans, and any other document your company uses to represent and manage its networks. Install the Visio Professional 5 30-day test drive and the sampling of over 100 Visio Network Equipment shapes included on the CD. To order a Visio product, obtain more information, or locate your nearest reseller, call (800) 248-4746, or visit Visio's Web site at www.visio.com for more information.

AGGroup NetTools and EtherPeek

Two AG Group products appear on the CD, which accompany this book. EtherPeek™ for Windows demonstration software, requiring a serial number, and the freeware version of AG NetTools™. To obtain a serial number for the EtherPeek demo, just send an e-mail to epwdemo@aggroup.com. EtherPeek is a full-featured, affordable packet and network analyzer. AG NetTools is an interface and menu-driven IP tool compilation.

IPCalc 2.0

Produced by Progression, Inc., IPCalc 2 is a TCP/IP address calculator designed to help you better understand the concepts behind IP addressing. It visually illustrates the bit patterns of an IP address and their behavior as you move from one addressing scheme to another. IPCalc 2 is a 32-bit application and will run on Windows 95/98 and NT. You can visit the Progression, Inc. Web site at www.progression-inc.com.

How to Contact the Authors

You can contact Todd Lammle through Globalnet System Solutions, Inc., a training and systems integration company in Colorado, or e-mail him at info@lammle.com.

To reach Don Porter, send him e-mail at don@uen.org.

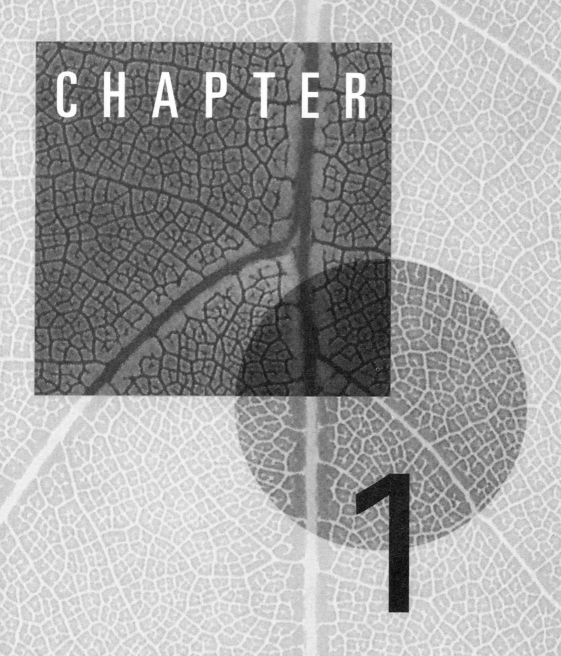

CHAPTER

1

Introduction to Internetworking

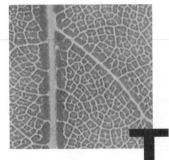

This opening chapter will examine internetworking and then establish how it evolved into the internetworking of today. We'll also cover the LAN and WAN equipment that's typically found in a modern internetworking environment.

A necessary prerequisite to this is to fully understand the OSI reference model and how the layered approach to application development has created the present internetworking standards that shape how modern internetworking takes place.

CCNA test objectives covered in this chapter include:

p 13
- Identify at least three reasons why the industry uses a layered model

p 15
- Identify and describe the functions of each of the seven layers of the OSI reference model

p 20
- Define flow control and describe the three basic methods used in networking

p 23
- List the key internetworking functions of the OSI Network layer and how they are performed in a router

p 23
- Define and explain the five conversion steps of data encapsulation

Internetworking Fundamentals

To understand Internetworking, we'll begin by going back to the origins of networking and following its evolutionary path. We'll look at how internetworks have developed along this path and finish with a discussion covering the demands of a typical, contemporary internetwork.

Evolution of Internetworking

As you might recall, network communications in the 1960s and 1970s were centered on the mainframe. Machines called dumb terminals would access the mainframe over low-speed lines. This arrangement was referred to as a centralized computing environment because all the processing took place in one central location. A classic example of a centralized computing environment is found in IBM's Systems Network Architecture using multi-drop lines and X.25 packet switching.

Through the dumb terminal, the user could run programs, access resources, and copy files. The mainframe would serve to authenticate the user, then coordinate the user and program. This method worked quite well and is actually very straightforward—with one computer. However, things become a little more complex when using multiple computers. When several machines need to be coordinated, you then have to be aware of things like:

- Addressing
- Error detection and correction
- Time synchronization
- Transmission coordination

Then the 1980s dawned. The PC became widely available and changed networking forever. At this point, printers were attached to PCs with serial cables that were typically shared with A/B switch boxes. This meant only two people could use the same printer. Pretty soon, boxes became available that would allow 5 or 10 users to be plugged into and share the same printer, but since printer queuing hadn't been developed yet, it still meant only one person could print at a given time. The necessity of having many printers to adequately service all the users' jobs was a pretty expensive reality indeed. So LANs (Local Area Networks) were born to help reduce costs. With the development of printer queuing—a directory created on a server that acts as a holding pen from which print jobs are stored and later printed in the order received—things got a lot better. But in order to make this process possible, the printers had to be connected to a LAN with that server. Only then could hundreds of users print to a printer (or printers) simultaneously.

Early LANs were small and isolated, and it wasn't long before the need to connect them became very apparent. As necessity is the mother of invention, soon, wide area networking evolved. In the late 1970s and early 1980s, minicomputers and shared Wide Area Networks (WANs) were created to address these growing business requirements.

Today, many businesses still have a mixture of mainframe and LAN technologies working side by side. Applications migrating from central hosts to distributed servers has complicated things considerably, resulting in new networking requirements and changing traffic patterns. The need for instant data transfer has increased the response to jump at new technologies to stay ahead of demand and remain competitive. MIS (management information system) jobs have become full-time positions now, where previously, network administration was simply the responsibility of whoever happened to be sitting next to the server. Both the people and equipment working in an internetworking environment must be flexible, scalable, and adaptable to remain useful and succeed.

Internetworks

Internetworks are the communication structures that work to tie LANs and WANs together. Their primary goal is to efficiently move information anywhere quickly, upon demand, and with complete integrity. Today's users have become increasingly dependent on their networks—watch the chaos that results around the office when a group of users' server or hub goes offline. Remember when fax machines came out? After a while, people stopped asking if you had a fax machine and just started asking for the number. Now, having Internet access is as common as having a fax. People used to ask me if I had e-mail, but now they just ask me for my e-mail address and Web page URL!

What this means is that in order for today's corporations to remain competitive in the global market, the networks they depend on now have to efficiently manage, on a daily basis, some or all of the following:

- Graphics and imaging

- Files in the gigabyte range

- Client-server computing

- High network traffic loads

To be able to amply meet these needs, the IS department must provide to users:

- Increased bandwidth

- Bandwidth on demand

- Low delays

- Data, voice, and video capabilities on the same media

Also, the network of today must be readily adaptable to the applications of tomorrow. In the not too distant future, networks will need to be equipped to handle:

- High-definition imaging

- Full-motion video

- Digitized audio

In short, for an internetwork to realize its purpose, it must be able to connect many different networks together to serve the organizations depending on it. And this connectivity must happen regardless of the type of physical media involved. Companies expanding their networks must overcome the limitations of physical and geographic boundaries. The Internet has served as a model to facilitate this growth.

LAN Devices

LANs were designed to operate in limited geographic areas, such as one floor of a building, or a single building. LANs connect PCs together so that they can access network resources like printers and files. A LAN connects physically adjacent devices on the network media or cable. Typical LAN devices include repeaters, bridges, hubs, switches, routers, and gateways.

Repeaters

These devices regenerate and propagate signals from one network segment to another. They don't change the address or data; they only pass the data on. Repeaters can't filter packets. Even though a repeater helps to extend network distance by regenerating weak signals, be aware that using one will result in combining network segments into a single network. Figure 1.1 shows what a repeater in a LAN looks like.

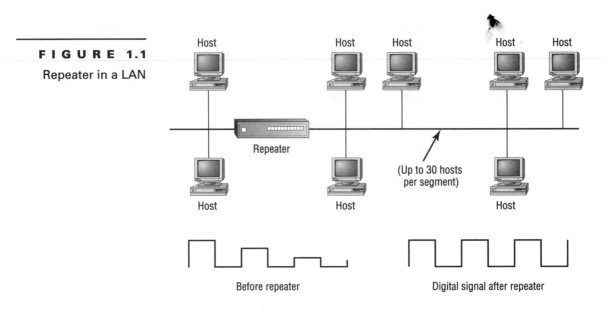

FIGURE 1.1

Repeater in a LAN

Before repeater   Digital signal after repeater

Sometimes repeaters are placed between source and destination hosts to help compensate for signal deterioration due to attenuation. This results in latency: a delay in the time it takes the signal to travel between source and destination hosts.

Bridges

These devices also regenerate signals, but they are more intelligent devices than repeaters. A bridge can read the destination MAC (Media Access Control) or hardware address from the data frame and determine if the destination computer is on the local segment—the segment from which it received the frame—or on other network segments. If the destination computer is on the local segment, it won't forward the frame. If the destination computer isn't on the local segment, the bridge will forward the frame to all other network segments. Figure 1.2 shows how a bridge in a LAN works.

When segmenting an Ethernet LAN, using a bridge instead of a repeater can give you more bandwidth per user because it translates into fewer users per segment. But again, you can end up experiencing latency problems of up to 20–30% due to processing and filtering frames. Also, since bridges forward broadcasts to all other attached segments, broadcast storms can result from the broadcast packets propagating throughout the network. A broadcast storm is a network segment event; during one, a broadcast packet is sent in a perpetual loop until that segment becomes overloaded.

FIGURE 1.2

Bridging a LAN

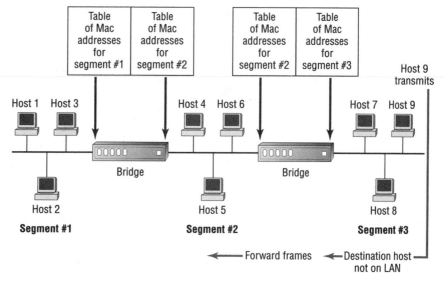

Hubs

Hubs connect all computer LAN connections into one device or concentrator. Hubs can be considered multiport repeaters. PCs can be connected using coax or twisted-pair cable, or even radio frequency (RF). When one computer transmits a digital signal onto the network media, the signal is transmitted to all other segments that are plugged into the hub. Figure 1.3 shows a typical hub working in a LAN.

Switches

Unlike hubs, switches can run in full duplex mode. This means that the computer and switch can both transmit and receive simultaneously. The biggest difference between a switch and a hub is that when a computer transmits a digital signal to a hub, it's then sent to all ports attached to that hub, whereas a switch will send it only to the specific port where the destination MAC address is located. Think of each switch port as being an extremely fast multiport bridge.

Routers

These devices are a step up from bridges. Bridges filter by MAC address, but routers can filter by both hardware and network address (IP address). When

FIGURE 1.3

LAN connections
in a hub

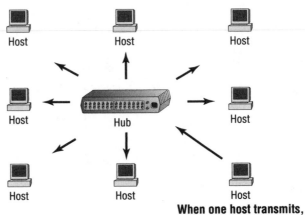

**When one host transmits,
all others must listen.**

a bridge forwards a packet, it sends it out to all segments that it's connected to, whereas a router only forwards packets to the network segment that the packet is destined for. Routers economically prevent unnecessary network traffic from being sent over the network's segments by opening up the data packet and reading the network address before forwarding it. Figure 1.4 shows a typical LAN with a router segmenting the network.

FIGURE 1.4

A router segmenting
a LAN

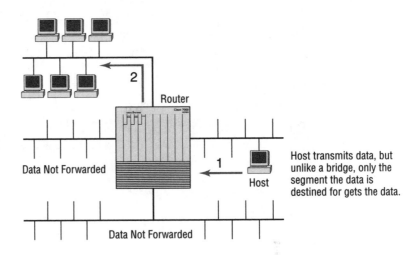

Gateways

These devices are created with software that can be run on PCs and even routers. They link different programs or protocols and examine the entire packet, including the data portion, in order to translate incompatible protocols. For example, to exchange mail between a CCMail server and an Exchange server, you would have to install a mail gateway. Another example would be gateway services that run on a router. These could link an IP network to an IPX network so the users on the IP network could communicate transparently with the users on the IPX network and vice versa.

ATM (Asynchronous Transfer Mode) Switches

These devices provide high-speed cell switching. ATM uses a cell relay technology that combines the advantages of both conventional circuit and packet-based systems.

WAN Devices

WANs extend beyond the LAN to connect networks located in different buildings, cities, states, and countries together. WANs are typically, but not necessarily, limited to using the services of Regional Bell Operating Companies (RBOCs) like Pacific Bell, AT&T, Sprint, MCI, and others. Figure 1.5 shows a WAN connecting offices in three cities.

WANs are connected over serial lines that operate at lower speeds than LANs. Typical WAN devices include:

- **Routers:** In the WAN environment, routers offer both internetworking and WAN interface controls.

- **ATM switches:** These provide high-speed cell switching between both LANs and WANs.

- **X.25 and frame relay switches:** These connect private data over public data circuits using digital signals.

- **Modems:** These connect private data over public telephone circuits using analog signals.

- **Channel Service Units/Data Service Units (CSU/DSU):** A component of customer premises equipment (CPE), which is used to terminate a digital circuit at the customer site. These connect to a central office

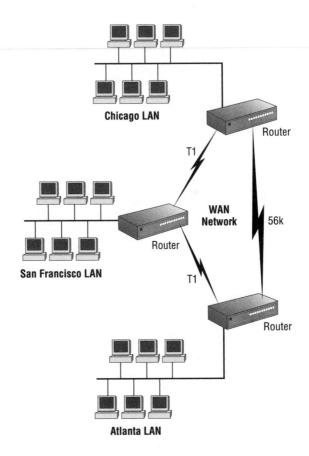

(CO), which is the closest telephone company switch located to the customer.

- **Communication servers:** These are typically dial in/out servers that allow users to dial in from remote locations and attach to the LAN. Cisco's AS5200 series of communication servers are an example of devices that provide such services.

- **Multiplexors:** These devices allow more then one signal to be sent out simultaneously over one physical circuit. The equipment is usually referred to as a *mux*.

The OSI Reference Model

When networks first came into being, computers could typically communicate only with computers from the same manufacturer. For example, companies ran either a complete DECnet solution or an IBM solution—not both together. In the early 1980s, The OSI (Open Systems Interconnection) model was created by the International Standards Organization (ISO) to break this barrier. This was meant to help vendors create interoperable network devices. Like world peace, it'll probably never happen completely, but it's still a great goal.

The OSI model is the primary architectural model for networks. It describes how data and network information is communicated from applications on one computer, through the network media, to an application on another computer. The OSI reference model breaks this approach into layers.

The Layered Approach

A *reference model* is a conceptual blueprint of how communications should take place. It addresses all the processes required for effective communication and divides these processes into logical groupings called *layers*. When a communication system is designed in this manner, it's known as *layered architecture*.

Think of it like this: You and some friends want to start a company. One of the first things you'd do is sit down and think through the things that must be done, who will do them, in what order, and how they relate to each other. Ultimately, you might group these tasks into departments. Let's say you decide to have an order-taking department, an inventory department, and a shipping department. Each of your departments has its own unique tasks, keeping its staff busy and requiring them to focus on only their own duties.

In this scenario, departments are a metaphor for the layers in a communication system. For things to run smoothly, the staff of each department will have to both trust and rely heavily on the others to do their jobs and competently handle their unique responsibilities. In your planning sessions, you would probably take notes, recording the entire process to facilitate later discussions about standards of operation that will serve as your business blueprint, or reference model.

Once your business is launched, your department heads, armed with the part of the blueprint relating to their department, will need to develop practical methods to implement the tasks assigned to them. These practical methods, or protocols, will need to be classified into a Standard Operating Procedures manual and followed closely. Each of the various procedures in your manual will have been included for different reasons and will have varying degrees of importance and implementation. If you form a partnership, or acquire another company, it will be imperative for its business protocols—its business blueprint—to match, or be compatible, with yours.

Similarly, software developers can use a reference model to understand computer communication processes and to see what types of functions need to be accomplished on any one layer. If they are developing a protocol for a certain layer, all they need to concern themselves with is their specific layer's functions, not those of any other layer. Some other layer and protocol will handle the other functions. The technical term for this idea is *binding*. The communication processes that are related to each other are bound, or grouped together, at a particular layer.

Advantages of Reference Models

There are many advantages to using a model. Remember, because developers know that another layer will handle functions they're not currently working on, they can confidently focus on just one layer's functions. This promotes specialization. Another benefit is that if changes are made to one layer, it doesn't necessarily change anything with the other layers.

Suppose an executive in your company in the management layer sends a letter. This person doesn't necessarily care if their company's shipping department, a different layer, changes from UPS to Federal Express, or vice versa. All they're concerned with is the letter and the recipient of the letter. It is someone else's job to see to its delivery. The technical phrase for this idea is *loose coupling*. You've probably heard phrases like this: "It's not *my* fault; it's not my department!" or "So-and-So's group always messes up stuff like this; we never do!" Loose coupling provides a *stable* protocol suite. Passing the buck doesn't.

Another big advantage is *compatibility*. If software developers adhere to the specifications outlined in the reference model, all the protocols written to conform to that model will work together. This is very good. Compatibility creates the foundation for a large number of protocols to be written and used.

In review of why the industry uses a layered model: Q 14, E4

- It clarifies the general functions, rather than specifics on how to do it

- It makes the complexity of networking into more manageable sublayers

- It uses standard interfaces to enable ease of interoperability

- Developers can change the features of one layer without changing all the code

- It allows specialization which helps industry progress

- It eases troubleshooting

Physical and Logical Data Movement

The two additional concepts that need to be addressed in a reference model are the *physical movement of data* and the *logical movement of data*.

As illustrated in Figure 1.6, the physical movement of data begins in the top layer and proceeds down the model, layer by layer. It works like this: Someone creates some information on an application at the top layer. Protocols there pass it down to a communication protocol that packages it, then hands it down to a transmission protocol for the data's actual physical transmission. The data then moves across the model, across some type of physical channel, like cable, fiber, radio frequencies, or microwaves.

FIGURE 1.6

Physical data flow through a model

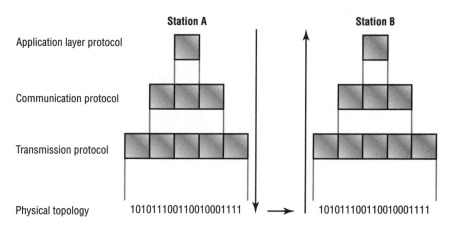

When the data reaches the destination computer, it moves up the model. Each layer at the destination sees and deals with only the data that was packaged by its counterpart on the sending side. Referring back to our analogy about the executive and the letter, the shipping department at the destination sees only the shipping packaging and the information provided by the sending side's shipping department. The destination's shipping department does not see the actual letter because peeking into mail addressed to someone else is a federal offense—it's against proper protocol. The destination company's executive up on the top layer is the one who will actually open and further process the letter.

The logical movement of data is another concept addressed in a reference model. From this perspective, each layer is communicating with only its counterpart layer on the other side (see Figure 1.7). Communication in the realm of humans flows best when it happens between peers—between people on the same level, or layer, in life. The more we have in common, the more similarities in our personalities, experiences, and occupations, the easier it is for us to relate to one another—for us to connect. It's the same with computers. This type of logical communication is called *peer-to-peer communication*. When more than one protocol is needed to successfully complete a communication process, they're grouped into a team called a *protocol stack*. Layers in a system's protocol stack communicate only with the corresponding layers in another system's protocol stack.

FIGURE 1.7

Logical data flow between peer layers

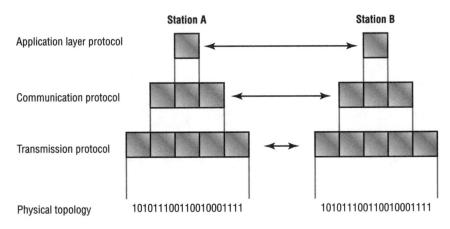

Station A   Station B

Application layer protocol

Communication protocol

Transmission protocol

Physical topology   1010111001100100001111   1010111001100100001111

The OSI Layers

The International Standards Organization (ISO) is the Emily Post of the network protocol world. Just like Ms. Post, who wrote the book setting the standards—or protocols—for human social interaction, the ISO developed the OSI reference model as the guide and precedent for an open network protocol set. Defining the etiquette of communication models, it remains today the most popular means of comparison for protocol suites. The OSI reference model has seven layers:

- Application
- Presentation
- Session
- Transport
- Network
- Data Link
- Physical

Figure 1.8 shows the way these "macrolayers" fit together.

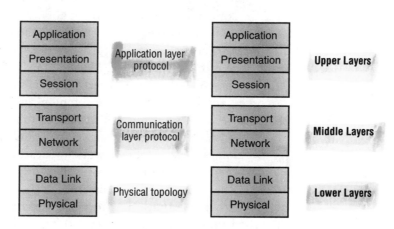

The ISO model's top three layers—Application, Presentation, and Session—deal with functions that aid applications in communicating with other applications. They specifically deal with tasks like file name formats, code sets, user interfaces, compression, encryption, and other functions relating to the exchange occurring between applications.

Figure 1.9 shows the functions defined at each layer of the OSI model. The following pages discuss this in detail.

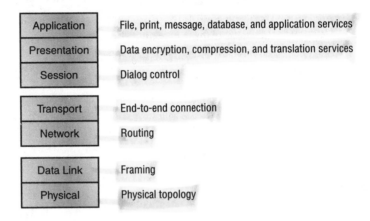

The Application Layer

The Application layer of the OSI model supports the components that deal with the communicating aspects of an application. The Application layer is responsible for identifying and establishing the availability of the intended communication partner. It is also responsible for determining if sufficient resources for the intended communication exists.

Although computer applications sometimes require only desktop resources, applications may unite communicating components from more than one network application: for example, things like file transfers, e-mail, remote access, network management activities, client/server processes, and information location. Many network applications provide services for communication over enterprise networks, but for present and future internetworking, the need is fast developing to reach beyond their limits. For the '90s and beyond, transactions and information exchanges between organizations are broadening to require internetworking applications like the following:

- **The World Wide Web (WWW):** Connects countless servers (the number seems to grow with each passing day) presenting diverse formats. Most are multimedia and include some or all of the following: graphics, text, video, even sound. Netscape Navigator, Internet Explorer, and other browsers like Mosaic simplify both accessing and viewing Web sites.

- **E-mail gateways:** E-mail gateways are versatile and can use Simple Mail Transfer Protocol (SMTP) or the X.400 standard to deliver messages between different e-mail applications.

- **Electronic Data Interchange (EDI):** This is a composite of specialized standards and processes that facilitates the flow of tasks such as accounting, shipping/receiving, and order and inventory tracking between businesses.

- **Special interest bulletin boards:** These include the many chat rooms on the Internet where people can connect and communicate with each other either by posting messages or by typing a live conversation. They can also share public domain software.

- **Internet navigation utilities:** Applications like Gopher and WAIS, as well as search engines like Yahoo!, Excite, and Alta Vista, help users locate the resources and information they need on the Internet.

- **Financial transaction services:** These are services that target the financial community. They gather and sell information pertaining to investments, market trading, commodities, currency exchange rates, and credit data to their subscribers.

The Presentation Layer

The Presentation layer gets its name from its purpose: It presents data to the Application layer. It's essentially a translator. A successful data transfer technique is to adapt the data into a standard format before transmission. Computers are configured to receive this generically formatted data and then convert the data back into its native format for actual reading (for example, EBCDIC to ASCII).

The OSI has protocol standards that define how standard data should be formatted. Tasks like data compression, decompression, encryption, and decryption are associated with this layer.

The Abstract Syntax Notation 1 (ASN.1) is the standard data syntax used by the Presentation layer. This kind of standardization is necessary when transmitting numerical data that's represented very differently by various computer systems' architectures. A good example is the Simple Network

Management Protocol that uses ASN.1 to depict the composition of objects in a network management database.

Some Presentation layer standards are involved in multimedia operations. The following serve to direct graphic and visual image presentation:

- **PICT:** A picture format used by Macintosh or PowerPC programs for transferring QuickDraw graphics.

- **TIFF:** The Tagged Image File Format is a standard graphics format for high-resolution, bitmapped images.

- **JPEG:** The Joint Photographic Experts Group bring these standards to us.

Others guide movies and sound:

- **MIDI:** The Musical Instrument Digital Interface is used for digitized music.

- **MPEG:** The Motion Picture Experts Group's standard for the compression and coding of motion video for CDs is increasingly popular. It provides digital storage and bit rates up to 1.5Mbps.

- **QuickTime:** This is for use with Macintosh or PowerPC programs; it manages audio and video applications.

The Session Layer

The Session layer's job can be likened to that of a mediator or referee. Its central concern is dialog control between devices, or *nodes*. Responsible for coordinating communication between systems, it serves to organize their communication by offering three different modes—simplex, half-duplex, and full-duplex. It also splits up a communication session into three different phases. These phases are connection establishment, data transfer, and connection release. In *simplex mode*, communication is actually a monologue with one device transmitting and another receiving. To get a picture of this, think of the telegraph machine's form of communication: .....--..----...---..-...

When in *half-duplex mode*, nodes take turns transmitting and receiving—the computer equivalent of talking on a speakerphone. Some of us have experienced the unique speakerphone phenomenon of forbidden interruption. The speakerphone's mechanism dictates that you may indeed speak your mind, but you have to wait until the person at the other end stops doing that first.

The only conversational proviso of *full-duplex mode* is *flow control*. This mitigates the problem of possible differences in the operating speeds of two nodes, where one may be transmitting faster than the other can receive. Other than that, communication between the two flows is unregulated, with both sides transmitting and receiving simultaneously.

Formal communication sessions occur in three phases. In the first, the connection-establishment phase, contact is secured and devices agree upon communication parameters and the protocols they'll use. Next, in the data transfer phase, these nodes engage in conversation, or dialog, and exchange information. Finally, when they're through communicating, nodes participate in a systematic release of their session.

A formal communications session is connection-oriented. In a situation where a large quantity of information is to be transmitted, the involved nodes agree upon rules for the creation of checkpoints along their transfer process. These are highly necessary in the case of an error occurring along the way. Among other things, they afford us humans the luxury of preserving our dignity in the face of our computers and co-workers. Let me explain. In the 44th minute of a 45-minute download, a loathsome error occurs...again! This is the third try, and the file-to-be-had is needed more than sunshine. Without your trusty checkpoints in place, you'd have to start all over again, potentially causing you to get more than just a little frustrated. To prevent this, we have checkpoints secured—something we call activity management—ensuring that the transmitting node has to retransmit only the data sent since the last checkpoint where the error occurred.

It's important to note that in some networking situations, devices send out simple, one-frame status reports that aren't sent in a formal session format. If they were, it would burden the network unnecessarily and result in lost economy. Instead, in these events, a *connectionless* approach is used, where the transmitting node simply sends off its data without establishing availability and without acknowledgment from its intended receiver. Think of connectionless communication like a message in a bottle: they're short and sweet, they go where the current takes them, and they arrive at an unsecured destination.

The following are some examples of session-layer protocols and interfaces:

- **Network File System (NFS):** This was developed by Sun Microsystems and used with TCP/IP and Unix workstations to allow transparent access to remote resources.

- **SQL:** The Structured Query Language developed by IBM provides users with a simpler way to define their information requirements on both local and remote systems.

- **RPC:** The Remote Procedure Call is a broad client/server redirection tool used for disparate service environments. Its procedures are created on clients and performed on servers.

- **X Window:** This is widely used by intelligent terminals for communicating with remote Unix computers. It allows them to operate as though they were locally attached monitors.

- **ASP:** Another client/server mechanism, the AppleTalk Session Protocol both establishes and maintains sessions amid AppleTalk client and server machines.

- **DNA SCP:** The Digital Network Architecture Session Control Protocol is a DECnet session layer protocol.

The Transport Layer

Services located in the Transport layer both segment and reassemble data from upper-layer applications and unite it onto the same data stream. They provide end-to-end data transport services and establish a logical connection between the sending host and destination host on an internetwork. The Transport layer is responsible for providing mechanisms for multiplexing upper-layer application, session establishment, and tear-down of virtual circuits. It also hides details of any network-dependent information from the higher layers by providing transparent data transfer.

Data integrity is ensured at this layer by maintaining flow control and by allowing users the option of requesting reliable data transport between systems. *Flow control* prevents the problem of a sending host on one side of the connection overflowing the buffers in the receiving host—an event that can result in lost data. Reliable data transport employs a connection-oriented communications session between systems, and the protocols involved ensure that the following will be achieved:

- The segments delivered are acknowledged back to the sender upon their reception.

- Any segments not acknowledged are retransmitted.

- Segments are sequenced back into their proper order upon arrival at their destination.

- A manageable data flow is maintained in order to avoid congestion, overloading, and the loss of any data.

An important reason for different layers to coexist within the OSI reference model is to allow for the sharing of a transport connection by more than one application. This sharing is available because the transport layer's functioning occurs segment by segment, and each segment is independent of the others. This allows different applications to send consecutive segments, processed on a first-come, first-served basis, that can be intended either for the same destination host or for multiple hosts.

Figure 1.10 shows how the transport layer sends the data of several applications originating from a source host to communicate with parallel applications on one or many destination host(s). The specific port number for each software application is set by software within the source machine before transmission. When it transmits a message, the source computer includes extra bits that encode the type of message, the program with which it was created, and the protocols that were used. Each software application transmitting a data stream segment uses the same preordained port number. When it receives the data stream, the destination computers are empowered to sort and reunite each application's segments, providing the Transport layer with all it needs to pass the data to its upper-layer peer application.

FIGURE 1.10

Transport layer data segments sharing a traffic stream

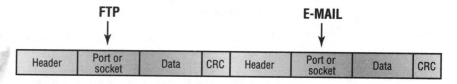

In reliable transport operation, one user first establishes a connection-oriented session with its peer system. Figure 1.11 portrays a typical connection-oriented session taking place between sending and receiving systems. In it, both hosts' application programs begin by notifying their individual operating systems that a connection is about to be initiated. The two operating systems communicate by sending messages over the network confirming that the transfer is approved and that both sides are ready for it to take place. Once the required synchronization is complete, a connection is fully established and the data transfer begins.

F I G U R E   1.11

Establishing a connection-oriented session

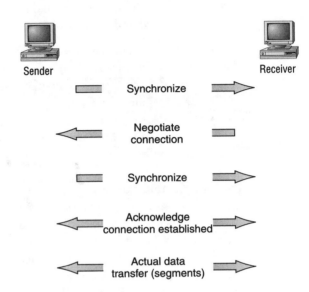

While the information is being transferred between hosts, the two machines periodically check in with each other, communicating through their protocol software, to ensure that all is going well and that the data is being received properly. The following summarizes the steps in a connection-oriented session pictured in Figure 1.11:

- The first "connection agreement" segment is a request for synchronization.

- The second and third segments acknowledge the request and establish connection parameters between hosts.

- The final segment is also an acknowledgment. It notifies the destination host that the connection agreement is accepted and that the actual connection has been established. Data transfer can now begin.

During a transfer, congestion can occur because a high-speed computer is generating data traffic faster than the network can transfer it or because many computers are simultaneously sending datagrams through a single gateway or destination. In the latter case, a gateway or destination can become congested even though no single source caused the problem. In either case, the problem is basically akin to a freeway bottleneck—too much traffic for too small a capacity. Usually, no one car is the problem, it's just that there are simply too many cars on that freeway.

When a machine receives a flood of datagrams too quickly for it to process, it stores them in memory. This buffering action solves the problem only if the datagrams are part of a small burst. However, if the datagram deluge continues, a device's memory will eventually be exhausted, its flood capacity will be exceeded, and it will discard any additional datagrams that arrive. But, no worries—because of transport function, network flood control systems work quite well. Instead of dumping resources and allowing data to be lost, the transport can issue a "not ready" indicator, as shown in Figure 1.12, to the sender, or source, of the flood. This mechanism works kind of like a stoplight, signaling the sending device to stop transmitting segment traffic to its overwhelmed peer. When the peer receiver has processed the segments already in its memory reservoir, it sends out a "ready" transport indicator. When the machine waiting to transmit the rest of its datagrams receives this "go" indictor, it can then resume its transmission.

FIGURE 1.12

Transmitting segments with flow control

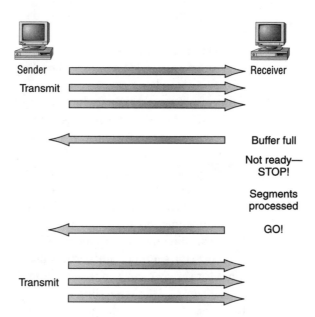

In fundamental, reliable, connection-oriented data transfer, datagrams are delivered to the receiving host in exactly the same sequence they're transmitted; the transmission fails if this order is breached. If any data segments are lost, duplicated, or damaged along the way, this will cause a failure to transmit. The answer to the problem is to have the receiving host acknowledge receiving each and every data segment.

Data throughput would be low if the transmitting machine had to wait for an acknowledgment after sending each segment, so because there's time available after the sender transmits the data segment and before it finishes processing acknowledgments from the receiving machine, the sender uses the break to transmit more data. How many data segments the transmitting machine is allowed to send without receiving an acknowledgment for them is called a *window*.

Windowing controls how much information is transferred from one end to the other. While some protocols quantify information by observing the number of packets, TCP/IP measures it by counting the number of bytes. In Figure 1.13, we show a window size of 1 and a window size of 3. When a window size of 1 is configured, the sending machine waits for an acknowledgment for each data segment it transmits before transmitting another. Configured to a window size of 3, it's allowed to transmit three data segments before an acknowledgment is received. In our simplified example, both the sending and receiving machines are workstations. Reality is rarely that simple, and most often acknowledgments and packets will commingle as they travel over the network and pass through routers. Routing complicates things, but not to worry, we'll be covering applied routing later in the book.

Reliable data delivery ensures the integrity of a stream of data sent from one machine to the other through a fully functional data link. It guarantees the data won't be duplicated or lost. The method that achieves this is known as *positive acknowledgment with retransmission*. This technique requires a receiving machine to communicate with the transmitting source by sending an acknowledgment message back to the sender when it receives data. The sender documents each segment it sends and waits for this acknowledgment before sending the next segment. When it sends a segment, the transmitting machine starts a timer and retransmits if it expires before an acknowledgment for the segment is returned from the receiving end.

In Figure 1.14, the sending machine transmits segments 1, 2, and 3. The receiving node acknowledges it has received them by requesting segment 4. When it receives the acknowledgment, the sender then transmits segments 4, 5, and 6. If segment 5 doesn't make it to the destination, the receiving node

FIGURE 1.13

Windowing

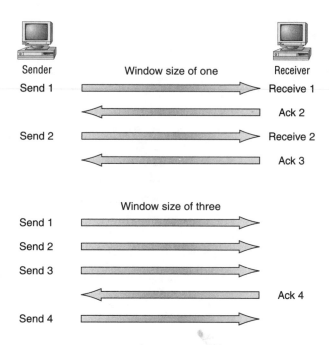

acknowledges that event with a request for the segment to be resent. The sending machine will then resend the lost segment and wait for an acknowledgment, which it must receive in order to move on to the transmission of segment 7.

The Network Layer

In life, there are lots of roads leading to Rome. The same holds true with the complicated cloud of networks. And the proper path through them is determined by protocols residing in layer 3: the Network layer. Path determination makes it possible for a router to appraise all available paths to a given destination and decide on the best one. Routers use network topology information when orienting themselves to the network and evaluating the different possible paths through it. These network "topo maps" can be configured by the network's administrator or be obtained through dynamic processes running on the network. The Network layer's interface is connected to networks, and it's employed by the Transport layer to provide the best end-to-end packet delivery services. The job of sending packets from the source network to the destination network is the Network layer's primary

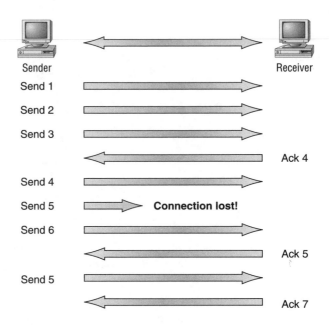

function. After the router decides on the best path from point A to point B, it proceeds with switching the packet onto it. This is known as *packet switching*. Essentially this is forwarding the packet received by the router on one network interface, or port, to the port that connects to the best path through the network cloud. That port will then send the packet to that particular packet's destination.

An internetwork must continually designate all paths of its media connections. In Figure 1.15, each line connecting routers is numbered, and those numbers are used by routers as network addresses. These addresses possess and convey important information about the path of media connections. They're used by routing protocols to pass packets from a source onward to its destination. The Network layer creates a composite "network map"—a communication strategy system—by combining information about the sets of links into an internetwork with path-determination, path-switching, and route-processing functions. It can also use these addresses to provide relay capability and to interconnect independent networks. Consistent across the entire internetwork, layer 3 addresses also streamline the network's performance by not forwarding unnecessary broadcasts that eat up precious bandwidth. Unnecessary broadcasts increase the network's overhead and waste capacity on any links and machines that don't need to receive them. Using consistent end-to-end addressing that accurately describes the path of media connections enables the Network layer to determine the best path to a destination without encumbering the device or links on the internetwork with unnecessary broadcasts.

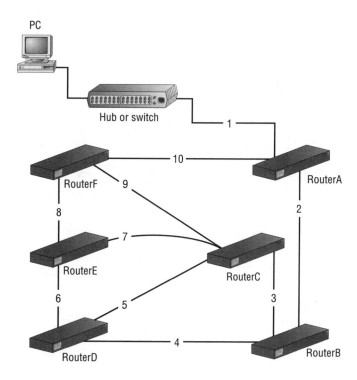

When an application on a host wants to send a packet to a destination device located on a different network, a data link frame is received on one of the router's network interfaces. The router proceeds to de-encapsulate, then examine, the frame to establish what kind of Network layer data is in tow. After this is determined, the data is sent on to the appropriate Network layer process; but the frame's mission is fulfilled, and it's simply discarded.

Detailed in Figure 1.16 is the Network layer process examining the packet's header to discover which network it's destined for. It then refers to the routing table to find the connections the current network has to foreign network interfaces. After one is selected, the packet is re-encapsulated in its data link frame with the selected interface's information and queued for delivery off to the next hop in the path toward its destination. This process is repeated every time the packet switches to another router. When it finally reaches the router connected to the network on which the destination host is located, the packet is encapsulated in the destination LAN's data link frame type. It's now properly packaged and ready for delivery to the protocol stack on the destination host.

FIGURE 1.16

The Network layer process

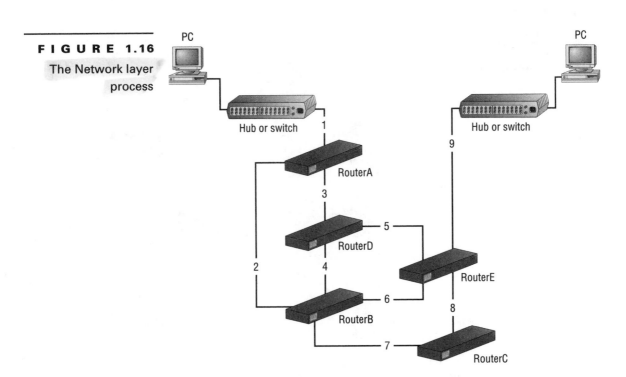

The following describes the Network layer process as shown in Figure 1.16.

- The sending PC sends a datagram to a PC located on Network 9.

- RouterA receives the datagram and checks the destination network. RouterA forwards the packet based on its knowledge of where the network is located.

- RouterB receives the packet and also checks the destination network. RouterB forwards this to RouterE after checking to find the best route to Network 9.

- RouterE receives the packet, puts it in a frame with the hardware destination of the receiving PC, and sends out the frame.

The Data Link Layer

The Data Link layer ensures that messages are delivered to the proper device and translates messages from up above into bits for the Physical layer to transmit. It formats the message into data frames and adds a customized header containing the hardware destination and source address. This added information forms a sort of capsule that surrounds the original message in much the same way as engines, navigational devices, and other tools were attached to the lunar modules of the Apollo project. These various pieces of equipment were useful only during certain stages of space flight and were stripped off the module and discarded when their designated stage was complete. Data traveling through networks is much the same. A data frame that's all packaged up and ready to go follows the format outlined in Figure 1.17.

The various elements of a data frame are described here:

- The *preamble* or *start indicator* is made up of a special bit pattern that alerts devices to the beginning of a data frame.

- The destination address (DA) is there for obvious reasons. The Data Link layer of every device on the network examines this to see if it matches its own address.

- The source address (SA) is the address of the sending device. It exists to facilitate replies to the message.

- In Ethernet_II frames, the two-byte field following the source address is a type field. This field specifies the upper-layer protocol that will receive the data after data link processing is complete.

- In 802.3 frames, the two-byte field following the source address is a length field. This indicates the number of bytes of data that is between this field and the Frame Check Sequence (FCS) field. Following the length field could be an 802.2 header for Logical Link Control (LLC) information. This information is needed to specify the upper layer

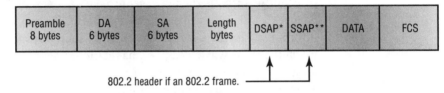

process, because 802.3 doesn't have a type field. Frame types will be discussed in detail in Chapter 3.

- The *data* is the actual message, plus all the information sent down to the sending device's Data Link layer from the layers above it.

- Finally, there's the FCS field. Its purpose corresponds to its name, and it houses the Cyclic Redundancy Checksum (CRC). The FCS allows the receiver to determine if a received frame was damaged or corrupted while in transit. CRCs work like this: The device sending the data determines a value summary for the CRC and stores it in the FCS field. The device on the receiving end performs the same procedure, then checks to see if its value matches the total, or sum, of the sending node; hence the term *checksum*.

Logical Link Control Sublayer   The LLC sublayer of the Data Link layer provides flexibility to the protocols running in the upper and lower layers. As shown in Figure 1.18, the LLC runs between the Network layer and the MAC sublayer of the Data Link layer. This allows protocols at the Network layer, for example IP, to operate without the burden of having to be concerned with what's happening at the Physical layer. Why? Because the Network layer's protocol knows that the LLC sublayer is responsible for making sure the MAC sublayer and the Physical layer are doing their job. The LLC acts as a managing buffer between the "executive" upper layers and the "shipping department" lower layers. In turn, the lower layer protocols don't need to be concerned about what's happening above.

FIGURE 1.18

The LLC sublayer of
the Data Link layer *(N I C - P H Y S I C A L)*

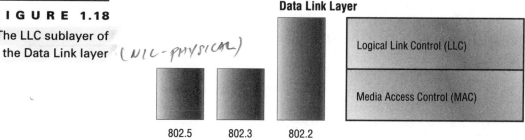

The LLC sublayer uses Source Service Access Points (SSAPs) and Destination Service Access Points (DSAPs) to help the lower layers communicate to the Network layer protocols.

This is important because the MAC sublayer must understand what to do with the data after the frame header is stripped off. It has to know who to hand the data to; this is where the DSAPs and SSAPs come in. Imagine someone coming to your door and asking if it's the correct address (hardware address). You respond, "Yes, what do you want?" The person (or data in the frame) responds, "I don't know." The service access points solve this problem by pointing to the upper-layer protocol, such as IP or IPX. In Figure 1.18, you can see that the 802.3 frame is not capable of handling DSAPs and SSAPs, so the 802.2 frame has to step in. The 802.2 frame is really an 802.3 frame with a DSAP and SSAP control field.

The LLC sublayer is also responsible for timing, flow control, and, with some protocol stacks, even connectionless and connection-oriented protocols.

Media Access Control (MAC) Sublayer   The MAC sublayer of the Data Link layer is responsible for framing. It builds frames from the 1s and 0s that the Physical layer picks up from the wire as a digital signal. It first checks the CRC to make sure nothing was damaged in transit, then it determines if the hardware address matches or not. If it does, the LLC then sends the data on to an upper layer protocol. This layer will also accept a frame if the destination address is a broadcast or multicast.

The MAC sublayer is also responsible for media access. Through it, the workstation is allowed to communicate over the network. This is partly a hardware operation, but it is also partially a software procedure as it's defined by both the network interface card (NIC) and the network card driver. We'll cover this more thoroughly soon; for now, here is a description of the three types of media access:

Contention: A good example of this is found in an Ethernet network where all devices communicate whenever they have something to say. It's pretty easy to imagine that in this scenario a data collision could easily occur if two devices were to "talk" at the same time. Because of this, in a contention network, the transmitting workstation must have control of the entire wire or network segment. Contention networks are great for small, bursty applications.

Token passing: Used in Token Ring, FDDI, and ArcNET networks, stations cannot transmit until they receive a special frame called a *token*. This arrangement also works to prevent the collision problem. Token passing networks work well if large, bandwidth-consuming applications are commonly used on the network.

Polling: Polling is generally used in large mainframe environments where hosts are polled to see if they need to transmit. Hosts (secondaries) aren't permitted to transmit until given permission from the primary host.

WAN Protocols at the Data Link Layer WAN Data Link protocols describe how frames are carried between systems on a single data link. They include protocols designed to operate over dedicated point-to-point facilities, multipoint facilities that are based on dedicated facilities, and multi-access switched services like Frame Relay.

The typical encapsulations for synchronous serial lines at the Data Link layer are

High-Level Data Link Control (HDLC): The ISO created the HDLC standard to support both point-to-point and multipoint configurations. It's too bad that most vendors implement HDLC in different ways, often making HDLC incompatible between vendors. HDLC is the Cisco default protocol for all serial links, and it won't communicate over a serial link with any other vendor's HDLC protocol.

Synchronous Data Link Control (SDLC): A protocol created by IBM to make it easier for their mainframes to connect to remote offices. Created for use in WANs, it became extremely popular in the 1980s because many companies were installing 327x controllers in their remote offices for communication with the mainframe in the corporate office. SDLC defines and uses a polling media-access method. This means the *Primary*, or front-end, asks (polls) the *Secondaries*, or 327x controllers, to find out if they need to communicate with it. Secondaries can't speak unless spoken to, nor can they speak to each other.

Link Access Procedure, Balanced (LAPB): Created for use with X.25, it defines frames as well as being capable of detecting out-of-sequence or missing frames. It also retransmits, exchanges, and acknowledges frames.

X.25: The first packet-switching network. This defines the point-to-point communication between a DTE and a DCE and supports both SVCs and PVCs. Cisco routers (DTEs) connect to modems or DSU/CSUs (DCEs).

Serial Line IP (SLIP): An industry standard developed in 1984 to support TCP/IP networking over low-speed serial interfaces in Berkeley Unix. With the Windows NT RAS service, Windows NT computers can use TCP/IP and SLIP to communicate with remote hosts.

Point-to-Point Protocol (PPP): Think of PPP as SLIP's big brother. It takes the specifications of SLIP and builds on it by adding login, password, and error correction capabilities. PPP is a Data Link protocol that can be used by many network protocols, such as IP, IPX, and AppleTalk. See RFC 1661 for more information, as described by the IETF.

Integrated Services Digital Network (ISDN): This operates through analog phone lines converted to use digital signaling. With ISDN you can transmit both voice and data.

Frame Relay: This is an upgrade from X.25 to be used where LAPB is no longer utilized. It's the fastest of the WAN protocols listed because of its simplified framing approach, which has no error correction. Frame Relay uses SVCs, PVCs, and DLCIs (Data Link Connection Identifiers) for addressing; plus, it requires access to the high-quality digital facilities of the phone company so it's not available everywhere.

The Physical Layer

The Physical layer has two responsibilities: it sends bits and receives bits. Bits come only in values of 1 or 0—a Morse code with numerical value. The Physical layer communicates directly with the various types of actual communication media. Different kinds of media represent these bit values in different ways. Some use audio tones, while others employ *state transitions*—changes in voltage from high to low and low to high. Specific protocols are needed for each type of media to describe the proper bit patterns to be used, how data is encoded into media signals, and the various qualities of the physical media's attachment interface.

At the Physical layer, the interface between the Data Terminal Equipment, or DTE, and the Data Circuit-Terminating Equipment, or DCE, is identified. The DCE is usually located at the service provider, while the DTE is the attached device. The services available to the DTE are most often accessed via a modem or channel service unit/data service unit (CSU/DSU).

The following Physical layer standards define this interface:

- EIA/TIA-232
- EIA/TIA-449
- V.24
- V.35
- X.21
- G.703
- EIA-530
- High-Speed Serial Interface (HSSI)

Data Encapsulation

Data encapsulation is the process in which the information in a protocol is wrapped, or contained, in the data section of another protocol. In the OSI reference model, each layer encapsulates the layer immediately above it as the data flows down the protocol stack.

The logical communication that happens at each layer of the OSI reference model doesn't involve many physical connections because the information each protocol needs to send is encapsulated in the layer of protocol information beneath it. This encapsulation produces a set of data called a packet (see Figure 1.19).

FIGURE 1.19

Data encapsulation at each layer of the OSI reference model

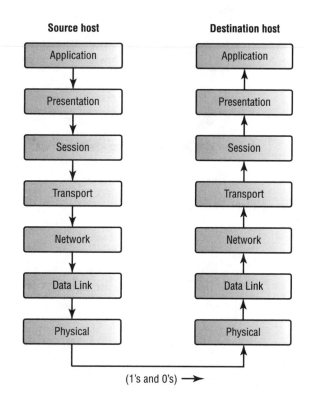

FIGURE 1.19

Data encapsulation at each layer of the OSI reference model

Looking at Figure 1.19, we can follow the data down through the model as it's encapsulated at each layer of the OSI reference model. Starting at the Application layer, data is encapsulated in Presentation layer information. When the Presentation layer receives this information, it looks like generic data being presented. The Presentation layer hands the data to the Session layer that's responsible for synchronizing the session with the destination host. The Session layer then passes this data to the Transport layer, which transports the data from the source host to the destination host. But before this happens, the Network layer adds routing information to the packet. It then passes the packet on to the Data Link layer for framing and for connection to the physical layer. The Physical layer sends the data as 1s and 0s to the destination host across fiber or copper wiring. Finally, when the destination host receives the 1s and 0s, the data passes back up through the model, one layer at a time. The data is de-encapsulated at each of the OSI model's peer layers.

At a transmitting device, the data encapsulation method is as follows:

1. User information is converted to data. *(upper layer)/APPLICATION PRESENTATION SESSION*

2. Data is converted to segments.

3. Segments are converted to packets or datagrams.

4. Packets or datagrams are converted to frames.

5. Frames are converted to bits.

LAN Technologies

It's time to describe the basic characteristics of Ethernet, Token Ring, FDDI, and ATM—four LAN technologies that account for virtually all deployed LANs—and take a look at the Data Link and Physical layer details of each of them.

- Ethernet: Though one of the very first LAN technologies, the largest installed LANs employ it.

- Token Ring: An IBM creation widely used in a large number of corporations that migrated from mainframes to LANs.

- FDDI: Was typically used as a backbone LAN between data closets. It's a popular campus LAN because it's very dependable and faster than Ethernet and Token Ring.

- ATM: Taking the place of FDDI in the campus backbone arena. It's gaining in popularity because it can run in both WAN and LAN environments at tremendous speeds.

Ethernet and IEEE 802.3

In 1980, Digital, Intel, and Xerox (DIX) created the original Ethernet_I. Predictably, Ethernet_II followed, and was released in 1984. Ethernet_II is also described as Carrier Sense, Multiple Access with Collision Detect (CSMA/CD). In response, the IEEE created the 802.3 subcommittee to come up with an Ethernet standard that happens to be almost identical to the Ethernet_II version of Ethernet. The two differ only in their descriptions of the Data Link layer. Ethernet_II has a Type field, whereas 802.3 has a Length field. Even so, they're both common in their Physical layer specifications, MAC addressing, and understanding of the LLC layer's responsibilities.

Ethernet_II and 802.3 both define a bus-topology LAN at 10Mbps, and the cabling defined in these standards are identical:

- 10Base2/Thinnet: Segments up to 185 meters using RG58 coax at 50 ohms.

- 10Base5/Thicknet: Segments up to 500 meters using RG8 or 11 at 50 ohms.

- 10BaseT/UTP: All hosts connect using unshielded twisted pair cable to a central device (a hub or switch). Category 3 UTP is specified to 10Mbps, category 5 to 100Mbps, category 6 to 155Mbps, and category 7 to 1 Gbps.

CSMA/CD

Carrier Sense Multiple Access with Collision Detect was created to overcome the problem of collisions that, as we said earlier, occur when packets are transmitted simultaneously from different nodes. Good collision management is important, because when a node transmits in a CSMA/CD network, all the other nodes on the network receive and examine that transmission. Only bridges and routers effectively prevent a transmission from propagating through the entire network.

The CSMA/CD protocol works like this: When a host wants to transmit over the network, it first checks for the presence of a digital signal on the wire. If all is clear (if no other host is transmitting), the host will then proceed with its transmission. And it doesn't stop there. The transmitting host constantly monitors the wire to make sure no other hosts begin transmitting. If the host detects another signal on the wire, it then sends out an extended jam signal that causes all nodes on the segment to stop sending data. The nodes respond to that jam signal by waiting a bit before attempting to transmit again. If after 15 tries collisions keep occurring, the nodes attempting to transmit will then time-out.

Broadcasts

A broadcast is a frame sent to all network stations at the same time. Remember that broadcasts are built into *all* protocols. Below, the dissected frame of an Etherpeek trace is displayed so you can see the destination hardware address, IP address, and more.

```
Ethernet Header
   Destination:   ff:ff:ff:ff:ff:ff Ethernet Broadcast
   Source:        02:07:01:22:de:a4
   Protocol Type:08-00   IP
IP Header - Internet Protocol Datagram
   Version:               4
   Header Length:         5
   Precedence:            0
   Type of Service:       %000
   Unused:                %00
   Total Length:          93
   Identifier:            62500
   Fragmentation Flags:   %000
   Fragment Offset:       0
   Time To Live:          30
   IP Type:               0x11  UDP
   Header Checksum:       0x9156
   Source IP Address:     10.7.1.9
   Dest. IP Address:      10.7.1.255
   No Internet Datagram Options
```

As this information shows, the source hardware and IP address are from the sending station that knows its own information. Its hardware address is 02:07:01:22:de:a4., and its source IP address is 10.7.1.9. The destination hardware address is FFFFFFFFFFFF, a MAC layer broadcast that is monitored by all stations on the network. The destination network address is 10.7.1.255—an IP broadcast for network 10.7.1.0—meaning all devices on network 10.7.1.0. We'll go over a lot more about addressing and binary numbers in Chapter 4, where we'll also examine and explain the rest of this network trace.

A frame addressed in this manner tells all the hosts on network 10.7.1.0 to receive it and process the data therein. This can be both a good thing and a bad thing. When servers or other hosts need to send data to all the other hosts on the network segment, network broadcasts are very useful indeed. But, if a lot of broadcasts are occurring on a network segment, network performance can be seriously impaired. This is one very big reason why it is so important to segment your network properly with bridges and/or routers.

Fiber Distributed Data Interface (FDDI)

Like Token Ring, Fiber Distributed Data Interface, as shown in Figure 1.20, is a token-passing media access topology. American National Standards Institute (ANSI) defines the standard (ANSI X3T9.5) for a dual Token Ring LAN operating at 100Mbps over fiber optics. Copper Distributed Data Interface can be used with UTP cable to connect servers or other stations directly into the ring (see Figure 1.20).

FIGURE 1.20

FDDI

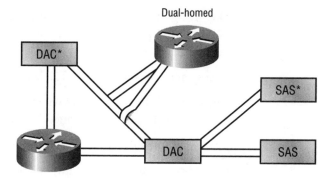

* Dual Attached Connection
* Single Attached Station

The advantages of FDDI include the following:

- FDDI can run very long distances and do so in electronically hostile environments where there's a lot of electromagnetic, or radio, frequency interference present.

- It runs at a high speed compared with 10Mbps Ethernet and 4/16Mbps Token Ring LANs

- FDDI employs a token-passing media access with dual counter-rotating rings, as shown in Figure 1.21. Typically, only one ring is active at any given time. That way, if a break or outage occurs, the FDDI ring will wrap back the other direction, keeping the ring intact.

Some stations can be attached to both rings for redundancy reasons. These are known as Dual Attachment Stations (DAS). These would be used mostly for high availability stations like servers.

- Cisco routers can attach with a technique called dual homing. This provides fault tolerance by providing a primary and backup path to the FDDI ring.

- FDDI is both a logical and physical ring—the only LAN that is an actual, physical ring. Like Token Ring, FDDI provides predictable deterministic delays and priorities.

- FDDI uses MAC addresses like other LANs do, but it uses a different numbering scheme. Instead of the eight-bit bytes that Ethernet and Token Ring uses, it applies four-bit symbols. FDDI has 12 four-bit symbols that make up its MAC addresses.

- Token Ring allows only one token on the ring at any given time, whereas FDDI permits several tokens to be present on the ring concurrently.

Some drawbacks of migrating to FDDI include the following:

- Relatively high latency occurs when Ethernet-to-FDDI and FDDI-to-Ethernet translation is performed between LANs.

- Capacity is still shared because FDDI dual ring is a shared LAN.

- There's no full duplex capability in shared networks.

- It's expensive—very expensive! FDDI components, i.e., hubs and NICs, aren't exactly bargain equipment.

Figure 1.21 shows how an FDDI LAN would wrap the primary ring back to the standby, secondary ring if a failure occurred.

When a station realizes that no tokens have been received from its nearest active upstream neighbor (NAUN) for a predetermined time period, it sends out a beacon as an alert and as an attempt to locate the failure. Once it starts to receive its own beacons, it assumes the ring is now up and running. If it doesn't receive its beacon back for a predetermined amount of time, the primary ring will wrap to the secondary ring as shown.

Token Ring

IBM created Token Ring in the 1970s; it was popular with true-blue customers needing to migrate from a mainframe environment. It lost to Ethernet in the

FIGURE 1.21

Dual-Ring Reliability

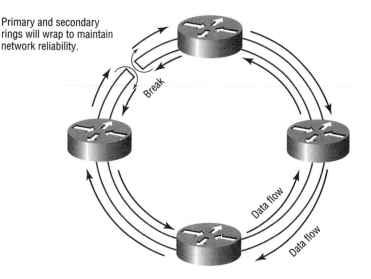

Primary and secondary rings will wrap to maintain network reliability.

Break

Data flow

Data flow

popularity polls because it's pricey by comparison. However, depending on what you're looking for, Token Ring is a more resilient network, especially under heavy loads. Sometimes you actually do get what you pay for.

Like Ethernet, the IEEE came out with its own standard for Token Ring, designated 802.5. This standard was so close to the IBM standard that the IEEE is now responsible for administrating both specifications.

At the physical layer, Token Ring runs as a star topology using shielded twisted pair (STP) wiring. Each station connects to a central hub called a Multistation Access Unit (MSAU). Logically, it runs in a ring where each station receives signals from its NAUN and repeats these signals to its downstream neighbors.

Token Ring uses MAC addresses like Ethernet does, but that's where the similarities end. Token Ring media access is described point by point below:

- Stations can't transmit whenever they want like Ethernet stations can. Instead, they have to wait to be given a special frame called a token. When a station receives a token, it does one of two things:

  - It appends the data it wants to send onto the end of the frame, then changes the T bit in the frame. Doing that alerts the receiving station that data is attached.

  - If the station that gets a token doesn't need to send any data, it simply passes on the token to the next station in the ring.

- The information frame circles the ring until it gets to the destination station. The destination station copies the frame and then tags the frame as being copied. The frame continues around until it reaches the originating station, which then removes it.

- Typically, only one frame can be on a ring at any given time. However, by using early token release, a station can transmit a new token onto the ring after transmitting its first frame.

- Collisions don't happen because stations can't transmit unless they have a token.

The frame in a Token Ring network is different from the frames in Ethernet. As shown in Figure 1.22, the token frame uses a priority system that permits certain user-designated, high-priority stations to use the network more frequently. The media access control field of the frame is shown below:

Access Control Field

FIGURE 1.22

Token Ring media access control field

P: Priority bits
T: Token bits
M: Monitor bits
R: Reservation bits

The two fields that control priority are predictably the priority field and the reservation field. If a priority token is transmitted, only stations with a priority equal to or higher than the priority of that token can claim it. Priority levels are configured by the network administrator. After the token is claimed and changed to an information frame, only stations with a priority rating higher than the transmitting station can reserve the token for the next pass around the network. When the next token is generated, it includes the highest priority for the reserving station. Stations that raise a token's priority level must reinstate the previous lower priority level after their transmission is complete.

The frame status field is shown in Figure 1.23. The address, or A bit, and the copied, or C bit, are used to indicate the status of an outstanding frame.

F I G U R E   1.23

Token Ring frame
status field

Frame Status Field

A	C	r	r	A	C	r	r

0	0	Destination not found
0	1	Copied but not acknowledged
1	0	Unable to copy data from frame
1	1	Station found or frame copied to another ring by a bridge

Both the bits are turned off when the sending station transmits the frame. When the sending station receives the frame back again, the station will read this information to ensure that the data was either received correctly by the destination computer or that it needs to be retransmitted.

Active Monitor

One station on a Token Ring network is always an Active Monitor. The Active Monitor makes sure that there isn't more then one token on the Ring at any given time. Also, if a transmitting station fails, it isn't able to remove the token as it makes it way back through the ring. Should this occur, the Active monitor would step in, remove the token, and then generate a new one. Also, many stations on the Ring will be designated as Standby Monitors (to act as backups) in case the Active Monitor goes offline.

ATM Technology

Asynchronous Transfer Mode (ATM) is a very high bandwidth, low delay technology that uses both switching and multiplexing. It uses 53-byte fixed size cells instead of frames like Ethernet. ATM is a very adaptable technology that works in both LANs and WANs. It can allocate bandwidth on demand, making it a great solution for bursty applications.

While ATM is not dependent on a Physical layer implementation, it does require a high-speed, high-bandwidth medium like fiber optics.

ATM can be used to support the following applications:

- Interactive multimedia
- Real-time video

- Client/server databases

- Interconnection of existing networks

The International Telecommunication Union—Telecomms Standardization Sector (ITU-T) and the ATM forum have worked in conjunction to create the standards for ATM.

Summary

In this chapter we covered the following key points:

- The reasons the industry uses a layered model instead of a flat model

- The specific functions of each layer of the ISO/OSI reference model

- The seven layers of the OSI reference model and the functions of each layer

- The Transport layer of the OSI reference model, flow control, and how it works in conjunction with positive acknowledgements and windowing to guarantee delivery of data

- The key internetworking functions of the OSI Network layer and how a router uses a datagram to send data through an internetwork

- The OSI model and the five conversion steps of data encapsulation as it moves down the model from the Application layer to the Physical layer

Review Questions

1. LAN stands for which of the following?

A. Long Area Network

B. Local Area Network

C. Local Arena Network

D. Local Area News

2. WAN stands for which of the following?

   A. WAN Area Network

   B. Wide Arena Network

   C. Wide Area Network

   D. Wide Area News

3. The two sublayers of the IEEE Data Link layer are which of the following?

   A. Data Link and MAC

   B. Data Link and LLC

   C. Logical Link Control and Media Access Control

   D. Logical and Link Control

4. Bridges work at which layer of the OSI reference model?

   A. Session

   B. Bridge

   C. Network

   D. Data Link

5. Repeaters work at which layer of the OSI reference model?

   A. Transport

   B. Presentation

   C. Physical

   D. Data Link

6. What is the Network layer of the OSI reference model responsible for?

   A. Bridging

   B. Regenerating the digital signal

   C. Routing packets through an internetwork

   D. Gateway services

7. List the seven layers of the OSI reference model and each of their functions.

8. Which three pairs of the following are Presentation layer standards?

   A. MPEG and MIDI

   B. PICT and JPEG

   C. ASCII and EBCDIC   *P18*

   D. NFS and SQL

9. Which of the following are Session layer standards?

   A. MPEG and MIDI

   B. NFS and SQL

   C. ASCII and EBCDIC   *P18-20*

   D. PICT and JPEG

10. Which three of the following are true statements about connection-oriented sessions?

   A. The segments delivered are acknowledged back to the sender upon their reception

   B. Any segments not acknowledged are dropped   *P20-21*

   C. Segments are sequenced back into their proper order upon arrival at their destination

   D. A manageable data flow is maintained in order to avoid congestion, overloading, and the loss of any data

11. CPE is an acronym for which of the following?

   A. Central Processing Engineering

   B. Central Processing Equipment

   C. Customer Processing Equipment   *P9*

   D. Customer Premise Equipment

12. CSU/DSU is an acronym for which of the following?

   A. Channel Service Unit/Digital Service Unit

   B. Channel Service Unit/Data Service Unit   *service provider*

   C. Channel Service Unite/Digital Service Unit   *P9, P34*

   D. Can't Send in Uniform/Don't Send another Unit

13. CO is an acronym for which of the following?

   A. Company Office

   B. Corporate Option

   C. Central Office   *P9-10*

   D. Central Option

14. Choose three reasons why the networking industry uses a layered model.

   A. It allows changes to occur in all layers when changing one protocol

   B. It allows changes in one layer to occur without changing other layers   *P13, p25*

   C. It clarifies what general function is to be done rather than how to do it

   D. It clarifies how to do it rather than what general functions should be done

   E. It facilitates systematic troubleshooting

15. Which layer defines bit synchronization?

   A. Application

   B. Presentation

   C. Session

   D. Transport

   E. Network

   F. Data Link   *P34*

   G. Physical

connector, wire

16. Which layer defines the physical topology?

   A. Application

   B. Presentation

   C. Session

   D. Transport

   E. Network

   F. Data Link   *p34, p15*

   G. Physical

17. Which layer is responsible for putting 1s and 0s into a logical group?

   A. Application

   B. Presentation   *↓ frames*

   C. Session

   D. Transport

   E. Network

   F. Data Link   *p29,*

   G. Physical

18. Which layer is responsible for framing?

   A. Application

   B. Presentation

   C. Session

   D. Transport

   E. Network

   F. Data Link   *p29*

   G. Physical

19. Which layer is responsible for addressing devices and <u>routing</u> through an internetwork?

A. Application

B. Presentation

C. Session

D. Transport

~~**E.**~~ Network

F. Data Link

G. Physical

20. Which layer hides details of any network-dependent information from the higher layers by providing transparent data transfer?

A. Application

B. Presentation

C. Session

~~**D.**~~ Transport

E. Network

F. Data Link

G. Physical

21. Which layer is responsible for flow control, acknowledgment, and windowing?

A. Application

B. Presentation

C. Session

~~**D.**~~ Transport

E. Network

F. Data Link

G. Physical

22. Which layer is responsible for providing mechanisms for multiplexing upper-layer application, session establishment, and tear-down of virtual circuits?

A. Application

B. Presentation

C. Session

D. Transport   *P 20*

E. Network

F. Data Link

G. Physical

23. Which layer is responsible for coordinating communication between systems?

A. Application

B. Presentation

C. Session   *P. 18*

D. Transport

E. Network

F. Data Link

G. Physical

24. Which layer is responsible for negotiating data transfer syntax?

A. Application

B. Presentation   *P. 17*

C. Session

D. Transport

E. Network

F. Data Link

G. Physical

format
encryption
compress

25. Which layer is responsible for synchronizing sending and receiving applications? *services, resources*

A. Application *p. 16*

B. Presentation

C. Session

D. Transport

E. Network

F. Data Link

G. Physical

26. Which layer is responsible for identifying and establishing the availability of the intended communication partner?

A. Application *p. 16*

B. Presentation

C. Session

D. Transport

E. Network

F. Data Link

G. Physical

27. Which layer is responsible for determining if sufficient resources for the intended communication exists?

A. Application *p. 16*

B. Presentation

C. Session

D. Transport

E. Network

F. Data Link

G. Physical

CHAPTER

2

LAN Segmentation

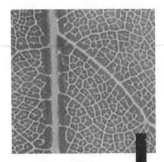

In this chapter, you'll learn to identify congestion and performance problems in a network and find some solutions for those problems. You'll discover the advantages or disadvantages of using a bridge, a router, or a LAN switch to segment a network. You'll also read about FastEthernet and the specification and implementation guidelines.

The CCNA test objectives covered in this chapter include:

Relieving Network Congestion

With a combination of powerful workstations, audio and video to the desktop, and network-intensive applications, 10Mbps Ethernet networks no longer offer enough bandwidth to fulfill the business requirements of the typical large business.

As more and more users are connected to the network, an Ethernet network's performance begins to lag as users fight for more bandwidth. Like too many cars getting onto a freeway at rush hour, this increased utilization forces an increase in network congestion as more users try to access the same network resources. Congestion causes users to scream for more bandwidth. However, simply increasing bandwidth can't always solve the problem. Things like having a slow server CPU or insufficient RAM on the workstations and servers can also be culprits and need to be considered.

A way to solve congestion problems and increase the networking performance of your LAN is to divide a single Ethernet segment into multiple network segments. This maximizes available bandwidth. Some of the technologies you can use to do that are:

Physical segmentation: You can segment the network with bridges and routers, thereby breaking up the collision domains. This minimizes packet collisions by decreasing the number of workstations on the same physical segment.

Network switching technology (microsegmenting): Like a bridge or router, switches can also provide LAN segmentation capabilities. LAN switches (for example, the Cisco Catalyst 5000) provide dedicated, point-to-point, packet-switched connections between their ports. Since this provides simultaneous switching of packets between the ports in the switch, it increases the amount of bandwidth open to each workstation.

Full-duplex Ethernet devices: Full-duplex Ethernet can provide almost twice the bandwidth of traditional Ethernet networks. However, for this to work, the network interface cards (NICs) must be able to run in full-duplex mode.

FastEthernet: Using FastEthernet switches can provide 10 times the amount of bandwidth available from 10BaseT.

▪ **FDDI:** An older, solid technology that can provide 100Mbps bandwidth. By running dual rings, it has the capability of up to 200Mbps. It's typically used between closets, floors, or in a campus environment.

It should be no surprise that reducing the number of users per collision domain increases the bandwidth on your network segment. By keeping the traffic local to the network segment, users have more available bandwidth and enjoy a noticeably better response time than if you simply had one large backbone in place.

Figure 2.1 shows an Ethernet network with repeaters. This network appears to be one large Ethernet network to all workstations, and basically it *is* one large collision domain. It's a good idea to segment your network with bridges and routers when it grows too large. But these devices use different technologies that can cause some delay and reduce communication efficiency, which is why it's so important to segment your network correctly.

FIGURE 2.1

Ethernet network with repeaters

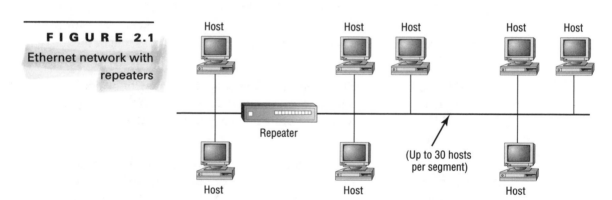

Segmentation with a Bridge

As discussed in Chapter 1, a bridge can segment or break up your network into smaller, more manageable pieces. But if it's incorrectly placed in your network, it can cause more harm than good!

Bridges do their work at the MAC sublayer of the Data Link layer. They create both physical and logical separate network segments to reduce traffic load. There are solid advantages to bridging: by segmenting a logical network into multiple physical pieces, it ensures network reliability, availability, scalability, and manageability.

As Figure 2.2 shows, bridges work by examining the MAC or hardware addresses in each frame and forwarding the frame to the other physical segments; but only if necessary. These devices dynamically build a forwarding table of information comprised of each MAC address and which segment that address is located on.

FIGURE 2.2

Segmentation with a bridge

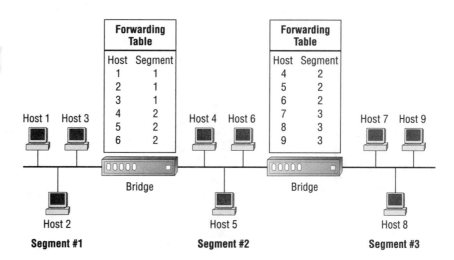

Forwarding Table	
Host	Segment
1	1
2	1
3	1
4	2
5	2
6	2

Forwarding Table	
Host	Segment
4	2
5	2
6	2
7	3
8	3
9	3

Host 1   Host 3   Host 4   Host 6   Host 7   Host 9

Bridge   Bridge

Host 2   Host 5   Host 8

Segment #1   **Segment #2**   **Segment #3**

Now for the bad news.... A drawback to using bridges is that if the destination MAC address is unknown to the bridge, the bridge will forward the frame to all segments except the port it received the frame from. Also, a 20–30% latency period to process frames can occur. Latency is the time is takes for a frame to get from the source host to the destination host. This delay can increase significantly if the frame cannot be immediately forwarded due to current activity on the destination segment.

Bridges will forward packets and multicast packets to all other segments that the bridge is attached to. Because the addresses from these broadcasts are never seen by the bridge, and therefore not filtered, broadcast storms can result. This same problem can happen with switches, as, theoretically, switch ports are bridge ports. A Cisco switch is really a multiport bridge that runs the Cisco IOS and performs the same functions as a bridge.

Segmentation with a Router

As you know, routers work at the Network layer and are used to route packets to destination networks. Routers, like bridges, use tables to make routing decisions. However, routers keep information only on how to get to remote networks in their tables, not to hosts; they use this information to route packets through an internetwork. For example, routers use IP addresses instead of hardware addresses when making routing decisions. The router keeps a routing table for each protocol on the network. A Cisco router will keep a routing table for AppleTalk, a different one for IPX, and still another for IP as shown in Figure 2.3

FIGURE 2.3

Routing tables are kept for each network layer routing protocol.

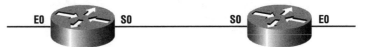

IP ROUTING TABLE			IP ROUTING TABLE	
Subnet	**Interface**		**Subnet**	**Interface**
172.16.10.0	E0		172.16.30.0	E0
172.16.20.0	S0		172.16.20.0	S0
172.16.30.0	S0		172.16.10.0	S0

IPX ROUTING TABLE			IPX ROUTING TABLE	
Subnet	**Interface**		**Subnet**	**Interface**
117	S0		10	S0
108	E0		108	E0
10	S0		117	S0

AppleTalk ROUTING TABLE			AppleTalk ROUTING TABLE	
Subnet	**Interface**		**Subnet**	**Interface**
2-2	E0		1-1	E0
10-10	S0		10-10	S0
1-1	S0		2-2	S0

The pros regarding routers:

- Manageability: Multiple routing protocols give the network manager who's creating an internetwork a lot of flexibility.

- Increased functionality: Cisco routers provide features addressing the issues of flow, error, and congestion control, plus fragmentation, reassembly, and control over packet lifetime.

- Multiple active paths: Using the protocol, DSAPs, SSAPs, and path metrics, routers can make informed routing decisions, as well as interpret the next layer protocol. Routers can have more than one active link between devices, which is a definite plus.

To provide these featured advantages, routers must be more complex and more software intensive than bridges. Routers provide a lower level of performance than bridges in terms of the number of frames or packets that can be processed per unit. A router must examine more fields in a packet than a bridge, resulting in a 30–40% loss of throughput for acknowledgment-oriented protocols and a 20–30% loss for sliding-window protocols.

Segmentation with LAN Switches

LAN switching is a great strategy for LAN segmentation. LAN switches improve performance by employing packet switching that permits high-speed data exchanges.

Just like bridges, switches use the destination MAC address in order to ensure that the packet is forwarded to the right outgoing port. Cut-through switches begin forwarding the packet before reception is complete, keeping latency to a minimum. The Catalyst 5505 switch uses a store-and-forward architecture. Figure 2.4 details a Cisco Catalyst 5505 series switch. It uses 10/100 full-duplex switching. Switch architecture will be covered later in this chapter.

F I G U R E   2.4

Cisco Catalyst
5505 switch

There are three different switching terms: port, frame switching, and cell switching (ATM).

- Port configuration switching allows a port to be assigned to a physical network segment under software control. It's the simplest form of switching.

- Frame switching is used to increase available bandwidth on the network. It allows multiple transmissions to occur in parallel. This is the type of switching performed by all catalyst switches.

- Cell switching (ATM) is similar to frame switching. ATM uses small, fixed-length cells that are switched on the network. It's the switching method used by all Cisco Lightstream switches.

A LAN switch supplies you with considerably higher port density at a lower cost than do standard bridges. Since LAN switches permit fewer users per segment, the average available bandwidth per user increases. This fewer-users-per-segment trend is known as microsegmentation, and it allows you to create dedicated segments. When you have one user per segment, each enjoys instant access to the full available bandwidth, instead of competing for it with other users. Because of this, the collisions so common with shared medium-sized networks that use hubs just don't happen.

A LAN switch bases the forwarding of frames on the frame's layer 2 address (layer 2 LAN switch) or on the frame's layer 3 address (multi-layer LAN switch). LAN switches are sometimes referred to as frame switches because they generally forward layer 2 frames, in contrast to an ATM switch that forwards cells.

As network use increases, we're seeing more Token Ring and FDDI LAN switches, but Ethernet LAN switches are still the most common type.

LAN switches uniquely support some very cool, new features including the following:

- Numerous, simultaneous conversations

- High-speed data exchanges

- Low latency and high frame-forwarding rates

- Dedicated communication between devices

- Full-duplex communication

- Media rate adaptation (both 10 and 100 Mbps hosts can work on the same network)

- An ability to work with existing 802.3-compliant network interface cards and cabling

Because of the dedicated, collision-free communication between network devices, file-transfer throughput is increased. Many conversations can occur simultaneously by forwarding or switching several packets at the same time, which expands the network capacity by the amount of supported conversations.

Full-duplex communication doubles throughput, and media rate adaptation allows the LAN switch to translate between 10 and 100 Mbps, to allocate bandwidth on an as-needed basis. Another benefit is that changing over to LAN switches often doesn't mean you have to change the existing hubs, network interface cards (NICs), or cabling.

Switching Modes

The latency for packet switching through the switch depends on the chosen switching mode. Options include: store-and-forward, cut-through, and fragment-free.

Store-and-Forward   Store-and-forward switching is one of two primary types of LAN switching. With this method, the LAN switch copies the entire frame into its onboard buffers and computes the cyclic redundancy check (CRC). The frame is discarded if it contains a CRC error, if it's a runt (less than 64 bytes including the CRC), or a giant (more than 1518 bytes, including the CRC). If the frame doesn't contain any errors, the LAN switch looks up the destination address in its forwarding, or switching, table and determines the outgoing interface. It then forwards the frame toward its destination. Because this type of switching copies the entire frame and runs a CRC, latency time can vary depending on frame length. This is the mode used by the Catalyst 5000 series switches.

Cut-Through (Real-Time)   Cut-through switching is the other main type of LAN switching. With it, the LAN switch copies only the destination address (the first 6 bytes following the preamble) into its onboard buffers. It then looks up the destination address in its switching table, determines the outgoing interface, and forwards the frame toward its destination. A cut-through switch provides reduced latency because it begins to forward the frame as soon as it reads the destination address and determines the outgoing interface. Some switches can be configured to perform cut-through switching on a per-port basis until a user-defined error threshold is reached. At that point, they automatically change over to store-and-forward mode. When the error rate falls below the threshold, the port automatically changes back to cut-through mode.

FragmentFree FragmentFree is a modified form of cut-through switching in which the switch waits for the collision windows, which are 64 bytes long, to pass before forwarding. If a packet has an error, it almost always occurs within the first 64 bytes. FragmentFree mode provides better error checking than the cut-through mode, with practically no increase in latency.

Figure 2.5 shows the different places that the switching mode takes place in the frame.

FIGURE 2.5

Different switching modes within a frame

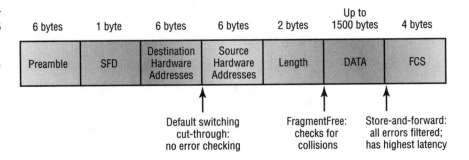

Spanning-Tree Protocol

IEEE 802.1d Spanning-Tree Protocol (STP) was developed to prevent routing loops in a network. If a router, switch, or hub has more then one path to the same destination, a routing problem could occur. To prevent this, the Spanning-Tree Protocol is executed between the devices to detect and logically block redundant paths from the network. The main function of the Spanning-Tree Protocol is to allow redundant network paths without suffering the effects of loops in the network.

The Spanning-Tree Algorithm (STA) implemented by STP prevents loops by calculating a stable Spanning-Tree network topology. When creating fault-tolerant internetworks, a loop-free path must exist between all Ethernet nodes in the network. The STA is used to calculate a loop-free path throughout a Catalyst 5000 series switched network. Spanning-Tree frames called bridge protocol data units (BPDUs) are sent and received by all switches in the network at regular intervals. The frames aren't forwarded by the switches participating in the spanning tree, instead, they're processed to determine the spanning tree topology itself. Catalyst 5000 series switches use STP 802.1d to perform this function as shown in the following Etherpeek trace:

```
Flags:          0x80  802.3
  Status:         0x00
  Packet Length:64
  Timestamp:      09:59:09.990000 02/19/1998
```

802.3 Header
```
  Destination:  01:80:c2:00:00:00
  Source:       08:00:02:0b:59:34
  LLC Length:   38
```
802.2 Logical Link Control (LLC) Header
```
  Dest. SAP:    0x42   802.1
  Source SAP:   0x42   802.1  Null LSAP
  Command:      0x03   Unnumbered Information
```
802.1 - Bridge Spanning Tree
```
  Protocol Identifier:   0
  Protocol Version ID:   0
  Message Type:          0  Configuration Message
  Flags:                 %00000000
  Root Priority/ID:      0x8000  /  08:00:02:0b:59:34
  Cost Of Path To Root: 0x00000000  (0)
  Bridge Priority/ID:    0x8000  / 08:00:02:0b:59:34
  Port Priority/ID:      0x80  /  0x01
  Message Age:              0/256 seconds (exactly 0 seconds)
  Maximum Age:             5120/256 seconds (exactly 20 seconds)
  Hello Time:              512/256 seconds (exactly 2 seconds)
  Forward Delay:           3840/256 seconds (exactly 15 seconds)
Extra bytes (Padding):
  .#..|ó..              02 23 00 07 7c f3 02 00
Frame Check Sequence:  0x00000000
```

VLAN (Virtual LAN)

To be able to have different ports on the switch that can be part of different subnetworks, you need to create virtual LANs within the switch.

Virtual Local Area Networks (VLANs) are a logical grouping of network users and resources connected to defined ports on the switch. A VLAN looks like, and is treated like, its own subnet. By using virtual LANs, you're no longer confined to physical locations. VLANs can be created by location, function, department—even by the application or protocol used—regardless of where the resources or users are located.

The benefits of VLANs are that they

- Simplify moves, adds, and changes
- Reduce administrative costs
- Have better control of broadcasts
- Tighten network security
- Microsegment with scalability
- Distribute traffic load
- Relocate server into secured locations

Frame Tagging

Frame identification (frame tagging) uniquely assigns a user-defined ID to each frame. This technique was chosen by the IEEE standards group because of its scalability.

VLAN frame identification is a relatively new approach that's been specifically developed for switched communications. In this approach, a unique user-defined identifier is placed in the header of each frame as it's forwarded throughout the switch fabric. The identifier is understood and examined by each switch prior to any broadcasts or transmissions to switch ports of other switches, routers, or end-station devices. When the frame exits the switch fabric, the switch removes the identifier before the frame is transmitted to the target end-station. All this means is that the switch tags a frame with a VLAN identifier that is only used within the switch fabric itself. Before that frame leaves the switch, it removes the VLAN ID, because nothing outside the switch will be able to understand the VLAN ID. The exception is when you run inter-switch link (ISL), then the VLAN ID is preserved as it passes over the ISL link.

The following points summarize frame tagging:

- Used by Catalyst 3000 and 5000 series switches

- Specifically developed for multi-VLAN, inter-switch communication

- Places a unique identifier in the header of each frame

- Identifier is removed before frame exits switch on non-trunk links

- Functions at layer 2

- Requires little processing or administrative overhead

Full-Duplex Ethernet

Full-duplex Ethernet can both transmit and receive simultaneously, but it requires a switch port, not a hub, to be able to do so.

Full duplex Ethernet uses point-to-point connections and is typically referred to as collision-free since it doesn't share bandwidth with any other devices. Frames sent by two nodes cannot collide because there are physically separate transmit and receive circuits between the nodes.

If you have a full-duplex 10Mbps Ethernet operating bi-directional on the same switch port, you can theoretically have 20Mbps aggregate throughput. Full-duplex can now be used in 10BaseT, 100BaseT, and 100BaseFL media, but all devices (NIC cards, for example), must be able to support full-duplex transmission.

Half-Duplex Ethernet Design

Figure 2.6 shows the circuitry involved in half-duplex Ethernet. When a station is sending to another station, the transmitting circuitry is active at the transmitting station, and the receive circuitry is active at the receiving station. This uses a single cable similar to a narrow one-way bridge.

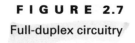

FIGURE 2.6

Half-duplex circuitry

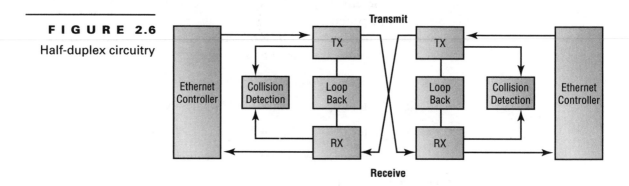

Full-Duplex Ethernet Design

Figure 2.7 shows full-duplex circuitry. Full-duplex Ethernet switch technology (FDES) provides a point-to-point connection between the transmitter of the transmitting station and the receiver of the receiving station. Half-duplex, standard Ethernet can usually provide 50–60% of the bandwidth available. In contrast, full-duplex Ethernet can provide a full 100%, because it can transmit and receive simultaneously, and because collisions don't occur.

FIGURE 2.7

Full-duplex circuitry

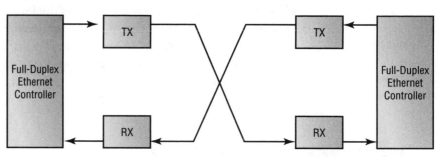

In order to run full-duplex, you must have the following:

- Two 10Mbps or 100Mbps paths
- Full-duplex NIC cards
- Loopback and collision detection disabled
- Software drivers supporting two simultaneous data paths

- Adherence to Ethernet distance standards
- 10BaseT/100BaseT: 100 meters
- 10BaseFL/100BaseFL: 2 kilometers

100BaseT Fast Ethernet

In 1995, the IEEE approved the IEEE 802.3u, the 100BaseT Ethernet standard. It defines the Physical and Data Link layers, uses the CSMA/CD protocol, and is 10 times faster than 10BaseT. Some of the new technology stars are:

100BaseFX: Ethernet over fiber at 100Mbps using 802.3 specs. It uses a two-strand, 50/125- or 62.5/125-micron multimode fiber-optic cable.

100BaseT4: Using 802.3 specs, 100Mbps over category 3, 4, or 5 cabling with a standard RJ-45 connector.

100BaseTX: Fast Ethernet over category 5 cabling. It's compatible with, and adheres to, 802.3 specifications. It can also use two-pair, 100 ohm shielded twisted pair (STP) cable or type 1 STP cable.

100BaseX: This refers to either the 100BaseTX or 100BaseFX media. This standard was approved to ensure compatibility between the Ethernet CSMA/CD and ANSI X3T9.5 standard.

100VG AnyLan: IEEE movement into fast Ethernet and Token Ring that appears to be going nowhere fast, mostly because it's not compatible with the 802.3 standards and Cisco doesn't support it.

Advantages of Fast Ethernet

Migrating or upgrading to 100BaseT from 10BaseT can substantially improve network throughput and overall performance. Because 100BaseT uses the same signaling techniques as 10BaseT, a gradual migration to 100BaseT doesn't have to be expensive or time consuming. Partially converting your LAN is a viable alternative to converting all clients simultaneously. The advantages of 100BaseT over 10BaseT are as follows:

- 100BaseT has 10 times the performance of 10BaseT

- Existing cabling and network equipment can be used

- It can use 10Mbps and 100Mbps together

- It uses tried-and-true CSMA/CD technology

- Migration is easy

And now, the catch: There can be some cost involved in replacing old NIC cards with new 10/100 cards, and it's possible that rewiring the building or floor might be necessary if the existing stuff's too old.

100BaseT Specifications

100BaseT networks use the same time slots that 10BaseT networks do. What do we mean by time slots? Time slots require a station to transmit all its bits before another station can transmit its packet. For 100BaseT networks to transmit in the same time slots, the distance must be reduced. This means that instead of the 5-4-3 rule that the standard Ethernet uses (5 network segments, 4 repeaters, only 3 segments populated) you can use only two Class II repeaters in a 100BaseT network. The timing in FastEthernet is shorter (10% of Ethernet). Max frame size or "time slot" is 1518 bytes. The physical distance is reduced because both Fast and regular Ethernet specifications state that the round trip time must not exceed 512 bit times. Since FastEthernet transmits faster, a signal of 512 bits covers a shorter distance.

100BaseT Repeaters

You can still use repeaters in your network to extend the distance of your shared Ethernet network or in switches with dedicated segments. Repeaters may actually reduce 100BaseFX max distances, because the repeater delays eat up the timing budget. It will, however, extend 100BaseTX distances. The different types of repeaters available are:

- Class 1: A translational repeater that can support both 100BaseX and 100BaseT4 signaling. The allowable delay for a class I repeater is 140 bit times.

- Class 2: A transparent repeater has shorter propagation delay, but only supports either 100BaseX or 100BaseT4, not both at the same time. The allowable delay for a class II repeater is only 92 bit times.

- FastHub 300: A repeater compatible with the IEEE 802.3u standard for FastEthernet. The FastHub 300 delivers 10 times the performance of a 10BaseT hub.

Table 2.1 shows the cable type, connector type, and maximum distance between end nodes.

T A B L E 2.1: Cable Type, Connector Type, and Max Distance Between End Nodes

Port Type	Cable	Connector Type	Distance
100BaseTX	Category 5	RJ 45	100 meters
100BaseFX	50/125 or 62.5/125	SC/ST/MIC	412 meters Half-duplex restricted to 412m. No restrictions for full-duplex (distance restrictions due to signal attenuation still applies).

Table 2.2 shows the maximum distance with repeaters.

T A B L E 2.2: Maximum Distance with Repeaters

Standard or Repeater Type	Number of Repeaters	UTP Medium	UTP and Fiber Media (TX/FX)
802.3u	one class I repeater	200 meters	261 meters
	one class II repeater	200 meters	308 meters
	two class II repeaters	205 meters	216 meters
FastHub 300	one class II repeater	200 meters	318 meters
	two class II repeaters	223 meters	236 meters
FastHub 300, plus one 3rd party 100BaseT class II repeater	two class II repeaters	214 meters	226 meters

Summary

In this chapter, we covered the following key points:

- Network congestion problems (and their solutions) in Ethernet networks. How segmenting your LAN can increase bandwidth for users on the network

- LAN segmentation using bridges

- The benefits of network segmentation using correct bridge placement

- LAN segmentation using routers

- The benefits of network segmentation with routers

- LAN segmentation using switches, which are really just bridges with multiple ports

- The benefits of network segmentation with switches

- The three switching methods (of which only two are used by Cisco)

- The difference between cut-through and store-and-forward LAN switching

- The difference between full- and half-duplex and the requirements to run full-duplex

- The features and benefits of FastEthernet

- The guidelines and distance limitations of FastEthernet

- The operation and benefits of the Spanning-Tree Protocol

- The benefits of VLANs and frame tagging described

Review Questions

1. The maximum distance of a 10Base5 network is which of the following?

   A. 200 meters

   B. 500 meters   *P 37*

   C. 1000 meters

   D. 1500 meters

2. The CSMA/CD Ethernet IEEE committee is defined as which of the following?

   A. 802.2

   B. 802.5

   C. 802.3   *P 36-37*

   D. 802.4

3. CSMA/CD stands for which of the following?

   A. Collision Sense, Multiple Access with Carrier Detect

   B. Collision Sense, Multiple Access with Collision Detect

   C. Carrier Sense, Multiple Access with Collision Detect   *P. 37*

   D. Carrier Sense, Mac Address with Collision Detect

4. Which of the following is a characteristic of a switch, but not of a repeater?

   A. Switches forward packets based on the IPX or IP address in the frame.

   B. Switches forward packets based only on the IP address in the packet.   *P59*

   C. Switches forward packets based on the IP address in the frame.

   D. Switches forward packets based on the MAC address in the frame.

5. How does the cut-through switching technique work?

    A. The LAN switch copies the entire frame into its onboard buffers and then looks up the destination address in its forwarding, or switching, table and determines the outgoing interface

    B. The switch waits only for the header to be received before it checks the destination address and starts forwarding the packets

    C. By using broadcast addresses as source addresses   *P.61*

    D. By using a Class II repeater in a collision domain

6. How do switches use store and forward?

    A. The switch waits only for the header to be received before it checks the destination address and starts forwarding the packets

    B. The LAN switch copies the entire frame into its onboard buffers and then looks up the destination address in its forwarding, or switching, table and determines the outgoing interface

    C. By using a class II repeater in a collision domain   *P61*

    D. By using broadcast addresses as source addresses

7. Choose all of the following that are needed to support full-duplex Ethernet.

    A. Multiple paths between multiple stations on a link

    B. Full-duplex NIC cards

    C. Loopback and collision detection disabled   *P65*

    D. Automatic detection of full-duplex operation by all connected stations

8. What two types of technology does 100BaseT use?

    A. Switching with 53-byte cells

    B. CSMA/CD

    C. IEEE 802.5   *P.67-68*

    D. 802.3u

9. Choose all of the following that are advantages to segmenting with routers.

~~A.~~ Manageability

~~B.~~ Flow control   *P 58 - ?*

~~C.~~ Explicit packet lifetime control

~~D.~~ Multiple active paths

10. Some advantages to segmenting with Bridges are_____

A. Datagram filtering

~~B.~~ Manageability   *P 29*

~~C.~~ Reliability

~~D.~~ Scalability

11. Which two of the following describe frame tagging?

A. Examines particular info about each frame

~~B.~~ A unique ID placed in the header of each frame as it traverses the switch fabric

~~C.~~ A user-assigned ID defined to each frame   *P 64 - 65*

D. The building of filter tables

12. Which of the following describes a full-duplex transmission?

A. Uses a single cable   *P 66*

~~B.~~ Uses a point-to-point connection from the transmitter of the transmitting station to the receiver of the receiving station

C. Data transmission in only both directions, but only one way at a time

D. Data transmission in only one direction

13. If a frame is received at a switch and only the destination hardware address is read before the frame is forwarded, what type of switching method are you using?

   A. Cut-through

   B. Store-and-forward

   C. Store-and-cut   *P 61*

   D. FragmentFree

14. Which of the following switching types is the default for Cisco 5505s?

   A. Cut-through

   B. Store-and-forward   *P 61*

   C. Store-and-cut

   D. FragmentFree

15. Which is true regarding store-and-forward switching method?

   A. It is default for all Cisco switches

   B. It only reads the destination hardware address before forwarding the frame

   C. Latency varies depending on frame length   *P 61*

   D. Latency is constant

16. What does the Spanning-Tree Algorithm (STA) do?

   A. STA is implemented by STP to prevent loops

   B. Forward packets through a switch   *P 62*

   C. Restores lost frames

   D. Prevents API duplication in bridged networks

17. Which can be true regarding VLANs? (Choose all that apply.)

   A. They are created by location

   B. They are created by function

   C. They are created by group   *P 64 ✓ switch.*

   D. They are created by department

18. What is the IEEE specification for Spanning Tree?

    A. 802.2u

    B. 802.3q

    ~~**C.** 802.1d~~   *p63*

    D. 802.6

19. Of the three switching types, which one has the lowest latency?

    ~~**A.** Cut-through~~

    B. FragmentFree

    C. Store-and-forward   *p61*

    D. None

20. Of the three switching types, which one has the highest latency?

    A. Cut-through

    B. FragmentFree

    ~~**C.** Store-and-forward~~   *p61*

    D. None

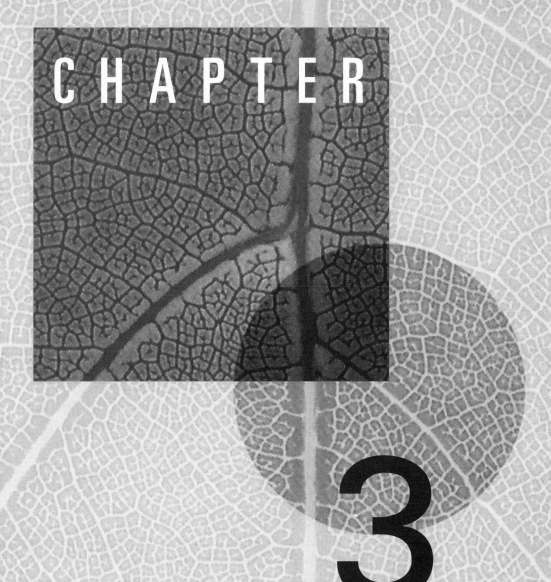

CHAPTER

3

TCP/IP and the DOD Reference Model

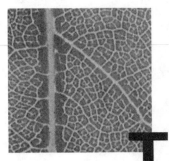

CP/IP was created by the Department of Defense as a protocol to ensure data integrity and preserve it as well as maintain communications in the event of catastrophic war. If designed and implemented correctly, a TCP/IP network can be a very dependable and resilient one. In this chapter, we'll cover the protocols of TCP/IP, and through this book, you'll learn how to create a marvelous TCP/IP network–using Cisco router, of course.

We'll start off by taking a look at the Department of Defense's version of TCP/IP, and then compare this version and protocols with the OSI reference model discussed in Chapter 1.

The CCNA test objectives covered in this chapter include:

- Identify the functions of the TCP/IP Transport-layer protocols

- Describe connection-oriented network service and connectionless network service, and identify the key differences between them

- Identify the functions of the TCP/IP Network-layer protocols

- Describe Data Link addresses and Network addresses, and identify the key differences between them

- Identify the functions performed by ICMP

- Describe the two parts of network addressing, then identify the parts in specific protocol address examples

- Define and describe the functions of a MAC address

The DOD Reference Model

The DOD model is a condensed version of the OSI model. It is comprised of four, instead of seven, layers:

- Process/Application
- Host-to-Host
- Internet
- Network Access

Figure 3.1 shows a comparison of the four-layer DOD model and the seven-layer OSI reference model. As you can see, the two are similar in concept, but each has a different number of layers with different names.

FIGURE 3.1

The DOD model and
the OSI model

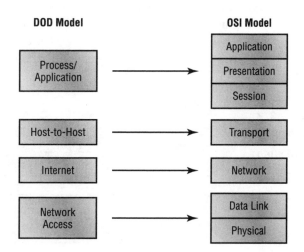

A vast array of protocols combine at the DOD model's Process/Application layer to integrate the various activities and duties spanning the focus of the OSI's corresponding top three (Session, Presentation, and Application) layers. (We'll be looking closely at those protocols in the next part of this chapter.) The Process/Application layer defines protocols for node-to-node application communication and also controls user interface specifications.

The Host-to-Host layer parallels the functions of OSI's Transport layer, defining protocols for setting up the level of transmission service for applications. It tackles issues like creating reliable end-to-end communication and ensuring the error-free delivery of data. It handles packet sequencing and maintains data integrity.

The *Internet layer* corresponds to the OSI's Network layer, designating the protocols relating to the logical transmission of packets over the entire network. It takes care of the addressing of hosts by giving them an IP (Internet Protocol) address, and handles the routing of packets among multiple networks. It also controls the communication flow between two hosts.

At the bottom of the model, the Network Access layer monitors the data exchange between the host and the network. The equivalent of the Data Link and Physical layers of the OSI model, it oversees hardware addressing and defines protocols for the physical transmission of data.

While the DOD and OSI models are alike in design and concept and have similar functions in similar places, *how* those functions occur are different. This difference requires the DOD model to have a very different suite of protocols than those of the OSI model. Figure 3.2 shows the TCP/IP protocol suite and how its protocols relate to the DOD model layers.

FIGURE 3.2

The TCP/IP
protocol suite

DOD Model

| Process/ Application | Telnet | FTP | LPD | SNMP |
| | TFTP | SMTP | NFS | X window |

| Host-to-Host | TCP | | UDP | |

| Internet | ICMP | BootP | ARP | RARP |
| | IP | | | |

| Network Access | Ethernet | Fast Ethernet | Token Ring | FDDI |

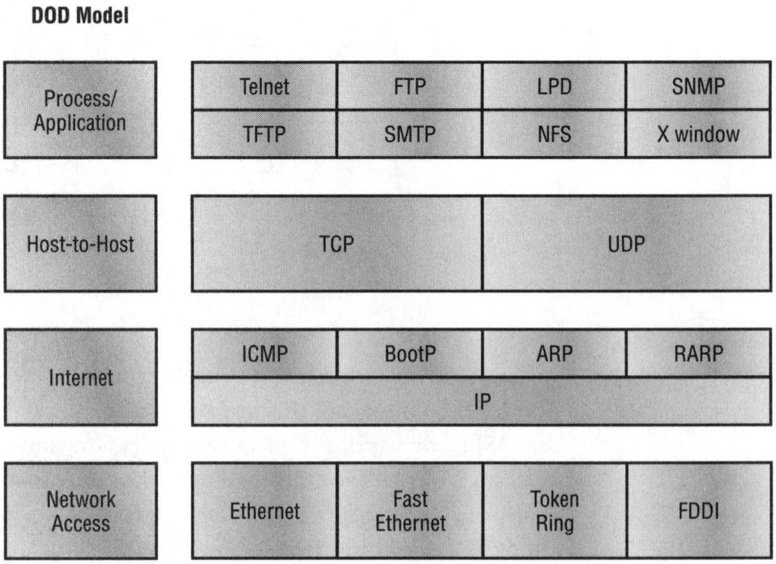

Process/Application Layer Protocols

As we explored earlier, one of the design goals of the original creators of the Internet was to have applications that could run on different computer platforms, in different places, and yet, somehow, still communicate. The answer came in the form of Process/Application layer protocols, which address the ability of one application to communicate with another, regardless of hardware platform, operating system, and other features of the two hosts.

Most applications written with TCP/IP protocols can be characterized as *client/server* applications. This means that there are two major parts to the software involved and that they are probably running on two different machines.

The server part of this software duo usually runs on the machine where the data is actually residing. It tends to be powerful, because much of the data processing and storage is done on it. It works like this: The client software sends requests to the server software for it to fulfill. Some typical requests include searches for information, printing, e-mailing, application services, and file transfers.

In addition to communicating with the server, another function of client software is to provide an interface for the user. It also permits you to tweak the data you've gotten from the server.

These matters explained, we'll move along and investigate the types of protocols that populate the DOD model's Process/Application layer and what they do.

Telnet

The chameleon of protocols, Telnet's specialty is terminal emulation. It allows a user on a remote client machine, called the Telnet client, to access the resources of another machine, the Telnet server. Telnet achieves this by pulling a fast one on the Telnet server and making the client machine appear as though it were a terminal directly attached to the local network. This projection is actually a software image, a virtual terminal that can interact with the chosen remote host. These emulated terminals are of the text-mode type and can execute refined procedures like displaying menus that give users the opportunity to choose options from them and access the applications on the duped server. Users begin a Telnet session by running the Telnet client software and then logging on to the Telnet server.

Telnet's capabilities are limited to running applications or snooping around on the server. It can't be used for file sharing functions like downloading information. To actually get the goods, you have to use the next protocol on the list: FTP.

FTP (File Transfer Protocol)

FTP is the protocol that actually lets us transfer files; it can facilitate this between any two machines that are using it. But FTP isn't just a protocol; it's also a program. Operating as a protocol, FTP is used by applications. As a program, it's employed by users to perform file tasks by hand. FTP also allows for access to both directories and files and can accomplish certain types of directory operations, like relocating into different ones. FTP teams up with Telnet to transparently log you in to the FTP server and then provides for the transfer of files.

Accessing a host through FTP is only the first step, though. Users must then be subjected to an authentication login that's probably secured with passwords and usernames placed there by system administrators to restrict access. But you can get around this somewhat by adopting the username "anonymous"—only what you'll gain access to once you are in there will be limited.

Even when being employed by users manually as a program, FTP's functions are limited to listing and manipulating directories, typing file contents, and copying files between hosts. It can't execute remote files as programs.

TFTP (Trivial File Transfer Protocol)

TFTP is the stripped-down, stock version of FTP, though it's the protocol of choice if you know exactly what you want and where it's to be found. It doesn't give you the abundance of functions that FTP does. TFTP has no directory browsing abilities; it can do nothing but send and receive files. This compact little protocol also skimps in the data department, sending much smaller blocks of data than FTP, and there's no authentication as there is with FTP, so it's insecure. Few sites support it due to the inherent security risks.

Later in this book you'll use TFTP to download a new Internetwork Operating System (IOS) to your Cisco router.

NFS (Network File System)

This is a jewel of a protocol specializing in file sharing. It allows two different types of file systems to interoperate. It's like this: Suppose the NFS server software is running on an NT server, and the NFS client software is running on a Unix host. NFS allows for a portion of the RAM on the NT server to transparently store Unix files, which can, in turn, be used by Unix users. Even though the NT file system and the Unix file system are unlike—they have different case sensitivity, file-name lengths, security, and so on—both Unix users and the NT users can access that same file with their normal file systems, in their normal way.

Where Telnet, FTP, and TFTP are limited, NFS goes the extra mile. NFS can execute remote files as programs and has the ability to import and export material. It's what you're using when you manipulate applications remotely.

SMTP (Simple Mail Transfer Protocol)

SMTP, answering our ubiquitous call to e-mail, uses a spooled, or queued, method of mail delivery. Once a message has been sent to a destination, the message is spooled to a device—usually a disk. The server software at the destination posts a vigil, regularly checking this queue for messages. When it detects them, it proceeds to deliver them to their destination.

LPD (Line Printer Daemon)

This protocol is designed for printer sharing. The LPD daemon, along with the LPR (Line Printer) program, allows print jobs to be spooled and sent to the network's printers.

X Window

Designed for client-server operations, *X Window* defines a protocol for the writing of graphical user interface-based client/server applications. The idea is to allow a program, called a client, to run on one computer, and then allow it to display a program called a window server on another computer.

SNMP (Simple Network Management Protocol)

Just as doctors are better equipped to maintain the health of their patients when they have the patient's history in hand, network managers are at an advantage if they possess performance histories of the network in their care. These case histories contain valuable information that enables the manager to anticipate future needs and analyze trends. By comparing the network's present condition to its past functioning patterns, managers can more easily isolate and troubleshoot problems.

SNMP is the protocol that provides for the collection and manipulation of this valuable network information. It gathers data by polling the devices on the network from a management station at fixed or random intervals, requiring them to disclose certain information. When all is well, SNMP receives something called a *baseline*—a report delimiting the operational traits of a healthy network. This protocol can also stand as a watchman over the network, quickly notifying managers of any sudden turn of events. These network watchmen are called *agents,* and when aberrations occur, agents send an alert called a *trap* to the management station.

The sensitivity of the agent, or threshold, can be increased or decreased by the network manager. An agent's threshold is like a pain threshold; the more sensitive it is, the sooner it screams an alert. Managers use baseline reports to aid them in deciding on agent threshold settings for their networks. The more sophisticated the management station's equipment is, the clearer the picture it can provide of the network's functioning. More powerful management stations have better record-keeping ability, as well as the added benefit of being able to provide enhanced graphic interfaces that can form logical portraits of network structure.

Two of Cisco's software applications that use SNMP are CiscoWorks (for both LAN and WAN monitoring of routers and switches) and CWSI, Cisco-Works for Switched Internetworks (for monitoring and managing switches and VLANs).

Host-to-Host Layer Protocols

The Host-to-Host layer's main purpose is to shield the upper-layer applications from the complexities of the network. This layer says to the upper layer, "Just give me your data, with any instructions, and I'll begin the process of getting your information ready for sending." The following sections describe the two main protocols at this layer.

TCP (Transmission Control Protocol)

TCP has been around since networking's early years, when WANs weren't very reliable. It was created to mitigate that problem, so reliability is TCP's strong point. It tests for errors, resends data if necessary, and reports the occurrence of an error to the upper layers if it can't manage to solve the problem itself.

This protocol takes large blocks of information from an application and breaks them down into segments. It numbers and sequences each segment so the destination's TCP protocol can put the segments back into the order that the application intended on the receiving end. After these segments have been sent, TCP waits for acknowledgment for each one from the receiving end's TCP, re-transmitting the ones that haven't been acknowledged.

Before it starts to send segments down the model, the sender's TCP protocol contacts the destination's TCP protocol in order to establish a connection. What is created is known as a *virtual circuit*. This type of communication is called *connection-oriented*. During this initial handshake, the two TCP layers also agree on the amount of information that's going to be sent before the recipient's TCP sends back an acknowledgment. With everything agreed upon in advance, the path is paved for reliable Application-layer communication to take place.

TCP is a full-duplex, connection-oriented, reliable, accurate protocol, and establishing all these terms and conditions, in addition to checking for errors, is no small task. It's very complicated and, not surprisingly, very costly in terms of network overhead. Using TCP should be reserved for use only in situations when reliability is of utmost importance. This is because today's networks are much more reliable than those of yore, so the added reliability is often unnecessary.

TCP Segment Format   Since the upper layers just send a data stream to the protocols in the Transport layers, we'll demonstrate how TCP segments a data stream and prepares it for the Network layer. Figure 3.3 shows the TCP segment format.

FIGURE 3.3

TCP segment format

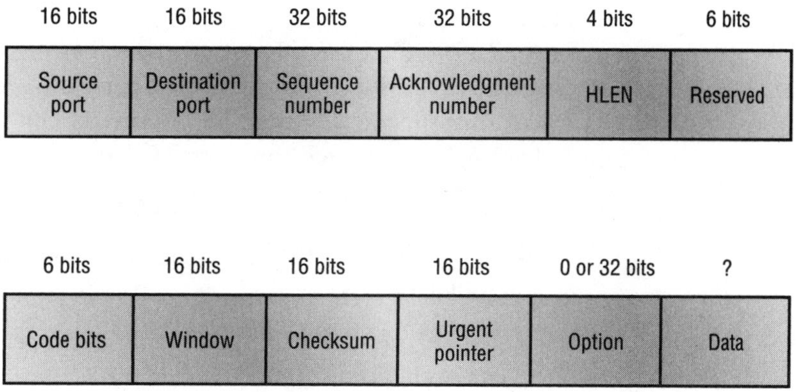

16 bits	16 bits	32 bits	32 bits	4 bits	6 bits
Source port	Destination port	Sequence number	Acknowledgment number	HLEN	Reserved

6 bits	16 bits	16 bits	16 bits	0 or 32 bits	?
Code bits	Window	Checksum	Urgent pointer	Option	Data

The definitions for the TCP segment are explained below:

- Source port: port or socket of the application that sent the data.

- Destination port: port or socket of application on the destination host.

- Sequence number: used to put the data back in the correct order, or to retransmit missing or damaged data.

- Acknowledgment number: defines which TCP octet is expected next.

- HLEN: header length defines the number of 32-bit words in the header.

- Reserved: always set to zero.

- Code bits: sets up and terminates a session.

- Window: the window size that the sender is willing to accept.

- Checksum: CRC, because TCP doesn't trust the lower layers and checks everything.

- Urgent Pointer: indicates the end of urgent data.

- Option: sets the maximum TCP segment size.

- Data: the data handed down to the TCP protocol at the Transport layer, which includes the upper-layer headers.

Port Numbers   TCP and UDP must use port numbers to communicate with the upper layers. Port numbers are used to keep track of different conversations crossing the network simultaneously. Originating source port numbers are dynamically assigned by the source host, usually some number greater than 1023.

RFC 1700 discusses what is called well-known port numbers. These are used by application developers in the network portion of their application. Check out Appendix E for more information on RFC 1700.

Figure 3.4 illustrates how both TCP and UDP use port numbers.

- Numbers 0–255 are used for public applications.

- Numbers 255–1023 are assigned to companies to use in their applications.

- Numbers above 1023 are used by the upper layers to set up sessions with other hosts, and by TCP to use as source and destination addresses in the TCP segment.

FIGURE 3.4

Port numbers for TCP and UDP

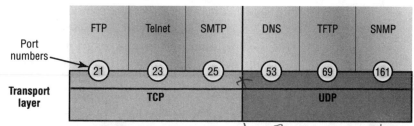

TCP can also access # 53, 69, 161   *UDP - can access also, port 21, 23, 25*

The following information shows a TCP session captured with Etherpeek.

```
TCP - Transport Control Protocol
   Source Port:       5973
   Destination Port: 1211
   Sequence Number:   1456389907
   Ack Number:        1242056456
   Offset:            5
   Reserved:          %000000
   Code:              %011000
            Ack is valid
            Push Request
   Window:            61320
   Checksum:          0x61a6
   Urgent Pointer:    0
   No TCP Options
   TCP Data Area:
   vL.5.+.5.+.5.+.5    76 4c 19 35 11 2b 19 35 11 2b 19 35 11
   2b 19 35
   .+.                 11 2b 19
   Frame Check Sequence:   0x0d00000f
```

As shown above, the source host makes up the source port, which in this case is 5972. The destination port is 1211, which was created by the destination station when it was first contacted for a session.

Okay, so why is it that the source and destination make up a port number? To differentiate between sessions with different hosts, that's why. How else would a server know where information is coming from if it didn't have a reservation number from a sending host? TCP and the upper layers don't use hardware and logical addresses to understand the sending host's address like the Data Link and Network layer protocols do. Instead, they use port numbers. It's easy to imagine the receiving host getting really confused if all the hosts used the same port number to get to FTP.

But there's an alternative to TCP's high overhead method of transmission—UDP.

UDP (User Datagram Protocol)

This protocol can be used in place of TCP. *UDP* is the scaled down economy model, and is considered a *thin protocol*. Like a thin person on a park bench, it doesn't take up a lot of room—in this case, on a network. It also doesn't offer all the bells and whistles of TCP, but it does do a fabulous job of transporting information that doesn't require reliable delivery—and it does it using far fewer network resources. (Please note that UDP is covered thoroughly in RFC 768.)

There are some situations where it would definitely be wise to opt for UDP rather than TCP. Remember the watchdog SNMP up there at the Process/Application layer? SNMP monitors the network sending intermittent messages and a fairly steady flow of status updates and alerts, especially when running on a large network. The cost in overhead necessary to establish, maintain, and close a TCP connection for each one of those little messages would reduce what would be an otherwise healthy, efficient network to a dammed-up bog in no time. Another circumstance calling for UDP over TCP is when the matter of reliability is already accomplished at the Process/Application layer. NFS handles its own reliability issues, making the use of TCP both impractical and redundant. However, this is decided by the application developer, not the user that wants to transfer data faster.

UDP receives upper-layer blocks of information, instead of streams of data like TCP, and breaks them into segments. Also like TCP, each segment is given a number for reassembly into the intended block at the destination. However, UDP does *not* sequence the segments and does not care in which order the segments arrive at the destination. At least it numbers them. But after that, UDP sends them off and forgets about them. It doesn't follow through, check up on, or even allow for an acknowledgment of safe arrival—complete abandonment. Because of this, it's referred to as an *unreliable* protocol. This does not mean that UDP is ineffective, only that it doesn't handle issues of reliability.

There are more things UDP doesn't do. It doesn't create a virtual circuit, and it doesn't contact the destination before delivering information to it. It is therefore also considered a *connectionless* protocol.

UDP Segment Format The very low overhead of UDP, which doesn't use windowing or acknowledgments, is shown in Figure 3.5.

FIGURE 3.5

UDP segment

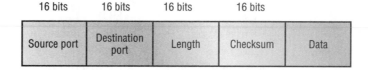

Since UDP assumes that the application will use its own reliability method, it doesn't use any. This gives an application developer a choice when running the Internet Protocol stack: TCP for reliability or UDP for faster transfers.

The UDP segment contains only the following information: source and destination ports, length of the segment, CRC, and data. UDP, like TCP, doesn't trust the lower layers and runs its own CRC. Remember that the Frame Check Sequence is the field that houses the CRC, which is why you can see the FCS information.

The following shows a UDP segment caught on a network analyzer:

```
UDP - User Datagram Protocol
   Source Port:          1085
   Destination Port:     5136
   Length:               41
   Checksum:             0x7a3c
   UDP Data Area:
   ..Z............    00 01 5a 96 00 01 00 00 00 00 00 11 00
00 00 00
   ...C..2...._C._C   2e 03 00 43 02 1e 32 0a 00 0a 00 80 43 00
80 43
        .                 00
Frame Check Sequence:   0x00000000
```

Notice the low overhead! Also, notice the ports are above 1023. This means that both the sending and receiving stations have had a previous session, so they already had port numbers set up to communicate with each other.

Take a look at the Sequence number, Ack number, and Window size. It is absent from the UDP segment. See, I wasn't making this stuff up!

Key Concepts of Host-to-Host Protocols

The following list highlights some of the key concepts that you should keep in mind regarding these two protocols.

TCP	UDP
Virtual circuit	Unsequenced
Sequenced	Unreliable
Acknowledgments	Connectionless
Reliable	Low overhead

Connection-Oriented and Connectionless Network Services

We've covered both connection-oriented and connectionless network services in the Transport layer and in the Host-to-Host layer. A telephone analogy might help you understand how TCP works. Most of us know that before you speak with someone on a phone, you must first establish a connection with that other person—wherever they might be. This is like a virtual circuit with the TCP protocol. If you were giving someone important information during your conversation, you might ask, "Did you get that?" A query like that is similar to a TCP acknowledgment. From time to time, for various reasons, people also ask, "Are you still there?" They end their conversations with a "goodbye" of some kind, putting closure on the phone call. These types of functions are also done by TCP.

Alternately, using UDP is like sending a postcard. To do that, you don't need to contact the other party first. You simply write your message, address it, and mail it. This is analogous to UDP's connectionless orientation. Since the message on the postcard is probably not a matter of life or death, you don't need an acknowledgment of its receipt. Similarly, UDP does not involve acknowledgments.

Internet Layer Protocols

There are two main reasons for the Internet layer's existence: routing, and providing a single network interface to the upper layers. None of the upper-layer protocols, and none of the ones on the lower layer, have any functions relating to routing. The complex and important task of routing is the job of the Internet layer. IP (Internet Protocol) essentially *is* the Internet layer. The other protocols found here merely exist to support it. IP contains the Big

Picture, and could be said to "see all," in that it is aware of all the interconnected networks. It can do this because all the machines on the network have a software, or logical, address called an IP address, which we'll cover more thoroughly later in this chapter.

IP looks at each packet's IP address. Then, using a routing table, it decides where a packet is to be sent next, choosing the best path. The Network Access-layer protocols at the bottom of the model don't possess IP's enlightened scope of the entire network; they deal only with physical links.

The second reason for the Internet layer is to provide a single network interface to the upper-layer protocols. Without this layer, application programmers would need to write "hooks" into every one of their applications for each different Network Access protocol. This would not only be a pain in the neck, but it would lead to different versions of each application—one for Ethernet, another one for Token Ring, and so on. To prevent this, IP provides one single network interface for the upper-layer protocols. That accomplished, it's then the job of IP and the various Network Access protocols to get along and work together.

All network roads don't lead to Rome—they lead to IP. And all the other protocols at this layer, as well as all those at the upper layers, use it. Never forget that. All paths through the model go through IP. The following sections describe the protocols at the Internet layer.

IP (Internet Protocol)

Identifying devices on networks requires answering these two questions: Which network is it on? And what is its ID on that network? The first answer is the *software, or logical address* (the correct street). The second answer is the *hardware address* (the correct mailbox). All hosts on a network have a logical ID called an IP address. This is the sofware, or logical, address and it contains valuable encoded information greatly simplifying the complex task of routing. (Please note that IP is discussed in RFC 791.)

IP receives segments from the Host-to-Host layer and fragments them into datagrams (packets). IP also reassembles datagrams back into segments on the receiving side. Each datagram is assigned the IP address of the sender and the IP address of the recipient. Each machine that receives a datagram makes routing decisions based upon the packet's destination IP address. Figure 3.6 shows an IP header.

The following fields make up the IP header:

- Version: IP version number.

FIGURE 3.6

IP Header

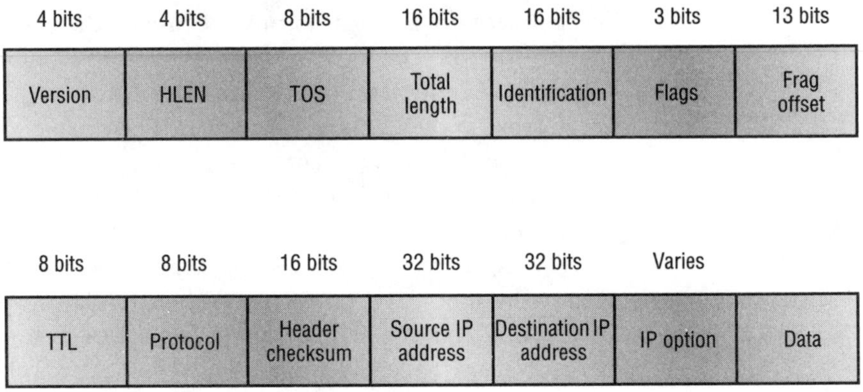

4 bits	4 bits	8 bits	16 bits	16 bits	3 bits	13 bits
Version	HLEN	TOS	Total length	Identification	Flags	Frag offset

8 bits	8 bits	16 bits	32 bits	32 bits	Varies	
TTL	Protocol	Header checksum	Source IP address	Destination IP address	IP option	Data

- HLEN: header length in 32-bit words.

- TOS: Type of Service tells how the datagram should be handled.

- Total Length: the length of the packet including header and data.

- Identification, Flags, Frag Offset: These provide fragmentation and reassembly if the packet is too large to put in a frame.

- TTL: Time to Live.

- Type or Protocol: port of upper-layer protocol (TCP is port 6 or UDP is port 17).

- Header checksum: Cyclic Redundancy Check or Frame Check Sequence (FCS).

- Source IP Address: 32-bit IP address of sending station.

- Destination IP address: the 32-bit IP address of the station this packet is destined for.

- IP Option: used for network testing, debugging, security, and more.

Here's a snapshot of an IP packet caught on a network analyzer (all the information discussed above is here):

```
IP Header - Internet Protocol Datagram
    Version:              4
    Header Length:        5
    Precedence:           0
```

```
Type of Service:        %000
Unused:                 %00
Total Length:           187
Identifier:             22486
Fragmentation Flags:    %010  Do Not Fragment
Fragment Offset:        0
Time To Live:           60
IP Type:                0x06  TCP
Header Checksum:        0xd031
Source IP Address:      10.7.1.30
Dest. IP Address:       10.7.1.10
No Internet Datagram Options
```

Notice we have logical, or IP addresses, in this header.

The type field—it's typically a protocol field, but this analyzer sees it as a type field—is important because if the header didn't carry the protocol information for the next layer, IP wouldn't know what to do with the data.

Figure 3.7 shows how IP sees the Transport layer.

FIGURE 3.7

The Protocol field in an IP header

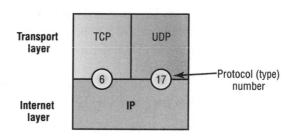

The protocol field tells IP to send the data to either TCP port 6 or UDP port 17.

ARP (Address Resolution Protocol)

When IP has a datagram to send, it has already been informed by upper-layer protocols of the destination's IP address. However, IP must also inform a Network Access protocol, such as Ethernet or Token Ring, of the destination's hardware address. If IP doesn't know the hardware address, it uses the ARP protocol to find this information. As IP's detective, ARP interrogates the network by sending out a broadcast asking the machine with the specified IP address to reply with its hardware address. In other words, ARP translates the software (IP) address into a hardware address—for example, the destination machine's Ethernet board address—and from it, deduces its whereabouts. This hardware address is technically referred to as the *media access control (MAC) address* or physical address. ARP is talked about in detail in IP address resolution at the end of this chapter.

RARP (Reverse Address Resolution Protocol)

When an IP machine happens to be a diskless machine, it has no way of initially knowing its IP address, but it does know its MAC address. The RARP protocol discovers the identity of these machines by sending out a packet that includes its MAC address, and a request to be informed of what IP address is assigned to that MAC address. A designated machine, called a RARP server, responds with the answer, and the identity crisis is over. RARP uses the information it does know about the machine's MAC address to learn its IP address and complete the machine's ID portrait.

BootP

BootP stands for *Bootstrap Protocol*. When a diskless workstation is powered on, it broadcasts a BootP request on the network. A BootP server hears the request and looks up the client's MAC address in its BootP file. If it finds an appropriate entry, it responds by telling the machine its IP address and the file—usually via the TFTP protocol—that it should boot from.

BootP is used by a diskless machine to learn the following:

- Its IP address

- The IP address of a server machine

- The name of a file that is to be loaded into memory and executed at boot up

ICMP (Internet Control Message Protocol)

ICMP is a management protocol and messaging service provider for IP. Its messages are carried as IP datagrams. *RFC 1256, ICMP Router Discovery Messages* is an annex to ICMP, which affords hosts extended capability in discovering routes to gateways. Periodically, router advertisements are announced over the network, reporting IP addresses for its network interfaces. Hosts listen for these network infomercials to acquire route information. A *router solicitation* is a request for immediate advertisements and may be sent by a host when it starts up. The following are some common events and messages that ICMP relates to:

- Destination unreachable: If a router can't send an IP datagram any further, it uses ICMP to send a message back to the sender advising it of the situation. For example, if a router receives a packet destined for a network that the router doesn't know about, it will send an ICMP Destination Unreachable message back to the sending station.

- Buffer full: If a router's memory buffer for receiving incoming datagrams is full, it will use ICMP to send out this message.

- Hops: Each IP datagram is allotted a certain number of routers that it may go through, called *hops*. If it reaches its limit of hops before arriving at its destination, the last router to receive that datagram deletes it. The executioner router then uses ICMP to send an obituary message, informing the sending machine of the demise of its datagram.

- Ping: Packet Internet Groper uses ICMP echo messages to check the physical connectivity of machines on an internetwork.

The following data is from a network analyzer catching an ICMP echo request. Notice that even though ICMP works at the Network layer, it still uses IP to do the ping request. The type field in the IP header is 0x01h for the ICMP protocol.

```
Flags:          0x00
Status:         0x00
Packet Length:78
Timestamp:      14:04:25.967000 05/06/1998
Ethernet Header
Destination:    00:a0:24:6e:0f:a8
Source:         00:80:c7:a8:f0:3d
Protocol Type:08-00   IP
IP Header - Internet Protocol Datagram
Version:             4
Header Length:       5
Precedence:          0
Type of Service:     %000
Unused:              %00
```

```
Total Length:           60
Identifier:             56325
Fragmentation Flags:    %000
Fragment Offset:        0
Time To Live:           32
IP Type:                0x01  ICMP
Header Checksum:        0x2df0
Source IP Address:      100.100.100.2
Dest. IP Address:       100.100.100.1
No Internet Datagram Options
```

<u>ICMP - Internet Control Messages Protocol</u>

```
ICMP Type:              8  Echo Request
Code:                   0
Checksum:               0x395c
Identifier:             0x0300
Sequence Number:        4352
ICMP Data Area:
abcdefghijklmnop    61 62 63 64 65 66 67 68 69 6a 6b 6c 6d
6e 6f 70
qrstuvwabcdefghi    71 72 73 74 75 76 77 61 62 63 64 65 66
67 68 69
Frame Check Sequence:   0x00000000
```

Network Access Layer Protocols

Programmers for the DOD model didn't define protocols for this layer; instead, their focus began at the Internet layer. In fact, this is exactly the quality that makes this model able to be implemented on almost any hardware platform. This versatility virtue is also one of the reasons the Internet protocol suite is so popular. Every protocol listed here relates to the physical transmission of data. The following are the Network Access layer's main duties:

- Receiving an IP datagram and framing it into a stream of bits—1s and 0s—for physical transmission. (The information at this layer is called a *frame*.) An example of a protocol that works at this level is CSMA/CD, or Carrier Sense, Multiple Access with Collision Detect. Again, purpose equals name. It checks the cable to see if there's already another

PC transmitting (Carrier Sense), allows all computers to share the same bandwidth (Multiple Access), and detects and retransmits collisions (Collision Detect). Essentially, it's the highway patrol of the Network Access layer.

- Specifying the MAC address. Even though the Internet layer determines the destination MAC address, it's the Network Access protocols that actually place the MAC address into the MAC frame.

- Ensuring that the stream of bits making up the frame has been accurately received by calculating a CRC (Cyclic Redundancy Checksum).

- Specifying the access methods to the physical network, such as *contention-based* for Ethernet (first come, first served), *token-passing* (wait for token before transmitting) for Token Ring and FDDI, and *polling* (wait to be asked) for IBM mainframes.

- Specifying the physical media, connectors, electrical signaling, and timing rules.

Frames

We caught some frames on our Etherpeek network analyzer for you. By looking at the different fields in the headers, you should be able to tell which type of frame you're looking at.

The frame below has only three fields: a destination, a source, and a type field. This is an Ethernet_II frame. Notice the Type field is IP or 08-00 in hexadecimal).

```
Destination:   00:60:f5:00:1f:27
Source:        00:60:f5:00:1f:2c
Protocol Type:08-00   IP
```

The next frame has the same fields, so it must also be an Ethernet_II frame. We put this one in so you could see that the frame can carry more than just IP. It can also carry IPX or 81-37h. Notice that this frame was a broadcast. You can tell because the destination hardware address is all 1s in binary, or all F's in hexadecimal.

```
Destination:   ff:ff:ff:ff:ff:ff Ethernet Broadcast
Source:        02:07:01:22:de:a4
Protocol Type:81-37   NetWare
```

Notice the length field. This must be an 802.3 frame. What protocol is this going to be handed to at the Network layer? It doesn't say in the frame, so it must be IPX. Why? Because when Novell created the 802.3 frame type (before the IEEE did), Novell was pretty much the only LAN server out there. So, Novell was assuming that if you're running a LAN, it must be IPX, there's nothing else, and why would we need a type or protocol field?

Times change, don't they?

```
Flags:          0x80   802.3
Status:         0x00
Packet Length:64
Timestamp:      12:45:45.192000 06/26/1998
Destination:    ff:ff:ff:ff:ff:ff Ethernet Broadcast
Source:         08:00:11:07:57:28
Length:         34
```

The next frame has a length field, so it's probably an 802.3, right? But look again, it also has a DSAP and a SSAP, so it has to be an 802.2 frame. (Remember that an 802.2 frame is an 802.3 frame with the LLC information in the header, so we know what the upper-layer protocol is.)

```
Flags:          0x80   802.3
Status:         0x02   Truncated
Packet Length:64
Slice Length:   51
Timestamp:      12:42:00.592000 03/26/1998
Destination:    ff:ff:ff:ff:ff:ff Ethernet Broadcast
Source:         00:80:c7:a8:f0:3d
LLC Length:     37
Dest. SAP:      0xe0   NetWare
Source SAP:     0xe0   NetWare  Individual LLC Sublayer
Management Function
Command:        0x03   Unnumbered Information
```

Take a look at Figure 3.8 and notice that the 802.2 frame type is specified to run through the LLC sublayer of the Data Link layer.

802.3 frames only go to the MAC sublayer and cannot use the LLC functions. 802.2 uses all the MAC sublayer specifications plus the management of the LLC to get the job done. One of the biggest differences is that the MAC

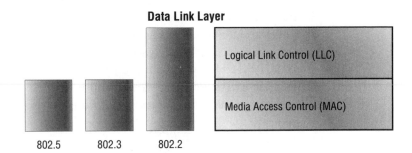

sublayer has error detection, while the LLC sublayer has error correction. This is why the 802.2 frame type is more efficient than the 802.3 frame type.

Physical and Logical Addressing

It's important to understand the difference between physical and logical addressing before getting into IP addressing in the Chapter 4.

Data-Link layer addressing, or physical (hardware) addressing, is a unique address that is burned into each NIC card by the manufacturer. Think of the hardware address like the address to your house. It's got to be different from the other addresses or your mail just isn't going to get to you. The hardware address is a 48-bit address expressed as six bytes as shown in Figure 3.9. The first three bytes, known as the vendor code, are given to the manufacturer by the IEEE. The IEEE administers this Organizational Unique Identifier (OUI) so there aren't any duplicate hardware addresses floating around. The second three bytes are made up by the manufacturer and are generally part of the serial number of the card.

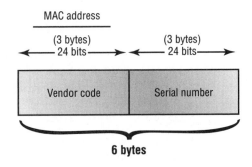

Logical addressing, sometimes referred to as virtual addressing, is used at the Network layer and is hierarchical in scheme, unlike physical addresses, which use a flat addressing scheme. The logical address defines more than the house on a street. The logical address can define the country, state, zip code, city, street, street address, and even the name. Examples of protocols that use logical addresses are IP and IPX.

Some of the technologies used to implement the Network Access layer are

- LAN-oriented protocols

  - Ethernet (thick coaxial cable, thin coaxial cable, twisted-pair cable)

  - FastEthernet

  - Token Ring

- WAN-oriented protocols

  - Point-to-Point Protocol (PPP)

  - X.25

  - Frame Relay

IP Address Resolution

The process of resolution involves asking a question and receiving an answer. In the case of IP address resolution, the question posed might be, "Which device is the owner of IP address 172.16.8.8?" The resolution, or answer, to that question would include the MAC address of the NIC, as encoded by the manufacturer. In essence, IP address resolution is the linking of an IP (or software address) to a hardware (or MAC) address.

Regardless of where the ultimate destination is located, ARP always uses a local broadcast to determine where data should be sent. If the destination happens to be on a remote network, the local default gateway's hardware address will be used to hop over to it. Once the mystery address has been resolved, it's recorded in a table called the ARP cache. If additional messages are sent to the same destination, the ARP cache will be checked first to prevent unnecessary network traffic generated by a broadcast.

You might also remember our discussion of RARP (Reverse Address Resolution Protocol). Like inductive vs. deductive reasoning, it is the inverse operation of ARP; it's used to get an IP address from a MAC address.

Local Resolution

Each subnet of the network can be thought of as an island that contains a city—say, Maui. So long as you never have to leave that island, you've remained local—or as is the case with computers, on the local network.

The process of resolving the IP address of a machine existing on the local network is shown in Figure 3.10 and outlined below. While reading through these steps, notice how ARP works in a way that minimizes network overhead.

FIGURE 3.10

Resolving a local
IP address

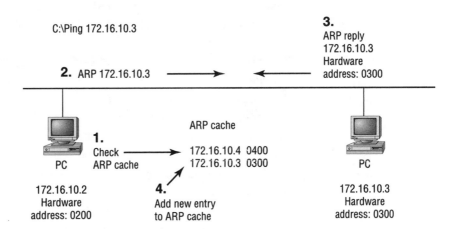

Step One: The destination machine's IP address is checked to see if it's on the local network. If so, the host system will then check its ARP cache for the machine's hardware address.

Step Two: Provided that the ARP address didn't find 172.16.10.3 in the host system's ARP cache, ARP will attempt to enter it by sending a message requesting the IP address's owner to send back its hardware address. Because the hardware address is still unknown, the ARP message is sent out as a broadcast that's read by each and every system on the local network. Like a self-addressed envelope that's sent inscribed with all the information necessary to get it back to its sender, both the IP address and the hardware address of the requesting system are included in the broadcast message.

Step Three: The reply message is sent directly to the hardware address of the requesting system. Only the owner of the requested IP address will respond. All other systems will disregard the request.

Step Four: Upon receiving the reply, the requesting machine will append the address into its ARP cache. Now we can begin to establish communication.

Let's take a look at an ARP request and reply captured with an Etherpeek network analyzer:

```
Flags:          0x00
  Status:         0x02  Truncated
  Packet Length:64     Slice Length:  42
  Timestamp:      14:04:25.966000 07/06/1998
Ethernet Header            ⌐oN
  Destination:  ff:ff:ff:ff:ff:ff Ethernet Broadcast
  Source:         00:80:c7:a8:f0:3d
  Protocol Type:08-06  IP ARP
ARP - Address Resolution Protocol
  Hardware:                  1  Ethernet (10Mb)
  Protocol:                  08-00  IP
  Hardware Address Length:   6
  Protocol Address Length:   4
  Operation:                 1  ARP Request
  Sender Hardware Address:   00:80:c7:a8:f0:3d
  Sender Internet Address:   100.100.100.2
  Target Hardware Address:   00:00:00:00:00:00  (ignored)
  Target Internet Address:   100.100.100.1
```

source { Sender Hardware Address / Sender Internet Address

Destination { Target Hardware Address / Target Internet Address

You should notice a few things right away:

- It used an Ethernet_II frame, and IP-ARP is the only Network layer protocol used, 08-06h—very efficient.

- The source hardware address is known, but the destination is a broadcast.

- The IP address for both the destination and source stations are known, but the destination's (target) hardware address is all 0s.

This is the ARP response to the ARP request. Notice that this next packet contains the hardware address of the source computer 100.100.100.1, which the computer ARP was trying to get the hardware address from.

```
Flags:          0x00
Status:         0x00
Packet Length:64
Timestamp:      14:04:25.966000 07/06/1998
Ethernet Header
  Destination:  00:80:c7:a8:f0:3d
  Source:       00:a0:24:6e:0f:a8
  Protocol Type:08-06  IP ARP
ARP - Address Resolution Protocol
  Hardware:                   1  Ethernet (10Mb)
  Protocol:                   08-00  IP
  Hardware Address Length:  6
  Protocol Address Length:  4
  Operation:                  2  ARP Response
  Sender Hardware Address:  00:a0:24:6e:0f:a8
  Sender Internet Address:  100.100.100.1
  Target Hardware Address:  00:80:c7:a8:f0:3d
  Target Internet Address:  100.100.100.2
Extra bytes (Padding):
  ...............  02 02 02 02 02 02 02 02 02 02 02 02 02
02 02 02
  ..                          02 02
Frame Check Sequence:  0x00000000
```

The router that I pinged from will then take this new hardware address and store it in its ARP cache as shown below:

```
Router# show arp
Protocol  Address         Age (min)   Hardware Addr   Type   Interface
Internet  100.100.100.1       0        00a0.246e.0fa8  ARPA   Ethernet0
Internet  100.100.100.2       0        0080.c7a8.f03d  ARPA   Ethernet0
Internet  100.100.100.3       -        00e0.1ea9.c418  ARPA   Ethernet0
```

At the router privilege mode prompt (#), I typed **show arp.** (We'll talk in detail about the different router commands in Chapters 5–12). This showed me the ARP cache. These entries were added into the cache after I pinged from 100.100.100.3 to IP addresses 100.100.100.1 and 100.100.100.2. Notice that I have three entries in my ARP cache: the router I pinged from and the two destination hosts. Let's talk about the ARP cache in a little more detail.

The ARP Cache

The ARP cache is a table used to store both IP addresses and their corresponding MAC addresses. Each time communication is initiated with another machine, it checks its ARP cache for a matching entry. If it doesn't find one, an ARP request is broadcasted, the address is resolved, and the resulting information is then entered into its ARP cache. The address is now handy for the next time communication with that device is necessary, much like an entry in your home address book would be. Additionally, the ARP cache maintains the hardware broadcast address (FFFFFFFF) for the local subnet as a permanent entry. Though it doesn't appear when the cache is viewed, this entry exists for the purpose of allowing a host to accept ARP broadcasts.

The ARP system is kind of like jail. Like all ARP entries (IP addresses have both a hardware address and a time stamp), every jail inmate has a number and exit date. In both cases, depending on the entry/inmate's behavior, the time spent "inside" will vary. Though lifetimes aren't definite for inmates, both ARP entries and inmates have them, along with maximum time periods for their duration. Old ARP entries are released early when the ARP cache becomes full, just as older inmates may be released early depending on the jail's capacity. Occasionally, a judge assigns the death penalty or consecutive lifetime sentences to an individual inmate—like making a manual entry into the ARP table. The only time these special inmates are released is when they die (are deleted from the ARP cache); a pardon is given, allowing the inmate to begin a new life (restarting the computer); or if the system discovers it has the wrong person (a broadcast notifying ARP of a new, corrected hardware address).

Remote Resolution

When it comes to computer operations, communications are usually much simpler if they involve devices within the local network. These processes can't always be simple, though. Complex internetworks with subnets have bridges or routers set up between them that connect them together. These devices are filters that serve to sort data according to its destination—they don't allow all data to cross indiscriminately.

To distinguish which data gets to pass through, routers look at the IP address destination located in the packet's header, whereas bridges look at a frame's header for the destination hardware address. Going back to our subnet island of Maui, let's say you find it necessary to contact someone or something that doesn't reside there, but exists on another island—Molokai. Since those who populate Molokai aren't Maui locals, by attempting to make contact with them, you are attempting remote communication. Let's pretend that to reach them, you must cross a drawbridge. Unless you arrive at the drawbridge with a specific remote Molokai address, the bridge operator will keep the bridge drawn, and you won't be allowed to cross.

Figure 3.11 and the steps immediately following it illustrate the process of resolving the IP address of a machine located on a remote network. These steps are repeated at every router the data encounters en route to its final destination.

FIGURE 3.11

Resolving a remote IP address

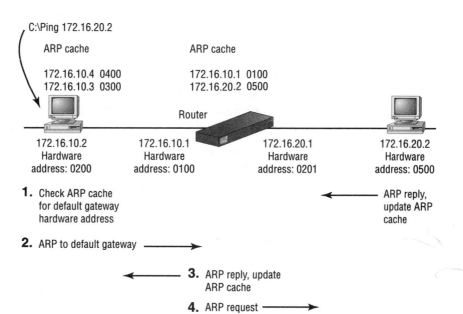

Step One: The destination IP address is checked to see if it's on the local network. Once determined otherwise, the system will check its local route table for a path to the remote network. If a path is found the ARP cache is checked for the hardware address of the default gateway specified in the routing path.

Step Two: When an entry for the default gateway isn't found, an ARP request is generated to determine the hardware address of the default gateway or router (see Figure 3.11). Since the only thing that is known about the destination is that it's on a remote network, the router will be used as the medium to reach the remote destination.

Step Three: The router will reply with its hardware address to the requesting host. The source host will then use ICMP to issue an echo request back to the router but addressed to the destination host, which will then deliver the echo request to the remote network, that will eventually reach the destination host. The router will then repeat Step One (that is, check if it's local or remote), and then take action accordingly. Generally, unless a routing path is found at the server, steps one through three are repeated until the client machine is on a local network. Note that the router can use either a broadcast or its cache in determining the hardware address of the destination host.

Step Four: The destination host will also respond to the ARP request with an ARP reply. Since the requesting system is on a remote network, that reply will be sent to the router. (It would respond to a ping request with an ICMP echo reply sent to the source host.) As with previous resolutions, if the router (default gateway) is not in the ARP cache, a local IP address resolution scenario will take place to determine the router's address.

Now, to validate this, we are going to ping from my station with an IP address of 100.100.100.2, with a default gateway of 100.100.100.3, to host 200.200.200.1, located on a remote subnet. First, let's take a look into the cache. I am at a Windows 95 workstation, so the command is arp –a. The output looks like this:

```
C:\>arp -a
No ARP Entries Found
```

Having no entries is typical because in a Windows environment, the ARP cache times out after only two minutes if a particular entry isn't used. By comparison, the ARP entries in a Cisco router last for four hours!

Let's ping the remote host of 200.200.200.1 and see what the ARP cache does.

```
C:\>ping 200.200.200.1
Pinging 200.200.200.1 with 32 bytes of data:
Reply from 200.200.200.1: bytes=32 time=25ms TTL=254
Reply from 200.200.200.1: bytes=32 time=22ms TTL=254
Reply from 200.200.200.1: bytes=32 time=22ms TTL=254
Reply from 200.200.200.1: bytes=32 time=22ms TTL=254
C:\>arp -a
Interface: 100.100.100.2
```

Internet Address	Physical Address	Type
100.100.100.3	00-e0-1e-a9-c4-18	dynamic

What's important to note here is that we received only the hardware address of our router, or default gateway: address 100.100.100.3. The router then "ARP'd" to the remote host and received the hardware address for IP address 200.200.200.1 as shown in the router's ARP cache:

```
Router# show arp
```

Protocol	Address	Age (min)	Hardware Addr	Type	Interface
Internet	200.200.200.1	0	0000.0c8d.5c9d	ARPA	Ethernet1
Internet	100.100.100.1	111	00a0.246e.0fa8	ARPA	Ethernet0
Internet	100.100.100.2	0	0080.c7a8.f03d	ARPA	Ethernet0
Internet	100.100.100.3	–	00e0.1ea9.c418	ARPA	Ethernet0

Summary

In this chapter, we covered the following key points:

- The functions of the TCP/IP Transport layer protocols. How the TCP/IP protocol stack protocols work at each layer of the DOD model and where they reside.

- Connection-oriented network service and connectionless network service and the key differences between them.

- The functions of the TCP/IP Network layer protocols. How the various protocols all work with IP at the Internet layer of the DOD stack.

- Data Link addresses and Network addresses and the key differences between them. How hardware addresses are assigned by the manufacturer and the difference between a hardware and a logical address.

- The functions performed by ICMP. The ICMP protocol specifics and how it works at the Internet layer of the DOD stack.

- The two parts of network addressing and the parts in specific protocol address examples.

Review Questions

1. What is the port number for TCP?

   A. 6

   B. 11

   C. 17   *P 92*

   D. 45

2. What is the port number for UDP?

   A. 6

   B. 11

   C. 17   *P93*

   D. 45

3. User Datagram Protocol works at which layer of the DOD model?

   A. Transport

   B. Internet

   C. Host-to-Host   *P 88, 90*

   D. Data Link

4. Which protocol works at the Internet layer and is responsible for making routing decisions?

   A. TCP

   B. UDP

   ~~**c.**~~ IP   *P 90*

   D. ARP

5. Which protocol will send a message to routers if a network outage or congestion occurs?

   A. IP

   B. ARP

   ~~**c.**~~ ICMP   *P94*

   D. TCP

6. Which port numbers are used by TCP and UDP to set up sessions with other hosts?

   A. 1-255

   B. 256-1022

   ~~**c.**~~ 10*2*3 and above *1024*   *P 86*

   D. 6 and 10 respectively

7. Which of the following is true?

   A. TCP is connection-orientated; UDP uses acknowledgements only

   B. Both TCP and UDP are connection-oriented, but only TCP uses windowing   *P. 85, 88,   P.90*

   ~~**c.**~~ TCP is connection-oriented, but UDP is connectionless

   D. TCP and UDP both have sequencing, but UDP is connectionless

8. Which protocol is used to manage and monitor the network?

   A. FTP

   B. SMTP

   C. SNMP   P 84

   D. IP

9. Which frame type use DSAPs and SSAPs to identify the upper-layer protocol?

   A. 802.3

   B. 802.5

   C. 802.2   P 98

   D. Ethernet_II

10. Which frame has a Type field to identify the upper-layer protocol?

   A. 802.2

   B. 802.5

   C. 802.3   P 97

   D. Ethernet_II

11. What does the acronym ARP stand for?

   A. ARP Resolution Protocol

   B. Address Restitution Protocol

   C. Address Resolution Phase   P 93

   D. Address Resolution Protocol

12. Ping uses which Internet layer protocol (besides IP)?

   A. ARP

   B. RARP

   C. DCMP

   D. ICMP   P 95

13. Which protocol sends redirects back to an originating router?

   A. ARP

   B. RARP

   C. ICMP *p95*

   D. BootP

   E. IP

   F. TCP

   G. UDP

14. Which of the following protocols are used to get an IP address from a known MAC address?

   A. ARP

   B. RARP *p94*

   C. ICMP

   D. BootP

   E. IP

   F. TCP

   G. UDP

15. Which of the following protocols is used to give an IP address to a diskless machine?

   A. ARP

   B. RARP

   C. ICMP

   D. BootP *p94*

   E. IP

   F. TCP

   G. UDP

16. Which two of the following protocols are used at the Transport layer?

    A. ARP

    B. RARP

    C. ICMP

    D. BootP

    E. IP

    F. TCP *p 84*

    G. UDP *p 88*

17. Which protocol gets a hardware address from a known IP address?

    A. ARP *p 93*

    B. RARP

    C. ICMP

    D. BootP

    E. IP

    F. TCP

    G. UDP

18. Which of the following is a connectionless protocol at the Transport layer?

    A. ARP

    B. RARP

    C. ICMP

    D. BootP

    E. IP

    F. TCP

    G. UDP *p 88*

19. If a router in your internetwork experienced congestion on serial port 0, which protocol will let the neighbor routers know?

   A. ARP

   B. RARP

   C. ICMP

   D. BootP

   E. IP

   F. TCP

   G. UDP

20. Which protocol is used for booting diskless workstations?

   A. ARP

   B. RARP

   C. ICMP

   D. BootP   *p 94*

   E. IP

   F. TCP

   G. UDP

CHAPTER

4

IP Addressing

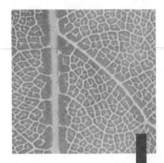

In this chapter, we'll probe further into the basics of TCP/IP and examine the supremely important subject of how accurate communication is achieved between specific networks and host systems through proper IP addressing. We'll discuss how and why that communication happens, the causes of failure when it does not, and how to configure devices on both LANs and WANs to ensure the solid performance of your network.

The CCNA test objectives covered in this chapter include:

119 • Describe the different classes of IP addresses (and subnetting)

119 • Configure IP addresses

119 • Verify IP addresses

What Is IP Addressing?

One of the most important topics in any discussion of TCP/IP is IP addressing. An *IP address* is a numeric identifier assigned to each machine on an IP network. It designates the location of the device it is assigned to on the network. As mentioned earlier, this type of address is a software address, not a hardware address—the latter is hard-coded in the machine or network interface card.

The Hierarchical IP Addressing Scheme

An IP address is made up of 32 bits of information. These bits are divided into four sections containing 1 byte (8 bits) each. These sections are referred to as *octets*. There are three methods for depicting an IP address:

- Dotted-decimal, as in 130.57.30.56

- Binary, as in 10000010.00111001.00011110.00111000

- Hexadecimal, as in 82 39 1E 38

All of these examples represent the same IP address.

The 32-bit IP address is a structured or hierarchical address, as opposed to a flat or nonhierarchical one. Although either type of addressing scheme could have been used, the hierarchical variety was chosen for a very good reason.

A good example of a flat addressing scheme is a social security number. There's no partitioning to it, meaning that each segment isn't allocated to numerically represent a certain area or characteristic of the object it's assigned to. The advantage of this scheme is that it can handle a large number of addresses, namely 4.2 billion (a 32-bit address space with two possible values for each position—either 0 or 1—gives you 2^{32}, or 4.2 billion). The disadvantage of this scheme, and the reason it's not used for IP addressing, relates to routing. If every address were unique, all routers on the Internet would need to store the address of each and every machine on the Internet. This would make efficient routing impossible even if only a fraction of the possible addresses were used.

The solution to this dilemma is to use a three-level, hierarchical addressing scheme that is structured by network, subnet, and host. An example of this is a telephone number. The first section of a telephone number, the area code, designates a very large area. The second section of the number, the prefix, narrows the scope to a local calling area. The final segment, the customer number, zooms in on the specific connection. IP addresses use the same type of layered structure. Rather than all 32 bits being treated as a unique identifier, as in flat addressing, a part of the address is designated as the network address, and the other part is designated as the node address.

The network address uniquely identifies each network. Every machine on the same network shares that network address as part of its IP address. In the IP address 172.16.30.56, for example, 172.16 is the network address.

The node address is assigned to, and uniquely identifies, each machine on a network. This part of the address must be unique because it identifies a particular machine—an individual—as opposed to a network, which is a group. This number can also be referred to as a host address. In the sample IP address 172.16.30.56, .30.56 is the node address.

The designers of the Internet decided to create classes of networks based on network size. For the small number of networks possessing a very large number of nodes, they created the rank *Class A network*. At the other extreme is the *Class C network*, reserved for the numerous networks with a small number of nodes. The class distinction for networks between very large and very small is predictably called the *Class B network*. Subdividing an IP address into a network and node address is determined by the class designation of one's network. Table 4.1 provides us with a summary of the three classes of networks, which will be described in much more detail throughout this chapter.

T A B L E 4.1: Summary of the Three Classes of Networks

Class	Format	Leading bit pattern	Decimal range of first byte of network address	Maximum networks	Maximum nodes per network
A	Net.Node.Node.Node	0	~~1–127~~ 1–126	127	16,777,214
B	Net.Net.Node.Node	10	128–191	16,384	65,534
C	Net.Net.Net.Node	110	192–223	2,097,152	254

To ensure efficient routing, Internet designers defined a mandate for the leading bits section of the address for each different network class. For example, since a router knows that a Class A network address always starts with a 0, the router might be able to speed a packet on its way after reading only the first bit of its address. Figure 4.1 illustrates how the leading bits of a network address are defined.

F I G U R E 4.1

Leading bits of a network address

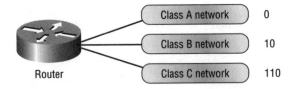

Some IP addresses are reserved for special purposes, and shouldn't be assigned to nodes by network administrators. Table 4.2 lists the members of this exclusive little club and why they're included in it.

T A B L E 4.2: Reserved IP Addresses

Address	Function — EXCEPTIONS
Network address of all 0s	Interpreted to mean "this network or segment."
Network address of all 1s	Interpreted to mean "all networks." Remember our broadcast examples of all Fs? All Fs is hexadecimal for all 1s in binary.
Network 127	Reserved for loopback tests. Designates the local node and allows that node to send a test packet to itself without generating network traffic.
Node address of all 0s	Interpreted to mean "this node."
Node address of all 1s	Interpreted to mean "all nodes" on the specified network; for example, 128.2.255.255 means "all nodes" on network 128.2 (Class B address). broadcast.
Entire IP address set to all 0s	Used by Cisco routers to designate the default route.
Entire IP address set to all 1s (same as 255.255.255.255)	Broadcast to all nodes on the current network; sometimes called an "all 1s broadcast."

Class A Networks

In a Class A network, the first byte is assigned to the network address, and the three remaining bytes are used for the node addresses. The Class A format is

Network.Node.Node.Node

For example, in the IP address 49.22.102.70, 49 is the network address, and 22.102.70 is the node address. Every machine on this particular network would have the distinctive network address of 49.

Class A network addresses are a byte long, with the first bit of that byte reserved (see Table 4.1) and the seven remaining bits available for manipulation. This means that the maximum number of Class A networks that can be created would be 128. Why? Because each of the seven bit positions can either be a 0 or a 1, thus 2^7 or 128. But to complicate things further, it was also decided that the network address of all 0s (0000 0000) would be reserved to designate the default route (see Table 4.2). This means the actual number of usable Class A network addresses is 128 minus 1, or 127.

Take a peek in the decimal-to-binary chart in Appendix D and see this for yourself. Start at binary 0 and view the first bit (the leftmost bit). Continue down through the chart until the first bit turns into the digit 1. See that? Sure enough, the decimal range of a Class A network is 0 through 127. Since the Much Ado About Nothing Address (all 0s) is one of those special clubmembers, the range of network addresses for a Class A network is 1 through 127. Table 4.2 shows us that another Class A number in that reserved club is number 127. This little revelation technically brings the total down to 126.

Each Class A network has three bytes (24-bit positions) for the node address of a machine. That means there are 2^{24}—or 16,777,216—unique combinations, and therefore precisely that many possible unique node addresses for each Class A network. Because addresses with the two patterns of all 0s and all 1s are reserved, the actual maximum usable number of nodes for a Class A network is 2^{24} minus 2, which equals 16,777,214.

Class B Networks

In a Class B network, the first two bytes are assigned to the network address, and the remaining two bytes are used for node addresses. The format is

Network.Network.Node.Node

For example, in the IP address 172.16.30.56, the network address is 172.16, and the node address is 30.56.

With a network address being two bytes of eight bits each, there would be 2^{16} unique combinations. But the Internet designers decided that all Class B networks should start with the binary digits 1 and 0. This leaves 14 bit positions to manipulate; therefore 16,384 (2^{14}) unique Class B networks.

If you take another peek at the decimal-to-binary chart in Appendix D, you will see that the first two bits of the first byte are 1 0, from decimal 128 up to 191. So, if you see a network address with the first byte in the range of decimal 128 to 191, you know it's a Class B network.

A Class B network has two bytes to use for node addresses. This is 2^{16} minus the two reserved patterns (all 0s and all 1s), for a total of 65,534 possible node addresses for each Class B network.

Class C Networks

The first three bytes of a Class C network are dedicated to the network portion of the address, with only one measly byte remaining for the node address. The format is

Network.Network.Network.Node

In the example IP address 192.168.100.102, the network address is 192.168.100, and the node address is 102.

In a Class C network, the first three bit positions are always the binary 110. The calculation is such: 3 bytes, or 24 bits, minus 3 reserved positions, leaves 21 positions. There are therefore 2^{21} or 2,097,152 possible Class C networks.

Referring again to that decimal-to-binary chart in Appendix D, you will see that the lead bit pattern of 110 starts at decimal 192 and runs through 223. Remembering our handy, non-calculatory, easy-recognition method, this means that although there are a total of 2,097,152 Class C networks possible, you can always spot a Class C address if the first byte is between 192 and 223.

Each unique Class C network has one byte to use for node addresses. This leads to 2^8 or 256, minus the two reserved patterns of all 0s and all 1s, for a total of 254 node addresses for each Class C network.

Additional Classes of Networks

Another class of networks is Class D. This range of addresses is used for multicast packets. The range of numbers is from 224.0.0.0 to 239.255.255.255.

There is also a Class E range of numbers starting at 240.0.0.0 and running to 255.255.255.255. These numbers are reserved for future use.

Unless you revel in chaos and desire to add stress to your life, both Class D and E addresses should not be assigned to nodes on your network.

Who Assigns Network Addresses?

If your network will be connected to the Internet, you have to petition the official Internet authorities for the assignment of a network address. An official Internet organization called the Network Information Center (NIC) can assist you in this process. For further information, contact:

Network Solutions
InterNIC Registration Services
505 Huntmar Park Drive
Herndon, VA 22070

You may also obtain help by sending e-mail to: hostmaster@internic.net.

If your network won't be connected to the Internet, you're free to assign any network address you wish.

For the most part, you're now able to obtain valid IP addresses from your Internet Service Provider (ISP). The NIC prefers you to do it that way, as it cuts down on the work it has to do.

Subnetting a Network

If an organization is large and has a lot of computers, or if its computers are geographically dispersed, it makes good sense to divide its huge network into smaller ones connected together by routers. The benefits to doing things this way include:

- Reduced network traffic. We all appreciate less traffic of any kind. Networks are no different. Without trusty routers, packet traffic could grind the entire network down to a near standstill. With routers, most traffic will stay on the local network; only packets destined for other networks will pass through the router.

- Optimized network performance. This is a bonus of reduced network traffic.

- Simplified management. It's easier to identify and isolate network problems in a group of smaller networks connected together than within one gigantic one.

- Facilitated spanning of large geographical distances. Because WAN links are considerably slower and more expensive than LAN links, having a single large network spanning long distances can create problems in every arena listed above. Connecting multiple smaller networks makes the system more efficient.

All this is well and good, but if an organization with multiple networks has been assigned only one network address by the NIC, that organization has a problem. As the saying goes, "Where there is no vision, the people perish." The original designers of the IP protocol envisioned a much smaller Internet with only tens of networks and hundreds of hosts. Their addressing scheme used a network address for each physical network.

As you can imagine, this scheme and the unforeseen growth of the Internet created a few problems. To name one, a single network address can be used to refer to multiple physical networks. However, an organization can request individual network addresses for each one of its physical networks. If every request were granted, there wouldn't be enough to go around.

Another problem relates to routers. If each router on the Internet needed to know about each existing physical network, routing tables would be impossibly huge. There would be an overwhelming amount of administrative overhead to maintain those tables, and the resulting physical overhead on the routers would be massive (CPU cycles, memory, disk space, and so on).

An additional consequence is that because routers exchange routing information with each other, a horrible overabundance of network traffic would result.

Although there's more than one way to approach this tangle, the principal solution is the one that we'll be covering in this chapter: subnetting.

What's subnetting? Subnetting is a TCP/IP software feature that allows for dividing a single IP network into smaller, logical subnetworks. This trick is achieved by using bits from the host portion of an IP address to create something called a subnet address.

Implementing Subnetting

As you know, the IP addressing scheme used for subnets is referred to as subnetting. Before you implement subnetting, you need to determine your current requirements and plan for future conditions. Follow these guidelines:

1. Determine the number of required network IDs.

   A. One for each subnet

   B. One for each wide area network connection

2. Determine the number of required host IDs per subnet.

   A. One for each TCP/IP host

   B. One for each router interface

3. Based on the above requirement, create

   A. One subnet mask for your entire network

   B. A unique subnet ID for each physical segment

   C. A range of host IDs for each subnet

Subnetting is network procreation. It is the act of creating little subnetworks from a single, large parent network. An organization with a single network address can have a subnet address for each individual physical network. Each subnet is still part of the shared network address, but it also has an additional identifier denoting its individual subnetwork number. This identifier is called a subnet address.

This practice solves several addressing problems. First, if an organization has several physical networks but only one IP network address, it can handle the situation by creating subnets. Next, because subnetting allows many physical networks to be grouped together, fewer entries in a routing table are required, notably reducing network overhead. Finally, all of the above combine to collectively yield greatly enhanced network efficiency.

For example, suppose that the Internet refers to Acme Inc. only by its single network address: 182.16. Suppose that Acme Inc. has several divisions, each dealing with a different department. Since Acme's network administrators have implemented subnetting, when packets come into its network, the Acme routers use the subnet addresses to route the packets to the correct internal subnet. Thus, the complexity of Acme Inc.'s network can be hidden from the rest of the Internet. This is called *information hiding*.

Information hiding also benefits the routers inside the Acme network. Without subnets, each Acme router would need to know the address of each machine on the entire Acme network—a bleak situation, creating additional overhead and poor routing performance. Because of the subnet scheme, which alleviates the need for each router to know about every machine on the entire Acme network, the company's routers need only two types of information:

- The addresses of each machine on the subnet to which it is attached

- The other subnet addresses

How to Implement Subnetting

Subnetting is implemented by assigning a subnet address to each machine on a given physical network. For example, in Figure 4.2, each machine on subnet 4 has a subnet address of 4.

Next, let's take a look at how a subnet address is incorporated into the rest of the IP address. The network portion of an IP address can't be altered. Every machine on a particular network must share the same network address. In Figure 4.3, you can see that all of Acme Inc.'s machines

FIGURE 4.2
The use of subnets

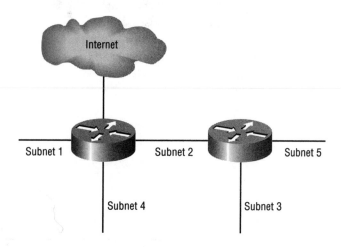

Subnet 1   Subnet 2   Subnet 5

Subnet 4   Subnet 3

Network Address 182.16.0.0
All hosts use network address 182.16

have a network address of 182.16. That principle is constant. In subnetting, it's the host address that's manipulated. The subnet address scheme takes a part of the host address and redesignates it as a subnet address. Bit positions are stolen from the host address to be used for the subnet identifier. Figure 4.3 shows how an IP address can be given a subnet address.

FIGURE 4.3
An IP address
can be given a
subnet address by
manipulating the
host address.

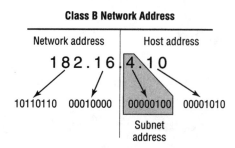

Class B Network Address

Network address   Host address

1 8 2 . 1 6 . 4 . 1 0

10110110   00010000   00000100   00001010

Subnet
address

Since the Acme Inc. network is of the Class B variety, the first two bytes refer to the network address, and are shared by all machines on the network—regardless of their particular subnet. Here, every machine's address on the subnet must have its third byte read 0000 0100. The fourth byte, the host address, is the unique number that identifies the actual host. So in reality, the IP address now has three parts: the network address, the subnet address, and the host address.

Figure 4.4 illustrates how a network address and a subnet address can be used. The same concepts and practices apply to each subnet created in the network.

FIGURE 4.4

A network address and
a subnet address

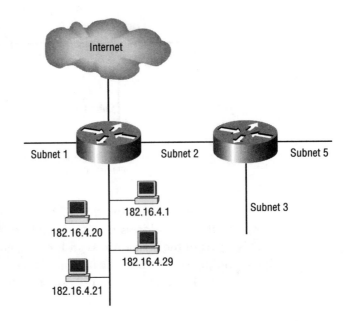

Subnet Masks

For the subnet address scheme to work, every machine on the network must know which part of the host address will be used as the subnet address. This is accomplished by assigning a subnet mask to each machine.

The network administrator creates a 32-bit subnet mask comprised of 1s and 0s. The 1s in the subnet mask represent the positions that refer to the network or subnet addresses. The 0s represent the positions that refer to the host part of the address. These concepts are illustrated in Figure 4.5.

In our Acme Inc. example, the first two bytes of the subnet mask are 1s because Acme's network address is a Class B address (formatted Net.Net .Node.Node). The third byte, normally assigned as part of the host address, is now used to represent the subnet address. Hence, those bit positions are represented with 1s in the subnet mask. The fourth byte is the only part in our example that represents the unique host address.

FIGURE 4.5

A subnet mask

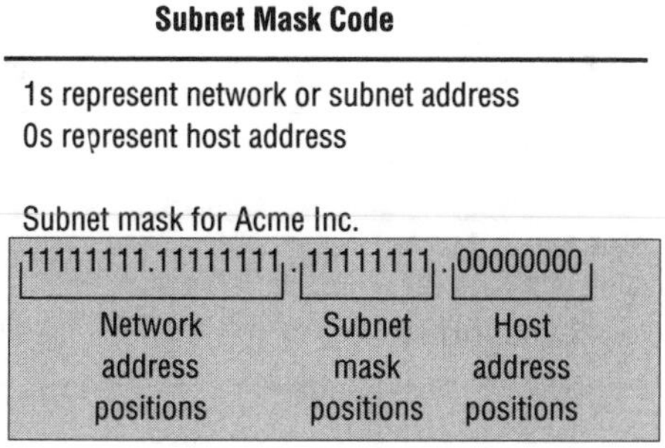

Subnet Mask Code

1s represent network or subnet address
0s represent host address

Subnet mask for Acme Inc.

11111111.11111111 . 11111111 . 00000000

Network	Subnet	Host
address	mask	address
positions	positions	positions

The subnet mask can also be denoted using the decimal equivalents of the binary patterns. The binary pattern of 1111 1111 is the same as decimal 255 (see the decimal-to-binary chart in Appendix D). Consequently, the subnet mask in our example can be denoted in two ways, as shown in Figure 4.6.

FIGURE 4.6

Subnet mask depiction

Subnet mask in binary:
11111111.11111111.11111111.00000000

Subnet mask in decimal:
255.255.255.0

All networks don't need to have subnets, meaning they don't need to use subnet masks. In this event, they are said to have a default subnet mask. This is basically the same as saying they don't have a subnet address. The default subnet masks for the different classes of networks are shown in Table 4.3. These cannot change. In other words, you cannot make a Class B subnet mask read 255.0.0.0. The host you try to assign this to will read this as invalid and typically won't even let you type it in. For a Class A network, you cannot change the first byte in a subnet mask; it must read 255.0.0.0 at a minimum. You also cannot assign 255.255.255.255, as this is all 1s and a broadcast address. A Class B address must start with 255.255.0.0, and a Class C must start with 255.255.255.

Once the network administrator has created the subnet mask and assigned it to each machine, the IP software views its IP address through the subnet mask to determine its subnet address. The IP software looks at its IP address through the lens of its subnet mask to see its subnet address. An illustration of an IP address being viewed through a subnet mask is shown in Figure 4.7.

T A B L E 4.3:   Default Subnet Mask

Class	Format	Default subnet mask
A	Net.Node.Node.Node	255.0.0.0
B	Net.Net.Node.Node	255.255.0.0
C	Net.Net.Net.Node	255.255.255.0

F I G U R E 4.7

IP address viewed through a subnet mask

Subnet Mask Code

1s represent network or subnet address
0s represent host address

Subnet mask   Subnet address positions
11111111.11111111 . 11111111 . 00000000

IP address of host on subnet 4
10110110 . 00010000 . 00000100 . 00010100
(182.16.4.20)
                      Bits related to subnet address

In this example, the IP software learns through the subnet mask that, instead of being part of the host address, the third byte of its IP address is now going to be used as a subnet address. The IP software then looks at the bit positions in its IP address that correspond to the mask, which are 0000 0100.

By using the entire third byte of a Class B address as the subnet address, it's easy to set and determine the subnet address. For example, if Acme Inc. wants to have a Subnet 12, the third byte of all machines on that subnet will be 0000 1100.

Using the entire third byte of a Class B network address for the subnet leaves room for a fair number of available subnet addresses. One byte dedicated to the subnet provides eight bit positions. Each position can be either a 1 or a 0, so the calculation is 2^8, or 256. But because you cannot use the two patterns of all 0s and all 1s, you must subtract two, for a total of 254. Thus, Acme Inc. can have up to 254 total subnetworks, each with 254 hosts.

Although the official IP specification (RFCs) limits the use of 0 as a subnet address, some products do permit it. For example, by adding special commands into your Cisco router it will allow you to use an all-0 subnet mask.

This allows one additional subnet number. For example, if the subnet mask was eight bits, instead of $2^8 = 256 - 2 = 254$, it would be $256 - 1 = 255$. But Cisco routers will not do this by default.

WARNING   Allowing a subnet address of 0 (all 0s) increases the number of subnet numbers by one. However, you shouldn't use this subnet address unless all of the software on your network recognizes this convention.

The formulas for calculating the maximum number of subnets and the maximum number of hosts per subnet are

$2^{\text{(number of masked bits in subnet mask)}} - 2 = $ maximum number of subnets

$2^{\text{(number of unmasked bits in subnet mask)}} - 2 = $ maximum number of hosts per subnet

In these formulas, *masked* refers to bit positions of 1, and *unmasked* refers to positions of 0. The 1s represent the subnet address and the 0s represent the host address. Figure 4.8 shows an example of how these formulas can be applied.

F I G U R E   4.8

Subnet and node
formulas

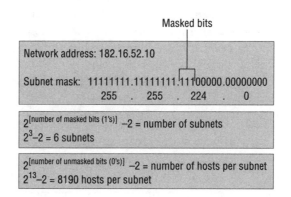

So if we were to take the number of masked bits (3) and use the above formula, we would have $2^3 - 2 = 6$. We then have six subnets. We have five bits left in the third octet and 8 bits from the fourth octet for addressing hosts. This is 13 bits for host addressing or $2^{13} - 2 = 8190$ hosts per subnet.

The downside to using an entire byte of a node address as your subnet address (255.255.255.0) is that you reduce the possible number of node addresses on each subnet. As explained earlier, without a subnet, a Class B address has 65,534 unique combinations of 1s and 0s that can be used for node addresses.

If you use an entire byte of the node address for a subnet, you then have only one byte for the host addresses, leaving only 254 possible host addresses. If any of your subnets will be populated with more than 254 machines, you have a problem. To solve it, you would either need to shorten the subnet mask, thereby lengthening the host address, or add a secondary IP address to your router interface, which would allow you more potential host addresses. But a side effect of this solution is that it reduces the number of possible subnets. Time to prioritize!

Figure 4.9 shows an example of using a smaller subnet address. Our company, Acme Inc., expects to need a maximum of 14 subnets. In this case, Acme does not need to take an entire byte from the host address (the third octet) for the subnet address. To get its 14 different subnet addresses, it only needs to snatch four bits from the host address ($2^4 - 2 = 14$). The host portion of the address has 12 usable bits remaining ($2^{12} - 2 = 4094$). Each of Acme's 14 subnets could then potentially have a total of 4094 host addresses or 4094 machines on each subnet.

Wait a minute, this is confusing! All those numbers—how can you ever remember them? Well, let's step back a minute and take a look at the different classes of networks and how to subnet each one. We'll start with Class C because it uses only eight bits and is the easiest to calculate.

Subnet Masks on Class C Networks

As you know, a Class C network uses the first three bytes (24 bits) to define the network address. This leaves us eight bits (1 byte) to address our hosts. If we want to create subnets, our options are limited because of the small number of bits available.

So, if you're going to break down your subnets smaller than the default Class C, figuring out the subnet mask, network number, broadcast address, and router address can get kind of confusing. Table 4.4 summarizes how you can break a Class C network down into one, two, four, or eight smaller subnets, with the subnet masks, network numbers, broadcast addresses, and router addresses. The first three bytes have simply been designated "x.y.z."

Suppose you want to chop up a Class C network, 192.168.100.x, into two subnets. As you see in the table, you'd use a subnet mask of 255.255.255.128 for each subnet. The first subnet would have network number 192.168.100.0, router

FIGURE 4.9

Using four bits of the
host address for a
subnet address

Acme, Inc.

Network Address:	132.8 (Class B; net.net.host.host)
Example IP Address:	1000 0100. 0000 1000. 0001 0010. 0011 1100
Decimal:	182 . 16 . 18 . 60

Subnet Mask Code

1s = Positions representing network or subnet addresses

0s = Positions representing the host address

Subnet Mask:

Binary:	1111 1111. 1111 1111. 1111 0000. 0000 0000
Decimal:	255 . 255 . 240 . 0

(The decimal '240' is equal to the binary '1111 0000.'
Refer to Appendix D: Decimal to Binary Chart.)

Positions relating to the subnet address.

Subnet Mask: 1111 1111. 1111 1111. 1111 0000. 0000 0000

IP address of a Acme machine: 1000 0100. 0000 1000. 0001 0010. 0011 1100
(Decimal: 182.16.18.60)

Bits relating to the subnet address.

Binary to Decimal Conversion for Subnet Address

Subnet Mask Positions:	1	1	1	1	0	0	0	0
Position / Value: ←— (continue)	128	64	32	16	8	4	2	1
Third Byte of IP address:	0	0	0	1	0	0	1	0
Decimal Equivalent:						0 + 16 = 16		
Subnet Address for this IP address:						16		

T A B L E 4.4:   Breaking a Class C Network into Subnets

Number of Desired Subnets	Subnet Mask	Network Number	Router Address	Broadcast Address	Remaining Number of IP Addresses
1	255.255.255.0	x.y.z.0	x.y.z.1	x.y.z.255	253
2	255.255.255.128	x.y.z.0	x.y.z.1	x.y.z.127	125
		x.y.z.128	x.y.z.129	x.y.z.255	125
4	255.255.255.192	x.y.z.0	x.y.z.1	x.y.z.63	61
		x.y.z.64	x.y.z.65	x.y.z.127	61
		x.y.z.128	x.y.z.129	x.y.z.191	61
		x.y.z.192	x.y.z.193	x.y.z.255	61
8	255.255.255.224	x.y.z.0	x.y.z.1	x.y.z.31	29
		x.y.z.32	x.y.z.33	x.y.z.63	29
		x.y.z.64	x.y.z.65	x.y.z.95	29
		x.y.z.96	x.y.z.97	x.y.z.127	29
		x.y.z.128	x.y.z.129	x.y.z.159	29
		x.y.z.160	x.y.z.161	x.y.z.191	29
		x.y.z.192	x.y.z.193	x.y.z.223	29
		x.y.z.224	x.y.z.225	x.y.z.255	29

address 192.168.100.1, and broadcast address 192.168.100.127. You could assign IP addresses 192.168.100.2 through 192.168.100.126 to 125 different IP addresses. The second subnet would have network number 192.168.100.128, router address 192.168.100.129, and broadcast address 192.168.100.255.

Now, you're probably wondering how can you subnet a Class C network like the ones we talked about in the table above? If you use the 2^x-2 calculation, the subnet 128 in the table doesn't make sense. Remember that subnet 0 is supposed to be a bad idea according to the RFCs; but by using subnet 0, you can subnet your Class C network with a subnet mask of 128. This uses only one bit, and by our trusty calculator, $2^1-2 = 0$ subnets. However, by putting in the ip subnet-zero command in your Cisco routers, you can then assign 1–127 for hosts in subnet zero and 129–254 for hosts in the 128 subnet as stated in the table. This saves you a lot of addresses. If you were to stick to the RFCs, then the best you'd be able to get is a subnet mask of 192

(2 bits). $2^2-2 = 2$. This gives you two subnets. What are these subnets anyway?

To figure out the actual valid subnets, use the following formula: 256 minus the subnet mask. In this example it would be 256–192 = 64, making 64 your first subnet. Keep adding the first subnet number to itself until you reach the subnet number. For example, 64 plus 64 equals 128. Your second subnet is 128. 128 plus 64 is 192. 192 is the subnet mask, so you can't use this as an actual subnet. This makes your valid subnets 64 and 128. What are the valid hosts you can assign in each subnet?

The numbers between the subnets are your valid hosts. For example, the valid host in a Class C network with a subnet mask of 192 are

Subnet 64: 65–126, which gives you 62 hosts per subnet. What happened to 127 as a valid host? Using 127 would mean your host bits would be all 1s—not allowed because it's used as the broadcast address for that subnet.

Subnet 128: 129–190. Huh? What happened to 191 through 254? The subnet mask is 192, which you can't use, and 191 would be all 1s and your broadcast address. Anything above 192 is also invalid for this subnet.

As you can see, this wastes a lot of precious addresses—130 to be exact. In a Class C network this would be hard to justify, and the 128 subnet is a much better solution if you need only two subnets.

What happens if you need four subnets in a Class C network? By using the calculation of $2^{\text{number of masked bits}}-2$, you would need 3 bits to get 6 subnets ($2^3-2 = 6$). What are the valid subnets and what are the valid hosts of each subnet? 11100000 is 224 in binary and would be the subnet mask. This must be the same on all workstations.

If a workstation has an incorrect mask, it could cause the router to assume that workstation is on a different subnet than it actually is. If this happens, the router won't forward packets to the workstation. Additionally, if the mask is incorrectly specified in the workstation's configuration, that workstation, which also looks at the mask, will send packets to the default gateway when it shouldn't.

To figure out the valid subnets, use: 256–224 = 32. This is your first subnet. The other subnets would be 64, 96, 128, 160, 192. The valid hosts are the numbers between the subnet numbers minus the all-1s address as shown in Table 4.5.

TABLE 4.5 Valid Hosts in Subnet 255.255.255.224	Subnet	Hosts
	32	33–62
	64	65–94
	96	97–126
	128	129–158
	160	161–190
	192	193–222

Let's add one more bit to the subnet mask and see what happens. We were using 3 bits, which gave us 224. By adding another bit, the mask now becomes 240 (11110000). By using 4 bits for the subnet mask, we get: $2^4-2 = 14$ subnets. This also gives us only 4 bits for the host addresses, or 14 hosts per subnet. As you can see, the amount of hosts per subnet decreases rather quickly when subnetting a Class C network. What are the valid subnets and hosts for each subnet?

254–240 = 14: The valid hosts are the numbers between the subnets, minus the all-1s address as shown in Table 4.6.

Let's do all this again, except with a Class B network.

Subnet Masks on Class B Networks

As you already know, a Class B network has 16 bits for host addresses. This gives us plenty of bits to play with when figuring out a subnet mask. Again, you must start with the leftmost bit and work toward the right when creating a subnet mask. For example, a Class B network would look like the following:

X.Y.0.0 with the default mask of 255.255.0.0.

Using the default mask would give you one network, with 65,534 hosts. The default mask in binary is

11111111.11111111.00000000.00000000.

TABLE 4.6	Subnet	Hosts
Valid Hosts in Subnet 240	16	17–30
	32	33–46
	48	49–62
	64	65–78
	80	81–94
	96	97–110
	112	113–126
	128	129–142
	144	145–158
	160	161–174
	176	177–190
	192	193–206
	208	209–222
	224	225–238

The 1s represent the network, and the 0s represent the hosts. So when you create a subnet mask, the leftmost unmasked bit(s) will be borrowed from the host's bits to become the subnet mask.

If we use only one bit, this would give us a mask of 255.255.128.0. With 16 bits, we typically don't need to worry about a shortage of host IDs, so using 128 isn't worth the trouble of putting the ip subnet-zero command in our router and figuring out our valid hosts. The first mask you should use is 255.255.192.0, or 11111111.11111111.11000000.00000000.

Throughout the rest of this chapter, we will bold the bits used for subnetting. This will help identify the difference between the three parts of an IP address: network, subnet, and hosts.

We now have our three parts of the IP address. The network address, the subnet address, and the host address. You figure out a 192 mask in the same way that you figure out a Class C 192 address—$2^2-2 = 2$ subnets—but you end up with a lot more hosts. The valid subnets would be 256–192 = 64 and 128. However, there are 14 bits (0s in the mask) left over for host addressing. This gives us $2^{14}-2 = 16,382$ hosts per subnet as shown in Table 4.7.

T A B L E 4.7	Subnet	Hosts
Valid Hosts in a 192 Subnetwork	64	X.Y.64.1 through X.Y.127.254
	128	X.Y.128.1 through X.Y. 191.254

Let's add another bit to our subnet mask. That would make it 11111111.11111111.**111**00000.00000000 or 255.255.224.0. $2^3-2 = 6$ subnets.

The valid subnets are 32 (256–224 = 32), 64, 96, 128,160, and 192. This gives us the valid hosts shown in Table 4.8:

T A B L E 4.8	Subnet	Hosts
Valid Hosts in a 224 Subnet	32	X.Y.32.1 through 63.254
	64	X.Y.64.1 through 95.254
	96	X.Y.96.1 through 127.254
	128	X.Y.128.1 through 159.254
	160	X.Y.160.1 through X.Y.191.254
	192	X.Y.192.1 through X.Y.223.254

So, the verdict is... we can get six subnets each with 8190 hosts if we use a 255.255.224.0 subnet mask.

Let's add a few more bits to the subnet mask and see what we get. If we use nine bits for the mask, this would give us $2^9-2 = 510$ subnets. With only seven bits for hosts we have $2^7-2 = 126$ hosts per subnet. The mask would look like this:

11111111.11111111.**11111111**.10000000 or 255.255.255.128.

Let's add even more bits and see what happens. If we use 14 bits for the subnet mask, we get $2^{14}-2 = 16,382$ subnets, but this gives us only $2^2-2 = 2$ hosts per subnet. The subnet mask would look like this:

11111111.11111111.**11111111**.11111100 or 255.255.255.252.

Why would you ever do this? Well believe it or not, this is very common Say you have a Class B network and are using a subnet mask of 255.255.255.0. This gives you 254 subnets and 254 hosts per subnet, right? But what if you have a network with many WAN links? Typically, you can have a direct connection between each site. Each of these links must be on their own subnet or network. How many hosts will be on these subnets? Two: one address for each router port. If you used the mask as described previously (255.255.255.0), you'd waste 252 host addresses per subnet. But by using the 255.255.255.252 subnet mask, you have tons of subnets available, each with only two hosts. However, you can do this only if you're running a routing algorithm like EIGRP or OSPF. The routing protocols allow what is called VLSM, or variable length subnet masks. This means you can run the 255.255.255.252 subnet mask on your interface to the WAN and run 255.255.255.0 on your router interfaces in your LAN. This works because the routing protocols like EIGRP and OSPF transmit the subnet mask information in the update packets that it sends to other routers. RIP and IGRP don't support this feature. This'll be covered in more detail later in the book.

Is this getting any better? Let's not stop now; we still have Class A networks to subnet!

Subnet Masks on Class A Networks

Class A networks have a huge number of addresses we can use to create subnets with. A default Class A network subnet mask is only eight bits or 255.0.0.0. This gives us 32 bits to play with.

If you use a mask of 11111111.1111111.00000000.00000000, or 255.255.0.0, this will give you eight bits for subnets or $2^8-2 = 254$ subnets. This leaves 16 bits for hosts, or $2^{16}-2 = 65,534$ hosts per subnet. That's a lot of hosts! So, what are the valid hosts anyway? The valid hosts are shown in Table 4.9.

How about if we split the subnets down the middle with 16 bits for the subnets and 16 bits for hosts? If you did, the mask would then look like this: 11111111.**11111111**.11110000.00000000 or 255.255.240.0.

T A B L E 4.9	Subnet	Hosts
Valid Hosts within a Class A Network	1	X.1.0.1 through X.1.255.254
	2	X.2.0.1 through X.2.255.254
	3	X.3.0.1 through X.3.255.254
This continues to...		
	252	X.252.0.1 through X.252.255.254
	253	X.253.0.1 through X.253.255.254
	254	X.254.0.1 through X.254.255.254
	0.16	X.0.16.1 through X.0.31.254
	0.32	X.0.32.1 through X.0.47.254
	0.48	X.0.48.1 through X.0.63.254
Etc., etc., etc...up to:		
	0.192	X.0.192.1 through X.0.207.254
	0.208	X.0.208.1 through X.0.223.254
	0.224	X.0.224.1 through X.0.239.254
	0.240	X.0.240.1 through X.0.255.254
Repeat for each second octet value:		
	1.0	X.1.0.1 through X.1.15.254
	1.16	X.1.16.1 through X.1.31.254
	1.32	X.1.32.1 through X.1.47.254
	1.48	X.1.48.1 through X.1.63.254
All the way up to:		
	255.192	X.255.192.1 through X.255.207.254
	255.208	X.255.208.1 through X.255.223.254
	255.224	X.255.224.1 through X.255.239.254

$2^{12}-2 = 4094$ subnets each with 4094 hosts. Sounds pretty good for a Class A network, don't you think? Did you figure out the valid hosts and subnets yet? It's a little more complicated than with our Class C examples. Well okay, it's a lot more complicated.

The second octet will be somewhere between 0 and 255. However, the third octet is something you need to figure out. Since the third octet has a 240 mask, you should get 256–240 = 16. The third octet has to start with 16, and it'll be the first subnet. The second subnet will be 32 and so on. This would make your valid subnets and hosts as shown in Table 4.10.

Subnets X.0.0 and X.255.240 are not valid because they are subnet-zero and broadcast address, respectively.

Can This Be Made Easier?

Now that we've been through the process of subnetting Class A, B, and C networks, you're probably wondering (hoping) if there's an easier way. Well, maybe. Because different people learn in different ways, I'm going to show you an alternate process, and you decide which works best for you.

Table 4.10 shows the different subnet masks available for a Class A network. This table starts off with 30 bits—the most that a subnet mask can be.

T A B L E 4.10: Subnet Masks Available for a Class A Network

Subnet Mask	Length of Subnet Mask (bits)	Number of Subnets	Number of Hosts Per Subnet
255.255.255.252	30	4,194,302	2
255.255.255.248	29	2,097,150	6
255.255.255.240	28	1,048,574	14
255.255.255.224	27	524,286	30
255.255.255.192	26	262,142	62
255.255.255.128	25	131,070	126
255.255.255.0	24	65,534	254
255.255.254.0	23	32,766	510

T A B L E 4.10:   Subnet Masks Available for a Class A Network *(cont.)*

Subnet Mask	Length of Subnet Mask (bits)	Number of Subnets	Number of Hosts Per Subnet
255.255.252.0	22	16,382	1,022
255.255.248.0	21	8,190	2,046
255.255.240.0	20	4,094	4,094
255.255.224.0	19	2,046	8,190
255.255.192.0	18	1,022	16,382
255.255.128.0	17	510	32,766
255.255.0.0	16	254	65,534
255.254.0.0	15	126	131,070
255.252.0.0	14	62	262,142
255.248.0.0	13	30	524,286
255.240.0.0	12	14	1,048,574
255.224.0.0	11	6	2,097,150
255.192.0.0	10	2	4,194,302

Remember that the default mask doesn't count against the bits used in the subnet mask. So even if the mask was 255.255.255.0, you are actually only using 16 bits for the subnet mask in a Class A network.

By using 30 bits, you have 4,194,302 subnets, each with only two hosts. This mask, 255.255.255.252, can be used for WAN connections (as we explained earlier when describing subnetting a Class B network). Of course, if you have more than 4 million WAN links, you'd be way too busy to be reading this book!

By following Table 4.11, which shows the different subnet masks available for a Class B network, you'll notice that the number of hosts increases as the number of bits used for subnetting decreases, and vice versa.

T A B L E 4.11:   Subnet Masks Available for a Class B Network

Subnet Mask	Length of Subnet Mask (bits)	Number of Subnets	Number of Hosts Per Subnet
255.255.255.252	30	16,382	2
255.255.255.248	29	8190	6
255.255.255.240	28	4094	14
255.255.255.224	27	2046	30
255.255.255.192	26	1022	62
255.255.255.128	25	510	126
255.255.255.0	24	254	254
255.255.254.0	23	126	510
255.255.252.0	22	62	1022
255.255.248.0	21	30	2046
255.255.240.0	20	14	4094
255.255.224.0	19	6	8190
255.255.192.0	18	2	16,382

Table 4.12 shows the different subnet masks available for a Class C network.

T A B L E 4.12: Subnet Masks Available for a Class C Network

Subnet Mask	Length of Subnet Mask (bits)	Number of Subnets	Number of Hosts Per Subnet
255.255.255.252	30	62	2
255.255.255.248	29	30	6
255.255.255.240	28	14	14
255.255.255.224	27	6	30
255.255.255.192	26	2	62

Test candidates should be aware that Cisco uses three notations when describing netmasks. One method we do not discuss in the book is called *prefix notation*, which is where you take the number of 1 bits starting from the most significant bit on the left, count right, and then sum them up to get the netmask. Prefix notation is always preceded by a forward slash "/". For example, the address 10.1.1.1/16 would mean that 16 bits are used for the netmask, giving you a result of 255.255.0.0. This method is more commonly used to describe VLSM configurations, such as 209.76.25.32/27, which would be a network address for the Class C address 209.76.25.0, using a netmask of 255.255.255.224.

Summary

In this chapter, we covered

- The different classes of networks and how to create subnetworks from an IP address and a subnet mask.
- How to find the valid IP addresses in a given subnet and then configure them to create subnets.
- How to verify the valid hosts within a subnet.

Review Questions

For questions 1–10, first examine all answers in binary.

1. You have a network ID of 172.16.0.0 and you need to divide it into multiple subnets. You need 600 host IDs for each subnet. Which subnet mask should you assign that will allow for growth?

   A. 255.255.224.0

   B. 255.255.240.0

   C. 255.255.248.0

   D. 255.255.252.0

2. You have a network ID of 172.16.0.0 with eight subnets. You need to allow for the largest possible number of host IDs per subnet. Which subnet mask should you assign?

   A. 255.255.224.0

   B. 255.255.240.0

   C. 255.255.248.0

   D. 255.255.252.0

3. You have a network ID of 192.168.55.0 and you need to divide it into multiple subnets. You need 25 host IDs for each subnet, with the largest amount of subnets available. Which subnet mask should you assign?

   A. 255.255.255.192

   B. 255.255.255.224

   C. 255.255.255.240

   D. 255.255.255.248

4. You have a Class A network address with 60 subnets. You need to add 40 new subnets in the next two years, but still allow for the largest possible number of host IDs per subnet. Which subnet mask should you assign?

A. 255.240.0.0

B. 255.248.0.0

C. 255.252.0.0

D. 255.254.0.0

5. You have a Class C network address of 192.168.19.0 with four subnets. You need the largest possible number of host IDs per subnet. Which subnet mask should you assign?

A. 255.255.255.192

B. 255.255.255.224

C. 255.255.255.240

D. 255.255.255.248

6. You have a Class B network address divided into 30 subnets. You will add 25 new subnets within the next two years. You need 600 host IDs for each subnet. Which subnet mask should you assign?

A. 255.192.0.0

B. 255.254.0.0

C. 255.255.248.0

D. 255.255.252.0

7. You have a network ID of 192.168.1.0 and you need to divide it into nine subnets. You need to provide for the largest possible number of host IDs per subnet. Which subnet mask should you assign?

A. 255.255.255.192

B. 255.255.255.224

C. 255.255.255.240

D. 255.255.255.248

8. You have a Class C network address divided into three subnets. You will need to add two subnets in the next two years. Each subnet will have 25 hosts. Which subnet mask should you assign?

A. 255.255.255.0

B. 255.255.255.192

C. 255.255.255.224

D. 255.255.255.248

9. You have a Class C network address of 192.168.88.0 and you need the largest possible number of subnets, with up to 12 hosts per subnet. Which subnet mask should you assign?

A. 255.255.255.192

B. 255.255.255.224

C. 255.255.255.240

D. 255.255.255.248

10. You need to come up with a TCP/IP addressing scheme for your company. How many network IDs must you allow for when you define the subnet mask for the network?

A. One for each subnet

B. One for each host ID

C. One for each router interface

D. One for each WAN connection

E. One for each network adapter installed on each host

11. You need to come up with a TCP/IP addressing scheme for your company. Which two factors must you consider when you define the subnet mask for the network?

A. The number of subnets on the network

B. The number of host IDs on each subnet

C. The volume of network traffic on each subnet

    D. The location of DNS servers

    E. The location of default gateways

12. You need to come up with a TCP/IP addressing scheme for your company. How many host IDs must you allow for when you define the subnet mask for the network?

    A. One for each subnet

    B. One for each router interface

    C. One for each WAN connection

    D. One for each network adapter installed on each host

13. You have an IP address of 172.16.3.57 with an 11-bit subnet mask. What are your valid hosts?

    A. 172.16.3.32 to 172.16.3.62

    B. 172.16.3.33 to 172.16.3.62

    C. 172.16.3.34 to 172.16.3.62

    D. 172.16.3.57 to 172.16.3.62

14. You have a subnet mask of 255.255.255.248. How many subnets and hosts do you have?

    A. 2,097,150 subnets with eight hosts

    B. 8190 subnets with six hosts

    C. 30 subnets with 14 hosts

    D. six subnets with 30 hosts

15. You have an IP address of 172.16.4.58 with a 12-bit subnet mask. What are your valid hosts?

    A. 172.16.4.48 to 172.16.4.63

    B. 172.16.4.49 to 172.16.4.63

    C. 172.16.4.49 to 172.16.4.62

    D. 172.16.4.55 to 172.16.4.62

16. You have an IP address of 172.16.13.5 with a 255.255.255.128 subnet mask. What is your class of address, subnet address, and broadcast address?

17. If you have a 22-bit subnet mask, how many subnets and how many hosts do you have?

   A. 8190 subnets, 4096 hosts

   B. 4,194,302 subnets, 2 hosts

   C. 2,096,138 subnets 6 hosts

   D. 16,384 subnets, 2046 hosts

18. If you have a 19-bit subnet mask, how many subnets and how many hosts do you have?

   A. 8190 subnets, 126 hosts

   B. 524,288 subnets, 32 hosts

   C. 524,286 subnets, 30 hosts

   D. 65,234 subnets, 62 hosts

19. If you have a class B network with a 10-bit subnet mask, how many subnets and how many hosts do you have?

   A. 1022 subnets, 62 hosts

   B. 62 subnets, 8190 hosts

   C. 8,190 subnets, 254 hosts

   D. 254 subnets, 126 hosts

20. If you have a class C network with a 6-bit subnet mask, how many subnets and how many hosts do you have?

   A. 254 subnets, 30 hosts

   B. 64 subnets, 8 hosts

   C. 62 subnets, 2 hosts

   D. 30 subnets, 2 hosts

CHAPTER

5

Getting Started with Cisco Routers

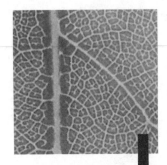

t's time to meet the Cisco interface. This chapter is going to help you understand the basics of the Cisco IOS (Internetworking Operating System) interface, which will prepare you for IP routing in Chapter 6.

In this chapter, you'll get an overview of the Cisco router and learn the different ways to connect to and configure it. You'll log in to a router and work with the help screens and the editing features. Next, you'll discover some common commands used to establish a router's status and examine and update the configuration file.

You'll finish by designing an IP addressing scheme, which you'll use in the labs throughout the rest of this book, and then use this design to configure Cisco routers.

The CCNA test objectives covered in this chapter include:

- *154* ■ Log into a router in both user and privileged modes

- *152* ■ Examine router elements (RAM, ROM, CDP, show)

- *150* ■ Use the context-sensitive help facility

- *160* ■ Use the command history and editing features

- *155* ■ Manage configuration files from the privileged Exec mode

- *164* ■ Control router passwords, identification, and banner

- *161/162* ■ Identify the main Cisco IOS commands for router startup

- *163* ■ Enter an initial configuration using the **setup** command

- *170* ■ Prepare the initial configuration of your router and enable IP

- *170* ■ Copy and manipulate configuration files

The Router

Cisco routers can be configured from many different sources and can be divided into external and internal components.

The first and probably most important port is the asynchronous serial port called the *console port*. Found on every Cisco router, the console port provides local access to a router through a laptop or console running terminal emulation software (for example, HyperTerminal in Windows 95).

Routers also have an auxiliary port that allows you to hook a modem up to the router and dial in to configure or troubleshoot it. Figure 5.1 shows the Cisco 2500 router.

FIGURE 5.1

Cisco 2500 router

Front view

Back view

You can configure a router through any of its interfaces—not just through its console or auxiliary port—but the interface must be connected to a network, IP protocol must be correctly configured, and the port must be active. The console port is really the starting point for configuring your interfaces. After that initial configuration, you can then telnet in through an interface like Ethernet 0.

A router can also be configured using external sources; setting up a router this way will be discussed in detail in Chapter 8. Here is a list of the external sources:

- TFTP servers

- Virtual terminals

- Network management stations

Internal Configuration Components

For the purposes of this chapter, our focus will remain on the internal configuration components of a router, which include the following:

- **ROM:** used by the router to store the bootstrap startup program, operating system software, and Power-On Self-Test (POST). The ROM chips are installed in sockets on the router's motherboard so that they can be replaced or upgraded.

- **Flash:** basically an erasable, re-programmable ROM that holds the operating system image and microcode. It allows you to "flash" the router and perform upgrades without removing and replacing chips on the motherboard. Flash is retained even when the router is turned off.

- **RAM:** provides caching and packet buffering, plus information like routing tables, which will be explained more in Chapter 6. RAM is used to hold the running operating system when the router is powered on; it is cleared when the router is reset or powered off.

- **NVRAM:** nonvolatile RAM that stores the router's startup configuration file. NVRAM retains its information even when the router is rebooted or shut down.

- **Interfaces:** located either on the motherboard or as separate modules that ease replacement or upgrading. The LAN interfaces are usually Ethernet, FastEthernet, or Token Ring. WANs are run from the synchronous serial interfaces. ISDN interfaces can be installed in the router separately.

The Router Startup Sequence

When the router powers up, it runs a routine that checks the hardware with a POST. This checks the CPU, memory, and all interface circuitry to make sure they're operational.

After the POST, events occur as shown in Figure 5.2.

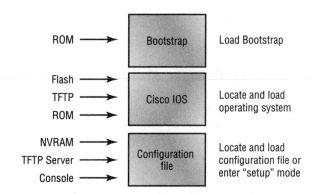

FIGURE 5.2

Startup sequence

1. The bootstrap program is stored in and executed from ROM on the CPU card; its purpose is to search for a valid Cisco IOS image. Why is it called "bootstrap"? Well, the term is derived from the data processing concept of a system "pulling itself up by its own bootstraps" and is similar to command.com searching in DOS. The router can search for the Cisco IOS image from ROM, but it can also do so from flash or from a TFTP server.

2. The operating system source is determined from the boot field setting in the router's configuration register. If the boot field indicates a flash, or network load, boot system commands on the configuration file indicate the exact location of the image the router needs to boot up. Flash memory is the default. Once a valid Cisco IOS image is loaded, it then searches for a configuration file.

3. The operating system image is loaded into low-addressed memory. Once loaded and operational, the operating system then determines the hardware and software components and lists its findings on the console terminal.

4. The saved configuration file in NVRAM is then loaded into main memory and executed one line at a time. These configuration commands start routing processes, supply addresses for interfaces, set media characteristics, and perform other preliminary functions.

5. If no valid configuration exists in NVRAM, the operating system will respond by deploying a "question-driven initial configuration dialog," referred to as the system configuration dialog. Sometimes this special

mode is also called the setup dialog. We'll go over this more thoroughly later in the chapter.

The User Interface

Cisco routers are configured from the user interface, which you can run either from the console port on the router or by telneting into the router from another host into any router interface.

The Exec Command Interpreter

Cisco IOS software has a command interpreter called the Exec. The Exec first interprets the command you type and then executes the operation you've commanded. (You have to log in to the router before an Exec command can be entered.)

The Exec has two levels of access: user and privileged. These two levels, sometimes referred to as modes, serve as security for access into the different levels of commands.

User Mode

User mode is used for ordinary tasks like checking the router's status, connecting to remote devices, making temporary changes to terminal settings, and viewing basic system information. But in this mode, visibility of the router's configuration and your troubleshooting capabilities are very limited.

Privileged Mode

This mode is used to change the configuration of the router. (From here, you can access the configuration mode we talk about next.) The commands in privileged mode include all those in user mode, plus those used to set operating system parameters, get detailed information on the router's status, test and run debug operations, and access global configuration modes.

Manual Configuration

To manually configure the router, you need to get into the configuration mode, which can be accessed only from within the privileged mode. In the configuration mode, you have access to configuration commands that will allow you to configure the router as a whole, as well as view other configuration modes.

By typing **config** and then pressing Enter, the router prompts you with the following options:

```
Router#config
Configuring from terminal, memory, or network [terminal]?
```

Config terminal (or config t) executes configuration commands from the terminal. From a console port or Telnet, you can make changes to your router. Press CTRL+Z to end the session and return to the console prompt.

```
Router#config t
Enter configuration commands, one per line.  End with
CRTL/Z.
Router(config)#^Z
```

- Config memory (config mem) executes configuration commands stored in NVRAM; this will copy the startup-config to the running-config.

- Config network (config net) is used to retrieve router configuration information from a network TFTP server.

```
Router#config net
Host or network configuration file [host]?
Address of remote host [255.255.255.255]? 172.16.10.1
Name of configuration file [router-confg]? RouterA-confg
Configure using RouterA-confg from 172.16.10.1? [confirm]
Loading RouterA-confg
```

When using config net, you must supply the IP address or hostname of the network TFTP server. We will talk more about TFTP servers in Chapter 8.

Logging In to the Router

When you first log in to a router, you see a user Exec mode prompt. You can type ? to get a list of commands at any time. (Throughout this book, we will bold the words you need to type.)

```
Router>?
Exec commands:
```

connect	Open a terminal connection
disable	Turn off privileged commands
disconnect	Disconnect an existing network connection
enable	Turn on privileged commands
exit	Exit from the EXEC
help	Description of the interactive help system
lock	Lock the terminal
login	Log in as a particular user
logout	Exit from the EXEC
mrinfo	Request neighbor and version information from a multicast router
mstat	Show statistics after multiple multicast traceroutes
mtrace	Trace reverse multicast path from destination to source
name-connection	Name an existing network connection
pad	Open a X.29 PAD connection
ping	Send echo messages
ppp	Start IETF Point-to-Point Protocol (PPP)
resume	Resume an active network connection
rlogin	Open an rlogin connection
show	Show running system information
slip	Start Serial-line IP (SLIP)
systat	Display information about terminal lines
telnet	Open a telnet connection
terminal	Set terminal line parameters
traceroute	Trace route to destination
tunnel	Open a tunnel connection
where	List active connections
x3	Set X.3 parameters on PAD

The --more-- prompt indicates there's more information to see. You can press Return to view the information line by line or press the space bar to see the next screen. To exit from user mode, you can type logout at any time. After a period of inactivity, the router will time-out and log you out automatically.

You go into privileged mode by typing **enable** at the Router prompt. You then must enter a password. As seen below, a hash sign is added to the Router prompt after you do this. Now, by typing **?**, you can view all the privileged mode commands.

```
Router>enable
Password:
[didn't show on screen]
Router#?
  bfe               For manual emergency modes setting
  clear             Reset functions
  clock             Manage the system clock
  configure         Enter configuration mode
  connect           Open a terminal connection
  copy              Copy configuration or image data
  debug             Debugging functions (see also 'undebug')
  disable           Turn off privileged commands
  disconnect        Disconnect an existing network connection
  enable            Turn on privileged commands
  erase             Erase flash or configuration memory
  exit              Exit from the EXEC
  help              Description of the interactive help system
  lock              Lock the terminal
  login             Log in as a particular user
  logout            Exit from the EXEC
  mbranch           Trace multicast route down tree branch
  mrbranch          Trace reverse multicast route up tree branch
  mrinfo            Request neighbor and version information
                    from a multicast router
  mstat             Show statistics after multiple multicast
                    traceroutes
  mtrace            Trace reverse multicast path from
                    destination to source
  name-connection   Name an existing network connection
  no                Disable debugging functions
  pad               Open a X.29 PAD connection
  ping              Send echo messages
```

ppp	Start IETF Point-to-Point Protocol (PPP)
reload	Halt and perform a cold restart
resume	Resume an active network connection
rlogin	Open an rlogin connection
rsh	Execute a remote command
send	Send a message to other tty lines
setup	Run the SETUP command facility
show	Show running system information
slip	Start Serial-line IP (SLIP)
start-chat	Start a chat-script on a line
systat	Display information about terminal lines
telnet	Open a telnet connection
terminal	Set terminal line parameters
test	Test subsystems, memory, and interfaces
traceroute	Trace route to destination
tunnel	Open a tunnel connection
undebug	Disable debugging functions (see also 'debug')
verify	Verify checksum of a Flash file
where	List active connections
write	Write running configuration to memory, network, or terminal
x3	Set X.3 parameters on PAD

To exit from privileged mode and return to user mode, type **disable**. Both exit and quit will take you out of both the privileged and user modes and log you out of the router.

Help

You can receive help on any command by typing **?** after the command. For example, if you need to set the clock on your router, but you don't know what the commands are, you could type clock ? as demonstrated below. Leaving one space between the word clock (or other command) and the question mark is important or it won't work.

Router#**clock ?**

Notice the space between clock and ?. You could also use clo ?.

set Set the time and date

This tells you the next command is set, and also informs you that it is used to set the date and time. This form of help is called command syntax help because it tells you which keywords or arguments are required to continue with a command.

Then you type **clock set ?**

```
Router#clock set ?
  hh:mm:ss  Current Time (hh:mm:ss)
```

Notice that doing this has given you even more information on how to set the clock. Now type in **clock set 10:29:30 ?**

```
Router#clock set 10:29:30 ?
  <1-31>  Day of the month
  MONTH   Month of the year
```

The router responds by giving you a message that it wants information about the day and month. So you need to type in more information.

```
RouterB#clock set 10:29:30 23 5
                               ^
% Invalid input detected at '^' marker
```

Notice that when you typed a number (**5**, in this case) instead of the name of the month (**May**), you received a % invalid input message. The router is very clear about what it considers invalid input—it includes a caret symbol (^) to indicate where the error is in the command.

To continue, type in **clock set 10:30:00 23 May ?**

```
Router#clock set 10:29:30 23 may ?
  <1993-2035>  Year
```

Okay, the router accepted "May" and now wants you to specify the year. So, to finish this command, type in **clock set 10:30:00 23 May 1998.**

The question mark (?) can be typed in at any time to find out the syntax required to complete your request. There is a difference between cl? and cl ?. Notice the space after cl on the second command. The command cl? gives you all the commands that start with cl. The command cl ? will give you an ambiguous command because it is looking for the next command, but you haven't specified a unique command like clo or cloc or clock.

Editing Commands

The user interface comes with an editing feature to help you type in repetitive commands. You can turn editing off at any time by typing the command **terminal no editing**. You can re-enable terminal editing by typing **terminal editing.**

The editing command provides a scrolling feature for commands that extend beyond a single line. When you reach the right margin when typing a command, the command line automatically shifts 10 spaces to the left. This is how it works: when you're typing on the router and you reach column 78, the router will shift everything that you have typed 10 characters to the left, opening up more space for you to type in.

Here is the command that we are trying to enter:

```
access-list 110 permit tcp 10.0.1.0 0.0.0.255 10.0.2.0 0.0.0.255
➥ eq ftp-data
```

```
Router#config t
Enter configuration commands, one per line.  End with CNTL/Z.
Router(config)#access-list 110 permit tcp 10.0.1.0 0.0.0.255
➥ 10.0.2.0 0.0.0.2
```

At this point, you are at column 77. As you continue to type the next character, "5," you will reach column 78 and the router will shift all that you have typed to the left by 10 character positions and insert a "$" at the beginning to indicate that there is text to the left that is not being displayed. This opens up space on the right side so that you can continue typing.

```
Router(config)#$ 110 permit tcp 10.0.1.0 0.0.0.255
➥ 10.0.2.0 0.0.0.255
Router(config)#$ 111 permit tcp 10.0.1.0 0.0.0.255
➥ 10.0.2.0 0.0.0.255 eq ftp-
```

As you continue typing, you get to column 78 again and the entire process repeats. As you type the letter "d," everything is shifted to the left by 10 characters. All of this activity happens on one line. We're showing it here on separate lines for clarity.

```
Router(config)#$t tcp 10.0.1.0 0.0.0.255 10.0.2.0 0.0.0.255
➥ eq ftp-d
Router(config)#$t tcp 10.0.1.0 0.0.0.255 10.0.2.0 0.0.0.255
➥ eq ftp-data
```

Below are the different commands used to edit and review the command history:

CTRL+A	Move to the beginning of the command line
CTRL+E	Move to the end of the command line
CTRL+F (or Right Arrow)	Move forward one character
CTRL+B (or Left Arrow)	Move back one character
CTRL+P (or Up Arrow)	Repeat previous command entry
CTRL+N (or Down Arrow)	Most recent command recall
ESC+B	Move backward one word
ESC+F	Move forward one word
`Router> show history`	Show command buffer
`Router> terminal history size`	Set command buffer size
`Router> terminal no editing`	Disable advanced editing features
`Router> terminal editing`	Re-enable advanced editing
Tab	Completes entry for you

For example:
Router#**sh run**
Router#**sh running-config**

We typed in **sh run,** and then pressed the Tab key. The router finished typing in sh running-config for us. Remember to use Tab for long commands.

Startup Commands

As you already know, the router's configuration files contain the configuration of the router. There are two basic configurations for each router: startup and running.

Startup Configuration

Startup configuration is held in NVRAM and accessed when the router is started and placed into DRAM. Type **show startup-config** to see the configuration.

```
Router#sh star
```

[If you type **sh star** and then press Tab button, the system will finish the command string.]

```
RouterB#sh startup-config
Using 661 out of 32762 bytes
!
version 11.0
service udp-small-servers
service tcp-small-servers
!
hostname RouterB
!
enable secret 5 $1$jMYk$21eDXo8XXwrBiVm5RR9wN.
enable password password
!
!
interface Ethernet0
 ip address 172.16.30.1 255.255.255.0
!
interface Serial0
 ip address 172.16.20.2 255.255.255.0
 no fair-queue
 clockrate 56000
!
interface Serial1
 ip address 172.16.40.1 255.255.255.0
 clockrate 56000
 --More-
```

Running Configuration

Running configuration is the configuration from NVRAM placed in DRAM at startup. By typing **config t**, any changes you make will amend this file. When you're happy with the new configuration, copy it to the startup-config by typing:

```
Router#copy running-config startup-config
Building configuration...
[OK]
```

Commands for Starting and Saving Configurations

Below is a list of commands to start and save configurations on your Cisco routers.

Show startup-config	This shows the configuration that'll be loaded when the router boots.
Show running-config	This shows the configuration that's currently loaded into RAM and running.
Erase startup-config	A really final-sounding command, yes—don't try this one at work! This will erase the configuration in the router's NVRAM and land it right back into the initial configuration dialog.
Reload	This reloads the startup-config into memory.
Setup	This starts the initial configuration dialog.

Software version 10.3 and earlier ran the following commands:

Show config	This is the same as show startup-config.
Write term	This is the same as show running-config.
Write erase	This is the same as erase startup-config.
Write mem	This is the same as copy running-config startup-config.

Sometimes we still use these commands out of habit, but the news from Cisco is that these won't be available in the future. So get into the habit of using the new commands—remember that using them with the Tab key can really help with the long ones.

Passwords

There are five different passwords used in securing your Cisco routers: enable secret, enable password, virtual terminal password, auxiliary password, and console password.

Enable Secret = encrypted

The enable secret is a one-way cryptographic secret password used in versions 10.3 and up. It has precedence over the enable password when it exists. You configure this password either during the setup mode of your router or by typing

```
Router#config t
Enter configuration commands, one per line.  End with CNTL/Z.
Router(config)#enable secret todd secret
Router(config)#^Z
```

Enable Password - Not ENCRYPTED

The enable password is used when there is no enable secret and when you are using older software and some boot images. It's manually encrypted (done by the administrator). You can set this up during the setup mode or by typing

```
Router#config t
Enter configuration commands, one per line.  End with CNTL/Z.
Router(config)#enable password todd enable
The enable password you have chosen is the same as your
enable secret.
This is not recommended.  Re-enter the enable password.
Router(config)#enable password lammle
Router(config)#^Z
```

Notice that when we typed the same password as the enable secret, it gave us a warning. If, however, you wanted to use the same password, you could type it in a second time and it would be accepted. We chose a different password instead.

Virtual Terminal Password - NOT ENCRYPTED

The virtual terminal password is used for Telnet sessions into the router. You can change the vty password at any time, but it must be specified or you won't be able to telnet into the router. You can set this up during the setup mode or by typing

```
Router#config t
Enter configuration commands, one per line.  End with CNTL/Z.
Router(config)#line vty 0 4
Router(config-line)#login
Router(config-line)#password todd
Router(config-line)#^Z
```

[handwritten: sub-mode of global] *[handwritten: virtual 5 terminals]*

line vty 0 4 specifies the number of Telnet sessions allowed in the router. You can also set up a different password for each line by typing **line vty [port number]**.

Auxiliary Password *[handwritten: — NOT ENCRYPTED]*

The auxiliary password is used to set a password for the auxiliary port. This port is used to connect a modem to a router for remote console connections.

```
Router#config t
Enter configuration commands, one per line.  End with CNTL/Z.
Router(config)#line aux 0
Router(config-line)#login
Router(config-line)#password todd
Router(config-line)#^Z
```

[handwritten: auxiliary]

Console Password *[handwritten: ↑ NOT ENCRYPTED]*

The console password is used to set the console port password. It can be set up manually only by typing

```
Router(config)#line con 0
Router(config-line)#login
Router(config-line)#password todd
Router(config-line)#^Z
```

[handwritten: console]

This sets up a password for anyone that connects directly to your router's console port.

Entering a Banner

You can add a banner that will be displayed whenever anyone logs in to your Cisco router. The command is **banner motd #**. motd stands for "message of the day." You must start an motd banner with a deliminating character of your choice.

```
Router(config)#banner motd #
Enter TEXT message.  End with the character '#'.
If you are not authorized to be in Acme.com router, log out
immediately!
# [enter]
RouterC(config)#end
```

The output will then look like this when either Telneting into the router or connecting to a console port:

```
Router con0 is now available


Press ENTER to get started.


If you are not authorized to be in Acme.com router, log out
immediately!


User Access Verification
Password:
```

Hostname

You can change the name your router displays by using the hostname command. For example, to change the name of our router to RouterC, we would type the following:

```
Router#config t
Enter configuration commands, one per line.  End with CNTL/Z.
Router(config)#hostname RouterC
RouterC(config-line)#^Z
```

Router Interfaces

The interfaces, also known as ports, on our Cisco 2500 routers are referred to as Serial0, Serial1, and Ethernet0 and are considered fixed configurations. When we are in configuration mode, we can type in S0, S1, and E0 to reference these ports. If we were using Token Ring, we would use T0; if we used FDDI, we would use F0.

Shutdown

To change the administrative state of a router interface to either up or down, you use the shutdown command. This will turn the administrative state of the interface down. The no shutdown command will turn the administrative state of an interface up.

Description

You can also add a description or text line to an interface by using the description command. This lets you document your interfaces for administrative purposes. For example, you can add circuit numbers to your serial links.

Switch and VIP interfaces

If the device is modular, like a Catalyst 5000 switch, the interfaces are numbered using the syntax type slot/port. For example, to configure a port on a 5000 switch, we would type **e 4/2** for Ethernet card 4, port 2.

The Cisco 7000 and 7500 series routers have cards called VIP or Versatile Interface Processor cards. These can have one or two slots for each port adapter, and each port adapter can have a number of interfaces. The numbering syntax is type slot/port adapter/port. For example, if you wanted to configure a port on the third Ethernet VIP card, first port (0), second Ethernet interface, you would type **e 2/0/1**.

Designing Our Internetwork

Before we continue configuring the routers we'll use for the rest of this book's labs, we need to create an IP addressing scheme. We'll set the network up as shown in Figure 5.3.

We have three routers named RouterA, RouterB, and RouterC. Each router has one Ethernet port and two serial ports. RouterA is connected to RouterB with a 56K line. A 56K line also connects RouterB to RouterC.

When designing an IP addressing scheme, it's a good idea to use the private or invalid addresses, because those addresses aren't valid on the Internet. No one can use them to communicate; this makes it difficult to gain access to the

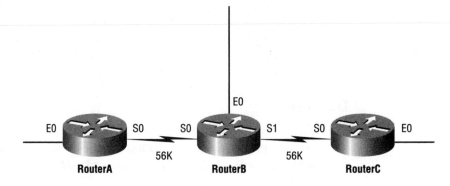

inside network of your company. Therefore, they can offer you some security. The private addresses are

Class A: 10.0.0.0

Class B: 172.16-31.0.0

Class C: 192.168.0.0

Let's use 172.16.0.0 as a network number. As Figure 5.3 shows, we have three Ethernet networks and two serial networks. This means we need to configure five networks as different subnetworks. If we use the mask 255.255.255.0, it will give us 254 subnets, each with 254 hosts. This design will work well for this book and the labs in it.

We'll designate our five networks as 172.16.10.0, 172.16.20.0, 172.16.30.0, 172.16.40.0, and 172.16.50.0, with all hosts having a 255.255.255.0 mask. Our internetwork will now look like the one in Figure 5.4.

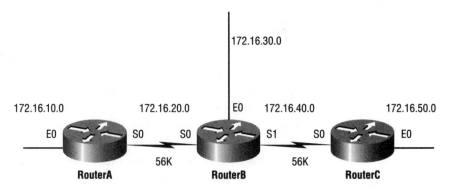

We now need to add actual host addresses to our router interfaces and to all the hosts on our network. The internetwork will now look like the one in Figure 5.5.

FIGURE 5.5

Our internetwork with host addressing

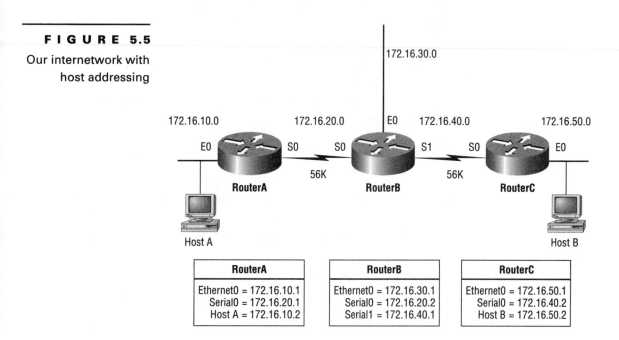

Now that we have our addressing scheme in place, we can configure the routers.

System Configuration Dialog

If you do a `write erase` or `erase startup-config` and a `reload` on your router, you'll see the system configuration dialog screen. You can type `setup` to get the dialog screen at any time, which is helpful in configuring your router.

RouterA

We did a `write erase` at the router prompt (you don't need to be in configuration mode to do this), then we did a `reload`. The router rebooted and gave us this response:

```
Notice: NVRAM invalid, possibly due to write erase.
        --- System Configuration Dialog ---
```

```
At any point you may enter a question mark '?' for help.
Use CTRL-c to abort configuration dialog at any prompt.
Default settings are in square brackets '[]'.
Would you like to enter the initial configuration dialog?
[yes][enter]
```

Let's press Enter at the [yes] prompt to continue with the configuration and see how the router responds:

```
First, would you like to see the current interface summary?
[yes][enter]

Any interface listed with OK? value "NO" does not have a
valid configuration
```

Interface	IP-Address	OK?	Method	Status	Protocol
Ethernet0	unassigned	NO	not set	up	down
Serial0	unassigned	NO	not set	up	down
Serial1	unassigned	NO	not set	up	down

```
Configuring global parameters:
```

We pressed Enter at the [yes] prompt to view the current interface summary, because that way we're assured that the POST has found all the interfaces.

We have two serial ports and one Ethernet port. They aren't okay (see the "NO not set" next to them?), because they aren't set up yet. They're designated "unassigned." The router now wants the name of the router we're trying configure, which will be RouterA. We'll enter that now and then press Enter. The router responds with

```
Enter host name [Router]: RouterA
The enable secret is a one-way cryptographic secret used
instead of the enable password when it exists.
Enter enable secret: todd
The enable password is used when there is no enable secret
and when using older software and some boot images.
Enter enable password: password
```

```
        Enter virtual terminal password: password2
        Configure SNMP Network Management? [yes]: n
        Configure IP? [yes][enter]
Configure IP? [yes][enter]
            Configure IGRP routing? [yes]: n
            Configure RIP routing? [no]:[enter]


Configuring interface parameters:

Configuring interface Ethernet0:
    Is this interface in use? [yes][enter]
    Configure IP on this interface? [yes][enter]
        IP address for this interface: 172.16.10.1
        Number of bits in subnet field [0]: 8
        Class B network is 172.16.0.0, 8 subnet bits; mask is
255.255.255.0

Configuring interface Serial0:
    Is this interface in use? [yes]:[enter]
    Configure IP on this interface? [yes]:[enter]
    Configure IP unnumbered on this interface? [no]:[enter]
        IP address for this interface: 172.16.20.1
        Number of bits in subnet field [8]:[enter]
        Class B network is 172.16.0.0, 8 subnet bits; mask is
255.255.255.0


Configuring interface Serial1:
    Is this interface in use? [yes]: n
```

Notice we indicated "no" to the routing commands like RIP and IGRP. Actually, we typed **n** indicating "no." We'll go over those commands in Chapter 6. Also notice that for the subnet mask, we typed in only eight bits. The router doesn't count the default masks in the number of bits, so even though we typed in only eight bits, it will still be realized as 255.255.255.0. The third byte is the only one used for subnetting. (If you're still wrestling with this concept, go back to Chapter 4 for a quick review.)

After we indicated "no" to configuring Serial1, the router showed us the configuration we created:

```
The following configuration command script was created:
hostname RouterA
enable secret 5 $1$KFHm$dvj9m3GnQzm9rsJ5lvw5D1
enable password password
line vty 0 4
password password2
no snmp-server
!
ip routing
!
interface Ethernet0
ip address 172.16.10.1 255.255.255.0
!
interface Serial0
ip address 172.16.20.1 255.255.255.0
!
interface Serial1
shutdown
no ip address
!
end
```

```
Use this configuration? [yes/no]:y
```

We typed a **y**, and then pressed Enter. The router then saved the configuration to NVRAM.

RouterB

Okay, onward to RouterB's configuration.

```
Notice: NVRAM invalid, possibly due to write erase.
        --- System Configuration Dialog ---

At any point you may enter a question mark '?' for help.
Use CTRL-c to abort configuration dialog at any prompt.
Default settings are in square brackets '[]'.
```

Would you like to enter the initial configuration dialog?
[yes]:**[enter]**

First, would you like to see the current interface summary?
[yes]:**[enter]**

Any interface listed with OK? value "NO" does not have a
valid configuration

Interface	IP-Address	OK?	Method	Status	Protocol
Ethernet0	unassigned	NO	not set	up	down
Serial0	unassigned	NO	not set	up	down
Serial1	unassigned	NO	not set	up	down

Configuring global parameters:

   Enter host name [Router]: **RouterB**

The enable secret is a one-way cryptographic secret used
instead of the enable password when it exists.

   Enter enable secret: **todd**

The enable password is used when there is no enable secret
and when using older software and some boot images.

   Enter enable password: **password**
   Enter virtual terminal password: **password2**
   Configure SNMP Network Management? [yes]: **n**
   Configure IP? [yes]:**[enter]**
     Configure IGRP routing? [yes]: **n**
     Configure RIP routing? [no]: **n**

Configuring interface parameters:
Configuring interface Ethernet0:
   Is this interface in use? [yes]:**[enter]**
   Configure IP on this interface? [yes]**[enter]**

```
    IP address for this interface: 172.16.30.1
    Number of bits in subnet field [0]: 8
    Class B network is 172.16.0.0, 8 subnet bits; mask is
255.255.255.0
```

```
Configuring interface Serial0:
  Is this interface in use? [yes]:[enter]
  Configure IP on this interface? [yes][enter]
  Configure IP unnumbered on this interface? [no]:[enter]
    IP address for this interface: 172.16.20.2
    Number of bits in subnet field [8]:[enter]
    Class B network is 172.16.0.0, 8 subnet bits; mask is
255.255.255.0
```

```
Configuring interface Serial1:
  Is this interface in use? [yes]:[enter]
  Configure IP on this interface? [yes]:[enter]
  Configure IP unnumbered on this interface? [no]:[enter]
    IP address for this interface: 172.16.40.1
    Number of bits in subnet field [8]:[enter]
    Class B network is 172.16.0.0, 8 subnet bits; mask is
255.255.255.0
```

```
The following configuration command script was created:
```

```
hostname RouterB
enable secret 5 $1$jMYk$21eDXo8XXwrBiVm5RR9wN.
enable password password
line vty 0 4
password password
no snmp-server
!
ip routing
!
interface Ethernet0
ip address 172.16.30.1 255.255.255.0
!
```

```
interface Serial0
ip address 172.16.20.2 255.255.255.0
!
interface Serial1
ip address 172.16.40.1 255.255.255.0
!
end


Use this configuration? [yes/no]:y
```

RouterC

Once we configure RouterC, we've completed the IP addressing of our routers. However, instead of doing the initial configuration through the setup program, let's manually configure this one. If you want to skip the automatic setup, you can press CTRL+C at any time, then type **config t** to get into the configuration mode.

```
router#config t
Enter configuration commands, one per line.  End with CNTL/Z.
router(config)#int e0
router(config-if)#description LAN Link to Sales
router(config-if)#ip address 172.16.50.1 255.255.255.0
router(config-if)#no shutdown
router(config-if)#int s0
router(config-if)#description WAN Link to SF
router(config-if)#ip address 172.16.40.2 255.255.255.0
router(config-if)#no shutdown
router(config-if)#exit
router(config)#hostname RouterC
RouterC(config)#enable ?
last-resort  Define enable action if no TACACS servers
respond
  password    Assign the privileged level password
  secret      Assign the privileged level secret
  use-tacacs  Use TACACS to check enable passwords
RouterC(config)#enable password simple1
RouterC(config)#enable secret todd
RouterC(config)#line vty 0 4
```

```
RouterC(config-line)#login
RouterC(config-line)#password telnettome
RouterC(config)#banner motd #
Enter TEXT message.  End with the character '#'.
If you are not me, then why are you here?
#
RouterC(config-line)#^Z
RouterC#
```

This is quite a shortcut compared with the initial configuration method, but you need to understand the interfaces to be able to do this.

First we typed **config t** and chose interface Ethernet0 by typing **int e0**. We typed in the description, IP address, subnet mask, then choosing to configure serial0 (s0), we put in the relevant description, IP address, and mask. Notice we needed to type the complete IP address and mask on one line.

That done, we changed the hostname of the router and typed **enable ?** to get the syntax to change our passwords. We then entered passwords for the enable password, enable secret, and vty (Telnet) ports. Line vty 0 4 is the number of Telnet ports defined; this can be seen by typing **sh running-config**. The bottom of the configuration shows the amount of vty ports available (0 through 4):

```
!
line con 0
line aux 0
 transport input all
line vty 0 4
 password telnettome
 login
!
end
```

We have one more password to enter: the console password. This is used when your terminal is directly connected to the console.

```
RouterC(config)#line console 0
RouterC(config-line)#login
RouterC(config-line)#password iamdirectlyconnected
RouterC(config-line)#^Z
```

Notice the con 0 password shows in the configuration:

```
line con 0
 password iamdirectlyconnected
 login
line aux 0
 transport input all
line vty 0 4
 password telnettome
 login
!
```

DTE/DCE Cable

We found the Ethernet ports on the router easily, but we'll need a little more configuration than just an IP address and subnet mask to find the serial ports.

We'll go into detail about WANs in Chapter 11, but some explanation on how the router should be configured for the labs is necessary now. We have connected a Cisco DTE/DCE (Data Terminal Equipment/Data Communication Equipment) cable, and we're simulating a WAN link between routers. Let us explain what we've done to simulate the WAN link.

By default, Cisco routers are DTE devices, but when you have routers connected together, simulating a WAN link, you can define a serial interface as a DCE device. Since Cisco routers use synchronous communications, which means a clock is required and is usually supplied from an external source, we need to add the `clock rate` command to the DCE serial ports on our routers. Why? Because we don't have a CSU/DSU that would normally handle the clocking on the line for us. You must specify the `clock rate` command on the DCE interfaces to simulate a clocking source. You should also specify the `bandwidth` command, because it's used by some routing protocols like IGRP to make routing decisions.

The Cisco serial port has 60 pins, and some of them are used for sensing whether the cable connected is DTE or DCE. The Cisco cable has a certain number of pins connected, or looped, together which gives the DCE and DTE cables a unique configuration. When you plug a DTE or DCE cable into a serial port, you can type the command **show controllers serial [port number]** to see if the interface sees a DCE or a DTE cable.

```
RouterC#sh controllers serial 0
HD unit 0, idb = 0x961FC, driver structure at 0x9A6C8
```

```
buffer size 1524  HD unit 0, V.35 DTE cable
cpb = 0x11, eda = 0x4940, cda = 0x4800
RX ring with 16 entries at 0x114800
```

Notice by looking at the second line that RouterC has found the V.35 DTE cable plugged into Serial0. Let's see what RouterB found:

```
RouterB#sh controllers serial 1
HD unit 1, idb = 0x9DAE8, driver structure at 0xA1FB0
buffer size 1524  HD unit 1, V.35 DCE cable
cpb = 0x22, eda = 0x3140, cda = 0x3000
RX ring with 16 entries at 0x223000

RouterB#sh controllers serial 0
HD unit 0, idb = 0x96138, driver structure at 0x9A600
buffer size 1524  HD unit 0, V.35 DCE cable
cpb = 0x21, eda = 0x4940, cda = 0x4800
RX ring with 16 entries at 0x214800
```

Since RouterB has two serial interfaces we typed the command twice—once for each interface. Notice the second line this time. RouterB has found a V.35 DCE cable on both of its serial interfaces.

RouterA offered this output:

```
RouterA#sh controllers serial 0
HD unit 0, idb = 0x961FC, driver structure at 0x9A6C8
buffer size 1524  HD unit 0, V.35 DTE cable
cpb = 0x11, eda = 0x4940, cda = 0x4800
RX ring with 16 entries at 0x114800
```

Both of the DCE ports are on RouterB, so the command and the resulting output would look like this:

```
RouterB#config t
Enter configuration commands, one per line.  End with CNTL/Z.
RouterB(config)#int s0
RouterB(config-if)#clock rate ?
        Speed (bits per second)
    1200
    2400
    4800
```

```
       9600
      19200
      38400
      56000
      64000
      72000
     125000
     148000
     250000
     500000
     800000
    1000000
    1300000
    2000000
    4000000
  <300-8000000>     Choose clock rate from list above
```

```
RouterB(config-if)#clock rate 56000
RouterB(config-if)#bandwidth ?
  <1-10000000>   Bandwidth in kilobits
RouterB(config-if)#bandwidth 56
RouterB(config-if)#int s1
RouterB(config-if)#clock rate 56000
RouterB(config-if)#bandwidth 56
RouterB(config-if)#^Z
RouterB#wr mem
```

Actually, we should have typed **copy running-config startup-config**, but old habits die hard. Anyway, the configuration for RouterB now looks like this:

```
RouterB#sh running-config
Building configuration...

Current configuration:
!
version 11.0
service udp-small-servers
```

```
service tcp-small-servers
!
hostname RouterB
!
enable secret 5 $1$jMYk$21eDXo8XXwrBiVm5RR9wN.
enable password password
!
interface Ethernet0
 ip address 172.16.30.1 255.255.255.0
!
interface Serial0
 ip address 172.16.20.2 255.255.255.0
 no fair-queue
 clockrate 56000
bandwidth 56
!
interface Serial1
 ip address 172.16.40.1 255.255.255.0
 clockrate 56000
bandwidth 56
!
!
line con 0
line aux 0
 transport input all
line vty 0 4
 password password
 login
!
end
```

Our three routers are now configured and we're ready for Chapter 6.

Summary

In this chapter, we covered the following key points:

- The main Cisco IOS commands for router startup
- How to log into a router in both user and privileged modes
- How to examine router elements (RAM, ROM, Flash, CDP, and show)
- How to use the context-sensitive help facility
- How to use the command history and editing features
- How to manage configuration files from the privileged Exec mode
- How to control router passwords, identification, and banner
- How to check an initial configuration using the setup command
- The initial configuration of your router and enable IP

Review Questions

1. What is the syntax for changing the name of a Cisco router?

   A. `host name newhostname`

   B. `hostname newhostname`   *P 166*

   C. `routername newhostname`

   D. You can't change the name

2. What is the syntax to add a banner to a Cisco router configuration?

   A. `# banner`

   B. `banner #`

   C. `banner motd #`   *P.165*

   D. `motd banner #`

3. What command can you use to copy the configuration from NVRAM into running RAM?

  A. `copy running-config startup-config`

  B. `copy startup-config running-config`

  C. `wr mem`

  D. `wr t`

4. What key do you use to view the last command that was entered into a Cisco router?

  A. The Down Arrow

  B. The Up Arrow   p161

  C. CTRL+6

  D. Type `sh last command`

5. Which other key command will give you the last command entered?

  A. CTRL+N

  B. CTRL+P   p161

  C. CTRL+A

  D. CTRL+Z

6. What key do you press to have the Cisco IOS finish typing a command for you?

  A. Enter

  B. CTRL

  C. Tab   p161

  D. Space bar

7. To exit from privileged mode back to user mode, what do you type at the privileged mode prompt (#)?

  A. `Exit`

  B. `Quit`

C. Disable   *p 156*

D. Goback

8. What does the `erase startup-config` command do?

    A. Loads the startup-config into RAM

    B. Loads the running-config into NVRAM

    C. Erases the startup-config and puts you in debug mode

    D. Erases the startup-config   *p 157*

9. If you have two Cisco routers connected with DTE/DCE cables, to which router would you add the command `clock rate` in order to facilitate a CSU/DSU?

    A. The serial interface running as a DCE   *p 177*

    B. The serial interface running as a DTE

    C. The Ethernet interface running as a DTE

    D. The Ethernet interface running as a DCE

10. What command do you use to change your enable password?

    A. Config t, enable secret *password*

    B. Config t, enable password *password*   *p 164*

    C. Config t, line vty 0 4, login, password *password*

    D. Config t, line con 0, login, password *password*

11. What is the command to set the clock rate on your DCE interfaces?

    A. clockrate 56

    B. clock rate 56

    C. clockrate 56000

    D. clock rate 56000   *p 179*

12. CTRL+A will provide what function?

    A. Take your cursor to the end of the line

    B. Take your cursor to the beginning of the line   *p 161*

    C. Exit you out of edit mode

    D. Move you down one line

13. The `terminal no editing` command will provide what function?

    A. Stop users from editing your configuration

    B. Provide password protection

    C. Stop the advanced editing features *p160*

    D. Allow the configuration to be configured only from the console port

14. What is the syntax you would use to configure a port on a Catalyst 5000 switch?

    A. slot port/type

    B. port type/slot

    C. type slot/port *p167*

    D. config t, int e4

15. What is the syntax to configure a port on a 7000 series router with a VIP card?

    A. slot card/port

    B. type slot/port adapter/port *p167*

    C. port type/slot port/adapter

    D. slot port/adapter

16. Which of the following will change your Telnet password?

    A. line aux 0

    B. line con 0

    C. line vty 1 *p165*

    D. line vty 5

17. How do you change your enable secret password?

    A. enable password <password>

    B. enable <password>

    C. enable secret password <password>

    D. enable secret <password> *p164*

18. When attaching a console cable to your router, how do you log in to user mode?

    A. Press return, type **password** if prompted *p187 #1*

    B. login <password>

    C. Press return, <login name>

    D. login <name, password>

19. If the advanced editing feature has been disabled, how do you then enable the advance editing features?

    A. enable editing

    B. terminal editing *p168*

    C. enable advanced editing

    D. terminal on editing

20. What is the AUX port used for?

    A. Authentication

    B. Backups

    C. Modem *p161, p165 = remote access for configuring router*

    D. Console

Laboratory Exercises

Initial Router Configuration

In this lab, you will configure your Cisco router with a simple IP configuration using some of the configuration commands learned in this chapter. (If you are in a classroom setting, ask your instructor for your IP addresses. If you are at home, be creative.)

1. Type **erase startup-config** and then restart your router, type setup, or turn on your router for the first time.

2. Globally configure your router using the System Configuration Dialog (also called Setup). Your router will automatically start the System Configuration Dialog script after it finishes booting.

3. Enter your hostname.

4. Enter your password, remembering it is case sensitive.

5. Enable only IP routine; say no to every other option when prompted.

6. Do not enable any other routed protocols or any other IP routing protocols.

7. Do not enable IP unnumbered.

8. Save the configuration.

9. Reload your router. As the router reboots, notice a series of r's and #'s across the screen. The r's denote the router, verifying that there is a complete image in flash. The #'s show the IOS being expanded from a compressed format from flash to RAM. If you are using a Cisco 2500, you will not see the #'s because the image is not expanded from flash to RAM, but rather executed from flash.

10. Log in to your router and go to configuration mode.

11. Set the console password.

12. Change your enable secret password.

13. Display the IP address information (logical address) for each interface using the sh ip int command.

EXERCISE 5.1 (CONTINUED)

14. Save the configuration.

15. Ping your routers to make sure IP is working.

EXERCISE 5.2

Console Login

In this lab, you will establish a console connection to the Cisco router, change your hostname, add a banner, and explore some of the context-sensitive help features.

1. After connecting a terminal to the router, press Enter. At the password prompt, type in your password; this will give you the greater-than prompt (>).

2. Type **?** to get a list of available commands.

3. After viewing the commands, type **enable**.

4. Enter your privileged-level password. You will then see a pound sign (#).

5. Type **?** and view the list of available commands. Press Enter at the --more-- prompt. This will take you through the available commands, one line at a time.

6. Press the space bar to scroll through the commands a screen at a time.

7. Press **Q** to quit and return to the privileged-level command prompt. Display the active configuration file stored in RAM.

8. Type **show run** then Tab at the router prompt. This will then complete the command show running-config. Press Enter.

9. Type **show ?** to see the list of available commands.

10. Change your hostname.

11. Add a banner to your router. (If you are in a classroom, be creative but professional.)

12. Save your configuration.

13. Type **sh history**. This will show you a list of the last commands you entered.

EXERCISE 5.2 (CONTINUED)

14. Press the Up and Down Arrows. (This is like the dos key in DOS.)

15. Exit from privileged mode by typing **disable**.

16. Type **exit** to log out of the router.

CHAPTER

6

Routing Basics

With the basics of TCP/IP covered and conquered in Chapters 1 through 4, and armed with a fundamental understanding of Cisco routers presented in Chapter 5, our focus now will both sharpen and shift. We'll begin by concentrating on IP routing, exploring both the basic and more complex issues related to it, and then move into a discussion on static routing and default routing.

What Is IP Routing?

IP *routing* is the process of sending data from a host on one network to a remote host on another network through a router or routers. The path that a router uses to deliver a packet is defined in its routing table. A routing table contains the IP addresses of router interfaces that connect to the other networks the router can communicate with. The routing table is consulted for a path to the network that's indicated by the packet's destination address. If a path isn't found, the packet is sent to the router's *default route* address—if one is configured. By default, a router can send packets to any network for which it has a configured interface. When one host attempts communication with another host on a different network, IP uses the host's default gateway address to deliver the packet to the corresponding router. When a route is found, the packet is sent to the proper network, then onward to the specified destination host. If a route isn't found, an error message is sent back to the source host.

The IP Routing Process

When a datagram's destination is located on a neighboring network, the IP routing process is fairly direct. With this kind of situation, a router follows a simple procedure as shown in Figure 6.1.

FIGURE 6.1

Simple routing

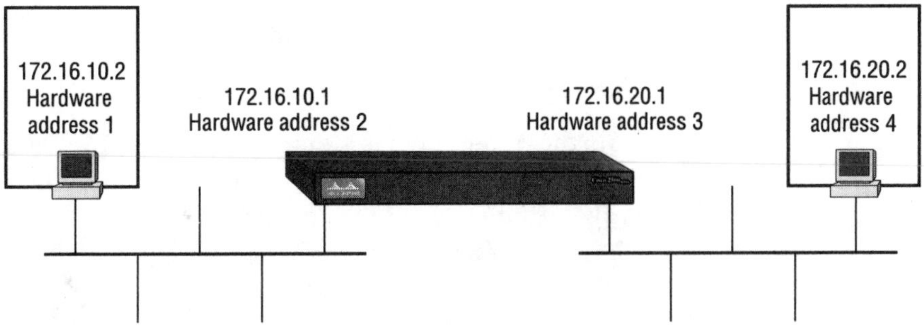

First, when a workstation wants to send a packet to a destination host (in this instance 172.16.10.2 transmitting to 172.16.20.2), host 172.16.10.2 checks the destination IP address. If it determines the address isn't on the local network, then it must be routed. Next, 172.16.10.2 calls on ARP to obtain the hardware address of its default gateway. The IP address of the default gateway is configured in machine 172.16.10.2's internal configuration (hopefully), but 172.16.10.2 still needs to find the hardware address of the default gateway. To do this, it checks the ARP cache, and if the hardware address isn't found, it then sends out an ARP request. IP then proceeds to address the packet with the newly obtained destination hardware address of its default router. The information utilized for addressing the packet includes:

- Source hardware address 1
- Source IP address 172.16.10.2
- Destination hardware address 2
- Destination IP address 172.16.20.2

IP, on the receiving router with the hardware address of 2, establishes that it's not the final, intended recipient by inspecting the packet's destination IP address. That address indicates that it must be forwarded to network 172.16.20.0. IP then uses ARP to determine the hardware address for 172.16.20.2. And the router puts the newly identified hardware address into its ARP cache for easy reference the next time it's called upon to route a packet to that destination.

This accomplished, the router sends the packet out to network 172.16.20.0 with a header that includes:

- Source hardware address 3

- Source IP address 172.16.10.2

- Destination hardware address 4

- Destination IP address 172.16.20.2

As the packet travels along network 172.16.20.0, it looks for hardware address 4, with the IP address of 172.16.20.2. When an NIC recognizes its hardware address, it grabs the packet.

It's important to note here that the source IP address is that of the host that created the packet originally (172.16.10.2). The source hardware address is now that of the router's connection interface to network 172.16.20.0. Also significant is that although the source and destination software IP address remains constant, both hardware addresses change at each hop the packet makes.

How did the router know how to forward the IP packet to 172.16.20.0? By consulting the routing tables maintained on IP routers. IP consults these to determine where the mystery network is so that it can send its packet there. The routing tables of very complex internetworks should designate all available routes to a destination network, plus provide an estimate advising the efficiency of each potential route. Routing tables maintain entries of where networks—not hosts—are located.

Static, Default, and Dynamic Routing

Routing tables store routing information. Routing algorithms initialize and maintain these routing tables. Initially, a router knows only how to reach networks or subnets that are directly connected to it.

Routers learn paths to other network in three different ways:

- Static routing

- Default routing

- Dynamic routing

Static Routing

Static routers require that routing tables be built and updated manually. If a route changes, static routers don't automatically share this information to inform each other of the event. An administrator must manually update the static route entry whenever an internetwork topology change requires it.

A benefit to creating static routes is that bandwidth is conserved. Why? Because broadcasts for updating routes aren't being continually sent over the network. Another advantage is security. With static routing, your routers know about only the networks that you want them to know about. This can prevent users from getting to resources you don't want them to access like Internet browsing.

It's a good idea to limit static routes to the remote destinations reachable through a single router. Static routing should also be used when a network is reachable by only one path (this is called a *stub network*). By configuring static routes to stub networks, the added overhead of dynamic updates is avoided.

Static routes can be configured on Cisco routers by using the `ip route` command. It uses the following command line:

```
ip route network mask address|interface [distance]
```

The following are the command line's arguments defined:

- Network: destination network or subnet

- Mask: subnet mask

- Address: IP address of next hop router

- Interface: name of interface to use to get to destination network

- Distance: the administrative distance

For example, to set up a static route for a remote network of 172.16.50.0, we would use the following command:

IP command	Remote network	Subnet mask	Default gateway
IP route	172.16.50.0	255.255.255.0	172.16.20.2

The router then knows to forward any packets with a destination IP address of network 172.16.50.0 to IP address 172.16.20.2. This router would then have to either forward the packet to its final destination or drop or discard the packet because it doesn't have a route to the final destination. Our job is to make sure that all routers know how to get to all networks so that packets do not get dropped.

The administrative distance, for example 120 for RIP networks, is applied to the source of routing information. It's a rating of the source's trustworthiness expressed as a numeric value from 0 to 255. The higher the number, the lower the trustworthiness rating. Table 7.1 in Chapter 7 shows the default administrative distances.

Configuring Static Routes

Figure 6.2 shows the network configuration we built in Chapter 5. RouterA is connected to networks 172.16.10.0 and network 172.16.20.0. RouterB is connected to networks 172.16.20.0, 172.16.30.0, and 172.16.40.0. RouterC is connected to network 172.16.40.0 and 172.16.50.0. All use a subnet mask of 255.255.255.0. Let's add static routes to each router in this internetwork.

FIGURE 6.2

Routers A, B, and C in our internetwork

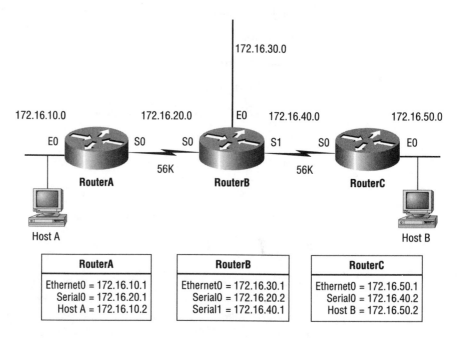

Take a look at each router's route table by typing **show ip route** at the router prompt.

Showing IP Routes for RouterA

Priviledge User mode
1) use show.

```
RouterA#sh ip route
Codes: C - connected, S - static, I - IGRP, R - RIP, M -
mobile, B - BGP, D - EIGRP, EX - EIGRP external, O - OSPF,
IA - OSPF inter area, E1 - OSPF external type 1, E2 - OSPF
external type 2, E - EGP,i - IS-IS, L1 - IS-IS level-1,
L2 - IS-IS level-2, * - candidate default
Gateway of last resort is not set
172.16.0.0 255.255.255.0 is subnetted, 2 subnets
C       172.16.20.0 is directly connected, Serial0
C       172.16.10.0 is directly connected, Ethernet0
```

Showing IP Routes for RouterB

```
RouterB#sh ip route
Codes: C - connected, S - static, I - IGRP, R - RIP, M -
mobile, B - BGP, D - EIGRP, EX - EIGRP external, O - OSPF,
IA - OSPF inter area, E1 - OSPF external type 1, E2 - OSPF
external type 2, E - EGP, i - IS-IS, L1 - IS-IS level-1, L2
- IS-IS level-2, * - candidate default
Gateway of last resort is not set
172.16.0.0 255.255.255.0 is subnetted, 3 subnets
C       172.16.30.0 is directly connected, Ethernet0
C       172.16.40.0 is directly connected, Serial1
C       172.16.20.0 is directly connected, Serial0
```

Showing IP Routes for RouterC

All routers see only their directly connected routes; this is evidenced below in the route table where "C" means "directly connected." At the end of each route entry is the interface where the IP address is configured; for example, Serial0.

```
RouterC#sh ip route
Codes: C - connected, S - static, I - IGRP, R - RIP, M -
mobile, B - BGP, D - EIGRP, EX - EIGRP external, O - OSPF,
IA - OSPF inter area, E1 - OSPF external type 1, E2 - OSPF
external type 2, E - EGP, i - IS-IS, L1 - IS-IS level-1,
L2 - IS-IS level-2, * - candidate default
Gateway of last resort is not set
172.16.0.0 255.255.255.0 is subnetted, 2 subnets
C       172.16.50.0 is directly connected, Ethernet0
C       172.16.40.0 is directly connected, Serial0
```

Let's try and ping from host 172.16.10.2 over to host 172.16.50.2. Doing that requires using a route that goes through three routers. Let's start now by pinging from host 172.16.10.2 and see how far we can get.

```
C:\>ping 172.16.10.2
Pinging 172.16.10.2 with 32 bytes of data:
Reply from 172.16.10.2: bytes=32 time<10ms TTL=128
Reply from 172.16.10.2: bytes=32 time<10ms TTL=128
Reply from 172.16.10.2: bytes=32 time<10ms TTL=128
Reply from 172.16.10.2: bytes=32 time<10ms TTL=128

C:\>ping 172.16.10.1
Pinging 172.16.10.1 with 32 bytes of data:
Reply from 172.16.10.1: bytes=32 time=2ms TTL=255
Reply from 172.16.10.1: bytes=32 time=2ms TTL=255
Reply from 172.16.10.1: bytes=32 time=2ms TTL=255
Reply from 172.16.10.1: bytes=32 time=2ms TTL=255
```

Notice that we can ping both 172.16.10.2 and 172.16.10.1—our host and our default gateway. So far, so good; but let's keep going.

```
C:\>ping 172.16.20.1
Pinging 172.16.20.1 with 32 bytes of data:
Reply from 172.16.20.1: bytes=32 time=10ms TTL=255
Reply from 172.16.20.1: bytes=32 time=2ms TTL=255
Reply from 172.16.20.1: bytes=32 time=2ms TTL=255
Reply from 172.16.20.1: bytes=32 time=3ms TTL=255

C:\>ping 172.16.20.2
Pinging 172.16.20.2 with 32 bytes of data:
Request timed out.
Request timed out.
Request timed out.
Request timed out.
```

Hmmm. Looks like 172.16.20.1 is as far as we can get. Why? After all, RouterA is directly connected to network 172.16.20.0. So why can't we ping 172.16.20.2 on RouterB from our host? Because RouterB does not have a route back to network 172.16.10.0. How do we add these routes, anyway?

There's more than one answer to that question. First, we'll explain it using static routes, then we'll apply default routes, and finally dynamic routing in Chapter 7 to solve the problem.

Configuring IP Routes for RouterA

In RouterA, the routing table shows that networks 172.16.10.0 and 172.16.20.0 are directly connected. That means we need to tell RouterA about networks 172.16.30.0, 172.16.40.0, and 172.16.50.0 by adding our routes into the Cisco router routing table as shown below.

We start by typing **config t**, which means "configure from my terminal," and then enter the required static routes. We proceed with CTRL+Z, then save to memory with copy run star.

```
RouterA#config t
Enter configuration commands, one per line.  End with CNTL/Z.
RouterA(config)#ip route 172.16.30.0 255.255.255.0 172.16.20.2
RouterA(config)#ip route 172.16.40.0 255.255.255.0 172.16.20.2
RouterA(config)#ip route 172.16.50.0 255.255.255.0 172.16.20.2
RouterA(config)#^Z
RouterA#copy run star
```

Basically, we told the router to get to network 172.16.30.0 with a subnet mask of 255.255.255.0, using interface 172.16.20.2 on RouterB. We did this for all three subnets. RouterB must forward these packets.

Configuring IP Routes for RouterB

Now, let's configure RouterB's IP routes to networks 172.16.10.0 and 172.16.50.0. RouterB is directly connected to subnets 20, 30, and 40, so we don't have to configure routes for those networks.

```
RouterB#config t
Enter configuration commands, one per line.  End with CNTL/Z.
RouterB(config)#ip route 172.16.10.0 255.255.255.0 172.16.20.1
RouterB(config)#ip route 172.16.50.0 255.255.255.0 172.16.40.2
RouterB(config)#^Z
RouterB#copy run star
```

We typed **config t**, then entered the route to 172.16.10.0 through 172.16.20.1. The route to 172.16.50.0 is through router interface 172.16.40.2.

Configuring IP Routes for RouterC

Now let's add the IP routes for RouterC. Since RouterC is directly connected to network 172.16.40.0 and 172.16.50.0, we need to add routes for subnets 10, 20, and 30.

```
RouterC#config t
Enter configuration commands, one per line.  End with CNTL/Z.
RouterC(config)#ip route 172.16.10.0 255.255.255.0 172.16.40.1
RouterC(config)#ip route 172.16.20.0 255.255.255.0 172.16.40.1
RouterC(config)#ip route 172.16.30.0 255.255.255.0 172.16.40.1
RouterC(config)#^Z
RouterC#copy run star
```

We told RouterC that to get to the 172.16.10.0 network with a mask of 255.255.255.0, it must use interface 172.16.40.1 on RouterB. We did this for all three networks.

Let's take a look at our new routing tables for Routers A, B, and C after adding all our routes.

RouterA

```
RouterA#sh ip route
Codes: C - connected, S - static, I - IGRP, R - RIP, M -
mobile, B - BGP, D - EIGRP, EX - EIGRP external, O - OSPF,
IA - OSPF inter area, E1 - OSPF external type 1, E2 - OSPF
external type 2, E - EGP, i - IS-IS, L1 - IS-IS level-1,
L2 - IS-IS level-2, * - candidate default
Gateway of last resort is not set
172.16.0.0 255.255.255.0 is subnetted, 5 subnets
S       172.16.50.0 [1/0] via 172.16.20.2
S       172.16.40.0 [1/0] via 172.16.20.2
S       172.16.30.0 [2/0] via 172.16.20.2
C       172.16.20.0 is directly connected, Serial0
C       172.16.10.0 is directly connected, Ethernet0
```

You can also type **sh ip route static** and receive a list of only the static entries. Here's an example from RouterA:

```
RouterA#sh ip route static
     172.16.0.0 255.255.255.0 is subnetted, 5 subnets
S       172.16.50.0 [1/0] via 172.16.20.2
```

```
S        172.16.40.0 [1/0] via 172.16.20.2
S        172.16.30.0 [1/0] via 172.16.20.2
```

RouterB

RouterB#**sh ip route**

Codes: C - connected, S - static, I - IGRP, R - RIP, M -
mobile, B - BGP, D - EIGRP, EX - EIGRP external, O - OSPF,
IA - OSPF inter area, E1 - OSPF external type 1, E2 - OSPF
external type 2, E - EGP, i - IS-IS, L1 - IS-IS level-1,
L2 - IS-IS level-2, * - candidate default

Gateway of last resort is not set

172.16.0.0 255.255.255.0 is subnetted, 5 subnets

```
C        172.16.30.0 is directly connected, Ethernet0
S        172.16.50.0 [1/0] via 172.16.40.2
C        172.16.40.0 is directly connected, Serial1
C        172.16.20.0 is directly connected, Serial0
S        172.16.10.0 [1/0] via 172.16.20.1
```

RouterC

RouterC#**sh ip route**

Codes: C - connected, S - static, I - IGRP, R - RIP, M -
mobile, B - BGP, D - EIGRP, EX - EIGRP external, O - OSPF,
IA - OSPF inter area, E1 - OSPF external type 1, E2 - OSPF
external type 2, E - EGP, i - IS-IS, L1 - IS-IS level-1,
L2 - IS-IS level-2, * - candidate default

Gateway of last resort is not set

172.16.0.0 255.255.255.0 is subnetted, 5 subnets

```
S        172.16.30.0 [1/0] via 172.16.40.1
C        172.16.50.0 is directly connected, Ethernet0
C        172.16.40.0 is directly connected, Serial0
S        172.16.20.0 [1/0] via 172.16.40.1
S        172.16.10.0 [1/0] via 172.16.40.1
```

Notice that all three routers possess paths to all five subnets. The "S" in the first column stands for static entries. Let's try and ping our host 172.16.50.2 now.

C:\>**ping 172.16.50.2**

Pinging 172.16.50.2 with 32 bytes of data:

```
Reply from 172.16.50.2: bytes=32 time=51ms TTL=29
Reply from 172.16.50.2: bytes=32 time=42ms TTL=29
Reply from 172.16.50.2: bytes=32 time=42ms TTL=29
Reply from 172.16.50.2: bytes=32 time=41ms TTL=29
```

It works! We just pinged from 172.16.10.2 to 172.16.50.2—yes! But it sure required a lot of work, didn't it? Just imagine doing that for dozens, if not hundreds, of routers! So if you're thinking there's got to be a better way, take a look at the next section on default routing—it just might make things easier.

Default Routing

First, a default route should be set in each router so that if a router doesn't know the path to a certain network, it can use that default route just like a host uses a default gateway. Setting the default route on Cisco routers is done in the same way as a static route; however, you create a default route entry using the network and subnet mask of all 0s. For example, to set the default route for RouterA in Figure 6.2, type:

```
RouterA(config)#ip route 0.0.0.0 0.0.0.0 172.16.20.2
```

Doing this tells RouterA that if it doesn't know what to do with a datagram, it should send it to 172.16.20.2 (the interface on RouterB).

For RouterB, we'll type in almost the same thing, only we'll designate a default route to RouterC and a default route to RouterA instead.

```
RouterB(config)#ip route 0.0.0.0 0.0.0.0 172.16.40.2
RouterB(config)#ip route 0.0.0.0 0.0.0.0 172.16.20.1
```

For RouterC, we'll set the default route to RouterB.

```
RouterC(config)#ip route 0.0.0.0 0.0.0.0 172.16.40.1
```

We've specified the default route for each of our routers, but there's still one more thing to discuss before this will work.

NOTE   The default route can also be referred to as a router or gateway of last resort.

IP Classless Command

Once in a while, a router receives packets destined for a subnet on a network that doesn't have a network default route. This can sometimes be a problem because, by default, if the subnet's number isn't in the routing table and there's no network default route, the Cisco IOS will simply toss out packets destined for a subnet that falls within its subnet-addressing scheme when they're received by a router. To get the Cisco IOS software to instead forward packets destined for the obscure subnets of directly connected networks onto the best route, you need the ip classless global configuration command.

The condition we just described is the reason we couldn't ping 172.16.20.2, even though the router was directly connected to network 20. Of course, if we'd had the ip classless command enabled, the Cisco IOS software would have forwarded those nebulous packets to the best route—in our case, the interface on RouterB.

The following example configures the router to forward packets destined for an unrecognized subnet to the best route possible:

```
RouterC#config t
Enter configuration commands, one per line.  End with CNTL/Z.
RouterC(config)#ip classless
RouterC(config)#^Z
RouterC#copy running-config startup-config
```

So, if you're using static routing, you should use the ip classless command.

Let's set the default routes on our routers and see if this will work without any static routes. We've taken out all the static routes and added ip classless commands to each router. To get a clear picture of what we did at RouterA, study the following:

```
RouterA#config t
Enter configuration commands, one per line.  End with CNTL/Z.
RouterA(config)#no ip route 172.16.50.0   △ SUBNET MASK.
RouterA(config)#no ip route 172.16.40.0
RouterA(config)#no ip route 172.16.30.0
RouterA(config)#ip route 0.0.0.0 0.0.0.0 172.16.20.2
RouterA(config)#ip classless
RouterA(config)#^Z
RouterA#copy run star
```

We did this at each router. The routing tables now look like this:

RouterA

```
RouterA#sh ip route
Codes: C - connected, S - static, I - IGRP, R - RIP, M -
mobile, B - BGP, D - EIGRP, EX - EIGRP external, O - OSPF,
IA - OSPF inter area, E1 - OSPF external type 1, E2 - OSPF
external type 2, E - EGP, i - IS-IS, L1 - IS-IS level-1,
L2 - IS-IS level-2, * - candidate default
Gateway of last resort is 172.16.20.2 to network 0.0.0.0
172.16.0.0 255.255.255.0 is subnetted, 2 subnets
C       172.16.20.0 is directly connected, Serial0
C       172.16.10.0 is directly connected, Ethernet0
S*    0.0.0.0 0.0.0.0 [1/0] via 172.16.20.2
```

RouterB

```
RouterB#sh ip route
Codes: C - connected, S - static, I - IGRP, R - RIP, M -
mobile, B - BGP, D - EIGRP, EX - EIGRP external, O - OSPF,
IA - OSPF inter area, E1 - OSPF external type 1, E2 - OSPF
external type 2, E - EGP, i - IS-IS, L1 - IS-IS level-1,
L2 - IS-IS level-2, * - candidate default
Gateway of last resort is 172.16.40.2 to network 0.0.0.0
172.16.0.0 255.255.255.0 is subnetted, 3 subnets
C       172.16.30.0 is directly connected, Ethernet0
C       172.16.40.0 is directly connected, Serial1
C       172.16.20.0 is directly connected, Serial0
S*    0.0.0.0 0.0.0.0 [1/0] via 172.16.40.2
                    [1/0] via 172.16.20.1
```

Notice the default route is set for both 172.16.40.2 and 172.16.20.1. If we set only the default route to RouterC, RouterB wouldn't know how to route packets back to network 10.

RouterC

```
RouterC#sh ip route
Codes: C - connected, S - static, I - IGRP, R - RIP, M -
mobile, B - BGP, D - EIGRP, EX - EIGRP external, O - OSPF,
IA - OSPF inter area, E1 - OSPF external type 1, E2 - OSPF
```

```
external type 2, E - EGP, i - IS-IS, L1 - IS-IS level-1,
L2 - IS-IS level-2, * - candidate default
Gateway of last resort is 172.16.40.1 to network 0.0.0.0
172.16.0.0 255.255.255.0 is subnetted, 2 subnets
C       172.16.50.0 is directly connected, Ethernet0
C       172.16.40.0 is directly connected, Serial0
S*   0.0.0.0 0.0.0.0 [1/0] via 172.16.40.1
```

The gateway of last resort is now set in all three routing tables. Let's check to see if we can ping from 172.16.10.2 to 172.16.50.2.

```
C:\>ping 172.16.50.2
Pinging 172.16.50.2 with 32 bytes of data:
Reply from 172.16.50.2: bytes=32 time=45ms TTL=29
Reply from 172.16.50.2: bytes=32 time=41ms TTL=29
Reply from 172.16.50.2: bytes=32 time=41ms TTL=29
Reply from 172.16.50.2: bytes=32 time=42ms TTL=29
```

Sure enough, it looks like things are working without the static routes. This method is a little easier than setting all the routes in each router. Also, if the routing tables aren't set correctly, this should help by forwarding the packets to the next router (but don't bet your job on it). It's best to have a working combination of both static and default routes, so we're going to explore dynamic routing in the next chapter. With that process, configuring static or default routes isn't necessary at all.

Summary

In this chapter, we covered the following key points:

- Understanding simple IP routing and how the IP and hardware address work and change as they go through a router.

- Understanding static routes and how a router uses them to make routing decisions.

- Configuring static routes and understanding how to update a Cisco router's routing table.

- Understanding default routes and the difference between a static route and a default route.

- Configuring default routes on a Cisco router.

Review Questions

1. Which Cisco IOS command can you use to see the routing table?

   A. sh ip config

   B. sh ip arp

   C. sh ip route   *p195*

   D. sh ip table

2. What is the command syntax for creating an IP static route in a Cisco Router?

   A. route IP *ip_address default_ gateway*

   B. IP route *destination_network subnet_mask default_gateway*   *p197*

   C. IP route *subnet_mask default_gateway network*

   D. IP route *default_gateway subnet_mask network*

3. What is the command syntax to set a gateway of last resort in your Cisco router?

   A. ip route 0.0.0.0 255.255.255.0 Next Hop Address

   B. route ip 0.0.0.0 255.255.255.0 Next Hop Address

   C. ip route 0.0.0.0 0.0.0.0 Next Hop Address   *p260*

   D. ip route 0.0.0.0 0.0.0.0 network

4. What is the command that you should use when using static and default routes with your Cisco routers?

   A. ip static

   B. ip default

   C. ip subnet-zero

   D. ip classless   *p201*

5. When should you use static routing instead of dynamic routing?

    A. Whenever you can

    B. When you have very few routers and want to save your bandwidth *p193*

    C. When you need the routing tables to be automatically updated

    D. When you want to use a default route

6. Static routes are used for which of the following?

    A. Defining a path to a router

    B. Defining a path to an IP destination network *p193*

    C. When you want to set a default gateway

    D. Updating the routing table dynamically

7. What are three ways that routers learn paths to destinations?

    A. Static routers

    B. Default routes

    C. Routing tables — *p192* *stores where it sends out*

    D. Dynamic routing

8. What is the administrative distance used for in static routes?

    A. Determining the network administrator for entering that route

    B. Creating a database *p227.*

    C. To rate the source's trustworthiness, expressed as a numeric value from 0 to 255

    D. To rate the source's trustworthiness, expressed as a numeric value from 0 to 1023

9. What is an administrative distance of 0?

    A. 0 is the default administrative distance for dynamic routing

    B. 0 is the default administrative distance for directly connected routes *P227*

    C. 0 means that there is no routing allowed on this router

    D. 0 means that there are 0 hops to the next destination

10. What does it mean if you have an administrative distance of 0?

    A. It means you can't get there from here

    B. 0 has the lowest trustworthiness rating

    C. 0 has the highest trustworthiness rating *P194*

    D. 0 means you are running RIP

11. What are three ways to build routing tables?

    A. Static

    B. Default

    C. Manual *P192*

    D. Dynamic

12. What is the default administrative distance of RIP?

    A. 0

    B. 100

    C. 120 *P228*

    D. 150

13. How do you create a default route?

    A. By using all 1s in place of the network and mask

    B. By defining a static route and using all 0s in place of the network and mask *P*

    C. By using 255 in place of the network and mask

    D. Login <name, password>

14. When looking at a routing table, what does the "S" mean?

    A. Dynamically connected

    B. Directly connected

    C. Statically connected   *p198*

    D. Sending packets

15. What is true about IP routing?

    A. The destination IP address changes at each hop

    B. The source IP address changes at each hop

    C. The frame does not change at each hop

    D. The frame changes at each hop   *192*

16. What static route parameter will tell a router the name of the interface to use to get to a destination network?

    A. Network

    B. Mask

    C. Interface   *p193*

    D. Address

17. When creating a static route, what is the gateway parameter used for?

    A. Defining the next hop

    B. Defining the weight

    C. Setting the static route   *p193*

    D. Updating the routing table

18. What does a router do with a received packet that is destined for an unknown network?

    A. Forwards the packet   *p201*

    B. Drops the packet — *1. prevent use gatoway.*

    C. Holds the packet till the next route update

    D. Sends a broadcast for the unknown network

19. What is true when creating static routes? (Choose all that apply.)

    A. The mask parameter is optional

    B. The gateway parameter is required

    C. The administrative distance is required *p.193*

    D. The administrative distance is optional

Best   worst
0 – 255 ⟶
NOT REQUIRED

20. When looking at the routing table, what does the "C" mean?

    A. Dynamic route

    B. Connected

    C. CLNS

    D. Directly connected *p195 – p198*

Laboratory Exercises

EXERCISE 6.1

Configuring Static Routes

This exercise will have you configure static routes into your Cisco routers.

1. Log in to your Cisco routers by either connecting a console cable to each router or using the Telnet utility.

2. Diagram the network as it is physically connected.

3. Create static routes to the remote subnets on your network by typing the command: **ip route destination_network subnet_mask default gateway**

4. Test connectivity to the remote networks with the ping command. (Does this work? Why not?)

EXERCISE 6.1 (CONTINUED)

5. Add the ip classless command to all your routers.

6. Test connectivity to the remote networks with the ping command. You should be able to ping all networks on your internetwork. If you can't, use the ping and ip route commands to troubleshoot where the problem lies.

EXERCISE 6.2

Configuring Default Routes

This next exercise will have you add default routes into your Cisco routers.

1. Log in to all your routers either by hooking up your console cable to each router or by using the Telnet utility.

2. Diagram your network as it is physically connected, or use the drawing you created from the exercise above.

3. Add the default routes in each of your routers by using the ip route 0.0.0.0 0.0.0.0 default_route command.

4. Test connectivity after removing your static routes.

5. Can you still ping to your remote networks? If not, use the ip route and ping utility to troubleshoot the problem.

CHAPTER

7

Dynamic IP Routing

On large internetworks, dynamic routing is generally the method of choice. Why? Because manually maintaining a static routing table would be overwhelmingly tedious (if not impossible) for a network administrator. Conversely, only minimal configuration is required with dynamic routing.

So let's really zoom in on dynamic routing and explore how routers communicate which protocols are used. We will also examine the different classes of dynamic routing protocols that are applied.

CCNA test objectives covered in this chapter include:

214 • Explain the services of separate and integrated multiprotocol routing

214 • List problems that each routing type encounters when dealing with topology changes and describe techniques to reduce the number of these problems

222 • Add the RIP routing protocol to your configuration

225 • Add the IGRP routing protocol to your configuration

Routed vs. Routing Protocols

First, we're going to talk about the confusion that can set in when talking about the terms "routed protocols" and "routing protocols." *Routed protocols* are used between routers to direct user traffic such as IP or IPX. Both IP and IPX can provide enough information in the network header of packets to enable a router to direct user traffic. Routed protocols specify the type of fields and how they're used within a packet. Packets that are defined as routed protocols can usually send data from end to end, that is, complete the path from sending to destination machines.

The only job that *routing protocols* have is to maintain routing tables that are used between routers. Examples of routing protocols are Routing Information Protocol (RIP), Open Shortest Path First (OSPF), Novell's Link-State Protocol (NLSP), a Cisco proprietary protocol called Interior Gateway Routing Protocol (IGRP), and Enhanced Interior Gateway Routing Protocol (EIGRP). These protocols provide a way of sharing route information with other routers for the purposes of updating and maintaining tables. These protocols don't send end-user data from network to network—routing protocols only pass routing information between routers.

Routers can support multiple independent routing protocols and can update and maintain routing tables for all routed protocols simultaneously. This allows us to create many networks over the same network media. Routers can do this because routed and routing protocols are focused—they pay no attention to each other's protocols. Thus it is called *ships-in-the-night routing*. Think of ships in a harbor, busy loading or unloading their freight. They pretty much ignore each other except to avoid colliding.

Most network communication occurs within small logical groups. Routing systems often mimic this behavior by designating logical groups of nodes as domains, autonomous systems, or areas.

A routing domain or autonomous system (AS) is a portion of an internetwork under common administrative authority. An AS consists of routers that share information using the same routing protocol. With certain protocols you can subdivide an AS into routing areas. Figure 7.1 shows how an AS could be set up.

FIGURE 7.1

Autonomous routing areas

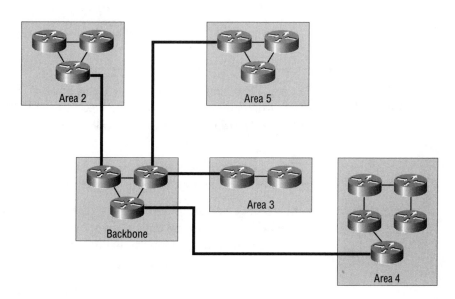

Figure 7.1 shows an autonomous system with a backbone and four areas. Areas 2, 3, 4, and 5 share information with the backbone and routers in their area only. This prevents unnecessary traffic, because most traffic occurs only within their own areas. Routing within a domain or area is called intra-domain routing. The routers that connect the areas to the backbone are called external, inter-domain, and inter-AS routers.

If you run your autonomous system on the Internet to connect your inter-network together, the Network Information Center (NIC) will assign you a unique 16-bit AS number that you use in configuring your system.

Exactly what interior routing protocols are and how they work within an autonomous system is what we'll explore next. After that, we'll define and examine exterior routing protocols.

Interior Routing Protocols

Interior routing is implemented at the Internet layer of the TCP/IP suite of protocols. An interior router can use an IP routing protocol and a specific routing algorithm to accomplish routing.

Examples of interior IP routing protocols include:

- RIP: a distance-vector routing protocol
- IGRP: Cisco's proprietary distance-vector routing protocol
- OSPF: a link-state routing protocol
- Enhanced IGRP: Cisco's balanced distance-vector routing protocol

OSPF and EIGRP are only introduced in this book. To get the detailed information you might need on OSFP and EIGRP, see *CCNP: Advanced Cisco Router Configuration Study Guide*, available through Sybex.

The interior routing protocols mentioned previously could be classified into two basic categories: distance-vector and link-state.

- Distance-vector understands the direction and distance to any network connection on the internetwork. Distance-vector listens to secondhand information to get its updates.

- Link-state, or shortest path first, understands the entire network better than distance-vector and never listens to secondhand information. Hence, it can make more accurate and informed routing decisions.

Well, okay then. Why not just use link-state? After all, it does seem to be the best choice. But is it? To really determine that, let's take a better look at the pros and cons of both and then decide.

Distance-Vector

What happens when a link drops or a connection gets broken? All routers must inform the other routers to update their routing tables. But sometimes you hear people complain about routing protocols slowing their network's performance. This can be because of convergence time—not the ubiquitous broadcast problem people love to gripe about regarding distance-vector protocols.

So what is convergence time? It's the time it takes for all the routers to update their tables when a reconfiguration, an outage, or a link drops—basically, when a change occurs. No data is passed during this time, and a slow-down is imminent. Once convergence is completed, all routers within the internetwork are operating with the same knowledge, and the internetwork is said to have converged. If convergence didn't happen, routers would possess outdated tables and make routing decisions based on potentially invalid information.

Distance-vector routing protocols update every 30 to 90 seconds. When they do this, it causes all routers to pass their entire routing tables to all other known routers.

Let's say you have three routers, A, B, and C, as shown in Figure 7.2. RouterA has direct connections to Networks 1 and 2. RouterB has direct connections to Networks 2 and 3. RouterC has direct connections to Networks 3 and 4.

FIGURE 7.2

Distance-vector routing tables

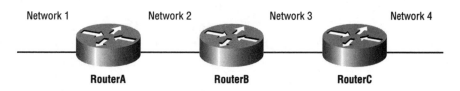

When distance-vector routers start up or get powered on, they get to know their neighbors; that is, they learn the metrics (hops) to the other routers on each of their interfaces. As the distance-vector network-discovery updates continue (every 30 seconds for RIP), routers discover the best path to destination networks. The paths are calculated by and based on the number of hops the routers are from each neighbor. In Figure 7.3, RouterC knows RouterB is connected to Network 1 by a metric of one. That means it must be a metric of two for RouterC to get to Network 1. RouterC will never be aware of the whole internetwork—it only knows secondhand what is "gossiped to it."

Remember convergence? Whenever the network topology changes for any reason, routing table updates must occur by each router sending out its entire routing table in the form of a broadcast to all the other routers. When a router receives the tables, it compares them with its own table. If it discovers a new network, or what it considers a faster way to get to one, it updates its table accordingly with that information.

Hop Count

What's the best way to a network? Distance-vector maintains that "the fewer hops, the better," and uses only hop counts when making its routing decisions. Take a look at Figure 7.3.

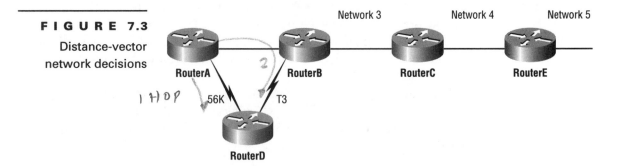

F I G U R E 7.3

Distance-vector network decisions

RouterA is getting to RouterD through a 56KB WAN link. RouterA can also reach RouterD via RouterB, which can get to RouterD through a T3. Which is faster? According to distance-vector, the fastest route would be through the 56KB pipe. Imagine sending 500MB files to a server plugged into a hub going to RouterD. It would take all day (and night)! So why in the world would it choose that path? Because distance-vector uses only metrics (hops) to base its routing decisions on, and in its opinion, one hop is better than two. The solution, of course, is to lie to RouterA that the metric to RouterD via the 56KB circuit is really three. This can be done manually and will cause RouterA to determine that two hops are better than three.

Routing Loops

A problem with distance-vector is routing loops. These can occur because every router is not updated at close to the same time. Let's say that the interface to Network 5 in Figure 7.3 fails. All routers know about Network 5 from RouterE. RouterA, in its tables, has a path to Network 5 through Routers B, C, and E. When Network 5 fails, RouterE tells RouterC. This causes RouterC to stop routing to Network 5 through RouterE. But Routers A, B, and D don't know about Network 5 yet, so they keep sending out update information. RouterC will eventually send out its update and cause B to stop routing to Network 5, but RouterA and RouterD are still not updated. To RouterA and RouterD, it appears that Network 5 is still available through RouterB with a metric of three.

So RouterA will send out its regular 30-second "Hello, I'm still here— these are the links I know about" message, which includes reachability for Network 5. Routers B and D then receive the wonderful news that Network 5 can be reached from RouterA. So Routers B and D send the information that Network 5 is available. Any packet destined for Network 5 will go to RouterA to B and then back to RouterA. This is a routing loop—what do you do to stop it?

Counting to Infinity

The routing loop problem just described is called *counting to infinity,* and it's caused by gossip and wrong information being communicated and propagated throughout the internetwork. Without some form of intervention, each time a packet passes though a router, the hop count would increase indefinitely.

One way of solving this problem is to define a maximum hop count. Distance-vector permits a hop count of up to 15, so anything that requires 16 hops is deemed unreachable. In other words, after a loop of 15 hops, Network 5 will be considered down. This means that counting to infinity, also known as exceeding TTL, will keep packets from going around the loop forever. Though a good solution, it won't remove the routing loop itself. Packets will still be attracted into the loop, but instead of traveling on it unchecked, they just whirl around for 16 bounces and then die.

Split Horizon

Another solution to the routing loop problem is called *split horizon*. It reduces incorrect routing information and routing overhead in a distance-vector network by enforcing the rule that information cannot be sent back in the direction from which that information was received. It would have prevented RouterA from sending the updated information it received from RouterB back to RouterB.

Route Poisoning

Another way to avoid problems caused by inconsistent updates is called *route poisoning*. When Network 5 goes down, RouterE initiates route poisoning by entering a table entry for Network 5 as 16 or unreachable (sometime referred to as *infinite*). By poisoning its route to Network 5, RouterE is not susceptible to incorrect updates about the route to Network 5. RouterE will keep this information in its tables until Network 5 comes up again, at which point it will trigger an update to notify its neighbors of the event.

Route poisoning and triggered updates will speed up convergence time, because neighboring routers don't have to wait 30 seconds (an eternity in computer land) before advertising the poisoned route.

Hold-Downs — for convergence

And then there are *hold-downs*. These work with route poisoning to prevent regular update messages from reinstating a route that's gone down. Hold-downs help prevent routes from changing too rapidly by allowing time for either the downed route to come back or for the network to stabilize somewhat before changing to the next best route. These also tell routers to restrict, for a specific time period, any changes that might affect recently removed routes. This prevents inoperative routers from being prematurely restored to other routers' tables.

Hold-downs use triggered updates, which reset the hold-down timer, to let the neighbor routers know of a change in the network. There are three instances that triggered updates will reset the hold-down timer:

1. HD timer expires

2. The router receives a processing task proportional to the number of links in the internetwork

3. Another update is received indicating the network status has changed

Link-State

Conversely, the link-state routing algorithm maintains a more complex table of topology information. Routers using the link-state concept are privileged to a complete understanding and view of all the links of distant routers, plus how they interconnect. The link-state routing process uses link-state packets (LSPs) or "hello packets" to inform other routers of distant links. In addition, it uses topological databases, the shortest path first (SPF) algorithm, and of course, a routing table.

Network discovery in link-state occurs quite differently than it does with distance-vector. First, routers exchange hello packets (LSPs) with one another giving them a bird's-eye view of the entire network. In this initial phase, each router communicates only its directly connected links. Second, all routers compile all of the LSPs received from the internetwork and build a topological database. After that, the SPF computes how each network can be reached, finding both the shortest and most efficient paths to each participating link-state network. Each router then creates a tree structure with itself representing the root.

The results are formed into a routing table, complete with a listing of the best paths—again, the best paths are not simply the shortest but the most efficient. Once these tasks are completed, the routers can use the table for switching packet traffic.

Unlike distance-vector, link-state understands that in order for a packet to get from RouterA to D most efficiently, the shortest path is via the T3—not through the painfully slow 56KB line. It knows this because it doesn't simply base its path choice decisions on hop count, it also analyzes things like available bandwidth and the amount of congestion on links to conclude what is truly the best path to a destination.

Convergence

Link-state routers also handle convergence in a completely different manner than distance-vector does. When the topology changes, the router or routers that first become aware of the event either send information to all other routers participating with the link-state algorithm, or send the news to a specific router that's designated to consult for table updates.

A router participating in a link-state network must do the following in order to converge:

1. Remember its neighbor's name, when it's up/down, and the cost of the path to that router.

2. Create an LSP that lists its neighbor's name and relative costs.

3. Send the newly created LSP to all other routers participating in the link-state network.

4. Receive LSPs from other routers and update its own database.

5. Build a complete map of the internetwork's topology from all the LSPs received, then compute the best route to each network destination.

Whenever a router receives an LSP packet, the router recalculates the best paths and updates the routing tables accordingly.

Power, Memory, and Bandwidth Needed

Some issues that must be considered when using link-state are processing power, memory usage, and bandwidth requirements.

To run the link-state algorithm, routers must have more power and memory available than what they require to run distance-vector. A Cisco router is designed specifically for this purpose.

In link-state, routers keep track of all their neighbors and all the networks they can reach. All that information—everything including various databases, the topology tree, and the routing table—must be stored in memory!

Dijkstra's algorithm states that a processing task proportional to the number of links in the internetwork multiplied by the number of routers in the network will compute the shortest path. What he means is that you need real processing power, ample memory, and a lot of bandwidth.

Why is the bandwidth requirement so important? Because when a link-state router comes online, it floods the internetwork with LSPs or hello packets and reduces the bandwidth available for actual data. You remember data, right? That stuff we're trying to get from point A to B.

The good news is that, unlike distance-vector, after this initial network deluge, link-state routers update their neighbors only every two hours on the average—unless a new router comes online or a link drops. And this two-hour period can be changed to be compatible with your bandwidth requirements. Let's say you have 56KB links to different continents. Would you use RIP (distance-vector) that updates every 30 seconds, or OSPF (link-state) that can be configured to update every 12 hours?

Another great thing about link-state is that with it, routers can be configured to use a designated router (DR) as the target to consult for all changes. All other routers on the same segment as the DR can contact this router directly for any pertinent network events instead of using the LSP broadcasts to communicate information.

You might be wondering what happens if the routers don't get an LSP packet? Or what happens if the link is slow and the network topology changes twice before some of the routers even receive the first LSP? Well, link-state routers can implement LSP time stamps, plus they can also use sequence numbers and aging schemes to avoid the spread of inaccurate LSP information. These features would be necessary only in large internetworks.

Comparing Distance-Vector to Link-State Routing

So, as you can see, there are quite a few major differences between the distance-vector and link-state routing algorithms. Let's take a moment to go over a few:

- Distance-vector routing gets all its topological data from secondhand information or network gossip, whereas link-state routing obtains a complete and accurate view of the internetwork by compiling LSPs.

- Distance-vector determines the best path by counting hops—by metrics. Link-state uses bandwidth analysis, plus other pertinent information to calculate the most efficient path.

- Distance-vector updates topology changes in 30-second intervals, adjustable in most cases, which can result in a slow convergence time. Link-state can be triggered by topology changes resulting in faster convergence times as LSPs are passed to other routers, sent to a multicast group of routers, or sent to a specific router.

All things considered, when it comes to routing protocols, there isn't any one solution for all networks. Routing choices shouldn't be based on fastest or cheapest as multivendor support or standards may well outweigh cost or other factors. Considerations like network simplicity, the need to set up and manage quickly and easily, or the ability to handle multiprotocols without complex configurations can be pivotal in making proper decisions for your network.

If you're still unclear on the best approach, how about a compromise? Utilizing the strengths of both, or hybrid routing, can be a great solution.

Balanced Hybrid

Balanced hybrid, or balanced routing, combines and uses the best of both distance-vector and link-state algorithms.

Although the hybrid approach does employ distance vectors with more accurate metric counts than those used by distance-vector alone to determine the path to an internetwork, it can converge quickly, thanks to the use of link-state triggers. Additionally, hybrid uses a more efficient link-state protocol that helps mitigate the problem of high bandwidth, processor power, and memory needs.

Some examples of hybrid protocols are OSI's IS-IS (Intermediate System to Intermediate System) and Cisco's EIGRP (Enhanced Interior Gateway Routing Protocol) talked about later in this chapter. But now, let's look at the Routing Information Protocol (RIP).

Routing Information Protocol (RIP)

RIP (and IGRP) always summarizes routing information by major network numbers. This is called *classfull routing. Classless* and *prefix routing protocols* allow contiguous blocks of hosts, subnets, or networks to be represented by a single route. RIP is a classfull routing protocol and does not support prefix routing.

RIP is a distance-vector routing protocol that practices classfull routing, which is used to discover the cost of a given route in terms of hops and store that information in the routing table.

The router can then consult the table in selecting the least costly, most efficient route to a destination. It gathers information by watching for routing table broadcasts by other routers and updating its own routing table in the event that a change occurs.

RIP is specified in RFC 1058 and updated with RFC 1723. Some of the differences defined in RFC 1723 are added security features. RIP messages are now allowed to carry more information in their updates.

RIP Routing Tables

At a minimum, RIP routing tables provide the following information:

- IP destination address
- A metric (numbered from 1 to 15) indicative of the total cost, in hops, of a particular route to a destination
- The IP address of the next router that a datagram would reach on the path to its destination
- A marker signaling recent changes to a route
- Timers, which are used to regulate performance
- Flags, which indicate whether the information about the route has recently changed
- Hold-downs used to prevent regular update messages from reinstating a route that's no longer functional
- Split horizon used to prevent routing loops
- A poison reverse update used to prevent larger routing loops

RIP sends out routing updates at regular intervals and whenever a network topology change occurs.

When a router that's running RIP receives new information indicating a better route to a destination, the new information replaces the older entry in its table. For example, if a router loses a link, it will recalculate the routes in its own tables and then send the revised information out to all its neighbors. Each router will receive this information, update its table accordingly, and then send the information out to all its neighbors.

Neighbors are routers with interfaces to a common network.

All of this sounds pretty cool, but there are a few drawbacks. For one thing, when a topology change takes place, it results in slow convergence. In a large network, this can very well lead to the counting to infinity problem, plus the routing loops that were talked about earlier.

RIP Packet Format

All things considered, you can see that RIP can be quite useful for routing within small- to moderate-sized homogenous internetworks. But, its small hop count limit and single metric don't really allow much flexibility in complex environments and, in fact, can cause a problem or two. Figure 7.4 shows the RIP packet format.

F I G U R E 7.4

RIP packet format

1 byte	1 byte	2 bytes	2 bytes	2 bytes	4 bytes	4 bytes	4 bytes	4 bytes
Command	Version number	Zero	Address family identifier	Zero	Address	Zero	Zero	Metric

The following bullet points summarize the fields in a RIP packet:

- The command field indicates whether the packet is a request or a response. A request is a packet from a router that asks another router to send all or part of its routing table. The response typically indicates that the packet is a reply to an unsolicited, regular routing update.

- The version number specifies which version of RIP is being implemented. Since there can be different versions of RIP implemented, this number can actually be specifying different, potentially incompatible implementations.

- The address family identifier field follows a field of 16 zeros. It identifies the type of addressing scheme used by a destination address for which update information is being given or sought in the RIP packet. The field will show a value of two when used with IP.

- Another field of 16 zeros precedes the address field. This field contains the address of a destination, and exists either as an update for the RIP packet's recipient or as a request by the packet's sender for update information about routes to it.

- The metric field follows two more 32-bit fields of zeros, and specifies the hop count to the destination whose address family and address were given in the preceding fields. Up to 25 destinations may be listed in a single RIP packet. If more than 25 entries need to be sent, the router will send its update in as many packets as necessary.

RIP Timers

RIP uses timers to regulate its performance:

- Routing Update Timer: This sets the interval (typically 30 seconds) between periodic routing updates in which the router sends a complete copy of its routing table out to all neighbors.

- Route Invalid Timer: This determines the length of time that must expire (90 seconds) before a router determines that a route has become invalid. It will come to this conclusion if it hasn't heard any updates about a particular route for that period. When that happens, the router will send out updates to all its neighbors letting them know that the route is invalid.

- Route Flush Timer: This sets the time between a route becoming invalid and its removal from the routing table (240 seconds). Before it's removed from the table, the router notifies its neighbors of that route's impending doom. The value of the route invalid timer must be less than that of the route flush timer. The reason for this is to provide the router with enough time to tell its neighbors about the invalid route before the routing table is updated.

Interior Gateway Routing Protocol (IGRP)

Interior Gateway Routing Protocol (IGRP) is also a distance-vector interior routing protocol that is proprietary to Cisco. Cisco developed the IGRP protocol in answer to RIP's shortcomings when used in larger autonomous systems. IGRP has a huge hop count limit—255 instead of RIP's measly 15.

IGRP Routing Tables

To build routing tables, IGRP can use the following:

- Metrics: These can be between 1 and 255; set by an administrator to influence route selection.

- Delay: The speed of the media in units of 10 milliseconds. For 10Mbps Ethernet, the delay is 100, or one ms.

- Bandwidth: These values reflect speed from 1200bps to 10Gbps.

- Reliability: Represented in fractions of 255 (where 255 is optimal).

- Load: Represents the saturation of the link in a fraction of 255 (where 0 equals no load).

IGRP can take all of these factors into consideration when making a routing decision, and administrators can adjust the settings of IGRP to help meet the individual performance needs of their internetwork.

To enhance operating stability, IGRP employs the following:

- Multipath routing: Dual lines of equal bandwidth may run a single stream of traffic in a round-robin fashion. This affords both performance and redundancy if a line goes down.

- Hold-downs: Used to prevent regular update messages from reinstating a downed link. If a route goes down during convergence, it will prevent routers that haven't heard the news of the downed link from misinforming other routers that they have a path to the route. Hold-downs tell routers to hold down any changes that might affect stated routes for a specific period of time. This period is slightly greater than the period of time necessary to update the entire network with a routing change.

- Split horizons: Information is never sent back to the router from which it came to prevent routing loops. Most often, hold-downs should effectively prevent routing loops, but IGRP uses split horizons as well because doing so provides extra algorithm stability.

- Poison reverse updates: Used to correct larger loops. Increases in routing metrics are generally indicative of routing loops. Poison reverse is used to remove the problem route and place it in hold-down.

IGRP Timers

To control performance, IGRP includes timers with default settings for each of the following:

- Update timers: These specify how frequently routing update messages should be sent. The default is 90 seconds.

- Invalid timers: These specify how long a router should wait before declaring a route invalid because it didn't receive a specific update about it. The default is three times the update period.

- Hold-Down timers: These specify the hold-down period. The default is three times the update timer period, plus 10 seconds.

- Flush timers: These indicate how much time should pass before a route should be flushed from the routing table. The default is seven times the routing update period.

IGRP Routes

IGRP advertises three types of routes:

- Interior: These are routes between subnets. If a network isn't subnetted, then IGRP doesn't advertise interior routes.

- System: These are routes to networks within an autonomous system. They are derived from directly connected interfaces, other IGRP routes, or access servers. They don't include subnet information.

- Exterior: These are routes to networks outside of the autonomous system. They are considered when identifying a gateway of last resort. The gateway of last resort is chosen from the list of exterior routes that IGRP provides.

As mentioned in Chapter 6, an administrative distance or metric can be used to represent the trustworthiness of the routing update source. Each type of route and routing protocol is assigned a particular administrative distance. The higher the value, the less trusted the source. Table 7.1 shows the current IOS software administrative distances.

T A B L E 7.1 Default administrative distances	Route Source	Default Distance
	Directly Connected Interface	0
	Static Route	1
	Enhanced IGRP Summary Route	5
	External BGP	20
	Internal Enhanced IGRP	90
	IGRP	100

TABLE 7.1 (cont.)	Route Source	Default Distance
Default administrative distances	OSPF	110
	IS-IS	115
	RIP	120
	EGP	140
	Internal BGP	200
	Unknown	255

Notice that the default RIP metric is 120 and that IGRP is 100. This means the router will trust a route entered by IGRP, prioritizing it over something entered by RIP.

Open Shortest Path First (OSPF)

Since OSPF is based on link-state algorithms, it's known as a link-state routing protocol. It's deployed within an *autonomous system,* a group of routers that share a routing protocol. When that protocol happens to be OSPF, each router retains its own database describing the topology of the autonomous system on which it's located.

This kind of system is much more flexible and has the following additional advantages:

- Network administrators are free to assign costs to a particular link. The total cost for a given path doesn't necessarily have to have a limit. It can accommodate huge networks since its upper metric limit is 65,535. Since each node creates a link-state database tree representing the network with itself as the tree's root, it's well equipped to choose the most direct path to a given destination. If more than one route of equal cost exists, OSPF routers can balance the load of network traffic between all available and equally cost-effective routes.

- Link-state routing advertisements are broadcasted much less often— only when a change is detected—thereby reducing network overhead.

- Link-state routing update packets can efficiently carry information for more than one router. This type of packet is sent only to adjacencies, or neighboring routers, that are selected to swap routing information. This is a "tell a friend" arrangement that further contributes to network efficiency.

- Even though OSPF is an interior routing protocol, it can receive and send routes to other autonomous systems.

Additional features offered by OSPF include:

- Type of service routing (TOS)

- Support for one or more metrics

- Variable-length subnet masks (VLSMs)

Enhanced Interior Gateway Routing Protocol (EIGRP)

The proprietary Cisco routing protocol, Enhanced IGRP (EIGRP), combines the advantages of link-state routing protocols with those of distance-vector protocols so it's considered a balanced hybrid routing protocol. It employs distance vectors to determine the best paths to destination networks, but resembles a link-state protocol in the way it uses topology changes to trigger routing database updates.

EIGRP includes the following features:

- Fast convergence

- Variable-length subnet masks

- Partial-bounded updates

- Multiprotocol support: IP/IPX/AppleTalk

Unlike RIP, EIGRP doesn't make periodic updates. When an EIGRP router first communicates with its neighbors, it receives complete routing tables from them. After this initial communication, it sends only routing changes (or partial updates). It also sends these changes only to the neighboring routers that would be affected by the changes. This yields improved bandwidth and accounts for the efficiency of Enhanced IGRP.

Exterior Routing Protocols

Exterior routing protocols were designed to communicate between autonomous systems (AS). These protocols are more complex than interior routing protocols, because they need to possess more information about a greater number of routers.

Exterior routing protocols are only introduced in this book. For a more detailed explanation on how EGP and BGP work please see *CCNP: Advanced Cisco Router Configuration Study Guide,* available through Sybex.

Exterior Gateway Protocol (EGP)

Even though Exterior Gateway Protocol (EGP) is a dynamic routing protocol, it uses a simple design. Its routing updates specify that only certain networks are accessible through specific routers. EGP doesn't use metrics like interior routing protocols, so it can't detect or correct routing loops.

EGP is a distance-vector protocol that allows ASs to communicate through a core routing network that connects the ASs together. These ASs have only one connection to the core, and can connect to each other only through the core. Figure 7.5 shows how this core EGP AS looks.

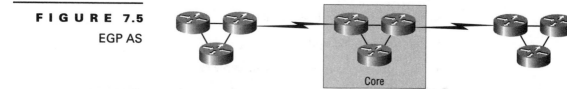

FIGURE 7.5
EGP AS

EGP Functions

EGP has three main functions:

- EGP routers establish a set of neighbors with which they share accessibility information.

- EGP routers send polls to their neighbors to see if they're "alive."

- EGP routers send update messages containing accessibility information on the network within their autonomous system.

EGP Message Types

EGP uses the following message types:

- Neighbor acquisition messages to test if neighbors are alive

- Neighbor reachability messages to determine when a neighbor is down

- Poll messages to acquire accessibility information about the networks on which remote hosts reside

- Error messages to identify various error conditions

Border Gateway Protocol (BGP)

Border Gateway Protocol (BGP) is an inter-autonomous system protocol created for use on the Internet. Unlike EGP, BGP can be used both between and within autonomous systems, and it can determine routing loops. For two BGP neighbors to communicate, they must be on the same physical network.

Routers within the same autonomous system ensure that all of the routers in that AS have a consistent view of it. The communication between routers in the same AS serves to determine the connection point to or from certain external autonomous systems. Figure 7.6 shows how a BGP can communicate between ASs.

FIGURE 7.6

A BGP AS

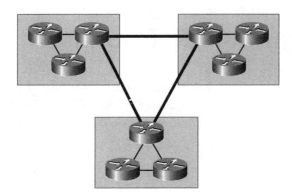

BGP doesn't use a core like EGP because with BGP, all areas can interconnect to each other and communicate without going through a central backbone core.

When a BGP router first comes online, it receives a complete BGP routing table from its neighbors. If a change occurs, updates are sent out incrementally.

The BGP metric specifies the degree of preference for a particular path. These preferences can be based on an autonomous system count, the type of link, and other factors. Metrics are typically assigned by the network administrator through configuration files.

BGP Message Types

One of BGP's features is that it keeps track of all the possible routes to a destination, but will advertise only what it considers to be the best or optimal route in its update messages. These update messages contain both a network number and an autonomous system path. The latter indicates the string of autonomous systems through which the specified networks can be reached. In other words, BGP lists the route to the destination. This precludes the counting to infinity and slow convergence problems associated with other distance-vector protocols.

In addition to update messages, BGP uses three other message types:

- Open: this is the first message sent after a transport protocol connection is established.

- Notification: this message is sent when an error is detected.

- Keepalive: these messages are sent often enough to keep the hold timer from expiring.

Configuring RIP Routing

It's time to learn how to turn on the dynamic routing protocol RIP. To teach you how, we'll add RIP routing to the three routers in our internetwork. First, you should know that adding RIP involves the following:

- Logging on to all local and remote routers

- Enabling RIP on the router

- Enabling the networks that you want RIP to advertise

Let's take another look at the lab setup. Figure 7.7 shows us our three routers.

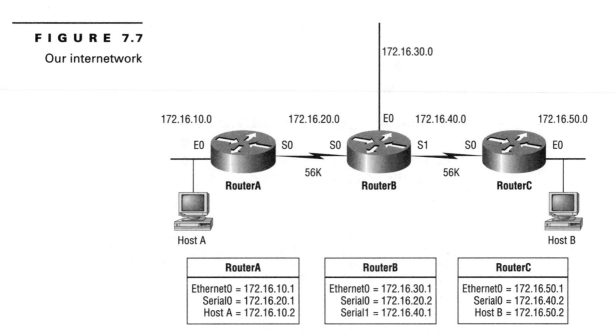

FIGURE 7.7

Our internetwork

Removing Existing Static and Default Entries

To begin, we're going to look at the three routing tables and take out all existing static and default entries.

RouterA

```
RouterA#sh ip route
Codes: C - connected, S - static, I - IGRP, R - RIP, M -
mobile, B - BGP, D - EIGRP, EX - EIGRP external, O - OSPF,
IA - OSPF inter area, E1 - OSPF external type 1, E2 - OSPF
external type 2, E - EGP, i - IS-IS, L1 - IS-IS level-1,
L2 - IS-IS level-2, * - candidate default

Gateway of last resort is 172.16.20.2 to network 0.0.0.0

     172.16.0.0 255.255.255.0 is subnetted, 5 subnets
S       172.16.50.0 [1/0] via 172.16.20.2
S       172.16.40.0 [1/0] via 172.16.20.2
```

```
S        172.16.30.0 [1/0] via 172.16.20.2
C        172.16.20.0 is directly connected, Serial0
C        172.16.10.0 is directly connected, Ethernet0
S*   0.0.0.0 0.0.0.0 [1/0] via 172.16.20.2
```

RouterA#**config t**

Enter configuration commands, one per line. End with CNTL/Z.

RouterA(config)#**no ip route 172.16.50.0**

RouterA(config)#**no ip route 172.16.40.0**

RouterA(config)#**no ip route 172.16.30.0**

RouterA(config)#**no ip route 0.0.0.0**

RouterA(config)#**exit**

RouterA#**sh ip route**

```
Codes: C - connected, S - static, I - IGRP, R - RIP, M -
mobile, B - BGP, D - EIGRP, EX - EIGRP external, O - OSPF,
IA - OSPF inter area, E1 - OSPF external type 1, E2 - OSPF
external type 2, E - EGP, i - IS-IS, L1 - IS-IS level-1,
L2 - IS-IS level-2, * - candidate default
```

Gateway of last resort is not set

```
     172.16.0.0 255.255.255.0 is subnetted, 2 subnets
C        172.16.20.0 is directly connected, Serial0
C        172.16.10.0 is directly connected, Ethernet0
```

RouterA#**wr mem**

Building configuration...

[OK]

RouterB

RouterB#**sh ip route**

```
Codes: C - connected, S - static, I - IGRP, R - RIP, M -
mobile, B - BGP, D - EIGRP, EX - EIGRP external, O - OSPF,
IA - OSPF inter area, E1 - OSPF external type 1, E2 - OSPF
external type 2, E - EGP, i - IS-IS, L1 - IS-IS level-1, L2
- IS-IS level-2, * - candidate default
```

Gateway of last resort is 172.16.20.1 to network 0.0.0.0

```
     172.16.0.0 255.255.255.0 is subnetted, 5 subnets
```

```
S        172.16.50.0 [1/0] via 172.16.40.2
C        172.16.30.0 is directly connected, Ethernet0
C        172.16.40.0 is directly connected, Serial1
C        172.16.20.0 is directly connected, Serial0
S        172.16.10.0 [1/0] via 172.16.20.1
S*   0.0.0.0 0.0.0.0 [1/0] via 172.16.20.1
             [1/0] via 172.16.40.2
```

RouterB#**config t**

Enter configuration commands, one per line. End with CNTL/Z.

RouterB(config)#**no ip route 172.16.50.0**

RouterB(config)#**no ip route 172.16.10.0**

RouterB(config)#**no ip route 0.0.0.0**

RouterB(config)#**exit**

RouterB#**sh ip route**

```
Codes: C - connected, S - static, I - IGRP, R - RIP, M -
mobile, B - BGP, D - EIGRP, EX - EIGRP external, O - OSPF,
IA - OSPF inter area, E1 - OSPF external type 1, E2 - OSPF
external type 2, E - EG, i - IS-IS, L1 - IS-IS level-1, L2 -
IS-IS level-2, * - candidate default


Gateway of last resort is not set


     172.16.0.0 255.255.255.0 is subnetted, 3 subnets
C        172.16.30.0 is directly connected, Ethernet0
C        172.16.40.0 is directly connected, Serial1
C        172.16.20.0 is directly connected, Serial0
```

RouterB#**copy runn star**

Building configuration...

[OK]

RouterC

RouterC#**sh ip route**

```
Codes: C - connected, S - static, I - IGRP, R - RIP, M -
mobile, B - BGP, D - EIGRP, EX - EIGRP external, O - OSPF,
IA - OSPF inter area, E1 - OSPF external type 1, E2 - OSPF
external type 2, E - EGP, i - IS-IS, L1 - IS-IS level-1,
L2 - IS-IS level-2, * - candidate default
```

Gateway of last resort is 172.16.40.1 to network 0.0.0.0

```
        172.16.0.0 255.255.255.0 is subnetted, 5 subnets
C       172.16.50.0 is directly connected, Ethernet0
C       172.16.40.0 is directly connected, Serial0
S       172.16.30.0 [1/0] via 172.16.40.1
S       172.16.20.0 [1/0] via 172.16.40.1
S       172.16.10.0 [1/0] via 172.16.40.1
S*    0.0.0.0 0.0.0.0 [1/0] via 172.16.40.1
RouterC#config t
Enter configuration commands, one per line.  End with CNTL/Z.
RouterC(config)#no ip route 172.16.30.0
RouterC(config)#no ip route 172.16.20.0
RouterC(config)#no ip route 172.16.10.0
RouterC(config)#no ip route 0.0.0.0
RouterC(config)#exit
RouterC#sh ip route
Codes: C - connected, S - static, I - IGRP, R - RIP, M -
mobile, B - BGP, D - EIGRP, EX - EIGRP external, O - OSPF,
IA - OSPF inter area, E1 - OSPF external type 1, E2 - OSPF
external type 2, E - EGP, i - IS-IS, L1 - IS-IS level-1, L2
- IS-IS level-2, * - candidate default

Gateway of last resort is not set

        172.16.0.0 255.255.255.0 is subnetted, 2 subnets
C       172.16.50.0 is directly connected, Ethernet0
C       172.16.40.0 is directly connected, Serial0
RouterC#wr mem
Building configuration...
[OK]
```

Adding RIP

Okay, now that we have our routing tables clear, we can add RIP so that our routing tables will be dynamically updated.

To do this, we first need to log in to all three routers. We do this by connecting the console cable to each router, one at a time. If we needed to connect remotely, we could telnet into each router, but we'd have to do that before we remove the static routes. If we don't remove the static routes, we wouldn't be able to communicate with the remote routers. Of course, you can always telnet into your closest neighbor, then telnet into their neighbor, and so on, but that's not very efficient.

We're going to add the RIP protocol in RouterA and then tell the router what networks we want it to advertise. Since we have only one network (172.16.0.0), that's the only entry we'll set in the router. An RIP router will accept only major networks. For example, if a specific address, such as 172.16.10.10 is entered, the router will accept it and discard the host portion, retaining only the major network information.

RouterA

```
RouterA#config t
Enter configuration commands, one per line.  End with CNTL/Z.
RouterA(config)#router rip
RouterA(config-router)#network 172.16.0.0
RouterA(config-router)#^Z
RouterA#wr mem
Building configuration...
[OK]
```

We'll do the same thing for RouterB.

RouterB

```
RouterB#config t
Enter configuration commands, one per line.  End with CNTL/Z.
RouterB(config)#router rip
RouterB(config-router)#network 172.16.0.0
RouterB(config-router)#^Z
RouterB#copy runn star
Building configuration...
[OK]
```

Notice we typed in copy runn star to save the running configuration to startup configuration. We are just showing alternative ways to do the same thing.

And for RouterC:

RouterC

```
RouterC#config t
Enter configuration commands, one per line.  End with CNTL/Z.
RouterC(config)#router rip
RouterC(config-router)#network 172.16.0.0
RouterC(config-router)#^Z
RouterC#wr mem
Building configuration...
[OK]
```

Testing RIP—Scenario 1

Let's test RIP to see if it's working by taking a look at our routing tables. Notice the "R" in the routing tables? That stands for RIP entries.

RouterA

```
RouterA#sh ip route
Codes: C - connected, S - static, I - IGRP, R - RIP, M -
mobile, B - BGP, D - EIGRP, EX - EIGRP external, O - OSPF,
IA - OSPF inter area, E1 - OSPF external type 1, E2 - OSPF
external type 2, E - EGP, i - IS-IS, L1 - IS-IS level-1,
L2 - IS-IS level-2, * - candidate default

Gateway of last resort is not set

     172.16.0.0 255.255.255.0 is subnetted, 5 subnets
R       172.16.50.0 [120/2] via 172.16.20.2, 00:00:12, Serial0
R       172.16.40.0 [120/1] via 172.16.20.2, 00:00:12, Serial0
R       172.16.30.0 [120/1] via 172.16.20.2, 00:00:12, Serial0
C       172.16.20.0 is directly connected, Serial0
C       172.16.10.0 is directly connected, Ethernet0
```

We can view only the RIP-found networks by typing **sh ip route rip**. From RouterA, the command output would look like this:

```
RouterA#sh ip route rip
        172.16.0.0 255.255.255.0 is subnetted, 5 subnets
R       172.16.50.0 [120/2] via 172.16.20.2, 00:00:12, Serial0
R       172.16.40.0 [120/1] via 172.16.20.2, 00:00:12, Serial0
R       172.16.30.0 [120/1] via 172.16.20.2, 00:00:12, Serial0
```

RouterB

```
RouterB#sh ip route
Codes: C - connected, S - static, I - IGRP, R - RIP, M -
mobile, B - BGP, D - EIGRP, EX - EIGRP external, O - OSPF,
IA - OSPF inter area, E1 - OSPF external type 1, E2 - OSPF
external type 2, E - EGP, i - IS-IS, L1 - IS-IS level-1,
L2 - IS-IS level-2, * - candidate default

Gateway of last resort is not set

        172.16.0.0 255.255.255.0 is subnetted, 5 subnets

R       172.16.50.0 [120/1] via 172.16.40.2, 00:00:06, Serial1
C       172.16.40.0 is directly connected, Serial1
C       172.16.30.0 is directly connected, Ethernet0
C       172.16.20.0 is directly connected, Serial0
R       172.16.10.0 [120/1] via 172.16.20.1, 00:00:03, Serial0
```

RouterC

```
RouterC#sh ip route
Codes: C - connected, S - static, I - IGRP, R - RIP, M -
mobile, B - BGP, D - EIGRP, EX - EIGRP external, O - OSPF,
IA - OSPF inter area, E1 - OSPF external type 1, E2 - OSPF
external type 2, E - EGP, i - IS-IS, L1 - IS-IS level-1, L2
- IS-IS level-2, * - candidate default

Gateway of last resort is not set

        172.16.0.0 255.255.255.0 is subnetted, 5 subnets
C       172.16.50.0 is directly connected, Ethernet0
C       172.16.40.0 is directly connected, Serial0
R       172.16.30.0 [120/1] via 172.16.40.1, 00:00:16, Serial0
```

```
R       172.16.20.0 [120/1] via 172.16.40.1, 00:00:16, Serial0
R       172.16.10.0 [120/2] via 172.16.40.1, 00:00:16, Serial0
```

All the networks are there. Let's make sure it works by pinging between our two hosts (172.16.10.2 to 172.16.50.2):

C:\>ping 172.16.50.2

```
Pinging 172.16.50.2 with 32 bytes of data:

Reply from 172.16.50.2: bytes=32 time=48ms TTL=29
Reply from 172.16.50.2: bytes=32 time=41ms TTL=29
Reply from 172.16.50.2: bytes=32 time=41ms TTL=29
Reply from 172.16.50.2: bytes=32 time=41ms TTL=29
```

Looks like RIP is enabled! It will work great for our small internetwork. Let's take a look at the Etherpeek trace to see the RIP updates in action.

```
    Flags:          0x00
    Status:         0x00
    Packet Length:110
    Timestamp:      14:55:10.075000 05/19/1998
Ethernet Header
    Destination:  ff:ff:ff:ff:ff:ff Ethernet Broadcast
    Source:         00:00:0c:8d:5c:9d
    Protocol Type:08-00   IP
IP Header - Internet Protocol Datagram
    Version:               4
    Header Length:         5
    Precedence:            0
    Type of Service:       %000
    Unused:                %00
    Total Length:          92
    Identifier:            0
    Fragmentation Flags:   %000
    Fragment Offset:       0
    Time To Live:          2
    IP Type:               0x11   UDP
    Header Checksum:       0x0281
```

Source IP Address: 172.16.10.1

Dest. IP Address: 255.255.255.255 IP Broadcast

No Internet Datagram Options

UDP - User Datagram Protocol

Source Port: 520 *RIP*

Destination Port: 520

Length: 72

Checksum: 0xd0fd

RIP - Routing Information Protocol

Command: 2 *Response containing network distance pairs*

Version: 1

Zero: 0x0000

Info on Net # 1

Network Number: 2

Zero: 0x0000

Net Address: 172.16.50.0

Zero: 0x0000000000000000

Distance: 3

Info on Net # 2

Network Number: 2

Zero: 0x0000

Net Address: 172.16.40.0

Zero: 0x0000000000000000

Distance: 2

Info on Net # 3

Network Number: 2

Zero: 0x0000

Net Address: 172.16.30.0

Zero: 0x0000000000000000

Distance: 2

Info on Net # 4

Network Number: 2

Zero: 0x0000

Net Address: 172.16.20.0

Zero: 0x0000000000000000

```
Distance:              1
Frame Check Sequence:  0x00000000
```

Sure enough—RIP is sending a broadcast of its whole table just as you learned it would earlier. And notice that within the RIP packet, the only information about the subnet is the distance (hop count).

Testing RIP—Scenario 2

Let's unplug an interface on RouterC and see what happens. We'll look at it from the console port in RouterA. We unplugged Ethernet0 on RouterC, and the interface to 172.16.50.0 went down.

RouterA

```
RouterA#sh ip route
Codes: C - connected, S - static, I - IGRP, R - RIP, M -
mobile, B - BGP, D - EIGRP, EX - EIGRP external, O - OSPF,
IA - OSPF inter area, E1 - OSPF external type 1, E2 - OSPF
external type 2, E - EGP, i - IS-IS, L1 - IS-IS level-1,
L2 - IS-IS level-2, * - candidate default

Gateway of last resort is not set

      172.16.0.0 255.255.255.0 is subnetted, 5 subnets
R        172.16.50.0 255.255.255.0 is possibly down,
            routing via 172.16.20.2, Serial0
R        172.16.40.0 [120/1] via 172.16.20.2, 00:00:19, Serial0
R        172.16.30.0 [120/1] via 172.16.20.2, 00:00:19, Serial0
C        172.16.20.0 is directly connected, Serial0
C        172.16.10.0 is directly connected, Ethernet0
RouterA#
```

Notice that RouterA thinks that Network 172.16.50.0 is down, and that it's holding down the table entry until it finds out for sure. The reason RouterA thinks Network 50 is down is because it hasn't received an RIP broadcast from RouterB telling RouterA that Network 172.16.50.0 is up and available through RouterB in three hops as shown in our Etherpeek trace.

```
Flags:    0x00
Status:   0x00
```

```
Packet Length:90
Timestamp:     15:06:17.081000 05/19/1998
Ethernet Header
  Destination:  ff:ff:ff:ff:ff:ff Ethernet Brdcast
  Source:       00:00:0c:8d:5c:9d
  Protocol Type:08-00   IP
IP Header - Internet Protocol Datagram
  Version:              4
  Header Length:        5
  Precedence:           0
  Type of Service:      %000
  Unused:               %00
  Total Length:         72
  Identifier:           0
  Fragmentation Flags:  %000
  Fragment Offset:      0
  Time To Live:         2
  IP Type:              0x11  UDP
  Header Checksum:      0x0295
  Source IP Address:    172.16.10.1
  Dest. IP Address:     255.255.255.255 IP Broadcast
  No Internet Datagram Options
UDP - User Datagram Protocol
  Source Port:          520  RIP
  Destination Port:     520
  Length:               52
  Checksum:             0xaf3b
RIP - Routing Information Protocol
  Command:              2  Response containing network distance
pairs
  Version:              1
  Zero:                 0x0000
Info on Net # 1
  Network Number:   2
  Zero:             0x0000
  Net Address:      172.16.40.0
```

```
       Zero:                0x0000000000000000
       Distance:            2
Info on Net # 2
   Network Number:          2
       Zero:                0x0000
   Net Address:             172.16.30.0
       Zero:                0x0000000000000000
       Distance:            2
Info on Net # 3
   Network Number:          2
       Zero:                0x0000
   Net Address:             172.16.20.0
       Zero:                0x0000000000000000
       Distance:            1
   Frame Check Sequence:    0x00000000
```

The RIP packet isn't updating the tables regarding Network 50, and since Network 50 is down, this is a good thing.

RouterA isn't telling RouterB about Network 50—it's still holding it down in its routing table. Let's plug Network 50 back in and see how long it takes for the network to converge.

```
Flags:          0x00
   Status:          0x00
   Packet Length:110
   Timestamp:      15:09:32.590000 05/19/1998
Ethernet Header
   Destination:    ff:ff:ff:ff:ff:ff Ethernet Broadcast
   Source:         00:00:0c:8d:5c:9d
   Protocol Type:08-00    IP
IP Header - Internet Protocol Datagram
   Version:               4
   Header Length:         5
   Precedence:            0
   Type of Service:       %000
   Unused:                %00
   Total Length:          92
   Identifier:            0
```

Fragmentation Flags:	%000
Fragment Offset:	0
Time To Live:	2
IP Type:	0x11 *UDP*
Header Checksum:	0x0281
Source IP Address:	172.16.10.1
Dest. IP Address:	255.255.255.255 IP Broadcast

No Internet Datagram Options
UDP - User Datagram Protocol

Source Port:	520 *RIP*
Destination Port:	520
Length:	72
Checksum:	0xd0fd

RIP - Routing Information Protocol

Command: 2 *Response containing network distance pairs*

Version:	1
Zero:	0x0000

Info on Net # 1

Network Number:	2
Zero:	0x0000
Net Address:	172.16.50.0
Zero:	0x0000000000000000
Distance:	3

Info on Net # 2

Network Number:	2
Zero:	0x0000
Net Address:	172.16.40.0
Zero:	0x0000000000000000
Distance:	2

Info on Net # 3

Network Number:	2
Zero:	0x0000
Net Address:	172.16.30.0
Zero:	0x0000000000000000
Distance:	2

```
Info on Net # 4
    Network Number:      2
    Zero:                0x0000
    Net Address:         172.16.20.0
    Zero:                0x0000000000000000
    Distance:            1
Frame Check Sequence:    0x00000000
```

RouterC immediately sent out an update to RouterB, which immediately sent out an update to RouterA telling it that Network 172.16.50.0 is up and available through RouterB to RouterC. Notice that because Routers A and B did a hold-down on Network 172.16.50.0 in their routing tables, we didn't end up with a routing loop.

Passive RIP

What if you wanted to run RIP on your local network, which is connected to the Internet, but you don't want to advertise your network on that route? No worries—you can use the passive command. This command stops the router from sending out any updates on the specified interface. For example, in Figure 7.8, our three routers are connected to the Internet through Serial1 on RouterC.

FIGURE 7.8

Route from our inter-network to the Internet

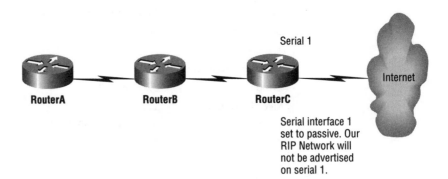

We'd then type in the following command:

RouterC#**config t**

```
Enter configuration commands, one per line.  End with CNTL/Z.
RouterC(config)#router rip
RouterC(config-router)#network 172.16.0.0
RouterC(config-router)#passive ?
  Ethernet  IEEE 802.3
  Null      Null interface
  Serial    Serial
RouterC(config-router)#passive serial 1
RouterC(config-router)#exit
```

Neighbor RIP

If you have a frame relay network that connects two sites of your company together, the frame relay network won't broadcast RIP updates by default—another good thing. This is the opposite of what we talked about above with the passive command.

We're *not* suggesting that you should run RIP over a WAN link. We're just telling you how to do it.

Remember that RIP is a broadcast protocol so the updates must reach all the routers that you want to advertise routes with.

To make RIP broadcast on non-broadcast networks, you use the neighbor command.

```
RouterC(config)#router rip
RouterC(config-router)#network 172.16.0.0
RouterC(config-router)#neighbor 172.18.3.10
RouterC(config-router)#^Z
RouterC#
```

This command will now encapsulate the RIP broadcasts into the format of the particular WAN (for example, frame relay) and send it to the router specified in the neighbor command.

Even if you don't have a network analyzer, there are ways to monitor RIP on your Cisco routers.

Monitoring RIP

These are some tools that you can use to help monitor your RIP network:

- Show IP Route

- Show IP Protocol

- Show IP Interfaces

- Debug IP RIP

- Trace

Show IP Route

You're already familiar with the sh ip route command, but let's go over the output that it gives you when it's running RIP:

```
RouterA#sh ip route
Codes: C - connected, S - static, I - IGRP, R - RIP, M -
mobile, B - BGP, D - EIGRP, EX - EIGRP external, O - OSPF,
IA - OSPF inter area, E1 - OSPF external type 1, E2 - OSPF
external type 2, E - EGP, i - IS-IS, L1 - IS-IS level-1,
L2 - IS-IS level-2, * - candidate default

Gateway of last resort is not set

     172.16.0.0 255.255.255.0 is subnetted, 5 subnets
R       172.16.50.0 [120/2] via 172.16.20.2, 00:00:06, Serial0
R       172.16.40.0 [120/1] via 172.16.20.2, 00:00:06, Serial0
R       172.16.30.0 [120/1] via 172.16.20.2, 00:00:06, serial0
C       172.16.20.0 is directly connected, Serial0
C       172.16.10.0 is directly connected, Ethernet0
```

Remember: The "R" is for RIP learned routes and the "C" is for directly connected networks.

The [120/1] equals the value of the administrative distance/the metric. The administrative distance is a value assigned to routing protocols. RIP has a value of 120, OSPF's value is 110, IGRP's value is 100, EIGRP's value is 90, static is 1, and directly connected is 0. The administrative distance is used if two routing protocols advertise the same route to the same router. The router prefers the route with the lowest administrative distance. This is because if you have multiple routing protocols running on your network, the router has to have some way of deciding which routing protocol is advertising the best route. Notice that the router prefers RIP last in determining a route to a remote network.

The 00:00:06 is the time since the router last received an advertisement for the route.

By typing in **sh ip route rip**, you can see only the RIP connected networks. For example, on RouterA:

```
RouterA#sh ip route rip
     172.16.0.0 255.255.255.0 is subnetted, 5 subnets
R    172.16.50.0 [120/2] via 172.16.20.2, 00:00:12, Serial0
R    172.16.40.0 [120/1] via 172.16.20.2, 00:00:12, Serial0
R    172.16.30.0 [120/1] via 172.16.20.2, 00:00:12, Serial0
```

Show IP Protocol

Show ip protocol will deliver information on RIP timers, the network to which RIP is assigned, and routing information sources.

```
RouterA#sh ip protocol
Routing Protocol is "rip"
  Sending updates every 30 seconds, next due in 5 seconds
  Invalid after 180 seconds, hold down 180, flushed after 240
  Outgoing update filter list for all interfaces is not set
  Incoming update filter list for all interfaces is not set
  Redistributing: rip
  Routing for Networks:
    172.16.0.0
  Routing Information Sources:
    Gateway         Distance      Last Update
    172.16.20.2        120        0:00:00
  Distance: (default is 120)
```

Notice all the information on the timers that we talked about earlier. Also notice that the updates are sent every 30 seconds with the next one due in five seconds.

Show IP Interfaces

This command shows you lots of statistics and how the interfaces on your Cisco router are configured.

```
RouterA#sh ip interface
Ethernet0 is up, line protocol is up
  Internet address is 172.16.10.1 255.255.255.0
  Broadcast address is 255.255.255.255
  Address determined by non-volatile memory
  MTU is 1500 bytes
  Helper address is not set
  Directed broadcast forwarding is enabled
  Outgoing access list is not set
  Inbound  access list is not set
  Proxy ARP is enabled
  Security level is default
  Split horizon is enabled
  ICMP redirects are always sent
  ICMP unreachables are always sent
  ICMP mask replies are never sent
  IP fast switching is enabled
  IP fast switching on the same interface is disabled
  IP multicast fast switching is enabled
  Router Discovery is disabled
  IP output packet accounting is disabled
  IP access violation accounting is disabled
  TCP/IP header compression is disabled
  Probe proxy name replies are disabled
  Gateway Discovery is disabled
  Policy routing is disabled
Serial0 is up, line protocol is up
  Internet address is 172.16.20.1 255.255.255.0
  Broadcast address is 255.255.255.255
  Address determined by non-volatile memory
  MTU is 1500 bytes
  Helper address is not set
```

```
    Directed broadcast forwarding is enabled
    Outgoing access list is not set
    Inbound  access list is not set
    Proxy ARP is enabled
    Security level is default
    Split horizon is enabled
    ICMP redirects are always sent
    ICMP unreachables are always sent
    ICMP mask replies are never sent
    IP fast switching is enabled
    IP fast switching on the same interface is enabled
    IP multicast fast switching is enabled
    Router Discovery is disabled
    IP output packet accounting is disabled
    IP access violation accounting is disabled
    TCP/IP header compression is disabled
    Probe proxy name replies are disabled
    Gateway Discovery is disabled
    Policy routing is disabled
Serial1 is administratively down, line protocol is down
    Internet protocol processing disabled
```

You can also see a particular interface by typing

```
RouterA#sh ip int ?
    Ethernet  IEEE 802.3
    Null      Null interface
    Serial    Serial
    brief     Brief summary of IP status and configuration
    <cr>
```

The Ethernet and serial ports can be seen individually by typing **sh ip int** s0, s1, or e0.

Debug ip rip

Debug ip rip will turn on RIP debugging. This'll give you an update list that shows the routing updates as they're sent and received. To stop debugging, type **undebug ip rip**.

```
RouterA#debug ip rip
RIP protocol debugging is on
RouterA#
RIP: received update from 172.16.20.2 on Serial0
      172.16.50.0 in 2 hops
      172.16.40.0 in 1 hops
RIP: sending update to 255.255.255.255 via Ethernet0
(172.16.10.1)
      subnet 172.16.50.0, metric 3
      subnet 172.16.40.0, metric 2
      subnet 172.16.20.0, metric 1
RIP: sending update to 255.255.255.255 via Serial0
(172.16.20.1)
      subnet 172.16.10.0, metric 1
RIP: received update from 172.16.20.2 on Serial0
      172.16.50.0 in 2 hops
      172.16.40.0 in 1 hops
RIP: sending update to 255.255.255.255 via Ethernet0
(172.16.10.1)
      subnet 172.16.50.0, metric 3
      subnet 172.16.40.0, metric 2
      subnet 172.16.20.0, metric 1
RouterA#undebug ip rip
RIP protocol debugging is off
RouterA#
```

Notice that network 172.16.30.0 isn't in the updates. We unplugged the hub that interface Ethernet0 was plugged into and the interface went down. Now RIP won't advertise that route. Debug ip rip is a great command to see what each router is advertising.

Trace

The trace command can be used to check the path a packet takes to get to the final destination.

```
RouterA#trace 172.16.50.2

Type escape sequence to abort.
```

Break Trace = ESC + CTRL + Z

```
Tracing the route to 172.16.50.2

1 172.16.20.2 20 msec 20 msec 20 msec
2 172.16.40.2 36 msec 36 msec 32 msec
3 172.16.50.2 36 msec 32 msec 32 msec
```

This showed us that to get from RouterA to the host on Network 50, it went through RouterB to RouterC—just what we thought. This is a great tool for checking path selection in a multirouter network.

Before we move on to configuring IGRP on our routers, let's remove the RIP entries from each router. We can do this by typing in only one command, no router rip, from within configuration mode.

```
RouterA#config t
Enter configuration commands, one per line.  End with CNTL/Z.
RouterA(config)#no router rip
RouterA(config)#^Z
RouterA# copy runn star
```

Configuring IGRP Routing

Configuring IGRP is not unlike configuring RIP. You add the router IGRP command followed by the network number you want the router to advertise. But there is one major difference—since you can have multiple IGRP routing protocols running between routers, you have to enter the autonomous system number. All the routers that you want to exchange router information must use this same number.

For example, in Figure 7.9, we have two sites connected with a WAN link. They won't update each other with routing information, because they're in different autonomous systems (Location A is using AS 10 and Location B is using AS 20). Location A and Location B would both have to use the same AS number in order to communicate and exchange route information.

Adding IGRP

Let's go ahead and configure our three routers.

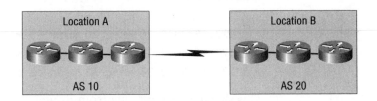

FIGURE 7.9

Different AS networks won't communicate with different AS numbers configured.

RouterA

```
RouterA#config t
Enter configuration commands, one per line.  End with CNTL/Z.
RouterA(config)#router ?
  bgp        Border Gateway Protocol (BGP)
  egp        Exterior Gateway Protocol (EGP)
  eigrp      Enhanced Interior Gateway Routing Protocol (EIGRP)
  igrp       Interior Gateway Routing Protocol (IGRP)
  isis       ISO IS-IS
  iso-igrp   IGRP for OSI networks
  mobile     Mobile routes
  ospf       Open Shortest Path First (OSPF)
  rip        Routing Information Protocol (RIP)
  static     Static routes

RouterA(config)#router igrp ?
  <1-65535>  Autonomous system number

RouterA(config)#router igrp 10
RouterA(config-router)#network 172.16.0.0
RouterA(config-router)#^Z
RouterA#wr mem
Building configuration...
[OK]
```

Notice that we typed router ? then received all the different types of routing protocols that we could enable. We chose IGRP and typed another ?.

This time it asked for our autonomous system number. We entered 10. You can choose any number between 1 and 65,655. That can be a lot of networks.

RouterB

```
RouterB#config t
Enter configuration commands, one per line.  End with CNTL/Z.
RouterB(config)#router igrp 10
RouterB(config-router)#network 172.16.0.0
RouterB(config-router)#^Z
RouterB#wr mem
Building configuration...
[OK]
```

RouterC

```
RouterC#config t
Enter configuration commands, one per line.  End with CNTL/Z.
RouterC(config)#router igrp 10
RouterC(config-router)#network 172.16.0.0
RouterC(config-router)#^Z
RouterC#wr mem
Building configuration...
[OK]
```

Verifying the Routing Tables

Okay, let's see what our routing tables found.

RouterA

```
RouterA#sh ip route
Codes: C - connected, S - static, I - IGRP, R - RIP, M -
mobile, B - BGP, D - EIGRP, EX - EIGRP external, O - OSPF,
IA - OSPF inter area, E1 - OSPF external type 1, E2 - OSPF
external type 2, E - EGP, i - IS-IS, L1 - IS-IS level-1,
L2 - IS-IS level-2, * - candidate default

Gateway of last resort is not set
```

```
          172.16.0.0 255.255.255.0 is subnetted, 5 subnets
I         172.16.50.0 [100/182671] via 172.16.20.2, 00:00:22, Serial0
I         172.16.40.0 [100/182571] via 172.16.20.2, 00:00:22, Serial0
I         172.16.30.0 [100/182571] via 172.16.20.2, 00:00:22, Serial0
C         172.16.20.0 is directly connected, Serial0
C         172.16.10.0 is directly connected, Ethernet0
```

RouterB

RouterB#**sh ip route**

Codes: C - connected, S - static, I - IGRP, R - RIP, M - mobile, B - BGP, D - EIGRP, EX - EIGRP external, O - OSPF, IA - OSPF inter area, E1 - OSPF external type 1, E2 - OSPF external type 2, E - EGP, i - IS-IS, L1 - IS-IS level-1, L2 - IS-IS level-2, * - candidate default

Gateway of last resort is not set

```
          172.16.0.0 255.255.255.0 is subnetted, 5 subnets
I         172.16.50.0 [100/8576] via 172.16.40.2, 00:01:03, Serial1
C         172.16.40.0 is directly connected, Serial1
C         172.16.30.0 is directly connected, Ethernet0
C         172.16.20.0 is directly connected, Serial0
I         172.16.10.0 [100/8576] via 172.16.20.1, 00:00:55, Serial0
```

RouterC

RouterC#**sh ip route**

Codes: C - connected, S - static, I - IGRP, R - RIP, M - mobile, B - BGP, D - EIGRP, EX - EIGRP external, O - OSPF, IA - OSPF inter area, E1 - OSPF external type 1, E2 - OSPF external type 2, E - EGP, i - IS-IS, L1 - IS-IS level-1, L2 - IS-IS level-2, * - candidate default

Gateway of last resort is not set

```
          172.16.0.0 255.255.255.0 is subnetted, 5 subnets
C         172.16.50.0 is directly connected, Ethernet0
C         172.16.40.0 is directly connected, Serial0
I         172.16.30.0 [100/10476] via 172.16.40.1, 00:00:36, Serial0
I         172.16.20.0 [100/10476] via 172.16.40.1, 00:00:36, Serial0
```

I   172.16.10.0 [100/10576] via 172.16.40.1, 00:00:36, Serial0

Notice that an "I" identifies the routes discovered by IGRP.

Let's catch some of the IGRP updates on an Etherpeek network analyzer.

```
Flags:          0x00
   Status:         0x00
   Packet Length:92
   Timestamp:      09:31:48.384000 05/20/1998
Ethernet Header
   Destination:  ff:ff:ff:ff:ff:ff Ethernet Broadcast
   Source:         00:00:0c:8d:5c:9d
   Protocol Type:08-00   IP
IP Header - Internet Protocol Datagram
   Version:              4
   Header Length:        5
   Precedence:           0
   Type of Service:      %000
   Unused:               %00
   Total Length:         74
   Identifier:           0
   Fragmentation Flags:  %000
   Fragment Offset:      0
   Time To Live:         2
   IP Type:              0x09  IGP
   Header Checksum:      0x029b
   Source IP Address:    172.16.10.1
   Dest. IP Address:     255.255.255.255 IP Broadcast
   No Internet Datagram Options
IGRP - Inter-Gateway Routing Protocol
   Protocol Version:     1
   Op Code:              1 Update
   Edition:              2
   Autonomous Sys:       10
   Local Subnets:        4
   Networks Inside AS:   0
   Networks Outside AS:  0
   Checksum:             21456
```

InteriorRouting Entry #1

Net Number:	16.50.0
Delay (microseconds):	41000
Bandwidth (Kbit/sec):	178571
Max. Transmission Unit:	1500
Reliability:	100%
Load:	0%
Hop Count:	2

InteriorRouting Entry #2

Net Number:	16.40.0
Delay (microseconds):	40000
Bandwidth (Kbit/sec):	178571
Max. Transmission Unit:	1500
Reliability:	100%
Load:	0%
Hop Count:	1

InteriorRouting Entry #3

Net Number:	16.30.0
Delay (microseconds):	40000
Bandwidth (Kbit/sec):	178571
Max. Transmission Unit:	1500
Reliability:	100%
Load:	0%
Hop Count:	1

InteriorRouting Entry #4

Net Number:	16.20.0
Delay (microseconds):	20000
Bandwidth (Kbit/sec):	178571
Max. Transmission Unit:	1500
Reliability:	100%
Load:	0%
Hop Count:	0

Frame Check Sequence: 0x00000000

There are some big differences between this IGRP packet and the RIP packet we looked at before. These are the delay, bandwidth, reliability, and load features not present in the RIP packets. These factors are all taken into consideration when a router is looking for the best route to a destination or if it's trying to load-balance.

Also, remember that the IGRP packet is sent out every 90 seconds by default—a much better time period than the 30-second timer RIP uses.

Monitoring IGRP

You can monitor IGRP on your Cisco routers with the same commands that you use to monitor RIP. Here's a list of them:

- Show IP Route
- Show IP Protocol
- Show IP Interfaces
- Debug IP IGRP
- Trace

The trace command is the same as it is with RIP—you won't see anything new—so we won't repeat that command.

Show IP Route IGRP

By typing **sh ip route igrp**, we can obtain the IGRP found routes exclusively.

```
RouterA#sh ip route igrp
     172.16.0.0 255.255.255.0 is subnetted, 5 subnets
I       172.16.50.0 [100/182671] via 172.16.20.2, 00:00:28, Serial0
I       172.16.40.0 [100/182571] via 172.16.20.2, 00:00:28, Serial0
I       172.16.30.0 [100/182571] via 172.16.20.2, 00:00:28, Serial0
```

Show IP Protocol

This command shows that the protocol in AS 10 is IGRP. Unlike RIP, which updates every 30 seconds, IGRP updates every 90 seconds, and we see here that the next broadcast is due in 65 seconds.

The metric weight is for calculating the composite metric as defined by Cisco. K1 and K2 indicate the weight to be assigned to bandwidth and delay. They are defined by the type of service requested for a packet.

```
RouterA#sh ip protocol
Routing Protocol is "igrp 10"
  Sending updates every 90 seconds, next due in 65 seconds
  Invalid after 270 seconds, hold down 280, flushed after 630
  Outgoing update filter list for all interfaces is not set
  Incoming update filter list for all interfaces is not set
  Default networks flagged in outgoing updates
  Default networks accepted from incoming updates
  IGRP metric weight K1=1, K2=0, K3=1, K4=0, K5=0
  IGRP maximum hopcount 100
  IGRP maximum metric variance 1
  Redistributing: igrp 10
  Routing for Networks:
    172.16.0.0
  Routing Information Sources:
    Gateway          Distance       Last Update
    172.16.20.2          100        0:00:02
  Distance: (default is 100)
```

By using the bandwidth command for each serial port, we can customize these values. For example, the Cisco IOS will decide by default that each serial link is using a T1. Using the sh int s1 command demonstrates this:

```
RouterB#sh int s1
Serial1 is up, line protocol is up
  Hardware is HD64570
  Internet address is 172.16.40.1 255.255.255.0
  MTU 1500 bytes, BW 1544 Kbit, DLY 20000 usec, rely 255/
255, load 1/255
```

Notice the BW is 1544Kb even through we are only using a 56KB link. Why is this important? Because IGRP can split traffic between paths that it "thinks" are equal. Since no adjustments are manually made to the router configuration, it can send the same amount of data down a real T1 link as it would a 56KB link if the bandwidth command isn't used.

Show IP Interface

This command doesn't just give you information about routing protocols, it presents you with much more. It shows you how the interfaces are configured, and it displays the status and global parameters associated with an interface.

```
RouterA#sh ip interface
Ethernet0 is up, line protocol is up
  Internet address is 172.16.10.1 255.255.255.0
  Broadcast address is 255.255.255.255
  Address determined by non-volatile memory
  MTU is 1500 bytes
  Helper address is not set
  Directed broadcast forwarding is enabled
  Outgoing access list is not set
  Inbound  access list is not set
  Proxy ARP is enabled
  Security level is default
  Split horizon is enabled
  ICMP redirects are always sent
  ICMP unreachables are always sent
  ICMP mask replies are never sent
  IP fast switching is enabled
  IP fast switching on the same interface is disabled
  IP multicast fast switching is enabled
  Router Discovery is disabled
  IP output packet accounting is disabled
  IP access violation accounting is disabled
  TCP/IP header compression is disabled
  Probe proxy name replies are disabled
  Gateway Discovery is disabled
  Policy routing is disabled
Serial0 is up, line protocol is up
  Internet address is 172.16.20.1 255.255.255.0
  Broadcast address is 255.255.255.255
  Address determined by non-volatile memory
  MTU is 1500 bytes
  Helper address is not set
  Directed broadcast forwarding is enabled
  Outgoing access list is not set
```

Inbound access list is not set

Proxy ARP is enabled

Security level is default

Split horizon is enabled

ICMP redirects are always sent

ICMP unreachables are always sent

ICMP mask replies are never sent

IP fast switching is enabled

IP fast switching on the same interface is enabled

IP multicast fast switching is enabled

Router Discovery is disabled

IP output packet accounting is disabled

IP access violation accounting is disabled

TCP/IP header compression is disabled

Probe proxy name replies are disabled

Gateway Discovery is disabled

Policy routing is disabled

Serial1 is administratively down, line protocol is down

Internet protocol processing disabled

Debug IP IGRP

Unlike debug ip rip, the debug ip igrp command has two options: events and transactions.

RouterA#**debug ip igrp events**

IGRP event debugging is on

RouterA#

IGRP: sending update to 255.255.255.255 via Ethernet0 (172.16.10.1)

IGRP: Update contains 3 interior, 0 system, and 0 exterior routes.

IGRP: Total routes in update: 3

IGRP: sending update to 255.255.255.255 via Serial0 (172.16.20.1)

IGRP: Update contains 1 interior, 0 system, and 0 exterior routes.

IGRP: Total routes in update: 1

IGRP: received update from 172.16.20.2 on Serial0

```
IGRP: Update contains 2 interior, 0 system, and 0 exterior
routes.
IGRP: Total routes in update: 2
RouterA#undebug ip igrp events
IGRP event debugging is off
RouterA#debug ip igrp transactions
IGRP protocol debugging is on
RouterA#
IGRP: received update from 172.16.20.2 on Serial0
      subnet 172.16.50.0, metric 182671 (neighbor 8576)
      subnet 172.16.40.0, metric 182571 (neighbor 8476)
      subnet 172.16.30.0, metric 182571 (neighbor 8476)
IGRP: sending update to 255.255.255.255 via Ethernet0
(172.16.10.1)
      subnet 172.16.50.0, metric=182671
      subnet 172.16.40.0, metric=182571
      subnet 172.16.30.0, metric=182571
      subnet 172.16.20.0, metric=180571
IGRP: sending update to 255.255.255.255 via Serial0
(172.16.20.1)
      subnet 172.16.10.0, metric=1100
IGRP: received update from 172.16.20.2 on Serial0
      subnet 172.16.50.0, metric 182671 (neighbor 8576)
      subnet 172.16.40.0, metric 182571 (neighbor 8476)
      subnet 172.16.30.0, metric 182571 (neighbor 8476)
RouterA#undebug ip igrp transactions
IGRP protocol debugging is off
```

Summary

In this chapter, we covered the following key points:

- We discussed the services of separate and integrated multiprotocol routing. We covered the different types of dynamic routing and how the algorithms work.

- We discussed problems that each routing type encounters when dealing with topology changes, and we described techniques to reduce the amount integrated multiprotocol routing.

- We added the RIP routing protocol to your configuration. We talked about in detail how the RIP protocol works and then gave examples of how to add the RIP protocol to your network.

- We added the IGRP routing protocol to your configuration. We talked in detail about how the IGRP protocol works and then gave examples of how to add the IGRP protocol to your network.

Review Questions

1. What is the routing algorithm used by RIP?

    A. Routed information

    B. Link together

    C. Link-state

    D. Distance-vector

2. What is the routing algorithm used by IGRP?

    A. Routed information

    B. Link together

    C. Link-state

    D. Distance-vector

3. Which command can you type at the router prompt to verify the broadcast frequency for IGRP?

    A. sh ip route

    B. sh ip protocol

    C. sh ip broadcast

    D. debug ip igrp

4. What is the routing metric used by RIP?

   A. Count to infinity

   B. Hop count   *p222*

   C. TTL

   D. Bandwidth, reliability, MTU, delay, and load

5. Which utility should you use to identify the path that a packet takes as it passes through the routers?

   A. ROUTE

   B. TRACE   *p252*

   C. IPCONFIG

   D. NETSTAT

6. What is the routing metric used by IGRP?

   A. Count to infinity

   B. Hop count   *p225*

   C. TTL

   D. Bandwidth, reliability, MTU, delay, and load

7. What does a metric of 16 hops represent in a RIP routing network?

   A. 16 ms

   B. Number of routers in the internetwork

   C. Number of hops

   D. 16 hops—unreachable   *p218*
        Poison

8. Hold-downs are used for what?

   A. To hold down the protocol from going to the next hop   *p226/218*

   B. To prevent regular update messages from reinstating a route that has gone down / *for Convergence*

C. To prevent regular update messages from reinstating a route that has just come up

D. To prevent irregular update messages from reinstating a route that has gone down

9. What is split horizon? *p 218*

A. Information received on an interface cannot be sent back out that same interface.

B. When you have a large bus (horizon) physical network, the routing protocol splits the traffic.

C. Split horizon holds the regular updates from broadcasting to a down link.

D. It prevents regular update messages from reinstating a route that has gone down.

10. What is poison reverse? *p 218, 226*

A. This sends back the protocol received from a router as a poison pill, which stops the regular updates.

B. This is information that is received from a router can't be sent back to that originating router.

C. Reverse poison prevents regular update messages from reinstating a route that has gone down.

D. When a router sets the metric for a down link to infinity.

11. What is the default administrative distance for IGRP?

A. 90

B. 100   *p 227*

C. 120

D. 220

12. What are the three types of routes that IGRP advertises?

A. Interior   *p 227*

    B. Dynamic

    C. System *p227*

    D. Exterior

13. What is the metric limit for link-state protocols?

    A. 16

    B. 255

    C. 6500 *p228*

    D. 65,533

14. Which of the following are distance-vector protocols?

    A. IGRP *p225*

    B. RIP *p222* *p214*

    C. OSPF

    D. NLSP

15. Which of the following routing protocols use AS?

    A. RIP

    B. RIP II

    C. IGRP *p225*

    D. OSPF *p228*

16. What commands are available for supporting RIP networks? (Choose all that apply.)

    A. sh ip route *p248*

    B. sh ip protocol

    C. sh rip network

    D. Sh ip int

    E. Debug ip rip

17. What is convergence time?

   A. The hold-down update time

   B. The time it takes for all routers to update their routing table when a change takes place   *p 219 - 220*

   C. The time it takes for a packet to get from a destination host to a receiving host

   D. The time it takes to boot a router

18. What is true about distance-vector–based networks? Choose the best answer.

   A. They send out partial updates every 60 seconds

   B. They send their complete routing table every 60 seconds

   C. They send their entire routing table every 30 seconds   *p 215, 216*

   D. They update every 90 seconds

19. What is true about link-state networks? Choose the best answer.

   A. They maintain a more complex table than distance-vector–based networks   *p 219*

   B. They maintain a less complex table than distance-vector–based networks

   C. They don't use convergence

   D. They use RIP timers

Laboratory Exercises

EXERCISE 7.1

RIP Routing

In this lab, you will add RIP routing to your routers.

1. Log in to your router and get the # prompt.

2. Type in **sh ip route** to get your directly connected networks.

3. Type in **config t** and turn on RIP routing. Use the following commands, but for the network number, use the directly connected network(s) discovered in Step 2.

   RouterA#**config t**
   Enter configuration commands, one per line. End with CNTL/Z.
   RouterA(config)#**router rip**
   RouterA(config-router)#**network 172.16.0.0**
   RouterA(config-router)#^Z
   RouterA#**wr mem**
   Building configuration...
   [OK]

4. Verify the RIP configuration by typing **sh ip protocol**.

5. Turn on RIP debugging and monitor the RIP routing updates by typing **debug ip rip**.

6. Turn off debugging by typing **undebug all**.

7. Display the IP routing table and verify that you have successfully received RIP updates from other routers using the sh ip route command.

8. Ping the other routers to verify that communication is taking place.

9. Use the trace command to verify the routes that packets take through your internetwork.

EXERCISE 7.2

IGRP Routing

In this lab, you will configure an IP network using the IGRP routing protocol.

1. Log in to your router and get the # prompt.

2. Remove RIP routing if it is configured.

3. Type **sh ip route** to get your directly connected routes.

4. Turn on IGRP routing by using the commands from the following example. Use the directly connected networks discovered in Step 3.

   Router#**config t**
   Enter configuration commands, one per line. End with CNTL/Z.
   Router(config)#**router igrp 10**
   Router(config-router)#**network 172.16.0.0**
   Router(config-router)#^Z
   Router#**wr mem**
   Building configuration. . .
   [OK]

5. Verify the IGRP configuration by typing **sh ip protocol**.

6. Turn on IGRP debugging by typing **debug ip igrp transactions**.

7. Turn off debugging and verify that you have received other IGRP updates from other routers by typing **sh ip route**.

8. Ping other routers to verify communication.

9. Use the trace command to verify the packet routes through your internetwork.

CHAPTER

8

Router Configuration

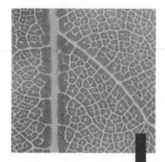

In this chapter, you're going to find out how to load the Cisco IOS from different sources. You'll also learn about the AutoInstall feature. In addition, we'll talk about the fallback routine and teach you how to back up and load the router configuration from both NVRAM and RAM to a TFTP server.

We'll finish by presenting you with some great Cisco IOS commands for examining the status of your routers and retrieving information.

CCNA test objectives covered in this chapter include:

273 ■ List the commands to load Cisco IOS software from flash memory, a TFTP server, or ROM

279 ■ Prepare to back up, upgrade, and load a backup Cisco IOS software image

281 ■ Examine router elements (RAM, ROM, CDP, show)

■ Copy and manipulate configuration files

■ Manage configuration files from the privileged Exec mode

■ Identify the functions performed by ICMP

Sources for Cisco IOS Software

As mentioned in Chapter 5, the Cisco IOS can be loaded into a Cisco router from many sources. The default source for the Cisco IOS depends mainly on hardware, but the Cisco IOS is typically loaded from EEPROM (Electronic Erasable Programmable Read Only Memory), also known as *flash memory*. You can use other sources, such as a TFTP server, or the router can use a fallback routine.

Remember that flash memory holds the binary executable IOS image known as the Cisco IOS. Do not confuse this with the router configuration held in NVRAM. The IOS image is the binary program that parses and executes the configuration, while the IOS configuration tells the device its current configuration.

TFTP Server

You can copy the contents of flash (the Cisco IOS) to a TFTP server by typing **copy flash tftp**. This can serve as a backup copy of the Cisco IOS and can also be used to verify that the copy in flash is the same as the original file.

```
RouterC#ping 172.16.10.2
Type escape sequence to abort.
Sending 5, 100-byte ICMP Echos to 172.16.10.2, timeout is 2
seconds:
.!!!!
Success rate is 80 percent (4/5), round-trip min/avg/max =
1/2/4 ms
```

We started with a ping from our router to our TFTP server to ensure that IP connectivity was working from the router that was targeted to copy the flash over to our TFTP host. After verifying connectivity, the flash can now be copied to our TFTP server.

```
RouterC#copy flash tftp

System flash directory:
File  Length   Name/status
  1   3621884  igs-i-1.110-18.bin
[3621948 bytes used, 572356 available, 4194304 total]
Address or name of remote host [255.255.255.255]?
172.16.10.2
Source file name? igs-i-1.110-18.bin
Destination file name [igs-i-1.110-18.bin]?
Verifying checksum for 'igs-i-1.110-18.bin' (file # 1)...  OK
Copy 'igs-i-1.110-18.bin' from Flash to server
   as 'igs-i-1.110-18.bin'? [yes/no]y
!!!!!!!!!!!!!!!!!!!!!!!!!!!!!!!!!!!!!!!!!!!!!!!!!!!!!!!!!!!!!!!!
!!!!!!!!!!!!!!!!!!!!!
```

```
!!!!!!!!!!!!!!!!!!!!!!!!!!!!!!!!!!!!!!!!!!!!!!!!!!!!!!!!!!!!!!!!!!!!!!
!!!!!!!!!!!!!!!!!!!!!!!
!!!!!!!!!!!!!!!!!!!!!!!!!!!!!!!!!!!!!!!!!!!!!!!!!!!!!!!!!!!!!!!!!!!!!!
!!!!!!!!!!!!!!!!!!!!!!!
!!!!!!!!!!!!!!!!!!!!!!!!!!!!!!!!!!!!!!!!!!!!!!!!!!!!!!!!!!!!!!!!!!!!!!
!!!!!!!!!!!!!!!!!!!!!!!
!!!!!!!!!!!!!!!!!!!!!!!!!!!!!!!!!!!!!!!!!!!!!!!!!!!!!!!!!!!!!!!!!!!!!!
!!!!!!!!!!!!!!!!!!!!!!!
!!!!!!!!!!!!!!!!!!!!!!!!!!!!!!!!!!!!!!!!!!!!!!!!!!!!!!!!!!!!!!!!!!!!!!
!!!!!!!!!!!!!!!!!!!!!!!
!!!!!!!!!!!!!!!!!!!!!!!!!!!!!!!!!!!!!!!!!!!!!!!!!!!!!!!!!!!!!!!!!!!!!!
!!!!!!!!!!!!!!!!!!!!!!!
!!!!!!!!!!!!!!!!!!!!!!!!!!!!!!!!!!!!!!!!!!!!!!!!!!!!!!!!!!!!!!!!!!!!!!
!!!!!!!!!!!!!!!!!!!!!!!
!!!!!!!!!!!!!!!!!!!!!!!!!!!!!!!!!!!!!!!!!!!!!!!!!!!!!!!!!!!!!!!!!!!!!!
!!!!!!!!!!
Upload to server done
Flash copy took 0:21:53 [hh:mm:ss]
RouterC#
```

Did you notice that it took almost 22 minutes to download the flash through our simulated WAN network? Keep this in mind when backing up your files from your remote locations.

You can copy from a TFTP server to flash anytime by typing **copy tftp flash.** This command is very useful for downloading new versions of the Cisco IOS into your router.

```
RouterC#copy tftp flash
                     ****  NOTICE  ****
Flash load helper v1.0
This process will accept the copy options and then terminate
the current system image to use the ROM based image for the
copy.
Routing functionality will not be available during that
time.
If you are logged in via telnet, this connection will
terminate.
Users with console access can see the results of the copy
operation.
                  ---- ******** ----
```

Proceed? [confirm]**return**

System flash directory:
File Length   Name/status
  1   3621884 igs-i-1.110-18.bin
[3621948 bytes used, 572356 available, 4194304 total]
Address or name of remote host [172.16.10.2]**return**
Source file name? **igs-i-1.110-18.bin**
Destination file name [igs-i-1.110-18.bin]?
Accessing file 'igs-i-1.110-18.bin' on 172.16.10.2...
Loading igs-i-1.110-18.bin from 172.16.10.2 (via Serial0): !
[OK]

Erase flash device before writing? [confirm]**return**
Flash contains files. Are you sure you want to erase?
[confirm]**return**

Copy 'igs-i-1.110-18.bin' from server
  as 'igs-i-1.110-18.bin' into Flash WITH erase? [yes/no]y

%SYS-5-RELOAD: Reload requested
%FLH: igs-i-1.110-18.bin from 172.16.10.2 to flash ...
System flash directory:
File Length   Name/status
  1   3621884 igs-i-1.110-18.bin
[3621948 bytes used, 572356 available, 4194304 total]
Accessing file 'igs-i-1.110-18.bin' on 172.16.10.2...
Loading igs-i-1.110-18.bin from 172.16.10.2 (via Serial0): !
[OK]

Erasing device... eeeeeeeeeeeeeeee ...erased
Loading igs-i-1.110-18.bin from 172.16.10.2 (via Serial0):
!!!!!!!!!!!!!!!!!!!!!!
!!
!!!!!!!!!!!!!!!!!!!!!!
!!
!!!!!!!!!!!!!!!!!!!!!!

```
!!!!!!!!!!!!!!!!!!!!!!!!!!!!!!!!!!!!!!!!!!!!!!!!!!!!!!!!!!!!!!!!
!!!!!!!!!!!!!!!!!!!!!!
!!!!!!!!!!!!!!!!!!!!!!!!!!!!!!!!!!!!!!!!!!!!!!!!!!!!!!!!!!!!!!!!
!!!!!!!!!!!!!!!!!!!!!!
!!!!!!!!!!!!!!!!!!!!!!!!!!!!!!!!!!!!!!!!!!!!!!!!!!!!!!!!!!!!!!!!
!!!!!!!!!!!!!!!!!!!!!!
!!!!!!!!!!!!!!!!!!!!!!!!!!!!!!!!!!!!!!!!!!!!!!!!!!!!!!!!!!!!!!!!
!!!!!!!!!!!!!!!!!!!!!!
!!!!!!!!!!!!!!!!!!!!!!!!!!!!!!!!!!!!!!!!!!!!!!!!!!!!!!!!!!!!!!!!
!!!!!!!!!!!!!!!!!!!!!!
!!!!!!!!!!!!!!!!!!!!!!!!!!!!!!!!!!!!!!!!!!!!!!!!!!!!!!!!!!!!!!!!
!!!!!!!!!!!!!!!!!!!!!!
!!!!!!!!!!!!!!!!!!!!!!!!!!!!!!!!!!!!!!!!!!!!!!!!!!!!!!!!
[OK - 3621884/4194304 bytes]

Verifying checksum...  OK (0xC248)
Flash copy took 0:21:34 [hh:mm:ss]
%FLH: Re-booting system after download
```

After confirming a few entries, you'll be asked if it's okay to erase the entire contents of flash memory. The programs asks the question because there's rarely room for more than one flash file. However, if there is room, you can have many different versions loaded in flash.

Each "e" stands for erase, and each exclamation point (!) represents the event that one UDP segment has been successfully transferred. The router must be rebooted to load the new image on a 2500 series router because the currently running IOS image is in flash memory. Use show flash to verify that the size matches that of the original file.

You can have some fun with your friends at work by using the erase flash command. Or, if you have more than one flash IOS loaded, you can use the delete command. If you have a device with an external flash card, the delete command will mark the flash image as deleted, but it doesn't actually delete the image. (For the image's annihilation to occur, you have to use the squeeze command that completes the deletion process.)

Fallback

You can specify sources where the router should look for the Cisco IOS software to create a fallback in case one configuration doesn't load or you just want the Cisco IOS to load from a TFTP server.

To have your router load the Cisco IOS from a TFTP server, use the following command string:

```
boot system TFTP ios_filename TFTP_ipaddress
```

Remember, there are three places a Cisco router can look for a valid Cisco IOS: flash, a TFTP server, or ROM. You can change the spot where a Cisco router looks for the IOS by adding boot commands in the configuration. The default action is defined by the Configuration Register setting and is normally set to load the first file found in flash memory.

```
RouterC(config)#boot ?
  bootstrap   Bootstrap image file
  buffersize  Specify the buffer size for netbooting a
config file
  host        Router-specific config file
  network     Network-wide config file
  system      System image file


RouterC(config)#boot system ?
  WORD   System image filename
  flash  Boot from flash memory
  mop    Boot from a Decnet MOP server
  rcp    Boot from a server via rcp
  rom    Boot from rom
  TFTP   Boot from a TFTP server
```

Typing the following will cause your router to try the other alternatives if the flash configuration doesn't come up:

```
boot system flash ios_filename
boot system TFTP ios_filename TFTP_address
boot system rom
```

The three examples above show how you can enter multiple boot commands for fallback purposes. The router will try to load from flash, then from a TFTP server, and finally from ROM.

Flash   This allows you to copy a system image without physically changing EEPROM. Flash memory is not vulnerable to network failures that can occur when loading system images from a TFTP server.

Network server Best used as a backup in case flash memory gets corrupted or lost.

ROM If flash memory is corrupted and a TFTP server can't load the image for some reason, booting from ROM is the final bootstrap option in software. Typically this lacks the protocols, features, and configurations of full Cisco IOS software.

TFTP Host

The TFTP host can be any system with TFTP loaded and operating that's able to contain files on the TCP/IP network. It comes in very handy when we're at a client site in need of either backing up an image or downloading a new one instead of trying to ferret out a Unix box to act as a TFTP server.

To prepare for using a TFTP host, make sure that the following conditions are met:

- Check the router to make sure you can see and write into flash. Check the size of the original flash so you can compare it after the copy is made.

- Check the TFTP server to make sure that IP is running and that you can ping both the router and the TFTP server.

- Check the TFTP server to make sure that you have room for the file and that you have the path to the default TFTP directory. This path is set by the TFTP server. If you have only one IOS in flash, you can get the file name of the flash code that is running by using the show flash command.

```
Router>sh flash

System flash directory:
File   Length    Name/status
  1    5394384   c2500-d-l_112-14.bin
[5394448 bytes used, 2994160 available, 8388608 total]
8192K bytes of processor board System flash (Read ONLY)
```

However, be aware that if you have more than one Cisco IOS in flash, you should type **show version**. Show flash lists all files in flash and does not indicate which one is currently running.

Using the TFTP Server for Backing Up and Restoring the Router Configuration

You can copy the router's current configuration from a router to a TFTP server by typing **copy running-config tftp**. Doing this gives you a backup of the router configuration and allows you to run the configuration from this server. You can also configure the router by making your changes to the configuration file stored on the TFTP server; when you're happy with the new configuration, copy the file to the router by using the copy tftp running-config command.

```
RouterC#copy run tftp
Remote host []? 172.16.10.1
Name of configuration file to write [routerc-confg]?return
Write file routerc-confg on host 172.16.10.1?
[confirm]return
Building configuration...
OK
```

Notice that by default it adds a -config to the end of the router's host name to create a default filename. When configuring an IOS device from a TFTP server, the device's default method is to try to load a file with the name of the device followed by the string -config.

For example, let's say a router in your Detroit office suddenly gasps its last and stops being a router forever. No worries—you, being unceasingly well prepared for life's little shakedowns, had the presence of mind to read this book, so you backed up your configuration! Because you did that, all that needs to be done is to have Cisco send a fresh router directly to the Detroit office and have someone there (even a user) simply put it into the network closet and plug it in. After that, you can talk someone through the configuring of one interface on the new router. When that's done, you can telnet in and update the configuration with the one that you backed up. How? Well, after you've telneted in, you just type in **copy tftp run**—that's it! Doing this will copy the stored configuration to running-config on the new router in a flash.

```
Router#copy TFTP run
Host or network configuration file [host]?return
Address of remote host [255.255.255.255]? 172.16.10.1
Name of configuration file []? detroit-confg return
```

```
Configure using detroit-confg from 172.16.10.1?
[confirm]return
Loading detroit-confg ..from 172.16.10.1 (via Ethernet0): !
[OK - 717/32723 bytes]
Detroit#
```

Notice that the host name of the router changed immediately after the configuration was loaded, because the configuration was loaded directly into DRAM. You will need to do a copy run star at this point.

Cisco AutoInstall Procedure

The Cisco AutoInstall procedure lets you configure your routers automatically and remotely over the network. It's typically used when you need to set up a router in a remote office where either there is no MIS staff or the staff has very limited knowledge and experience.

To configure the router automatically, the router must be connected to your LAN or WAN through one of its interfaces. The router can be configured by its Ethernet, Token Ring, FDDI, or any serial interfaces.

The router will act as a BootP (bootstrap protocol) workstation and connect to an existing router that is acting as a BootP or RARP (reverse address resolution protocol) server. This existing router will be used to give the new router its IP address and point the new router to the TFTP server by way of its helper address.

A helper address is defined on a router to forward UDP broadcasts to a server; in this case, a TFTP broadcast will be forwarded to a TFTP server. The helper address can also be used to forward DHCP requests to a DHCP server.

After the BootP server (existing router) gives the new router its IP address the new router will look for a DNS server to resolve the IP address to its host name. The router configuration will then be downloaded from the TFTP server to the new router.

The steps below outline the procedure a new router will take when trying to download a configuration from a TFTP server.

1. Upon bootup, the new router will send out a BootP request for an IP address, and it'll take the first IP address received from a BootP server.

2. After it has received an IP address, it'll attempt to resolve the IP address to a hostname, whether from the TFTP server or a DNS

server. If the hostname is resolved from the TFTP server, the TFTP server sends a file named *network-config*, which contains the new hostname of the router. The network-config file contains commands that apply to all routers and terminal servers on the network.

3. After the hostname is resolved, the router will request a configuration file from the TFTP server that contains the configuration information named *hostname-config*. The hostname-config file contains commands that apply to one router in particular. If the TFTP server can't send the hostname-config file, it'll send out a generic file named *router-config*. At that point, you have to telnet into the new router and make the necessary configurations manually.

4. The TFTP server sends this file to the new router. The new router then loads it into running config.

When naming your files, remember that the Cisco IOS understands two naming conventions: DOS and Unix. The DOS names are limited to eight characters, plus a three-letter extension, and the Unix conventions are limited to hostname-config for the host file and network-config for the network configuration file.

Cisco IOS Commands

To examine the status of a router, there are several different commands available. Each command allows you to configure and examine different components of the router. Figure 8.1 shows where the router status commands take place.

Show Version

Show version allows you to display the current version of the Cisco IOS. This is shown highlighted below. (You can use sh ver as an abbreviation for show version.)

```
Router#sh ver
Cisco Internetwork Operating System Software
```

FIGURE 8.1

Router status commands

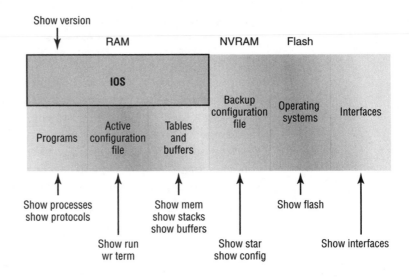

IOS (tm) 3000 Software (IGS-I-L), **Version 11.1(11)**, RELEASE
➡ SOFTWARE (fc1)

Copyright (c) 1986-1997 by cisco Systems, Inc.

Compiled Tue 24-Jun-97 12:20 by jaturner

Image text-base: 0x0301E644, data-base: 0x00001000

ROM: System Bootstrap, Version 11.0(10c), SOFTWARE

ROM: 3000 Bootstrap Software (IGS-BOOT-R), Version 11.0(10c),
➡ RELEASE SOFTWARE (

fc1)

Show version also indicates to you how long the router has been up:

    RouterB uptime is 31 minutes

how the system was started:

    System restarted by power-on

and where the system was loaded from:

System image file is "flash:igs-i-l.110-16", **booted via flash**

cisco 2500 (68030) processor (revision N) with 2048K/2048K bytes
➡ of memory.

Processor board ID 06262774, with hardware revision 00000000

Bridging software.
X.25 software, Version 2.0, NET2, BFE and GOSIP compliant.

In addition, show version will reveal the interfaces the POST found.

1 Ethernet/IEEE 802.3 interface.
2 Serial network interfaces.
32K bytes of non-volatile configuration memory.
8192K bytes of processor board System flash (Read ONLY)

The configuration register is also displayed:

Configuration register is 0x2102

Show Processes

Show processes will display the active processes on your router (sh proc will work).

Router#**sh proc**

This shows you CPU utilization for five seconds, one minute, and five minutes.

CPU utilization for five seconds: 0%/0%; one minute: 0%;
five minutes: 0%

PID

PID shows the ID number of each process.

Q

Q is the queue (high, medium, low) priority.

TY

TY is a status of the process.

PC

PC is the Program Counter.

Runtime

Runtime is the CPU time in milliseconds for the process.

Invoked

Invoked equals the total time the process has been invoked.

uSecs

uSecs is the CPU time in microseconds for each process invocation.

Stacks

Stacks shows you the low watermark/total stack space available in bytes.

TTY

TTY tells which terminal controls the process.

Process

Process displays the name of the process:

PID	QTy	PC	Runtime (ms)	Invoked	uSecs	Stacks	TTY	Process
1	M*	0	560	79	7088	2268/4000	0	Exec
2	Lst	30D2066	2356	85	27717	1832/2000	0	Check heaps
3	Mst	30FA1A2	0	2	0	1764/2000	0	Timers
4	Lwe	3154CFC	0	43	0	1760/2000	0	ARP Input
5	Lwe	316EF3E	0	1	0	1764/2000	0	Probe Input
6	Mwe	316E8BA	0	1	0	1776/2000	0	RARP Input
7	Hwe	31605A4	4	43	93	3752/4000	0	IP Input
8	Mwe	3189D8E	4	506	7	1652/2000	0	TCP Timer
9	Lwe	318BB58	0	1	0	3752/4000	0	TCP Protocols
10	Mwe	31D87AA	0	255	0	1664/2000	0	CDP Protocol
11	Mwe	31A2A60	144	2562	56	3792/4000	0	IP Background
12	Lsi	31BB1E6	4	43	93	1828/2000	0	IP Cache Ager

PID	QTy	PC	Runtime (ms)	Invoked	uSecs	Stacks	TTY	Process
13	Mwe	316B29A	4	1	4000	1580/2000	0	BOOTP Server
14	Cwe	30C7786	0	1	0	1788/2000	0	Critical Bkgnd
15	Mwe	30C7622	8	171	46	1504/2000	0	Net Background
16	Lwe	30F3D38	4	8	500	3672/4000	0	Logger
17	Msp	30EC62C	380	2520	150	1644/2000	0	TTY Background
18	Msp	30C7544	12	2522	4	1844/2000	0	Per-Second Jobs
19	Msp	30C74DA	1376	2522	545	1436/2000	0	Net Periodic
20	Hwe	30C79B4	0	1	0	1764/2000	0	Net Input
21	Msp	30C756A	1176	43	27348	1840/2000	0	Per-minute Jobs

--More–

Show Memory

Show memory is used to see how the management system allocated memory for different purposes (sh mem).

Router#**sh mem**

	Head	Total(b)	Used(b)	Free(b)	Lowest(b)	Largest(b)
Processor	4CD18	1778408	638664	1139744	1136952	1133220
I/O	200000	2097152	336336	1760816	1760816	1760560

The chart above displays the summarized statistics of the system memory allocator's activities. With it, we can discover the amount of memory in use, for example, or the size of the largest available free block.

The chart below is a block-by-block listing of memory use.

Processor memory

Address	Bytes	Prev.	Next	REF	PrevF	NextF	Alloc PC	What
4CD18	1056	0	4D160	1			30D240C	List Elements
4D160	2656	4CD18	4DBE8	1			30D240C	List Headers
4DBE8	2548	4D160	4E604	1			30E1E38	TTY data
4E604	2000	4DBE8	4EDFC	1			30E3FD8	TTY Input Buf
4EDFC	512	4E604	4F024	1			30E4008	TTY Output Buf
4F024	3000	4EDFC	4FC04	1			30D34C2	*Init*
4FC04	1056	4F024	5004C	1			30D240C	messages
5004C	1032	4FC04	5047C	1			3110872	*Init*
5047C	4636	5004C	516C0	0	0	0	312840A	(coalesced)
516C0	2548	5047C	520DC	1			3114A42	*Init*
520DC	84	516C0	52158	1			3115C40	Init
52158	84	520DC	521D4	1			3115C40	Init
521D4	84	52158	52250	1			3115C40	Init
52250	3456	521D4	52FF8	1			30D240C	Reg Service
52FF8	2056	52250	53828	1			30D240C	Reg Function
53828	1216	52FF8	53D10	1			30D981A	Registry
53D10	1216	53828	541F8	1			30D981A	Registry
541F8	1216	53D10	546E0	1			30D981A	Registry

--More—

Show Stacks

Show stacks monitors the stack use of processes and interrupts routines, and if the reboot was the result of a crash, displays the reason for the last system reboot.

```
RouterC#sh stacks
Minimum process stacks:
Free/Size  Name
2860/4000  Init
1652/2000  Router Init
2268/4000  Virtual Exec
2272/4000  Exec

Interrupt level stacks:
Level    Called Unused/Size  Name
  3           0  3000/3000   Serial interface state change
interrupt
  4       20198  2560/3000   Network interfaces
  5       32195  2796/3000   Console Uart
```

Show Buffers

Show buffers reveals the size of the Small, Middle, Big, VeryBig, Large, and Huge buffers (sh buff).

```
Router#sh buff
Buffer elements:
     500 in free list (500 max allowed)
     726 hits, 0 misses, 0 created

Public buffer pools:
Small buffers, 104 bytes (total 50, permanent 50):
     50 in free list (20 min, 150 max allowed)
     357 hits, 0 misses, 0 trims, 0 created
     0 failures (0 no memory)
Middle buffers, 600 bytes (total 25, permanent 25):
     25 in free list (10 min, 150 max allowed)
     20 hits, 0 misses, 0 trims, 0 created
     0 failures (0 no memory)
```

> **Big buffers**, 1524 bytes (total 50, permanent 50):
>
> 50 in free list (5 min, 150 max allowed)
>
> 0 hits, 0 misses, 0 trims, 0 created
>
> 0 failures (0 no memory)
>
> **VeryBig buffers**, 4520 bytes (total 10, permanent 10):
>
> 10 in free list (0 min, 100 max allowed)
>
> 0 hits, 0 misses, 0 trims, 0 created
>
> 0 failures (0 no memory)
>
> **Large buffers**, 5024 bytes (total 0, permanent 0):
>
> 0 in free list (0 min, 10 max allowed)
>
> 0 hits, 0 misses, 0 trims, 0 created
>
> 0 failures (0 no memory)
>
> **Huge buffers**, 18024 bytes (total 0, permanent 0):
>
> 0 in free list (0 min, 4 max allowed)
>
> 0 hits, 0 misses, 0 trims, 0 created
>
> 0 failures (0 no memory

Show Flash

Show flash describes our flash memory and reveals both the size of our files and the amount of free flash memory (sh fla).

Router#**sh fla**

System flash directory:
File   Length   Name/status
  1   3612396   igs-i-1.110-16
[3612460 bytes used, 4776148 available, 8388608 total]
8192K bytes of processor board System flash (Read ONLY)

Show Running-Config

Show running-config (write term on version 10.3 and earlier) details the running configuration file.

Show Startup-Config

Show startup-config (show config on version 10.3 and earlier) reveals the configuration stored in NVRAM.

Show Interfaces

Show interfaces (sh int) shows us the hardware interfaces installed on our router plus their status. It begins with the first interface and continues through all of them. You can type **sh int e0** to see the status of that particular interface.

```
Router#sh int
Ethernet0 is up, line protocol is down
```

Notice that the next line shows us the hardware address:

```
Hardware is Lance, address is 00e0.1ea9.c418 (bia 00e0.1ea9.c418)
Internet address is 172.16.30.1 255.255.255.0
MTU 1500 bytes, BW 10000 Kbit, DLY 1000 usec, rely 128/255,
load 1/255
Encapsulation ARPA, loopback not set, keepalive set (10 sec)
ARP type: ARPA, ARP Timeout 4:00:00
Last input never, output 0:00:01, output hang never
Last clearing of "show interface" counters never
Output queue 0/40, 0 drops; input queue 0/75, 0 drops
5 minute input rate 0 bits/sec, 0 packets/sec
5 minute output rate 0 bits/sec, 0 packets/sec
   0 packets input, 0 bytes, 0 no buffer
   Received 0 broadcasts, 0 runts, 0 giants
   0 input errors, 0 CRC, 0 frame, 0 overrun, 0 ignored, 0 abort
   0 input packets with dribble condition detected
   384 packets output, 23049 bytes, 0 underruns
   384 output errors, 0 collisions, 1 interface resets, 0 restarts
   0 output buffer failures, 0 output buffers swapped out
--More--
```

Show Protocols

Show protocols details which protocols are configured on the router (sh prot). You can see that only IP is configured on interfaces e0, s0, and s1.

```
Router#sh prot
Global values:
   Internet Protocol routing is enabled
Ethernet0 is up, line protocol is down
```

```
          Internet address is 172.16.30.1 255.255.255.0
       Serial0 is down, line protocol is up
          Internet address is 172.16.20.2 255.255.255.0
       Serial1 is down, line protocol is up
          Internet address is 172.16.40.1 255.255.255.0
```

Show IP Protocol

To see the protocol in more detail, use the show ip protocol command (sh ip prot).

```
RouterC#sh ip prot
Routing Protocol is "rip"
   Sending updates every 30 seconds, next due in 22 seconds
   Invalid after 180 seconds, hold down 180, flushed after
240
   Outgoing update filter list for all interfaces is not set
   Incoming update filter list for all interfaces is not set
   Redistributing: rip
   Routing for Networks:
     172.16.0.0
   Routing Information Sources:
     Gateway          Distance        Last Update
     172.16.40.1            120        0:00:02
   Distance: (default is 120)
```

Accessing Other Routers

We're now going to take a look at the different ways we can connect to and retrieve information about remote routers. We'll get the details on how to get information using the Cisco Discovery Protocol and virtual terminal connections, and we'll learn the basics on connectivity testing.

Cisco Discovery Protocol (CDP)

The proprietary protocol CDP allows you to access configuration information on other routers with a single command. By running Subnetwork Access

Protocol (SNAP) at the Data Link layer, two devices running different Network layer protocols can still communicate and learn about each other. These devices can include all LANs and most WANs. *later*

CDP starts by default on any router version 10.3 or ~~earlier~~ and discovers neighboring Cisco routers running CDP by doing a Data Link broadcast. It doesn't matter which protocol is running at the Network layer.

Once CDP has discovered a router, it can then display information about the upper-layer protocols such as IP and IPX. A router caches the information it receives from its CDP neighbors. Anytime a router receives updated information that a CDP neighbor has changed, it discards the old information in favor of the new broadcast.

Let's take a look at a network trace and examine a CDP frame:

```
Flags:          0x80  802.3
  Status:         0x00
  Packet Length:305
  Timestamp:      12:09:42.623000 06/09/1998
802.3 Header
  Destination:   01:00:0c:cc:cc:cc
  Source:        00:00:0c:8d:5c:9d
  LLC Length:    287
802.2 Logical Link Control (LLC) Header
  Dest. SAP:     0xaa  SNAP
  Source SAP:    0xaa  SNAP
  Command:       0x03  Unnumbered Information
  Protocol:      00-00-0c-20-00  Cisco DP
  Packet Data:
  .´.}....RouterA.   01 b4 9f 7d 00 01 00 0b 52 6f 75 74 65 72 41 00
  ............¬...    02 00 11 00 00 00 01 01 01 cc 00 04 ac 10 0a 01
  ....Ethernet0...   00 03 00 0d 45 74 68 65 72 6e 65 74 30 00 04 00
  ........ÔCisco I   08 00 00 00 01 00 05 00 d4 43 69 73 63 6f 20 49
  nternetwork Oper   6e 74 65 72 6e 65 74 77 6f 72 6b 20 4f 70 65 72
  ating System Sof   61 74 69 6e 67 20 53 79 73 74 65 6d 20 53 6f 66
  tware .IOS (tm)    74 77 61 72 65 20 0a 49 4f 53 20 28 74 6d 29 20
  3000 Software (I   33 30 30 30 20 53 6f 66 74 77 61 72 65 20 28 49
  GS-I-L), Version   47 53 2d 49 2d 4c 29 2c 20 56 65 72 73 69 6f 6e
  11.0(18), RELEA    20 31 31 2e 30 28 31 38 29 2c 20 52 45 4c 45 41
  SE SOFTWARE (fc1   53 45 20 53 4f 46 54 57 41 52 45 20 28 66 63 31
```

```
).Copyright (c)     29 0a 43 6f 70 79 72 69 67 68 74 20 28 63 29 20
1986-1997 by cis    31 39 38 36 2d 31 39 39 37 20 62 79 20 63 69 73
co Systems, Inc.    63 6f 20 53 79 73 74 65 6d 73 2c 20 49 6e 63 2e
.Compiled Mon 01    0a 43 6f 6d 70 69 6c 65 64 20 4d 6f 6e 20 30 31
-Dec-97 18:09 by    2d 44 65 63 2d 39 37 20 31 38 3a 30 39 20 62 79
jaturner....cis     20 6a 61 74 75 72 6e 65 72 00 06 00 0e 63 69 73
co 2500             63 6f 20 32 35 30 30
Frame Check Sequence:    0x00000000
```

Notice in the Etherpeek trace that the frame is a SNAP frame and the protocol is a Cisco DP. Also notice that Network layer information isn't present in the frame.

CDP Commands

The commands to display the results of the CDP broadcast can be viewed by connecting a console port to a router that's configured to run CDP on its interfaces—but you can see only the directly connected routers as shown in Figure 8.2. To see RouterD, you would have to telnet into that router to get CDP information.

F I G U R E 8.2

CDP neighbors

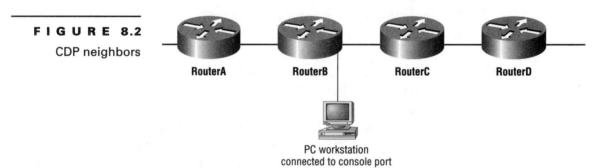

RouterA   RouterB   RouterC   RouterD

PC workstation
connected to console port

By typing **sh cdp ?**, we receive a list of commands available on our router.

```
RouterB#sh cdp ?
    entry       Information for specific neighbor entry
    interface   CDP interface status and configuration
    neighbors   CDP neighbor entries
    traffic     CDP statistics
    <cr>
```

By typing **sh cdp int,** we can see the interface information plus the encapsulation. This is the default encapsulation used by the interface. It also shows us the timers—60 seconds for an update and 180 seconds for hold time.

```
RouterB#sh cdp int
Ethernet0 is up, line protocol is up, encapsulation is ARPA
  Sending CDP packets every 60 seconds
  Holdtime is 180 seconds
Serial0 is up, line protocol is up, encapsulation is HDLC
  Sending CDP packets every 60 seconds
  Holdtime is 180 seconds
Serial1 is up, line protocol is up, encapsulation is HDLC
  Sending CDP packets every 60 seconds
  Holdtime is 180 seconds
```

The sh cdp entry command can give you the CDP information received from all routers by typing an asterisk (*) or a specific router by typing the router name.

```
RouterB#sh cdp entry ?
  *     all CDP neighbor entries
  WORD  Name of CDP neighbor entry
  <cr>


RouterB#sh cdp entry RouterA
-------------------------
Device ID: RouterA
Entry address(es):
  IP address: 172.16.20.1
Platform: cisco 2500,  Capabilities: Router
Interface: Serial0,  Port ID (outgoing port): Serial0
Holdtime : 130 sec

Version :
Cisco Internetwork Operating System Software
IOS (tm) 3000 Software (IGS-I-L), Version 11.0(18), RELEASE
SOFTWARE (fc1)
Copyright (c) 1986-1997 by cisco Systems, Inc.
Compiled Mon 01-Dec-97 18:09 by jaturner
```

The show cdp neighbors command will reveal the information being exchanged among neighbors.

```
RouterB#sh cdp neighbors
Capability Codes: R - Router, T - Trans Bridge, B - Source
Route Bridge, S - Switch, H - Host, I - IGMP, r - Repeater

Device ID  Local Intrfce  Holdtme  Capability  Platform  Port ID
RouterC    Ser 1          158      R           2500      Ser 0
RouterA    Ser 0          150      R           2500      Ser 0
```

For each neighbor it displays the following:

- Neighbor Device ID: the name of the neighbor router that this router exchanges CDP information with

- Local interface: the interface on which this neighbor is heard

- Holdtime: decremental hold time in seconds

- Capability: router's capability code—R for router, S for switch, etc.

- Platform: which type of device the neighbor is

- Port ID: the interface of the remote neighbor router you receive CDP information from

sh cdp neighbor detail gives the same information as well as information from the sh cdp entry command.

```
RouterB#sh cdp neighbor detail
-------------------------
Device ID: RouterC
Entry address(es):
  IP address: 172.16.40.2
Platform: cisco 2500,  Capabilities: Router
Interface: Serial1,  Port ID (outgoing port): Serial0
Holdtime : 123 sec

Version :
Cisco Internetwork Operating System Software
IOS (tm) 3000 Software (IGS-I-L), Version 11.0(18), RELEASE
SOFTWARE (fc1)
```

```
Copyright (c) 1986-1997 by cisco Systems, Inc.
Compiled Mon 01-Dec-97 18:09 by jaturner


-------------------------
Device ID: RouterA
Entry address(es):
  IP address: 172.16.20.1
Platform: cisco 2500,  Capabilities: Router
Interface: Serial0,  Port ID (outgoing port): Serial0
Holdtime : 174 sec


Version :
Cisco Internetwork Operating System Software
IOS (tm) 3000 Software (IGS-I-L), Version 11.0(18), RELEASE
SOFTWARE (fc1)
Copyright (c) 1986-1997 by cisco Systems, Inc.
Compiled Mon 01-Dec-97 18:09 by jaturner
```

The sh cdp traffic command reveals the amount of packets sent and received among neighbors.

```
RouterB#sh cdp traffic
CDP counters :
        Packets output: 206, Input: 202
        Hdr syntax: 0, Chksum error: 0, Encaps failed: 0
        No memory: 0, Invalid packet: 0, Fragmented: 0
```

Virtual Terminal Connections (Telnet)

Telnet, part of the TCP/IP protocol suite, is a virtual terminal protocol that allows you to connect to remote hosts, including routers, without being physically attached to them. Cisco routers can support up to five simultaneous incoming telnet sessions (vty 0 4).

To access a remote router, type **telnet**, along with the IP address of the remote host. For a Cisco router, this can be the IP address of any active interface on the router.

```
RouterB#telnet 172.16.50.1
Trying 172.16.50.1 ... Open
```

```
User Access Verification

Password:
RouterC>exit
[Connection to 172.16.50.1 closed by foreign host]
```

Notice that we telneted into RouterC from RouterB by using its Ethernet0 interface. Remember—we're directly connected through a simulated 56K WAN link into RouterC's Serial0 port (172.16.40.2), but we can use any interface on the router to make a connection. To close the session type **exit**. If you want to return to your originating router without terminating the session to the remote router, you can enter an escape sequence of CTRL+Shift+6 then **X**. It's kind of like playing twister with your fingers, but it works.

```
RouterC#telnet routerb
Trying RouterB (172.16.40.1)... Open

User Access Verification

Password:
RouterB> (We typed ctrl-shift-6 then X, but it didn't show
on the screen)
RouterC#sh sessions
Conn Host            Address        Byte  Idle  Conn Name
*   1 routerb        172.16.40.1    0     0     routerb

RouterC#1
[Resuming connection 1 to routerb ... ](return)
RouterB>
```

After typing CTRL+Shift+6 then **X**, we typed **sh sessions**. This showed us the telnet sessions open and their connection number. We then typed a **1** and pressed Return and were reconnected to RouterB.

At this point you can type **end** or disconnect to terminate the sessions, or you can add unlimited sessions.

Hostnames

You can configure your router to resolve IP addresses to hostnames—which can be configured on each router like a hosts table in Unix—or you can use a DNS server to resolve names. That way, you don't have to remember IP addresses, and you can connect to a remote router by using its hostname.

To configure your routers to use hostnames, use the ip host command.

```
RouterB#config t
Enter configuration commands, one per line.  End with CNTL/Z.
RouterB(config)#ip host ?
  WORD  Name of host

RouterB(config)#ip host RouterC ?
  <0-65535>  Default telnet port number
  A.B.C.D    Host IP address (maximum of 8)

RouterB(config)#ip host RouterC 172.16.40.2
RouterB(config)#^Z
RouterB#
```

We typed **ip host** ? and received the Help screen telling us to enter the name of the host. We then typed **RouterC** ? and received the next Help screen telling us to give the IP address of the host and an optional number to set when telneting. The default port is 23. Notice that you can have up to eight IP addresses for the host name. We put in the IP address of 172.16. 40.2, which is our closest interface for that router, but remember, you can use any interface address.

Now, we should be able to just type the word **RouterC**, and it should set up a session with us.

```
RouterB#routerc
Trying RouterC (172.16.40.2)... Open

User Access Verification

Password:
RouterC>exit

[Connection to routerc closed by foreign host]
RouterB#
```

This sure makes things easier.

To display all the hostnames and their related IP addresses that your router knows about, you can use the sh hosts command (both sh hosts and sh host work).

```
RouterB#sh hosts
Default domain is not set
Name/address lookup uses domain service
Name servers are 255.255.255.255


Host                    Flags       Age Type    Address(es)
RouterC                 (perm, OK)  0   IP      172.16.40.2
RouterA                 (perm, OK)  0   IP      172.16.20.1
RouterB#
```

The parameters for the show host command are shown below:

- Hosts shows the names of learned hosts.

- Flags describes how the name was learned.

  - Perm means it was manually configured.

  - Temp refers to whether it was resolved by DNS.

  - OK means it's current.

  - EX means that the entry has timed out.

- Age refers to the time in hours the name has been resolved.

- Type refers to the protocol.

- Address(es) refers to the logical address of the host.

To configure your router to use a DNS server—it's easier than configuring hostnames on each router or configuring the router not to use a DNS lookup—you can use the ip domain-lookup command.

```
RouterB#routera
Translating "routera"...domain server (255.255.255.255)
% Unknown command or computer name, or unable to find
computer address
RouterB#config t
Enter configuration commands, one per line.  End with CNTL/Z.
RouterB(config)#no ip domain-lookup
```

```
RouterB(config)#^Z
RouterB#
```

The `ip domain-lookup` command is enabled by default. If you were to type in a hostname that it couldn't resolve, it would try to broadcast for a DNS server to resolve the name. This can be annoying—at best—when you're in a hurry because you not only have a router down, you have to wait for the DNS broadcast to time-out before you can continue (of course you can play twister with your fingers as described earlier at any time). You can type **no ip domain-lookup** to stop the router from looking for a DNS server and to receive an immediate response back from the router.

To configure your router for a DNS server, use both the `ip domain-lookup` and `ip name-server` commands.

```
RouterB#config t
Enter configuration commands, one per line.  End with CNTL/Z.
RouterB(config)#ip domain-lookup
RouterB(config)#ip name-server ?
  A.B.C.D  Domain server IP address (maximum of 6)
RouterB(config)#ip name-server 172.16.30.8
RouterB(config)#^Z
```

The router will now use a DNS server to try to resolve hostnames.

Basic Testing

To perform basic testing on your internetwork, you can follow the layers of the OSI reference model. Figure 8.3 shows the OSI reference model and the commands associated at each layer.

Let's start out by telneting to a remote router. This way we'll know that all layers (the upper and bottom) must be working.

Testing with Telnet

Let's look at an Etherpeek network trace and see why Telnet is a great tool for testing all layers of the OSI reference model.

```
Flags:        0x00
  Status:        0x00
  Packet Length:68
  Timestamp:    12:16:05.495000 06/09/1998
```

FIGURE 8.3

Testing commands at each layer of the OSI reference model

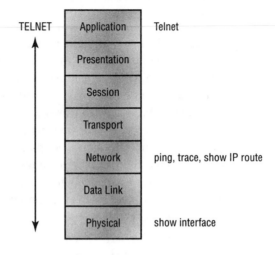

```
Ethernet Header
    Destination:    00:80:c7:a8:f0:3d
    Source:         00:00:0c:8d:5c:9d
    Protocol Type:08-00   IP
IP Header - Internet Protocol Datagram
    Version:                4
    Header Length:          5
    Precedence:             0
    Type of Service:        %000
    Unused:                 %00
    Total Length:           50
    Identifier:             23
    Fragmentation Flags:    %000
    Fragment Offset:        0
    Time To Live:           254
    IP Type:                0x06   TCP
    Header Checksum:        0x468a
    Source IP Address:      172.16.20.2
    Dest. IP Address:       172.16.10.2
    No Internet Datagram Options
```

```
TCP - Transport Control Protocol
  Source Port:       23  TELNET
  Destination Port: 1032
  Sequence Number:  2665776445
  Ack Number:       17009601
  Offset:           5
  Reserved:         %000000
  Code:             %011000
            Ack is valid
            Push Request
  Window:           2093
  Checksum:         0xffe7
  Urgent Pointer:   0
  No TCP Options
TELNET - Network Virtual Terminal
  TELNET Data:
  ..                      0d 0a
  TELNET Data:
  RouterB#                52 6f 75 74 65 72 42 23
Frame Check Sequence:  0x00000000
```

Not only does Telnet use Ethernet_II frames at the Data Link layer, it also uses IP at the Network layer and TCP at the Transport layer. It goes all the way up to the application layer. If we can telnet, then we must have solid network communication between two hosts.

Testing with Ping

If you can't Telnet into a host, or if you want to test physical network connectivity between two or more hosts, using ping is a great choice. Packet InterNet Groper (PING) isn't just used for IP networks; it can be used with almost any type of Network layer protocol including IPX, AppleTalk, Apollo, VINES, and DECnet.

```
RouterC#ping 172.16.10.1
Type escape sequence to abort.
Sending 5, 100-byte ICMP Echos to 172.16.10.1, timeout is 2
seconds:
.!!!!
```

```
Success rate is 80 percent (5/5), round-trip min/avg/max =
64/65/68 ms
RouterC#
```

Below are some responses you might receive, plus their explanations.

TABLE 8.1 Ping Responses	Ping Responses	Explanations
	!	successful receipt of an echo reply
	.	time-out
	U	destination unreachable
	C	congested experience packet
	I	ping interrupted (CTRL-Shift-6 X)
	?	packet type unknown
	&	packet time-to-live exceeded

The ping command sends ICMP echo packets as shown below in the Etherpeek trace:

```
Flags:        0x00
  Status:        0x00
  Packet Length:78
  Timestamp:    12:27:04.513000 06/09/1998
Ethernet Header
  Destination:  00:00:0c:8d:5c:9d
  Source:       00:80:c7:a8:f0:3d
  Protocol Type:08-00  IP
IP Header - Internet Protocol Datagram
  Version:             4
  Header Length:       5
  Precedence:          0
  Type of Service:     %000
  Unused:              %00
```

```
Total Length:          60
Identifier:            48646
Fragmentation Flags:   %000
Fragment Offset:       0
Time To Live:          32
IP Type:               0x01  ICMP
Header Checksum:        0x7097
Source IP Address:     172.16.10.2
Dest. IP Address:      172.16.10.1
No Internet Datagram Options
ICMP - Internet Control Messages Protocol
ICMP Type:             8  Echo Request
Code:                  0
Checksum:              0x415c
Identifier:            0x0300
Sequence Number:       2304
ICMP Data Area:
abcdefghijklmnop   61 62 63 64 65 66 67 68 69 6a 6b 6c 6d
6e 6f 70
qrstuvwabcdefghi   71 72 73 74 75 76 77 61 62 63 64 65 66
67 68 69
Frame Check Sequence:   0x00000000
```

Notice that doing this checks only up to the Network layer.

Extended ping gives you more options and is supported only in privileged mode. Extended ping can also use IP, AppleTalk, and IPX.

```
RouterC#ping
Protocol [ip]:
Target IP address: 172.16.10.2
Repeat count [5]:
Datagram size [100]:
Timeout in seconds [2]:
Extended commands [n]: y
Source address or interface: 172.16.40.2
Type of service [0]:
Set DF bit in IP header? [no]: y
Validate reply data? [no]: y
Data pattern [0xABCD]:
```

```
Loose, Strict, Record, Timestamp, Verbose[none]: v
Loose, Strict, Record, Timestamp, Verbose[V]:
Sweep range of sizes [n]:
Type escape sequence to abort.
Sending 5, 100-byte ICMP Echos to 172.16.10.2, timeout is 2
seconds:
Reply to request 0 (68 ms)
Reply to request 1 (64 ms)
Reply to request 2 (68 ms)
Reply to request 3 (68 ms)
Reply to request 4 (64 ms)
Success rate is 100 percent (5/5), round-trip min/avg/max =
64/66/68 ms
RouterC#
```

Notice all the options available. We like to use extended ping just to be able to make packets larger than the default 100 bytes.

Testing with the Trace Command

The trace command was covered in Chapter 6: we already know that the trace command can be used to discover routes to remote destinations and that it's similar to the ping command. Not completely, however. Unlike ping, the trace command takes advantage of the error messages when a packet exceeds its TTL (time-to-live).

The trace command will start out by sending a TTL of 1. This will cause the first router to receive the packet and send back an error. It keeps sending new probes with incrementing TTL, with each packet reaching one hop further than the last, until it understands the complete path, distance, and time between each router.

```
RouterA#trace ?
  WORD      Trace route to destination address or hostname
  appletalk AppleTalk Trace
  clns      ISO CLNS Trace
  ip        IP Trace
  oldvines  Vines Trace (Cisco)
  vines     Vines Trace (Banyan)
  <cr>
```

```
RouterA#trace ip ?
  WORD  Trace route to destination address or hostname
  <cr>

RouterA#trace ip 172.16.40.2

Type escape sequence to abort.
Tracing the route to 172.16.40.2

  1 172.16.20.2 24 msec 24 msec 28 msec
  2 172.16.40.2 44 msec 44 msec *
RouterA#
```

Trace can use IP, CLNS, VINES, and AppleTalk.

When the trace reaches the target destination, an asterisk (*) is reported in the display. In response to the probe packet, it's typically reported because of a port-unreachable packet plus the time-out.

Some other responses might include:

TABLE 8.2 Trace Responses	**Trace Responses**	**Explanations**
	!H	The router received the probe but didn't forward it because of an access list.
	P	The protocol was unreachable.
	N	The network was unreachable.
	U	The port was unreachable.
	*	There was a time-out.

Notice in the Etherpeek trace that ICMP is used to send back an error message to the sending router and that the TTL is only 125.

```
Ethernet Header
```

```
      Destination:   00:80:c7:a8:f0:3d
      Source:        00:00:0c:8d:5c:9d
      Protocol Type:08-00   IP
   IP Header - Internet Protocol Datagram
      Version:              4
      Header Length:        5
      Precedence:           0
      Type of Service:      %000
      Unused:               %00
      Total Length:         56
      Identifier:           2892
      Fragmentation Flags:  %000
      Fragment Offset:      0
      Time To Live:         223
      IP Type:              0x01   ICMP
      Header Checksum:      0x2854
      Source IP Address:    172.16.40.2
      Dest. IP Address:     172.16.10.2
      No Internet Datagram Options
   ICMP - Internet Control Messages Protocol
      ICMP Type:            3  Destination Unreachable
      Code:                 3  Port Unreachable
      Checksum:             0xd078
      Unused (must be zero):0x00000000

   Header of packet that caused error follows.
   IP Header - Internet Protocol Datagram
      Version:              4
      Header Length:        5
      Precedence:           0
      Type of Service:      %000
      Unused:               %00
      Total Length:         78
      Identifier:           59654
      Fragmentation Flags:  %000
      Fragment Offset:      0
```

```
Time To Live:          125
IP Type:               0x11  UDP
Header Checksum:       0xc074
Source IP Address:     172.16.10.2
Dest. IP Address:      172.16.50.1
No Internet Datagram Options
```

(This is the only time we like seeing an error!)

Testing with the Show Interface Command

Another command we've already used is the sh int command. One of the most important elements of the show interface serial command is that it displays the line and data link protocol status.

```
RouterC#sh int s0
Serial0 is up, line protocol is up
    Hardware is HD64570
    Internet address is 172.16.40.2 255.255.255.0
    MTU 1500 bytes, BW 1544 Kbit, DLY 20000 usec, rely 255/
255, load 1/255
    Encapsulation HDLC, loopback not set, keepalive set (10 sec)
    Last input 0:00:03, output 0:00:02, output hang never
    Last clearing of "show interface" counters never
    Output queue 0/40, 0 drops; input queue 0/75, 0 drops
    5 minute input rate 0 bits/sec, 0 packets/sec
    5 minute output rate 0 bits/sec, 0 packets/sec
       6000 packets input, 424701 bytes, 0 no buffer
       Received 3177 broadcasts, 0 runts, 0 giants
       0 input errors, 0 CRC, 0 frame, 0 overrun, 0 ignored, 0
abort
       6185 packets output, 1400825 bytes, 0 underruns
       0 output errors, 0 collisions, 2 interface resets, 0
restarts
       0 output buffer failures, 0 output buffers swapped out
       0 carrier transitions
       DCD=up  DSR=up  DTR=up  RTS=up  CTS=up
```

Carrier detect brings up the serial port, and keepalives bring up the line protocol. Why is this important? Because if the carrier detect is up, it means your physical layer connection is working. The line protocol refers to the data link framing and means you have the correct frame type and are communicating end to end.

If the interface is up but the line protocol is down, there's a problem with the connection or clocking. If the interface is down and so is the line protocol, it means there's an interface problem. If the interface shows administratively down and the line protocol is also down, the interface is disabled.

The sh int command lets you see the real-time statistics of an interface. For example, if you have many input errors, it's possible there's a problem with the link or the equipment is faulty. You can clear the counters by typing **clear counters**. This can give you a clear picture of the current status of the interface.

Testing with the Debug Command

We used the debug command in Chapter 6 when looking at RIP and IGRP. We can also use the debug command to help track problems with the network and discover which protocol messages are being sent and received by the router.

WARNING It's important to note that debugging a live network could cause a severe slowdown. Do not leave debugging on: use it only to diagnose a problem—then turn it off.

```
RouterC#debug all
This may severely impact network performance. Continue?
[confirm]
All possible debugging has been turned on
RouterC#
Serial0: HDLC myseq 2139, mineseen 2139, yourseen 2139, line up
CDP-PA: Packet received from RouterB on interface Serial0
**Entry  found in cache**
RIP: sending update to 255.255.255.255 via Ethernet0
(172.16.50.1)
        subnet 172.16.40.0, metric 1
        subnet 172.16.20.0, metric 2
        subnet 172.16.10.0, metric 3
RIP: Update contains 3 routes
RIP: Update queued
```

```
RIP: Update sent via Ethernet0
IP: s=172.16.50.1 (local), d=255.255.255.255 (Ethernet0),
len 67, sending broad/
multicast
RIP: sending update to 255.255.255.255 via Serial0
(172.16.40.2)
     subnet 172.16.50.0, metric 1
RIP: Update contains 1 routes
RIP: Update queued
RIP: Update sent via Serial0
IP: s=172.16.40.2 (local), d=255.255.255.255 (Serial0), len
65, sending broad/mu
lticast
RouterC#undebug all
All possible debugging has been turned off
RouterC#
```

Wow, we ran this for only five seconds on our not-very-busy network. Can you imagine running this with hundreds of routers? It would be better to run debug with some options, wouldn't it? Well, you can get a whole list of options by typing **debug ?**.

By default, debug posts all messages on the console terminal. If you'd like to log these messages to a log file on a Unix or Windows NT host, you can use the logging configuration command.

```
RouterC#config t
Enter configuration commands, one per line.  End with CNTL/Z.
RouterC(config)#logging 172.16.10.1
RouterC(config)#^Z
RouterC#sh log
Syslog logging: enabled (0 messages dropped, 0 flushes, 0
overruns)
     Console logging: level debugging, 39 messages logged
     Monitor logging: level debugging, 0 messages logged
     Trap logging: level informational, 16 message lines
logged
        Logging to 172.16.10.1, 1 message lines logged
RouterC#
```

Summary

In this chapter, we covered the following:

- The commands from which to load Cisco IOS software: flash memory, a TFTP server, or ROM. We talked about where the IOS is stored and how to load it.

- How to prepare to back up, upgrade, and load a backup Cisco IOS image. We gave examples on how to flash your Cisco IOS.

- How to examine router elements (RAM, ROM, CDP, show). We talked about how the ROM, flash, and RAM work. We also talked about and gave details for the CDP protocol.

- How to copy and manipulate configuration files. We talked in detail about the startup-config and the running-config and how to use each one.

- How to manage configuration files from the privileged exec mode. We learned to configure both the startup-config and running-config.

- How to identify the functions performed by ICMP. We talked about how ICMP can be used to see if a host is alive (ping) and how the routers find their way through the internetwork to this host (trace).

Review Questions

1. What's the default CDP update broadcast rate for routers in seconds?

   A. 60   p293

   B. 90

   C. 180

   D. 240

2. What's the default CDP hold time in seconds?

   A. 60

   B. 90

C. 180   *p293*

D. 240

3. What command will allow you to load a Cisco router configuration that is stored on a TFTP server?

A. config t, tftp ip addresses of `tftp` server

B. config net, ip address of `tftp` server   *p155*

C. config mem, ip address of `tftp` server

D. config net, ip address of router

4. You just received an output that states the CDP hold time, hardware, port ID, and local interface. What was the command you typed in?

A. `sh int`

B. `sh cdp int`

C. `sh cdp neighbor`   *p294*

D. `sh cdp info`

5. Which command will load the Cisco router configuration into RAM (choose three)?

A. `reload`   *– p163*

B. `copy star run`   *p163*

C. `copy run star`

D. `copy TFTP run`   *p279*

6. Which command do you type to view the hostnames configured in your router (choose two)?

A. `sh hostnames`

B. `sh hosts`   *p298*

C. `sh host`

D. `hostnames`

7. If you type **copy tftp flash,** which event did you cause?

   A. erased your router configuration

   B. erased the configuration on your TFTP host   *P 274*

   C. copied a file from your TFTP server to your router flash

   D. copied your router's configuration from your TFTP server to your router

8. If you want to type in the hostname Bob instead of the IP address 172.16.10.1 to access the remote router named Bob, what should you do?

   A. `config t, hostname Router bob 172.16.10.1`

   B. `config t, ip hostname 172.16.10.1 router bob`

   C. `config t, ip host 172.16.10.1 bob`

   D. `config t, ip host bob 172.16.10.1`   *p 297*

9. What does it mean if you're running a trace and receive a "P" as a response?

   A. it passed through the first router

   B. positive response

   C. protocol responded

   D. protocol unreachable   *p 385*

10. How can you view the CDP information received from all routers?

   A. `sh cdp received`

   B. `sh cdp entry *`   *p 293*

   C. `cdp entry *`

   D. `sh cdp route`

11. What command should you use to have your router load the valid Cisco IOS from a TFTP server?

   A. `copy TFTP run`

   B. `copy run TFTP`

C. boot TFTP flash

D. boot system TFTP   *p 277*

12. What command will copy your router configuration to a TFTP server?

A. copy TFTP run

B. copy star TFTP   *p 279*

C. boot system run

D. copy flash TFTP

13. Which protocols can you use when testing with Trace (choose all that apply)?

A. AppleTalk   *p 304*

B. DECnet

C. CLNS

D. IP

E. TCP

F. Vines

G. Old Vines

14. Which command will you use to disable DNS lookup?

A. no DNS-lookup

B. domain no-lookup

C. no domain-lookup

D. no ip domain-lookup   *p 298, 299*

15. Which command do you use to configure your router to do a domain lookup?

A. DNS-server 10.10.10.10

B. 10.10.10.10 DNS-lookup

C. IP DNS-server 10.10.10.10

D. IP name-server 10.10.10.10   *p 299*

16. How can you telnet into multiple routers but keep the sessions open all at the same time?

   A. CTRL+Shift+^   *p296*

   B. CTRL+Shift+%

   C. CTRL+Alt+^

   D. Return

17. After telneting into multiple routers simultaneously, what command can you type to see these connections?

   A. sh telnet

   B. sh ports open

   C. sh sessions   *p296*

   D. sh hosts

18. If you want to configure the router configuration stored in NVRAM, which command should you use?

   A. config t

   B. config mem   *p155*

   C. config TFTP

   D. config startup-config

19. If you want to load a new Cisco IOS into your router's memory, which command should you use?

   A. copy star run

   B. copy run star

   C. copy flash TFTP

   D. copy TFTP flash   *p274*

20. What type of frame does CDP use to gather information about its directly connected neighbors?

   A. Subnetwork Access Protocol   *p291*

   B. TCP/IP

   C. 802.2

   D. Ethernet II

Laboratory Exercises

EXERCISE 8.1

CDP and Telnet

In this first lab, you will use CDP to discover other routers, then use Telnet as a local and remote management tool.

1. Log in to your router and get to privilege mode.

2. Discover the IP addresses of your directly connected Cisco neighbors by typing **sh cdp neighbor detail**.

3. Telnet to the routers you have discovered.

4. From the remote router, type **sh cdp neighbor**. Write down the difference, if any, of any new routers found.

5. Telnet to the new routers found.

6. Keep doing this until you have a complete map of your internetwork.

EXERCISE 8.2

Copying Configuration Files to a TFTP Server

In this next lab you will copy your active configuration file out to a TFTP server.

1. Log in to your router and get to your privilege mode prompt.

2. Type **copy run TFTP**.

3. Type in the IP address of your TFTP server (you can use the TFTP server from the CD in the front of this book or download it from the Cisco Web site and run it on your Windows 98 workstation).

4. Press Enter at the "Name of configuration file to write" prompt.

5. Log out.

EXERCISE 8.3

IP Host Table

In this next lab, you will add an IP host table to your router's active configuration.

1. Log in to your router and get to the private mode prompt.

2. View your host table by typing **sh hosts.**

3. Add a remote router to your host table by typing **ip host router name Ip_address** where router name is the name of the remote router and the IP address is the interface you will connect to the remote router through.

4. View your host table by typing **sh hosts**.

5. Test your host table by connecting to the remote router by using the hostname.

6. Log out.

EXERCISE 8.4

Loading a New IOS into Flash

In this exercise, you will copy a new IOS into your router's flash memory from a TFTP server.

1. Log in to your router and get to the privileged mode prompt.

2. Record the current version and name of the IOS that is currently running by typing **sh version**.

3. Check your TFTP directory for the name of the file that you will copy from the TFTP server to flash. If you have copied a new version from the Cisco Web site, put this file in the default TFTP directory of your server.

4. Verify TCP/IP connectivity to your TFTP server by using the ping command.

5. Type **copy TFTP flash**.

6. Type in the IP address of your TFTP server at the "Address or name of remote host" prompt.

7. Enter the name of the new Cisco IOS file name.

8. At the "Destination file name" prompt, press Enter.

9. At the Erase flash device before writing prompt, press Enter.

10. At the "copy file_name from server into flash with erase" prompt, press Enter.

11. Reload your router when the copy is complete.

12. Check to see your if your new version is running by typing **sh version**.

CHAPTER

9

Configuring Novell IPX

Most network administrators have, at some point, encountered IPX for two reasons: first, Novell NetWare uses IPX as its default protocol; second, it was the most popular network operating system during the late 1980s and early 1990s. As a result, millions of IPX networks have been installed. But Novell is changing things with the release of NetWare 5.0. Now, TCP/IP is the default communications protocol instead of IPX, even though Novell still supports IPX. Why? Well, considering the multitude of installed IPX clients and servers, it would be pretty impractical to yank the support for it. No—there's little doubt—IPX will be around for a while! And considering that, it's no surprise that the Cisco IOS provides full support for large IPX internetworks. But to really take advantage of its functions and features, we first need to review the operation and addressing of Novell IPX because it varies significantly from the TCP/IP method we've covered so far. Armed with a solid grasp of things IPX, we'll explore the configuration of IPX in the Cisco IOS, and from there cover the monitoring of IPX traffic.

The CCNA test objectives covered in this chapter include:

329 ■ List the required IPX address and encapsulation type

332 ■ Enable the Novell IPX protocol and configure interfaces

348 ■ Monitor Novell IPX operation on the router

321 ■ Describe the two parts of network addressing, then identify the parts in specific protocol address examples

Introduction to Novell IPX

Novell IPX (Internetwork Packet Exchange) has been in use since its release in the early 1980s. It's quite similar to XNS (Xerox Network Systems), developed by Xerox at its Palo Alto Research Center in the 1960s; it even shares a likeness with TCP/IP. IPX is really a family of protocols that coexist and interact to empower sound network communications.

Novell IPX Protocol Stack

IPX doesn't map directly to the OSI model, but its protocols still function in layers. When designing IPX, engineers were more concerned with performance than with strict compliance to existing standards or models. Even so, comparisons can be made.

Figure 9.1 illustrates the IPX protocols, layers, and functions relative to those of the OSI model:

FIGURE 9.1

IPX protocol stack and the OSI model

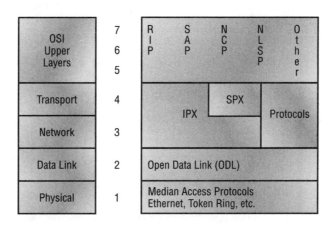

IPX

IPX performs functions at layers 3 and 4 of the OSI model. It controls the assignment of IPX addresses (software addressing) on individual nodes, governs packet delivery across internetworks, and makes routing decisions based on information provided by the routing protocols, RIP or NLSP. IPX is a connectionless protocol (similar to TCP/IP's UDP), so it doesn't require any acknowledgement that packets were received from the destination node. To communicate with the upper-layer protocols, IPX uses *sockets*. These are similar to TCP/IP ports in that they're used to address multiple, independent applications running on the same machine.

SPX

SPX (Sequence Packet eXchange) adds connection-oriented communications to the otherwise connectionless IPX. Through it, upper-layer protocols can ensure data delivery between source and destination nodes. SPX works by creating *virtual circuits* or *connections* between machines, with each connection having a specific *connection ID* included in the SPX header.

RIP

RIP (Routing Information Protocol) is a distance-vector routing protocol used to discover IPX routes through internetworks. It employs ticks (1/18 of a second) and hop count (number of routers between nodes) as metrics for determining preferred routes.

SAP

SAP (Service Advertising Protocol) is used to advertise and request services— servers use it to advertise the services they offer, and clients use it to locate network services.

NLSP

NLSP (NetWare Link Services Protocol) is an advanced link-state routing protocol developed by Novell. It's intended to replace both RIP and SAP.

NCP

NCP (NetWare Core Protocol) provides clients with access to server resources— functions such as file access, printing, synchronization, and security are all handled by NCP.

What does the presence of routing protocols, connection and connectionless transport protocols, and application protocols indicate to you? All of those factors add up to the fact that IPX is capable of supporting large internetworks running many applications. Understanding how Novell uses these protocols clears the way for you to include third-party devices (such as Cisco routers) into an IPX network.

Client-Server Communication

Novell NetWare follows a strict client-server model (there's no overlap): a NetWare node is either a client or a server, and that is that. You won't find *peer* machines that both provide and consume network resources here. Clients can be workstations running MacOS, DOS, MS Windows, WindowsNT, OS/2, Unix, or VMS. Servers generally run Novell NetWare. NetWare servers provide the following services to clients:

- file

- print

- message

- application

- database

As you would think, NetWare clients are dependent on servers to locate all network resources. Every NetWare server builds a SAP table comprised of all the network resources that it's aware of. (We'll explain how they do this a bit later in the chapter.) When clients require access to a certain resource, they issue an IPX broadcast called a GNS (GetNearestServer request) so they can locate a NetWare server that provides the particular resource the client needs. In turn, the servers receiving the GNS check their SAP tables to locate a NetWare server that matches the specific request, then respond to the client with another GNS (GetNearestServer response). The response GNS points the client to a specific server to contact for the resource it requested. If none of the servers hearing the client's GNS request have the requested service, or know of a server that does in their SAP tables, they simply don't respond, leaving the requesting client without the ability to access the requested resource.

Why do we care? Because Cisco routers build SAP tables, too, and they can respond to client GNS requests just as if they were NetWare servers. This doesn't mean they *offer* the services that NetWare servers do, just that their responses are identical when it comes to locating services. The *GetNearest-Server* response to a client can come from a local NetWare server, a remote NetWare server, or a Cisco router, and generally, if there are local NetWare servers present, they should respond to the client's request. But if there are no local NetWare servers, the local Cisco router that connects the client's segment to the IPX internetwork can respond to the client's GNS. This saves the client from having to wait for remote NetWare servers to respond. A second advantage of this arrangement is that precious WAN bandwidth isn't occupied with GNS conversations between clients on a segment with no local NetWare server and remote NetWare servers, as shown in Figure 9.2.

FIGURE 9.2

Remote IPX clients on a serverless network

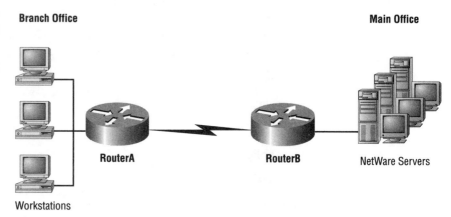

Here we see client workstations at the remote office site: they require access to server resources at the main office. In this situation, RouterA would answer client GNS requests from its SAP table rather than forwarding the request across the WAN to the main office servers. The clients never realize or care that there isn't a NetWare server present on their LAN.

This communication insulates the client from the task of locating and tracking available network resources—it places that burden on the server instead. The client simply broadcasts a GNS and waits for a response. From the client's perspective, all network resources respond as though they were local, regardless of their physical location in the internetwork.

Server-Server Communication

Communications between two NetWare servers is a bit more complicated than client-server communications. As was mentioned earlier, servers are responsible for maintaining tables of all available network resources, regardless of whether those resources are local to the server. Plus, keep in mind that each server must be able to locate *any* resource on the internetwork.

Servers exchange two types of information using two separate protocols: SAP (Service Advertising Protocol) and RIP (Routing Information Protocol).

As their names suggest, SAP communicates service information, and RIP communicates routing information.

WARNING Please don't confuse RIP in IPX with RIP in TCP/IP. They're both routing protocols, but they're not the same routing protocol.

NetWare servers use SAP to advertise the services they offer by sending out a SAP broadcast every 60 seconds. The broadcast includes all services that the server has learned about from other servers—not just the ones they furnish. All servers receiving the SAP broadcast incorporate the information into their own SAP tables; it then rebroadcast it in their own SAP updates. Because SAP information is shared among all servers, all servers eventually become aware of all available services and are thereby equipped to respond to client GNS requests. As new services are introduced, they're added to SAP tables on local servers, then rebroadcast until every server knows they exist and where to get them.

So how does a Cisco router fit in here? Well, as far as SAP is concerned, that router acts just like another NetWare server. By default, a SAP broadcast won't cross a Cisco router. A Cisco router catalogs all SAPs heard on any of its IPX-enabled interfaces in its SAP table; it then broadcasts the whole table from each of those interfaces at 60-second intervals, unless you change the settings—just as NetWare servers do. This is an important point, especially with WAN links. The router isolates SAP broadcasts to individual segments and passes along only the summarized information to each segment. Let's take a look at a SAP broadcast with our Etherpeek analyzer.

```
Flags:          0x00
   Status:        0x00
   Packet Length:306
   Timestamp:     23:48:36.362000 06/28/1998
Ethernet Header
   Destination:   ff:ff:ff:ff:ff:ff Ethernet Brdcast
   Source:        00:80:5f:ad:14:e4
   Protocol Type:81-37   NetWare
IPX - NetWare Protocol
   Checksum:            0xffff
   Length:             288
```

```
Transport Control:
   Reserved:              %0000
   Hop Count:             %0000
   Packet Type:           4  PEP
Destination Network:      0xcc715b00
   Destination Node:      ff:ff:ff:ff:ff:ff Ethernet Brdcast
   Destination Socket:    0x0452  Service Advertising Protocol
   Source Network:        0xcc715b00
   Source Node:           00:80:5f:ad:14:e4
   Source Socket:         0x0452  Service Advertising Protocol
SAP - Service Advertising Protocol
   Operation:             2  NetWare General Service Response
Service Advertising Set #1
   Service Type:          263  NetWare 386
   Service Name:          BORDER3..................................
Network Number:          0x12db8494
   Node Number:           00:00:00:00:00:01
Socket Number:           0x8104
Hops to Server:          1
Service Advertising Set #2
   Service Type:          4  File Server
   Service Name:          BORDER3.................................
Network Number:          0x12db8494
   Node Number:           00:00:00:00:00:01
Socket Number:           0x0451
Hops to Server:          1
Service Advertising Set #3
   Service Type:          632
   Service Name:          BORDER_____R.S.I@@@@@D.PJ..
Network Number:          0x12db8494
   Node Number:           00:00:00:00:00:01
Socket Number:           0x4006
Hops to Server:          1
Service Advertising Set #4
   Service Type:          993
   Service Name:          BORDER3..................................
```

```
    Network Number:    0x12db8494
    Node Number:       00:00:00:00:00:01
    Socket Number:     0x9056
    Hops to Server:    1
Frame Check Sequence:  0x00000000
```

This SAP is from a NetWare server named BORDER3. Notice that it is advertising four separate services that it offers. These services—their address and socket information—will be included in the SAP table of all IPX-enabled devices attached to this network (including our routers) and rebroadcast throughout the internetwork.

RIP information is exchanged between servers much the same way that SAP information is. Servers build routing tables that contain entries for the networks they're directly connected to, then broadcast this information on to all IPX-enabled interfaces. Other servers on those segments receive those updates and broadcast their RIP tables on their IPX interfaces. Just as SAP information travels from server to server until all servers are enlightened, RIP information is proliferated until all servers and routers know of the internetwork's routes. RIP information is also broadcast at 60-second intervals, as is SAP information. Let's take a look at an IPX RIP packet with our Etherpeek analyzer.

```
    Flags:          0x80  802.3
      Status:         0x00
      Packet Length:94
      Timestamp:      15:23:05.642000 06/28/1998
    802.3 Header
      Destination:  ff:ff:ff:ff:ff:ff Ethernet Brdcast
      Source:       00:00:0c:8d:5c:9d
      LLC Length:   76
    802.2 Logical Link Control (LLC) Header
      Dest. SAP:    0xe0  NetWare
      Source SAP:   0xe0  NetWare  Null LSAP
      Command:      0x03  Unnumbered Information
    IPX - NetWare Protocol
      Checksum:               0xffff
      Length:                 72
      Transport Control:
```

```
          Reserved:          %0000
          Hop Count:         %0000
        Packet Type:         1 RIP
    Destination Network:     0x00002300
    Destination Node:        ff:ff:ff:ff:ff:ff Ethernet Brdcast
    Destination Socket:      0x0453  Routing Information Protocol
    Source Network:          0x00002300
    Source Node:             00:00:0c:8d:5c:9d
    Source Socket:           0x0453  Routing Information Protocol
RIP - Routing Information Protocol
    Operation:               2 Response
Network Number Set # 1
    Network Number:      0x00005200
    Number of Hops:      3
    Number of Ticks:     14
Network Number Set # 2
    Network Number:      0x00004100
    Number of Hops:      2
    Number of Ticks:     8
Network Number Set # 3
    Network Number:      0x00003200
    Number of Hops:      1
    Number of Ticks:     2
Network Number Set # 4
    Network Number:      0x00002200
    Number of Hops:      1
    Number of Ticks:     2
Network Number Set # 5
    Network Number:      0x00002100
    Number of Hops:      1
    Number of Ticks:     2
Extra bytes (Padding):
    r                        72
```

See that? It looks a lot like an IP RIP packet, only it's missing the IP addresses. In their place, we have IPX addresses and network numbers instead. We have only three routers, and this packet is sent out every 60 seconds—imagine this happening on a large network with hundreds of routers!

IPX Addressing

After sweating through IP addressing, IPX addressing should seem like a day at the beach. The IPX addressing scheme has several features that make it a whole lot easier to understand and administer than the TCP/IP scheme is.

IPX addresses use 80 bits, or 10 bytes, of data. As with TCP/IP addresses, they are hierarchical and divided into a network and node portion. The first four bytes always represent the network address, and the last six bytes always represent the node address. There's none of that Class A, Class B, or Class C TCP/IP stuff in IPX addressing—the network and node portions of the address are always the same length. So after subnet masking, this is sweet indeed!

Just as it is with IP network addresses, the network portion of the address is assigned by administrators and must be unique on the entire IPX internetwork. Node addresses are automatically assigned to every node. In most cases, the MAC address of the machine is used as the node portion of the address. This offers several notable advantages over TCP/IP addressing. Since client addressing is dynamic (automatic), you don't have to run DHCP or manually configure each individual workstation with an IPX address. Also, since the hardware address (layer 2) is included as part of the software address (layer 3), there's no need for a TCP/IP ARP equivalent in IPX.

As with TCP/IP addresses, IPX addresses can be written in several formats. Most often, they're written in hex, such as 00007C80.0000.8609.33E9.

The first eight hex digits (00007C80) represent the network portion of the address; the remaining 12 hex digits (0000.8609.33E9) represent the node portion and are the MAC address of the workstation. When referring to the IPX network, it's a common IPX custom to drop leading 0s. This done, the above network address would simply be referred to as IPX network 7C80. The node portion is commonly divided into three sections of four hex digits divided by periods, as shown above.

On networks running both TCP/IP and IPX, administrators frequently associate network addresses from one protocol with the other. To do this, take a TCP/IP network address, convert it to hexadecimal, and use those eight digits as the IPX network address on that segment. This ensures that your IPX network addresses will be unique—assuming your TCP/IP is already working, of course!

Encapsulation

Encapsulation, or framing, is the process of taking packets from upper-layer protocols and building frames to transmit across the network. As you probably recall, frames live at layer 2 of the OSI model. When you're dealing with IPX, encapsulation is the specific process of taking IPX datagrams (layer 3) and building frames (layer 2) for one of the supported media. We'll cover IPX encapsulation on the following physical networks:

- Ethernet
- Token Ring
- FDDI

Why is this significant? Well, for the very good reason that NetWare supports multiple, *incompatible* framing methods, and it does so on the same media. For instance, take Ethernet. NetWare has four different *frame types* to choose from depending on your needs (see Table 9.1), and each one of those frame types is incompatible with the other ones. It's like this: Say your servers are using Ethernet_802.2 and your clients are configured for Ethernet_II. No worries? Maybe. If they're communicating with each other via a router that supports both frame types, you're set. If not—you're cooked—they just won't talk! When configuring any IPX device (including a router) on a network, the frame type has to be consistent for things to work.

T A B L E 9.1	NetWare Frame Type	Features
Novell Ethernet Encapsulations	Ethernet_802.3	Default up to NetWare 3.11
	Ethernet_802.2	Default since NetWare 3.12
	Ethernet_II	Supports both TCP/IP and IPX
	Ethernet_SNAP	AppleTalk, IPX, and TCP/IP

Sometimes—and only sometimes—you could intentionally have multiple frame types present on the same network. An example is in Figure 9.3.

FIGURE 9.3

Multiple frame types
on a single Ethernet
segment

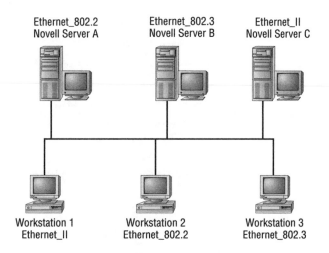

Ethernet_802.2
Novell Server A

Ethernet_802.3
Novell Server B

Ethernet_II
Novell Server C

Workstation 1
Ethernet_II

Workstation 2
Ethernet_802.2

Workstation 3
Ethernet_802.3

Notice that each frame type in Figure 9.3 has a unique IPX network address. Even though there's a single Ethernet segment, there are three *virtual* IPX networks and therefore three unique IPX network addresses. Here, Workstation 1 would be able to communicate only with Server C because they're both running Ethernet_II. Workstation 2 would be able to communicate only with Server A, and Workstation 3, only with Server B. But what if you wanted all the workstations to communicate with all the servers—what would you do? Just add a router that supports all three frame types. Doing that would allow any workstation to communicate with any of the servers, but that router would have to route all packets among all the servers and clients with dissimilar frame types.

When configuring a router, you'll need to know both the frame type and the IPX network address information for each segment that you plan to attach that router to. To find this information, go to one of the NetWare servers and type config at the server console. The response to this command is shown on the following page.

You can see that each section reports frame types and IPX network numbers. If you have a network like the one above, it's important to realize that you may need to visit a bunch of servers to get all the frame types and IPX network address information you need for a particular segment.

```
File server name: SERVERA
IPX internal network number: 35F0753D
     Node address: 000000000001
     Frame type: VIRTUAL_LAN
     LAN protocol: IPX network AAAAAAAA
Server Up Time:  4 Minutes 2 Seconds

Intel EtherExpress(TM) PRO/100 adapter
     Version 1.22    July 5, 1995
     Hardware setting: Slot 11, I/O ports E000h to E01Fh, Interrupt Ah
     Node address: 00AA0062E93D
     Frame type: ETHERNET_802.2
     Board name: E100_1_E82
     LAN protocol: IPX network 22222222

Intel EtherExpress(TM) PRO/100 adapter
     Version 1.22    July 5, 1995
     Hardware setting: Slot 11, I/O ports E000h to E01Fh, Interrupt Ah
     Node address: 00AA0062E93D
     Frame type: ETHERNET_802.3
     Board name: E100_1_E83
     LAN protocol: IPX network 11111111

Intel EtherExpress(TM) PRO/100 adapter
     Version 1.22    July 5, 1995
     Hardware setting: Slot 11, I/O ports E000h to E01Fh, Interrupt Ah
     Node address: 00AA0062E93D
     Frame type: ETHERNET_II
     Board name: E100_1_ETI
     LAN protocol: ARP
     LAN protocol: IP  address 172.16.10.15  mask FF.FF.FF.0  interfaces 1

Tree Name: ABC_CORP
Bindery Context(s):
     Corp

SERVERA:
```

Enabling IPX on Cisco Routers

Cool—with the basics behind you, it's *finally* time to configure IPX on the router! There are two main tasks to activate IPX across Cisco routers:

- enable IPX routing
- enable IPX on each individual interface

Enabling IPX Routing

Before we talk about IPX routing with Cisco, let's take another look at our internetwork. Figure 9.4 shows the three routers plus our addressing.

FIGURE 9.4

Our internetwork

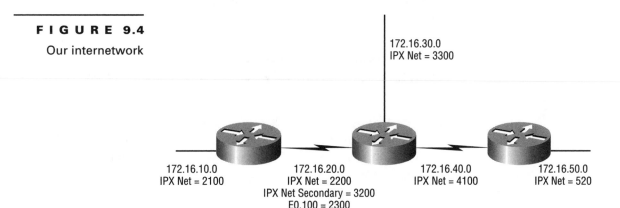

FIGURE 9.4

Our internetwork

Notice that in this figure we added the IPX network numbers for all network segments. This is how we will configure our routers.

The IPX routing command is entered in global configuration mode. As the
command implies, it enables IPX routing on the router.

```
RouterA#sh prot
Global values:
  Internet Protocol routing is enabled
Ethernet0 is up, line protocol is up
  Internet address is 172.16.10.1/24
Serial0 is up, line protocol is up
  Internet address is 172.16.20.1/24
Serial1 is administratively down, line protocol is down
RouterA#config t
Enter configuration commands, one per line.  End with CNTL/Z.
RouterA(config)#ipx routing
RouterA(config)#^Z
RouterA#
%SYS-5-CONFIG_I: Configured from console by console
RouterA#sh prot
Global values:
  Internet Protocol routing is enabled
  IPX routing is enabled
```

```
Ethernet0 is up, line protocol is up
   Internet address is 172.16.10.1/24
Serial0 is up, line protocol is up
   Internet address is 172.16.20.1/24
Serial1 is administratively down, line protocol is down
RouterA#
```

We started off by taking a look at the protocols running on the router. It showed us only the Internet Protocol. We then did a config t and enabled IPX by typing ipx routing. IPX routing now shows active, but we still need to configure our interfaces.

Enabling IPX on Individual Interfaces

Once you have IPX routing enabled on the router, the next step is to enable IPX on individual interfaces. To enable IPX on an interface, first enter the interface configuration mode, then issue the following command:

```
ipx network number [encapsulation encapsulation-type]
[secondary]
```

The various parts are defined as follows:

- *Number* is the IPX network address.

- Encapsulation *encapsulation-type* is optional. Table 9.2 shows the default encapsulation-type on different media.

- Secondary is used to indicate a secondary encapsulation (frame type) and network address on the same interface.

T A B L E   9.2:   Novell IPX Frame Types

Interface Type	Novell Frame Type	Cisco Keyword
Ethernet	Ethernet_802.3	novell-ether (default)
	Ethernet_802.2	sap
	Ethernet_II	arpa
	Ethernet_snap	snap

[handwritten: × Application Printing.]

[handwritten: sap = advertise services available in FileServer]

[handwritten: HDLC = default encapsulation of serial port.]

TABLE 9.2.   Novell IPX Frame Types   *(continued)*

Interface Type	Novell Frame Type	Cisco Keyword
Token Ring	Token-Ring	sap (default)
	Token-Ring_snap	snap
FDDI	Fddi_snap	snap (default)
	Fddi_802.2	sap
	Fddi_raw	novell-fddi

You'll need the IPX network address and frame type information from the "config" screen of your NetWare servers for this step. When specifying encapsulation type on the router, make sure to use the Cisco keyword, *not* the Novell frame type. The Cisco keywords are shown in the table above and in the help screen below:

```
RouterA(config-if)#ipx network 3100 encapsulation ?
    arpa          IPX Ethernet_II
    hdlc          HDLC on serial links
    novell-ether  IPX Ethernet_802.3
    novell-fddi   IPX FDDI RAW
    sap           IEEE 802.2 on Ethernet, FDDI, Token Ring
    snap          IEEE 802.2 SNAP on Ethernet, Token Ring,
                  and FDDI
```

Let's configure our routers to route IPX.

```
RouterA#config t
Enter configuration commands, one per line.  End with CNTL/Z.
RouterA(config)#int e0
RouterA(config-if)#ipx ?

    access-group       Apply an access list to inbound or out-
                       bound packets
    accounting         Enable IPX accounting on this interface
    advertise-default  Only advertise the IPX/RIP default route
    route-only         out onto this network
```

bandwidth-percent	Set EIGRP bandwidth limit
compression	Select IPX compression commands
delay	Set an IPX delay on the interface, in 'ticks'
down	Bring an IPX network administratively down
encapsulation	IPX encapsulation
gns-reply-disable	Disable Get Nearest Server replies on this interface
gns-response-delay	Delay in answering GNS on this interface
hello-interval	Configures IPX EIGRP hello interval
helper-address	Forward broadcasts to a specific address
helper-list	Filter helpered IPX packets on input
hold-down	Configures IPX EIGRP routes hold down time
hold-time	Configures IPX EIGRP hold time
input-network-filter	Filter incoming routing updates
input-sap-filter	Filter services learned from the Service Advertising Protocol
ipxwan	Configure IPXWAN on this interface
link-delay	Set an IPX link delay on the interface, in microseconds
netbios	Setup IPX NetBIOS filters and caching on this interface
network	Assign an IPX network & enable IPX routing
nlsp	Select NLSP commands
output-gns-filter	Filter services reported in response to Get Nearest Server
output-network-filter	Filter outgoing routing updates
output-rip-delay	Interpacket delay for RIP updates
output-sap-delay	Interpacket delay for SAP updates
output-sap-filter	Filter services reported via SAP
pad-process-switched-packets	Pad odd-length packets on output (pro-cess-switched only)
rip-max-packetsize	Maximum size of RIP packets being sent on interface

rip-multiplier	Multiple of RIP update interval for aging of RIP routes
route-cache	Enable fast switching
router-filter	Filter sources of routing updates
router-sap-filter	Select source router and service type of SAP updates
sap-incremental	Send incremental SAP updates - for IPX EIGRP networks only
sap-interval	Set SAP update period
sap-max-packetsize	Maximum size of SAP packets being sent on interface
sap-multiplier	Multiple of SAP update interval for aging of SAP routes
split-horizon	Perform split horizon
spx-idle-time	Set an SPX idle time on the interface, in seconds
spx-spoof	Spoof SPX keepalives packets
throughput	Set IPX link throughput in bit per second
triggered-rip-delay	Interpacket delay for triggered RIP updates (override output-rip-delay for triggered updates only)
triggered-sap-delay	Interpacket delay for triggered SAP updates (override output-rip-delay for triggered updates only)
type-20-propagation	Forward IPX type 20 propagation packets
update-time	Set IPX routing update timer
watchdog	Special handling for IPX server watchdog packets

```
RouterA(config-if)#ipx network ?
  <1-FFFFFFFD>  IPX network number (default route enabled)

RouterA(config-if)#ipx network 2100
RouterA(config-if)#int s0
RouterA(config-if)#ipx network 2200
RouterA(config-if)#^Z
RouterA#
```

Other than making sure your Novell servers are running the same network number as your router's interface, you're done. IPX is pretty easy.

Adding Secondary Addresses

But suppose you need to add multiple frame types to the same interface, as in the network we saw in Figure 9.3. There are two methods for adding additional frame types to an interface. The first is to use the secondary option as shown below:

```
RouterA#config t
Enter configuration commands, one per line.  End with CNTL/Z.
RouterA(config)#int s0
RouterA(config-if)#ipx network 3200 encap hdlc sec
RouterA(config-if)#exit
RouterA#sh prot s0
Serial0 is up, line protocol is up
   Internet address is 172.16.20.1/24
   IPX address is 2200.0000.0c8d.5c9d (HDLC)
   IPX address is 3200.0000.0c8d.5c9d (HDLC)
```

This configuration would permit communication among all workstations and servers, but Cisco has stated ominously that this method won't be supported in future IOS releases.

A better way is to use subinterfaces, which are detailed below. This does the same thing as the configuration above, but it's also forward compatible with future IOS releases!

Subinterfaces allow us to create virtual interfaces on a Cisco router and are the new way to run secondary IP, IPX, etc. addresses on the same interface. To define subinterfaces, use the interface ethernet slot/port.number command. The number you can use for the interface is between e0.0 and e0.4292967295—that's a lot of subinterfaces! An example is shown below:

```
RouterA(config)#int e0.100
RouterA(config-subif)#ipx network 2300 encap sap
RouterA(config-subif)#^Z
RouterA#
%SYS-5-CONFIG_I: Configured from console by console
RouterA#sh prot e0
```

```
Ethernet0 is up, line protocol is up
  Internet address is 172.16.10.1/24
  IPX address is 2100.0000.0c8d.5c9d
RouterA#sh prot e0.100
Ethernet0.100 is up, line protocol is up
  IPX address is 2300.0000.0c8d.5c9d
RouterA#wr t
Building configuration...

Current configuration:
!
version 11.2
no service password-encryption
service udp-small-servers
service tcp-small-servers
!
hostname RouterA
!
enable secret 5 $1$iEbq$4zS1yXIkb3HxJNQVlWC39/
enable password simple1
!
ipx routing 0000.0c8d.5c9d
!
interface Ethernet0
 ip address 172.16.10.1 255.255.255.0
 ipx network 2100
!
interface Ethernet0.100
 arp timeout 0
 ipx network 2300 encapsulation SAP
!
interface Serial0
 ip address 172.16.20.1 255.255.255.0
 bandwidth 56
 --More--
```

Notice that it looks like we have two Ethernet ports instead of one. You can define a limitless number of subinterfaces on a given physical interface—but keep memory limitations in mind when doing this.

Monitoring IPX on Cisco Routers

Once you have IPX configured and running, you have several ways to verify and track that your router is communicating correctly.

Show IPX Servers

This command is a lot like the display servers command in NetWare—it displays the contents of the SAP table in the Cisco router, so you should see the names of all SAP services here. Remember that if the router doesn't have entries for remote servers in its own SAP table, local clients will never see those servers. So, if you have servers missing from this table that should be here, double check your IPX network addresses and encapsulation settings.

```
RouterA#sho ipx servers
Codes: S - Static, P - Periodic, E - EIGRP, N - NLSP,
H - Holddown, + = detail
9 Total IPX Servers

Table ordering is based on routing and server info
```

Type	Name	Net	Address	Port	Route	Hops	Itf
P	4 BORDER1	350ED6D2.0000.0000.0001:0451			2/01	1	Et0
P	4 BORDER3	12DB8494.0000.0000.0001:0451			2/01	1	Et0
P	107 BORDER1	350ED6D2.0000.0000.0001:8104			2/01	1	Et0
P	107 BORDER3	12DB8494.0000.0000.0001:8104			2/01	1	Et0
P	26B BORDER	350ED6D2.0000.0000.0001:0005			2/01	1	Et0
P	278 BORDER	12DB8494.0000.0000.0001:4006			2/01	1	t0
P	278 BORDER	350ED6D2.0000.0000.0001:4006			2/01	1	Et0
P	3E1 BORDER1	350ED6D2.0000.0000.0001:9056			2/01	1	Et0
P	3E1 BORDER3	12DB8494.0000.0000.0001:9056			2/01	1	Et0

Show IPX Route

This command displays the IPX routing table entries that the router knows about. The router reports networks to which it is directly connected, then reports networks that it has learned of since the router has come online.

```
RouterA#sh ipx route
Codes: C - Connected primary network,    c - Connected
secondary network, S - Static, F - Floating static, L -
Local (internal), W - IPXWAN, R - RIP, E - EIGRP, N - NLSP,
X - External, A - Aggregate, s - seconds, u - uses

6 Total IPX routes. Up to 1 parallel paths and 16 hops
allowed.

No default route known.

C       2100 (NOVELL-ETHER),   Et0
C       2200 (HDLC),           Se0
C       2300 (SAP),            Et0.100
c       3200 (HDLC),           Se0
R       4100 [07/01] via       2200.00e0.1ea9.c418,    13s, Se0
R       5200 [13/02] via       2200.00e0.1ea9.c418,    13s, Se0
RouterA#
```

Every NetWare server runs an "internal" IPX network that you should see listed along with "external" networks on this screen. You can reference the internal IPX network address from the config screen at the server console.

If you were to set up parallel IPX paths between routers, by default, the Cisco IOS will not learn about these paths. The router will learn a single path to a destination and discard information about alternative, parallel, equal-cost paths. This shows in the output above with the phrase "up to 1 parallel paths and 16 hops allowed." You need to add the command ipx maximum-paths 2 (up to 512), which will allow the router to accept the possibility that there might be more than one path to the same destination.

The Cisco IOS will perform per-packet load-sharing by default over these parallel lines. Packets will be sent on a round-robin basis between all equal-cost lines, without regard to the destination. However, if you want to ensure that all packets sent to a destination or host will always go over the same line, use the IPX per-host-load-share command.

Show IPX Traffic

This command gives you a summary of the number and type of IPX packets received and transmitted by the router. Notice that this command will show you both the IPX RIP and SAP update packets.

```
RouterA#sh ipx traffic
System Traffic for 0.0000.0000.0001 System-Name: RouterA
Rcvd:   15 total, 0 format errors, 0 checksum errors, 0 bad
hop count, 0 packets pitched, 15 local destination, 0
multicast
Bcast:  10 received, 249 sent
Sent:   255 generated, 0 forwarded
        0 encapsulation failed, 0 no route
SAP:    1 SAP requests, 0 SAP replies, 0 servers
        0 SAP Nearest Name requests, 0 replies
        0 SAP General Name requests, 0 replies
        0 SAP advertisements received, 0 sent
        0 SAP flash updates sent, 0 SAP format errors
RIP:    1 RIP requests, 0 RIP replies, 6 routes
        8 RIP advertisements received, 230 sent
        12 RIP flash updates sent, 0 RIP format errors
Echo:   Rcvd 0 requests, 5 replies
        Sent 5 requests, 0 replies
        0 unknown: 0 no socket, 0 filtered, 0 no helper
        0 SAPs throttled, freed NDB len 0
Watchdog:
        0 packets received, 0 replies spoofed
Queue lengths:
        IPX input: 0, SAP 0, RIP 0, GNS 0
        SAP throttling length: 0/(no limit), 0 nets pending
lost route reply
 --More-
```

Show IPX Interfaces

This command gives you the interface settings.

```
RouterA#sh ipx int e0
Ethernet0 is up, line protocol is up
    IPX address is 2100.0000.0c8d.5c9d, NOVELL-ETHER [up]
    Delay of this IPX network, in ticks is 1 throughput 0 link
delay 0
    IPXWAN processing not enabled on this interface.
    IPX SAP update interval is 1 minute(s)
    IPX type 20 propagation packet forwarding is disabled
    Incoming access list is not set
    Outgoing access list is not set
    IPX helper access list is not set
    SAP GNS processing enabled, delay 0 ms, output filter list
is not set
    SAP Input filter list is not set
    SAP Output filter list is not set
    SAP Router filter list is not set
    Input filter list is not set
    Output filter list is not set
    Router filter list is not set
    Netbios Input host access list is not set
    Netbios Input bytes access list is not set
    Netbios Output host access list is not set
    Netbios Output bytes access list is not set
    Updates each 60 seconds, aging multiples RIP: 3 SAP: 3
    SAP interpacket delay is 55 ms, maximum size is 480 bytes
    RIP interpacket delay is 55 ms, maximum size is 432 bytes
--More-
```

Debug IPX

The debug IPX command shows you IPX as it's running through your internetwork. It's noteworthy that you can see the IPX IRP and SAP updates with this command, but be careful—it can consume your precious CPU if you don't use it wisely.

```
RouterA#debug ipx ?
  compression     IPX compression
  eigrp           IPX EIGRP packets
  ipxwan          Novell IPXWAN events
  nlsp            IPX NLSP activity
  packet          IPX activity
  redistribution  IPX route redistribution
  routing         IPX RIP routing information
  sap             IPX Service Advertisement information
  spoof           IPX and SPX Spoofing activity
RouterA#debug ipx routing ?
  activity  IPX RIP routing activity
  events    IPX RIP routing events
RouterA#debug ipx routing act
IPX routing debugging is on
RouterA#
IPXRIP: update from 2200.00e0.1ea9.c418
    5200 in 2 hops, delay 13
    4100 in 1 hops, delay 7
IPXRIP: positing full update to 2100.ffff.ffff.ffff via
Ethernet0 (broadcast)
IPXRIP: src=2100.0000.0c8d.5c9d, dst=2100.ffff.ffff.ffff,
packet sent
    network 5200, hops 3,  delay 14
    network 4100, hops 2,  delay 8
    network 2300, hops 1,  delay 2
    network 3200, hops 1,  delay 2
    network 2200, hops 1,  delay 2
IPXRIP: positing full update to 3200.ffff.ffff.ffff via
Serial0 (broadcast)
IPXRIP: src=3200.0000.0c8d.5c9d, dst=3200.ffff.ffff.ffff,
packet sent
    network 5200, hops 3,  delay 19
    network 4100, hops 2,  delay 13
    network 2300, hops 1,  delay 7
    network 2200, hops 1,  delay 7
    network 2100, hops 1,  delay
```

```
RouterA#undebug ipx routing act
IPX routing debugging is off
RouterA#
```

Extended Ping

Examine the readout on the following page. With extended ping, you can also ping IPX nodes and interfaces.

```
RouterC#sh prot e0
Ethernet0 is up, line protocol is up
   Internet address is 172.16.50.1/24
   IPX address is 5200.0000.0c3f.1d86
RouterA#ping
Protocol [ip]: ipx
Target IPX address: 5200.0000.0c3f.1d86
Repeat count [5]:
Datagram size [100]:
Timeout in seconds [2]:
Verbose [n]:
Novell Standard Echo [n]: y
Type escape sequence to abort.
Sending 5, 100-byte IPX Novell Echoes to
5200.0000.0c3f.1d86, timeout is 2 seconds:!!!!!
Success rate is 100 percent (5/5), round-trip min/avg/max =
4/7/12 ms
```

We first did a sh prot on router C to get its IPX address. After that, we pinged that address from RouterA with complete success.

Summary

In this chapter, we covered the following points:

- The required IPX address and encapsulation types. We covered in detail the frame types that Cisco routers can use when running IPX.

- How to enable the Novell IPX protocol and configure router interfaces. We talked about and gave examples of how to configure IPX on Cisco routers and its interfaces.

- How to monitor the Novell IPX operation on the router. We covered some basic tools for monitoring IPX on your routers.

- The two parts of network addressing, then we identified the parts in specific protocol address examples. We talked about an IPX host address and identified the different parts of this address.

Review Questions

1. Which of the following provides connection-oriented transport to upper-layer protocols?

   A. RIP

   B. NLSP

   C. SPX   *p-322*

   D. NCP

2. Which of the following can respond to a client GNS request (choose all that apply)?

   A. local NetWare server   *p 323*

   B. remote NetWare server

   C. local client

   D. Cisco router

3. How often do servers exchange SAP information unless set otherwise?

   A. every 15 seconds

   B. every 30 seconds

   C. every 60 seconds   *p 325*

   D. every 120 seconds

4. How can you configure a secondary subinterface on your Ethernet interface?

   A. Config t, int e0.24000 *p 352*

   B. Config t, int e100.0 *p 338*

   C. config t, 24000 e0

   D. config t, 24000 e100

5. Given the IPX address 00007C81.00A0.2494.E939, which of the following is the associated IPX network and node address?

   A. Net 00a0. node 2494 E939

   B. Net 00007C81 node 00a0.2494.e939 *p 329*

   C. Net 00A0.2494. node E939

   D. Net 7C81 00a0 Node 2494.e939

6. What was the default Ethernet encapsulation on NetWare 3.11?

   A. Ethernet_II

   B. Ethernet_802.3 *p 330*

   C. Ethernet_802.2

   D. Ethernet_snap

7. Which of the following are valid methods of including multiple encapsulations on a single interface?

   A. secondary networks

   B. subinterfaces *p 338*

   C. additional physical interfaces

   D. There is no method to use multiple encapsulations on a single interface.

8. Which command would you use to see if you were receiving SAP and RIP information on an interface?

    A. sho ipx route

    B. sho ipx traffic

    C. sho ipx interface *p 343*

    D. sho ipx servers

9. Which command would you use to see if the router is hearing your server SAPs?

    A. sho ipx route

    B. sho ipx traffic

    C. sho ipx interface

    D. sho ipx servers *p 340*

10. Which commands will allow you to display the IPX address of an interface (choose all that apply)?

    A. sh ipx route

    B. sh int

    C. sh prot *p 333*

    D. debug ipx int

11. You want to forward IPX packets over multiple paths. What command do you use?

    A. ipx forward maximum-paths

    B. ipx maximum-paths

    C. ipx forward

    D. ipx forward-paths

12. Which of the following are valid Cisco encapsulation names (choose all that apply)? *p 334, p 335*

    A. arpa = IPX Ethernet

    B. hdlc = HDLC on serial links

    C. novell-ether = IPX Ethernet_802.3

    D. novell-fddi = IPX Fddi_Raw

    E. sap = IEEE 802.2 on Ethernet, FDDI and Token Ring

    F. snap = IEEE 802.2 SNAP on Ethernet, FDDI, and Token Ring

13. Which commands must be used to enable IPX networking?

    A. IPX routing, IPX number, network 790

    B. IPX routing, int e0, IPX network number 980   *p 334, 335*

    C. IPX routing, int e0, IPX network 77790, encapsulation arpa

    D. IPX routing, IPX encapsulation SAP, int e0, network 789

14. What is the default encapsulation and frame type on an Ethernet interface when enabling Novell?

    A. SAP

    B. 802.2

    C. SNAP

    D. Token_SNAP

    E. 802.3   *p 330*

    F. Ethernet_II

15. If you are running Token Ring with Novell IPX routing, which encapsulation should you use?

    A. 802.5

    B. SAP

    C. 802.2

    D. SNAP   *p 335*

16. If you want to run the 802.2 frame type on your Ethernet interface, which encapsulation type should you choose?

    A. SNAP

    B. 802.2

    C. Ethernet_II

    D. SAP *p334*

    E. Novell-Ether

17. If you want to enable Ethernet_II frame type on your Ethernet interface, which encapsulation should you use?

    A. ARPA *p334*

    B. RARPA

    C. SAP

    D. RIP

    E. SNAP

    F. Novell-Ether

18. Which of the following is the correct syntax for configuring a subinterface?

    A. config t, int e0, ipx network 100, encap sap

    B. config t, int e0, sub 100, ipx 100

    C. config t, int e0.100, ipx network 100 encap arpa sec

    D. config t, int e0.100, ipx network 100 encap arpa *p338*

19. Which command will show the network servers advertising on your network?

    A. sh novell

    B. sh ipx sap

    C. sh ipx servers *p340*

    D. sh servers

20. Which command displays the status of the IPX interfaces configured in the router and the parameters configured on each interface?

A. sh ipx int   *p343*

B. sh int

C. sh ipx stat

D. sh ip config

Laboratory Exercises

EXERCISE 9.1

Enable IPX Routing

In this lab you'll log into the router, enter **enable mode,** and configure IPX routing.

1. Press Return to get started and enter your password.

2. Type **enable** at the router prompt and enter your password.

3. Enter global configuration mode by typing **configure terminal**.

4. Type **ipx routing**, then hit Return.

5. Type **CTRL+Z** to exit configuration mode.

6. Type **show config** and verify that IPX routing is enabled. What was used as your node address? Where did this come from?

7. Type **exit** to log out of the router.

EXERCISE 9.2

Enabling IPX on the Router's Interfaces

In this lab, you'll add IPX network numbers to your router's interfaces.

1. Log in to your router and enter **privilege mode**.

2. Type **config t**, then specify your router interface.

3. Type **ipx network** (network number).

EXERCISE 9.2 (CONTINUED)

4. Type **CTRL+Z**.

5. Type **sh prot**. Is IPX enabled on your interface?

6. Type **exit**.

EXERCISE 9.3

Enabling Subinterfaces on Your Router's Interfaces

In this lab, you'll add a subinterface to your router's Ethernet interface.

1. Log in to your router and enter **privilege mode**.

2. Type **config t**.

3. Type **int e0.200** (or any number you want).

4. Type **ipx network 4000** (or your network number).

5. Type **CTRL+Z**.

6. Type **sh prot e0.200**. Is your interface enabled?

7. Exit out of your router.

CHAPTER

10

Managing Traffic with Access Lists

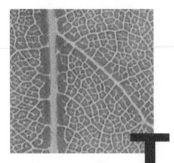

The proper use and configuration of access lists is a vital part of router configuration because access lists are such a vital networking accessory. Contributing mightily to the efficiency and optimization of your network, access lists give network managers a huge amount of control over traffic flow throughout the internetwork. With them, managers can gather basic statistics on packet flow, and security policies can be implemented. Sensitive devices can also be protected from unauthorized access.

We're going to discuss access lists for both TCP/IP and IPX as well as cover some of the tools available to test and monitor the functionality of applied access lists.

The CCNA Test Objectives covered in this chapter include:

- Configure standard and extended access lists to filter IP traffic
- Configure IPX access lists and SAP filters to control basic Novell traffic
- Monitor and verify selected access list operations on the router

Access Lists

Access lists are essentially lists of conditions that control access. They're powerful tools that control access both to and from network segments. They can filter unwanted packets and be used to implement security policies. With the right combination of access lists, a network manager is armed with the power to enforce nearly any access policy he or she can invent.

The IP and IPX access lists work similarly—they're both packet filters that packets are compared with, categorized by, and acted upon. Once the lists are built, they can be applied to either inbound or outbound traffic on any interface. Applying an access list will then cause the router to analyze every packet crossing that interface in the specified direction and take action accordingly.

There are a few important rules a packet follows when it's being compared with an access list:

- It's always compared with each line of the access list in sequential order—it'll always start with line 1, then line 2, then line 3, and so on.

- It's compared with lines of the access list only until a match is made. Once the packet matches a line of the access list, it's acted upon, and no further comparisons take place.

- There is an implicit "deny" at the end of each access list—it means that if a packet doesn't match up to any lines in the access list, it'll be discarded.

Each of these rules has some powerful implications when filtering IP and IPX packets with access lists.

Standard IP Access Lists

There are two steps to configuring standard IP access lists:

1. Configure the access list.

2. Apply the access list to an interface.

The two steps mentioned above are the same two steps used to configure extended IP access lists, standard and extended IPX access lists, and IPX SAP filters. We'll talk about the IPX lists later in this chapter.

Configuring the Access List

Standard IP access lists have the ability to analyze the source IP addresses of TCP/IP packets, then take action based upon that analysis. Each line of a standard IP access list uses the following format:

access-list {number} {permit or deny} {source address}

To define access lists, use the access-list command in configuration mode. Each access list is assigned a unique number to distinguish it from the other lists. IP standard access lists are given numbers between 1 and 99, but other access list types require different number ranges:

```
RouterA#config t
Enter configuration commands, one per line.   End with CNTL/Z.
RouterA(config)#access-list ?
   <1-99>       IP standard access list
   <100-199>    IP extended access list
   <1000-1099>  IPX SAP access list
   <1100-1199>  Extended 48-bit MAC address access list
   <1200-1299>  IPX summary address access list
   <200-299>    Protocol type-code access list
   <300-399>    DECnet access list
   <600-699>    Appletalk access list
   <700-799>    48-bit MAC address access list
   <800-899>    IPX standard access list
   <900-999>    IPX extended access list
```

The *permit* or *deny* keyword indicates whether to allow or discard matching packets, and the *source address* is used to define which source IP addresses should be acted upon. We'll soon discuss the syntax of these options.

Let's suppose that we have the network diagrammed as shown in Figure 10.1.

F I G U R E   10.1

Our internetwork

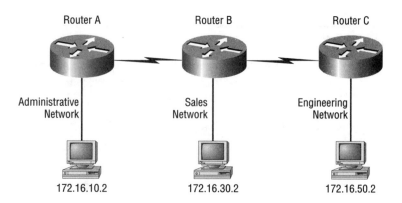

What we have here are three machines, each on its own network, so if we wanted to allow external access to the Admin server only from the Sales workstation, we could write an access list that looks like:

```
RouterA#config t
Enter configuration commands, one per line. End with CNTL/Z.
RouterA(config)#access-list 10 permit 172.16.30.2
RouterA(config)#^Z
RouterA#
```

We randomly selected 10 for a value within the appropriate range of 1 through 99. The first and only line of access list 10 permits packets with a source address of 172.16.30.2—the Sales workstation. Here's how the line in our one-line access list above maps against our template:

access-list	{number}	{permit/deny}	{source}
access-list	10	permit	172.16.30.2

Applying the Access List to an Interface

Looks great, but we're not there yet. Even though we've configured the access list, it won't filter anything until we apply it to an interface. Here's how we'll do that:

```
RouterA#config t
Enter configuration commands, one per line.  End with CNTL/Z.
RouterA(config)#int e0
RouterA(config-if)#ip access-group 10 out
RouterA(config-if)#^Z
RouterA#
```

First, we'll enter configuration mode and then select the ethernet0 interface. Then, we'll use the `ip access-group` command to specify 10 `out`.

Use the *access-list* keyword to enter the access list, but use the *access-group* keyword to apply that access list to an interface.

The 10 refers to access list 10 that we created above. The out tells the router to compare outbound packets—not inbound packets—with the list. This can get a bit confusing. It helps to remember that the command is being applied to the router, not the network, so the out and in designations refer to the router's perspective, not that of the nodes on the network. To the router, out means packets leaving its interface(s) and going out to the network; in means packets arriving at the router's interface(s) from the network. In our example, we're seeking to control the outbound packets leaving from the router, so we'll use the out command.

Here's our effective access list applied to all packets outbound to the Ethernet interface, network 172.16.10.0:

```
permit 172.16.30.2
deny    any
```

Notice the implicit deny any we've added to the end of the list. Your router won't show that, but it's important to remember that it'll act as though it's there. IP packets arriving from the Sales workstation will be forwarded to the Admin network, but packets arriving from any other device won't match line 1, so they'll be dropped because of implicit line 2. The access list won't affect any nodes already on the Admin network—they'll be able to communicate normally—but the list will affect any nodes that have to send packets across RouterA to reach the Admin network. The only node not in the Admin network still able to communicate with the Admin network is the workstation at 172.16.30.2.

When applying access lists to individual interfaces, remember that only one access list per protocol is allowed inbound and that only one access list per protocol is allowed outbound.

Wildcard Masking

We're going to complicate things a bit. What if we wanted to allow the entire Sales network access—not just that one workstation? And what if we also wanted to allow the one workstation in the Engineering network access but deny access to the rest of the Engineering nodes? Here's how we'd do it:

```
RouterA#config t
Enter configuration commands, one per line.  End with CNTL/Z.
```

```
RouterA(config)#access-list 11 permit 172.16.50.2 0.0.0.0
RouterA(config)#access-list 11 permit 172.16.30.0 0.0.0.255
RouterA(config)#int e0
RouterA(config-if)#ip access-group 11 out
```

```
RouterA(config-if)#^Z
RouterA#
```

Once again, let's map each of the above lines against our template:

access-list	{number}	{permit/deny}	{source}
access-list	11	permit	172.16.50.2 0.0.0.0
access-list	11	permit	172.16.30.0 0.0.0.255

This is just like the example above, with one exception. We've used a wildcard mask to specify the source address: the 0.0.0.255 following the 172.16.30.0 above. It consists of a 32-bit binary string of 0s followed by 1s, broken into octets, and written in decimal. 1s are considered "throwaway bits," meaning that their corresponding positions in the address are irrelevant. By specifying the source address and mask as

Address:	172.	16.	30.	0
MASK:	0.	0.	0.	255

we're saying that the 172, 16, and 30 are required to match up, but the last octet of the IP address can be any value (remember that 255 is 1111 1111 in decimal). Likewise, when we specify it as follows

Address:	172.	16.	50.	2
MASK:	0.	0.	0.	0

we're requiring 172, 16, 50, and 2 to all match up exactly, because we've set all mask values to 0. We didn't really need to specify the 0.0.0.0 mask in the second line, but it was much easier to use the 0.0.0.255 mask in the first line than it would have been to enter every workstation on the 172.16.30.0 network. (Doing that would have required 255 entries!)

Now that we've explained the masking, let's look at the results of the above access list. Again, our effective access list is

```
permit 172.16.50.2, wildcard bits 0.0.0.0
```

```
permit 172.16.30.0, wildcard bits 0.0.0.255
deny any
```

Now any machine from the Sales network (172.16.30.*) can access the Admin network, and so can that one workstation (172.16.50.2) in the Engineering network. All other machines will be denied access by the implicit deny any at the end of the list.

When modifying access lists, it's a common practice to enter a new list, apply it to the interface, then remove the old list. Why? Because doing that prevents you from accidentally messing up a running access list. Here we've moved from 10 to 11. On the next modification we would move from 11 back to 10, and so on.

Extended IP Access Lists

With standard IP access lists covered, it's time to take a look into extended IP access lists. Their function is pretty much the same—the difference centers on what can be filtered. In standard IP access lists, our decisions to permit or deny packets are limited to comparisons with the packets' source address information. But with extended IP access lists, we can act on any of the following:

- Source address
- Destination address
- IP protocol (TCP, udp, icmp, etc.)
- Port information (www, dns, ftp, etc.)

So with extended access lists, our abilities are extended. We can make much more detailed lists than we can with the standard type. The syntax for each line on extended access lists is similar to that of standard access lists. The first three fields—access-list, number, and permit or deny—are exactly the same. But we can additionally specify a protocol before the source and create destination and port fields after the source address. Here's a template for each line of an extended IP access list:

access-list {number} {permit or deny} {protocol} {source} {destination} {port}

Let's continue with the example we already have going and change things again. Let's say that now we want only the workstation in Engineering to be able to access a proxy server in the Admin network with the IP address 172.16.10.2 and port address 8080. We also want any machine in the sales network to access this same proxy server. Plus, we want anyone to be able to access all the Web servers located in the Admin network. Got any ideas? Here's how we'd do that:

```
RouterA#config t
Enter configuration commands, one per line.  End with CNTL/Z.
RouterA(config)#access-list 110 permit tcp host 172.16.50.2
host 172.16.10.2 eq 8080
RouterA(config)#access-list 110 permit tcp 172.16.30.0
0.0.0.255 host 172.16.10.2  eq 8080
RouterA(config)#access-list 110 permit tcp any any eq www
RouterA(config)#int e0
RouterA(config-if)#ip access-group 110 out
RouterA(config-if)#^Z
RouterA#
```

(handwritten annotations: coming in; source/access)

As we said, the first three fields here are the same as what we did with the standard IP access lists, but we've changed our access list number to 110 instead—part of the 100–199 range reserved for extended IP access lists. Okay, let's focus on the last four fields. Here's how the three lines map to our new template for extended IP access lists:

protocol	source	destination	port
tcp	host 172.16.50.2	host 172.16.10.2	eq 8080
tcp	172.16.30.0 0.0.0.255	host 172.16.10.2	eq 8080
tcp	any	any	eq www

Our new field is protocol, and it's specified as TCP. In this case, we chose to allow TCP connections to our proxy on port 8080. We could have specified any of the other protocols as shown here:

```
RouterA#config t
Enter configuration commands, one per line.  End with CNTL/Z.
RouterA(config)#access-list 110 permit ?
  <0-255>  An IP protocol number
```

ahp	Authentication Header Protocol
eigrp	Cisco's EIGRP routing protocol
esp	Encapsulation Security Payload
gre	Cisco's GRE tunneling
icmp	Internet Control Message Protocol
igmp	Internet Gateway Message Protocol
igrp	Cisco's IGRP routing protocol
ip	Any Internet Protocol
ipinip	IP in IP tunneling
nos	KA9Q NOS compatible IP over IP tunneling
ospf	OSPF routing protocol
pcp	Payload Compression Protocol
tcp	Transmission Control Protocol
udp	User Datagram Protocol

We've used three different methods of specifying source and destination addresses, and we've seen wildcard masking before, but there are two new methods presented here. In reality, we're just using some keywords to save ourselves the effort of typing in the masks.

- *host 172.16.10.2* is the same as saying 172.16.10.2 0.0.0.0 with wild-card masking. Setting all the bits in the wildcard mask to 0s basically says there are no wildcards, so we can be referring to only a single machine or host. This means we can use the *host* keyword instead of the mask of 0.0.0.0.

- *any* is equivalent to saying 0.0.0.0 255.255.255.255 with wildcard masking. When we set all bits in a wildcard mask to 1s, we get 255.255.255.255, so we're saying that none of the bits really matter. We use this here because we don't care about source or destination addresses; we're filtering based on some other parameter. In our example, we're filtering based upon port.

Finally, we can specify the port to be acted upon. How well do you remember your TCP ports? (Again, we have many options at this point.) Here we go:

```
RouterA#config t
Enter configuration commands, one per line.  End with CNTL/Z.
```

```
RouterA(config)#access-list 110 permit tcp host 172.16.50.2
host 172.16.10.2 ?
  eq           Match only packets on a given port number
  established  Match established connections
  gt           Match only packets with a greater port number
  log          Log matches against this entry
  log-input    Log matches against this entry, including
               input interface
  lt           Match only packets with a lower port number
  neq          Match only packets not on a given port number
  precedence   Match packets with given precedence value
  range        Match only packets in the range of port
               numbers
  tos          Match packets with given TOS value
  <cr>
```

At this point, we could have just ended the command without specifying any port information, and if we did that, all ports would have been allowed. We chose to use the eq operator, but there are other numeric comparisons available that we could have selected instead to specify more than one port. Once we selected eq, we again had many options available:

```
RouterA#config t
RouterA(config)#access-list 110 permit tcp host 172.16.50.2
host 172.16.10.2 eq ?
  <0-65535>   Port number
  bgp         Border Gateway Protocol (179)
  chargen     Character generator (19)
  cmd         Remote commands (rcmd, 514)
  daytime     Daytime (13)
  discard     Discard (9)
  domain      Domain Name Service (53)
  echo        Echo (7)
  exec        Exec (rsh, 512)
  finger      Finger (79)
  ftp         File Transfer Protocol (21)
  ftp-data    FTP data connections (used infrequently, 20)
  gopher      Gopher (70)
```

hostname	NIC hostname server (101)
ident	Ident Protocol (113)
irc	Internet Relay Chat (194)
klogin	Kerberos login (543)
kshell	Kerberos shell (544)
login	Login (rlogin, 513)
lpd	Printer service (515)
nntp	Network News Transport Protocol (119)
pim-auto-rp	PIM Auto-RP (496)
pop2	Post Office Protocol v2 (109)
pop3	Post Office Protocol v3 (110)
smtp	Simple Mail Transport Protocol (25)
sunrpc	Sun Remote Procedure Call (111)
syslog	Syslog (514)
tacacs	TAC Access Control System (49)
talk	Talk (517)
telnet	Telnet (23)
time	Time (37)
uucp	Unix-to-Unix Copy Program (540)
whois	Nicname (43)
www	World Wide Web (HTTP, 80)

E-MAIL { pop2, pop3 }

You can either specify the number of the port or use one of the keywords listed above. Notice that in the description, the port that's actually filtered is listed. If you can't remember that SMTP uses port 25, just enter smtp. This can make reading long access lists a whole lot easier.

After all this, what exactly is it that those three little lines do? They do the following:

- The first line permits one workstation at address 172.16.50.2 to establish TCP connections to port 8080 with the machine at 172.16.10.2.

- The second line allows the entire Sales network (172.16.30.*) to access this same proxy server, using TCP connections to port 8080.

- The third line allows any source machine to establish TCP connections to port 80 with any machine in the Admin network. Functionally, it says just ignore source and destination addresses. What does this line evaluate, then? The eq www is the key here—we don't care where packets are coming from or where they're going, but if they're not destined for port 80 (that's default for WWW), they don't match this line.

Remember, the implicit deny at the end of the access list will prohibit any connections that aren't allowed in one of the three previous lines. It does not appear in the list, but it is so important!

Monitoring Extended IP Access Lists

Now that we have our extended access list operating, let's take a look at monitoring the operation of it. We'll start with the show access-list command:

```
RouterA#show access-1
Extended IP access list 110
    permit tcp host 172.16.50.2 host 172.16.10.2 eq 8080 (34 matches)
    permit tcp 172.16.30.0 0.0.0.255 host 172.16.10.2 eq 8080 (11 matches)
    permit tcp any any eq www (33 matches)
```

This command will list all of the access lists running on the router. On RouterA, we currently have access list 110 running. Notice that the command will list each line of the access list and that it also reports the number of packets that matched each line. This information is priceless when troubleshooting access lists. If you configure an access list then use this command, you should be able to see the counters incremented as packets hit the access list.

Immediately after typing in the above command, I went to the machine set up at 172.16.50.2 and hit Reload on my browser. Notice the counters in the next screen:

```
RouterA#sho access-1
Extended IP access list 110
    permit tcp host 172.16.50.2 host 172.16.10.2 eq 8080 (47 matches)
    permit tcp 172.16.30.0 0.0.0.255 host 172.16.10.2 eq 8080 (11 matches)
    permit tcp any any eq www (33 matches)
```

The counters for both lines 2 and 3 stayed the same, but notice that the one for line 1 went from 34 to 47. Why? Well, there were obviously multiple objects in that one Web page! So, not only do we know that my access list is working, we know which lines are used the most.

As access lists are executed top to bottom, administrators will frequently move the most commonly matched lines up in the access list. This gives most packets a match in the first few lines of the access list rather than forcing them to go through most of the list before finding a match. If you do this, be careful that you don't inadvertently change the functionality of your access list!

We are going to make one more change to our extended access list and add a line to enable logging:

```
RouterA#config t
Enter configuration commands, one per line.  End with CNTL/Z.
RouterA(config)#access-list 110 permit tcp host 172.16.50.2 host
➥ 172.16.10.2 eq 8080
RouterA(config)#access-list 110 permit tcp 172.16.30.0 0.0.0.255
➥ host 172.16.10.2 eq 8080
RouterA(config)#access-list 110 permit tcp any any eq www
RouterA(config)#access-list 110 deny ip any any log
RouterA(config)#^Z
RouterA#
```

We added a last line that denies all IP traffic not previously filtered. This was done implicitly before, but we get a couple of things by including the line that we didn't have before. First of all, now when we use the show access-list command, we get to see the number of matches on the denied line:

```
RouterA#sho access-l
Extended IP access list 110
  permit tcp host 172.16.50.2 host 172.16.10.2 eq 8080 (15 matches)
  permit tcp 172.16.30.0 0.0.0.255 host 172.16.10.2 eq 8080 (4 matches)
  permit tcp any any eq www (8 matches)
  deny ip any any log (4 matches)
RouterA#
```

Here we see that there were actually four matches against the deny line. The *log* keyword tells the router to make an entry into the log anytime that line of the access list is matched. By default, the router will log to the console:

```
    RouterA#
```

```
%SEC-6-IPACCESSLOGP: list 110 denied tcp 172.16.30.2(2024) -
> 172.16.10.2(21), 1 packet
```

The following information is included in the log:

- Access list number

- Source address

- Source port

- Destination address

- Destination port

- Number of packets

All of this log information could be redirected to the syslog server and stored for security purposes.

Displaying Access List Information

There are two additional commands used in monitoring IP access lists that we should mention here: show ip access-list and clear access-list counter.

- Show ip access-list: this command shows only the IP access lists.

- Clear access-list counter: this command clears the counters for the show access-list commands.

The following shows the additional IP access-list commands in use:

```
RouterA#show ip access-list
Extended IP access list 110
    permit tcp host 172.16.50.2 host 172.16.10.2 eq 8080 (15
matches)
    permit tcp 172.16.30.0 0.0.0.255 host 172.16.10.2 eq
8080 (4 matches)
    permit tcp any any eq www (8 matches)
    deny ip any any log (4 matches)
RouterA#clear access-list counters 110
RouterA#sho access-l
Extended IP access list 110
    permit tcp host 172.16.50.2 host 172.16.10.2 eq 8080
    permit tcp 172.16.30.0 0.0.0.255 host 172.16.10.2 eq 8080
```

```
              permit tcp any any eq www
              deny ip any any log
RouterA#
```

When monitoring access lists, it's often important to find which interfaces have which access lists applied to them. There are two commands that we can use to display this information: show ip interface and show running config.

Here's how the output of these two commands looks on our RouterA:

```
RouterA#sho ip interface e0
Ethernet0 is up, line protocol is up
    Internet address is 172.16.10.1/24
    Broadcast address is 255.255.255.255
    Address determined by non-volatile memory
    MTU is 1500 bytes
    Helper address is not set
    Directed broadcast forwarding is enabled
    Multicast reserved groups joined: 224.0.0.9
    Outgoing access list is 110
    Inbound  access list is not set
    Proxy ARP is enabled
    Security level is default
    Split horizon is enabled
    ICMP redirects are always sent
    ICMP unreachables are always sent
    ICMP mask replies are never sent
    IP fast switching is enabled
    IP fast switching on the same interface is disabled
    IP multicast fast switching is enabled
    Router Discovery is disabled
    IP output packet accounting is disabled
    IP access violation accounting is disabled
    TCP/IP header compression is disabled
    Probe proxy name replies are disabled
    Gateway Discovery is disabled
    Policy routing is disabled
    Network address translation is disabled
```

```
RouterA#
```

The outbound and incoming access lists are shown:

```
RouterA#show running-config
Building configuration...

Current configuration:
!
version 11.3
no service password-encryption
!
hostname RouterA
!
enable secret 5 $1$YMNO$Pz1r4tEg1E91wcKrNUIOHO
enable password password
!
!
interface Ethernet0
 ip address 172.16.10.1 255.255.255.0
 ip access-group 110 out
 no mop enabled
!
interface Serial0
 ip address 172.16.20.1 255.255.255.0
 no ip mroute-cache
!
interface Serial1
 no ip address
 shutdown
!
router rip
 redistribute connected
 network 172.16.0.0
!
ip classless
```

```
access-list 110 permit tcp host 172.16.50.2 host 172.16.10.2
eq 8080
access-list 110 permit tcp 172.16.30.0 0.0.0.255 host
172.16.10.2 eq 8080
access-list 110 permit tcp any any eq www
access-list 110 deny    ip any any log
!
line con 0
line aux 0
line vty 0 4
 password password2
 login
!
end
RouterA#
```

Standard IPX Access Lists

After getting through IP access lists, IPXs should be a breeze. Most of what we have already learned about IP access lists still applies here, but there are some important changes.

IPX access lists are covered in much more depth in the Advanced Cisco Router Configuration courseware.

Standard IPX access lists allow or deny packets based on source and destination IPX addresses. With standard IP access lists, we looked only at source addresses. Our template for each line of an IPX standard access list is as follows:

access-list {number} {permit/deny} {source} {destination}

Let's say we have IPX configured in our network as outlined in Figure 10.2.
Let's set up an IPX access list allowing IPX network 30 to access IPX network 10, but disallowing IPX network 50 from accessing the same network. Here's what we'll do:

RouterA#**config t**

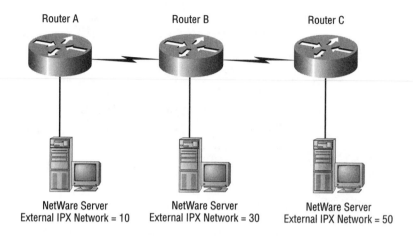

FIGURE 10.2

Our IPX internetwork

Router A   Router B   Router C

NetWare Server   NetWare Server   NetWare Server
External IPX Network = 10   External IPX Network = 30   External IPX Network = 50

```
Enter configuration commands, one per line.  End with CNTL/Z.
RouterA(config)#access-list 810 permit 30 10
RouterA(config)#access-list 810 deny 50 10
RouterA(config)#int e0
RouterA(config-if)#ipx access-group 810 out
RouterA(config-if)#^Z
RouterA#
```

And again, let's map these two lines against our template to see what's happening:

access-list	number	permit/deny	source	destination
access-list	810	permit	30	10
access-list	810	deny	50	10

The number 810 corresponds to the range 800–899 that's reserved for IPX standard access lists. Permit/deny is the same as it is with IP packets. Here we have specified source and destination based on IPX network addresses from our diagram. No wildcard masking is required to specify an entire IPX network, just list the network address and you are done!

Just as there is with IP access lists, there's an implicit deny at the end of the access list. In this case, any networks other than 30 will be denied access to network 10. If we wanted to allow all IPX networks except 50, we'd proceed as follows:

```
RouterA#config t
Enter configuration commands, one per line.  End with CNTL/Z.
RouterA(config)#access-list 811 deny 50 10
RouterA(config)#access-list 811 permit -1 -1
RouterA(config)#int e0
RouterA(config-if)#ipx access-group 811 out
 RouterA(config-if)#^Z
RouterA#
```

Once again, let's put these two lines into our template to see what we have:

access-list	number	permit/deny	source	destination
access-list	811	deny	50	10
access-list	811	permit	-1	-1

Important here is the use of the –1 network address, because in IPX access lists, the –1 network address refers to any IPX network address. It's just like using the *any* keyword when referring to network addresses in IP access lists to specify any IP network.

If this syntax gets confusing (and it certainly can), just remember that online help is always available to help you remember the next parameter. Here is an example of how one line from the above example could be entered using the online help:

```
RouterA(config)#access-list ?
  <1-99>       IP standard access list
  <100-199>    IP extended access list
  <1000-1099>  IPX SAP access list
  <1100-1199>  Extended 48-bit MAC address access list
  <1200-1299>  IPX summary address access list
  <200-299>    Protocol type-code access list
  <300-399>    DECnet access list
  <600-699>    Appletalk access list
  <700-799>    48-bit MAC address access list
```

```
                <800-899>     IPX standard access list
                <900-999>     IPX extended access list

RouterA(config)#access-list 810 ?
  deny     Specify packets to reject
  permit   Specify packets to permit

RouterA(config)#access-list 810 permit ?
  -1             Any IPX net
  <0-FFFFFFFF>   Source net
  N.H.H.H        Source net.host address
  <cr>

RouterA(config)#access-list 810 permit 30 ?
  -1             Any IPX net
  <0-FFFFFFFF>   Destination net
  N.H.H.H        Destination net.host address
  <cr>

RouterA(config)#access-list 810 permit 30 10 ?
  <cr>

RouterA(config)#access-list 810 permit 30 10
```

Extended IPX Access Lists

Extended IPX access lists can filter based on any of the following:

- Source network/node
- Destination network/node
- IPX protocol (SAP, SPX, etc.)
- IPX socket

These are access lists in the range 900–999 and are configured just like standard access lists, with the addition of protocol and socket information. Let's take a look at a template for building lines in an IPX extended access list.

access-list {number} {permit/deny} {protocol} {source} {socket}

{destination} {socket}

Here again, when we move from standard into extended access lists, we're simply adding the ability to filter based on protocol and socket (port for IP).

Let's take access list 811 from our above example and implement it as an extended access list so we can log attempts to access network 10 from network 50:

```
RouterA#config t
Enter configuration commands, one per line.  End with CNTL/Z.
RouterA(config)#access-list 910 deny -1 50 0 10 0
RouterA(config)#access-list 910 permit -1 -1 0 -1 0
RouterA(config)#int e0

RouterA(config-if)#ipx access-group 910 out
RouterA(config-if)#^Z
RouterA#
```

The log command could be used to log any attempts from network 50 to access network 10 and record the following information:

- Source address

- Source socket

- Destination address

- Destination socket

- Protocol type

Once again, use the online help if you need it to wade through the syntax. Here is a look at the online help while entering one of the above lines:

```
RouterA(config)#access-list ?
    <1-99>       IP standard access list
    <100-199>    IP extended access list
    <1000-1099>  IPX SAP access list
    <1100-1199>  Extended 48-bit MAC address access list
    <1200-1299>  IPX summary address access list
    <200-299>    Protocol type-code access list
    <300-399>    DECnet access list
    <600-699>    Appletalk access list
```

```
            <700-799>    48-bit MAC address access list
            <800-899>    IPX standard access list
            <900-999>    IPX extended access list

RouterA(config)#access-list 910 ?
  deny    Specify packets to reject
  permit  Specify packets to permit

RouterA(config)#access-list 910 permit ?
  -1       Any IPX protocol type
  <0-255>  Protocol type number (DECIMAL)
  <cr>

RouterA(config)#access-list 910 permit -1 ?
  -1             Any IPX net
  <0-FFFFFFFF>   Source net
  N.H.H.H        Source net.host address
  <cr>

RouterA(config)#access-list 910 permit -1 -1 ?
  <0-FFFFFFFF>  Source Socket (0 for all sockets)
HEXIDECIMAL
  <cr>

RouterA(config)#access-list 910 permit -1 -1

RouterA(config)#
```

IPX SAP Filters

IPX SAP filters are implemented using the same tools we've been discussing all along in this chapter. They have an important place in controlling IPX SAP traffic, as discussed in Chapter 9. Why is this important? Because if you can control the SAPs, you can control the access to IPX devices. We'll use access lists in the 1000–1099 range to specify IPX SAP filters. Here's the template for each line of an IPX SAP filter:

  access-list {number} {permit/deny} {source} {service type}

On our Admin network, we have three NetWare servers but we want only the one with internal IPX network address 11.0000.0000.0001 to be seen by the outside world. To accomplish that, we'd configure and apply an access list as follows:

```
RouterA#config t
Enter configuration commands, one per line.  End with CNTL/Z.
RouterA(config)#access-list 1010 permit 11.0000.0000.0001 0
RouterA(config)#int e0
RouterA(config-if)#ipx input-sap-filter 1010
RouterA(config-if)#^Z
RouterA#
```

And here's how the one line in the above access list maps to the template:

access-list	number	permit/deny	source	service type
access-list	1010	permit	11.0000.0000.0001	0

Our number, 1010, falls into the range 1000–1099 reserved for IPX SAP filters. The source network is the network/node address of the server. The resulting access list allows packets from 11.0000.0000.0001 to enter the Ethernet interface and be included in SAP updates across the network. As with other access lists, there's an implicit deny that blocks all other SAP updates arriving at the router on the Ethernet interface. Finally, we entered a 0 for service type indicating that all services should be allowed:

```
RouterA#config t
Enter configuration commands, one per line.  End with CNTL/Z.
RouterA(config)#access-list 1010 permit 11.0000.0000.0001 ?
  <0-FFFF>  Service type-code (0 matches all services)
  N.H.H.H   Source net.host mask
  <cr>

RouterA(config)#
```

As before, here is the above line entered using the online help:

```
RouterA(config)#access-list ?
  <1-99>     IP standard access list
  <100-199>  IP extended access list
```

```
<1000-1099>  IPX SAP access list
<1100-1199>  Extended 48-bit MAC address access list
<1200-1299>  IPX summary address access list
<200-299>    Protocol type-code access list
<300-399>    DECnet access list
<600-699>    Appletalk access list
<700-799>    48-bit MAC address access list
<800-899>    IPX standard access list
<900-999>    IPX extended access list

RouterA(config)#access-list 1010 ?
deny    Specify packets to reject
permit  Specify packets to forward

RouterA(config)#access-list 1010 permit ?
-1            Any IPX net
<0-FFFFFFFF>  Source net
N.H.H.H       Source net.host address

RouterA(config)#access-list 1010 permit 11.0000.0000.0001 ?
<0-FFFFFFFF>  Service type-code (0 matches all services)
N.H.H.H       Source net.host mask
<cr>

RouterA(config)#access-list 1010 permit 11.0000.0000.0001 0 ?
WORD   A SAP server name
<cr>

RouterA(config)#access-list 1010 permit 11.0000.0000.0001 0

RouterA(config)#
```

Summary

In this chapter, we covered the following points:

- How to configure standard access lists to filter IP traffic. We learned what a standard access list is and how to apply it to a Cisco router to add security to our network.

- How to configure extended access lists to filter IP traffic. We learned the difference between a standard and extended access list and how to apply these lists to Cisco routers.

- How to configure IPX access lists and SAP filters to control basic Novell traffic. We learned the difference between a standard and extended IPX access list and how to apply the lists to a Cisco router.

- How to monitor and verify selected access list operations on the router. We went over some basic monitoring commands to verify and test out IP and IPX access lists.

Review Questions

1. IP standard access lists use which of the following as a basis for permitting or denying packets?

   A. Source address   *p 356*

   B. Destination address

   C. Protocol

   D. Port

2. IP extended access lists use which of the following as a basis for permitting or denying packets?

   A. Source address

   B. Destination address

   C. Protocol

D. Port

E. All of the above

3. To specify all hosts in the class B IP network 172.16.0.0, which wildcard access list mask would you use?

A. 255.255.0.0

B. 255.255.255.0

C. 0.0.255.255

D. 0.255.255.255

E. 0.0.0.255

4. Which of the following are valid ways to refer only to host 172.16.30.55 in an IP access list?

A. 172.16.30.55 0.0.0.255

B. 172.16.30.55 0.0.0.0

C. any 172.16.30.55

D. host 172.16.30.55

E. 0.0.0.0 172.16.30.55

F. ip any 172.16.30.55

5. Which of the following access lists will allow only WWW traffic into network 196.15.7.0?

A. access-list 100 permit tcp any 196.15.7.0 0.0.0.255 eq www

B. access-list 10 deny tcp any 196.15.7.0 eq www

C. access-list 100 permit 196.15.7.0 0.0.0.255 eq www

D. access-list 10 permit tcp any 196.15.7.0 0.0.0.255

E. access-list 10 permit www 196.15.7.0 0.0.0.255

6. Which of the following will show which ports have IP access lists applied?

 A. show ip port

 B. show access-list

 C. show ip interface

 D. show access-list interface

 E. show running config

7. Which of the following are logged when IP access list logging is enabled?

 A. Source address

 B. Source port

 C. Destination address

 D. Destination port

 E. Time

 F. Protocol

 G. Access list line number

 H. Access list number

8. Which of the following is a valid IPX standard access list?

 A. access-list 800 permit 30 50

 B. access-list 900 permit 30 50

 C. access-list permit all 30 50

 D. access-list 800 permit 30 50 eq SAP

 E. access-list 900 permit -1 50

9. Which of the following can be logged by IPX extended access lists?

 A. Source address

 B. Source socket

C. Destination address

D. Destination socket

E. Access list line number

F. Time

G. Interface

H. Access list number

I. Protocol

10. Which of the following will apply IPX SAP access list 1050 for incoming traffic, assuming you're already at interface configuration?

    A. `ipx access-group 1050 in`

    B. `ipx input-sap-filter 1050`

    C. `ipx access-list 1050 in`

    D. `ipx input-sap-filter 1050 in`

    E. `ipx access-group 1050`

11. Which of the following commands will show an extended access list 187?

    A. `sh ip int`

    B. `sh ip access-list`

    C. `sh access-list 187`

    D. `sh access-list 187 extended`

12. What is the IP extended access list range?

    A. 1–99

    B. 200–299

    C. 1000–1999

    D. 100–199

13. Which of the following commands is valid for creating an extended IP access list?

   A. access-list 101 permit ip host 172.16.30.0 any eq 21 log

   B. access-list 101 permit tcp host 172.16.30.0 any eq 21 log

   C. access-list 101 permit icmp 172.16.30.0 any ftp log

   D. access-list 101 permit ip any eq 172.16.30.0 21 log

14. What is the extended IPX access list range?

   A. 100–199

   B. 900–999

   C. 1000–1999

   D. 700–799

15. What does the -1 mean in an extended IPX access list?

   A. Deny this host

   B. Deny any network or host

   C. Local network only, no hops

   D. Any host or any network

16. What are three ways to monitor IP access lists?

   A. sh int

   B. sh ip interface

   C. sh run

   D. sh access-lists

17. Which of the following can be used to monitor IPX access lists (choose all that apply)?

   A. sh int

   B. sh access-lists

   C. sh flash

D. sh ver

~~**E.** sh ipx int~~

~~**F.** sh run~~

18. Which access configuration allows only traffic from network 172.16.0.0 to enter int s0?

A. Access-list 10 permit 172.16.0.0 0.0255.255, int s0, ip access-list 10 in

B. Access-group 10 permit 172.16.0.0 0.0.255.255, int s0, ip access-list 10 out

C. Access-list 10 permit 172.16.0.0 0.0.255.255, int s0, ip access-group 10 in

D. Access-list 10 permit 172.16.0.0 0.0.255.255, int s0, ip access-group 10 out

19. If you want to capture IPX access lists being hit, what command parameter do you add to your extended IPX access list?

A. Logging

B. Log

C. Enable log

D. Capture list

20. In an IP access list, you want to refer to host 172.16.50.1. What mask would you use to make the list as specific as possible?

A. 255.255.0.0

B. 0.0.0.0

C. 0.0.255.255

D. 0.255.255.255

Laboratory Exercises

EXERCISE 10.1

IP Standard Access Lists

In this lab, you'll configure and apply an IP standard access list to your router.

1. Configure your router's Ethernet interface with an IP address.

2. Configure a standard IP access list to prevent all machines on network 172.16.0.0 from accessing your Ethernet network.

3. Apply the access list to your Ethernet interface.

4. Now, add a second line to your access list that denies host 196.22.15.5 access to your Ethernet network.

5. Type the show access-list command to verify that you've entered the access list correctly.

6. Type the show running-config command to verify that the access list was properly applied to the Ethernet interface.

EXERCISE 10.2

IP Extended Access Lists

In this lab, you'll further configure your router from Exercise 10.1 to log inappropriate requests, plus allow access to your mail and WWW server.

1. Remove the access list that you configured in Exercise 10.1 from your router by removing it from all interfaces and then removing the access list itself.

2. Verify step 1 by using the show running-config command.

3. Re-create the access list that you created in Exercise 10.1, but this time create it as an extended access list rather than as a standard list.

4. Add two lines to your new list to allow access to any e-mail and WWW services running on your Ethernet network.

EXERCISE 10.2 (CONTINUED)

5. Add a final line that denies all access and logs to the console.

6. From some machine that's not on your Ethernet network, ping a host that is attached to an Ethernet interface to generate a log message.

EXERCISE 10.3

IPX SAP Access Lists

In this exercise, you'll configure an IPX SAP access list and apply it to your Ethernet interface.

1. Configure your Ethernet interface for IPX and assign it an IPX network number.

2. Configure an IPX SAP access list that prevents any SAP messages other than those from IPX address 45.0000.0000.0001 from leaving the Ethernet network.

3. Apply the IPX SAP access list to the Ethernet interface, using the appropriate keyword *input-sap-filter*.

4. Verify that the access list is applied by using the show running-config and show ipx interface commands.

5. Verify that the access list is entered correctly using the show access-list command.

CHAPTER

11

Wide Area Networking

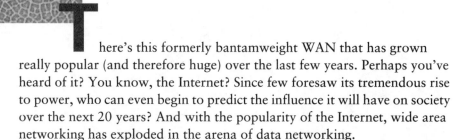

here's this formerly bantamweight WAN that has grown really popular (and therefore huge) over the last few years. Perhaps you've heard of it? You know, the Internet? Since few foresaw its tremendous rise to power, who can even begin to predict the influence it will have on society over the next 20 years? And with the popularity of the Internet, wide area networking has exploded in the arena of data networking.

This chapter's focus will be on the technologies used in wide area networking, and in it, we'll explore some of the most popular WAN technologies such as Frame Relay and ISDN.

The CCNA Test Objectives covered in this chapter include:

390
- Differentiate among the following WAN services: Frame Relay, ISDN/LAPD, HDLC, and PPP

401
- Recognize key Frame Relay and features

403
- List commands to configure Frame Relay LMIs, maps, and subinterfaces

407
- List commands to monitor Frame Relay operation in the router

409
- Identify PPP operations to encapsulate WAN data on Cisco routers

412
- State a relevant use and context for ISDN networking

412
- Identify ISDN protocols, function groups, reference points, and channels

413
- Describe Cisco's implementation of ISDN BRI

We could easily expand this chapter to fill an entire book—indeed, many volumes have been devoted to the topic. Wide area networking is a very broad term that includes literally hundreds of methods of data transfer. WAN protocols are similar to their LAN cousins (Ethernet, Token Ring, etc.) in that they primarily convey upper-layer protocol information across actual networks. In terms of the OSI model, we're mostly focusing on layers 1 and 2 here. And just as there are with LANs, many potential methods are available to get from point A to B. WAN protocols can be, well, a bit diverse. Let's begin by taking a look at the most popular WAN.

Plain Old Telephone Service (POTS)

POTS stands for Plain Old Telephone Service—the voice network we use every time we pick up the telephone and place a call. POTS just also happens to be the largest network in the world. Worldwide, there are still more telephone users than Internet users, making POTS the most commonly used WAN service today. It's no surprise, considering the incredible installed-base of the large telephone companies. It is important to understand how POTS is used in internetworking and the Internet. Cisco routers can use this network to traverse the world to deliver data to remote sites and branches.

There are a few terms you will use frequently in wide area networking with Cisco routers. The following terms deserve a thorough explanation.

Demarc: The boundary between the customer's in-house wiring and the service provider's wiring. It's the demarcation point, or the end of responsibility, for the service provider.

CPE: Customer premise equipment refers to all wiring and equipment on the customer's side of the demarc.

Local loop: The wiring running from the demarc to the CO.

CO (Central Office): The point where the local loop gains access to the service provider's high-speed trunk lines. This is often referred to as a POP (point of presence).

Synchronous Data-Link Control (SDLC)

IBM originally developed SDLC (Synchronous Data-Link Control) for use by its SNA protocol. SDLC was the predecessor to HDLC and is a bit-synchronous Data Link layer protocol. Cisco routers can be configured to use the SDLC protocol on their serial interfaces for connecting remote buildings or offices with the SNA protocol suite.

SDLC was developed by IBM during the mid-1970s for use in Systems Network Architecture (SNA) environments. Subsequent to the implementation of SDLC by IBM, SDLC formed the basis for numerous similar protocols, including HDLC and LAPB.

Bit-synchronous protocols owe their success to their expanded efficiency, flexibility, and (in some cases) greater speed, with SDLC in the lead as the chief SNA link layer protocol for WAN links. Versatile SDLC supports many link types and topologies such as the following:

- Point-to-point and multipoint links

- Bounded and unbounded media

- Half-duplex and full-duplex transmission facilities

- Circuit and packet-switched networks

And SDLC supports two network node types:

- **Primary stations** control the operation of other stations, poll secondaries in a predetermined order, and set up, tear down, and manage links.

- **Secondary stations** are controlled by a primary station. If a secondary is polled, it can transmit outgoing data. An SDLC secondary can send information only to the primary, and even then, it can send the information only after the primary grants permission.

High-Level Data-Link Control (HDLC)

The High-Level Data-Link Control protocol (HDLC) is a popular ISO-standard, bit-oriented, link layer protocol that specifies an encapsulation method for data on synchronous serial data links. The International Organization for Standardization (ISO) modified SDLC to come up with HDLC. Thereafter, the International Telecommunication Union Telecommunication Standardization Sector (ITU-T) tweaked HDLC a bit to create Link Access Procedure (LAP) and then Link Access Procedure Balanced

(LAPB). After that, the Institute of Electrical and Electronic Engineers (IEEE) went to work on HDLC and the result was the IEEE 802.2 specification.

HDLC is the default encapsulation used by Cisco routers over synchronous serial links. Cisco's HDLC is proprietary—it won't communicate with any other vendor's HDLC implementation—but don't give Cisco grief for it; everyone's HDLC implementation is proprietary. When we brought up our routers in Chapter 5, we were using HDLC encapsulation on all of our serial links. Here's a peek at a serial interface on our router configured with the default encapsulation, HDLC:

```
RouterA#show int s0
Serial0 is up, line protocol is up
 Hardware is HD64570
 Internet address is 172.16.20.1/24
 MTU 1500 bytes, BW 1544 Kbit, DLY 20000 usec, rely 255/255,
load 1/255
 Encapsulation HDLC, loopback not set, keepalive set (10
sec)
 Last input 00:00:05, output 00:00:01, output hang never
 Last clearing of "show interface" counters never
 Input queue: 0/75/0 (size/max/drops); Total output drops: 0
 Queueing strategy: weighted fair
 Output queue: 0/1000/64/0 (size/max total/threshold/drops)
    Conversations 0/2/256 (active/max active/max total)
    Reserved Conversations 0/0 (allocated/max allocated)
 5 minute input rate 0 bits/sec, 2 packets/sec
 5 minute output rate 0 bits/sec, 1 packets/sec
    1363 packets input, 59515 bytes, 0 no buffer
    Received 1242 broadcasts, 0 runts, 0 giants, 0 throttles
    0 input errors, 0 CRC, 0 frame, 0 overrun, 0 ignored, 0
abort
    1403 packets output, 59222 bytes, 0 underruns
    0 output errors, 0 collisions, 24 interface resets
    0 output buffer failures, 0 output buffers swapped out
    25 carrier transitions
    DCD=up DSR=up DTR=up RTS=up CTS=up
RouterA#
```

Notice that, just as expected, the fifth line reports our encapsulation as HDLC.

Transfer Modes Supported by HDLC

HDLC uses transfer modes to define media access on the WAN. HDLC supports the following transfer modes:

Normal response mode (NRM): This transfer mode is implemented with SDLC. Under NRM, secondaries can't communicate with a primary until the primary asks it to.

Asynchronous response mode (ARM): This mode allows secondaries to communicate with a primary without its permission.

Asynchronous balanced mode (ABM): This mode introduced the combined node—one that can act as either a primary or secondary station. All ABM communications take place between a number of combined nodes, and combined stations can originate transmissions without permission.

Link Access Procedure Balanced (LAPB): This mode is integrated into the X.25 protocol stack. LAPB shares the same frame format, frame types, and field functions as both SDLC and HDLC. It's confined to the ABM transfer mode with which you can establish circuits with either data terminal equipment (DTE) or data circuit-terminating equipment (DCE). Devices that initiate communication are deemed primaries and those that respond are called secondaries.

Dial-on-Demand Routing (DDR)

DDR (dial-on-demand routing) allows wide area links to be used selectively. With it, the administrator has the ability to define interesting traffic on the router and initiate WAN links based upon that traffic. Interesting traffic is defined by access lists (see Chapter 10), so there's a great deal of flexibility afforded to the administrator. For instance, an expensive ISDN connection to the Internet could be initiated to retrieve e-mail but not for a WWW request. DDR is an effective tool when WAN access is charged by an ISP or telephone company in some time interval, and it's best to use it when WAN access is infrequent.

Dial-on-demand routing (DDR) provides the missing software ingredient for creating a fully functional backup system. Versatile DDR can be used over several different types of connections and is supported in Cisco IOS version 9 and later. It supports the following networking protocols: IP, IPX, AppleTalk, DECnet, OSI/CLNS, and others. And DDR's flexibility reaches even further—it can be used over several different types of interfaces (synchronous and asynchronous serial interfaces as well as ISDN).

If you opt to use DDR as a backup connection, there are a few details to keep in mind. Since DDR interfaces are usually inactive, no dynamic routing information can be learned from those interfaces. This means that you will need static routes (and zones if using AppleTalk) configured so the router will know which of the available routes is on the other side of the backup link. And here's another issue: remember that static routes have an administrative distance of 0, and will override any dynamically learned route. Why does this matter? Well, if the router was configured with a plain static route, then the DDR would become that router's primary link instead of a backup link. Yikes! We definitely do not want that to happen. But there is a way to avoid this disturbing event: you must weight the static routes. You can do that with the following command:

```
ip route 10.1.2.3 255.255.255.0 10.5.6.7 <1-255>
```

Here, the <1-255> is the distance metric specified to weight the static route. BGP routes usually have an administrative distance of 20, internal EIGRP routes have a distance of 90 by default, and external EIGP routes have a default distance of 170. With a specified distance greater than 200, the static route won't be used to initiate a DDR connection unless all other routes are absent or they're unreachable via the interface from which they were discovered.

It's not a good idea to use OSPF, BGP, or IS-IS in a DDR environment. These protocols require an acknowledgement from their neighbor in order for routing updates to be sent, and due to the nature of DDR links, it's very possible that the interface won't be active when a response needs to be sent. This really isn't a big deal when using DDR as a backup connection because with it, static routes are used to establish routes to desired destinations instead of routing protocols anyway.

With the proper static routes set so that the backup line is activated only when the dynamic routes become unreachable, DDR follows four steps to establish communication with the other site. At this point, it's important to remember that the routers on both sides of the backup line have DDR set up on the interfaces. Before a DDR link can be established, the following four criteria have to be met:

1. The router verifies that there's a route to the intended destination.

2. Via the static route, the router finds the DDR interface that is connected to the desired destination.

3. The router checks to see if the DDR interface is already active and connected to the destination.

4. Finally, the router determines if the packet is either interesting or uninteresting. This decision is based upon the access lists applied to the DDR interface. Interesting packets pass through the access list, but the uninteresting ones won't be allowed passage.

If the packet is an interesting one and there is not already a connection, the router will establish a connection and the packets will be sent through that interface. If the packet is uninteresting and doesn't pass the access list, no connection will be made and the packet will be dropped.

X.25

The X.25 protocol was born in a different world than today's digital networks. Originally designed in the 1970s when circuits were both analog and noisy, X.25 is way overbuilt for today's needs.

X.25 uses addressing defined by X.121, in which addresses are between one and 14 decimal digits long. The first four bits are used for the DNIC (Data Network Identifier Code), and the remaining bits can be assigned by the administrator.

X.25 defines point-to-point communications between DTEs and DCEs. DTE stands for *data terminal equipment* and is usually a router of some sort. DCE stands for *data circuit-terminating equipment* and is usually a modem or CSU/DSU. The DCE connects to the X.25 service provider's network with the goal of establishing a virtual circuit between two DTE devices. X.25 supports both switched and permanent virtual circuits.

Regardless of the type of system connected to the network, versatile X.25 works well. It's heavily used in the packet-switched networks (PSNs) of telephone companies that charge their customers based on how much they use the network. So it makes sense that the development of the X.25 standard was created by common carriers. In the 1970s, there was a need for WAN protocols that could provide connectivity across public data networks (PDNs), and X.25 is now administered as an international standard by the ITU-T.

There are three categories that X.25 network devices can typically be placed in:

Data Terminal Equipment (DTE): End systems that communicate over an X.25 network (such as host systems, terminals, and PCs that belong to the individual subscriber) and are present at the same site.

Data Circuit-Terminating Equipment (DCE): Specific communications equipment such as packet switches that interface between a packet switching exchange (PSE) and DTE devices. They're typically found in carrier facilities.

Packet Switching Exchange (PSE): Switches that constitute the majority of a carrier's network and handle the transfer of data between DTE devices via the X.25 packet-switched network.

X.25 Sessions

X.25 sessions, which are used for DTE to DTE communication, are established using the following process:

1. One DTE device contacts another to request a communication session.

2. The receiving DTE device either accepts or refuses the connection.

3. If the request is accepted, the two systems begin full-duplex information transfer.

4. Either DTE device can terminate the connection.

After the session has been terminated, any further communication requires establishing a new session.

Virtual Circuits over an X.25 Network

Virtual circuits are logical, not physical, connections that are formed so that reliable communication between network devices can take place. A virtual circuit represents a logical, bi-directional path from one DTE device to another over an X.25 network. The connection can physically pass through *x* amount of transitional nodes such as PSEs and DCE devices. Additionally, a whole bunch of virtual circuits can be multiplexed onto one physical circuit, then demultiplexed at the remote end where the data is then sent to the proper destinations.

There are two types of virtual circuits that X.25 uses: SVC and PVC.

SVC

SVC stands for switched virtual circuit. An SVC is a temporary connection that is used for intermittent data transfers and requires two DTE devices to establish, maintain, and then terminate a session every time they need to talk.

PVC

PVCs (permanent virtual circuits) are established and used for recurrent, steady data transfer. Since they don't need sessions to be established and terminated, a DTE can transmit data whenever necessary. The session is already set up and active, and it remains that way.

X.25 Protocol Suite

The X.25 protocol suite maps to the lowest three layers (Physical through Network layers) of the OSI reference model. The following protocols are typically used in X.25 implementations:

- Packet Layer Protocol (PLP)

- Link Access Procedure Balanced (LAPB)

- X.21bis and other physical layer serial interfaces (such as EIA/TIA-232, EIA/TIA-449, EIA-530, G.703, and so forth)

Packet Layer Protocol (PLP)

The Packet Layer Protocol (PLP) is X.25's network layer protocol. It manages packet exchanges between DTE devices across virtual circuits, but PLP can also run over Logical Link Control 2 (LLC2) implementations on LANs and over Integrated Services Digital Network (ISDN) interfaces running Link Access Procedure on the D channel (LAPD).

Here are PLP's five modes of operation:

Call Setup Mode: Used to institute SVCs between DTE devices. To initially set up a virtual circuit, PLP uses X.121's addressing scheme. Different virtual circuits can be in different modes at the same time because call setup mode is deployed as individual virtual circuits require it. This mode is for use only with SVCs, not with PVCs.

Data Transfer Mode: Used for data transfer between two DTE devices via a virtual circuit. Tasks like segmentation, reassembly, bit padding, and error and flow control occur in this mode. Just like call setup mode, data transfer mode is also deployed on a per-virtual-circuit basis, but unlike call setup, it's used with both SVCs and PVCs.

Idle Mode: Used when a virtual circuit is established, but there isn't any transfer of data occurring. It's deployed on a per-virtual-circuit basis and only with SVCs.

Call Clearing Mode: Used to terminate communication sessions between DTE devices as well as SVCs. It's also deployed on a per-virtual-circuit basis and only with SVCs.

Restarting Mode: Used to synchronize the transmission between a DCE device (that is locally connected) and a DTE device. Tasks like communication and packet framing between DTE and DCE devices happen here. Since it affects all the DTE device's established virtual circuits, it isn't deployed on a per-virtual-circuit basis.

Link Access Procedure Balanced (LAPB)

LAPB's job is to make sure that frames are error free and properly sequenced. It's a bit-oriented protocol, and we've listed the three different LAPB's frame types:

Information Frames (I-Frames): These transport upper-layer information and a bit (no pun intended) of control information. I-frames both send and receive sequence numbers and relate to jobs such as sequencing, flow control, error detection, and recovery.

Supervisory Frames (S-Frames): Bearing control information, S-frames schlep receive sequence numbers and handle both requests for and the suspension of transmission. In addition, they report on the status and acknowledge when I-frames have been received.

Unnumbered Frames (U-Frames): Also bearing control information, they handle things like link setup and disconnection as well as error reporting. U-frames don't schlep any sequence numbers around at all.

X.21bis

Used in X.25 at the physical layer, the X.21bis protocol specifies the electrical and mechanical processes for the use of the physical media. It oversees both activation and deactivation of whatever physical media connect the DTE and DCE devices. At a speed of up to 19.2Kbps, X21bis supports point-to-point connections and synchronous, full-duplex transmission over four-wire media.

X.25 on Cisco Routers

Cisco routers support X.25 encapsulation via the encap x25 command that you can apply while in interface configuration mode. There are many configuration parameters with X.25, as shown below:

```
RouterA#config t
Enter configuration commands, one per line. End with CNTL/Z.
RouterA(config)#int s0
RouterA(config-if)#encap x25
RouterA(config-if)#x25 ?
  accept-reverse   Accept all reverse charged calls
  address          Set interface X.121 address
  alias            Define an alias address pattern
  default          Set protocol for calls with unknown Call
                   User Data
  facility         Set explicit facilities for originated calls
  hic              Set highest incoming channel
  hoc              Set highest outgoing channel
  hold-queue       Set limit on packets queued per circuit
  hold-vc-timer    Set time to prevent calls to a failed
                   destination
```

htc	Set highest two-way channel
idle	Set inactivity time before clearing SVC
ip-precedence	Open one virtual circuit for each IP TOS
ips	Set default maximum input packet size
lic	Set lowest incoming channel
linkrestart	Restart when LAPB resets
loc	Set lowest outgoing channel
ltc	Set lowest two-way channel
map	Map protocol addresses to X.121 address
modulo	Set operating standard
nvc	Set maximum VCs simultaneously open to one host per protocol
ops	Set default maximum output packet size
pad-access	Accept only PAD connections from statically mapped X25 hosts
pvc	Configure a Permanent Virtual Circuit
suppress-called-address	Omit destination address in outgoing calls
suppress-calling-address	Omit source address in outgoing calls
t20	Set DTE Restart Request retransmission timer
t21	Set DTE Call Request retransmission timer
t22	Set DTE Reset Request retransmission timer
t23	Set DTE Clear Request retransmission timer
threshold	Set packet count acknowledgement threshold
use-source-address	Use local source address for forwarded calls
win	Set default input window (maximum unacknowledged packets)
wout	Set default output window (maximum unacknowledged packets)

X.121 addresses aren't burned into ROM like LAN addresses, so you need to tell your Cisco router about the local X.121 address on an X.25 serial interface. The way you do this is with the x25 address command as shown below:

```
RouterA(config)#int s0
RouterA(config-if)#x25 address ?
 X.121 Addr X.121 address
RouterA(config-if)#x25 address 12345678
```

The default packet size of 128 bytes doesn't work with every vendor's implementation of X.25. But no worries—you can configure your Cisco routers with the correct input packet size (IPS) and output packet size (OPS) using the commands x25 ips and x25 ops as shown below:

```
RouterA(config-if)#x25 ips ?
 <16-4096> Bytes (power of two)
RouterA(config-if)#x25 ips 256
RouterA(config-if)#x25 ops 256
```

Also, you just might need to adjust your window size for packets that are used by flow control mechanisms. The default window size is 2, but you can change this with the commands X.25 win (window input size) and the X.25 wout (window output size) as follows:

```
RouterA(config-if)#x25 win ?
 <1-127> Packets
RouterA(config-if)#x25 win 7
RouterA(config-if)#x25 wout 7
```

The Show Interfaces output displays the X.25 encapsulation in the fourth line. The three lines after that will give you the following LAPB stats:

```
RouterA#sh int s0
Serial0 is administratively down, line protocol is down
 Hardware is HD64570
 MTU 1500 bytes, BW 1544 Kbit, DLY 20000 usec, rely 255/255,
load 1/255
 Encapsulation X25, loopback not set
 LAPB DTE, modulo 8, k 7, N1 12056, N2 20
   T1 3000, interface outage (partial T3) 0, T4 0
   State DISCONNECT, VS 0, VR 0, Remote VR 0,
Retransmissions 0
   Queues: U/S frames 0, I frames 0, unack. 0, reTx 0
   IFRAMEs 0/0 RNRs 0/0 REJs 0/0 SABM/Es 0/0 FRMRs 0/0 DISCs
0/0
```

```
    X25 DTE, address 12345678, state R1, modulo 8, timer 0
       Defaults: cisco encapsulation, idle 0, nvc 1
        input/output window sizes 7/7, packet sizes 256/256
       Timers: T20 180, T21 200, T22 180, T23 180, TH 0
       Channels: Incoming-only none, Two-way 1-1024, Outgoing-
  only none
       RESTARTs 0/0 CALLs 0+0/0+0/0+0 DIAGs 0/0
  Last input never, output never, output hang never
  Last clearing of "show interface" counters never
  Queueing strategy: fifo
  Output queue 0/40, 0 drops; input queue 0/75, 0 drops
  5 minute input rate 0 bits/sec, 0 packets/sec
  5 minute output rate 0 bits/sec, 0 packets/sec
     0 packets input, 0 bytes, 0 no buffer
     Received 0 broadcasts, 0 runts, 0 giants, 0 throttles
  --More--
```

Frame Relay

Frame relay has become one of the most popular WAN protocols available over the past few years. For a number of reasons, frame relay has been attractive as an inexpensive way to connect a large number of sites.

One of the reasons frame relay has become attractive is the concept of shared bandwidth. For example, if you need to connect a remote site in Salt Lake City with one in Denver, you could use a dedicated leased line. If you leased a T1, the telephone company would need to deliver a pipe of 1.5Mbps between Salt Lake City and Denver. That bandwidth would remain available to you, even when you were not sending any traffic across! Now consider hundreds or even thousands of these leased lines running from Salt Lake City to Denver, all of them only using a portion of their total bandwidth. (There must be some way to turn all that unused bandwidth into money....)

Enter frame relay. Instead of giving everyone their own dedicated bandwidth between Salt Lake City and Denver, all customers share access to the total bandwidth available through the frame relay cloud. Remember that data traffic is bursty by nature. With hundreds of customers sharing the total pipe, utilization is much more efficient and, thus, less expensive than leased lines for both telephone companies and customers. Your sites in Salt Lake City and Denver could both be installed with T1 access to the frame relay cloud and could communicate at up to T1 speeds, as long as the frame relay cloud was not saturated.

You may recall that the reason that we saved all that money over a leased line is that we were sharing the bandwidth with hundreds of other customers. If many customers transmitted simultaneously, although statistically unlikely, there could be a situation in which no bandwidth was available. There is, fortunately, a safety net. It is called a CIR (committed information rate). In the previous scenario where you installed 1.5Mbps frame-relay access between Salt Lake City and Denver, you have the ability to burst to T1 speeds. You could specify a CIR of say, 56Kbps, which would guarantee the ability to pass at least 56Kbps between your two sites. You could send 1.5Mbps if the bandwidth were available on the network, but you could get 56Kbps through no matter what. While you could specify a CIR of 1.5Mbps, you would generally lose the advantage (pricewise) of frame relay over a leased line. This model is so attractive because you pay for what you absolutely need, but can still burst well beyond that level, so long as the network bandwidth is available. Some telephone companies will even allow you to purchase a CIR of 0, meaning that you have no *guaranteed* bandwidth, but can still send frames through the cloud.

Frame Relay Features

Frame relay is a high-performance WAN protocol that operates at the Physical and Data Link layers of the OSI reference model. It was originally designed for use across Integrated Services Digital Network (ISDN) interfaces, but today it's also used over a variety of other network interfaces.

Frame relay gives us a communications interface between DTE and DCE devices. DTE consists of terminals, PCs, routers, and bridges—all are customer-owned end-node and internetworking devices. DCE devices such as packet switches are carrier-owned internetworking devices.

Popular opinion is that frame relay is faster and more efficient than X.25 because it assumes that error checking will be done through higher-layer protocols and application services. Frame relay provides connection-oriented Data Link layer communication by using virtual circuits like X.25. A frame relay virtual circuit is a logical connection between two DTEs across a packet-switched network (PSN) and is identified by a DLCI. We will talk about DLCIs shortly. Like X.25, frame relay uses both PVCs and SVCs, but most frame relay networks use PVCs.

Frame Relay with Cisco Routers

When configuring frame relay on Cisco routers, we specify it as an encapsulation on serial interfaces. There are only two encapsulation types: Cisco and IETF.

```
RouterA(config)#int s0
RouterA(config-if)#encapsulation frame-relay ?
 ietf Use RFC1490 encapsulation
 <cr>
```

Cisco is the default encapsulation unless you type IETF. You use the Cisco encapsulation when connecting between two Cisco devices. You will use the IETF (Internet Engineering Task Force) encapsulation when connecting your Cisco device to a non-Cisco device by using frame relay. Check with your service provider to find out which encapsulation type to use. If they don't know, call a different provider.

Data-Link Connection Identifiers

Frame relay virtual circuits are identified by data-link connection identifiers (DLCIs). A frame relay service provider, like a telephone company, typically assigns DLCI values that are used by frame relay to distinguish between different virtual circuits on the network. Because many virtual circuits can be terminated on a multipoint frame relay interface, many DLCIs are affiliated with it. For the IP devices at each end of a virtual circuit to communicate, their IP addresses are mapped to DLCIs. This is so that a multipoint device can point out the appropriate destination virtual circuit to the frame relay network to each packet sent over the single physical interface.

Frame relay uses DLCIs the same way that X.25 uses X.121 addresses. Every DLCI number can have global or local meaning everywhere in the frame-relay network. But the customary implementation is to give each DLCI local meaning. What does this do? It makes two DTE devices connected via a virtual circuit use different DLCI values when referring to the same connection.

Configuring a DLCI number to an interface is shown below:

```
RouterA(config-if)#frame-relay interface-dlci ?
<16-1007> Define a DLCI as part of the current subinterface
RouterA(config-if)#frame-relay interface-dlci 16
```

Local Management Interface (LMI)

The LMI was developed in 1990 by Cisco Systems, StrataCom, Northern Telecom, and Digital Equipment Corporation. The group became known as the "Gang-of-Four LMI" or "Cisco LMI." This "gang" took the basic frame relay protocol from the CCIT and added extensions to the protocol features that allowed internetworking devices to communicate easily with a frame relay network.

LMI messages provide information about the current DLCI values, the global or local significance of the DLCI values, and the status of virtual circuits.

You will need to check with your frame relay provider to find out which type to use. The default type is Cisco, but you may need to change to ANSI or Q.933A. The three LMI types are shown below:

```
RouterA(config-if)#frame-relay lmi-type ?
 cisco
 ansi
 q933a
```

All standard LMI signaling formats are supported by the following:

ANSI: Annex D defined by ANSI standard T1.617

ITU-T (Q.933A): Annex A defined by Q.933A

Cisco: LMI defined by the gang of four (default)

 Starting with Cisco IOS version 11.2, the LMI type is autodetected.

Subinterfaces

You can have multiple virtual circuits on a single serial interface and treat each virtual circuit as a separate interface, called a subinterface. Think of a subinterface as a hardware interface defined by the IOS software.

The advantages to using subinterfaces is that you can assign different network-layer characteristics to each subinterface and virtual circuit, such as IP routing on one virtual circuit and IPX on another.

You define subinterfaces with the `interface s0.subinterface number` command as shown below:

```
RouterA(config)#int s0.?
 <0-4294967295> Serial interface number
RouterA(config)#int s0.16 ?
 multipoint    Treat as a multipoint link
 point-to-point Treat as a point-to-point link
```

You can define a limitless number of subinterfaces on a given physical interface, keeping router memory in mind. In the above example, we chose to use subinterface 16 because that is the DLCI number of that interface. You can choose any number between 0 and 4292967295.

The two types of subinterfaces are point-to-point and multipoint. Point-to-point subinterfaces are used when a single virtual circuit connects one router to another. Multipoint subinterfaces are used when the router is the center of a star of virtual circuits.

An example of a production router running multiple subinterfaces is shown below. Notice that the subinterface number matches the DLCI number. This is not a requirement but helps in the administration of the interfaces. Also notice that there is no LMI type defined, which means they are running either the default of Cisco or using autodetect if running Cisco IOS version 11.2 or newer.

```
interface Serial0.16 point-to-point
ip address 192.168.2.22 255.255.255.252
 ipx network 101
 frame-relay interface-dlci 16
!
interface Serial0.17 point-to-point
ip address 192.168.2.101 255.255.255.252
 ipx network 102
 frame-relay interface-dlci 17
!
interface Serial0.18 point-to-point
ip address 192.168.2.113 255.255.255.252
```

```
    ipx network 103
    frame-relay interface-dlci 18
!
interface Serial0.19 point-to-point
ip address 192.168.2.109 255.255.255.252
 ipx network 104
 frame-relay interface-dlci 19
!
interface Serial0.20 point-to-point
ip address 192.168.2.105 255.255.255.252
 ipx network 105
 frame-relay interface-dlci 20
```

Mapping Frame Relay

As we explained earlier, in order for IP devices at the ends of virtual circuits to communicate, their addresses must be mapped to the DLCIs. There are two ways to make this mapping happen:

1. Use the frame relay map command

2. Use the inverse-arp function

Here's an example using the frame relay map command:

```
RouterA(config)#int s0.16
RouterA(config-if)#encap frame-relay ietf
RouterA(config-if)#no inverse-arp
RouterA(config-if)#ip address 172.16.30.1 255.255.255.0
RouterA(config-if)#frame-relay map ip 172.16.30.17 30 cisco broadcast
RouterA(config-if)#frame-relay map ip 172.16.30.18 50 broadcast
RouterA(config-if)#frame-relay map ip 172.16.30.19 40
```

Here's what we did: First, we chose our subinterface, and we added the encapsulation command using IETF. We then turned off inverse arp and mapped three virtual circuits and their corresponding DLCI numbers. Notice the Cisco encapsulation on the first virtual circuit. The other two virtual circuits use the encapsulation type specified in the interface command (IETF). The frame relay map command is the only way to mix both Cisco and IETF encapsulation types. The broadcast keyword at the end of the map command tells the router to forward broadcasts for this interface to this specific virtual circuit.

Instead of putting in map commands for each virtual circuit, you can use the `inverse-arp` function to perform dynamic mapping of the IP address to the DLCI number. This makes our configuration look like this:

```
RouterA(config)#int s0.16
RouterA(config-if)#encap frame-relay ietf
RouterA(config-if)#ip address 172.16.30.1 255.255.255.0
```

Yes, it's a whole lot easier, but it's not as stable as using the map command. Why? Sometimes, when using the `inverse-arp` function, configuration errors occur because virtual circuits can be insidiously and dynamically mapped to unknown devices.

Monitoring Frame Relay

There are several ways to check the status of your interfaces and PVCs once you have frame relay encapsulation set up and running:

```
RouterA>sho frame ?
  ip      show frame relay IP statistics
  lmi     show frame relay lmi statistics
  map     Frame-Relay map table
  pvc     show frame relay pvc statistics
  route   show frame relay route
  traffic Frame-Relay protocol statistics
```

The show frame pvc will list all configured PVCs and DLCIs:

```
RouterA#sho frame pvc

PVC Statistics for interface Serial0 (Frame Relay DTE)

DLCI = 16, DLCI USAGE = LOCAL, PVC STATUS = ACTIVE,
INTERFACE = Serial0.1

 input pkts 50977876    output pkts 41822892    in bytes
3137403144
 out bytes 3408047602    dropped pkts 5       in FECN pkts 0
 in BECN pkts 0       out FECN pkts 0      out BECN pkts 0
```

```
   in DE pkts 9393     out DE pkts 0
   pvc create time 7w3d, last time pvc status changed 7w3d


DLCI = 18, DLCI USAGE = LOCAL, PVC STATUS = ACTIVE,
INTERFACE = Serial0.3

  input pkts 30572401    output pkts 31139837    in bytes
1797291100
  out bytes 3227181474    dropped pkts 5       in FECN pkts 0
  in BECN pkts 0         out FECN pkts 0      out BECN pkts 0
  in DE pkts 28         out DE pkts 0
  pvc create time 7w3d, last time pvc status changed 7w3d


DLCI = 20, DLCI USAGE = LOCAL, PVC STATUS = ACTIVE,
INTERFACE = Serial0.5

  input pkts 33059904    output pkts 33381448    in bytes
2016627916
  out bytes 4244863762    dropped pkts 6       in FECN pkts 0
  in BECN pkts 0         out FECN pkts 0      out BECN pkts 0
  in DE pkts 301        out DE pkts 0
  pvc create time 7w3d, last time pvc status changed 3d02h


DLCI = 21, DLCI USAGE = LOCAL, PVC STATUS = ACTIVE,
INTERFACE = Serial0.6

  input pkts 27326898    output pkts 28340038    in bytes
1635295444
  out bytes 2708333259    dropped pkts 5       in FECN pkts 0
  in BECN pkts 1013     out FECN pkts 0      out BECN pkts 0
  in DE pkts 4927       out DE pkts 0
  pvc create time 7w3d, last time pvc status changed 7w0d
```

We can also use the show interface command to check for LMI traffic:

```
RouterA#sho int s0
Serial0 is up, line protocol is up
  Hardware is HD64570
```

MTU 1500 bytes, BW 1544 Kbit, DLY 20000 usec, rely 255/255, load 2/255

Encapsulation FRAME-RELAY, loopback not set, keepalive set (10 sec)

LMI enq sent 451751, LMI stat recvd 451750, LMI upd recvd 164, DTE LMI up

LMI enq recvd 0, LMI stat sent 0, LMI upd sent 0

LMI DLCI 1023 LMI type is CISCO frame relay DTE

Broadcast queue 0/64, broadcasts sent/dropped 0/0, interface broadcasts 839294

7

Last input 00:00:02, output 00:00:00, output hang never

Last clearing of "show interface" counters never

Input queue: 0/75/0 (size/max/drops); Total output drops: 0

Queueing strategy: weighted fair

Output queue: 0/64/0 (size/threshold/drops)

  Conversations 0/19 (active/max active)

  Reserved Conversations 0/0 (allocated/max allocated)

5 minute input rate 13000 bits/sec, 30 packets/sec

5 minute output rate 16000 bits/sec, 28 packets/sec

  142390130 packets input, 5033149 bytes, 0 no buffer

  Received 0 broadcasts, 0 runts, 0 giants

  0 input errors, 0 CRC, 0 frame, 0 overrun, 0 ignored, 0 abort

  135137047 packets output, 709476803 bytes, 0 underruns

  0 output errors, 0 collisions, 7 interface resets

  0 output buffer failures, 0 output buffers swapped out

  0 carrier transitions

  DCD=up DSR=up DTR=up RTS=up CTS=up

Point-to-Point Protocol (PPP)

Point-to-Point Protocol (PPP) is a Data Link protocol that can be used over either asynchronous (dial-up) or synchronous (ISDN) media. It uses

LCP (Link Control Protocol) to build and maintain Data Link connections. LCP is packed with a number of features, including:

- Authentication using either PAP (Password Authentication Protocol) or CHAP (Challenge-Handshake Authentication Protocol)

- Compression of data for transmission across media

These features weren't available in PPP's predecessor, SLIP (Serial Line Internet Protocol), so this is progress.

Another new feature is the support for multiple protocols. SLIP supported only IP, but through NCP (Network Control Protocol), PPP supports IP, IPX, AppleTalk, DECnet, OSI/CLNS and Transparent bridging. NCP is actually a family of protocols, one for each layer 3 protocol that is supported by PPP.

Configuring PPP encapsulation on an interface is a fairly straightforward process as follows:

```
RouterA#config t
Enter configuration commands, one per line. End with CNTL/Z.
RouterA(config)#int s0
RouterA(config-if)#encapsulation ppp
RouterA(config-if)#^Z
RouterA#
```

Of course, PPP encapsulation must be enabled on both interfaces that are connected to a serial line to work, and there are several additional configuration options available by using the help command as follows:

```
RouterA#config t
Enter configuration commands, one per line. End with CNTL/Z.
RouterA(config)#int s0
RouterA(config-if)#ppp ?
  authentication Set PPP link authentication method
  bridge      Enable PPP bridge translation
  chap        Set CHAP authentication parameters
  compression   Enable PPP Compression control negotiation
  max-bad-auth  Allow multiple authentication failures
  multilink    Make interface multilink capable
  pap         Set PAP authentication parameters
  quality      Set minimum Link Quality before link is down
```

```
reliable-link  Use LAPB with PPP to provide a reliable link
timeout        Set PPP timeout parameters
use-tacacs     Use TACACS to verify PPP authentications
```

RouterA(config-if)#

See? There are a lot of options to control the compression, authentication, and other features of PPP in the Cisco IOS.

Now that we have PPP encapsulation enabled, let's take a look to verify that it's up and running:

```
RouterA#show int s0
Serial0 is up, line protocol is up
 Hardware is HD64570
 Internet address is 172.16.20.1/24
 MTU 1500 bytes, BW 1544 Kbit, DLY 20000 usec, rely 255/255,
load 1/255
 Encapsulation PPP, loopback not set, keepalive set (10 sec)
 LCP Open
 Listen: IPXCP
 Open: IPCP, CDPCP, ATCP
 Last input 00:00:05, output 00:00:05, output hang never
 Last clearing of "show interface" counters never
 Input queue: 0/75/0 (size/max/drops); Total output drops: 0
 Queueing strategy: weighted fair
 Output queue: 0/1000/64/0 (size/max total/threshold/drops)
   Conversations 0/2/256 (active/max active/max total)
   Reserved Conversations 0/0 (allocated/max allocated)
 5 minute input rate 0 bits/sec, 0 packets/sec
 5 minute output rate 0 bits/sec, 0 packets/sec
   670 packets input, 31845 bytes, 0 no buffer
   Received 596 broadcasts, 0 runts, 0 giants, 0 throttles
   0 input errors, 0 CRC, 0 frame, 0 overrun, 0 ignored, 0
abort
   707 packets output, 31553 bytes, 0 underruns
   0 output errors, 0 collisions, 18 interface resets
   0 output buffer failures, 0 output buffers swapped out
 21 carrier transitions
```

```
         DCD=up DSR=up DTR=up RTS=up CTS=up
RouterA#
```

Notice that the fifth line lists encapsulation as PPP, and the sixth line tells us that LCP is open. Remember that LCP's job is to build and maintain connections. The eighth line tells us that IPCP, CDPCP, and ATCP are open. This shows the IP, CDP, and AppleTalk support from NCP. Now, the seventh line reports that we are listening for IPXCP. This interface on RouterA is configured for IPX, but it's not receiving IPX traffic from the interface on RouterB that isn't configured for IPX.

ISDN

ISDN (Integrated Services Digital Network) is a digital service designed to run over existing telephone networks. Being able to deliver a true digital service across your existing local loop is very cool indeed. ISDN can support both data and voice—a telecommuter's dream. But ISDN applications require bandwidth. Typical ISDN applications and implementations include high-speed image applications (such as Group IV facsimile), high-speed file transfer, videoconferencing, and multiple links into homes of telecommuters.

ISDN is actually a set of communication protocols proposed by telephone companies that allows them to carry a group of digital services that simultaneously convey data, text, voice, music, graphics, and video to end users, and it was designed to achieve this over the telephone systems already in place. ISDN is referenced by a suite of ITU-T standards that encompass the OSI model's Physical, Data Link, and Network layers.

ISDN Terminals

Devices connecting to the ISDN network are known as terminals and have the following two types:

- **TE1:** Terminal equipment type 1 understand ISDN standards.

- **TE2:** Terminal equipment type 2 predate ISDN standards. To use a TE2, you have to use a terminal adapter (TA).

ISDN Reference Points

ISDN uses four different reference points to define logical interfaces. They are as follows:

- **R reference point**: Defines the reference point between non-ISDN equipment and a TA.

- **S reference point**: Defines the reference point between user terminals and an NT2.

- **T reference point**: Defines the reference point between NT1 and NT2 devices.

- **U reference point**: Defines the reference point between NT1 devices and line-termination equipment in a carrier network. (This is only in North America where the NT1 function isn't provided by the carrier network.)

ISDN Protocols

ISDN protocols are defined by the ITU, and there are three protocols that deal with diverse issues:

- Protocols beginning with the letter *E* specify ISDN on the existing telephone network.

- Protocols beginning with the letter *I* specify concepts, terminology, and services.

- Protocols beginning with the letter *Q* specify switching and signaling.

Basic Rate Interface

ISDN Basic Rate Interface (BRI, also known as 2B+1D) service provides two B channels and one D channel. The BRI B-channel service operates at 64Kbps and carries data, while the BRI D-channel service operates at 16Kbps and usually carries control and signaling information. The D-channel signaling protocol spans the OSI reference model's Physical, Data Link, and Network layers. BRI also provides framing control for a total bit rate of up to 192Kbps.

When configuring ISDN BRI, you will need to obtain SPIDs (Service Profile Identifiers), and you should have one SPID for each B channel and two for BRI. SPIDs can be thought of as the telephone number of each B channel.

The ISDN device gives the SPID to the ISDN switch, which then allows the device to access the network for BRI or PRI service. Without a SPID, many IDSN switches don't allow an ISDN device to place a call on the network.

Primary Rate Interface

In North America and Japan, the ISDN Primary Rate Interface (PRI, also known as 23B+D1) service delivers 23 B channels and one 64Kbps D channel for a total bit rate of up to 1.544Mbps.

In Europe, Australia, and other parts of the world, ISDN provides 30 B channels and one 64Kbps D channel for a total bit rate of up to 2.048Mbps.

ISDN with Cisco Routers

Accessing ISDN with a Cisco router means that you will need to purchase either a Network Termination 1 (NT1) or an ISDN modem. If your router has a BRI interface, you're ready to rock. Otherwise, you can use one of your router's serial interfaces if you can get a hold of a TA. A router with a BRI interface is called a TE (Terminal End-point 1), and one that requires a TA is called a TE2 (Terminal End-point 2).

ISDN supports virtually every upper-layer network protocol (IP, IPX, AppleTalk, you name it), and you can choose PPP, HDLC, or LAPD as your encapsulation protocol.

When configuring ISDN, you'll need to know the type of switch that your service provider is using. To see which switches your router will support, use the isdn switch-type ? command in global configuration mode. You need to do this because each manufacturer has a proprietary protocol for signaling.

For each ISDN BRI interface, you need to specify the SPIDs that are using the isdn spid1 and isdn spid2 interface subcommands. An example is shown below:

```
RouterA#config t
Enter configuration commands, one per line. End with CNTL/Z.
RouterA(config)#isdn switch-type basic-dms100
RouterA(config)#int bri0
```

```
RouterA(config-if)#encap ppp
RouterA(config-if)#isdn spid1 775456721
RouterA(config-if)#isdn spid2 775456722
```

The encapsulation is PPP because ISDN specifies this method used to establish the digital phone call.

For each ISDN PRI interface, you need to specify the data-link-specific information for the T1 controller. This is how the PRI communicates with the ISDN switch. Information such as framing and line coding is essential. An example of this follows:

```
RouterA(config)#controller T1 1/0
RouterA(config-if)#framing esf
RouterA(config-if)#linecode b8zs
RouterA(config-if)#pri-group timeslots 1-24
```

Extended Superframe Framing (ESF) is used on T1 circuits. It consists of 24 frames of 192 data bits each, with bit 193 providing timing and other functions.

B8ZS is a binary eight-zero substitution line-coding mechanism that guarantees the density of 1s over a link by substituting a special code whenever eight consecutive 0s are sent and then removing the special code at the remote end of the connection.

That last entry, "timeslots 1–24," defines ISDN PRI timeslots. It has a value between 1 and 24.

Summary

In this chapter, we covered the following key points:

- The difference between the following WAN services: X.25/LAPB, frame relay, ISDN/LAPD, SDLC, HDLC, PPP, and DDR

- Key frame relay and X.25 terms and features

- The commands to configure frame relay LMIs, maps, and subinterfaces

- The commands to monitor frame relay operation in the router

- How to identify PPP operations to encapsulate WAN data on Cisco routers

- How to state a relevant use and context for ISDN networking

- How to identify ISDN protocols, function groups, reference points, and channels

- How to describe Cisco's implementation of ISDN BRI

Review Questions

1. Which of the following best describes X.21bis?

   A. Used for X.25 service in Europe

   B. The Physical layer protocol used in X.25

   C. Specifies packet switching type

   D. Used in PLP call setup mode

2. When would you use ISDN?

   A. To connect IBM mainframes

   B. To connect local area networks (LANs) using digital service with dissimilar media

   C. To support applications requiring high-speed voice, video, and data communications

   D. When you need both a consistent and very high rate of data speed and transfer

3. How many frame relay encapsulation types are available with Cisco routers?

   A. Three

   B. Two

   C. Four

   D. Five

4. How many LMI types are available?

   A. Two

   B. Three

   C. Four

   D. Five

5. Regarding frame relay, which of the following statements are true?

   A. You must use Cisco encapsulation if connecting to non-Cisco equipment

   B. You must use ANSI encapsulation if connecting to non-Cisco equipment

   C. You must use IETF encapsulation if connecting to non-Cisco equipment

   D. You must use Q.933A encapsulation if connecting to non-Cisco equipment

6. What is the default LMI type?

   A. Q.933A

   B. ANSI

   C. IETF

   D. Cisco

7. Which of the following uses a PVC at layer 2?

   A. X.25

   B. ISDN

   C. Frame relay

   D. HDLC

8. Which ISDN protocol prefix specifies switching?

   A. I

   B. E

   C. S

   D. Q

9. If you wanted to view the DLCI and line speed for your frame relay network, which command would you use?

   A. `sh frame-relay`

   B. `sh run`

   C. `sh frame-relay dlci/speed`

   D. `sh frame-relay pvc`

10. Which of the following are valid WAN terms (choose all that apply)?

   A. DTE

   B. CPE

   C. demarc

   D. DCE

11. What does the ISDN Basic Rate Interface (BRI) provide?

   A. 23 B channels and one 64Kbps D channel

   B. Total bit rate of up to 1.544Mbps

   C. Two 56Kbps B channels and one 64Kbps D channel

   D. Two 64Kbps B channels and one 16Kbps D channel

12. What is true about frame relay DLCI?

   A. DLCI is optional in a frame-relay network

   B. DLCI represents a single physical circuit

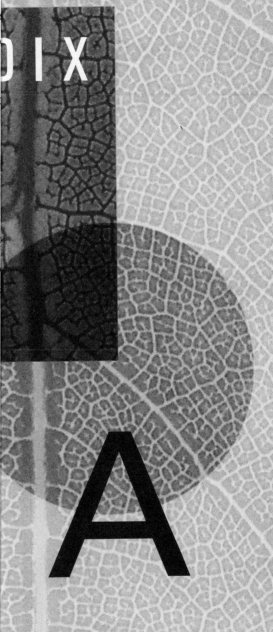

C. DLCI identifie

D. DLCI is used t
relay

13. Which ISDN proto

A. I

B. T

C. Q

D. E

14. What does ISDN

A. One 64Kbps B

B. Two 64Kbps

C. 24 B channels

D. 23 B channels

15. Which command

A. sh frame pvc

B. sh frame

C. sh frame lmi

D. sh pvc

16. What is the default
Cisco routers?

A. SDLC

B. HDLC

C. Cisco

D. ANSI

Chapter 1

1. LAN stands for which of the following?

   A. Long Area Network

   B. Local Area Network

   C. Local Arena Network

   D. Local Area News

Answer: B

2. WAN stands for which of the following?

   A. WAN Area Network

   B. Wide Arena Network

   C. Wide Area Network

   D. Wide Area News

Answer: C

3. The two sublayers of the IEEE Data Link layer are which of the following?

   A. Data Link and MAC

   B. Data Link and LLC

   C. Logical Link Control and Media Access Control

   D. Logical and Link Control

Answer: C

4. Bridges work at which layer of the OSI reference model?

   A. Session

   B. Bridge

   C. Network

D. Data Link

Answer: D. Because bridges use MAC or hardware addresses for filtering networks, they work at the MAC sublayer of the Data Link layer.

5. Repeaters work at which layer of the OSI reference model?

A. Transport

B. Presentation

C. Physical

D. Data Link

Answer: C. Repeaters work at the Physical layer and only regenerate or repeat the digital signal. There is no filtration of the network.

6. What is the Network layer of the OSI reference model responsible for?

A. Bridging

B. Regenerating the digital signal

C. Routing packets through an internetwork

D. Gateway services

Answer: C. Even though a router can handle all of the functions listed, the Network layer is *mostly* responsible for routing. Bridging occurs at the Data Link layer, and regenerating the digital signal happens mostly at the Physical layer. Gateway services occur at all layers of the OSI reference model.

7. List the seven layers of the OSI reference model and each of their functions.

Answer:

- Application: file, print, message, application, and database services
- Presentation: encryption, decryption, compression, and expansion
- Session: dialog control
- Transport: end-to-end connection

- Network: routing
- Data Link: framing
- Physical: transmitting 1s and 0s across the wire

8. Which three pairs of the following are Presentation layer standards?

   A. MPEG and MIDI

   B. PICT and JPEG

   C. ASCII and EBCDIC

   D. NFS and SQL

   Answer: A, B, C. The Presentation layer standards are MPEG, MIDI, and QuickTime for movies and sound; PICT, TIFF, and JPEG for direct graphic and visual image presentation; and ASCII and EBCDIC for data standards.

9. Which of the following are Session layer standards?

   A. MPEG and MIDI

   B. NFS and SQL

   C. ASCII and EBCDIC

   D. PICT and JPEG

   Answer: B

10. Which three of the following are true statements about connection-oriented sessions?

    A. The segments delivered are acknowledged back to the sender upon their reception

    B. Any segments not acknowledged are dropped

    C. Segments are sequenced back into their proper order upon arrival at their destination

D. A manageable data flow is maintained in order to avoid congestion, overloading, and the loss of any data

Answer: A, C, D. Connection-oriented sessions take place at the Transport layer. The protocol TCP is responsible for segments being delivered and acknowledged. Any segments not acknowledged are resent. Segments are sequenced and put back into their proper order upon arrival. TCP is also responsible for flow control and congestion management.

11. CPE is an acronym for which of the following?

 A. Central Processing Engineering

 B. Central Processing Equipment

 C. Customer Processing Equipment

 D. Customer Premise Equipment

Answer: D

12. CSU/DSU is an acronym for which of the following?

 A. Channel Service Unit/Digital Service Unit

 B. Channel Service Unit/Data Service Unit

 C. Channel Service Unite/Digital Service Unit

 D. Can't Send in Uniform/Don't Send another Unit

Answer: B

13. CO is an acronym for which of the following?

 A. Company Office

 B. Corporate Option

 C. Central Office

 D. Central Option

Answer: C

14. Choose three reasons why the networking industry uses a layered model.

    A. It allows changes to occur in all layers when changing one protocol

    B. It allows changes in one layer to occur without changing other layers

    C. It clarifies what general function is to be done rather than how to do it

    D. It clarifies how to do it rather than what general functions should be done

    E. It facilitates systematic troubleshooting

Answer: B, C, E

15. Which layer defines bit synchronization?

    A. Application

    B. Presentation

    C. Session

    D. Transport

    E. Network

    F. Data Link

    G. Physical

Answer: G

16. Which layer defines the physical topology?

    A. Application

    B. Presentation

    C. Session

    D. Transport

    E. Network

    F. Data Link

    G. Physical

Answer: G

17. Which layer is responsible for putting 1s and 0s into a logical group?

    A. Application

    B. Presentation

    C. Session

    D. Transport

    E. Network

    F. Data Link

    G. Physical

Answer: F

18. Which layer is responsible for framing?

    A. Application

    B. Presentation

    C. Session

    D. Transport

    E. Network

    F. Data Link

    G. Physical

Answer: F

19. Which layer is responsible for addressing devices and routing through an internetwork?

    A. Application

    B. Presentation

    C. Session

    D. Transport

    E. Network

    F. Data Link

    G. Physical

Answer: E

20. Which layer hides details of any network-dependent information from the higher layers by providing transparent data transfer?

    A. Application

    B. Presentation

    C. Session

    D. Transport

    E. Network

    F. Data Link

    G. Physical

Answer: D

21. Which layer is responsible for flow control, acknowledgment, and windowing?

    A. Application

    B. Presentation

    C. Session

    D. Transport

    E. Network

    F. Data Link

    G. Physical

Answer: D

22. Which layer is responsible for providing mechanisms for multiplexing upper-layer application, session establishment, and tear-down of virtual circuits?

   A. Application

   B. Presentation

   C. Session

   D. Transport

   E. Network

   F. Data Link

   G. Physical

   Answer: D

23. Which layer is responsible for coordinating communication between systems?

   A. Application

   B. Presentation

   C. Session

   D. Transport

   E. Network

   F. Data Link

   G. Physical

   Answer: C

24. Which layer is responsible for negotiating data transfer syntax?

   A. Application

   B. Presentation

   C. Session

   D. Transport

    E. Network

    F. Data Link

    G. Physical

Answer: B

25. Which layer is responsible for synchronizing sending and receiving applications?

    A. Application

    B. Presentation

    C. Session

    D. Transport

    E. Network

    F. Data Link

    G. Physical

Answer: A

26. Which layer is responsible for identifying and establishing the availability of the intended communication partner?

    A. Application

    B. Presentation

    C. Session

    D. Transport

    E. Network

    F. Data Link

    G. Physical

Answer: A

27. Which layer is responsible for determining if sufficient resources for the intended communication exists?

    A. Application

    B. Presentation

    C. Session

    D. Transport

    E. Network

    F. Data Link

    G. Physical

Answer: A

Chapter 2

1. The maximum distance of a 10Base5 network is which of the following?

    A. 200 meters

    B. 500 meters

    C. 1000 meters

    D. 1500 meters

Answer: B

2. The CSMA/CD Ethernet IEEE committee is defined as which of the following?

    A. 802.2

    B. 802.5

    C. 802.3

    D. 802.4

Answer: C

3. CSMA/CD stands for which of the following?

A. Collision Sense, Multiple Access with Carrier Detect

B. Collision Sense, Multiple Access with Collision Detect

C. Carrier Sense, Multiple Access with Collision Detect

D. Carrier Sense, Mac Address with Collision Detect

Answer: C

4. Which of the following is a characteristic of a switch, but not of a repeater?

A. Switches forward packets based on the IPX or IP address in the frame.

B. Switches forward packets based only on the IP address in the packet.

C. Switches forward packets based on the IP address in the frame.

D. Switches forward packets based on the MAC address in the frame.

Answer: D

5. How does the cut-through switching technique work?

A. The LAN switch copies the entire frame into its onboard buffers and then looks up the destination address in its forwarding, or switching, table and determines the outgoing interface

B. The switch waits only for the header to be received before it checks the destination address and starts forwarding the packets

C. By using broadcast addresses as source addresses

D. By using a Class II repeater in a collision domain

Answer: B

6. How do switches use store and forward?

A. The switch waits only for the header to be received before it checks the destination address and starts forwarding the packets

    B. The LAN switch copies the entire frame into its onboard buffers and then looks up the destination address in its forwarding, or switching, table and determines the outgoing interface

    C. By using a class II repeater in a collision domain

    D. By using broadcast addresses as source addresses

Answer: B

7. Choose all of the following that are needed to support full-duplex Ethernet.

    A. Multiple paths between multiple stations on a link

    B. Full-duplex NIC cards

    C. Loopback and collision detection disabled

    D. Automatic detection of full-duplex operation by all connected stations

Answer: B, C

8. What two types of technology does 100BaseT use?

    A. Switching with 53-byte cells

    B. CSMA/CD

    C. IEEE 802.5

    D. 802.3u

Answer: B, D

9. Choose all of the following that are advantages to segmenting with routers.

    A. Manageability

    B. Flow control

    C. Explicit packet lifetime control

    D. Multiple active paths

Answer: All of the above

10. Some advantages to segmenting with Bridges are_____

    A. Datagram filtering

    B. Manageability

    C. Reliability

    D. Scalability

Answer: B, C and D

11. Which two of the following describe frame tagging?

    A. Examines particular info about each frame

    B. A unique ID placed in the header of each frame as it traverses the switch fabric

    C. A user-assigned ID defined to each frame

    D. The building of filter tables

Answer: B and C

12. Which of the following describes a full-duplex transmission?

    A. Uses a single cable

    B. Uses a point-to-point connection from the transmitter of the transmitting station to the receiver of the receiving station

    C. Data transmission in only both directions, but only one way at a time

    D. Data transmission in only one direction

Answer: B

13. If a frame is received at a switch and only the destination hardware address is read before the frame is forwarded, what type of switching method are you using?

    A. Cut-through

    B. Store-and-forward

    C. Store-and-cut

    D. FragmentFree

Answer: A

14. Which of the following switching types is the default for Cisco 5505s?

    A. Cut-through

    B. Store-and-forward

    C. Store-and-cut

    D. FragmentFree

Answer: B

15. Which is true regarding store-and-forward switching method?

    A. It is default for all Cisco switches

    B. It only reads the destination hardware address before forwarding the frame

    C. Latency varies depending on frame length

    D. Latency is constant

Answer: C

16. What does the Spanning-Tree Algorithm (STA) do?

    A. STA is implemented by STP to prevent loops

    B. Forward packets through a switch

    C. Restores lost frames

    D. Prevents API duplication in bridged networks

Answer: A

17. Which can be true regarding VLANs? (Choose all that apply.)

    A. They are created by location

B. They are created by function

C. They are created by group

D. They are created by department

Answer: All of the above

18. What is the IEEE specification for Spanning Tree?

   A. 802.2u

   B. 802.3q

   C. 802.1d

   D. 802.6

Answer: C

19. Of the three switching types, which one has the lowest latency?

   A. Cut-through

   B. FragmentFree

   C. Store-and-forward

   D. None

Answer: A

20. Of the three switching types, which one has the highest latency?

   A. Cut-through

   B. FragmentFree

   C. Store-and-forward

   D. None

Answer: C

Chapter 3

1. What is the port number for TCP?

    A. 6

    B. 11

    C. 17

    D. 45

Answer: A

2. What is the port number for UDP?

    A. 6

    B. 11

    C. 17

    D. 45

Answer: C

3. User Datagram Protocol works at which layer of the DOD model?

    A. Transport

    B. Internet

    C. Host-to-Host

    D. Data Link

Answer: C

4. Which protocol works at the Internet layer and is responsible for making routing decisions?

    A. TCP

    B. UDP

    C. IP

    D. ARP

Answer: C. IP works at the Internet layer. It looks at the destination network address in the packet and forwards the packet, based on routing tables and what it determines to be the best route to the destination.

5. Which protocol will send a message to routers if a network outage or congestion occurs?

    A. IP

    B. ARP

    C. ICMP

    D. TCP

Answer: C. Internet Control Message Protocol alerts routers if a network outage or congestion occurs so they can make different routing decision based on that information.

6. Which port numbers are used by TCP and UDP to set up sessions with other hosts?

    A. 1-255

    B. 256-1022

    C. 1023 and above

    D. 6 and 10 respectively

Answer: C

7. Which of the following is true?

    A. TCP is connection-orientated; UDP uses acknowledgements only

    B. Both TCP and UDP are connection-oriented, but only TCP uses windowing

    C. TCP is connection-oriented, but UDP is connectionless

D. TCP and UDP both have sequencing, but UDP is connectionless

Answer: C. TCP is a connection-oriented, reliable protocol that uses sequencing and acknowledgments to make sure packets are delivered properly. UDP is connectionless, unreliable, and doesn't use sequencing or acknowledgements.

8. Which protocol is used to manage and monitor the network?

A. FTP

B. SMTP

C. SNMP

D. IP

Answer: C

9. Which frame type use DSAPs and SSAPs to identify the upper-layer protocol?

A. 802.3

B. 802.5

C. 802.2

D. Ethernet_II

Answer: C

10. Which frame has a Type field to identify the upper-layer protocol?

A. 802.2

B. 802.5

C. 802.3

D. Ethernet_II

Answer: D. Ethernet_II has a type field to identify the upper-layer protocol. 802.3 only has a length field and can't identify the upper-layer protocol.

11. What does the acronym ARP stand for?

    A. ARP Resolution Protocol

    B. Address Restitution Protocol

    C. Address Resolution Phase

    D. Address Resolution Protocol

Answer: D

12. Ping uses which Internet layer protocol (besides IP)?

    A. ARP

    B. RARP

    C. DCMP

    D. ICMP

Answer: D

13. Which protocol sends redirects back to an originating router?

    A. ARP

    B. RARP

    C. ICMP

    D. BootP

    E. IP

    F. TCP

    G. UDP

Answer: C

14. Which of the following protocols are used to get an IP address from a known MAC address?

    A. ARP

    B. RARP

C. ICMP

D. BootP

E. IP

F. TCP

G. UDP

Answer: B

15. Which of the following protocols is used to give an IP address to a diskless machine?

A. ARP

B. RARP

C. ICMP

D. BootP

E. IP

F. TCP

G. UDP

Answer: D

16. Which two of the following protocols are used at the Transport layer?

A. ARP

B. RARP

C. ICMP

D. BootP

E. IP

F. TCP

G. UDP

Answer: F, G

17. Which protocol gets a hardware address from a known IP address?

    A. ARP

    B. RARP

    C. ICMP

    D. BootP

    E. IP

    F. TCP

    G. UDP

Answer: A

18. Which of the following is a connectionless protocol at the Transport layer?

    A. ARP

    B. RARP

    C. ICMP

    D. BootP

    E. IP

    F. TCP

    G. UDP

Answer: G

19. If a router in your internetwork experienced congestion on serial port 0, which protocol will let the neighbor routers know?

    A. ARP

    B. RARP

    C. ICMP

    D. BootP

    E. IP

F. TCP

G. UDP

Answer: C

---

20. Which protocol is used for booting diskless workstations?

A. ARP

B. RARP

C. ICMP

D. BootP

E. IP

F. TCP

G. UDP

Answer: D

Chapter 4

For questions 1–10, first examine all answers in binary.

1. You have a network ID of 172.16.0.0 and you need to divide it into multiple subnets. You need 600 host IDs for each subnet. Which subnet mask should you assign that will allow for growth?

A. 255.255.224.0

B. 255.255.240.0

C. 255.255.248.0

D. 255.255.252.0

Answer: D

224.0: 11100000.00000000: 224 gives us three bits, or six subnets, each with 8190 hosts.

240.0: 11110000.00000000: 240 gives us four bits, or 14 subnets, each with 4094 hosts.

248.0: 11111000.00000000: 248 gives us five bits, or 30 subnets, each with 2046 hosts.

252.0: 11111100.00000000: 252 gives us six bits, or 62 subnets, each with 1022 hosts.

Answer D gives us 62 subnets with more than twice the amount of hosts required per subnet.

2. You have a network ID of 172.16.0.0 with eight subnets. You need to allow for the largest possible number of host IDs per subnet. Which subnet mask should you assign?

   A. 255.255.224.0

   B. 255.255.240.0

   C. 255.255.248.0

   D. 255.255.252.0

Answer: B

224.0: 11100000.00000000: 224 gives us three bits, or six subnets, each with 8190 hosts.

240.0: 11110000.00000000: 240 gives us four bits, or 14 subnets, each with 4094 hosts.

248.0: 11111000.00000000: 248 gives us five bits, or 30 subnets, each with 2046 hosts.

252.0: 11111100.00000000: 252 gives us six bits, or 62 subnets, each with 1022 hosts.

By using only eight subnets, we can use 240.0 as a mask, giving us 14 subnets, each with 4094 hosts.

3. You have a network ID of 192.168.55.0 and you need to divide it into multiple subnets. You need 25 host IDs for each subnet, with the largest amount of subnets available. Which subnet mask should you assign?

A. 255.255.255.192

B. 255.255.255.224

C. 255.255.255.240

D. 255.255.255.248

Answer: B

192: 11000000: 192 gives us 2 bits, or 2 subnets, each with 62 hosts.

224: 11100000: 224 gives us three bits, or six subnets, each with 30 hosts.

240: 11110000: 240 gives us four bits, or 14 subnets, each with 14 hosts.

248: 11111000: 248 gives us five bits, or 30 subnets, each with 6 hosts.

Subnet mask 224 and mask 192 each gives us more than 25 hosts, but mask 224 gives us the most subnets.

4. You have a Class A network address with 60 subnets. You need to add 40 new subnets in the next two years, but still allow for the largest possible number of host IDs per subnet. Which subnet mask should you assign?

A. 255.240.0.0

B. 255.248.0.0

C. 255.252.0.0

D. 255.254.0.0

Answer: D

240.0.0: 11110000.00000000.00000000: 240 gives us four bits, or 14 subnets, each with 1,048,574 hosts.

248.0.0: 11111000.00000000.00000000: 248 gives us five bits, or 30 subnets, each with 524,286 hosts.

252.0.0: 11111100.00000000.00000000: 252 gives us six bits, or 62 subnets, each with 262,142 hosts.

254.0.0: 11111110.00000000.00000000: 254 gives us seven bits, or 126 subnets, each with 131,070 hosts.

Only mask 254.0.0 gives us the amount of subnets we need to allow for maximum growth.

5. You have a Class C network address of 192.168.19.0 with four subnets. You need the largest possible number of host IDs per subnet. Which subnet mask should you assign?

   A. 255.255.255.192

   B. 255.255.255.224

   C. 255.255.255.240

   D. 255.255.255.248

Answer: B

192: 11000000: 192 gives us 2 bits, or 2 subnets, each with 62 hosts.

224: 11100000: 224 gives us three bits, or six subnets, each with 30 hosts.

240: 11110000: 240 gives us four bits, or 14 subnets, each with 14 hosts.

248: 11111000: 248 gives us five bits, or 30 subnets, each with six hosts.

Only mask 224 gives us more than four subnets with the largest amount of hosts.

6. You have a Class B network address divided into 30 subnets. You will add 25 new subnets within the next two years. You need 600 host IDs for each subnet. Which subnet mask should you assign?

   A. 255.192.0.0

   B. 255.254.0.0

   C. 255.255.248.0

   D. 255.255.252.0

Answer: D

248.0: 11111000.00000000: 248 gives us five bits, or 30 subnets, each with 2046 hosts.

252.0: 11111100.00000000: 252 gives us six bits, or 62 subnets, each with 1022 hosts.

Answers A and B were from a Class A network and therefore not valid. Mask 252.0 gives us 62 subnets, each with 1022 hosts—enough to meet business requirements.

7. You have a network ID of 192.168.1.0 and you need to divide it into nine subnets. You need to provide for the largest possible number of host IDs per subnet. Which subnet mask should you assign?

   A. 255.255.255.192

   B. 255.255.255.224

   C. 255.255.255.240

   D. 255.255.255.248

Answer: C

192: 11000000: 192 gives us two bits, or two subnets, each with 62 hosts.

224: 11100000: 224 gives us three bits, or six subnets, each with 30 hosts.

240: 11110000: 240 gives us four bits, or 14 subnets, each with 14 hosts.

248: 11111000: 248 gives us five bits, or 30 subnets, each with six hosts.

Only mask 240 can give us the amount of subnets needed.

8. You have a Class C network address divided into three subnets. You will need to add two subnets in the next two years. Each subnet will have 25 hosts. Which subnet mask should you assign?

   A. 255.255.255.0

   B. 255.255.255.192

   C. 255.255.255.224

   D. 255.255.255.248

Answer: C

0: 00000000: 0 gives us 1 network with 254 hosts.

192: 11000000: 192 gives us two bits, or two subnets, each with 62 hosts.

224: 11100000: 224 gives us three bits, or six subnets, each with 30 hosts.

248: 11111000: 248 gives us five bits, or 30 subnets, each with six hosts.

The business requirements require five subnets, each with 25 hosts. Only mask 224 gives us this answer.

9. You have a Class C network address of 192.168.88.0 and you need the largest possible number of subnets, with up to 12 hosts per subnet. Which subnet mask should you assign?

A. 255.255.255.192

B. 255.255.255.224

C. 255.255.255.240

D. 255.255.255.248

Answer: C

192: 11000000: 192 gives us two bits, or two subnets, each with 62 hosts.

224: 11100000: 224 gives us three bits, or six subnets, each with 30 hosts.

240: 11110000: 240 gives us four bits, or 14 subnets, each with 14 hosts.

248: 11111000: 248 gives us five bits, or 30 subnets, each with six hosts.

Mask 248 gives us the largest number of subnets out of all the answers; however, 240 gives us 14 hosts.

10. You need to come up with a TCP/IP addressing scheme for your company. How many network IDs must you allow for when you define the subnet mask for the network?

A. One for each subnet

B. One for each host ID

C. One for each router interface

D. One for each WAN connection

E. One for each network adapter installed on each host

Answer: A and D. Each host on the network must have a unique IP address. However, you are required to have only one network ID per network. Each set of hosts must share a common network ID, as well as connections between networks, which are the WAN connections.

11. You need to come up with a TCP/IP addressing scheme for your company. Which two factors must you consider when you define the subnet mask for the network?

    A. The number of subnets on the network

    B. The number of host IDs on each subnet

    C. The volume of network traffic on each subnet

    D. The location of DNS servers

    E. The location of default gateways

    Answer: A and B

12. You need to come up with a TCP/IP addressing scheme for your company. How many host IDs must you allow for when you define the subnet mask for the network?

    A. One for each subnet

    B. One for each router interface

    C. One for each WAN connection

    D. One for each network adapter installed on each host

    Answer: B and D

13. You have an IP address of 172.16.3.57 with an 11-bit subnet mask. What are your valid hosts?

    A. 172.16.3.32 to 172.16.3.62

    B. 172.16.3.33 to 172.16.3.62

    C. 172.16.3.34 to 172.16.3.62

    D. 172.16.3.57 to 172.16.3.62

Answer: B. 11 bits gives you 255.255.255.224; 2,046 subnets, each with 30 hosts. 172.16.3.57 is in the 32 subnet range, and the valid hosts for subnet 32 are 33–62. The broadcast address is 63.

14. You have a subnet mask of 255.255.255.248. How many subnets and hosts do you have?

    A. 2,097,150 subnets with eight hosts

    B. 8190 subnets with six hosts

    C. 30 subnets with 14 hosts

    D. six subnets with 30 hosts

Answer: B. This question is not as hard as it seems. With 248 in the fourth octet, you can have a maximum of six hosts per subnet, regardless of the number of subnets or the class of address.

15. You have an IP address of 172.16.4.58 with a 12-bit subnet mask. What are your valid hosts?

    A. 172.16.4.48 to 172.16.4.63

    B. 172.16.4.49 to 172.16.4.63

    C. 172.16.4.49 to 172.16.4.62

    D. 172.16.4.55 to 172.16.4.62

Answer: C. A 12-bit subnet mask gives us 255.255.255.240; 4094 subnets, each with 4,194,302 subnets, 2 hosts. 172.16.4.58 is in the 48 subnet range, and the valid range is 49 through 62. Address 63 is a broadcast address.

16. You have an IP address of 172.16.13.5 with a 255.255.255.128 subnet mask. What is your class of address, subnet address, and broadcast address?

Answer: Class B, Subnet 13, Broadcast address 255.255.255.127. The valid range for hosts is 172.16.13.1 to 172.16.13.126.

17. If you have a 22-bit subnet mask, how many subnets and how many hosts do you have?

    A. 8190 subnets, 4096 hosts

    B. 4,194,302 subnets, 2 hosts

    C. 2,096,138 subnets 6 hosts

    D. 16,384 subnets, 2046 hosts

Answer: B

18. If you have a 19-bit subnet mask, how many subnets and how many hosts do you have?

    A. 8190 subnets, 126 hosts

    B. 524,288 subnets, 32 hosts

    C. 524,286 subnets, 30 hosts

    D. 65,234 subnets, 62 hosts

Answer: C

19. If you have a class B network with a 10-bit subnet mask, how many subnets and how many hosts do you have?

    A. 1022 subnets, 62 hosts

    B. 62 subnets, 8190 hosts

    C. 8,190 subnets, 254 hosts

    D. 254 subnets, 126 hosts

Answer: A

20. If you have a class C network with a 6-bit subnet mask, how many subnets and how many hosts do you have?

    A. 254 subnets, 30 hosts

    B. 64 subnets, 8 hosts

    C. 62 subnets, 2 hosts

    D. 30 subnets, 2 hosts

Answer: C

Chapter 5

  1. What is the syntax for changing the name of a Cisco router?

    A. host name newhostname

    B. hostname newhostname

    C. routername newhostname

    D. You can't change the name

Answer: B

  2. What is the syntax to add a banner to a Cisco router configuration?

    A. # banner

    B. banner #

    C. banner motd #

    D. motd banner #

Answer: C

  3. What command can you use to copy the configuration from NVRAM into running RAM?

    A. copy running-config startup-config

    B. copy startup-config running-config

    C. wr mem

    D. wr t

Answer: B

  4. What key do you use to view the last command that was entered into a Cisco router?

    A. The Down Arrow

B. The Up Arrow

C. CTRL+6

D. Type sh last command

Answer: B

5. Which other key command will give you the last command entered?

A. CTRL+N

B. CTRL+P

C. CTRL+A

D. CTRL+Z

Answer: B. By pressing CTRL+P, you can scroll through the last commands entered in the same way that you can by pressing the Up Arrow.

6. What key do you press to have the Cisco IOS finish typing a command for you?

A. Enter

B. CTRL

C. Tab

D. Space bar

Answer: C

7. To exit from privileged mode back to user mode, what do you type at the privileged mode prompt (#)?

A. Exit

B. Quit

C. Disable

D. Goback

Answer: C

8. What does the `erase startup-config` command do?

    A. Loads the startup-config into RAM

    B. Loads the running-config into NVRAM

    C. Erases the startup-config and puts you in debug mode

    D. Erases the startup-config

Answer: D

9. If you have two Cisco routers connected with DTE/DCE cables, to which router would you add the command `clock rate` in order to facilitate a CSU/DSU?

    A. The serial interface running as a DCE

    B. The serial interface running as a DTE

    C. The Ethernet interface running as a DTE

    D. The Ethernet interface running as a DCE

Answer: A. Cisco routers, by default, run as DTE devices. CSU/DSUs will connect to the serial interfaces of a router and give clocking. When connecting two routers together, you must add the `clock rate` command to the router that has the DCE interface. You can see which router has the DCE interface by typing `sh controller's serial [serial interface number]`.

10. What command do you use to change your enable password?

    A. `Config t, enable secret` *password*

    B. `Config t, enable password` *password*

    C. `Config t, line vty 0 4, login, password` *password*

    D. `Config t, line con 0, login, password` *password*

Answer: B. All of the answers change a different password on Cisco routers; however, only answer B will change the enable password.

11. What is the command to set the clock rate on your DCE interfaces?

    A. `clockrate 56`

   B. clock rate 56

   C. clockrate 56000

   D. clock rate 56000

Answer: D

12. CTRL+A will provide what function?

   A. Take your cursor to the end of the line

   B. Take your cursor to the beginning of the line

   C. Exit you out of edit mode

   D. Move you down one line

Answer: B

13. The `terminal no editing` command will provide what function?

   A. Stop users from editing your configuration

   B. Provide password protection

   C. Stop the advanced editing features

   D. Allow the configuration to be configured only from the console port

Answer: C

14. What is the syntax you would use to configure a port on a Catalyst 5000 switch?

   A. slot port/type

   B. port type/slot

   C. type slot/port

   D. config t, int e4

Answer: C

15. What is the syntax to configure a port on a 7000 series router with a VIP card?

   A. slot card/port

   B. type slot/port adapter/port

   C. port type/slot port/adapter

   D. slot port/adapter

Answer: B

16. Which of the following will change your Telnet password?

   A. line aux 0

   B. line con 0

   C. line vty 1

   D. line vty 5

Answer: C

17. How do you change your enable secret password?

   A. enable password <password>

   B. enable <password>

   C. enable secret password <password>

   D. enable secret <password>

Answer: D

18. When attaching a console cable to your router, how do you log in to user mode?

   A. Press return, type **password** if prompted

   B. login <password>

   C. Press return, <login name>

D. login <name, password>

Answer: A

19. If the advanced editing feature has been disabled, how do you then enable the advance editing features?

A. enable editing

B. terminal editing

C. enable advanced editing

D. terminal on editing

Answer: B

20. What is the AUX port used for?

A. Authentication

B. Backups

C. Modem

D. Console

Answer: C

Chapter 6

1. Which Cisco IOS command can you use to see the routing table?

A. sh ip config

B. sh ip arp

C. sh ip route

D. sh ip table

Answer: C

2. What is the command syntax for creating an IP static route in a Cisco Router?

A. route IP *ip_address default_ gateway*

B. IP route *destination_network subnet_mask default_gateway*

C. IP route *subnet_mask default_gateway network*

D. IP route *default_gateway subnet_mask network*

Answer: B

3. What is the command syntax to set a gateway of last resort in your Cisco router?

A. `ip route 0.0.0.0 255.255.255.0 Next Hop Address`

B. `route ip 0.0.0.0 255.255.255.0 Next Hop Address`

C. `ip route 0.0.0.0 0.0.0.0 Next Hop Address`

D. `ip route 0.0.0.0 0.0.0.0 network`

Answer: C

4. What is the command that you should use when using static and default routes with your Cisco routers?

A. `ip static`

B. `ip default`

C. `ip subnet-zero`

D. `ip classless`

Answer: D

5. When should you use static routing instead of dynamic routing?

A. Whenever you can

B. When you have very few routers and want to save your bandwidth

C. When you need the routing tables to be automatically updated

   D. When you want to use a default route

Answer: B

6. Static routes are used for which of the following?

   A. Defining a path to a router

   B. Defining a path to an IP destination network

   C. When you want to set a default gateway

   D. Updating the routing table dynamically

Answer: B

7. What are three ways that routers learn paths to destinations?

   A. Static routers

   B. Default routes

   C. Routing tables

   D. Dynamic routing

Answer: A, B, D

8. What is the administrative distance used for in static routes?

   A. Determining the network administrator for entering that route

   B. Creating a database

   C. To rate the source's trustworthiness, expressed as a numeric value from 0 to 255

   D. To rate the source's trustworthiness, expressed as a numeric value from 0 to 1023

Answer: C

9. What is an administrative distance of 0?

   A. 0 is the default administrative distance for dynamic routing

    B. 0 is the default administrative distance for directly connected routes

    C. 0 means that there is no routing allowed on this router

    D. 0 means that there are 0 hops to the next destination

Answer: B

10. What does it mean if you have an administrative distance of 0?

    A. It means you can't get there from here.

    B. 0 has the lowest trustworthiness rating.

    C. 0 has the highest trustworthiness rating.

    D. 0 means you are running RIP.

Answer: C

11. What are three ways to build routing tables?

    A. Static

    B. Default

    C. Manual

    D. Dynamic

Answer: A, B, D

12. What is the default administrative distance of RIP?

    A. 0

    B. 100

    C. 120

    D. 150

Answer: C

13. How do you create a default route?

    A. By using all 1's in place of the network and mask

    B. By defining a static route and using all 0's in place of the network and mask

    C. By using 255 in place of the network and mask

    D. login <name, password>

Answer: B

14. When looking at a routing table, what does the "S" mean?

    A. Dynamically connected

    B. Directly connected

    C. Statically connected

    D. Sending packets

Answer: C

15. What is true about IP routing?

    A. The destination IP address changes at each hop

    B. The source IP address changes at each hop

    C. The frame does not change at each hop

    D. The frame changes at each hop

Answer: D

16. What static route parameter will tell a router the name of the interface to use to get to a destination network?

    A. Network

    B. Mask

    C. Interface

    D. Address

Answer: C

17. When creating a static route, what is the gateway parameter used for?

    A. Defining the next hop

    B. Defining the weight

    C. Setting the static route

    D. Updating the routing table

Answer: A

18. What does a router do with a received packet that is destined for an unknown network?

    A. Forwards the packet

    B. Drops the packet

    C. Holds the packet till the next route update

    D. Sends a broadcast for the unknown network

Answer: B

19. What is true when creating static routes? (choose all that apply)

    A. The mask parameter is optional

    B. The gateway parameter is required

    C. The administrative distance is required

    D. The administrative distance is optional

Answer: B, D

20. When looking at the routing table, what does the "C" mean?

    A. Dynamic route

    B. Connected

    C. CLNS

    D. Directly connected

Answer: D

Chapter 7

1. What is the routing algorithm used by RIP?

   A. Routed information

   B. Link together

   C. Link-state

   D. Distance-vector

Answer: D

2. What is the routing algorithm used by IGRP?

   A. Routed information

   B. Link together

   C. Link-state

   D. Distance-vector

Answer: D

3. Which command can you type at the router prompt to verify the broadcast frequency for IGRP?

   A. `sh ip route`

   B. `sh ip protocol`

   C. `sh ip broadcast`

   D. `debug ip igrp`

Answer: B

4. What is the routing metric used by RIP?

   A. Count to infinity

   B. Hop count

   C. TTL

D. Bandwidth, reliability, MTU, delay, and load

Answer: B

5. Which utility should you use to identify the path that a packet takes as it passes through the routers?

   A. ROUTE

   B. TRACE

   C. IPCONFIG

   D. NETSTAT

Answer: B

6. What is the routing metric used by IGRP?

   A. Count to infinity

   B. Hop count

   C. TTL

   D. Bandwidth, reliability, MTU, delay, and load

Answer: D

7. What does a metric of 16 hops represent in a RIP routing network?

   A. 16 ms

   B. Number of routers in the internetwork

   C. Number of hops

   D. 16 hops—unreachable

Answer: D

8. Hold-downs are used for what?

   A. To hold down the protocol from going to the next hop

   B. To prevent regular update messages from reinstating a route that has gone down

C. To prevent regular update messages from reinstating a route that has just come up

D. To prevent irregular update messages from reinstating a route that has gone down

Answer: B

9. What is split horizon?

A. Information received on an interface cannot be sent back out that same interface.

B. When you have a large bus (horizon) physical network, the routing protocol splits the traffic.

C. Split horizon holds the regular updates from broadcasting to a down link.

D. It prevents regular update messages from reinstating a route that has gone down.

Answer: A

10. What is poison reverse?

A. This sends back the protocol received from a router as a poison pill, which stops the regular updates.

B. This is information that is received from a router can't be sent back to that originating router.

C. Reverse poison prevents regular update messages from reinstating a route that has gone down.

D. When a router sets the metric for a down link to infinity.

Answer: D

11. What is the default administrative distance for IGRP?

A. 90

B. 100

  C. 120

  D. 220

Answer: B

12. What are the three types of routes that IGRP advertises?

  A. Interior

  B. Dynamic

  C. System

  D. Exterior

Answer: A, C, D

13. What is the metric limit for link-state protocols?

  A. 16

  B. 255

  C. 6500

  D. 65,533

Answer: D

14. Which of the following are distance-vector protocols?

  A. IGRP

  B. RIP

  C. OSPF

  D. NLSP

Answer: A, B

15. Which of the following routing protocols use AS?

  A. RIP

  B. RIP II

C. IGRP

D. OSPF

Answer: C, D

16. What commands are available for supporting RIP networks (choose all that apply)?

A. sh ip route

B. sh ip protocol

C. sh rip network

D. Sh ip int

E. Debug ip rip

Answer: A, B, D, E

17. What is convergence time?

A. The hold down update time

B. The time it takes for all routers to update their routing table when a change takes place

C. The time it takes for a packet to get from a destination host to a receiving host

D. The time it takes to boot a router

Answer: B

18. What is true about distance-vector–based networks?

A. They send out partial updates every 60 seconds

B. They send their complete routing table every 60 seconds

C. They send their entire routing table every 30 seconds

D. They update every 90 seconds

Answer: C

19. What is true about link-state networks?

A. They maintain a more complex table than distance-vector–based networks

B. They maintain a less complex table than distance-vector–based networks

C. They don't use convergence

D. They use RIP timers

Answer: A

Chapter 8

1. What's the default CDP update broadcast rate for routers in seconds?

A. 60

B. 90

C. 180

D. 240

Answer: A

2. What's the default CDP hold time in seconds?

A. 60

B. 90

C. 180

D. 240

Answer: C

3. What command will allow you to load a Cisco router configuration that is stored on a TFTP server?

A. config t, tftp ip addresses of tftp server

B. config net, ip address of `tftp` server

C. config mem, ip address of `tftp` server

D. config net, ip address of router

Answer: B

4. You just received an output that states the CDP hold time, hardware, port ID, and local interface. What was the command you typed in?

A. `sh int`

B. `sh cdp int`

C. `sh cdp neighbor`

D. `sh cdp info`

Answer: C. The `show cdp neighbor` command will show you the hardware platform (Cisco 2500, for example), the local interface the routers are connected through, the hold time the router is configured for, as well as the port id port ID of the remote router. It'll also reveal the neighbor device ID and its capability.

5. Which command will load the Cisco router configuration into RAM (choose three)?

A. `reload`

B. `copy star run`

C. `copy run star`

D. `copy TFTP run`

Answer: A, B, D

6. Which command do you type to view the hostnames configured in your router (choose two)?

A. `sh hostnames`

B. `sh hosts`

C. `sh host`

    D. hostnames

Answer: B and C

7. If you type **copy tftp flash,** which event did you cause?

    A. erased your router configuration

    B. erased the configuration on your TFTP host

    C. copied a file from your TFTP server to your router flash

    D. copied your router's configuration from your TFTP server to your router

Answer: C

8. If you want to type in the hostname Bob instead of the IP address 172.16.10.1 to access the remote router named Bob, what should you do?

    A. `config t, hostname Router bob 172.16.10.1`

    B. `config t, ip hostname 172.16.10.1 router bob`

    C. `config t, ip host 172.16.10.1 bob`

    D. `config t, ip host bob 172.16.10.1`

Answer: D

9. What does it mean if you're running a trace and receive a "P" as a response?

    A. it passed through the first router

    B. positive response

    C. protocol responded

    D. protocol unreachable

Answer: D

10. How can you view the CDP information received from all routers?

    A. `sh cdp received`

B. `sh cdp entry *`

C. `cdp entry *`

D. `sh cdp route`

Answer: B

11. What command should you use to have your router load the valid Cisco IOS from a TFTP server?

   A. `copy TFTP run`

   B. `copy run TFTP`

   C. `boot TFTP flash`

   D. `boot system TFTP`

Answer: D

12. What command will copy your router configuration to a TFTP server?

   A. `copy TFTP run`

   B. `copy star TFTP`

   C. `boot system run`

   D. `copy flash TFTP`

Answer: B

13. Which protocols can you use when testing with Trace (choose all that apply)?

   A. AppleTalk

   B. DECnet

   C. CLNS

   D. IP

   E. TCP

   F. Vines

G. Old Vines

Answer: A, C, D, F, G

14. Which command will you use to disable DNS lookup?

   A. no DNS-lookup

   B. domain no-lookup

   C. no domain-lookup

   D. no ip domain-lookup

Answer: D

15. Which command do you use to configure your router to do a domain lookup?

   A. DNS-server 10.10.10.10

   B. 10.10.10.10 DNS-lookup

   C. IP DNS-server 10.10.10.10

   D. IP name-server 10.10.10.10

Answer: D

16. How can you telnet into multiple routers but keep the sessions open all at the same time?

   A. CTRL+Shift+^

   B. CTRL+Shift+%

   C. CTRL+Alt+^

   D. Return

Answer: A

17. After telneting into multiple routers simultaneously, what command can you type to see these connections?

   A. sh telnet

B. sh ports open

C. sh sessions

D. sh hosts

Answer: C

18. If you want to configure the router configuration stored in NVRAM, which command should you use?

A. config t

B. config mem

C. config TFTP

D. config startup-config

Answer: B

19. If you want to load a new Cisco IOS into your router's memory, which command should you use?

A. copy star run

B. copy run star

C. copy flash TFTP

D. copy TFTP flash

Answer: D

20. What type of frame does CDP use to gather information about its directly connected neighbors?

A. Subnetwork Access Protocol

B. TCP/IP

C. 802.2

D. Ethernet II

Answer: A

Chapter 9

1. Which of the following provides connection-oriented transport to upper-layer protocols?

   A. RIP

   B. NLSP

   C. SPX

   D. NCP

   Answer: C

2. Which of the following can respond to a client GNS request (choose all that apply)?

   A. local NetWare server

   B. remote NetWare server

   C. local client

   D. Cisco router

   Answer: A, B, and D

3. How often do servers exchange SAP information unless set otherwise?

   A. every 15 seconds

   B. every 30 seconds

   C. every 60 seconds

   D. every 120 seconds

   Answer: C

4. How can you configure a secondary subinterface on your Ethernet interface?

   A. Config t, int e0.24000

   B. Config t, int e100.0

C. config t, 24000 e0

D. config t, 24000 e100

Answer: A

---

5. Given the IPX address 00007C81.00A0.2494.E939, which of the following is the associated IPX network and node address?

   A. Net 00a0. node 2494 E939

   B. Net 00007C81 node 00a0.2494.e939

   C. Net 00A0.2494. node E939

   D. Net 7C81 00a0 Node 2494.e939

Answer: B

6. What was the default Ethernet encapsulation on NetWare 3.11?

   A. Ethernet_II

   B. Ethernet_802.3

   C. Ethernet_802.2

   D. Ethernet_snap

Answer: B

7. Which of the following are valid methods of including multiple encapsulations on a single interface?

   A. secondary networks

   B. subinterfaces

   C. additional physical interfaces

   D. There is no method to use multiple encapsulations on a single interface.

Answer: A, B

8. Which command would you use to see if you were receiving SAP and RIP `information on an interface?`

    A. `sho ipx route`

    B. `sho ipx traffic`

    C. `sho ipx interface`

    D. `sho ipx servers`

Answer: C

9. Which command would you use to see if the router is hearing your server SAPs?

    A. `sho ipx route`

    B. `sho ipx traffic`

    C. `sho ipx interface`

    D. `sho ipx servers`

Answer: D

10. Which commands will allow you to display the IPX address of an interface (choose all that apply)?

    A. `sh ipx route`

    B. `sh int`

    C. `sh prot`

    D. `debug ipx int`

Answer: C. The `sh int` command shows only the hardware address of the interface. However, by adding the network number of the segment in front of that address, you can figure out the IPX address. The `sh ipx int e0` command will show you the complete IPX address of that interface.

11. You want to forward IPX packets over multiple paths. What command do you use?

    A. `ipx forward maximum-paths`

    B. `ipx maximum-paths`

C. ipx forward

D. ipx forward-paths

Answer: B

12. Which of the following are valid Cisco encapsulation names (choose all that apply)?

   A. arpa = IPX Ethernet

   B. hdlc = HDLC on serial links

   C. novell-ether = IPX Ethernet_802.3

   D. novell-fddi = IPX Fddi_Raw

   E. sap = IEEE 802.2 on Ethernet, FDDI and Token Ring

   F. snap = IEEE 802.2 SNAP on Ethernet, FDDI, and Token Ring

Answer: All of the above

13. Which commands must be used to enable IPX networking?

   A. IPX routing, IPX number, network 790

   B. IPX routing, int e0, IPX network number 980

   C. IPX routing, int e0, IPX network 77790, encapsulation arpa

   D. IPX routing, IPX encapsulation SAP, int e0, network 789

Answer: C

14. What is the default encapsulation and frame type on an Ethernet interface when enabling Novell?

   A. SAP

   B. 802.2

   C. SNAP

   D. Token_SNAP

   E. 802.3

    F. Ethernet_II

Answer: E

15. If you are running Token Ring with Novell IPX routing, which encapsulation should you use?

    A. 802.5

    B. 802.3

    C. 802.2

    D. SNAP

Answer: B

16. If you want to run the 802.2 frame type on your Ethernet interface, which encapsulation type should you choose?

    A. SNAP

    B. 802.2

    C. Ethernet_II

    D. SAP

    E. Novell-Ether

Answer: D

17. If you want to enable Ethernet_II frame type on your Ethernet interface, which encapsulation should you use?

    A. ARPA

    B. RARPA

    C. SAP

    D. RIP

    E. SNAP

    F. Novell-Ether

Answer: A

18. Which of the following is the correct syntax for configuring a subinterface?

    A. config t, int e0, ipx network 100, encap sap

    B. config t, int e0, sub 100, ipx 100

    C. config t, int e0.100, ipx network 100 encap arpa sec

    D. config t, int e0.100, ipx network 100 encap arpa

Answer: D

19. Which command will show the network servers advertising on your network?

    A. sh novell

    B. sh ipx sap

    C. sh ipx servers

    D. sh servers

Answer: C

20. Which command displays the status of the IPX interfaces configured in the router and the parameters configured on each interface?

    A. sh ipx int

    B. sh int

    C. sh ipx stat

    D. sh ip config

Answer: A

Chapter 10

1. IP standard access lists use which of the following as a basis for permitting or denying packets?

    A. Source address

    B. Destination address

    C. Protocol

    D. Port

Answer: A

2. IP extended access lists use which of the following as a basis for permitting or denying packets?

    A. Source address

    B. Destination address

    C. Protocol

    D. Port

    E. All of the above

Answer: E

3. To specify all hosts in the class B IP network 172.16.0.0, which wildcard access list mask would you use?

    A. 255.255.0.0

    B. 255.255.255.0

    C. 0.0.255.255

    D. 0.255.255.255

    E. 0.0.0.255

Answer: C

4. Which of the following are valid ways to refer only to host 172.16.30.55 in an IP access list?

    A. 172.16.30.55 0.0.0.255

    B. 172.16.30.55 0.0.0.0

    C. any 172.16.30.55

    D. host 172.16.30.55

E. 0.0.0.0 172.16.30.55

F. ip any 172.16.30.55

Answer: B, D

5. Which of the following access lists will allow only WWW traffic into network 196.15.7.0?

   A. access-list 100 permit tcp any 196.15.7.0 0.0.0.255 eq www

   B. access-list 10 deny tcp any 196.15.7.0 eq www

   C. access-list 100 permit 196.15.7.0 0.0.0.255 eq www

   D. access-list 10 permit tcp any 196.15.7.0 0.0.0.255

   E. access-list 10 permit www 196.15.7.0 0.0.0.255

Answer: A

6. Which of the following will show which ports have IP access lists applied?

   A. show ip port

   B. show access-list

   C. show ip interface

   D. show access-list interface

   E. show running config

Answer: C, E

7. Which of the following are logged when IP access list logging is enabled?

   A. Source address

   B. Source port

   C. Destination address

   D. Destination port

   E. Time

F. Protocol

G. Access list line number

H. Access list number

Answer: A, B, C, D, F, H

8. Which of the following is a valid IPX standard access list?

A. `access-list 800 permit 30 50`

B. `access-list 900 permit 30 50`

C. `access-list permit all 30 50`

D. `access-list 800 permit 30 50 eq SAP`

E. `access-list 900 permit -1 50`

Answer: A

9. Which of the following can be logged by IPX extended access lists?

A. Source address

B. Source socket

C. Destination address

D. Destination socket

E. Access list line number

F. Time

G. Interface

H. Access list number

I. Protocol

Answer: A, B, C, D, H, I

10. Which of the following will apply IPX SAP access list 1050 for incoming traffic, assuming you're already at interface configuration?

A. `ipx access-group 1050 in`

B. `ipx input-sap-filter 1050`

C. `ipx access-list 1050 in`

D. `ipx input-sap-filter 1050 in`

E. `ipx access-group 1050`

Answer: B

11. Which of the following commands will show an extended access list 187?

A. `sh ip int`

B. `sh ip access-list`

C. `sh access-list 187`

D. `sh access-list 187 extended`

Answer: B, C (B will show ALL ip access lists, including 187.)

12. What is the IP extended access list range?

A. 1–99

B. 200–299

C. 1000–1999

D. 100–199

Answer: D

13. Which of the following commands is valid for creating an extended IP access list?

A. `access-list 101 permit ip host 172.16.30.0 any eq 21 log`

B. `access-list 101 permit tcp host 172.16.30.0 any eq 21 log`

C. `access-list 101 permit icmp 172.16.30.0 any ftp log`

D. `access-list 101 permit ip any eq 172.16.30.0 21 log`

Answer: B. IP doesn't have port associations, TCP does.

14. What is the extended IPX access list range?

    A. 100–199

    B. 900–999

    C. 1000–1999

    D. 700–799

Answer: B

15. What does the -1 mean in an extended IPX access list?

    A. Deny this host

    B. Deny any network or host

    C. Local network only, no hops

    D. Any host or any network

Answer: D

16. What are three ways to monitor IP access lists?

    A. `sh int`

    B. `sh ip interface`

    C. `sh run`

    D. `sh access-lists`

Answer: B, C, D

17. Which of the following can be used to monitor IPX access lists (choose all that apply)?

    A. `sh int`

    B. `sh access-lists`

    C. `sh flash`

    D. `sh ver`

    E. `sh ipx int`

    F. `sh run`

Answer: B, E, F

18. Which access configuration allows only traffic from network 172.16.0.0 to enter int s0?

A. Access-list 10 permit 172.16.0.0 0.0255.255, int s0, ip access-list 10 in

B. Access-group 10 permit 172.16.0.0 0.0.255.255, int s0, ip access-list 10 out

C. Access-list 10 permit 172.16.0.0 0.0.255.255, int s0, ip access-group 10 in

D. Access-list 10 permit 172.16.0.0 0.0.255.255, int s0, ip access-group 10 out

Answer: C

19. If you want to capture IPX access lists being hit, what command parameter do you add to your extended IPX access list?

A. Logging

B. Log

C. Enable log

D. Capture list

Answer: B

20. In an IP access list, you want to refer to host 172.16.50.1. What mask would you use to make the list as specific as possible?

A. 255.255.0.0

B. 0.0.0.0

C. 0.0.255.255

D. 0.255.255.255

Answer: B

Chapter 11

1. Which of the following best describes X.21bis?

A. Used for X.25 service in Europe

B. The Physical layer protocol used in X.25

C. Specifies packet switching type

D. Used in PLP call setup mode

Answer: B

2. When would you use ISDN?

A. To connect IBM mainframes

B. To connect local area networks (LANs) using digital service with dissimilar media

C. To support applications requiring high-speed voice, video, and data communications

D. When you need both a consistent and very high rate of data speed and transfer

Answer: C

3. How many frame relay encapsulation types are available with Cisco routers?

A. Three

B. Two

C. Four

D. Five

Answer: B

4. How many LMI types are available?

A. Two

B. Three

C. Four

D. Five

Answer: B. There are three LMI types: Cisco, Ansi, and Q.933A.

5. Regarding frame relay, which of the following statements are true?

    A. You must use Cisco encapsulation if connecting to non-Cisco equipment

    B. You must use ANSI encapsulation if connecting to non-Cisco equipment

    C. You must use IETF encapsulation if connecting to non-Cisco equipment

    D. You must use Q.933A encapsulation if connecting to non-Cisco equipment

Answer: C

6. What is the default LMI type?

    A. Q.933A

    B. ANSI

    C. IETF

    D. Cisco

Answer: D

7. Which of the following uses a PVC at layer 2?

    A. X.25

    B. ISDN

    C. Frame relay

    D. HDLC

Answer: C

8. Which ISDN protocol prefix specifies switching?

    A. I

    B. E

    C. S

    D. Q

Answer: D

9. If you wanted to view the DLCI and line speed for your frame relay network, which command would you use?

    A. `sh frame-relay`

    B. `sh run`

    C. `sh frame-relay dlci/speed`

    D. `sh frame-relay pvc`

Answer: D

10. Which of the following are valid WAN terms (choose all that apply)?

    A. DTE

    B. CPE

    C. demarc

    D. DCE

Answer: A, B, C, D

11. What does the ISDN Basic Rate Interface (BRI) provide?

    A. 23 B channels and one 64Kbps D channel

    B. Total bit rate of up to 1.544Mbps

    C. Two 56Kbps B channels and one 64Kbps D channel

    D. Two 64-Kbps B channels and one 16Kbps D channel

Answer: D

12. What is true about frame relay DLCI?

    A. DLCI is optional in a frame-relay network

    B. DLCI represents a single physical circuit

    C. DLCI identifies a logical connection between DTE devices

    D. DLCI is used to tag the beginning of a frame when using frame relay

Answer: C

13. Which ISDN protocol specifies basic telephone service?

    A. I

    B. T

    C. Q

    D. E

Answer: D

14. What does ISDN PRI support?

    A. One 64Kbps B channels and one 16Kbps D channel

    B. Two 64Kbps B channels and one 16Kbps D channel

    C. 24 B channels and one 64Kbps D channel

    D. 23 B channels and one 64Kbps D channel

Answer: D

15. Which command will list all configured PVCs and DLCIs?

    A. sh frame pvc

    B. sh frame

    C. sh frame lmi

    D. sh pvc

Answer: A

16. What is the default encapsulation on point-to-point links between two Cisco routers?

    A. SDLC

    B. HDLC

    C. Cisco

    D. ANSI

Answer: B

17. What are HDLC transfer modes used for?

   A. Connection-orientated services

   B. Connectionless services

   C. Media access

   D. Data transfer

Answer: C

18. What is true when using DDR?

   A. You should use dynamic routing

   B. You must use static routing

   C. You should use ISDN

   D. SDLC is the preferred encapsulation

Answer: B

19. What information is provided by the local management interface (choose all that apply)?

   A. The status of virtual circuits

   B. The current DLCI values

   C. The global or local significance of the DLCI values

   D. LMI encapsulation type

Answer: A, B, C

20. What ISDN protocol specifies concepts, terminology, and services?

   A. I

   B. S

   C. Q

   D. E

Answer: A

APPENDIX

B

Configuring AppleTalk

This appendix introduces AppleTalk and describes the basics of enabling AppleTalk traffic to cross your internetwork. First, we'll cover the AppleTalk protocol stack and discuss the protocols relevant to communication across an internetwork. After that, we'll jump into AppleTalk addressing because it's quite different from both the IPX and IP methods. We'll finish by adding AppleTalk to the routers we've already used for IP and IPX. We'll enable an AppleTalk routing protocol called RTMP, assign our router interfaces AppleTalk addresses and zones, then discuss monitoring the AppleTalk traffic on those interfaces.

Introduction to AppleTalk Configuration

For quite some time, many a network administrator has believed that AppleTalk is an unworthy internetwork protocol that's best confined to the LAN. Even though Apple has made some significant improvements to it, this belief continues among network staff today. But the fact that there are entire industries dependent on the capabilities of these machines and given the profound loyalty of many Macintosh users, a network staffer's opinion can be pretty irrelevant sometimes. Few end users are as devoted to their platform as Mac users are. Let's face it, when the new CEO stacks a PC in the hall outside their office saying, "I use a Mac," or your newest client wants you to integrate their graphics department into the company's internetwork, you'll need the information presented in this appendix!

AppleTalk Protocol Stack

Let's begin by taking a look at the AppleTalk protocol stack in Figure B.1.

FIGURE B.1

AppleTalk compared
with the OSI reference
model

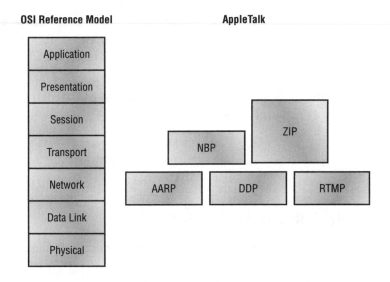

Because all of the protocols listed above aren't used in internetworking, we'll focus on those that are the most relevant.

EtherTalk, TokenTalk, FDDITalk

AppleTalk supports Ethernet, Token Ring, and FDDI at the Physical layer.

There's another Apple network called LocalTalk that is common on older Apple networks. LocalTalk was designed to run over regular telephone cable—it's very slow and unsupported on Cisco equipment.

AARP: AppleTalk Address Resolution Protocol is similar in function to ARP in TCP/IP in that it maps to layer 3 and addresses to layer 2 (hardware) addresses. AppleTalk also uses AARP in the dynamic assignment of node addresses.

DDP: Datagram Delivery Protocol provides unique addressing of all nodes on the AppleTalk internetwork and handles connectionless delivery of datagrams between any nodes.

NBP: Name Binding Protocol is similar to DNS in TCP/IP because it maps hostnames to layer 3 (Network) addresses, but NBP is more dynamic because instead of just translating names, it'll search the network and build a list of hostnames matching user or application needs.

RTMP: Routing Table Maintenance Protocol is a distance-vector routing protocol that uses split-horizon methods to control routing loops. RTMP updates are exchanged between routers at 10-second intervals.

ZIP: Zone Information Protocol is used to implement AppleTalk zones. ZIP maps zone names to network addresses allowing for the creation of logical networks.

AppleTalk Communication

AppleTalk communications occur in both zones and through location of service.

AppleTalk Zones

Zone—what's a zone? And how do zones work on the internetwork? Technically, a zone is a logical network segment independent of your physical network segment's constraints that AppleTalk gives you the option of creating. A logical network is a network that you define based on your users instead of your wiring. Why would you want to do that? Figure B.2 shows an example of how it's useful.

Just suppose that on each floor of your building you have a single network, meaning that you have to cross a router to communicate floor to floor as shown in Figure B.2, and that each floor has a unique network address (don't worry, we'll discuss addressing next). The physical network on each floor is the *broadcast domain*, and all users on a given floor share that one broadcast domain. AppleTalk uses broadcasts to locate services, which implies that your users on each floor can locate services on that floor using broadcasts—right? But we're going to complicate things a bit. Let's suppose that because of space considerations, marketing has offices on the first, third, and fifth floors. It gets worse: engineering has offices on the first and second floor. So, to summarize things: your *physical networks* are segmented by

FIGURE B.2

AppleTalk zone
example

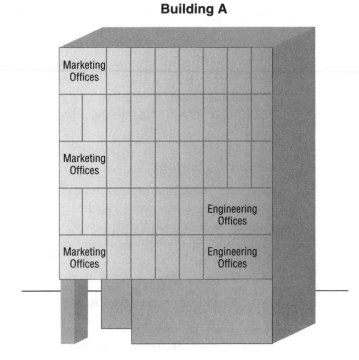

Building A

floor, but your *departments* segment your users, and you've got a problem because your physical network doesn't match your departmental needs.

AppleTalk is a wonderfully dynamic protocol for users locating network services, but as we said, it depends on broadcasts. End nodes within a department such as marketing need to be able to send and receive broadcast traffic to every other end node in marketing *regardless of the physical topology of the network*. What's a network administrator to do? Use AppleTalk zones, that's what.

The idea behind zones is to group users and network resources together into a logical zone that's independent of physical network constraints allowing all users within those zones to exchange broadcast traffic. Referring to the above example, you'd want to create a zone called marketing, then ensure that all broadcasts to the marketing zone reached the first-, third-, and fifth-floor segments. For your logical engineering zone, broadcasts would need to reach the first and second floors. With things set up like that, your users in marketing could exchange broadcast traffic and locate network services even though they span three separate segments—and AppleTalk takes care of this for you!

When you define the marketing zone and tell the router interfaces on the first, third, and fifth floors that they're part of the marketing zone, the routers build tables of zones and associated network addresses. In marketing's case, there would be three networks. The routers then take care of forwarding broadcast requests to the other network segments within the zone and of forwarding the replies back to the source workstation's network segment.

Location of Services

Mac users launch an application called Chooser to locate resources on the internetwork. Once users launch the Chooser application, they select an AppleTalk zone and type of resource (file server, printer, etc.). Chooser then builds a list of workstation names that offer the selected service in the selected zone. The user selects one of the names, then proceeds with their task. Let's get a more detailed idea of how this works:

1. The user launches the Chooser application.

2. The Chooser queries the router for available zones and presents the list of available zones to the user.

3. The user selects a zone and the type of resource requested.

4. The user's Mac issues an NBP request identifying the requested type of resource and zone.

5. The routers ensure that the NBP broadcast is forwarded to all specified network segments for that zone.

6. All nodes in the requested zone receive the NBP broadcast, and the nodes that provide the requested service reply to the requesting workstation.

7. Routers forward the responses to the requesting workstation's segment.

8. The Chooser builds a list of available services.

9. The user selects a service and proceeds with the task.

With this arrangement, it's pretty obvious that the proper forwarding of broadcasts is crucial to locating resources on the internetwork. From the users' perspective, they can just use the dynamic Chooser to find out which resources are available on the internetwork. And if you get a new laser printer, you simply plug it in, tell it which zone it's in, and Chooser will automatically let users looking for that type of printer know that it's available.

Okay—so let's take a look at how this works in an actual network. We are going to configure our internetwork as outlined in Figure B.3.

FIGURE B.3

Our internetwork with AppleTalk

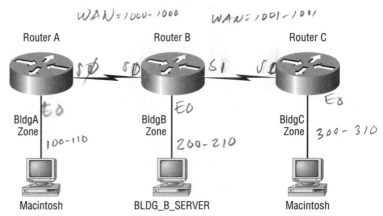

We have the workstation located on the BldgA zone, and we want to attach to the server BLDG_B_SERVER on the BldgB zone. Here is what Etherpeek sees on the BldgA zone, starting with step 2 from above:

Flags:	0x80 *802.3*
Status:	0x00
Packet Length:	64
Timestamp:	14:44:52.508000 06/18/1998

802.3 Header

Destination:	00:00:0c:5d:6e:c8
Source:	08:00:07:7f:62:cf
LLC Length:	29

802.2 Logical Link Control (LLC) Header

Dest. SAP:	0xaa SNAP
Source SAP:	0xaa SNAP *Group LLC Sublayer Management Function*
Command:	0x03 *Unnumbered Information*
Protocol:	08-00-07-80-9b ETalkPh2

Long DDP Header - Datagram Delivery Protocol

```
Unused:              %00
Hop Count:           %0000
Datagram Length:     21
DDP Checksum:        0x0000
Dest. Network:       107
Source Network:      101
Dest Node:           1
Source Node:         217
Dest. Socket:        6  Zone Information
Source Socket:       245
DDP Type:            3  ATP
```

ATP Header - AppleTalk Transaction Protocol

```
Function Code:           1  TReq
Control Information:     %000  ALO
TRel Timeout Indicator:  %000  30 seconds
Bitmap:                  %00000001  Need Packet(s) 0
Transaction ID:          2374
```

ZIP - Zone Information Protocol

```
Function:                8  GetZoneList
Unused:                  0
Start Index:             1
```

Extra bytes (Padding):

```
................  00 00 00 00 00 00 00 00 00 00 00 00 00
00 00 00
        .                        00
```

         Frame Check Sequence: 0x00000000

We can see in the ZIP header at the end of this packet that it's a type 8 (GetZoneList). So the workstation is requesting the zone list from the router. Notice that this is not a broadcast—it's a directed request between the workstation and router. Now let's take a look at the router's response:

```
Flags:          0x80  802.3
Status:         0x00
Packet Length:  69
Timestamp:      14:44:52.513000 06/18/1998
```

802.3 Header

Destination: 08:00:07:7f:62:cf
Source: 00:00:0c:5d:6e:c8
LLC Length: 51

802.2 Logical Link Control (LLC) Header

Dest. SAP: 0xaa   SNAP
Source SAP: 0xaa   SNAP
Command: 0x03   *Unnumbered Information*
Protocol: 08-00-07-80-9b   ETalkPh2

Long DDP Header - Datagram Delivery Protocol

Unused: %00
Hop Count: %0000
Datagram Length: 43
DDP Checksum: 0xe151
Dest. Network: 101
Source Network: 107
Dest Node: 217
Source Node: 1
Dest. Socket: 245
Source Socket: 6   *Zone Information*
DDP Type: 3   *ATP*

ATP Header - AppleTalk Transaction Protocol

Function Code: 2   *TResp*
Control Information: %010   *ALO   EOM*
TRel Timeout Indicator: %000   *30 seconds*
Sequence Number: 0   *Here is Packet 0*
Transaction ID: 2374

ZIP - Zone Information Protocol

Last Flag: 1
Unused: 0
Number of Zones: 4
Zone: BldgA
Zone: BldgB
Zone: BldgC
Zone: WAN
Frame Check Sequence: 0x00000000

Again, in the ZIP header, we can see that the router has listed the four zones on our internetwork for the requesting workstation. This information will be presented to the user by the Chooser application.

After the user selects a type of service and a zone, we can capture the packet described in step 4:

Flags:	0x80	*802.3*
Status:	0x00	
Packet Length:	64	
Timestamp:	14:44:55.319000 06/18/1998	

802.3 Header

Destination:	00:00:0c:5d:6e:c8
Source:	08:00:07:7f:62:cf
LLC Length:	46

802.2 Logical Link Control (LLC) Header

Dest. SAP:	0xaa	SNAP
Source SAP:	0xaa	SNAP *Group LLC Sublayer Management Function*
Command:	0x03	*Unnumbered Information*
Protocol:	08-00-07-80-9b	ETalkPh2

Long DDP Header - Datagram Delivery Protocol

Unused:	%00	
Hop Count:	%0000	
Datagram Length:	38	
DDP Checksum:	0x0000	
Dest. Network:	107	
Source Network:	101	
Dest Node:	1	
Source Node:	217	
Dest. Socket:	2	*Name Information*
Source Socket:	253	
DDP Type:	2	*NBP*

NBP - Name Binding Protocol

Function:	1	*BrRq - Broadcast Request*
Tuple Count:	1	
NBP ID:	6	

NBP Tuple # 1

Node Address:	101.217

Socket Number:253
Enumerator: 0
Object: =
Type: AFPServer
Zone: BldgB
Frame Check Sequence: 0x00000000

In this packet, we can tell from the NBP header that the request was for an AFPServer (AppleShare File Protocol Server) in the BldgB zone. Since the current segment isn't part of that zone, the router forwards the request to the appropriate segment. Finally, we can see the response from the server on the remote segment coming back to the requesting workstation as described in step 7:

Flags: 0x80 802.3
Status: 0x00
Packet Length:72
Timestamp: 14:44:58.547000 06/18/1998
802.3 Header
Destination: 08:00:07:7f:62:cf
Source: 00:00:0c:5d:6e:c8
LLC Length: 54
802.2 Logical Link Control (LLC) Header
Dest. SAP: 0xaa SNAP
Source SAP: 0xaa SNAP Group LLC Sublayer Management
Function
Command: 0x03 Unnumbered Information
Protocol: 08-00-07-80-9b ETalkPh2
Long DDP Header - Datagram Delivery Protocol
Unused: %00
Hop Count: %0010
Datagram Length: 46
DDP Checksum: 0x0000
Dest. Network: 101
Source Network: 204
Dest Node: 217
Source Node: 1
Dest. Socket: 253

```
       Source Socket:    2  Name Information
       DDP Type:         2  NBP
NBP - Name Binding Protocol
   Function:      3  LkUp-Reply
   Tuple Count:   1
   NBP ID:        6
NBP Tuple # 1
   Node Address: 204.1
   Socket Number:251
   Enumerator:    1
   Object:        BLDG_B_SERVER
   Type:          AFPServer
   Zone:          *
Frame Check Sequence:   0x00000000
```

Here we can see in the NBP response the network address of the responding device (204.1), the device's type (an AFPServer), and its name (BLDG_B_SERVER). The requesting workstation now knows everything it needs to know to communicate across the internetwork with the server.

AppleTalk Addressing

AppleTalk uses a 24-bit address written in dotted decimal format network.node. The network portion is always 16 bits long and the node portion is always eight bits long, so like IPX, there's no subnetting and no classes. And there are two versions of AppleTalk—Phase 1 and Phase 2. In Phase 1, there were some rather nasty limitations in addressing. See Table B.1.

T A B L E B.1 AppleTalk Phase 1 Addressing	**AppleTalk Phase 1**	
	Number of network addresses per segment	1
	Number of host addresses per network	127
	Number of server addresses per network	127
	Number of zones per network	1

Wow—we're limited to 127 host addresses per segment because the node address is defined in only eight bits! And since you can have only one network address per segment, the number of nodes per segment is also really limited. As if that weren't enough, there's also a limitation of one zone per network imposed on us, obliterating an administrator's ability to create multiple logical networks within the same segment! Yikes—there's gotta be a better way! Thankfully, Apple thought so too. Let's take a look at some changes made for AppleTalk Phase 2 in Table B.2.

T A B L E B.2 AppleTalk Phase 2 Addressing	**AppleTalk Phase 2**	
	Number of network addresses per segment	unlimited
	Number of host addresses per network	unlimited
	Number of server addresses per network	unlimited
	Number of zones per network	255

Okay, now we're talking—with Phase 2 there can be an unlimited number of network addresses per segment! Plus, there are ample node addresses available, despite the fact that network addresses are still only eight bits long.

There really isn't an unlimited number of networks available per segment—you're still limited by the 16-bit network portion of the address, giving you approximately 65,000 potential networks. But it's highly unlikely you'd ever need anywhere near 65,000 network addresses for a single network!

Also, we can now have multiple zones per network, allowing us to create multiple logical networks (zones) within a single AppleTalk network.

As is the case with IP, there are a few reserved network and node addresses. Network address 0 (zero) is reserved for use by nodes that haven't yet learned their segment's address, so it can't be assigned. Node addresses 254 and 255 are also reserved and can't be assigned to nodes.

The technique used by AppleTalk Phase 2 to assign multiple network addresses to a single segment is called *extended addressing*. Instead of having a single network address on a segment, you can assign a range—an extension—of addresses to a segment. Here's an example: a non-extended address for a segment could be network 100, and an extended address for the same segment could be network 100–110—a range of 11 network addresses (100, 101, . . ., 110). But what if you have even more node addresses? Well, how about network 100–1000 (901 network addresses). Need fewer node addresses? Try network 100–100 (one network address). All you have to do is specify a range of network addresses you want included on the segment in the extended address. Pretty easy, huh?

AppleTalk nodes dynamically obtain node addresses upon start-up. When a new machine starts up, it sends out a ZIP to find the network address, or the address range if extended addressing is being used. The machine then selects a random node address and issues an AARP to see if anyone is using that particular network node address. If there's no response, the machine will continue using that address. Node addressing is completely dynamic and requires no administration.

When an AppleTalk node starts up, it sets up a provisional address. If the node is being started for the very first time, it chooses, at random, a network number between 65,280 and 65,534. This range is referred to as the *start-up range*. The node number is also chosen at random. If the node has been started before, it will use its previous address as a "hint." In either case, the node will use AARP to check whether the selected provisional address is in use. If the address is in use, it will select another node number and check again. If the node is using a "hint" and subsequently exhausts all available node numbers without finding an unused address, it will choose a new network address from the start-up range and a new node number and then repeat the check for an unused address.

Once the node has selected an unused provisional address, it can send a ZIP GetNetInfo request to a router to determine the actual segment's cable range. If the network number for the provisional address falls between the segment's cable range, it is kept. Otherwise, a new network number is chosen from this cable range and the resulting node address will be checked using AARP. If the address is in use, the node will select another node number. If it runs out of node numbers, it will choose another network number from within the segment's cable range and repeat the node address check process. Once the node has found an unused network number and node number combination, these will become its final node address. The address will be saved and used as a future "hint."

Enabling AppleTalk on Cisco Routers

The configuration tasks for AppleTalk are similar to those required for IPX configuration. First, we'll enable AppleTalk routing in global configuration mode and then configure each individual interface with the appropriate network and zone information.

Enabling AppleTalk Routing

Okay—let's get started configuring our test network. We'll set up the networks and zones as illustrated in Figure B.3.

Notice we're using an extended network address on all segments. The Ethernet networks will be assigned a range of 11 network addresses, and the serial networks will be assigned one. Also every segment, including the serial networks, is assigned to a zone. Assigning all serial interfaces to a single WAN zone is fairly common practice.

Without this first step, enabling AppleTalk routing from global configuration mode, we couldn't move on to configure individual interfaces:

```
RouterA#config t
Enter configuration commands, one per line.  End with CNTL/Z.
RouterA(config)#appletalk routing
RouterA(config)#^Z
RouterA#
```

Configuring AppleTalk on Interfaces

Our next step is to configure AppleTalk on each individual interface. We'll be configuring both network and zone information:

```
RouterA#config t
Enter configuration commands, one per line.  End with CNTL/Z.
RouterA(config)#int e0
RouterA(config-if)#appletalk cable-range 100-110
RouterA(config-if)#appletalk zone BldgA
RouterA(config-if)#int s0
RouterA(config-if)#appletalk cable-range 1000-1000
RouterA(config-if)#appletalk zone WAN
RouterA(config-if)#^Z
```

```
RouterA#
```

The command to assign extended network addresses is

```
appletalk cable-range <range>
```

If we wanted to assign non-extended network addresses we could use the `appletalk address <address>` command. As detailed above, it's still possible to assign a single network address when using extended addressing. Here, we've used the cable-range command for consistency.

That's it! The router is now configured. But before we go into monitoring AppleTalk, here are the configurations for RouterB and RouterC:

RouterB

```
RouterB#config t
Enter configuration commands, one per line.  End with CNTL/Z.
RouterB(config)#appletalk routing
RouterB(config)#int e0
RouterB(config-if)#appletalk cable-range 200-210
RouterB(config-if)#appletalk zone BldgB
RouterB(config-if)#int s0
RouterB(config-if)#appletalk cable-range 1000-1000
RouterB(config-if)#appletalk zone WAN
RouterB(config-if)#int s1
RouterB(config-if)#appletalk cable-range 1001-1001
RouterB(config-if)#appletalk zone WAN
RouterB(config-if)#^Z
RouterB#
```

RouterC

```
RouterC#config t
Enter configuration commands, one per line.  End with CNTL/Z.
RouterC(config)#appletalk routing
RouterC(config)#int e0
RouterC(config-if)#appletalk cable-range 300-310
RouterC(config-if)#appletalk zone BldgC
RouterC(config-if)#int s0
RouterC(config-if)#appletalk cable-range 1001-1001
```

```
RouterC(config-if)#appletalk zone WAN
RouterC(config-if)#^Z
RouterC#
```

Notice when we configured the two serial interfaces on a common segment, they received identical cable-range and zone information. Whenever you have multiple interfaces on a common segment, their network and zone configuration must be identical for AppleTalk to function properly. There's an exception called *discovery mode* that we will discuss shortly.

At this point, you may be wondering when we're going to configure a routing protocol. The answer is that we already have! When we entered the command

```
RouterA(config)#appletalk routing
```

in global configuration mode, we automatically enabled RTMP on all interfaces that we configured subsequently for AppleTalk. RTMP is the default routing protocol, and it can be changed. Take a look at the following command:

```
RouterA#config t
Enter configuration commands, one per line.  End with CNTL/Z.
RouterA(config)#int e0
RouterA(config-if)#appletalk protocol ?
  eigrp  Enable AT/EIGRP processing on this interface
  rtmp   Enable RTMP processing on this interface
RouterA(config-if)#^Z
```

Notice that we have two routing protocol choices on each interface. Once again, RTMP is enabled by default on each interface unless we manually change it.

NOTE Additional AppleTalk routing protocols, such as AURP and EIGRP, will be covered in *CCNP: Advanced Cisco Router Configuration* by Sybex.

Now that the network is set up and running, here is an Etherpeek look at an RTMP update from RouterA's Ethernet interface:

```
Flags:          0x80  802.3
Status:         0x00
Packet Length:73
```

Timestamp:	20:56:30.689000 06/18/1998

802.3 Header

Destination:	09:00:07:ff:ff:ff
Source:	00:00:0c:5d:6e:c8
LLC Length:	55

802.2 Logical Link Control (LLC) Header

Dest. SAP:	0xaa	SNAP	
Source SAP:	0xaa	SNAP	*Null LSAP*
Command:	0x03	*Unnumbered Information*	
Protocol:	08-00-07-80-9b	*ETalkPh2*	

Long DDP Header - Datagram Delivery Protocol

Unused:	%00	
Hop Count:	%0000	
Datagram Length:	47	
DDP Checksum:	0xd978	
Dest. Network:	0	
Source Network:	106	
Dest Node:	255	
Source Node:	74	
Dest. Socket:	1	*RTMP*
Source Socket:	1	*RTMP*
DDP Type:	1	*RTMP Response or Data*

RTMP - Routing Table Maintenance Protocol

Router's Net:	106
ID Length:	8
Router's Node ID:	74

RTMP Tuple # 1

Range Start:	100	
Range Flag:	%100	*Extended*
Distance:	0	
Range End:	110	
Version:	0x82	

RTMP Tuple # 2

Range Start:	200	
Range Flag:	%100	*Extended*
Distance:	1	

Range End:	210	
Version:	0x82	

RTMP Tuple # 3

Range Start:	300	
Range Flag:	%100	*Extended*
Distance:	2	
Range End:	310	
Version:	0x82	

RTMP Tuple # 4

Range Start:	1000	
Range Flag:	%100	*Extended*
Distance:	0	
Range End:	1000	
Version:	0x82	

RTMP Tuple # 5

Range Start:	1001	
Range Flag:	%100	*Extended*
Distance:	1	
Range End:	1001	
Version:	0x82	
Frame Check Sequence:	0x00000000	

Notice that, just as we expected, each of our network cable-ranges is listed in the RTMP update. Take a look at Figure B.4. Notice that the time stamps on each of the RTMP updates received from RouterA are at equal 10-second intervals—again, just as we expected.

Before we go on, let's take a look at our final router configurations:

RouterA

```
RouterA#wr t
Building configuration...

Current configuration:
!
version 11.3
no service password-encryption
!
```

FIGURE B.4

AppleTalk RTMP
updates

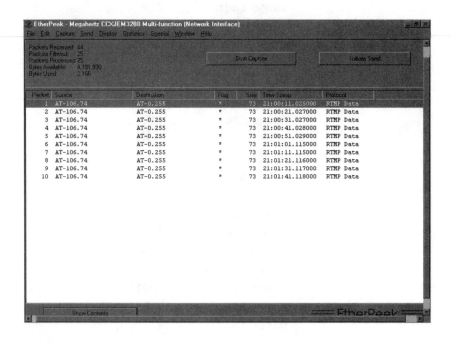

```
hostname RouterA
!
enable secret 5 $1$YMNO$Pz1r4tEg1E91wcKrNUIOHO
enable password password
!
appletalk routing
!
interface Ethernet0
 ip address 172.16.10.1 255.255.255.0
 appletalk cable-range 100-110 101.83
 appletalk zone BldgA
 no mop enabled
!
interface Serial0
 ip address 172.16.20.1 255.255.255.0
 no ip mroute-cache
 appletalk cable-range 1000-1000 1000.5
```

```
 appletalk zone WAN
!
interface Serial1
 no ip address
 shutdown
!
router rip
 redistribute connected
 network 172.16.0.0
!
ip classless
!
line con 0
line aux 0
line vty 0 4
 password password2
 login
!
end

RouterA#
```

RouterB

```
RouterB#wr t
Building configuration...

Current configuration:
!
version 11.3
no service password-encryption
!
hostname RouterB
!
enable secret 5 $1$hbRx$RuNTv6S.oJYs6L/OEEcey/
enable password password
!
```

```
appletalk routing
!
interface Ethernet0
 ip address 172.16.30.1 255.255.255.0
 appletalk cable-range 200-210 204.210
 appletalk zone BldgB
 no mop enabled
!
interface Serial0
 ip address 172.16.20.2 255.255.255.0
 no ip mroute-cache
 bandwidth 56
 appletalk cable-range 1000-1000 1000.77
 appletalk zone WAN
 clockrate 56000
!
interface Serial1
 ip address 172.16.40.1 255.255.255.0
 bandwidth 56
 appletalk cable-range 1001-1001 1001.79
 appletalk zone WAN
 clockrate 56000
!
router rip
 redistribute connected
 network 172.16.0.0
!
ip classless
!
line con 0
line aux 0
line vty 0 4
 password password2
 login
!
end

RouterB#
```

RouterC

```
RouterC#wr t
Building configuration...

Current configuration:
!
version 11.3
no service password-encryption
!
hostname RouterC
!
enable secret 5 $1$D6/k$SDGQc4haThdggG1I7LOWM1
enable password password
!
appletalk routing
!
interface Ethernet0
 ip address 172.16.50.1 255.255.255.0
 appletalk cable-range 300-310 306.192
 appletalk zone BldgC
!
interface Serial0
 ip address 172.16.40.2 255.255.255.0
 no ip mroute-cache
 appletalk cable-range 1001-1001 1001.216
 appletalk zone WAN
!
interface Serial1
 no ip address
 shutdown
!
router rip
 redistribute connected
 network 172.16.0.0
!
```

```
ip classless
!
line con 0
line aux 0
line vty 0 4
 password password2
 login
!
end

RouterC#
```

Discovery Mode

Suppose we have a single Ethernet segment with three attached Cisco routers on our AppleTalk internetwork. We've already mentioned that we're required to have the same network and zone information configured on each interface sharing the common segment. Now we could configure this by hand, but there is another way (see Figure B.5).

FIGURE B.5

Configuring AppleTalk using a seed router

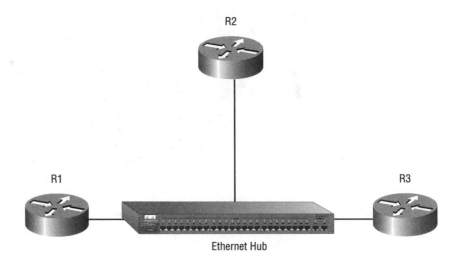

R2

R1

R3

Ethernet Hub

R1's Ethernet will be configured as normal, with cable-range and zone information. It'll be used as the *seed router*—the router that provides cable-range and zone information to other routers on the network. R2's and R3's Ethernet interfaces will be placed in discovery mode, meaning they'll learn cable-range and zone information from R1. There are two ways to configure R2 or R3:

- Enter a cable range of 0–0. This tells the router to learn its address from a seed router on the network.

- Enter the command `appletalk discovery` at the interface configuration instead of cable-range and zone information.

Discovery mode cannot be used on serial interfaces.

Below are examples of this configuration:

```
R1#config t
Enter configuration commands, one per line.  End with CNTL/Z.
R1(config)#int e0
R1(config-if)#appletalk cable-range 100-101
R1(config-if)#appletalk zone Information Systems
R1(config-if)#^Z
R1#


R2#config t
Enter configuration commands, one per line.  End with CNTL/Z.
R2(config)#int e0
R2(config-if)#appletalk cable-range 0-0
R2(config-if)#^Z
R2#


R3#config t
Enter configuration commands, one per line.  End with CNTL/Z.
R3(config)#int e0
```

```
R3(config-if)#appletalk cable-range 5-5
R3(config-if)#appletalk discovery
R3(config-if)#^Z
R3#
```

Now, both R2 and R3 will learn network and zone information from R1. Even though R3 has a defined cable-range of 5–5, the `appletalk discovery` command will force the router to learn its network and zone from the seed router. If we need to reconfigure this segment, we just need to modify R1 (the seed router), and R2 and R3 will then learn the new information from it the next time R2 and R3 are rebooted or when AppleTalk is restarted on the interface.

Any router will function as a seed router once it has obtained its node address information.

Monitoring AppleTalk Traffic

There are several useful commands used to monitor AppleTalk once the interfaces have been configured. As always, remember to use the context-sensitive help when exploring IOS commands.

To verify zone information, we'll use the `show appletalk zone` command on RouterA:

```
RouterA#show appletalk zone
Name                              Network(s)
BldgA                             100-110
BldgB                             200-210
BldgC                             300-310
WAN                               1001-1001 1000-1000
Total of 4 zones
RouterA#
```

Notice that all zones are listed by the router along with corresponding network cable-range information.

Next, let's check out the AppleTalk routing table on RouterA by using the `show appletalk route` command.

```
RouterA#show appletalk route
Codes: R - RTMP derived, E - EIGRP derived, C - connected, A
- AURP, S - static  P - proxy
5 routes in internet
```

The first zone listed for each entry is its default (primary) zone.

```
C Net 100-110 directly connected, Ethernet0, zone BldgA
R Net 200-210 [1/G] via 1000.77, 0 sec, Serial0, zone BldgB
R Net 300-310 [2/G] via 1000.77, 0 sec, Serial0, zone BldgC
C Net 1000-1000 directly connected, Serial0, zone WAN
R Net 1001-1001 [1/G] via 1000.77, 0 sec, Serial0, zone WAN
RouterA#
```

Here we have Net 100–110 and 1000–1000 directly connected, with the remaining networks accessible via Serial0. The "R" in the first column indicates that the routes were learned via RTMP.

NOTE

RTMP uses hop count as a metric and reports the number of hops to remote networks. For the route to Net 300-310, the [2/G] indicates that network 300–310 is 2 hops away, as seen in the above output. The maximum number of hops allowed by RTMP is 30.

There are several ways to view AppleTalk interface information. The first is to use the show appletalk interface brief command, as follows:

```
RouterA#show appletalk interface brief
Interface        Address      Config         Status/Line
Protocol    Atalk Protocol
Ethernet0        101.83       Extended       up        up
Serial0          1000.5       Extended       up        up
Serial1          unassigned   not config'd   administratively
down n/a
RouterA#
```

This command summarizes each interface's AppleTalk configuration on a single line, and it's helpful to get a quick look at all of the router's interfaces. Now, let's use the show appletalk interface command to get some more detailed information.

```
RouterA#show appletalk interface
Ethernet0 is up, line protocol is up
  AppleTalk cable range is 100-110
  AppleTalk address is 101.83, Valid
  AppleTalk zone is "BldgA"
  AppleTalk address gleaning is disabled
  AppleTalk route cache is enabled
Serial0 is up, line protocol is up
  AppleTalk cable range is 1000-1000
  AppleTalk address is 1000.5, Valid
  AppleTalk zone is "WAN"
  AppleTalk port configuration verified by 1000.77
  AppleTalk address gleaning is not supported by hardware
  AppleTalk route cache is enabled
Serial1 is administratively down, line protocol is down
  AppleTalk protocol processing disabled
RouterA#
```

We now have more detailed information about each interface, including cable-range and zone information. Let's get a look at the overall AppleTalk configuration using the show appletalk globals command, which summarizes the overall AppleTalk activities of the router:

```
RouterA#show appletalk globals
AppleTalk global information:
  Internet is incompatible with older, AT Phase1, routers.
  There are 5 routes in the internet.
  There are 4 zones defined.
  Logging of significant AppleTalk events is disabled.
  ZIP resends queries every 10 seconds.
  RTMP updates are sent every 10 seconds.
  RTMP entries are considered BAD after 20 seconds.
  RTMP entries are discarded after 60 seconds.
  AARP probe retransmit count: 10, interval: 200 msec.
  AARP request retransmit count: 5, interval: 1000 msec.
  DDP datagrams will be checksummed.
  RTMP datagrams will be strictly checked.
```

```
        RTMP routes may not be propagated without zones.
        Routes will not be distributed between routing protocols.
        Routing between local devices on an interface will not be
performed.
        IPTalk uses the udp base port of 768 (Default).
        AppleTalk EIGRP is not enabled.
        Alternate node address format will not be displayed.
        Access control of any networks of a zone hides the zone.
    RouterA#
```

Anyone who has used the `ping` command when troubleshooting an IP network knows how valuable this function can be. You can ping using AppleTalk from your Cisco router. As we saw above, on RouterA the Ethernet interface has AppleTalk address 101.83. Let's ping the Mac at address 107.183:

```
RouterA#ping appletalk
Target AppleTalk address: 107.183
Repeat count [5]:
Datagram size [100]:
Timeout in seconds [2]:
Verbose [n]:
Sweep range of sizes [n]:
Type escape sequence to abort.
Sending 5, 100-byte AppleTalk Echos to 107.183, timeout is 2
seconds:
!!!!!
Success rate is 100 percent (5/5), round-trip min/avg/max = 8/8/
12 ms
RouterA#
```

The ! marks indicate a successful Ping.

There are several debug options for AppleTalk. Below is a list of context-sensitive help for apple debug options:

```
RouterA#debug apple ?
    arp                 Appletalk address resolution protocol
    aurp-connection     AURP connection
    aurp-packet         AURP packets
    aurp-update         AURP routing updates
```

domain	AppleTalk Domain function
eigrp-all	All AT/EIGRP functions
eigrp-external	AT/EIGRP external functions
eigrp-hello	AT/EIGRP hello functions
eigrp-packet	AT/EIGRP packet debugging
eigrp-query	AT/EIGRP query functions
eigrp-redistribution	AT/EIGRP route redistribution
eigrp-request	AT/EIGRP external functions
eigrp-target	Appletalk/EIGRP for targeting address
eigrp-update	AT/EIGRP update functions
errors	Information about errors
events	Appletalk special events
fs	Appletalk fast-switching
iptalk	IPTalk encapsulation and functionality
load-balancing	AppleTalk load-balancing
macip	MacIP functions
nbp	Name Binding Protocol (NBP) functions
packet	Per-packet debugging
redistribution	Route Redistribution
remap	AppleTalk Remap function
responder	AppleTalk responder debugging
routing	(RTMP&EIGRP) functions
rtmp	(RTMP) functions
zip	Zone Information Protocol functions

Many of these are beyond the scope of this book. However, there are several that could prove useful in troubleshooting. For example, here is the output of debug apple rtmp on RouterA:

```
RouterA#debug apple rtmp
AppleTalk RTMP routing debugging is on
RouterA#
AT: src=Serial0:1000.5, dst=1000-1000, size=16, 1 rte, RTMP pkt sent
AT: src=Ethernet0:101.83, dst=100-110, size=34, 4 rtes, RTMP pkt sent
AT: Route ager starting on Main AT RoutingTable (5 active nodes)
AT: Route ager finished on Main AT RoutingTable (5 active nodes)
AT: RTMP from 1000.77 (new 0,old 3,bad 0,ign 0, dwn 0)
```

```
AT: src=Serial0:1000.5, dst=1000-1000, size=16, 1 rte, RTMP pkt sent
AT: src=Ethernet0:101.83, dst=100-110, size=34, 4 rtes, RTMP pkt sent
AT: Route ager starting on Main AT RoutingTable (5 active nodes)
AT: Route ager finished on Main AT RoutingTable (5 active nodes)
AT: RTMP from 1000.77 (new 0,old 3,bad 0,ign 0, dwn 0)
AT: src=Serial0:1000.5, dst=1000-1000, size=16, 1 rte, RTMP pkt sent
AT: src=Ethernet0:101.83, dst=100-110, size=34, 4 rtes, RTMP pkt sent
```

Here we can see information on RTMP broadcasts originating at this
router (the first two lines beginning "AT: src="). Notice the split horizon
working on the two interfaces—there are four routes advertised to the
Ethernet interface, and only one route advertised to the serial interface.
Remember the rule: Never advertise a route out on the interface you learned
it from. There's only one route not learned of via the serial interface, so it's
only that one route sent to the serial interface, and so on.

We can also see RTMP broadcasts arriving from RouterB—the lines
beginning "AT: RTMP from." From this, we can determine that there are no
new routes and three old routes being learned from the update.

Summary

We introduced the AppleTalk protocol stack and looked at the protocols most relevant to networking. They were AARP, DDP, NBP, RTMP,
and ZIP. We discussed addressing, how AppleTalk nodes locate network
resources, and how zones work.

We then discussed configuration of routing and interfaces. We mentioned
discovery mode and looked at several of the monitoring and debugging
options available.

APPENDIX

C

Password Recovery

At times it may be necessary to recover lost or forgotten passwords. The following procedure works for all routers running Cisco IOS release 10.0 and later. It also works for all routers that have a software configuration register, regardless of the IOS version.

Step 1

Enter ROM monitor mode. Power cycle the router, and within 60 seconds after the router comes up, press the Break key. This can be ALT+Break or CTRL+Break. The exact key sequence is dependent upon the terminal emulator. Some emulators use ALT+B while others use a pull-down menu.

```
RouterA#
System Bootstrap, Version 5.2(8a), RELEASE SOFTWARE
Copyright (c) 1986-1995 by cisco Systems
2500 processor with 6144 Kbytes of main memory

Abort at 0x106D0D4 (PC)
>
```

If you are using Windows Terminal or HyperTerminal, use CTRL+Break. (The Break key is all the way to the top right of our keyboard.)

Step 2

Enter the o command to read the configuration register's original value.

```
>o
Configuration register = 0xFFFF2102 at last boot
Bit#    Configuration register option settings:
15      Diagnostic mode disabled
```

14	IP broadcasts do not have network numbers
13	Boot default ROM software if network boot fails
12-11	Console speed is 9600 baud
10	IP broadcasts with ones
08	Break disabled
07	OEM disabled
06	Ignore configuration disabled
03-00	Boot file is cisco2-2500 (or 'boot system' command)

```
>
```

Notice that your configuration register settings are in the top line: remember the last four digits for later. Ours show 2102.

Step 3

Set bit 6 by typing **o/r 0x2142**. → *bypass password.*

```
>o/r 0x2142
```

Step 4

Initialize and reboot the router by typing an **i**.

```
>i

System Bootstrap, Version 5.2(8a), RELEASE SOFTWARE
Copyright (c) 1986-1995 by cisco Systems
```

We typed an **i** and the router rebooted. The router will then go into setup mode. Answer NO to all questions in setup mode.

Step 5

Enter privileged mode by typing **en**.

Step 6

Restore the configuration file stored in NVRAM to active RAM using the `copy star run` command. This will restore the original configuration file.

Step 7

> 7 Sh △ Ver   ⟍ — verify Configuration - register

Get into configuration mode, then change the virtual configuration register back to the original contents. Remember the 2102?

```
RouterA#config t
Enter configuration commands, one per line.  End with CNTL/Z.
RouterA(config)#config-register 0x2102   — Normal boot
```

Step 8

Type **sh run** to see the passwords. If they are encrypted, create new passwords by using the following commands:

```
RouterA#config t
Enter configuration commands, one per line.  End with CNTL/Z.
RouterA(config)#enable secret todd
RouterA(config)#enable password lammle
RouterA(config)#line con 0
RouterA(config-line)#login
RouterA(config-line)#password todd
RouterA(config-line)#line vty 0 4
RouterA(config-line)#login
RouterA(config-line)#password todd
RouterA(config-line)#end
```

Step 9

Make sure your configuration register is set to the original settings by typing a **sh ver.**

```
Configuration register is 0x2142 (will be 0x2102 at next
reload)
```

If you do not see your original settings in the will be 0xNNNN at next reload section, execute step 7 again.

APPENDIX

D

Decimal-to-Binary Table

T A B L E D.1: Decimal-to-Binary Table *(continued)*

Decimal	Hex	Binary	Decimal	Hex	Binary	Decimal	Hex	Binary	Decimal	Hex	Binary
168	A8	10101000	190	BE	10111110	212	D4	11010100	234	EA	11101010
169	A9	10101001	191	BF	10111111	213	D5	11010101	235	EB	11101011
170	AA	10101010	192	C0	11000000	214	D6	11010110	236	EC	11101100
171	AB	10101011	193	C1	11000001	215	D7	11010111	237	ED	11101101
172	AC	10101100	194	C2	11000010	216	D8	11011000	238	EE	11101110
173	AD	10101101	195	C3	11000011	217	D9	11011001	239	EF	11101111
174	AE	10101110	196	C4	11000100	218	DA	11011010	240	F0	11110000
175	AF	10101111	197	C5	11000101	219	DB	11011011	241	F1	11110001
176	B0	10110000	198	C6	11000110	220	DC	11011100	242	F2	11110010
177	B1	10110001	199	C7	11000111	221	DD	11011101	243	F3	11110011
178	B2	10110010	200	C8	11001000	222	DE	11011110	244	F4	11110100
179	B3	10110011	201	C9	11001001	223	DF	11011111	245	F5	11110101
180	B4	10110100	202	CA	11001010	224	E0	11100000	246	F6	11110110
181	B5	10110101	203	CB	11001011	225	E1	11100001	247	F7	11110111
182	B6	10110110	204	CC	11001100	226	E2	11100010	248	F8	11111000
183	B7	10110111	205	CD	11001101	227	E3	11100011	249	F9	11111001
184	B8	10111000	206	CE	11001110	228	E4	11100100	250	FA	11111010
185	B9	10111001	207	CF	11001111	229	E5	11100101	251	FB	11111011
186	BA	10111010	208	D0	11010000	230	E6	11100110	252	FC	11111100
187	BB	10111011	209	D1	11010001	231	E7	11100111	253	FD	11111101
188	BC	10111100	210	D2	11010010	232	E8	11101000	254	FE	11111110
189	BD	10111101	211	D3	11010011	233	E9	11101001	255	FF	11111111

T A B L E D.1: Decimal-to-Binary Table *(continued)*

Decimal	Hex	Binary	Decimal	Hex	Binary	Decimal	Hex	Binary	Decimal	Hex	Binary
84	54	01010100	105	69	01101001	126	7E	01111110	147	93	10010011
85	55	01010101	106	6A	01101010	127	7F	01111111	148	94	10010100
86	56	01010110	107	6B	01101011	128	80	10000000	149	95	10010101
87	57	01010111	108	6C	01101100	129	81	10000001	150	96	10010110
88	58	01011000	109	6D	01101101	130	82	10000010	151	97	10010111
89	59	01011001	110	6E	01101110	131	83	10000011	152	98	10011000
90	5A	01011010	111	6F	01101111	132	84	10000100	153	99	10011001
91	5B	01011011	112	70	01110000	133	85	10000101	154	9A	10011010
92	5C	01011100	113	71	01110001	134	86	10000110	155	9B	10011011
93	5D	01011101	114	72	01110010	135	87	10000111	156	9C	10011100
94	5E	01011110	115	73	01110011	136	88	10001000	157	9D	10011101
95	5F	01011111	116	74	01110100	137	89	10001001	158	9E	10011110
96	60	01100000	117	75	01110101	138	8A	10001010	159	9F	10011111
97	61	01100001	118	76	01110110	139	8B	10001011	160	A0	10100000
98	62	01100010	119	77	01110111	140	8C	10001100	161	A1	10100001
99	63	01100011	120	78	01111000	141	8D	10001101	162	A2	10100010
100	64	01100100	121	79	01111001	142	8E	10001110	163	A3	10100011
101	65	01100101	122	7A	01111010	143	8F	10001111	164	A4	10100100
102	66	01100110	123	7B	01111011	144	90	10010000	165	A5	10100101
103	67	01100111	124	7C	01111100	145	91	10010001	166	A6	10100110
104	68	01101000	125	7D	01111101	146	92	10010010	167	A7	10100111

T A B L E D.1: Decimal-to-Binary Table

Decimal	Hex	Binary	Decimal	Hex	Binary	Decimal	Hex	Binary	Decimal	Hex	Binary
0	00	00000000	21	15	00010101	42	2A	00101010	63	3F	00111111
1	01	00000001	22	16	00010110	43	2B	00101010	64	40	01000000
2	02	00000010	23	17	00010111	44	2C	00101011	65	41	01000001
3	03	00000011	24	18	00011000	45	2D	00101100	66	42	01000010
4	04	00000100	25	19	00011001	46	2E	00101101	67	43	01000011
5	05	00000101	26	1A	00011010	47	2F	00101110	68	44	01000100
6	06	00000110	27	1B	00011011	48	30	00101111	69	45	01000101
7	07	00000111	28	1C	00011100	49	31	00110000	70	46	01000110
8	08	00001000	29	1D	00011101	50	32	00110001	71	47	01000111
9	09	00001001	30	1E	00011110	51	33	00110010	72	48	01001000
10	0A	00001010	31	1F	00011111	52	34	00110011	73	49	01001001
11	0B	00001011	32	20	00100000	53	35	00110100	74	4A	01001010
12	0C	00001100	33	21	00100001	54	36	00110101	75	4B	01001011
13	0D	00001101	34	22	00100010	55	37	00110110	76	4C	01001100
14	0E	00001110	35	23	00100011	56	38	00110111	77	4D	01001101
15	0F	00001111	36	24	00100100	57	39	00111000	78	4E	01001110
16	10	00010000	37	25	00100101	58	3A	00111001	79	4F	01001111
17	11	00010001	38	26	00100110	59	3B	00111010	80	50	01010000
18	12	00010010	39	27	00100111	60	3C	00111011	81	51	01010001
19	13	00010011	40	28	00101000	61	3D	00111100	82	52	01010010
20	14	00010100	41	29	00101001	62	3E	00111101	83	53	01010011

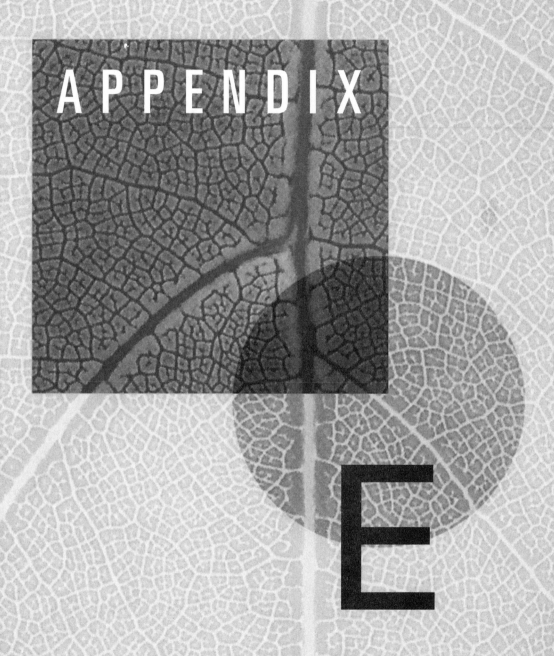

APPENDIX

E

RFC 1700

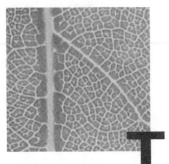

he well-known ports are controlled and assigned by the IANA, and on most systems can be used only by system (or root) processes or by programs executed by privileged users.

Ports are used in the TCP RFC793 to name the ends of logical connections that carry long-term conversations. For the purpose of providing services to unknown callers, a service contact port is defined. This list specifies the port used by the server process as its contact port. The contact port is sometimes called the *well-known port*.

To the extent possible, these same port assignments are used with the UDP RFC768. The assigned ports use a small portion of the possible port numbers. For many years the assigned ports were in the range 0–255. Recently, the range for assigned ports managed by the IANA has been expanded to the range 0–1023. The following table lists the well-known port numbers.

T A B L E E.1: Well-Known Port Numbers

Keyword	Decimal	Description
	0/tcp	Reserved
	0/udp	Reserved
tcpmux	1/tcp	TCP Port Service Multiplexer
tcpmux	1/udp	TCP Port Service Multiplexer
compressnet	2/tcp	Management Utility
compressnet	2/udp	Management Utility
compressnet	3/tcp	Compression Process
compressnet	3/udp	Compression Process

TABLE E.1: Well-Known Port Numbers *(continued)*

Keyword	Decimal	Description
#	4/tcp	Unassigned
#	4/udp	Unassigned
rje	5/tcp	Remote Job Entry
rje	5/udp	Remote Job Entry
#	6/tcp	Unassigned
#	6/udp	Unassigned
echo	7/tcp	Echo
echo	7/udp	Echo
#	8/tcp	Unassigned
#	8/udp	Unassigned
discard	9/tcp	Discard
discard	9/udp	Discard
#	10/tcp	Unassigned
#	10/udp	Unassigned
systat	11/tcp	Active Users
systat	11/udp	Active Users
#	12/tcp	Unassigned
#	12/udp	Unassigned
daytime	13/tcp	Daytime
daytime	13/udp	Daytime

T A B L E E.1: Well-Known Port Numbers *(continued)*

Keyword	Decimal	Description
#	14/tcp	Unassigned
#	14/udp	Unassigned
#	15/tcp	Unassigned (was netstat)
#	15/udp	Unassigned
#	16/tcp	Unassigned
#	16/udp	Unassigned
qotd	17/tcp	Quote of the Day
qotd	17/udp	Quote of the Day
msp	18/tcp	Message Send Protocol
msp	18/udp	Message Send Protocol
chargen	19/tcp	Character Generator
chargen	19/udp	Character Generator
ftp-data	20/tcp	File Transfer (Default Data)
ftp-data	20/udp	File Transfer (Default Data)
ftp	21/tcp	File Transfer (Control)
ftp	21/udp	File Transfer (Control)
#	22/tcp	Unassigned
#	22/udp	Unassigned
telnet	23/tcp	Telnet
telnet	23/udp	Telnet

T A B L E E.1:   Well-Known Port Numbers   *(continued)*

Keyword	Decimal	Description
	24/tcp	Any private mail system
	24/udp	Any private mail system
smtp	25/tcp	Simple Mail Transfer
smtp	25/udp	Simple Mail Transfer
#	26/tcp	Unassigned
#	26/udp	Unassigned
nsw-fe	27/tcp	NSW User System FE
nsw-fe	27/udp	NSW User System FE
#	28/tcp	Unassigned
#	28/udp	Unassigned
msg-icp	29/tcp	MSG ICP
msg-icp	29/udp	MSG ICP
#	30/tcp	Unassigned
#	30/udp	Unassigned
msg-auth	31/tcp	MSG Authentication
msg-auth	31/udp	MSG Authentication
#	32/tcp	Unassigned
#	32/udp	Unassigned
dsp	33/tcp	Display Support Protocol
dsp	33/udp	Display Support Protocol

T A B L E E.1: Well-Known Port Numbers *(continued)*

Keyword	Decimal	Description
#	34/tcp	Unassigned
#	34/udp	Unassigned
	35/tcp	Any private printer server
	35/udp	Any private printer server
#	36/tcp	Unassigned
#	36/udp	Unassigned
time	37/tcp	Time
time	37/udp	Time
rap	38/tcp	Route Access Protocol
rap	38/udp	Route Access Protocol
rlp	39/tcp	Resource Location Protocol
rlp	39/udp	Resource Location Protocol
#	40/tcp	Unassigned
#	40/udp	Unassigned
graphics	41/tcp	Graphics
graphics	41/udp	Graphics
nameserver	42/tcp	Hostname Server
nameserver	42/udp	Hostname Server
nicname	43/tcp	Who Is
nicname	43/udp	Who Is

T A B L E E.1: Well-Known Port Numbers *(continued)*

Keyword	Decimal	Description
mpm-flags	44/tcp	MPM FLAGS Protocol
mpm-flags	44/udp	MPM FLAGS Protocol
mpm	45/tcp	Message Processing Module (recv)
mpm	45/udp	Message Processing Module (recv)
mpm-snd	46/tcp	MPM (default send)
mpm-snd	46/udp	MPM (default send)
ni-ftp	47/tcp	NI FTP
ni-ftp	47/udp	NI FTP
auditd	48/tcp	Digital Audit Daemon
auditd	48/udp	Digital Audit Daemon
login	49/tcp	Login Host Protocol
login	49/udp	Login Host Protocol
re-mail-ck	50/tcp	Remote Mail Checking Protocol
re-mail-ck	50/udp	Remote Mail Checking Protocol
la-maint	51/tcp	IMP Logical Address Maintenance
la-maint	51/udp	IMP Logical Address Maintenance

T A B L E E.1: Well-Known Port Numbers *(continued)*

Keyword	Decimal	Description
xns-time	52/tcp	XNS Time Protocol
xns-time	52/udp	XNS Time Protocol
domain	53/tcp	Domain Name Server
domain	53/udp	Domain Name Server
xns-ch	54/tcp	XNS Clearinghouse
xns-ch	54/udp	XNS Clearinghouse
isi-gl	55/tcp	ISI Graphics Language
isi-gl	55/udp	ISI Graphics Language
xns-auth	56/tcp	XNS Authentication
xns-auth	56/udp	XNS Authentication
	57/tcp	Any private terminal access
	57/udp	Any private terminal access
xns-mail	58/tcp	XNS Mail
xns-mail	58/udp	XNS Mail
	59/tcp	Any private file service
	59/udp	Any private file service
	60/tcp	Unassigned
	60/udp	Unassigned
ni-mail	61/tcp	NI MAIL
ni-mail	61/udp	NI MAIL

T A B L E E.1:   Well-Known Port Numbers   *(continued)*

Keyword	Decimal	Description
acas	62/tcp	ACA Services
acas	62/udp	ACA Services
#	63/tcp	Unassigned
#	63/udp	Unassigned
covia	64/tcp	Communications Integrator (CI)
covia	64/udp	Communications Integrator (CI)
tacacs-ds	65/tcp	TACACS-Database Service
tacacs-ds	65/udp	TACACS-Database Service
sql*net	66/tcp	Oracle SQL*NET
sql*net	66/udp	Oracle SQL*NET
bootps	67/tcp	Bootstrap Protocol Server
bootps	67/udp	Bootstrap Protocol Server
bootpc	68/tcp	Bootstrap Protocol Client
bootpc	68/udp	Bootstrap Protocol Client
tftp	69/tcp	Trivial File Transfer
tftp	69/udp	Trivial File Transfer
gopher	70/tcp	Gopher
gopher	70/udp	Gopher
netrjs-1	71/tcp	Remote Job Service
netrjs-1	71/udp	Remote Job Service

T A B L E E.1: Well-Known Port Numbers *(continued)*

Keyword	Decimal	Description
netrjs-2	72/tcp	Remote Job Service
netrjs-2	72/udp	Remote Job Service
netrjs-3	73/tcp	Remote Job Service
netrjs-3	73/udp	Remote Job Service
netrjs-4	74/tcp	Remote Job Service
netrjs-4	74/udp	Remote Job Service
	75/tcp	Any private dial-out service
	75/udp	Any private dial-out service
deos	76/tcp	Distributed External Object Store
deos	76/udp	Distributed External Object Store
	77/tcp	Any private RJE service
	77/udp	Any private RJE service
vettcp	78/tcp	vettcp
vettcp	78/udp	vettcp
finger	79/tcp	Finger
finger	79/udp	Finger
www-http	80/tcp	World Wide Web HTTP
www-http	80/udp	World Wide Web HTTP
hosts2-ns	81/tcp	HOSTS2 Name Server

T A B L E E.1: Well-Known Port Numbers *(continued)*

Keyword	Decimal	Description
hosts2-ns	81/udp	HOSTS2 Name Server
xfer	82/tcp	XFER Utility
xfer	82/udp	XFER Utility
mit-ml-dev	83/tcp	MIT ML Device
mit-ml-dev	83/udp	MIT ML Device
ctf	84/tcp	Common Trace Facility
ctf	84/udp	Common Trace Facility
mit-ml-dev	85/tcp	MIT ML Device
mit-ml-dev	85/udp	MIT ML Device
mfcobol	86/tcp	Micro Focus Cobol
mfcobol	86/udp	Micro Focus Cobol
	87/tcp	Any private terminal link
	87/udp	Any private terminal link
kerberos	88/tcp	Kerberos
kerberos	88/udp	Kerberos
su-mit-tg	89/tcp	SU/MIT Telnet Gateway
su-mit-tg	89/udp	SU/MIT Telnet Gateway
dnsix	90/tcp	DNSIX Securit Attribute Token Map
dnsix	90/udp	DNSIX Securit Attribute Token Map

T A B L E E.1: Well-Known Port Numbers *(continued)*

Keyword	Decimal	Description
mit-dov	91/tcp	MIT Dover Spooler
mit-dov	91/udp	MIT Dover Spooler
npp	92/tcp	Network Printing Protocol
npp	92/udp	Network Printing Protocol
dcp	93/tcp	Device Control Protocol
dcp	93/udp	Device Control Protocol
objcall	94/tcp	Tivoli Object Dispatcher
objcall	94/udp	Tivoli Object Dispatcher
supdup	95/tcp	SUPDUP
supdup	95/udp	SUPDUP
dixie	96/tcp	DIXIE Protocol Specification
dixie	96/udp	DIXIE Protocol Specification
swift-rvf	97/tcp	Swift Remote Virtual File Protocol
swift-rvf	97/udp	Swift Remote Virtual File Protocol
tacnews	98/tcp	TAC News
tacnews	98/udp	TAC News
metagram	99/tcp	Metagram Relay
metagram	99/udp	Metagram Relay
newacct	100/tcp	Unauthorized use

T A B L E E.1:   Well-Known Port Numbers   *(continued)*

Keyword	Decimal	Description
hostname	101/tcp	NIC Hostname Server
hostname	101/udp	NIC Hostname Server
iso-tsap	102/tcp	ISO-TSAP
iso-tsap	102/udp	ISO-TSAP
gppitnp	103/tcp	Genesis Point-to-Point Trans Net
gppitnp	103/udp	Genesis Point-to-Point Trans Net
acr-nema	104/tcp	ACR-NEMA Digital Imag. & Comm. 300
acr-nema	104/udp	ACR-NEMA Digital Imag. & Comm. 300
csnet-ns	105/tcp	Mailbox Name Nameserver
csnet-ns	105/udp	Mailbox Name Nameserver
3com-tsmux	106/tcp	3COM-TSMUX
3com-tsmux	106/udp	3COM-TSMUX
rtelnet	107/tcp	Remote Telnet Service
rtelnet	107/udp	Remote Telnet Service
snagas	108/tcp	SNA Gateway Access Server
snagas	108/udp	SNA Gateway Access Server
pop2	109/tcp	Post Office Protocol, Version 2

T A B L E   E.1:   Well-Known Port Numbers   *(continued)*

Keyword	Decimal	Description
pop2	109/udp	Post Office Protocol, Version 2
pop3	110/tcp	Post Office Protocol, Version 3
pop3	110/udp	Post Office Protocol, Version 3
sunrpc	111/tcp	SUN Remote Procedure Call
sunrpc	111/udp	SUN Remote Procedure Call
mcidas	112/tcp	McIDAS Data Transmission Protocol
mcidas	112/udp	McIDAS Data Transmission Protocol
auth	113/tcp	Authentication Service
auth	113/udp	Authentication Service
audionews	114/tcp	Audio News Multicast
audionews	114/udp	Audio News Multicast
sftp	115/tcp	Simple File Transfer Protocol
sftp	115/udp	Simple File Transfer Protocol
ansanotify	116/tcp	ANSA REX Notify
ansanotify	116/udp	ANSA REX Notify
uucp-path	117/tcp	UUCP Path Service
uucp-path	117/udp	UUCP Path Service
sqlserv	118/tcp	SQL Services
sqlserv	118/udp	SQL Services

T A B L E E.1: Well-Known Port Numbers *(continued)*

Keyword	Decimal	Description
nntp	119/tcp	Network News Transfer Protocol
nntp	119/udp	Network News Transfer Protocol
cfdptkt	120/tcp	CFDPTKT
cfdptkt	120/udp	CFDPTKT
erpc	121/tcp	Encore Expedited Remote Pro.Call
erpc	121/udp	Encore Expedited Remote Pro.Call
smakynet	122/tcp	SMAKYNET
smakynet	122/udp	SMAKYNET
ntp	123/tcp	Network Time Protocol
ntp	123/udp	Network Time Protocol
ansatrader	124/tcp	ANSA REX Trader
ansatrader	124/udp	ANSA REX Trader
locus-map	125/tcp	Locus PC-Interface Net Map Ser
locus-map	125/udp	Locus PC-Interface Net Map Ser
unitary	126/tcp	Unisys Unitary Login
unitary	126/udp	Unisys Unitary Login

T A B L E E.1:   Well-Known Port Numbers   *(continued)*

Keyword	Decimal	Description
locus-con	127/tcp	Locus PC-Interface Conn Server
locus-con	127/udp	Locus PC-Interface Conn Server
gss-xlicen	128/tcp	GSS X License Verification
gss-xlicen	128/udp	GSS X License Verification
pwdgen	129/tcp	Password Generator Protocol
pwdgen	129/udp	Password Generator Protocol
cisco-fna	130/tcp	Cisco FNATIVE
cisco-fna	130/udp	Cisco FNATIVE
cisco-tna	131/tcp	Cisco TNATIVE
cisco-tna	131/udp	Cisco TNATIVE
cisco-sys	132/tcp	Cisco SYSMAINT
cisco-sys	132/udp	Cisco SYSMAINT
statsrv	133/tcp	Statistics Service
statsrv	133/udp	Statistics Service
ingres-net	134/tcp	INGRES-NET Service
ingres-net	134/udp	INGRES-NET Service
loc-srv	135/tcp	Location Service
loc-srv	135/udp	Location Service
profile	136/tcp	PROFILE Naming System

T A B L E E.1: Well-Known Port Numbers *(continued)*

Keyword	Decimal	Description
profile	136/udp	PROFILE Naming System
netbios-ns	137/tcp	NETBIOS Name Service
netbios-ns	137/udp	NETBIOS Name Service
netbios-dgm	138/tcp	NETBIOS Datagram Service
netbios-dgm	138/udp	NETBIOS Datagram Service
netbios-ssn	139/tcp	NETBIOS Session Service
netbios-ssn	139/udp	NETBIOS Session Service
emfis-data	140/tcp	EMFIS Data Service
emfis-data	140/udp	EMFIS Data Service
emfis-cntl	141/tcp	EMFIS Control Service
emfis-cntl	141/udp	EMFIS Control Service
bl-idm	142/tcp	Britton-Lee IDM
bl-idm	142/udp	Britton-Lee IDM
imap2	143/tcp	Interim Mail Access Protocol v2
imap2	143/udp	Interim Mail Access Protocol v2
news	144/tcp	News
news	144/udp	News
uaac	145/tcp	UAAC Protocol
uaac	145/udp	UAAC Protocol

T A B L E E.1: Well-Known Port Numbers *(continued)*

Keyword	Decimal	Description
iso-tp0	146/tcp	ISO-IP0
iso-tp0	146/udp	ISO-IP0
iso-ip	147/tcp	ISO-IP
iso-ip	147/udp	ISO-IP
cronus	148/tcp	CRONUS-SUPPORT
cronus	148/udp	CRONUS-SUPPORT
aed-512	149/tcp	AED 512 Emulation Service
aed-512	149/udp	AED 512 Emulation Service
sql-net	150/tcp	SQL-NET
sql-net	150/udp	SQL-NET
hems	151/tcp	HEMS
hems	151/udp	HEMS
bftp	152/tcp	Background File Transfer Program
bftp	152/udp	Background File Transfer Program
sgmp	153/tcp	SGMP
sgmp	153/udp	SGMP
netsc-prod	154/tcp	NETSC
netsc-prod	154/udp	NETSC
netsc-dev	155/tcp	NETSC

T A B L E E.1: Well-Known Port Numbers *(continued)*

Keyword	Decimal	Description
netsc-dev	155/udp	NETSC
sqlsrv	156/tcp	SQL Service
sqlsrv	156/udp	SQL Service
knet-cmp	157/tcp	KNET/VM Command/Message Protocol
knet-cmp	157/udp	KNET/VM Command/Message Protocol
pcmail-srv	158/tcp	PCMail Server
pcmail-srv	158/udp	PCMail Server
nss-routing	159/tcp	NSS-Routing
nss-routing	159/udp	NSS-Routing
sgmp-traps	160/tcp	SGMP-TRAPS
sgmp-traps	160/udp	SGMP-TRAPS
snmp	161/tcp	SNMP
snmp	161/udp	SNMP
snmptrap	162/tcp	SNMPTRAP
snmptrap	162/udp	SNMPTRAP
cmip-man	163/tcp	CMIP/TCP Manager
cmip-man	163/udp	CMIP/TCP Manager
cmip-agent	164/tcp	CMIP/TCP Agent
smip-agent	164/udp	CMIP/TCP Agent

T A B L E E.1:   Well-Known Port Numbers *(continued)*

Keyword	Decimal	Description
xns-courier	165/tcp	Xerox
xns-courier	165/udp	Xerox
s-net	166/tcp	Sirius Systems
s-net	166/udp	Sirius Systems
namp	167/tcp	NAMP
namp	167/udp	NAMP
rsvd	168/tcp	RSVD
rsvd	168/udp	RSVD
send	169/tcp	SEND
send	169/udp	SEND
print-srv	170/tcp	Network PostScript
print-srv	170/udp	Network PostScript
multiplex	171/tcp	Network Innovations Multiplex
multiplex	171/udp	Network Innovations Multiplex
cl/1	172/tcp	Network Innovations CL/1
cl/1	172/udp	Network Innovations CL/1
xyplex-mux	173/tcp	Xyplex
xyplex-mux	173/udp	Xyplex
mailq	174/tcp	MAILQ

T A B L E E.1: Well-Known Port Numbers *(continued)*

Keyword	Decimal	Description
mailq	174/udp	MAILQ
vmnet	175/tcp	VMNET
vmnet	175/udp	VMNET
genrad-mux	176/tcp	GENRAD-MUX
genrad-mux	176/udp	GENRAD-MUX
xdmcp	177/tcp	X Display Manager Control Protocol
xdmcp	177/udp	X Display Manager Control Protocol
nextstep	178/tcp	NextStep Window Server
NextStep	178/udp	NextStep Window Server
bgp	179/tcp	Border Gateway Protocol
bgp	179/udp	Border Gateway Protocol
ris	180/tcp	Intergraph
ris	180/udp	Intergraph
unify	181/tcp	Unify
unify	181/udp	Unify
audit	182/tcp	Unisys Audit SITP
audit	182/udp	Unisys Audit SITP
ocbinder	183/tcp	OCBinder
ocbinder	183/udp	OCBinder

T A B L E E.1: Well-Known Port Numbers *(continued)*

Keyword	Decimal	Description
ocserver	184/tcp	OCServer
ocserver	184/udp	OCServer
remote-kis	185/tcp	Remote-KIS
remote-kis	185/udp	Remote-KIS
kis	186/tcp	KIS Protocol
kis	186/udp	KIS Protocol
aci	187/tcp	Application Communication Interface
aci	187/udp	Application Communication Interface
mumps	188/tcp	Plus Five's MUMPS
mumps	188/udp	Plus Five's MUMPS
qft	189/tcp	Queued File Transport
qft	189/udp	Queued File Transport
gacp	190/tcp	Gateway Access Control Protocol
cacp	190/udp	Gateway Access Control Protocol
prospero	191/tcp	Prospero Directory Service
prospero	191/udp	Prospero Directory Service
osu-nms	192/tcp	OSU Network Monitoring System

T A B L E   E.1:   Well-Known Port Numbers   *(continued)*

Keyword	Decimal	Description
osu-nms	192/udp	OSU Network Monitoring System
srmp	193/tcp	Spider Remote Monitoring Protocol
srmp	193/udp	Spider Remote Monitoring Protocol
irc	194/tcp	Internet Relay Chat Protocol
irc	194/udp	Internet Relay Chat Protocol
dn6-nlm-aud	195/tcp	DNSIX Network Level Module Audit
dn6-nlm-aud	195/udp	DNSIX Network Level Module Audit
dn6-smm-red	196/tcp	DNSIX Session Mgt Module Audit Redir
dn6-smm-red	196/udp	DNSIX Session Mgt Module Audit Redir
dls	197/tcp	Directory Location Service
dls	197/udp	Directory Location Service
dls-mon	198/tcp	Directory Location Service Monitor
dls-mon	198/udp	Directory Location Service Monitor
smux	199/tcp	SMUX

T A B L E E.1: Well-Known Port Numbers *(continued)*

Keyword	Decimal	Description
smux	199/udp	SMUX
src	200/tcp	IBM System Resource Controller
src	200/udp	IBM System Resource Controller
at-rtmp	201/tcp	AppleTalk Routing Maintenance
at-rtmp	201/udp	AppleTalk Routing Maintenance
at-nbp	202/tcp	AppleTalk Name Binding
at-nbp	202/udp	AppleTalk Name Binding
at-3	203/tcp	AppleTalk Unused
at-3	203/udp	AppleTalk Unused
at-echo	204/tcp	AppleTalk Echo
at-echo	204/udp	AppleTalk Echo
at-5	205/tcp	AppleTalk Unused
at-5	205/udp	AppleTalk Unused
at-zis	206/tcp	AppleTalk Zone Information
at-zis	206/udp	AppleTalk Zone Information
at-7	207/tcp	AppleTalk Unused
at-7	207/udp	AppleTalk Unused

T A B L E E.1: Well-Known Port Numbers *(continued)*

Keyword	Decimal	Description
at-8	208/tcp	AppleTalk Unused
at-8	208/udp	AppleTalk Unused
tam	209/tcp	Trivial Authenticated Mail Protocol
tam	209/udp	Trivial Authenticated Mail Protocol
z39.50	210/tcp	ANSI Z39.50
z39.50	210/udp	ANSI Z39.50
914c/g	211/tcp	Texas Instruments 914C/G Terminal
914c/g	211/udp	Texas Instruments 914C/G Terminal
anet	212/tcp	ATEXSSTR
anet	212/udp	ATEXSSTR
ipx	213/tcp	IPX
ipx	213/udp	IPX
vmpwscs	214/tcp	VM PWSCS
vmpwscs	214/udp	VM PWSCS
softpc	215/tcp	Insignia Solutions
softpc	215/udp	Insignia Solutions
atls	216/tcp	Access Technology License Server

TABLE E.1: Well-Known Port Numbers *(continued)*

Keyword	Decimal	Description
atls	216/udp	Access Technology License Server
dbase	217/tcp	dBASE Unix
dbase	217/udp	dBASE Unix
mpp	218/tcp	Netix Message Posting Protocol
mpp	218/udp	Netix Message Posting Protocol
uarps	219/tcp	Unisys ARPs
uarps	219/udp	Unisys ARPs
imap3	220/tcp	Interactive Mail Access Protocol v3
imap3	220/udp	Interactive Mail Access Protocol v3
fln-spx	221/tcp	Berkeley rlogind with SPX auth
fln-spx	221/udp	Berkeley rlogind with SPX auth
rsh-spx	222/tcp	Berkeley rshd with SPX auth
rsh-spx	222/udp	Berkeley rshd with SPX auth
cdc	223/tcp	Certificate Distribution Center
cdc	223/udp	Certificate Distribution Center
#	224-241	Reserved

T A B L E E.1:   Well-Known Port Numbers *(continued)*

Keyword	Decimal	Description
#	242/tcp	Unassigned
#	242/udp	Unassigned
sur-meas	243/tcp	Survey Measurement
sur-meas	243/udp	Survey Measurement
#	244/tcp	Unassigned
#	244/udp	Unassigned
link	245/tcp	LINK
link	245/udp	LINK
dsp3270	246/tcp	Display Systems Protocol
dsp3270	246/udp	Display Systems Protocol
#	247-255	Reserved
#	256-343	Unassigned
pdap	344/tcp	Prospero Data Access Protocol
pdap	344/udp	Prospero Data Access Protocol
pawserv	345/tcp	Perf Analysis Workbench
pawserv	345/udp	Perf Analysis Workbench
zserv	346/tcp	Zebra server
zserv	346/udp	Zebra server
fatserv	347/tcp	Fatmen Server

T A B L E E.1: Well-Known Port Numbers *(continued)*

Keyword	Decimal	Description
fatserv	347/udp	Fatmen Server
csi-sgwp	348/tcp	Cabletron Management Protocol
csi-sgwp	348/udp	Cabletron Management Protocol
#	349-370	Unassigned
clearcase	371/tcp	Clearcase
clearcase	371/udp	Clearcase
ulistserv	372/tcp	Unix Listserv
ulistserv	372/udp	Unix Listserv
legent-1	373/tcp	Legent Corporation
legent-1	373/udp	Legent Corporation
legent-2	374/tcp	Legent Corporation
legent-2	374/udp	Legent Corporation
hassle	375/tcp	Hassle
hassle	375/udp	Hassle
nip	376/tcp	Amiga Envoy Network Inquiry Proto
nip	376/udp	Amiga Envoy Network Inquiry Proto
tnETOS	377/tcp	NEC Corporation

T A B L E E.1:   Well-Known Port Numbers *(continued)*

Keyword	Decimal	Description
tnETOS	377/udp	NEC Corporation
dsETOS	378/tcp	NEC Corporation
dsETOS	378/udp	NEC Corporation
is99c	379/tcp	TIA/EIA/IS-99 modem client
is99c	379/udp	TIA/EIA/IS-99 modem client
is99s	380/tcp	TIA/EIA/IS-99 modem server
is99s	380/udp	TIA/EIA/IS-99 modem server
hp-collector	381/tcp	hp performance data collector
hp-collector	381/udp	hp performance data collector
hp-managed-node	382/tcp	hp performance data managed node
hp-managed-node	382/udp	hp performance data managed node
hp-alarm-mgr	383/tcp	hp performance data alarm manager
hp-alarm-mgr	383/udp	hp performance data alarm manager
arns	384/tcp	A Remote Network Server System
arns	384/udp	A Remote Network Server System

T A B L E   E.1:   Well-Known Port Numbers   *(continued)*

Keyword	Decimal	Description
ibm-app	385/tcp	IBM Application
ibm-app	385/tcp	IBM Application
asa	386/tcp	ASA Message Router Object Def.
asa	386/udp	ASA Message Router Object Def.
aurp	387/tcp	Appletalk Update-Based Routing Pro.
aurp	387/udp	Appletalk Update-Based Routing Pro.
unidata-ldm	388/tcp	Unidata LDM Version 4
unidata-ldm	388/udp	Unidata LDM Version 4
ldap	389/tcp	Lightweight Directory Access Protocol
ldap	389/udp	Lightweight Directory Access Protocol
uis	390/tcp	UIS
uis	390/udp	UIS
synotics-relay	391/tcp	SynOptics SNMP Relay Port
synotics-relay	391/udp	SynOptics SNMP Relay Port
synotics-broker	392/tcp	SynOptics Port Broker Port
synotics-broker	392/udp	SynOptics Port Broker Port

T A B L E E.1: Well-Known Port Numbers *(continued)*

Keyword	Decimal	Description
dis	393/tcp	Data Interpretation System
dis	393/udp	Data Interpretation System
embl-ndt	394/tcp	EMBL Nucleic Data Transfer
embl-ndt	394/udp	EMBL Nucleic Data Transfer
netcp	395/tcp	NETscout Control Protocol
netcp	395/udp	NETscout Control Protocol
netware-ip	396/tcp	Novell Netware over IP
netware-ip	396/udp	Novell Netware over IP
mptn	397/tcp	Multi Protocol Trans. Net.
mptn	397/udp	Multi Protocol Trans. Net.
kryptolan	398/tcp	Kryptolan
kryptolan	398/udp	Kryptolan
#	399/tcp	Unassigned
#	399/udp	Unassigned
work-sol	400/tcp	Workstation Solutions
work-sol	400/udp	Workstation Solutions
ups	401/tcp	Uninterruptible Power Supply
ups	401/udp	Uninterruptible Power Supply
genie	402/tcp	Genie Protocol
genie	402/udp	Genie Protocol

T A B L E E.1: Well-Known Port Numbers *(continued)*

Keyword	Decimal	Description
decap	403/tcp	decap
decap	403/udp	decap
nced	404/tcp	nced
nced	404/udp	nced
ncld	405/tcp	ncld
ncld	405/udp	ncld
imsp	406/tcp	Interactive Mail Support Protocol
imsp	406/udp	Interactive Mail Support Protocol
timbuktu	407/tcp	Timbuktu
timbuktu	407/udp	Timbuktu
prm-sm	408/tcp	Prospero Resource Manager Sys. Man.
prm-sm	408/udp	Prospero Resource Manager Sys. Man.
prm-nm	409/tcp	Prospero Resource Manager Node Man.
prm-nm	409/udp	Prospero Resource Manager Node Man.
decladebug	410/tcp	DECLadebug Remote Debug Protocol
decladebug	410/udp	DECLadebug Remote Debug Protocol

T A B L E E.1.   Well-Known Port Numbers *(continued)*

Keyword	Decimal	Description
rmt	411/tcp	Remote MT Protocol
rmt	411/udp	Remote MT Protocol
synoptics-trap	412/tcp	Trap Convention Port
synoptics-trap	412/udp	Trap Convention Port
smsp	413/tcp	SMSP
smsp	413/udp	SMSP
infoseek	414/tcp	InfoSeek
infoseek	414/udp	InfoSeek
bnet	415/tcp	BNet
bnet	415/udp	BNet
silverplatter	416/tcp	Silverplatter
silverplatter	416/udp	Silverplatter
onmux	417/tcp	Onmux
onmux	417/udp	Onmux
hyper-g	418/tcp	Hyper-G
hyper-g	418/udp	Hyper-G
ariel1	419/tcp	Ariel
ariel1	419/udp	Ariel
smpte	420/tcp	SMPTE
smpte	420/udp	SMPTE

T A B L E E.1: Well-Known Port Numbers *(continued)*

Keyword	Decimal	Description
ariel2	421/tcp	Ariel
ariel2	421/udp	Ariel
ariel3	422/tcp	Ariel
ariel3	422/udp	Ariel
opc-job-start	423/tcp	IBM Operations Planning and Control Start
opc-job-start	423/udp	IBM Operations Planning and Control Start
opc-job-track	424/tcp	IBM Operations Planning and Control Track
opc-job-track	424/udp	IBM Operations Planning and Control Track
icad-el	425/tcp	ICAD
icad-el	425/udp	ICAD
smartsdp	426/tcp	smartsdp
smartsdp	426/udp	smartsdp
svrloc	427/tcp	Server Location
svrloc	427/udp	Server Location
ocs_cmu	428/tcp	OCS_CMU
ocs_cmu	428/udp	OCS_CMU
ocs_amu	429/tcp	OCS_AMU
ocs_amu	429/udp	OCS_AMU

T A B L E E.1: Well-Known Port Numbers *(continued)*

Keyword	Decimal	Description
utmpsd	430/tcp	UTMPSD
utmpsd	430/udp	UTMPSD
utmpcd	431/tcp	UTMPCD
utmpcd	431/udp	UTMPCD
iasd	432/tcp	IASD
iasd	432/udp	IASD
nnsp	433/tcp	NNSP
nnsp	433/udp	NNSP
mobileip-agent	434/tcp	MobileIP-Agent
mobileip-agent	434/udp	MobileIP-Agent
mobilip-mn	435/tcp	MobilIP-MN
mobilip-mn	435/udp	MobilIP-MN
dna-cml	436/tcp	DNA-CML
dna-cml	436/udp	DNA-CML
comscm	437/tcp	comscm
comscm	437/udp	comscm
dsfgw	438/tcp	dsfgw
dsfgw	438/udp	dsfgw
dasp	439/tcp	dasp
dasp	439/udp	dasp

T A B L E E.1: Well-Known Port Numbers *(continued)*

Keyword	Decimal	Description
sgcp	440/tcp	sgcp
sgcp	440/udp	sgcp
decvms-sysmgt	441/tcp	decvms-sysmgt
decvms-sysmgt	441/udp	decvms-sysmgt
cvc_hostd	442/tcp	cvc_hostd
cvc_hostd	442/udp	cvc_hostd
https	443/tcp	https
https	443/udp	https
snpp	444/tcp	Simple Network Paging Protocol
snpp	444/udp	Simple Network Paging Protocol
microsoft-ds	445/tcp	Microsoft-DS
microsoft-ds	445/udp	Microsoft-DS
ddm-rdb	446/tcp	DDM-RDB
ddm-rdb	446/udp	DDM-RDB
ddm-dfm	447/tcp	DDM-RFM
ddm-dfm	447/udp	DDM-RFM
ddm-byte	448/tcp	DDM-BYTE
ddm-byte	448/udp	DDM-BYTE
as-servermap	449/tcp	AS Server Mapper

T A B L E   E.1:   Well-Known Port Numbers   *(continued)*

Keyword	Decimal	Description
as-servermap	449/udp	AS Server Mapper
tserver	450/tcp	TServer
tserver	450/udp	TServer
#	451-511	Unassigned
exec	512/tcp	Remote process execution; authentication performed using passwords and Unix login names.
biff	512/udp	Used by mail system to notify users of new mail received; currently receives messages only from processes on the same machine.
login	513/tcp	Remote login a la telnet; automatic authentication. Performed based on privileged port numbers and distributed databases that identify "authentication domains."
who	513/udp	Maintains databases showing who's logged in to machines on a local net and the load average of the machine.
cmd	514/tcp	Like exec, but automatic authentication is performed as for login server.
syslog	514/udp	

T A B L E E.1: Well-Known Port Numbers *(continued)*

Keyword	Decimal	Description
printer	515/tcp	Spooler
printer	515/udp	Spooler
#	516/tcp	Unassigned
#	516/udp	Unassigned
talk	517/tcp	Like tenex link, but across machine—unfortunately, doesn't use link protocol (this is actually just a rendezvous port from which a tcp connection is established).
talk	517/udp	Like tenex link, but across machine—unfortunately, doesn't use link protocol (this is actually just a rendezvous port from which a tcp connection is established).
ntalk	518/tcp	
ntalk	518/udp	
utime	519/tcp	unixtime
utime	519/udp	unixtime
efs	520/tcp	Extended file name server
router	520/udp	Local routing process (on site); uses variant of Xerox XNS routing information protocol.
#	521-524	Unassigned

T A B L E   E.1:   Well-Known Port Numbers   *(continued)*

Keyword	Decimal	Description
timed	525/tcp	timeserver
timed	525/udp	timeserver
tempo	526/tcp	newdate
tempo	526/udp	newdate
#	527-529	Unassigned
courier	530/tcp	rpc
courier	530/udp	rpc
conference	531/tcp	chat
conference	531/udp	chat
netnews	532/tcp	readnews
netnews	532/udp	readnews
netwall	533/tcp	For emergency broadcasts
netwall	533/udp	For emergency broadcasts
#	534-538	Unassigned
apertus-ldp	539/tcp	Apertus Technologies Load Determination
apertus-ldp	539/udp	Apertus Technologies Load Determination
uucp	540/tcp	uucpd
uucp	540/udp	uucpd

T A B L E E.1: Well-Known Port Numbers *(continued)*

Keyword	Decimal	Description
uucp-rlogin	541/tcp	uucp-rlogin
uucp-rlogin	541/udp	uucp-rlogin
#	542/tcp	Unassigned
#	542/udp	Unassigned
klogin	543/tcp	
klogin	543/udp	
kshell	544/tcp	krcmd
kshell	544/udp	krcmd
#	545-549	Unassigned
new-rwho	550/tcp	new-who
new-rwho	550/udp	new-who
#	551-555	Unassigned
dsf	555/tcp	
dsf	555/udp	
remotefs	556/tcp	rfs server
remotefs	556/udp	rfs server
#	557-559	Unassigned
rmonitor	560/tcp	rmonitord
rmonitor	560/udp	rmonitord
monitor	561/tcp	

T A B L E E.1: Well-Known Port Numbers *(continued)*

Keyword	Decimal	Description
monitor	561/udp	
chshell	562/tcp	chcmd
chshell	562/udp	chcmd
#	563/tcp	Unassigned
#	563/udp	Unassigned
9pfs	564/tcp	Plan 9 file service
9pfs	564/udp	Plan 9 file service
whoami	565/tcp	whoami
whoami	565/udp	whoami
#	566-569	Unassigned
meter	570/tcp	demon
meter	570/udp	demon
meter	571/tcp	udemon
meter	571/udp	udemon
#	572-599	Unassigned
ipcserver	600/tcp	Sun IPC server
ipcserver	600/udp	Sun IPC server
nqs	607/tcp	nqs
nqs	607/udp	nqs
urm	606/tcp	Cray Unified Resource Manager

T A B L E E.1: Well-Known Port Numbers *(continued)*

Keyword	Decimal	Description
urm	606/udp	Cray Unified Resource Manager
sift-uft	608/tcp	Sender-Initiated/Unsolicited File Transfer
sift-uft	608/udp	Sender-Initiated/Unsolicited File Transfer
npmp-trap	609/tcp	npmp-trap
npmp-trap	609/udp	npmp-trap
npmp-local	610/tcp	npmp-local
npmp-local	610/udp	npmp-local
npmp-gui	611/tcp	npmp-gui
npmp-gui	611/udp	npmp-gui
ginad	634/tcp	ginad
ginad	634/udp	ginad
mdqs	666/tcp	
mdqs	666/udp	
doom	666/tcp	Doom Id Software
doom	666/tcp	Doom Id Software
elcsd	704/tcp	errlog copy/server daemon
elcsd	704/udp	errlog copy/server daemon
entrustmanager	709/tcp	EntrustManager

T A B L E E.1: Well-Known Port Numbers *(continued)*

Keyword	Decimal	Description
entrustmanager	709/udp	EntrustManager
netviewdm1	729/tcp	IBM NetView DM/6000 Server/Client
netviewdm1	729/udp	IBM NetView DM/6000 Server/Client
netviewdm2	730/tcp	IBM NetView DM/6000 send/tcp
netviewdm2	730/udp	IBM NetView DM/6000 send/tcp
netviewdm3	731/tcp	IBM NetView DM/6000 receive/tcp
netviewdm3	731/udp	IBM NetView DM/6000 receive/tcp
netgw	741/tcp	netGW
netgw	741/udp	netGW
netrcs	742/tcp	Network-based Rev. Cont. Sys.
netrcs	742/udp	Network-based Rev. Cont. Sys.
flexlm	744/tcp	Flexible License Manager
flexlm	744/udp	Flexible License Manager
fujitsu-dev	747/tcp	Fujitsu Device Control
fujitsu-dev	747/udp	Fujitsu Device Control
ris-cm	748/tcp	Russell Info Sci Calendar Manager
ris-cm	748/udp	Russell Info Sci Calendar Manager

T A B L E E.1: Well-Known Port Numbers *(continued)*

Keyword	Decimal	Description
kerberos-adm	749/tcp	Kerberos administration
kerberos-adm	749/udp	Kerberos administration
rfile	750/tcp	
loadav	750/udp	
pump	751/tcp	
pump	751/udp	
qrh	752/tcp	
qrh	752/udp	
rrh	753/tcp	
rrh	753/udp	
tell	754/tcp	send
tell	754/udp	send
nlogin	758/tcp	
nlogin	758/udp	
con	759/tcp	
con	759/udp	
ns	760/tcp	
ns	760/udp	
rxe	761/tcp	
rxe	761/udp	

T A B L E E.1:   Well-Known Port Numbers   *(continued)*

Keyword	Decimal	Description
quotad	762/tcp	
quotad	762/udp	
cycleserv	763/tcp	
cycleserv	763/udp	
omserv	764/tcp	
omserv	764/udp	
webster	765/tcp	
webster	765/udp	
phonebook	767/tcp	Phone
phonebook	767/udp	Phone
vid	769/tcp	
vid	769/udp	
cadlock	770/tcp	
cadlock	770/udp	
rtip	771/tcp	
rtip	771/udp	
cycleserv2	772/tcp	
cycleserv2	772/udp	
submit	773/tcp	
notify	773/udp	

T A B L E E.1: Well-Known Port Numbers *(continued)*

Keyword	Decimal	Description
rpasswd	774/tcp	
acmaint_dbd	774/udp	
entomb	775/tcp	
acmaint_transd	775/udp	
wpages	776/tcp	
wpages	776/udp	
wpgs	780/tcp	
wpgs	780/udp	
concert	786/tcp	Concert
concert	786/udp	Concert
mdbs_daemon	800/tcp	
mdbs_daemon	800/udp	
device	801/tcp	
device	801/udp	
xtreelic	996/tcp	Central Point Software
xtreelic	996/udp	Central Point Software
maitrd	997/tcp	
maitrd	997/udp	
busboy	998/tcp	
puparp	998/udp	

T A B L E   E.1:   Well-Known Port Numbers   *(continued)*

Keyword	Decimal	Description
garcon	999/tcp	
applix	999/udp	Applix ac
puprouter	999/tcp	
puprouter	999/udp	
cadlock	1000/tcp	
ock	1000/udp	
	1023/tcp	Reserved
	1024/udp	Reserved

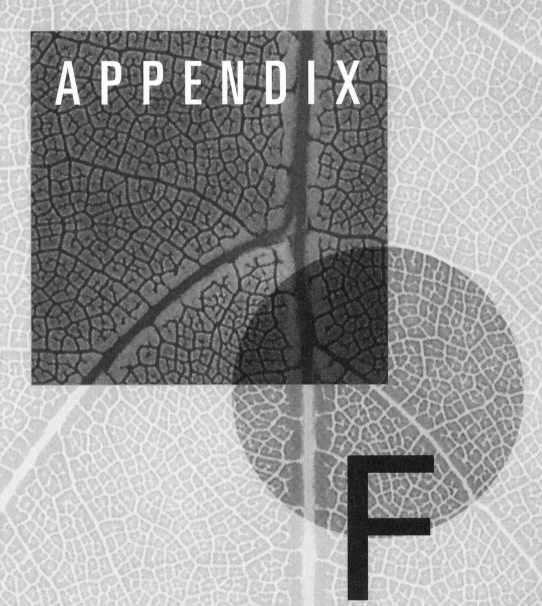

APPENDIX

F

Glossary

10Base2 10Mbps baseband Ethernet specification using 50-ohm thin coaxial cable. 10Base2, which is part of the IEEE 802.3 specification, has a distance limit of 185 meters per segment. *See also* Cheapernet, Ethernet, IEEE 802.3, and Thinnet.

10Base5 10Mbps baseband Ethernet specification using standard (thick) 50-ohm baseband coaxial cable. 10Base5, which is part of the IEEE 802.3 baseband Physical layer specification, has a distance limit of 500 meters per segment. *See also* Ethernet and IEEE 802.3.

10BaseF 10Mbps baseband Ethernet specification that refers to the 10BaseFB, 10BaseFL, and 10BaseFP standards for Ethernet over fiber-optic cabling. *See also* 10BaseFB, 10BaseFL, 10BaseFP, and Ethernet.

10BaseFB 10Mbps baseband Ethernet specification using fiber-optic cabling. 10BaseFB is part of the IEEE 10BaseF specification. It is not used to connect user stations, but instead provides a synchronous signaling backbone that allows additional segments and repeaters to be connected to the network. 10BaseFB segments can be up to 2000 meters long. *See also* 10BaseF and Ethernet.

10BaseFL 10Mbps baseband Ethernet specification using fiber-optic cabling. 10BaseFL is part of the IEEE 10BaseF specification and, while able to interoperate with FOIRL, is designed to replace the FOIRL specification. 10BaseFL segments can be up to 1000 meters long if used with FOIRL, and up to 2000 meters if 10BaseFL is used exclusively. *See also* 10BaseF, Ethernet, and FOIRL.

10BaseFP 10Mbps fiber-passive baseband Ethernet specification using fiber-optic cabling. 10BaseFP is part of the IEEE 10BaseF specification. It organizes a number of computers into a star topology without the use of repeaters. 10BaseFP segments can be up to 500 meters long. *See also* 10BaseF and Ethernet.

10BaseT 10Mbps baseband Ethernet specification using two pairs of twisted-pair cabling (Category 3, 4, or 5): one pair for transmitting data and the other for receiving data. 10BaseT, which is part of the IEEE 802.3 specification, has a distance limit of approximately 100 meters per segment. *See also* Ethernet and IEEE 802.3.

10Broad36 10Mbps broadband Ethernet specification using broadband coaxial cable. 10Broad36, which is part of the IEEE 802.3 specification, has a distance limit of 3600 meters per segment. *See also* Ethernet and IEEE 802.3.

100BaseFX 100Mbps baseband Fast Ethernet specification using two strands of multimode fiber-optic cable per link. To guarantee proper signal timing, a 100BaseFX link cannot exceed 400 meters in length. Based on the IEEE 802.3 standard. *See also* 100BaseX, Fast Ethernet, and IEEE 802.3.

100BaseT 100Mbps baseband Fast Ethernet specification using UTP wiring. Like the 10BaseT technology on which it is based, 100BaseT sends link pulses over the network segment when no traffic is present. However, these link pulses contain more information than those used in 10BaseT. Based on the IEEE 802.3 standard. *See also* 10BaseT, Fast Ethernet, and IEEE 802.3.

100BaseT4   100Mbps baseband Fast Ethernet specification using four pairs of Category 3, 4, or 5 UTP wiring. To guarantee proper signal timing, a 100BaseT4 segment cannot exceed 100 meters in length. Based on the IEEE 802.3 standard. *See also* Fast Ethernet and IEEE 802.3.

100BaseTX   100Mbps baseband Fast Ethernet specification using two pairs of either UTP or STP wiring. The first pair of wires is used to receive data; the second is used to transmit. To guarantee proper signal timing, a 100BaseTX segment cannot exceed 100 meters in length. Based on the IEEE 802.3 standard. *See also* 100BaseX, Fast Ethernet, and IEEE 802.3.

100BaseX   100Mbps baseband Fast Ethernet specification that refers to the 100BaseFX and 100BaseTX standards for Fast Ethernet over fiber-optic cabling. Based on the IEEE 802.3 standard. *See also* 100BaseFX, 100BaseTX, Fast Ethernet, and IEEE 802.3.

100VG-AnyLAN   100Mbps Fast Ethernet and Token Ring media technology using four pairs of Category 3, 4, or 5 UTP cabling. This high-speed transport technology, developed by Hewlett-Packard, can be made to operate on existing 10BaseT Ethernet networks. Based on the IEEE 802.12 standard. *See also* IEEE 802.12.

4B/5B local fiber   4-byte/5-byte local fiber. Fiber channel physical media used for FDDI and ATM. Supports speeds of up to 100Mbps over multimode fiber. *See also* TAXI 4B/5B.

8B/10B local fiber   8-byte/10-byte local fiber. Fiber channel physical media that supports speeds up to 149.76Mbps over multimode fiber.

A&B bit signaling   Procedure used in T1 transmission facilities in which each of the 24 T1 subchannels devotes one bit of every sixth frame to the carrying of supervisory signaling information. Also called 24th channel signaling.

AAL   ATM adaptation layer. Service-dependent sublayer of the Data Link layer. The AAL accepts data from different applications and presents it to the ATM layer in the form of 48-byte ATM payload segments. AALs consist of two sublayers, CS and SAR. AALs differ on the basis of the source-destination timing used, whether they use CBR or VBR, and whether they are used for connection-oriented or connectionless mode data transfer. At present, the four types of AAL recommended by the ITU-T are AAL1, AAL2, AAL3/4, and AAL5. See AAL1, AAL2, AAL3/4, AAL5, CS, and SAR. *See also* ATM and ATM layer.

AAL1   ATM adaptation layer 1. One of four AALs recommended by the ITU-T. AAL1 is used for connection-oriented, delay-sensitive services requiring constant bit rates, such as uncompressed video and other isochronous traffic. *See also* AAL.

AAL2   ATM adaptation layer 2. One of four AALs recommended by the ITU-T. AAL2 is used for connection-oriented services that support a variable bit rate, such as some isochronous video and voice traffic. *See also* AAL.

AAL3/4   ATM adaptation layer 3/4. One of four AALs (merged from two initially distinct adaptation layers) recommended by the ITU-T. AAL3/4 supports both connectionless and connection-oriented links, but is primarily used for the transmission of SMDS packets over ATM networks. *See also* AAL.

AAL5 ATM adaptation layer 5. One of four AALs recommended by the ITU-T. AAL5 supports connection-oriented, VBR services, and is used predominantly for the transfer of classical IP over ATM and LANE traffic. AAL5 uses SEAL and is the least complex of the current AAL recommendations. It offers low bandwidth overhead and simpler processing requirements in exchange for reduced bandwidth capacity and error-recovery capability. *See also* AAL and SEAL.

AARP AppleTalk Address Resolution Protocol. Protocol in the AppleTalk protocol stack that maps a data-link address to a network address.

AARP probe packets Packets transmitted by AARP that determine if a randomly selected node ID is being used by another node in a nonextended AppleTalk network. If the node ID is not being used, the sending node uses that node ID. If the node ID is being used, the sending node chooses a different ID and sends more AARP probe packets. *See also* AARP.

ABM Asynchronous Balanced Mode. An HDLC (and derivative protocol) communication mode supporting peer-oriented, point-to-point communications between two stations, where either station can initiate transmission.

ABR 1. available bit rate. QOS class defined by the ATM Forum for ATM networks. ABR is used for connections that do not require timing relationships between source and destination. ABR provides no guarantees in terms of cell loss or delay, providing only best-effort service. Traffic sources adjust their transmission rate in response to information they receive describing the status of the network and its capability to successfully deliver data. Compare with CBR, UBR, and VBR. 2. Area border router. Router located on the border of one or more OSPF areas that connects those areas to the backbone network. ABRs are considered members of both the OSPF backbone and the attached areas. They therefore maintain routing tables describing both the backbone topology and the topology of the other areas.

Abstract Syntax Notation One See ASN.1.

access list List kept by routers to control access to or from the router for a number of services (for example, to prevent packets with a certain IP address from leaving a particular interface on the router).

access method 1. Generally, the way in which network devices access the network medium. 2. Software within an SNA processor that controls the flow of information through a network.

access server Communications processor that connects asynchronous devices to a LAN or WAN through network and terminal emulation software. Performs both synchronous and asynchronous routing of supported protocols. Sometimes called a network access server. Compare with communication server.

accounting management One of five categories of network management defined by ISO for management of OSI networks. Accounting management subsystems are responsible for collecting network data relating to resource usage. *See also* configuration management, fault management, performance management, and security management.

ACD   automatic call distribution. Device or service that automatically reroutes calls to customers in geographically distributed locations served by the same CO. *See also* CO.

ACF   Advanced Communications Function. A group of SNA products that provides distributed processing and resource sharing. *See also* ACF/NCP.

ACF/NCP   Advanced Communications Function/Network Control Program. The primary SNA NCP. ACF/NCP resides in the communications controller and interfaces with the SNA access method in the host processor to control network communications. *See also* ACF and NCP.

acknowledgment   Notification sent from one network device to another to acknowledge that some event (for example, receipt of a message) has occurred. Sometimes abbreviated ACK. Compare to NAK.

ACR   allowed cell rate. Parameter defined by the ATM Forum for ATM traffic management. ACR varies between the MCR and the PCR, and is dynamically controlled using congestion control mechanisms. *See also* MCR and PCR.

ACSE   association control service element. An OSI convention used to establish, maintain, or terminate a connection between two applications.

active hub   Multiported device that amplifies LAN transmission signals.

active monitor   Device responsible for managing a Token Ring. A network node is selected to be the active monitor if it has the highest MAC address on the ring. The active monitor is responsible for such management tasks as ensuring that tokens are not lost, or that frames do not circulate indefinitely. *See also* ring monitor and standby monitor.

ADCCP   Advanced Data Communications Control Protocol. An ANSI standard bit-oriented data link control protocol.

address   Data structure or logical convention used to identify a unique entity, such as a particular process or network device.

addressed call mode   Mode that permits control signals and commands to establish and terminate calls in V.25bis. *See also* V.25bis.

address mapping   Technique that allows different protocols to interoperate by translating addresses from one format to another. For example, when routing IP over X.25, the IP addresses must be mapped to the X.25 addresses so that the IP packets can be transmitted by the X.25 network. *See also* address resolution.

address mask   Bit combination used to describe which portion of an address refers to the network or subnet and which part refers to the host. Sometimes referred to simply as mask. *See also* subnet mask.

address resolution   Generally, a method for resolving differences between computer addressing schemes. Address resolution usually specifies a method for mapping

Network layer (Layer 3) addresses to Data Link layer (Layer 2) addresses. *See also* address mapping.

Address Resolution Protocol   See ARP.

adjacency   Relationship formed between selected neighboring routers and end nodes for the purpose of exchanging routing information. Adjacency is based upon the use of a common media segment.

adjacent nodes   1. In SNA, nodes that are connected to a given node with no intervening nodes. 2. In DECnet and OSI, nodes that share a common network segment (in Ethernet, FDDI, or Token Ring networks).

ADM   Add Drop Multiplexer. In OSS, a multiplexer that allows a signal to be added into or dropped out of a SONET span. *See also* SONET.

administrative distance   A rating of the trustworthiness of a routing information source. Administrative distance is often expressed as a numerical value between 0 and 255. The higher the value, the lower the trustworthiness rating.

administrative weight   A value set by the network administrator to indicate the desirability of a network link. One of four link metrics exchanged by PTSPs to determine the available resources of an ATM network. See PTSP.

ADPCM   adaptive differential pulse code modulation. Process by which analog voice samples are encoded into high-quality digital signals.

ADSL   asymmetric digital subscriber line. One of four DSL technologies. ADSL is designed to deliver more bandwidth downstream (from the central office to the customer site) than upstream. Downstream rates range from 1.5Mbps to 9Mbps, while upstream bandwidth ranges from 16Kbps to 640Kbps. ADSL transmissions work at distances up to 18,000 feet over a single copper twisted pair. Compare with HDSL, SDSL, and VDSL.

ADSU   ATM DSU. Terminal adapter used to access an ATM network via an HSSI-compatible device. *See also* DSU.

advertising   Router process in which routing or service updates are sent at specified intervals so that other routers on the network can maintain lists of usable routes.

AEP   AppleTalk Echo Protocol. Used to test connectivity between two AppleTalk nodes. One node sends a packet to another node and receives a duplicate, or echo, of that packet.

AFI   authority and format identifier. The portion of an NSAP format ATM address that identifies the type and format of the IDI portion of an ATM address. *See also* IDI and NSAP.

AFP   AppleTalk Filing Protocol. A presentation-layer protocol that allows users to share data files and application programs that reside on a file server. AFP supports AppleShare and Mac OS File Sharing.

agent   1. Generally, software that processes queries and returns replies on behalf of an application. 2. In NMSs, process that resides in all managed devices and reports the values of specified variables to management stations.

AIN   Advanced Intelligent Network. In SS7, an expanded set of network services made available to the user and under user control that requires improvement in network switch architecture, signaling capabilities, and peripherals. *See also* SS7.

AIP   ATM Interface Processor. ATM network interface for Cisco 7000 series routers designed to minimize performance bottlenecks at the UNI. The AIP supports AAL3/4 and AAL5. *See also* AAL3/4 and AAL5.

AIS   alarm indication signal. In a T1 transmission, an all-ones signal transmitted in lieu of the normal signal to maintain transmission continuity and to indicate to the receiving terminal that there is a transmission fault that is located either at, or upstream from, the transmitting terminal. *See also* T1.

alarm   SNMP message notifying an operator or administrator of a network problem. *See also* event and trap.

a-law   The ITU-T companding standard used in the conversion between analog and digital signals in PCM systems. A-law is used primarily in European telephone networks and is similar to the North American mu-law standard. *See also* companding and mu-law.

algorithm   Well-defined rule or process for arriving at a solution to a problem. In networking, algorithms are commonly used to determine the best route for traffic from a particular source to a particular destination.

alignment error   In IEEE 802.3 networks, an error that occurs when the total number of bits of a received frame is not divisible by eight. Alignment errors are usually caused by frame damage due to collisions.

all-rings explorer packet   See all-routes explorer packet.

all-routes explorer packet   Explorer packet that traverses an entire SRB network, following all possible paths to a specific destination. Sometimes called all-rings explorer packet. *See also* explorer packet, local explorer packet, and spanning explorer packet.

ALO transaction   An ATP transaction in which the request is repeated until a response is received by the requester or until a maximum retry count is reached. This recovery mechanism ensures that the transaction request is executed at least once. *See also* ATP.

AM   amplitude modulation. Modulation technique whereby information is conveyed through the amplitude of the carrier signal.Compare with FM and PAM. *See also* modulation.

AMA   Automatic Messaging Accounting. In OSS, the automatic collection, recording, and processing of information relating to calls for billing purposes.

AMADNS   AMA Data Networking System. In OSS, the next generation Bellcore system for the collection and transport of AMA data from central office switches to a billing system. *See also* AMA.

AMATPS   AMA Teleprocessing System. In OSS, the Bellcore legacy system for collecting and transporting AMA data from central office switches to a billing system. The AMATPS consists of an AMA Transmitter and a collector. *See also* AMA.

AMI   alternate mark inversion. Line-code type used on T1 and E1 circuits. In AMI, zeros are represented by 01 during each bit cell, and ones are represented by 11 or 00, alternately, during each bit cell. AMI requires that the sending device maintain ones density. Ones density is not maintained independent of the data stream. Sometimes called binary coded alternate mark inversion. Compare with B8ZS. *See also* ones density.

amplitude   Maximum value of an analog or a digital waveform.

analog transmission   Signal transmission over wires or through the air in which information is conveyed through variation of some combination of signal amplitude, frequency, and phase.

ANSI   American National Standards Institute. Voluntary organization comprised of corporate, government, and other members that coordinates standards-related activities, approves U.S. national standards, and develops positions for the United States in international standards organizations. ANSI helps develop international and U.S. standards relating to, among other things, communications and networking. ANSI is a member of the IEC and the ISO. *See also* IEC and ISO.

anycast   In ATM, an address that can be shared by multiple end systems. An anycast address can be used to route a request to a node that provides a particular service.

API   application programming interface. Specification of function-call conventions that defines an interface to a service.

Apollo Domain   Proprietary network protocol suite developed by Apollo Computer for communication on proprietary Apollo networks.

APPC   Advanced Program-to-Program Communication. IBM SNA system software that allows high-speed communication between programs on different computers in a distributed computing environment. APPC establishes and tears down connections between communicating programs, and consists of two interfaces, a programming interface and a data-exchange interface. The former replies to requests from programs requiring communication; the latter establishes sessions between programs. APPC runs on LU 6.2 devices. *See also* LU 6.2.

AppleTalk   Series of communications protocols designed by Apple Computer. Two phases currently exist. Phase 1, the earlier version, supports a single physical network that can have only one network number and be in one zone. Phase 2, the more recent version, supports multiple logical networks on a single physical network and allows networks to be in more than one zone. *See also* zone.

Application layer   Layer 7 of the OSI reference model. This layer provides services to application processes (such as electronic mail, file transfer, and terminal emulation) that are outside of the OSI model. The Application layer identifies and establishes the availability of intended communication partners (and the resources required to connect with them), synchronizes cooperating applications, and establishes agreement on procedures for error recovery and control of data integrity. Corresponds roughly with the transaction services layer in the SNA model. *See also* Data Link layer, Network layer, Physical layer, Presentation layer, Session layer, and Transport layer.

APPN   Advanced Peer-to-Peer Networking. Enhancement to the original IBM SNA architecture. APPN handles session establishment between peer nodes, dynamic transparent route calculation, and traffic prioritization for APPC traffic. Compare with APPN+. *See also* APPC.

APPN+   Next-generation APPN that replaces the label-swapping routing algorithm with source routing. Also called high-performance routing. *See also* APPN.

APaRT   automated packet recognition/translation. Technology that allows a server to be attached to CDDI or FDDI without requiring the reconfiguration of applications or network protocols. APaRT recognizes specific Data Link layer encapsulation packet types and, when these packet types are transferred from one medium to another, translates them into the native format of the destination device.

ARA   AppleTalk Remote Access. Protocol that provides Macintosh users direct access to information and resources at a remote AppleTalk site.

ARCnet   Attached Resource Computer Network. A 2.5Mbps token-bus LAN developed in the late 1970s and early 1980s by Datapoint Corporation.

area   Logical set of network segments (either CLNS-, DECnet-, or OSPF-based) and their attached devices. Areas are usually connected to other areas via routers, making up a single autonomous system. *See also* autonomous system.

ARM   asynchronous response mode. HDLC communication mode involving one primary station and at least one secondary station, where either the primary or one of the secondary stations can initiate transmissions. *See also* primary station and secondary station.

ARP   Address Resolution Protocol. Internet protocol used to map an IP address to a MAC address. Defined in RFC 826. Compare with RARP. *See also* proxy ARP.

ARPA   Advanced Research Projects Agency. Research and development organization that is part of DoD. ARPA is responsible for numerous technological advances in communications and networking. ARPA evolved into DARPA, and then back into ARPA again (in 1994). *See also* DARPA.

ARPANET   Advanced Research Projects Agency Network. Landmark packet-switching network established in 1969. ARPANET was developed in the 1970s by BBN and funded by ARPA (and later DARPA). It eventually evolved into the Internet. The term ARPANET was officially retired in 1990. *See also* ARPA, BBN, DARPA, and Internet.

ARQ automatic repeat request. Communication technique in which the receiving device detects errors and requests retransmissions.

ASBR autonomous system boundary router. ABR located between an OSPF autonomous system and a non-OSPF network. ASBRs run both OSPF and another routing protocol, such as RIP. ASBRs must reside in a nonstub OSPF area. *See also* ABR, non-stub area, and OSPF.

ASCII American Standard Code for Information Interchange. 8-bit code for character representation (7 bits plus parity).

ASN.1 Abstract Syntax Notation One. OSI language for describing data types independent of particular computer structures and representation techniques. Described by ISO International Standard 8824. *See also* BER (basic encoding rules).

ASP AppleTalk Session Protocol. Protocol that uses ATP to provide session establishment, maintenance, and teardown, as well as request sequencing. *See also* ATP.

associative memory Memory that is accessed based on its contents, not on its memory address. Sometimes called content addressable memory (CAM).

AST automatic spanning tree. Function that supports the automatic resolution of spanning trees in SRB networks, providing a single path for spanning explorer frames to traverse from a given node in the network to another. AST is based on the IEEE 802.1 standard. See IEEE 802.1 and SRB.

ASTA Advanced Software Technology and Algorithms. Component of the HPCC program intended to develop software and algorithms for implementation on high-performance computer and communications systems. *See also* HPCC.

asynchronous transmission Term describing digital signals that are transmitted without precise clocking. Such signals generally have different frequencies and phase relationships. Asynchronous transmissions usually encapsulate individual characters in control bits (called start and stop bits) that designate the beginning and end of each character. Compare with isochronous transmission, plesiochronous transmission, and synchronous transmission.

ATCP AppleTalk Control Protocol. The protocol that establishes and configures AppleTalk over PPP, as defined in RFC 1378. *See also* PPP.

ATDM asynchronous time-division multiplexing. Method of sending information that resembles normal TDM, except that time slots are allocated as needed rather than preassigned to specific transmitters. Compare with FDM, statistical multiplexing, and TDM.

ATG address translation gateway. Cisco DECnet routing software function that allows a router to route multiple, independent DECnet networks and to establish a user-specified address translation for selected nodes between networks.

ATM Asynchronous Transfer Mode. International standard for cell relay in which multiple service types (such as voice, video, or data) are conveyed in fixed-length (53-byte) cells. Fixed-length cells allow cell processing to occur in hardware, thereby reducing transit delays. ATM is designed to take advantage of high-speed transmission media such as E3, SONET, and T3.

ATM ARP server   A device that provides address-resolution services to LISs when running classical IP over ATM.

ATM endpoint   The point in an ATM network where an ATM connection is initiated or terminated. ATM endpoints includes ATM-attached workstations, ATM-attached servers, ATM-to-LAN switches, and ATM routers.

ATM Forum   International organization jointly founded in 1991 by Cisco Systems, NET/ADAPTIVE, Northern Telecom, and Sprint that develops and promotes standards-based implementation agreements for ATM technology. The ATM Forum expands on official standards developed by ANSI and ITU-T, and develops implementation agreements in advance of official standards.

ATM layer   Service-independent sublayer of the Data Link layer in an ATM network. The ATM layer receives the 48-byte payload segments from the AAL and attaches a 5-byte header to each, producing standard 53-byte ATM cells. These cells are passed to the Physical layer for transmission across the physical medium. *See also* AAL.

ATMM   ATM management. Process that runs on an ATM switch that controls VCI translation and rate enforcement. *See also* ATM and VCI.

ATM user-user connection   Connection created by the ATM layer to provide communication between two or more ATM service users, such as ATMM processes. Such communication can be unidirectional, using one VCC, or bidirectional, using two VCCs. *See also* ATM layer, ATMM, and VCC.

ATP   AppleTalk Transaction Protocol. Transport-level protocol that provides a loss-free transaction service between sockets. This service allows exchanges between two socket clients in which one client requests the other to perform a particular task and to report the results; ATP binds the request and response together to ensure the reliable exchange of request-response pairs.

attenuation   Loss of communication signal energy.

AU   Access unit. Device that provides ISDN access to PSNs. *See also* PSN.

AUI   attachment unit interface. IEEE 802.3 interface between an MAU and a NIC (network interface card). The term AUI can also refer to the rear panel port to which an AUI cable might attach. Also called transceiver cable. *See also* IEEE 802.3, MAU, and NIC.

AURP   AppleTalk Update-Based Routing Protocol. Method of encapsulating AppleTalk traffic in the header of a foreign protocol, allowing the connection of two or more discontiguous AppleTalk internetworks through a foreign network (such as TCP/IP) to form an AppleTalk WAN. This connection is called an AURP tunnel. In addition to its encapsulation function, AURP maintains routing tables for the entire AppleTalk WAN by exchanging routing information between exterior routers. *See also* AURP tunnel and exterior router.

AURP tunnel   Connection created in an AURP WAN that functions as a single, virtual data link between AppleTalk internetworks physically separated by a foreign network (a TCP/IP network, for example). *See also* AURP.

authority zone   Associated with DNS, an authority zone is a section of the domain-name tree for which one name server is the authority. *See also* DNS.

automatic call reconnect   Feature permitting automatic call rerouting away from a failed trunk line.

autonomous confederation   Group of autonomous systems that rely on their own network reachability and routing information more than they rely on that received from other autonomous systems or confederations.

autonomous switching   Feature on Cisco routers that provides faster packet processing by allowing the ciscoBus to switch packets independently without interrupting the system processor.

autonomous system   Collection of networks under a common administration sharing a common routing strategy. Autonomous systems are subdivided by areas. An autonomous system must be assigned a unique 16-bit number by the IANA. Sometimes abbreviated AS. *See also* area and IANA.

autoreconfiguration   Process performed by nodes within the failure domain of a Token Ring network. Nodes automatically perform diagnostics in an attempt to reconfigure the network around the failed areas. *See also* failure domain.

average rate   The average rate, in kilobits per second (kbps), at which a given virtual circuit will transmit.

B8ZS   binary 8-zero substitution. Line-code type, used on T1 and E1 circuits, in which a special code is substituted whenever 8 consecutive zeros are sent over the link. This code is then interpreted at the remote end of the connection. This technique guarantees ones density independent of the data stream. Sometimes called bipolar 8-zero substitution. Compare with AMI. *See also* ones density.

backbone   The part of a network that acts as the primary path for traffic that is most often sourced from, and destined for, other networks.

back end   Node or software program that provides services to a front end. *See also* client, front end, and server.

backoff   The (usually random) retransmission delay enforced by contentious MAC protocols after a network node with data to transmit determines that the physical medium is already in use.

backplane   Physical connection between an interface processor or card and the data buses and power distribution buses inside a chassis.

back pressure   Propagation of network congestion information upstream through an internetwork.

backward learning   Algorithmic process used for routing traffic that surmises information by assuming symmetrical network conditions. For example, if node A receives a packet from node B through intermediate node C, the backward-learning routing algorithm will assume that A can optimally reach B through C.

balanced configuration   In HDLC, a point-to-point network configuration with two combined stations.

balun   balanced, unbalanced. Device used for matching impedance between a balanced and an unbalanced line, usually twisted-pair and coaxial cable.

bandwidth   The difference between the highest and lowest frequencies available for network signals. The term is also used to describe the rated throughput capacity of a given network medium or protocol.

bandwidth reservation   Process of assigning bandwidth to users and applications served by a network. Involves assigning priority to different flows of traffic based on how critical and delay-sensitive they are. This makes the best use of available bandwidth, and if the network becomes congested, lower-priority traffic can be dropped. Sometimes called bandwidth allocation. *See also* call priority.

BARRNet   Bay Area Regional Research Network. Regional network serving the San Francisco Bay Area. The BARRNet backbone is composed of four University of California campuses (Berkeley, Davis, Santa Cruz, and San Francisco), Stanford University, Lawrence Livermore National Laboratory, and NASA Ames Research Center. BARRNET is now part of BBN Planet. *See also* BBN Planet.

baseband   Characteristic of a network technology where only one carrier frequency is used. Ethernet is an example of a baseband network. Also called narrowband. Contrast with broadband.

bash   Bourne-again shell. Interactive UNIX shell based on the traditional Bourne shell, but with increased functionality. *See also* root account.

baud   Unit of signaling speed equal to the number of discrete signal elements transmitted per second. Baud is synonymous with bits per second (bps), if each signal element represents exactly 1 bit.

BBN   Bolt, Beranek, and Newman, Inc. High-technology company located in Massachusetts that developed and maintained the ARPANET (and later, the Internet) core gateway system. *See also* BBN Planet.

BBN Planet   Subsidiary company of BBN that operates a nationwide Internet access network composed in part by the former regional networks BARRNET, NEARNET, and SURAnet. *See also* BARRNet, BBN, NEARNET, and SURAnet.

Bc   Committed Burst. Negotiated tariff metric in Frame Relay internetworks. The maximum amount of data (in bits) that a Frame Relay internetwork is committed to accept and transmit at the CIR. *See also* Be and CIR.

B channel   bearer channel. In ISDN, a full-duplex, 64Kbps channel used to send user data. Compare to D channel, E channel, and H channel.

BDCS Broadband Digital Cross-Connect System. A SONET DCS capable of cross connecting DS-3, STS-1 and STS-3c signals. *See also* DCS.

Be Excess Burst. Negotiated tariff metric in Frame Relay internetworks. The number of bits that a Frame Relay internetwork will attempt to transmit after Bc is accommodated. Be data is, in general, delivered with a lower probability than Bc data because Be data can be marked as DE by the network. *See also* Bc and DE.

beacon Frame from a Token Ring or FDDI device indicating a serious problem with the ring, such as a broken cable. A beacon frame contains the address of the station assumed to be down. *See also* failure domain.

BECN backward explicit congestion notification. Bit set by a Frame Relay network in frames traveling in the opposite direction of frames encountering a congested path. DTE receiving frames with the BECN bit set can request that higher-level protocols take flow control action as appropriate. Compare with FECN.

Bellcore Bell Communications Research. Organization that performs research and development on behalf of the RBOCs.

BER 1. bit error rate. The ratio of received bits that contain errors. 2. basic encoding rules. Rules for encoding data units described in the ISO ASN.1 standard. *See also* ASN.1.

BERT bit error rate tester. Device that determines the BER on a given communications channel. *See also* BER (bit error rate).

best-effort delivery Describes a network system that does not use a sophisticated acknowledgment system to guarantee reliable delivery of information.

BGP Border Gateway Protocol. Interdomain routing protocol that replaces EGP. BGP exchanges reachability information with other BGP systems. It is defined by RFC 1163. *See also* BGP4 and EGP.

BGP4 BGP Version 4. Version 4 of the predominant interdomain routing protocol used on the Internet. BGP4 supports CIDR and uses route aggregation mechanisms to reduce the size of routing tables. *See also* BGP and CIDR.

BICI Broadband Inter-Carrier Interface. An ITU-T standard that defines the protocols and procedures needed for establishing, maintaining, and terminating broadband switched virtual connections between public networks.

BIGA Bus Interface Gate Array. Technology that allows the Catalyst 5000 to receive and transmit frames from its packet-switching memory to its MAC local buffer memory without the intervention of the host processor.

big-endian Method of storing or transmitting data in which the most significant bit or byte is presented first. Compare with little-endian.

binary A numbering system characterized by ones and zeros (1 = on, 0 = off).

BinHex Binary Hexadecimal. A method for converting binary files into ASCII for transmission by applications, such as e-mail, that can only handle ASCII.

BIP   bit interleaved parity. In ATM, a method used to monitor errors on a link. A check bit or word is sent in the link overhead for the previous block or frame. Bit errors in the payload can then be detected and reported as maintenance information.

biphase coding   Bipolar coding scheme originally developed for use in Ethernet. Clocking information is embedded into and recovered from the synchronous data stream without the need for separate clocking leads. The biphase signal contains no direct current energy.

BIND   Berkeley Internet Name Domain. Implementation of DNS developed and distributed by the University of California at Berkeley. Many Internet hosts run BIND, and it is the ancestor of many commercial BIND implementations.

bipolar   Electrical characteristic denoting a circuit with both negative and positive polarity. Contrast with unipolar.

BISDN   Broadband ISDN. ITU-T communication standards designed to handle high-bandwidth applications such as video. BISDN currently uses ATM technology over SONET-based transmission circuits to provide data rates from 155 to 622Mbps and beyond. Contrast with N-ISDN. *See also* BRI, ISDN, and PRI.

bit   Binary digit used in the binary numbering system. Can be 0 or 1.

BITNET   "Because It's Time" Networking Services. Low-cost, low-speed academic network consisting primarily of IBM mainframes and 9600-bps leased lines. BITNET is now part of CREN. *See also* CREN.

BITNET III   Dial-up service providing connectivity for members of CREN. *See also* CREN.

bit-oriented protocol   Class of Data Link layer communication protocols that can transmit frames regardless of frame content. Compared with byte-oriented protocols, bit-oriented protocols provide full-duplex operation and are more efficient and reliable. Compare with byte-oriented protocol.

bit rate   Speed at which bits are transmitted, usually expressed in bits per second (bps).

bits per second   Abbreviated bps.

black hole   Routing term for an area of the internetwork where packets enter, but do not emerge, due to adverse conditions or poor system configuration within a portion of the network.

blocking   In a switching system, a condition in which no paths are available to complete a circuit. The term is also used to describe a situation in which one activity cannot begin until another has been completed.

block multiplexer channel   IBM-style channel that implements the FIPS-60 channel, a U.S. channel standard. This channel is also referred to as OEMI channel and 370 block mux channel.

blower   Internal cooling fan used in larger router and switch chassis.

BLSR Bidirectional Line Switch Ring. A SONET ring architecture that provides working and protection fibers between nodes. If the working fiber between nodes is cut, traffic is automatically routed onto the protection fiber. *See also* SONET.

BNC connector Standard connector used to connect IEEE 802.3 10Base2 coaxial cable to an MAU.

BNN boundary network node. In SNA terminology, a subarea node that provides boundary function support for adjacent peripheral nodes. This support includes sequencing, pacing, and address translation. Also called boundary node.

BOC Bell operating company. Twenty-two local phone companies formed by the breakup of AT&T. See RBOC.

BOOTP Bootstrap Protocol. Protocol used by a network node to determine the IP address of its Ethernet interfaces, in order to affect network booting.

boot PROM boot programmable read-only memory. Chip mounted on a printed circuit board used to provide executable boot instructions to a computer device.

border gateway Router that communicates with routers in other autonomous systems.

boundary function Capability of SNA subarea nodes to provide protocol support for attached peripheral nodes. Typically found in IBM 3745 devices.

BPDU bridge protocol data unit. Spanning-Tree Protocol hello packet that is sent out at configurable intervals to exchange information among bridges in the network. *See also* PDU.

BRHR Basic Research and Human Resources. Component of the HPCC program designed to support research, training, and education in computer science, computer engineering, and computational science. *See also* HPCC.

BRI Basic Rate Interface. ISDN interface composed of two B channels and one D channel for circuit-switched communication of voice, video, and data. Compare with PRI. *See also* BISDN, ISDN, and N-ISDN.

bridge Device that connects and passes packets between two network segments that use the same communications protocol. Bridges operate at the Data Link layer (Layer 2) of the OSI reference model. In general, a bridge will filter, forward, or flood an incoming frame based on the MAC address of that frame. *See also* relay.

bridge forwarding Process that uses entries in a filtering database to determine whether frames with a given MAC destination address can be forwarded to a given port or ports. Described in the IEEE 802.1 standard. *See also* IEEE 802.1.

bridge group Bridging feature that assigns network interfaces to a particular spanning-tree group. Bridge groups can be compatible with the IEEE 802.1 or the DEC specification.

bridge number Number that identifies each bridge in an SRB LAN. Parallel bridges must have different bridge numbers.

bridge static filtering   Process in which a bridge maintains a filtering database consisting of static entries. Each static entry equates a MAC destination address with a port that can receive frames with this MAC destination address and a set of ports on which the frames can be transmitted. Defined in the IEEE 802.1 standard. *See also* IEEE 802.1.

broadband   Transmission system that multiplexes multiple independent signals onto one cable. In telecommunications terminology, any channel having a bandwidth greater than a voice-grade channel (4 kHz). In LAN terminology, a coaxial cable on which analog signaling is used. Also called wideband. Contrast with baseband.

broadcast   Data packet that will be sent to all nodes on a network. Broadcasts are identified by a broadcast address. Compare with multicast and unicast. *See also* broadcast address.

broadcast address   Special address reserved for sending a message to all stations. Generally, a broadcast address is a MAC destination address of all ones. Compare with multicast address and unicast address. *See also* broadcast.

broadcast domain   The set of all devices that will receive broadcast frames originating from any device within the set. Broadcast domains are typically bounded by routers because routers do not forward broadcast frames.

broadcast search   Propagation of a search request to all network nodes if the location of a resource is unknown to the requester. *See also* directed search.

broadcast storm   Undesirable network event in which many broadcasts are sent simultaneously across all network segments. A broadcast storm uses substantial network bandwidth and, typically, causes network time-outs.

browser   GUI-based hypertext client application, such as Internet Explorer, Mosaic, and Netscape Navigator, used to access hypertext documents and other services located on innumerable remote servers throughout the WWW and Internet. *See also* hypertext, Internet, Mosaic, and WWW.

BSC   binary synchronous communication. Character-oriented Data Link layer protocol for half-duplex applications. Often referred to simply as bisync.

BSD   Berkeley Standard Distribution. Term used to describe any of a variety of UNIX-type operating systems based on the UC Berkeley BSD operating system.

BT   burst tolerance. Parameter defined by the ATM Forum for ATM traffic management. For VBR connections, BT determines the size of the maximum burst of contiguous cells that can be transmitted. *See also* VBR.

buffer   Storage area used for handling data in transit. Buffers are used in internetworking to compensate for differences in processing speed between network devices. Bursts of data can be stored in buffers until they can be handled by slower processing devices. Sometimes referred to as a packet buffer.

US   broadcast and unknown server. Multicast server used in ELANs that is used to flood traffic addressed to an unknown destination, and to forward multicast and broadcast traffic to the appropriate clients. *See also* ELAN.

bus   1. Common physical signal path composed of wires or other media across which signals can be sent from one part of a computer to another. Sometimes called highway. 2. See bus topology.

bus and tag channel   IBM channel, developed in the 1960s, incorporating copper multiwire technology. Replaced by the ESCON channel. *See also* ESCON channel and parallel channel.

bus topology   Linear LAN architecture in which transmissions from network stations propagate the length of the medium and are received by all other stations. Compare with ring topology, star topology, and tree topology.

BX.25   An AT&T implementation of X.25. *See also* X.25.

bypass mode   Operating mode on FDDI and Token Ring networks in which an interface has been removed from the ring.

bypass relay   Allows a particular Token Ring interface to be shut down and thus effectively removed from the ring.

byte   Term used to refer to a series of consecutive binary digits that are operated upon as a unit (for example, an 8-bit byte).

byte-oriented protocol   Class of data-link communications protocols that use a specific character from the user character set to delimit frames. These protocols have largely been replaced by bit-oriented protocols. Compare with bit-oriented protocol.

byte reversal   Process of storing numeric data with the least-significant byte first. Used for integers and addresses on devices with Intel microprocessors.

cable   Transmission medium of copper wire or optical fiber wrapped in a protective cover.

cable range   Range of network numbers that is valid for use by nodes on an extended AppleTalk network. The cable range value can be a single network number or a contiguous sequence of several network numbers. Node addresses are assigned based on the cable range value.

CAC   Connection Admission Control. The set of actions taken by each ATM switch during connection setup in order to determine whether a connection's request QOS will violate the QOS guarantees for established connections. CAC is also used when routing a connection request through an ATM network.

call admission control   Traffic management mechanism used in ATM networks that determines whether the network can offer a path with sufficient bandwidth for a requested VCC.

CAC   Connection admission control. In ATM, the set of actions taken by the network during the call setup phase (or call renegotiation phase) in order to determine whether a connection request can be accepted or should be rejected.

call priority   Priority assigned to each origination port in circuit-switched systems. This priority defines the order in which calls are reconnected. Call priority also defines which calls can or cannot be placed during a bandwidth reservation. *See also* bandwidth reservation.

call setup time   The time required to establish a switched call between DTE devices.

CAM   content-addressable memory. See associative memory.

CAP   Competitive Access Provider. An independent company providing local telecommunications services mainly to business customers in competition with an area's BOC or IOC. Teleport and MFS are the two major CAPs operating in major metropolitan areas in the US. *See also* BOC and IOC.

carrier   Electromagnetic wave or alternating current of a single frequency, suitable for modulation by another, data-bearing signal. *See also* modulation.

Category 1 cabling   One of five grades of UTP cabling described in the EIA/TIA-586 standard. Category 1 cabling is used for telephone communications and is not suitable for transmitting data. Compare with Category 2 cabling, Category 3 cabling, Category 4 cabling, and Category 5 cabling. *See also* EIA/TIA-586 and UTP.

Category 2 cabling   One of five grades of UTP cabling described in the EIA/TIA-586 standard. Category 2 cabling is capable of transmitting data at speeds up to 4Mbps. Compare with Category 1 cabling, Category 3 cabling, Category 4 cabling, and Category 5 cabling. *See also* EIA/TIA-586 and UTP.

Category 3 cabling   One of five grades of UTP cabling described in the EIA/TIA-586 standard. Category 3 cabling is used in 10BaseT networks and can transmit data at speeds up to 10Mbps. Compare with Category 1 cabling, Category 2 cabling, Category 4 cabling, and Category 5 cabling. *See also* EIA/TIA-586 and UTP.

Category 4 cabling   One of five grades of UTP cabling described in the EIA/TIA-586 standard. Category 4 cabling is used in Token Ring networks and can transmit data at speeds up to 16Mbps. Compare with Category 1 cabling, Category 2 cabling, Category 3 cabling, and Category 5 cabling. *See also* EIA/TIA-586 and UTP.

Category 5 cabling   One of five grades of UTP cabling described in the EIA/TIA-586 standard. Category 5 cabling can transmit data at speeds up to 100Mbps. Compare with Category 1 cabling, Category 2 cabling, Category 3 cabling, and Category 4 cabling. *See also* EIA/TIA-586 and UTP.

catenet   Network in which hosts are connected to diverse networks, which themselves are connected with routers. The Internet is a prominent example of a catenet.

CATV   cable television. Communication system where multiple channels of programming material are transmitted to homes using broadband coaxial cable. Formerly called Community Antenna Television.

CBDS   Connectionless Broadband Data Service. European high-speed, packet-switched, datagram-based WAN networking technology. Similar to SMDS. *See also* SMDS.

CBR   constant bit rate. QOS class defined by the ATM Forum for ATM networks. CBR is used for connections that depend on precise clocking to ensure undistorted delivery. Compare with ABR, UBR, and VBR.

CCITT   Consultative Committee for International Telegraph and Telephone. International organization responsible for the development of communications standards. Now called the ITU-T. See ITU-T.

CCS   common channel signaling. Signaling system used in telephone networks that separates signaling information from user data. A specified channel is exclusively designated to carry signaling information for all other channels in the system. *See also* SS7.

CD   Carrier Detect. Signal that indicates whether an interface is active. Also, a signal generated by a modem indicating that a call has been connected.

CDDI   Copper Distributed Data Interface. Implementation of FDDI protocols over STP and UTP cabling. CDDI transmits over relatively short distances (about 100 meters), providing data rates of 100Mbps using a dual-ring architecture to provide redundancy. Based on the ANSI Twisted-Pair Physical Medium Dependent (TPPMD) standard. Compare with FDDI.

CDP   Cisco Discovery Protocol. Media- and protocol-independent device-discovery protocol that runs on all Cisco-manufactured equipment including routers, access servers, bridges, and switches. Using CDP, a device can advertise its existence to other devices and receive information about other devices on the same LAN or on the remote side of a WAN. Runs on all media that support SNAP, including LANs, Frame Relay, and ATM media.

CDPD   Cellular Digital Packet Data. Open standard for two-way wireless data communication over high-frequency cellular telephone channels. Allows data transmissions between a remote cellular link and a NAP. Operates at 19.2Kbps.

CDV   cell delay variation. A component of cell transfer delay, which is induced by buffering and cell scheduling. CDV is a QOS delay parameter associated with CBR and VBR service. *See also* CBR and VBR.

CDVT   cell delay variation tolerance. In ATM, a QOS parameter for managing traffic that is specified when a connection is setup. In CBR transmissions, CDVT determines the level of jitter that is tolerable for the data samples taken by the PCR. *See also* CBR and PCR.

cell   The basic data unit for ATM switching and multiplexing. Cells contain identifiers that specify the data stream to which they belong. Each cell consists of a 5-byte header and 48 bytes of payload. *See also* cell relay.

cell payload scrambling   Technique used an ATM switch to maintain framing on some medium-speed edge and trunk interfaces.

cell relay   Network technology based on the use of small, fixed-size packets, or cells. Because cells are fixed-length, they can be processed and switched in hardware at high speeds. Cell relay is the basis for many high-speed network protocols including ATM, IEEE 802.6, and SMDS. *See also* cell.

cellular radio   Technology that uses radio transmissions to access telephone company networks. Service is provided in a particular area by a low-power transmitter.

Centrex   An LEC service that provides local switching applications similar to those provided by an on-site PBX. With Centrex, there is no on-site switching; all customer connections go back to the CO. *See also* CO and LEC (local exchange carrier).

CEPT   Conférence Européenne des Postes et des Télécommunications. Association of the 26 European PTTs that recommends communication specifications to the ITU-T.

CER   cell error ratio. In ATM, the ratio of transmitted cells that have errors to the total cells sent in a transmission for a specific period of time.

CERFnet   California Education and Research Federation Network. TCP/IP network, based in Southern California, that connects hundreds of higher-education centers internationally while also providing Internet access to subscribers. CERFnet was founded in 1988 by the San Diego Supercomputer Center and General Atomics and is funded by the NSF.

CGI   Common Gateway Interface. A set of rules that describe how a Web server communicates with another application running on the same computer and how the application (called a "GI program") communicates with the Web server. Any application can be a CGI program if it handles input and output according to the CGI standard.

chaining   SNA concept in which RUs are grouped together for the purpose of error recovery.

channel   1. A communication path. Multiple channels can be multiplexed over a single cable in certain environments. 2. In IBM, the specific path between large computers (such as mainframes) and attached peripheral devices.

channel-attached   Pertaining to attachment of devices directly by data channels (input/output channels) to a computer.

channelized E1   Access link operating at 2.048Mbps that is subdivided into 30 B-channels and 1 D-channel. Supports DDR, Frame Relay, and X.25. Compare with channelized T1.

channelized T1   Access link operating at 1.544Mbps that is subdivided into 24 channels (23 B-channels and 1 D-channel) of 64Kbps each. The individual channels or groups of channels connect to different destinations. Supports DDR, Frame Relay, and X.25. Also referred to as fractional T1. Compare with channelized E1.

CHAP   Challenge Handshake Authentication Protocol. Security feature supported on lines using PPP encapsulation that prevents unauthorized access. CHAP does not itself prevent unauthorized access, it merely identifies the remote end. The router or access server then determines whether that user is allowed access. Compare to PAP.

chat script   String of text that defines the login "conversation" that occurs between two systems. Consists of expect-send pairs that define the string that the local system expects to receive from the remote system and what the local system should send as a reply.

Cheapernet   Industry term used to refer to the IEEE 802.3 10Base2 standard or the cable specified in that standard. Compare with Thinnet. *See also* 10Base2, Ethernet, and IEEE 802.3.

checksum   Method for checking the integrity of transmitted data. A checksum is an integer value computed from a sequence of octets taken through a series of arithmetic operations. The value is recomputed at the receiving end and compared for verification.

choke packet   Packet sent to a transmitter to tell it that congestion exists and that it should reduce its sending rate.

CICNet   Regional network that connects academic, research, nonprofit, and commercial organizations in the Midwestern United States. Founded in 1988, CICNet was a part of the NSFNET and was funded by the NSF until the NSFNET dissolved in 1995. *See also* NSFNET.

CICS   Customer Information Control System. IBM application subsystem allowing transactions entered at remote terminals to be processed concurrently by user applications.

CID   Craft Interface Device. A terminal or PC-based interface that enables the performance of local maintenance operations.

CIDR   classless interdomain routing. Technique supported by BGP4 and based on route aggregation. CIDR allows routers to group routes together in order to cut down on the quantity of routing information carried by the core routers. With CIDR, several IP networks appear to networks outside the group as a single, larger entity. With CIDR, IP addresses and their subnet masks are written as 4 octets, separated by periods, followed by a forward slash and a two-digit number that represents the subnet mask. *See also* BGP4.

child peer group   A peer group for which another peer group is the parent peer group. *See also* logical group node, peer group, and parent peer group.

CIP   Channel Interface Processor. Channel attachment interface for Cisco 7000 series routers. The CIP is used to connect a host mainframe to a control unit, eliminating the need for an FEP for channel attachment.

CIR   committed information rate. The rate at which a Frame Relay network agrees to transfer information under normal conditions, averaged over a minimum increment of time. CIR, measured in bits per second, is one of the key negotiated tariff metrics. *See also* Bc.

circuit   Communications path between two or more points.

circuit group   Grouping of associated serial lines that link two bridges. If one of the serial links in a circuit group is in the spanning tree for a network, any of the serial links in the circuit group can be used for load balancing. This load-balancing strategy avoids data ordering problems by assigning each destination address to a particular serial link.

circuit steering   A mechanism used by some ATM switches to eavesdrop on a virtual connection and copy its cells to another port where an ATM analyzer is attached. Also known as port snooping.

circuit switching   Switching system in which a dedicated physical circuit path must exist between sender and receiver for the duration of the "call." Used heavily in the telephone company network. Circuit switching can be contrasted with contention and token passing as a channel-access method, and with message switching and packet switching as a switching technique.

Cisco FRAD   Cisco Frame Relay access device. Cisco product that supports Cisco IOS Frame Relay SNA services and can be upgraded to be a full-function multiprotocol router. The Cisco FRAD connects SDLC devices to Frame Relay without requiring an existing LAN. However, the Cisco FRAD does support attached LANs and can perform conversion from SDLC to Ethernet and Token Ring. *See also* FRAD.

CiscoFusion   Cisco internetworking architecture that "fuses" together the scalability, stability, and security advantages of the latest routing technologies with the performance benefits of ATM and LAN switching, and the management benefits of VLANs. *See also* Cisco IOS software.

Cisco IOS software   Cisco Internetwork Operating System software. Cisco system software that provides common functionality, scalability, and security for all products under the CiscoFusion architecture. The Cisco IOS software allows centralized, integrated, and automated installation and management of internetworks, while ensuring support for a wide variety of protocols, media, services, and platforms. *See also* CiscoFusion.

CiscoView   GUI-based device-management software application that provides dynamic status, statistics, and comprehensive configuration information for Cisco internetworking devices. In addition to displaying a physical view of Cisco device chassis, CiscoView also provides device monitoring functions and basic troubleshooting capabilities, and can be integrated with several leading SNMP-based network management platforms

classical IP over ATM   Specification for running IP over ATM in a manner that takes full advantage of the features of ATM. Defined in RFC 1577. Sometimes called CIA.

CLAW   Common Link Access for Workstations. Data link layer protocol used by channel-attached RISC System/6000 series systems and by IBM 3172 devices running TCP/IP off-load. CLAW improves efficiency of channel use and allows the CIP to provide the functionality of a 3172 in TCP/IP environments and support direct channel attachment. The output from TCP/IP mainframe processing is a series of IP datagrams that the router can switch without modifications.

clear channel A channel that uses out-of-band signaling (as opposed to in-band signaling) so that the channel's entire bit rate is available.

CLI command line interface. An interface that allows the user to interact with the operating system by entering commands and optional arguments. The UNIX operating system and DOS provide CLIs. Compare with GUI.

client Node or software program (front-end device) that requests services from a server. *See also* back end, front end, and server.

client/server computing Term used to describe distributed computing (processing) network systems in which transaction responsibilities are divided into two parts: client (front end) and server (back end). Both terms (client and server) can be applied to software programs or actual computing devices. Also called distributed computing (processing). Compare with peer-to-peer computing. *See also* RPC.

CLNP Connectionless Network Protocol. OSI Network layer protocol that does not require a circuit to be established before data is transmitted. *See also* CLNS.

CLNS Connectionless Network Service. OSI Network layer service that does not require a circuit to be established before data is transmitted. CLNS routes messages to their destinations independently of any other messages. *See also* CLNP.

CLP cell loss priority. Field in the ATM cell header that determines the probability of a cell being dropped if the network becomes congested. Cells with CLP = 0 are insured traffic, which is unlikely to be dropped. Cells with CLP = 1 are best-effort traffic, which might be dropped in congested conditions in order to free up resources to handle insured traffic.

CLR cell loss ratio. In ATM, the ratio of discarded cells to cells that are successfully transmitted. CLR can be set as a QOS parameter when a connection is set up.

CLS Cisco Link Services. A front-end for a variety of data-link control services.

CLSI Cisco Link Services Interface. The messages that are exchanged between CLS and data-link users such as APPN, SNA service point, and DLSw+.

cluster controller 1. Generally, an intelligent device that provides the connections for a cluster of terminals to a data link. 2. In SNA, a programmable device that controls the input/output operations of attached devices. Typically, an IBM 3174 or 3274 device.

CMI coded mark inversion. ITU-T line coding technique specified for STS-3c transmissions. Also used in DS-1 systems. *See also* DS-1 and STS-3c.

CMIP Common Management Information Protocol. OSI network management protocol created and standardized by ISO for the monitoring and control of heterogeneous networks. *See also* CMIS.

CMIS Common Management Information Services. OSI network management service interface created and standardized by ISO for the monitoring and control of heterogeneous networks. *See also* CMIP.

CMNS   Connection-Mode Network Service. Extends local X.25 switching to a variety of media (Ethernet, FDDI, Token Ring). *See also* CONP.

CMT   connection management. FDDI process that handles the transition of the ring through its various states (off, active, connect, and so on), as defined by the ANSI X3T9.5 specification.

CO   central office. Local telephone company office to which all local loops in a given area connect and in which circuit switching of subscriber lines occurs.

CO-IPX   Connection Oriented IPX. A native ATM protocol based on IPX under development by Novell.

coaxial cable   Cable consisting of a hollow outer cylindrical conductor that surrounds a single inner wire conductor. Two types of coaxial cable are currently used in LANs: 50-ohm cable, which is used for digital signaling, and 75-ohm cable, which is used for analog signaling and high-speed digital signaling.

CODEC   coder-decoder. Device that typically uses pulse code modulation to transform analog signals into a digital bit stream, and digital signals back into analog.

coding   Electrical techniques used to convey binary signals.

collapsed backbone   Nondistributed backbone in which all network segments are interconnected by way of an internetworking device. A collapsed backbone might be a virtual network segment existing in a device such as a hub, a router, or a switch.

collision   In Ethernet, the result of two nodes transmitting simultaneously. The frames from each device impact and are damaged when they meet on the physical media. *See also* collision domain.

collision domain   In Ethernet, the network area within which frames that have collided are propagated. Repeaters and hubs propagate collisions; LAN switches, bridges and routers do not. *See also* collision.

common carrier   Licensed, private utility company that supplies communication services to the public at regulated prices.

communication   Transmission of information.

communication controller   In SNA, a subarea node (such as an IBM 3745 device) that contains an NCP.

communication server   Communications processor that connects asynchronous devices to a LAN or WAN through network and terminal emulation software. Performs only asynchronous routing of IP and IPX. Compare with access server.

communications line   The physical link (such as wire or a telephone circuit) that connects one or more devices to one or more other devices.

community   In SNMP, a logical group of managed devices and NMSs in the same administrative domain.

Community Antenna Television   Now known as CATV. See CATV.

community string   Text string that acts as a password and is used to authenticate messages sent between a management station and a router containing an SNMP agent. The community string is sent in every packet between the manager and the agent. Also called a community name.

companding   Contraction derived from the opposite processes of compression and expansion. Part of the PCM process whereby analog signal values are logically rounded to discrete scale-step values on a nonlinear scale. The decimal step number is then coded in its binary equivalent prior to transmission. The process is reversed at the receiving terminal using the same nonlinear scale. Compare with compression and expansion. *See also* a-law and mu-law.

compression   The running of a data set through an algorithm that reduces the space required to store or the bandwidth required to transmit the data set. Compare with companding and expansion.

configuration direct VCC   In ATM, a bi-directional point-to-point VCC set up by a LEC to an LES. One of three control connections defined by Phase 1 LANE. Compare with control distribute VCC and control direct VCC.

configuration management   One of five categories of network management defined by ISO for management of OSI networks. Configuration management subsystems are responsible for detecting and determining the state of a network. *See also* accounting management, fault management, performance management, and security management.

configuration register   In Cisco routers, a 16-bit, user-configurable value that determines how the router functions during initialization. The configuration register can be stored in hardware or software. In hardware, the bit position is set using a jumper. In software, the bit position is set by specifying a hexadecimal value using configuration commands.

congestion   Traffic in excess of network capacity.

congestion avoidance   The mechanism by which an ATM network controls traffic entering the network to minimize delays. In order to use resources most efficiently, lower-priority traffic is discarded at the edge of the network if conditions indicate that it cannot be delivered.

congestion collapse   A condition in which the re-transmission of frames in an ATM network results in little or no traffic successfully arriving at the destination. Congestion collapse frequently occurs in ATM networks composed of switches that do not have adequate and effective buffering mechanisms complimented by intelligent packet discard or ABR congestion feedback mechanisms.

connectionless   Term used to describe data transfer without the existence of a virtual circuit. Compare with connection-oriented. *See also* virtual circuit.

connection-oriented   Term used to describe data transfer that requires the establishment of a virtual circuit. *See also* connectionless and virtual circuit.

CONP   Connection-Oriented Network Protocol. OSI protocol providing connection-oriented operation to upper-layer protocols. *See also* CMNS.

console   DTE through which commands are entered into a host.

contention   Access method in which network devices compete for permission to access the physical medium. Compare with circuit switching and token passing.

control direct VCC   In ATM, a bidirectional VCC set up by a LEC to a LES. One of three control connections defined by Phase 1 LANE. Compare with configuration direct VCC and control distribute VCC.

control distribute VCC   In ATM, a unidirectional VCC set up from a LES to a LEC. One of three control connections defined by Phase 1LANE. Typically, the VCC is a point-to-multipoint connection. Compare with configuration direct VCC and control direct VCC.

convergence   The speed and ability of a group of internetworking devices running a specific routing protocol to agree on the topology of an internetwork after a change in that topology.

conversation   In SNA, an LU 6.2 session between two transaction programs.

cookie   A piece of information sent by a Web server to a Web browser that the browser is expected to save and send back to the Web server whenever the browser makes additional requests of the Web server.

core gateway   The primary routers in the Internet.

core router   In a packet-switched star topology, a router that is part of the backbone and that serves as the single pipe through which all traffic from peripheral networks must pass on its way to other peripheral networks.

COS   1. class of service. Indication of how an upper-layer protocol requires that a lower-layer protocol treat its messages. In SNA subarea routing, COS definitions are used by subarea nodes to determine the optimal route to establish a given session. A COS definition comprises a virtual route number and a transmission priority field. Also called TOS (type of service). 2. Corporation for Open Systems. Organization that promulgates the use of OSI protocols through conformance testing, certification, and related activities.

COSINE   Cooperation for Open Systems Interconnection Networking in Europe. European project financed by the European Community (EC) to build a communication network between scientific and industrial entities in Europe. The project ended in 1994.

cost   Arbitrary value, typically based on hop count, media bandwidth, or other measures, that is assigned by a network administrator and used to compare various paths through an internetwork environment. Cost values are used by routing protocols to determine the most favorable path to a particular destination: the lower the cost, the better the path. Sometimes called path cost. *See also* routing metric.

count to infinity   Problem that can occur in routing algorithms that are slow to converge, in which routers continuously increment the hop count to particular networks. Typically, some arbitrary hop-count limit is imposed to prevent this problem.

CP   control point. In SNA networks, element that identifies the APPN networking components of a PU 2.1 node, manages device resources, and can provide services to other devices. In APPN, CPs are able to communicate with logically adjacent CPs by way of CP-to-CP sessions. *See also* EN and NN.

CPCS   common part convergence sublayer. One of the two sublayers of any AAL. The CPCS is service-independent and is further divided into the CS and the SAR sublayers. The CPCS is responsible for preparing data for transport across the ATM network, including the creation of the 48-byte payload cells that are passed to the ATM layer. *See also* AAL, ATM layer, CS, SAR, and SSCS.

CPE   customer premises equipment. Terminating equipment, such as terminals, telephones, and modems, supplied by the telephone company, installed at customer sites, and connected to the telephone company network.

CPI-C   Common Programming Interface for Communications. Platform-independent API developed by IBM and used to provide portability in APPC applications. *See also* APPC.

cps   cells per second.

crankback   A mechanism used by ATM networks when a connection setup request is blocked because a node along a selected path cannot accept the request. In this case, the path is rolled back to an intermediate node, which attempts to discover another path to the final destination using GCAC. *See also* GCAC.

CRC   cyclic redundancy check. Error-checking technique in which the frame recipient calculates a remainder by dividing frame contents by a prime binary divisor and compares the calculated remainder to a value stored in the frame by the sending node.

CREN   Corporation for Research and Educational Networking. The result of a merger of BITNET and CSNET. CREN is devoted to providing Internet connectivity to its members, which include the alumni, students, faculty, and other affiliates of participating educational and research institutions, via BITNET III. *See also* BITNET, BITNET III, and CSNET.

CRM   cell rate margin. One of three link attributes exchanged using PTSPs to determine the available resources of an ATM network. CRM is a measure of the difference between the effective bandwidth allocation per traffic class as the allocation for sustainable cell rate.

CRV   call reference value. A number carried in all Q.931 (I.451) messages that provides an identifier for each ISDN call.

cross talk   Interfering energy transferred from one circuit to another.

CS   convergence sublayer. One of the two sublayers of the AAL CPCS, responsible for padding and error checking. PDUs passed from the SSCS are appended with an

8-byte trailer (for error checking and other control information) and padded, if necessary, so that the length of the resulting PDU is divisible by 48. These PDUs are then passed to the SAR sublayer of the CPCS for further processing. *See also* AAL, CPCS, SAR, and SSCS.

CSA   Canadian Standards Association. Agency within Canada that certifies products that conform to Canadian national safety standards.

CSLIP   Compressed Serial Link Internet Protocol. Extension of SLIP that, when appropriate, allows just header information to be sent across a SLIP connection, reducing overhead and increasing packet throughput on SLIP lines. *See also* SLIP.

CSMA/CD   carrier sense multiple access collision detect. Media-access mechanism wherein devices ready to transmit data first check the channel for a carrier. If no carrier is sensed for a specific period of time, a device can transmit. If two devices transmit at once, a collision occurs and is detected by all colliding devices. This collision subsequently delays retransmissions from those devices for some random length of time. CSMA/CD access is used by Ethernet and IEEE 802.3.

CSNET   Computer Science Network. Large internetwork consisting primarily of universities, research institutions, and commercial concerns. CSNET merged with BITNET to form CREN. *See also* BITNET and CREN.

CSNP   complete sequence number PDU. PDU sent by the designated router in an OSPF network to maintain database synchronization.

CSU   channel service unit. Digital interface device that connects end-user equipment to the local digital telephone loop. Often referred to together with DSU, as CSU/DSU. *See also* DSU.

CTD   cell transfer delay. In ATM, the elapsed time between a cell exit event at the source UNI and the corresponding cell entry event at the destination UNI for a particular connection. The CTD between the two points is the sum of the total inter-ATM node transmission delay and the total ATM node processing delay.

CTS   1. Clear To Send. Circuit in the EIA/TIA-232 specification that is activated when DCE is ready to accept data from DTE. 2. common transport semantic. Cornerstone of the IBM strategy to reduce the number of protocols on networks. CTS provides a single API for developers of network software and enables applications to run over APPN, OSI, or TCP/IP.

cut-through packet switching   Packet switching approach that streams data through a switch so that the leading edge of a packet exits the switch at the output port before the packet finishes entering the input port. A device using cut-through packet switching reads, processes, and forwards packets as soon as the destination address is looked up, and the outgoing port determined. Also known as on-the-fly packet switching. Compare with store and forward packet switching.

CxBus   Cisco Extended Bus. Data bus for interface processors on Cisco 7000 series routers. *See also* SP.

DAC   dual-attached concentrator. FDDI or CDDI concentrator capable of attaching to both rings of an FDDI or CDDI network. It can also be dual-homed from the master ports of other FDDI or CDDI concentrators.

DACS   Digital Access and Cross-connect System. AT&T's term for a digital cross-connect system.

DARPA   Defense Advanced Research Projects Agency. U.S. government agency that funded research for and experimentation with the Internet. Evolved from ARPA, and then, in 1994, back to ARPA. *See also* ARPA.

DARPA Internet   Obsolete term referring to the Internet. See Internet.

DAS   1. dual attachment station. Device attached to both the primary and the secondary FDDI rings. Dual attachment provides redundancy for the FDDI ring: if the primary ring fails, the station can wrap the primary ring to the secondary ring, isolating the failure and retaining ring integrity. Also known as a Class A station. Compare with SAS. 2. dynamically assigned socket. A socket that is dynamically assigned by DDP upon request by a client. In an AppleTalk network, the sockets numbered 128 to 254 are allocated as DASs.

database object   A piece of information that is stored in a database.

data direct VCC   In ATM, a bi-directional point-to-point VCC set up between two LECs. One of three data connections defined by Phase 1 LANE. Data direct VCCs do not offer any type of QOS guarantee, so they are typically used for UBR and ABR connections. Compare with control distribute VCC and control direct VCC.

data flow control layer   Layer 5 of the SNA architectural model. This layer determines and manages interactions between session partners, particularly data flow. Corresponds to the Session layer of the OSI model. *See also* data link control layer, path control layer, physical control layer, presentation services layer, transaction services layer, and transmission control layer.

datagram   Logical grouping of information sent as a Network layer unit over a transmission medium without prior establishment of a virtual circuit. IP datagrams are the primary information units in the Internet. The terms cell, frame, message, packet, and segment are also used to describe logical information groupings at various layers of the OSI reference model and in various technology circles.

Datakit   An AT&T proprietary packet switching system widely deployed by the RBOCs.

data link control layer   Layer 2 in the SNA architectural model. Responsible for the transmission of data over a particular physical link. Corresponds roughly to the Data Link layer of the OSI model. *See also* data flow control layer, path control layer, physical control layer, presentation services layer, transaction services layer, and transmission control layer.

Data Link layer   Layer 2 of the OSI reference model. This layer provides reliable transit of data across a physical link. The Data Link layer is concerned with physical addressing, network topology, line discipline, error notification, ordered delivery of frames, and flow control. The IEEE has divided this layer into two sublayers: the MAC sublayer and the LLC sublayer. Sometimes simply called link layer. Roughly corresponds to the data link control layer of the SNA model. *See also* Application layer, LLC, MAC, Network layer, Physical layer, Presentation layer, Session layer, and Transport layer.

data sink   Network equipment that accepts data transmissions.

data stream   All data transmitted through a communications line in a single read or write operation.

DB connector   data bus connector. Type of connector used to connect serial and parallel cables to a data bus. DB connector names are of the format DB-x, where x represents the number of wires within the connector. Each line is connected to a pin on the connector, but in many cases, not all pins are assigned a function. DB connectors are defined by various EIA/TIA standards.

DCA   Defense Communications Agency. U.S. government organization responsible for DDN networks such as MILNET. Now called DISA. See DISA.

DCC   Data Country Code. One of two ATM address formats developed by the ATM Forum for use by private networks.Adapted from the subnetwork model of addressing in which the ATM layer is responsible for mapping Network layer addresses to ATM addresses. Compare with ICD.

DCE   data communications equipment (EIA expansion) or data circuit-terminating equipment (ITU-T expansion). The devices and connections of a communications network that comprise the network end of the user-to-network interface. TheDCE provides a physical connection to the network, forwards traffic, and provides a clocking signal used to synchronize data transmission between DCE and DTE devices. Modems and interface cards are examples of DCE. Compare with DTE.

DCS   Digital Cross-connect System. A network element providing automatic cross connection of a digital signal or its constituent parts.

D channel   1. data channel. Full-duplex, 16Kbps (BRI) or 64Kbps (PRI) ISDN channel. Compare to B channel, E channel, and H channel. 2. In SNA, a device that connects a processor and main storage with peripherals.

DDM   Distributed Data Management. Software in an IBM SNA environment that provides peer-to-peer communication and file sharing. One of three SNA transaction services. *See also* DIA and SNADS.

DDN   Defense Data Network. U.S. military network composed of an unclassified network (MILNET) and various secret and top-secret networks. DDN is operated and maintained by DISA. *See also* DISA and MILNET.

DDP   Datagram Delivery Protocol. AppleTalk Network layer protocol that is responsible for the socket-to-socket delivery of datagrams over an AppleTalk internetwork.

DDR   dial-on-demand routing. Technique whereby a router can automatically initiate and close a circuit-switched session as transmitting stations demand. The router spoofs keepalives so that end stations treat the session as active. DDR permits routing over ISDN or telephone lines using an external ISDN terminal adapter or modem.

DE   discard eligible. See tagged traffic.

deadlock   1. Unresolved contention for the use of a resource. 2. In APPN, when two elements of a process each wait for action by or a response from the other before they resume the process.

decibels   Abbreviated dB.

DECnet   Group of communications products (including a protocol suite) developed and supported by Digital Equipment Corporation. DECnet/OSI (also called DECnet Phase V) is the most recent iteration and supports both OSI protocols and proprietary Digital protocols. Phase IV Prime supports inherent MAC addresses that allow DECnet nodes to coexist with systems running other protocols that have MAC address restrictions. *See also* DNA.

DECnet routing   Proprietary routing scheme introduced by Digital Equipment Corporation in DECnet Phase III. In DECnet Phase V, DECnet completed its transition to OSI routing protocols (ES-IS and IS-IS).

decryption   The reverse application of an encryption algorithm to encrypted data, thereby restoring that data to its original, unencrypted state. *See also* encryption.

dedicated LAN   Network segment allocated to a single device. Used in LAN switched network topologies.

dedicated line   Communications line that is indefinitely reserved for transmissions, rather than switched as transmission is required. *See also* leased line.

de facto standard   Standard that exists by nature of its widespread use. Compare with de jure standard. *See also* standard.

default route   Routing table entry that is used to direct frames for which a next hop is not explicitly listed in the routing table.

de jure standard   Standard that exists because of its approval by an official standards body. Compare with de facto standard. *See also* standard.

delay   The time between the initiation of a transaction by a sender and the first response received by the sender. Also, the time required to move a packet from source to destination over a given path.

demand priority   Media access method used in 100VG-AnyLAN that uses a hub that can handle multiple transmission requests and can process traffic according to priority, making it useful for servicing time-sensitive traffic such as multimedia and video. Demand priority eliminates the overhead of packet collisions, collision recovery, and broadcast traffic typical in Ethernet networks. *See also* 100VG-AnyLAN.

demarc   Demarcation point between carrier equipment and CPE.

demodulation   Process of returning a modulated signal to its original form. Modems perform demodulation by taking an analog signal and returning it to its original (digital) form. *See also* modulation.

demultiplexing   The separating of multiple input streams that have been multiplexed into a common physical signal back into multiple output streams. *See also* multiplexing.

DES   Data Encryption Standard. Standard cryptographic algorithm developed by the U.S. NBS.

designated bridge   The bridge that incurs the lowest path cost when forwarding a frame from a segment to the route bridge.

designated router   OSPF router that generates LSAs for a multiaccess network and has other special responsibilities in running OSPF. Each multiaccess OSPF network that has at least two attached routers has a designated router that is elected by the OSPF Hello protocol. The designated router enables a reduction in the number of adjacencies required on a multiaccess network, which in turn reduces the amount of routing protocol traffic and the size of the topological database.

destination address   Address of a network device that is receiving data. *See also* source address.

deterministic load distribution   Technique for distributing traffic between two bridges across a circuit group. Guarantees packet ordering between source-destination pairs and always forwards traffic for a source-destination pair on the same segment in a circuit group for a given circuit-group configuration.

DHCP   Dynamic Host Configuration Protocol. Provides a mechanism for allocating IP addresses dynamically so that addresses can be reused when hosts no longer needs them.

DIA   Document Interchange Architecture. Defines the protocols and data formats needed for the transparent interchange of documents in an SNA network. One of three SNA transaction services. *See also* DDM and SNADS.

dial backup   Feature that provides protection against WAN downtime by allowing the network administrator to configure a backup serial line through a circuit-switched connection.

dial-up line   Communications circuit that is established by a switched-circuit connection using the telephone company network.

differential encoding   Digital encoding technique whereby a binary value is denoted by a signal change rather than a particular signal level.

differential Manchester encoding   Digital coding scheme where a mid-bit-time transition is used for clocking, and a transition at the beginning of each bit time denotes a zero. The coding scheme used by IEEE 802.5 and Token Ring networks.

DIN   Deutsche Industrie Norm. German national standards organization.

DIN connector   Deutsche Industrie Norm connector. Multipin connector used in some Macintosh and IBM PC-compatible computers, and on some network processor panels.

directed search   Search request sent to a specific node known to contain a resource. A directed search is used to determine the continued existence of the resource and to obtain routing information specific to the node. *See also* broadcast search.

directed tree   A logical construct used to define data streams or flows. The origin of a data stream is the root. Data streams are unidirectional branches directed away from the root and toward targets, and targets are the leaves of the directed tree.

directory services   Services that help network devices locate service providers.

DISA   Defense Information Systems Agency. U.S. military organization responsible for implementing and operating military information systems, including the DDN. *See also* DDN.

discovery architecture   APPN software that enables a machine configured as an APPN EN to automatically find primary and backup NNs when the machine is brought onto an APPN network.

discovery mode   Method by which an AppleTalk interface acquires information about an attached network from an operational node and then uses this information to configure itself. Also called dynamic configuration.

distance vector routing algorithm   Class of routing algorithms that iterate on the number of hops in a route to find a shortest-path spanning tree. Distance vector routing algorithms call for each router to send its entire routing table in each update, but only to its neighbors. Distance vector routing algorithms can be prone to routing loops, but are computationally simpler than link state routing algorithms. Also called Bellman-Ford routing algorithm. *See also* link-state routing algorithm and SPF.

distortion delay   Problem with a communication signal resulting from nonuniform transmission speeds of the components of a signal through a transmission medium. Also called group delay.

DLCI   data-link connection identifier. Value that specifies a PVC or SVC in a Frame Relay network. In the basic Frame Relay specification, DLCIs are locally significant (connected devices might use different values to specify the same connection). In the LMI extended specification, DLCIs are globally significant (DLCIs specify individual end devices). *See also* LMI.

DLSw   data-link switching. Interoperability standard, described in RFC 1434, that provides a method for forwarding SNA and NetBIOS traffic over TCP/IP networks using Data Link layer switching and encapsulation. DLSw uses SSP (Switch-to-Switch Protocol) instead of SRB, eliminating the major limitations of SRB, including hop-count limits, broadcast and unnecessary traffic, timeouts, lack of flow control, and lack of prioritization schemes. *See also* DLSw+, SRB, and SSP.

DLSw+   Data Link Switching Plus. Cisco implementation of the DLSw standard for SNA and NetBIOS traffic forwarding. DLSw+ goes beyond the standard to include the advanced features of the current Cisco RSRB implementation, and provides additional functionality to increase the overall scalability of data-link switching. *See also* DLSw.

DLU   Dependent LU. An LU that depends on the SSCP to provide services for establishing sessions with other LUs. *See also* LU and SSCP.

DLUR   Dependent LU Requester. The client half of the Dependent LU Requestor/Server enhancement to APPN. The DLUR component resides in APPN ENs and NNs that support adjacent DLUs by securing services from the DLUS. *See also* APPN, DLU, and DLUS.

DLUR node   In APPN networks, an EN or NN that implements the DLUR component. *See also* DLUR.

DLUS   Dependent LU Server. The server half of the Dependent LU Requestor/Server enhancement to APPN. The DLUS component provides SSCP services to DLUR nodes over an APPN network. *See also* APPN, DLU, and DLUR.

DLUS node   In APPN networks, a NN that implements the DLUS component. *See also* DLUS.

DMA   direct memory access. The transfer of data from a peripheral device, such as a hard disk drive, into memory without that data passing through the microprocessor. DMA transfers data into memory at high speeds with no processor overhead.

DMAC   destination MAC. The MAC address specified in the Destination Address field of a packet. Compare with SMAC. *See also* MAC address.

DMP   Data Movement Processor. Processor on the Catalyst 5000 that, along with the multiport packet buffer memory interface, performs the frame-switching function for the switch. The DMP also handles translational bridging between the Ethernet and FDDI interfaces, IP segmentation, and intelligent bridging with protocol-based filtering.

DNA   Digital Network Architecture. Network architecture developed by Digital Equipment Corporation. The products that embody DNA (including communications protocols) are collectively referred to as DECnet. *See also* DECnet.

DNIC   Data Network Identification Code. Part of an X.121 address. DNICs are divided into two parts: the first specifying the country in which the addressed PSN is located and the second specifying the PSN itself. *See also* X.121.

DNS   Domain Name System. System used in the Internet for translating names of network nodes into addresses. *See also* authority zone.

DNSIX   Department of Defense Intelligence Information System Network Security for Information Exchange. Collection of security requirements for networking defined by the U.S. Defense Intelligence Agency.

DoD   Department of Defense. U.S. government organization that is responsible for national defense. The DoD has frequently funded communication protocol development.

domain   1. In the Internet, a portion of the naming hierarchy tree that refers to general groupings of networks based on organization-type or geography. 2. In SNA, an SSCP and the resources it controls. 3. In IS-IS, a logical set of networks.

Domain   Networking system developed by Apollo Computer (now part of Hewlett-Packard) for use in its engineering workstations.

dot address   Refers to the common notation for IP addresses in the form n.n.n.n where each number n represents, in decimal, 1 byte of the 4-byte IP address. Also called dotted notation or four-part dotted notation.

DQDB   Distributed Queue Dual Bus. Data link layer communication protocol, specified in the IEEE 802.6 standard, designed for use in MANs. DQDB, which permits multiple systems to interconnect using two unidirectional logical buses, is an open standard that is designed for compatibility with carrier transmission standards, and is aligned with emerging standards for BISDN. SIP (SMDS Interface Protocol) is based on DQDB. *See also* MAN.

DRAM   dynamic random-access memory. RAM that stores information in capacitors that must be periodically refreshed. Delays can occur because DRAMs are inaccessible to the processor when refreshing their contents. However, DRAMs are less complex and have greater capacity than SRAMs. *See also* SRAM.

drop   Point on a multipoint channel where a connection to a networked device is made.

drop cable   Generally, a cable that connects a network device (such as a computer) to a physical medium. A type of AUI. *See also* AUI.

DS-0   digital signal level 0. Framing specification used in transmitting digital signals over a single channel at 64Kbps on a T1facility. Compare with DS-1 and DS-3.

DS-1   digital signal level 1. Framing specification used in transmitting digital signals at 1.544Mbps on a T1 facility (in the United States) or at 2.108Mbps on an E1 facility (in Europe). Compare with DS-0 and DS-3. *See also* E1 and T1.

DS-1/DTI   DS-1 domestic trunk interface. Interface circuit used for DS-1 applications with 24 trunks.

DS-3   digital signal level 3. Framing specification used for transmitting digital signals at 44.736Mbps on a T3 facility. Compare with DS-0 and DS-1. *See also* E3 and T3.

DSAP   destination service access point. The SAP of the network node designated in the Destination field of a packet. Compare to SSAP. *See also* SAP (service access point).

DSL   digital subscriber line. A public network technology that delivers high band-width over conventional copper wiring at limited distances. There are four types of DSLs: ADSL, HDSL, SDSL, and VDSL. All are provisioned via modem pairs, with one modem located at a central office and the other at the customer site. Because most DSL technologies don't use the whole bandwidth of the twisted pair, there is room left for a voice channel. *See also* ADSL, HDSL, SDSL, and VDSL.

DSP   domain specific part. The part of an NSAP-format ATM address that contains an area identifier, a station identifier, and a selector byte. *See also* NSAP.

DSPU   downstream physical unit. In SNA, a PU that is located downstream from the host. *See also* DSPU concentration in the Cisco Systems section.

DSPU concentration   Cisco IOS software feature that enables a router to function as a PU concentrator for SNA PU 2 nodes. PU concentration at the router simplifies the task of PU definition at the upstream host while providing additional flexibility and mobility for downstream PU devices.

DSR   data set ready. EIA/TIA-232 interface circuit that is activated when DCE is powered up and ready for use.

DSU   data service unit. Device used in digital transmission that adapts the physical interface on a DTE device to a transmission facility such as T1 or E1. The DSU is also responsible for such functions as signal timing. Often referred to together with CSU, as CSU/DSU. *See also* CSU.

DSX-1   Cross-connection point for DS-1 signals.

DTE   data terminal equipment. Device at the user end of a user-network interface that serves as a data source, destination, or both. DTE connects to a data network through a DCE device (for example, a modem) and typically uses clocking signals generated by the DCE. DTE includes such devices as computers, protocol translators, and multiplexers. Compare with DCE.

DTL   designated transit list. A list of nodes and optional link IDs that completely specify a path across a single PNNI peer group.

DTMF   dual tone multifrequency. Use of two simultaneous voice-band tones for dialing (such as touch tone).

DTR   data terminal ready. EIA/TIA-232 circuit that is activated to let the DCE know when the DTE is ready to send and receive data.

DUAL   Diffusing Update Algorithm. Convergence algorithm used in Enhanced IGRP that provides loop-free operation at every instant throughout a route computation. Allows routers involved in a topology change to synchronize at the same time, while not involving routers that are unaffected by the change. *See also* Enhanced IGRP.

dual counter-rotating rings   Network topology in which two signal paths, whose directions are opposite one another, exist in a token-passing network. FDDI and CDDI are based on this concept.

dual-homed station   Device attached to multiple FDDI rings to provide redundancy.

dual homing   Network topology in which a device is connected to the network by way of two independent access points (points of attachment). One access point is the primary connection, and the other is a standby connection that is activated in the event of a failure of the primary connection.

DVMRP   Distance Vector Multicast Routing Protocol. Internetwork gateway protocol, largely based on RIP, that implements a typical dense mode IP multicast scheme. DVMRP uses IGMP to exchange routing datagrams with its neighbors. *See also* IGMP.

DXI   Data Exchange Interface. ATM Forum specification, described in RFC 1483, that defines how a network device such as a bridge, router, or hub can effectively act as an FEP to an ATM network by interfacing with a special DSU that performs packet segmentation and reassembly.

dynamic address resolution   Use of an address resolution protocol to determine and store address information on demand.

Dynamic IISP   Dynamic Interim-Interswitch Signaling Protocol. A basic call routing protocol that automatically reroutes ATM connections in the event of link failures. Dynamic IISP is an interim solution until PNNI Phase 1 is completed. Contrast with IISP.

dynamic routing   Routing that adjusts automatically to network topology or traffic changes. Also called adaptive routing.

E1   Wide-area digital transmission scheme used predominantly in Europe that carries data at a rate of 2.048Mbps. E1 lines can be leased for private use from common carriers. Compare with T1. *See also* DS-1.

E.164   1. ITU-T recommendation for international telecommunication numbering, especially in ISDN, BISDN, and SMDS. An evolution of standard telephone numbers. 2. The name of the field in an ATM address that contains numbers in E.164 format.

E2A   Legacy protocols for providing OAM&P functions between a network element and an operations support system. *See also* OAM&P.

E3   Wide-area digital transmission scheme used predominantly in Europe that carries data at a rate of 34.368Mbps. E3 lines can be leased for private use from common carriers. Compare with T3. *See also* DS-3.

early token release   Technique used in Token Ring networks that allows a station to release a new token onto the ring immediately after transmitting, instead of waiting for the first frame to return. This feature can increase the total bandwidth on the ring. *See also* Token Ring.

EARN   European Academic Research Network. European network connecting universities and research institutes. EARN merged with RARE to form TERENA. *See also* RARE and TERENA.

EBCDIC   extended binary coded decimal interchange code. Any of a number of coded character sets developed by IBM consisting of 8-bit coded characters. This character code is used by older IBM systems and telex machines. Compare with ASCII.

E channel   echo channel. 64Kbps ISDN circuit-switching control channel. The E channel was defined in the 1984 ITU-T ISDN specification, but was dropped in the 1988 specification. Compare with B channel, D channel, and H channel.

echoplex   Mode in which keyboard characters are echoed on a terminal screen upon return of a signal from the other end of the line indicating that the characters were received correctly.

ECMA   European Computer Manufacturers Association. Group of European computer vendors who have done substantial OSI standardization work.

edge device   1. A physical device that is capable of forwarding packets between legacy interfaces (such as Ethernet and Token Ring) and ATM interfaces based on data-link and Network layer information. An edge device does not participate in the running of any Network layer routing protocol, but it obtains forwarding descriptions using the route distribution protocol. 2. Any device that isn't an ATM switch that can connect to an ATM switch.

EDI   electronic data interchange. The electronic communication of operational data such as orders and invoices betweenorganizations.

EDIFACT   Electronic Data Interchange for Administration, Commerce, and Transport. Data exchange standard administered by the United Nations to be a multi-industry EDI standard.

EEPROM   electrically erasable programmable read-only memory. EPROM that can be erased using electrical signals applied to specific pins. *See also* EPROM.

EFCI   Explicit Forward Congestion Indication. In ATM, one of the congestion feedback modes allowed by ABR service. A network element in an impending congestion state or in a congested state may set the EFCI. The destination end-system can implement a protocol that adaptively lowers the cell rate of the connection based on the value of the EFCI. *See also* ABR.

EGP   Exterior Gateway Protocol. Internet protocol for exchanging routing information between autonomous systems. Documented in RFC 904. Not to be confused with the general term exterior gateway protocol. EGP is an obsolete protocol that has been replaced by BGP. *See also* BGP.

EIA   Electronic Industries Association. Group that specifies electrical transmission standards. The EIA and TIA have developed numerous well-known communications standards, including EIA/TIA-232 and EIA/TIA-449. *See also* TIA.

EIA-530   Refers to two electrical implementations of EIA/TIA-449: RS-422 (for balanced transmission) and RS-423 (for unbalanced transmission). *See also* RS-422, RS-423, and EIA/TIA-449.

EIA/TIA-232   Common Physical layer interface standard, developed by EIA and TIA, that supports unbalanced circuits at signal speeds of up to 64Kbps. Closely resembles the V.24 specification. Formerly known as RS-232.

EIA/TIA-449 Popular Physical layer interface developed by EIA and TIA. Essentially, a faster (up to 2Mbps) version of EIA/TIA-232 capable of longer cable runs. Formerly called RS-449. *See also* EIA-530.

EIA/TIA-586 Standard that describes the characteristics and applications for various grades of UTP cabling. *See also* Category 1cabling, Category 2 cabling, Category 3 cabling, Category 4 cabling, Category 5 cabling, and UTC.

EIP Ethernet Interface Processor. Interface processor card on the Cisco 7000 series routers. The EIP provides high-speed (10Mbps) AUI ports that support Ethernet Version 1 and Ethernet Version 2 or IEEE 802.3 interfaces, and a high-speed data path to other interface processors.

EISA Extended Industry-Standard Architecture. 32-bit bus interface used in PCs, PC-based servers, and some UNIX workstations and servers. *See also* ISA.

ELAN emulated LAN. ATM network in which an Ethernet or Token Ring LAN is emulated using a client-server model. ELANs are composed of an LEC, an LES, a BUS, and an LECS. Multiple ELANs can exist simultaneously on a single ATM network. ELANs are defined by the LANE specification. *See also* BUS, LANE, LEC, LECS, and LES.

ELAP EtherTalk Link Access Protocol. The link-access protocol used in an EtherTalk network. ELAP is built on top of the standard Ethernet Data Link layer.

electronic mail Widely used network application in which text messages are transmitted electronically between end users over various types of networks using various network protocols. Often called e-mail.

EMA 1. Enterprise Management Architecture. Digital Equipment Corporation network management architecture, based on the OSI network management model. 2. Electronic Messaging Association. Forum devoted to standards and policy work, education, and development of electronic messaging systems such as electronic mail, voice mail, and facsimile.

EMI electromagnetic interference. Interference by electromagnetic signals that can cause reduced data integrity and increased error rates on transmission channels.

EMIF ESCON Multiple Image Facility. Mainframe I/O software function that allows one ESCON channel to be shared among multiple logical partitions on the same mainframe. *See also* ESCON.

EMP electromagnetic pulse. Caused by lightning and other high-energy phenomena. Capable of coupling enough energy into unshielded conductors to destroy electronic devices. *See also* Tempest.

emulation mode Function of an NCP that enables it to perform activities equivalent to those performed by a transmission control unit.

EN end node. APPN end system that implements the PU 2.1, provides end-user services, and supports sessions between local and remote CPs. ENs are not capable of routing traffic and rely on an adjacent NN for APPN services. Compare with NN. *See also* CP.

encapsulation   The wrapping of data in a particular protocol header. For example, Ethernet data is wrapped in a specific Ethernet header before network transit. Also, when bridging dissimilar networks, the entire frame from one network is simply placed in the header used by the Data Link layer protocol of the other network. *See also* tunneling.

encapsulation bridging   Carries Ethernet frames from one router to another across disparate media, such as serial and FDDI lines. Contrast with translational bridging.

encoder   Device that modifies information into the required transmission format.

encryption   The application of a specific algorithm to data so as to alter the appearance of the data making it incomprehensible to those who are not authorized to see the information. *See also* decryption.

end point   Device at which a virtual circuit or virtual path begins or ends.

Enhanced Monitoring Services   Set of analysis tools on the Catalyst 5000 switch, consisting of an integrated RMON agent and the SPAN. These tools provide traffic monitoring, and network segment analysis and management. *See also* RMON and span.

Enhanced IGRP   Enhanced Interior Gateway Routing Protocol. Advanced version of IGRP developed by Cisco. Provides superior convergence properties and operating efficiency, and combines the advantages of link state protocols with those of distance vector protocols. Compare with IGRP. *See also* IGP, OSPF, and RIP.

enterprise network   Large and diverse network connecting most major points in a company or other organization. Differs from a WAN in that it is privately owned and maintained.

entity   Generally, an individual, manageable network device. Sometimes called an alias.

entity identifier   The unique address of an NVE's socket in a node on an Apple-Talk network. The specific format of an entity identifier is network-dependent. *See also* NVE.

entity name   A name that an NVE may assign to itself. Although not all NVEs have names, NVEs can possess several names (or aliases). An entity name is made up of three character strings: object, entity type, and zone. For example: Bldg 2 LaserJet 5:LaserWriter@Bldg 2 Zone. *See also* NVE.

entity type   The part of an entity name that describes the entity's class; for example, LaserWriter or AFPServer. *See also* entity name.

EOM   end of message. An indicator in the AAL that identifies the last ATM cell containing information from a data packet that has been segmented.

EOT   end of transmission. Generally, a character that signifies the end of a logical group of characters or bits.

EPD   early packet discard. A mechanism used by some ATM switches to allow a complete AAL5 frame to be discarded when a threshold condition is met, such as one indicating that congestion is imminent. Useful for avoiding unwanted congestion that jeopardize the switch's ability to properly support existing connections with a guaranteed service. Compare with TPD.

EPROM   erasable programmable read-only memory. Nonvolatile memory chips that are programmed after they are manufactured, and, if necessary, can be erased by some means and reprogrammed. Compare with EEPROM and PROM.

equalization   Technique used to compensate for communications channel distortions.

ER   explicit rate. In ATM, an RMcell used to limit the ACR for a transmission to a specific value. It is initially set by the source to a requested rate , such as the PCR. Later, it may be reduced by any network element in the path to a value that the element can sustain. *See also* ACR, PCR, and RM.

error control   Technique for detecting and correcting errors in data transmissions.

error-correcting code   Code having sufficient intelligence and incorporating sufficient signaling information to enable the detection and correction of many errors at the receiver.

error-detecting code   Code that can detect transmission errors through analysis of received data based on the adherence of the data to appropriate structural guidelines.

ES   1. end system. Generally, an end-user device on a network. 2. end system. Non-routing host or node in an OSI network.

ESI   end system identifier. An identifier that distinguishes multiple nodes at the same level when the lower level peer group is partitioned. (Usually an IEEE 802 address.)

ESCON   Enterprise System Connection. IBM channel architecture that specifies a pair of fiber-optic cables, with either LEDs or lasers as transmitters and a signaling rate of 200Mbps.

ESCON channel   IBM channel for attaching mainframes to peripherals such as storage devices, backup units, and network interfaces. This channel incorporates fiber channel technology. The ESCON channel replaces the bus and tag channel. Compare with parallel channel. *See also* bus and tag channel.

ESD   electrostatic discharge. Discharge of stored static electricity that can damage electronic equipment and impair electrical circuitry, resulting in complete or intermittent failures.

ESF   Extended Superframe. Framing type used on T1 circuits that consists of 24 frames of 192 bits each, with the 193rd bit providing timing and other functions. ESF is an enhanced version of SF. *See also* SF.

ES-IS   End System-to-Intermediate System. OSI protocol that defines how end systems (hosts) announce themselves to intermediate systems (routers). *See also* IS-IS.

ESnet Energy Sciences Network. Data communications network managed and funded by the U.S. Department of Energy Office of Energy Research (DOE/OER). Interconnects the DOE to educational institutions and other research facilities.

ESS Electronic Switching System. AT&T's term for an electronic central office switch. A 5ESS is AT&T's digital central office for end office applications and a 4ESS is its digital central office for toll center application.

Ethernet Baseband LAN specification invented by Xerox Corporation and developed jointly by Xerox, Intel, and Digital Equipment Corporation. Ethernet networks use CSMA/CD and run over a variety of cable types at 10Mbps. Ethernet is similar to the IEEE 802.3 series of standards. *See also* 10Base2, 10Base5, 10BaseF, 10BaseT, 10Broad36, FastEthernet, and IEEE 802.3.

EtherTalk Apple Computer's data-link product that allows an AppleTalk network to be connected by Ethernet.

ETSI European Telecommunication Standards Institute. Organization created by the European PTTs and the European Community (EC) to propose telecommunications standards for Europe.

EUnet European Internet. European commercial Internet service provider. EUnet is designed to provide electronic mail, news, and other Internet services to European markets.

event Network message indicating operational irregularities in physical elements of a network or a response to the occurrence of a significant task, typically the completion of a request for information. *See also* alarm and trap.

excess rate In ATM, traffic in excess of the insured rate for a given connection. Specifically, the excess rate equals the maximum rate minus the insured rate. Excess traffic is delivered only if network resources are available and can be discarded during periods of congestion. Compare with insured rate and maximum rate.

EXEC The interactive command processor of the Cisco IOS software.

expansion The process of running a compressed data set through an algorithm that restores the data set to its original size. Compare with companding and compression.

expedited delivery Option set by a specific protocol layer telling other protocol layers (or the same protocol layer in another network device) to handle specific data more rapidly.

explicit route In SNA, a route from a source subarea to a destination subarea, as specified by a list of subarea nodes and transmission groups that connect the two.

explorer frame Frame sent out by a networked device in a SRB environment to determine the optimal route to another networked device.

explorer packet Generated by an end station trying to find its way through a SRB network. Gathers a hop-by-hop description of a path through the network by being marked (updated) by each bridge that it traverses, thereby creating a complete topological map. *See also* all-routes explorer packet, local explorer packet, and spanning explorer packet.

exterior gateway protocol   Any internetwork protocol used to exchange routing information between autonoous systems. Not to be confused with Exterior Gateway Protocol (EGP), which is a particular instance of an exterior gateway protocol.

exterior router   Router connected to an AURP tunnel, responsible for the encapsulation and deencapsulation of AppleTalk packets in a foreign protocol header (for example, IP). *See also* AURP and AURP tunnel.

failure domain   Area in which a failure has occurred in a Token Ring, defined by the information contained in a beacon. When a station detects a serious problem with the network (such as a cable break), it sends a beacon frame that includes the station reporting the failure, its NAUN, and everything in between. Beaconing in turn initiates a process called autoreconfiguration. *See also* autoreconfiguration, beacon, and NAUN.

fallback   A mechanism used by ATM networks when rigorous path selection does not generate an acceptable path. The fallback mechanism attempts to determine a path by selectively relaxing certain attributes, such as delay, in order to find a path that meets some minimal set of desired attributes.

fan-out unit   Device that allows multiple devices on a network to communicate using a single network attachment.

fantail   Panel of I/O connectors that attaches to an equipment rack, providing easy access for data connections to a networking.

Fast Ethernet   Any of a number of 100Mbps Ethernet specifications. Fast Ethernet offers a speed increase ten times that of the 10BaseT Ethernet specification, while preserving such qualities as frame format, MAC mechanisms, and MTU. Such similarities allow the use of existing 10BaseT applications and network management tools on Fast Ethernet networks. Based on an extension to the IEEE 802.3 specification. Compare with Ethernet. *See also* 100BaseFX, 100BaseT, 100BaseT4, 100BaseTX, 100BaseX, and IEEE 802.3.

fast switching   Cisco feature whereby a route cache is used to expedite packet switching through a router. Contrast with process switching.

fault management   One of five categories of network management defined by ISO for management of OSI networks. Fault management attempts to ensure that network faults are detected and controlled. *See also* accounting management, configuration management, performance management, and security management.

FCC   Federal Communications Commission. U.S. government agency that supervises, licenses, and controls electronic and electromagnetic transmission standards.

FCS   frame check sequence. Refers to the extra characters added to a frame for error control purposes. Used in HDLC, Frame Relay, and other Data Link layer protocols.

FDDI   Fiber Distributed Data Interface. LAN standard, defined by ANSI X3T9.5, specifying a 100Mbps token-passing network using fiber-optic cable, with transmission distances of up to 2 km. FDDI uses a dual-ring architecture to provide redundancy. Compare with CDDI and FDDI II.

FDDI II   ANSI standard that enhances FDDI. FDDI II provides isochronous transmission for connectionless data circuits and connection-oriented voice and video circuits. Compare with FDDI.

FDDITalk   Apple Computer's data-link product that allows an AppleTalk network to be connected by FDDI cable.

FDM   frequency-division multiplexing. Technique whereby information from multiple channels can be allocated bandwidth on a single wire based on frequency. Compare with ATDM, statistical multiplexing, and TDM.

FECN   forward explicit congestion notification. Bit set by a Frame Relay network to inform DTE receiving the frame that congestion was experienced in the path from source to destination. DTE receiving frames with the FECN bit set can request that higher-level protocols take flow-control action as appropriate. Compare with BECN.

FEP   front-end processor. Device or board that provides network interface capabilities for a networked device. In SNA, typically an IBM 3745 device.

FEIP   Fast Ethernet Interface Processor. Interface processor on the Cisco 7000 series routers. The FEIP supports up to two 100Mbps 100BaseT ports.

fiber-optic cable   Physical medium capable of conducting modulated light transmission. Compared with other transmission media, fiber-optic cable is more expensive, but is not susceptible to electromagnetic interference, and is capable of higher data rates. Sometimes called optical fiber.

FID0   format indicator 0. One of several formats that an SNA TH can use. An FID0 TH is used for communication between an SNA node and a non-SNA node. *See also* TH.

FID1   format indicator 1. One of several formats that an SNA TH can use. An FID1 TH encapsulates messages between two subarea nodes that do not support virtual and explicit routes. *See also* TH.

FID2   format indicator 2. One of several formats that an SNA TH can use. An FID2 TH is used for transferring messages between a subarea node and a PU 2, using local addresses. *See also* TH.

FID3   format indicator 3. One of several formats that an SNA TH can use. An FID3 TH is used for transferring messages between a subarea node and a PU 1, using local addresses. *See also* TH.

FID4   format indicator 4. One of several formats that an SNA TH can use. An FID4 TH encapsulates messages between two subarea nodes that are capable of supporting virtual and explicit routes. *See also* TH.

field-replaceable unit   Hardware component that can be removed and replaced on-site. Typical field-replaceable units include cards, power supplies, and chassis components.

file transfer Category of popular network applications that allow files to be moved from one network device to another.

filter Generally, a process or device that screens network traffic for certain characteristics, such as source address, destination address, or protocol, and determines whether to forward or discard that traffic based on the established criteria.

finger An software tool for determining whether a person has an account at a particular Internet site. Many sites do not allow incoming finger requests, but some do.

firewall Router or access server, or several routers or access servers, designated as a buffer between any connected public networks and a private network. A firewall router uses access lists and other methods to ensure the security of the private network.

firmware Software instructions set permanently or semipermanently in ROM.

FIP FDDI Interface Processor. Interface processor on the Cisco 7000 series routers. The FIP supports SASs, DASs, dual homing, and optical bypass, and contains a 16-mips processor for high-speed (100Mbps) interface rates. The FIP complies with ANSI and ISO FDDI standards.

flapping Routing problem where an advertised route between two nodes alternates (flaps) back and forth between two paths due to a network problem that causes intermittent interface failures.

Flash memory Nonvolatile storage that can be electrically erased and reprogrammed developed by Intel and licensed to other semiconductor companies. Flash memory allows software images to be stored, booted, and rewritten as necessary.

flash update Routing update sent asynchronously in response to a change in the network topology. Compare with routing update.

flat addressing A scheme of addressing that does not use a logical hierarchy to determine location. For example, MAC addresses are flat; bridging protocols must flood packets throughout the network in order to deliver the packet to the appropriate location. Compare with hierarchical addressing.

flooding Traffic passing technique used by switches and bridges in which traffic received on an interface is sent out all of the interfaces of that device except the interface on which the information was originally received.

flow Stream of data traveling between two endpoints across a network (for example, from one LAN station to another). Multiple flows can be transmitted on a single circuit.

flow control Technique for ensuring that a transmitting entity, such as a modem, does not overwhelm a receiving entity with data. When the buffers on the receiving device are full, a message is sent to the sending device to suspend the transmission until the data in the buffers has been processed. In IBM networks, this technique is called pacing.

flowspec The traffic parameters of a flow.

FLT   Full Line Terminal. A multiplexer that terminates a SONET span. *See also* SONET.

FM   frequency modulation. Modulation technique in which signals of different frequencies represent different data values. Compare with AM and PAM. *See also* modulation.

FNC   Federal Networking Council. Group responsible for assessing and coordinating U.S. federal agency networking policies and needs.

FOIRL   fiber-optic interrepeater link. Fiber-optic signaling methodology based on the IEEE 802.3 fiber-optic specification. FOIRL is a precursor of the 10BaseFL specification, which is designed to replace it. *See also* 10BaseFL.

forward channel   Communications path carrying information from the call initiator to the called party.

forward delay interval   Amount of time an interface spends listening for topology change information after that interface has been activated for bridging and before forwarding actually begins.

forwarding   Process of sending a frame toward its ultimate destination by way of an internetworking device.

FOTS   Fiber Optics Transmission Systems. Vendor-proprietary fiber optic transmission equipment.

Fourier transform   Technique used to evaluate the importance of various frequency cycles in a time series pattern.

FRAD   Frame Relay access device. Any network device that provides a connection between a LAN and a Frame Relay WAN. *See also* Cisco FRAD and FRAS in the Cisco Systems section.

fragment   Piece of a larger packet that has been broken down to smaller units.

fragmentation   Process of breaking a packet into smaller units when transmitting over a network medium that cannot support the original size of the packet. *See also* reassembly.

frame   Logical grouping of information sent as a Data Link layer unit over a transmission medium. Often refers to the header and trailer, used for synchronization and error control, that surround the user data contained in the unit. The terms cell, datagram, message, packet, and segment are also used to describe logical information groupings at various layers of the OSI reference model and in various technology circles.

frame forwarding   The mechanism by which frame-based traffic, such as HDLC and SDLC, traverses an ATM network.

Frame Relay   Industry-standard, switched Data Link layer protocol that handles multiple virtual circuits using HDLC encapsulation between connected devices. Frame Relay is more efficient than X.25, the protocol for which it is generally considered a replacement. *See also* X.25.

Frame Relay bridging   Bridging technique, described in RFC 1490, that uses the same spanning-tree algorithm as other bridging functions, but allows packets to be encapsulated for transmission across a Frame Relay network.

FRAS   Frame Relay Access Support. Cisco IOS software feature that allows SDLC, Token Ring, Ethernet, and Frame Relay-attached IBM devices to connect to other IBM devices across a Frame Relay network. *See also* FRAD.

free-trade zone   Part of an AppleTalk internetwork that is accessible by two other parts of the internetwork that are unable to directly access one another.

frequency   Number of cycles, measured in hertz, of an alternating current signal per unit time.

front end   Node or software program that requests services of a back end. *See also* back end, client, and server.

FSIP   Fast Serial Interface Processor. The default serial interface processor for Cisco 7000 series routers. The FSIP provides four or eight high-speed serial ports

FST   Fast Sequenced Transport. Connectionless, sequenced transport protocol that runs on top of the IP protocol. SRB traffic is encapsulated inside of IP datagrams and is passed over an FST connection between two network devices (such as routers). Speeds up data delivery, reduces overhead, and improves the response time of SRB traffic.

FTAM   File Transfer, Access, and Management. In OSI, an Application layer protocol developed for network file exchange and management between diverse types of computers.

FTP   File Transfer Protocol. Application protocol, part of the TCP/IP protocol stack, used for transferring files between network nodes. FTP is defined in RFC 959.

full duplex   Capability for simultaneous data transmission between a sending station and a receiving station. Compare with half duplex and simplex.

full mesh   Term describing a network in which devices are organized in a mesh topology, with each network node having either a physical circuit or a virtual circuit connecting it to every other network node. A full mesh provides a great deal of redundancy, but because it can be prohibitively expensive to implement, it is usually reserved for network backbones. *See also* mesh and partial mesh.

Fuzzball   Digital Equipment Corporation LSI-11 computer system running IP gateway software. The NSFnet used these systems as backbone packet switches.

G.703/G.704   ITU-T electrical and mechanical specifications for connections between telephone company equipment and DTE using BNC connectors and operating at E1 data rates.

G.804   ITU-T framing standard that defines the mapping of ATM cells into the physical medium.

gateway   In the IP community, an older term referring to a routing device. Today, the term router is used to describe nodes that perform this function, and gateway refers to a special-purpose device that performs an Application layer conversion of information from one protocol stack to another. Compare with router.

gateway host   In SNA, a host node that contains a gateway SSCP.

gateway NCP   NCP that connects two or more SNA networks and performs address translation to allow cross-network session traffic.

GB   gigabyte. Approximately 1,000,000,000 bytes.

GBps   gigabytes per second.

Gb   gigabit. 1,000,000,000 bits.

Gbps   gigabits per second.

GCAC   generic call admission control. In ATM, a PNNI algorithm designed for CBR and VBR connections.. Any node can use GCAC to calculate the expected CAC behavior of another node given than node's advertised link metrics and the QOS of a connection setup request. *See also* CAC.

GCRA   generic cell rate algorithm. An algorithm that defines conformance with respect to the traffic contract of the connection. For each cell arrival, the GCRA determines whether the cell conforms to the traffic contract.

GDP   Gateway Discovery Protocol. Cisco protocol that allows hosts to dynamically detect the arrival of new routers as well as determine when a router goes down. Based on UDP. *See also* UDP in the main glossary.

GGP   Gateway-to-Gateway Protocol. MILNET protocol specifying how core routers (gateways) should exchange reachability and routing information. GGP uses a distributed shortest-path algorithm.

GHz   gigahertz.

gigabit   Abbreviated Gb.

gigabits per second   Abbreviated Gbps.

gigabyte   Abbreviated GB.

gigabytes per second   Abbreviated GBps.

gigahertz   Abbreviated GHz.

gleaning   The process by which a router automatically derives AARP table entries from incoming packets. Gleaning speeds up the process of populating the AARP table. *See also* AARP.

GNS   Get Nearest Server. Request packet sent by a client on an IPX network to locate the nearest active server of a particular type. An IPX network client issues a GNS request to solicit either a direct response from a connected server or a response from a router that tells it where on the internetwork the service can be located. GNS is part of the IPX SAP. *See also* IPX and SAP (Service Advertisement Protocol).

GOSIP   Government OSI Profile. U.S. government procurement specification for OSI protocols. Through GOSIP, the government has mandated that all federal agencies standardize on OSI and implement OSI-based systems as they become commercially available.

grade of service   Measure of telephone service quality based on the probability that a call will encounter a busy signal during the busiest hours of the day.

graphical user interface   See GUI.

GRE   generic routing encapsulation. Tunneling protocol developed by Cisco that can encapsulate a wide variety of protocol packet types inside IP tunnels, creating a virtual point-to-point link to Cisco routers at remote points over an IP internetwork. By connecting multiprotocol subnetworks in a single-protocol backbone environment, IP tunneling using GRE allows network expansion across a single-protocol backbone environment

ground station   Collection of communications equipment designed to receive signals from (and usually transmit signals to) satellites. Also called a downlink station.

guard band   Unused frequency band between two communications channels that provides separation of the channels to prevent mutual interference.

GUI   graphical user interface. User environment that uses pictorial as well as textual representations of the input and output of applications and the hierarchical or other data structure in which information is stored. Conventions such as buttons, icons, and windows are typical, and many actions are performed using a pointing device (such as a mouse). Microsoft Windows and the Apple Macintosh are prominent examples of platforms utilizing a GUI.

half duplex   Capability for data transmission in only one direction at a time between a sending station and a receiving station. BSC is an example of a half-duplex protocol. *See also* BSC. Compare with full duplex and simplex.

handshake   Sequence of messages exchanged between two or more network devices to ensure transmission synchronization.

HBD3   Line code type used on E1 circuits.

H channel   high-speed channel. Full-duplex ISDN primary rate channel operating at 384Kbps. Compare with B channel, D channel, and E channel.

HDLC   High-Level Data Link Control. Bit-oriented synchronous Data Link layer protocol developed by ISO. Derived from SDLC, HDLC specifies a data encapsulation method on synchronous serial links using frame characters and checksums. *See also* SDLC.

HDSL   High-data-rate digital subscriber line. One of four DSL technologies. HDSL delivers 1.544Mbps of bandwidth each way over two copper twisted pairs. Because HDSL provides T1 speed, telephone companies have been using HDSL to provision local access to T1 services whenever possible. The operating range of HDSL is limited to 12,000 feet, so signal repeaters are installed to extend the service. HDSL requires two twisted pairs, so it is deployed primarily for PBX network connections, digital loop carrier systems, interexchange POPs, Internet servers, and private data networks. Compare with ADSL, SDSL, and VDSL.

headend   The end point of a broadband network. All stations transmit toward the headend; the headend then transmits toward the destination stations.

header   Control information placed before data when encapsulating that data for network transmission. Compare with trailer. *See also* PCI.

HEC   header error control. An algorithm for checking and correcting an error in an ATM cell. Using the fifth octet in the ATM cell header, ATM equipment may check for an error and correct the contents of the header. The check character is calculated using a CRC algorithm allowing a single bit error in the header to be corrected or multiple errors to be detected.

HELLO   Interior routing protocol used principally by NSFnet nodes. HELLO allows particular packet switches to discover minimal delay routes. Not to be confused with the Hello protocol.

hello packet   Multicast packet that is used by routers for neighbor discovery and recovery. Hello packets also indicate that a client is still operating and network-ready.

Hello protocol   Protocol used by OSPF systems for establishing and maintaining neighbor relationships. Not to be confused with HELLO.

helper address   Address configured on an interface to which broadcasts received on that interface will be sent.

HEPnet   High-Energy Physics Network. Research network that originated in the United States, but that has spread to most places involved in high-energy physics. Well-known sites include Argonne National Laboratory, Brookhaven National Laboratory, Lawrence Berkeley Laboratory, and the Stanford Linear Accelerator Center (SLAC).

hertz   Measure of frequency, abbreviated Hz. Synonymous with cycles per second.

heterogeneous network   Network consisting of dissimilar devices that run dissimilar protocols and in many cases support dissimilar functions or applications.

hierarchical addressing   A scheme of addressing that uses a logical hierarchy to determine location. For example, IP addresses consist of network numbers, subnet numbers, and host numbers, which IP routing algorithms use to route the packet to the appropriate location. Compare with flat addressing.

HIP   HSSI Interface Processor. Interface processor on the Cisco 7000 series routers. The HIP provides one HSSI port that supports connections to ATM, SMDS, Frame Relay, or private lines at speeds up to T3 or E3.

HIPPI   High-Performance Parallel Interface. High-performance interface standard defined by ANSI. HIPPI is typically used to connect supercomputers to peripherals and other devices.

holddown   State into which a route is placed so that routers will neither advertise the route nor accept advertisements about the route for a specific length of time (the holddown period). Holddown is used to flush bad information about a route from all routers in the network. A route is typically placed in holddown when a link in that route fails.

homologation   Conformity of a product or specification to international standards, such as ITU-T, CSA, TUV, UL, or VCCI. Enables portability across company and international boundaries.

hop   Term describing the passage of a data packet between two network nodes (for example, between two routers). *See also* hop count.

hop count   Routing metric used to measure the distance between a source and a destination. RIP uses hop count as its sole metric. *See also* hop and RIP.

host   Computer system on a network. Similar to the term node except that host usually implies a computer system, whereas node generally applies to any networked system, including access servers and routers. *See also* node.

host node   SNA subarea node that contains an SSCP. *See also* SSCP.

host number   Part of an IP address that designates which node on the subnetwork is being addressed. Also called a host address.

HPCC   High Performance Computing and Communications. U.S. government funded program advocating advances in computing, communications, and related fields. The HPCC is designed to ensure U.S. leadership in these fields through education, research and development, industry collaboration, and implementation of high-performance technology. The five components of the HPCC are ASTA, BRHR, HPCS, IITA, and NREN.

HPCS   High Performance Computing Systems. Component of the HPCC program designed to ensure U.S. technological leadership in high-performance computing through research and development of computing systems and related software. *See also* HPCC.

HPR   High Performance Routing. Second-generation routing algorithm for APPN. HPR provides a connectionless layer with nondisruptive routing of sessions around link failures, and a connection-oriented layer with end-to-end flow control, error control, and sequencing. Compare to ISR. *See also* APPN.

HSCI   High-Speed Communications Interface. Single-port interface, developed by Cisco, providing full-duplex synchronous serial communications capability at speeds up to 52Mbps.

HSRP   Hot Standby Router Protocol. Provides high network availability and transparent network topology changes. HSRP creates a Hot Standby router group with a lead router that services all packets sent to the Hot Standby address. The lead router is monitored by other routers in the group, and if it fails, one of these standby routers inherits the lead position and the Hot Standby group address

HSSI   High-Speed Serial Interface. Network standard for high-speed (up to 52Mbps) serial connections over WAN links.

HTTP   Hypertext Transfer Protocol. The protocol used by Web browsers and Web servers to transfer files, such as text and graphic files.

HTML Hypertext Markup Language. Simple hypertext document formatting language that uses tags to indicate how a given part of a document should be interpreted by a viewing application, such as a Web browser. *See also* hypertext and web browser.

hub 1. Generally, a term used to describe a device that serves as the center of a star-topology network. 2. Hardware or software device that contains multiple independent but connected modules of network and internetwork equipment. Hubs can be active (where they repeat signals sent through them) or passive (where they do not repeat, but merely split, signals sent through them). 3. In Ethernet and IEEE 802.3, an Ethernet multiport repeater, sometimes referred to as a concentrator.

hybrid network Internetwork made up of more than one type of network technology, including LANs and WANs.

hypertext Electronically-stored text that allows direct access to other texts by way of encoded links. Hypertext documents can be created using HTML, and often integrate images, sound, and other media that are commonly viewed using a browser. *See also* HTML and browser.

IAB Internet Architecture Board. Board of internetwork researchers who discuss issues pertinent to Internet architecture. Responsible for appointing a variety of Internet-related groups such as the IANA, IESG, and IRSG. The IAB is appointed by the trustees of the ISOC. *See also* IANA, IESG, IRSG, and ISOC.

IANA Internet Assigned Numbers Authority. Organization operated under the auspices of the ISOC as a part of the IAB. IANA delegates authority for IP address-space allocation and domain-name assignment to the InterNIC and other organizations. IANA also maintains a database of assigned protocol identifiers used in the TCP/IP stack, including autonomous system numbers. *See also* IAB, ISOC, and InterNIC.

ICD International Code Designator. One of two ATM address formats developed by the ATM Forum for use by private networks. Adapted from the subnetwork model of addressing in which the ATM layer is responsible for mapping Network layer addresses to ATM addresses. Compare with DCC.

ICMP Internet Control Message Protocol. Network layer Internet protocol that reports errors and provides other information relevant to IP packet processing. Documented in RFC 792.

IDI initial domain identifier. The portion of an NSAP or NSAP-format ATM address that specifies the address allocation and administration authority. *See also* NSAP.

IDN International Data Number. See X.121.

IDP initial domain part. The part of a CLNS address that contains an authority and format identifier and a domain identifier.

IDPR Interdomain Policy Routing. Interdomain routing protocol that dynamically exchanges policies between autonomous systems. IDPR encapsulates interautonomous system traffic and routes it according to the policies of each autonomous system along the path. IDPR is currently an IETF proposal. *See also* policy-based routing.

IDRP   IS-IS Interdomain Routing Protocol. OSI protocol that specifies how routers communicate with routers in different domains.

IEC   International Electrotechnical Commission. Industry group that writes and distributes standards for electrical products and components.

IEEE   Institute of Electrical and Electronics Engineers. Professional organization whose activities include the development of communications and network standards. IEEE LAN standards are the predominant LAN standards today.

IEEE 802.1   IEEE specification that describes an algorithm that prevents bridging loops by creating a spanning tree. The algorithm was invented by Digital Equipment Corporation. The Digital algorithm and the IEEE 802.1 algorithm are not exactly the same, nor are they compatible. *See also* spanning tree, spanning-tree algorithm, and Spanning-Tree Protocol.

IEEE 802.12   IEEE LAN standard that specifies the Physical layer and the MAC sublayer of the Data Link layer. IEEE 802.12 uses the demand priority media-access scheme at 100Mbps over a variety of physical media. *See also* 100VG-AnyLAN.

IEEE 802.2   IEEE LAN protocol that specifies an implementation of the LLC sublayer of the Data Link layer. IEEE 802.2 handles errors, framing, flow control, and the Network layer (Layer 3) service interface. Used in IEEE 802.3 and IEEE 802.5 LANs. *See also* IEEE 802.3 and IEEE 802.5.

IEEE 802.3   IEEE LAN protocol that specifies an implementation of the Physical layer and the MAC sublayer of the Data Link layer. IEEE 802.3 uses CSMA/CD access at a variety of speeds over a variety of physical media. Extensions to the IEEE 802.3 standard specify implementations for Fast Ethernet. Physical variations of the original IEEE 802.3 specification include 10Base2, 10Base5, 10BaseF, 10BaseT, and 10Broad36. Physical variations for Fast Ethernet include 100BaseT, 100BaseT4, and 100BaseX.

IEEE 802.4   IEEE LAN protocol that specifies an implementation of the Physical layer and the MAC sublayer of the Data Link layer. IEEE 802.4 uses token-passing access over a bus topology and is based on the token bus LAN architecture. *See also* token bus.

IEEE 802.5   IEEE LAN protocol that specifies an implementation of the Physical layer and MAC sublayer of the Data Link layer. IEEE 802.5 uses token passing access at 4 or 16Mbps over STP cabling and is similar to IBM Token Ring. *See also* Token Ring.

IEEE 802.6   IEEE MAN specification based on DQDB technology. IEEE 802.6 supports data rates of 1.5 to 155Mbps. *See also* DQDB.

IESG   Internet Engineering Steering Group. Organization, appointed by the IAB, that manages the operation of the IETF. *See also* IAB and IETF.

IETF Internet Engineering Task Force. Task force consisting of over 80 working groups responsible for developing Internet standards. The IETF operates under the auspices of ISOC. *See also* ISOC.

IFIP International Federation for Information Processing. Research organization that performs OSI prestandardization work. Among other accomplishments, IFIP formalized the original MHS model. *See also* MHS.

I-frame Information frame. One of three SDLC frame formats. *See also* S-frame and U-frame.

IGMP Internet Group Management Protocol. Used by IP hosts to report their multicast group memberships to an adjacent multicast router. *See also* multicast router.

IGP Interior Gateway Protocol. Internet protocol used to exchange routing information within an autonomous system. Examples of common Internet IGPs include IGRP, OSPF, and RIP. *See also* IGRP in the Cisco Systems section, OSPF, and RIP.

IIH IS-IS Hello. Message sent by all IS-IS systems to maintain adjacencies. *See also* IS-IS.

IISP Interim-Interswitch Signaling Protocol. Formerly known as PNNI Phase 0, IISP is an ATM signaling protocol for inter-switch communication. using manually configured prefix tables. When a signaling request is received by a switch, the switch checks the destination ATM address against the prefix table and notes the port with the longest prefix match. It then forwards the signaling request across that port using UNI procedures. IISP is an interim solution until PNNI Phase 1 is completed. Contrast with Dynamic IISP. (Reviewers: this is a new term and definition.)

IITA Information Infrastructure Technology and Applications. Component of the HPCC program intended to ensure U.S. leadership in the development of advanced information technologies. *See also* HPCC.

ILMI Interim Local Management Interface. Specification developed by the ATM Forum for incorporating network-management capabilities into the ATM UNI.

IMP interface message processor. Old name for ARPANET packet switches. *See also* packet switch.

INA Information Networking Architecture. A Bellcore object-oriented architecture for the management of ATM and SONET equipment and services in an operating company environment.

INASoft The Bellcore implementation of INA. *See also* INA.

in-band signaling Transmission within a frequency range normally used for information transmission. Compare with out-of-band signaling.

information element Used in signaling messages.

infrared Electromagnetic waves whose frequency range is above that of microwaves, but below that of the visible spectrum. LAN systems based on this technology represent an emerging technology.

INE   Intelligent Network Element. A network element that can be provisioned from a remote OSS.

INOC   Internet Network Operations Center. BBN group that in the early days of the Internet monitored and controlled the Internet core gateways (routers). INOC no longer exists in this form.

insured burst   In an ATM network, the largest burst of data above the insured rate that will be temporarily allowed on a PVC and not tagged by the traffic policing function for dropping in the case of network congestion. The insured burst is specified in bytes or cells. Compare with maximum burst. *See also* insured rate.

insured rate   The long-term data throughput, in bits or cells per second, that an ATM network commits to support under normal network conditions. The insured rate is 100 percent allocated; the entire amount is deducted from the total trunk bandwidth along the path of the circuit. Compare with excess rate and maximum rate. *See also* insured burst.

insured traffic   Traffic within the insured rate specified for an ATM PVC. This traffic should not be dropped by the network under normal network conditions. *See also* CLP and insured rate.

Integrated IS-IS   Routing protocol based on the OSI routing protocol IS-IS, but with support for IP and other protocols. Integrated IS-IS implementations send only one set of routing updates, making it more efficient than two separate implementations. Formerly referred to as Dual IS-IS. Compare with IS-IS.

Integrated Services Internet   An IETF proposal for enhancing IP to allow it to support integrated or multimedia services, including traffic management mechanisms that closely match the traffic management mechanisms of ATM. An example is RSVP.

interarea routing   Term used to describe routing between two or more logical areas. Compare with intra-area routing.

interface   1. Connection between two systems or devices. 2. In routing terminology, a network connection. 3. In telephony, a shared boundary defined by common physical interconnection characteristics, signal characteristics, and meanings of interchanged signals. 4. The boundary between adjacent layers of the OSI model.

interface processor   Any of a number of processor modules used in the Cisco 7000 series routers. See AIP, CIP, EIP, FEIP, FIP, FSIP, HIP, MIP, SIP (Serial Interface Processor), and TRIP.

interference   Unwanted communication channel noise.

International Standards Organization   Erroneous expansion of the acronym ISO. See ISO.

Internet   Term used to refer to the largest global internetwork, connecting tens of thousands of networks worldwide and having a "culture" that focuses on research and standardization based on real-life use. Many leading-edge network technologies come from the Internet community. The Internet evolved in part from ARPANET. At one time, called the DARPA Internet. Not to be confused with the general term internet. *See also* ARPANET.

internet   Short for internetwork. Not to be confused with the Internet. See internetwork.

Internet protocol   Any protocol that is part of the TCP/IP protocol stack. See TCP/IP.

internetwork   Collection of networks interconnected by routers and other devices that functions (generally) as a single network. Sometimes called an internet, which is not to be confused with the Internet.

internetworking   General term used to refer to the industry that has arisen around the problem of connecting networks together. The term can refer to products, procedures, and technologies.

InterNIC   Organization that serves the Internet community by supplying user assistance, documentation, training, registration service for Internet domain names, and other services. Formerly called Network Information Center (NIC).

interoperability   Ability of computing equipment manufactured by different vendors to communicate with one another successfully over a network.

intra-area routing   Term used to describe routing within a logical area. Compare with interarea routing.

Inverse ARP   Inverse Address Resolution Protocol. Method of building dynamic routes in a network. Allows an access server to discover the network address of a device associated with a virtual circuit.

I/O   input/output.

IOC   Independent Operating Company. An independently owned company providing local telephone services to residential and business customers in a geographic area not served by an RBOC.

IP   Internet Protocol. Network layer protocol in the TCP/IP stack offering a connectionless internetwork service. IP provides features for addressing, type-of-service specification, fragmentation and reassembly, and security. Documented in RFC 791.

IP address   32-bit address assigned to hosts using TCP/IP. An IP address belongs to one of five classes (A, B, C, D, or E) and is written as 4 octets separated by periods (dotted decimal format). Each address consists of a network number, an optional subnetwork number, and a host number. The network and subnetwork numbers together are used for routing, while the host number is used to address an individual host within the network or subnetwork. A subnet mask is used to extract network and subnetwork information from the IP address. Classless interdomain routing (CIDR) provides a new way of representing IP addresses and subnet masks. Also called an Internet address. *See also* CIDR, IP, and subnet mask.

IPCP   IP Control Protocol. The protocol that establishes and configures IP over PPP. *See also* IP and PPP.

IP multicast   Routing technique that allows IP traffic to be propagated from one source to a number of destinations or from many sources to many destinations. Rather than sending one packet to each destination, one packet is sent to a multicast group identified by a single IP destination group address.

IPv6   IP Version 6. A replacement for the current version of IP (Version 4). IPv6 includes support for flow ID in the packet header, which can be used to identify flows. Formerly known as IPng (next generation).

IPSO   IP Security Option. U.S. government specification that defines an optional field in the IP packet header that defines hierarchical packet security levels on a per interface basis.

IPX   Internetwork Packet Exchange. NetWare Network layer (Layer 3) protocol used for transferring data from servers to workstations. IPX is similar to IP and XNS.

IPXCP   IPX Control Protocol. The protocol that establishes and configures IPX over PPP. *See also* IPX and PPP.

IPXWAN   Protocol that negotiates end-to-end options for new links. When a link comes up, the first IPX packets sent across are IPXWAN packets negotiating the options for the link. When the IPXWAN options have been successfully determined, normal IPX transmission begins. Defined by RFC 1362.

IRDP   ICMP Router Discovery Protocol. Enables a host to determine the address of a router that it can use as a default gateway. Similar to ESIS, but used with IP. *See also* ES-IS.

IRN   intermediate routing node. In SNA, a subarea node with intermediate routing capability.

IRSG   Internet Research Steering Group. Group that is part of the IAB and oversees the activities of the IRTF. *See also* IAB and IRTF.

IRTF   Internet Research Task Force. Community of network experts that consider Internet-related research topics. The IRTF is governed by the IRSG and is considered a subsidiary of the IAB. *See also* IAB and IRSG.

IS   intermediate system. Routing node in an OSI network.

ISA   Industry-Standard Architecture. 16-bit bus used for Intel-based personal computers. *See also* EISA.

isarithmic flow control   Flow control technique that permits travel through the network. Possession of these permits grants the right to transmit. Isarithmic flow control is not commonly implemented.

ISDN   Integrated Services Digital Network. Communication protocol, offered by telephone companies, that permits telephone networks to carry data, voice, and other source traffic. *See also* BISDN, BRI, N-ISDN, and PRI.

IS-IS Intermediate System-to-Intermediate System. OSI link-state hierarchical routing protocol based on DECnet Phase V routing whereby ISs (routers) exchange routing information based on a single metric to determine network topology. Compare with Integrated IS-IS. *See also* ES-IS and OSPF.

ISO International Organization for Standardization. International organization that is responsible for a wide range of standards, including those relevant to networking. ISO developed the OSI reference model, a popular networking reference model.

ISL Inter-Switch Link. A Cisco-proprietary protocol that maintains VLAN information as traffic flows between switches and routers

ISO 3309 HDLC procedures developed by ISO. ISO 3309:1979 specifies the HDLC frame structure for use in synchronous environments. ISO 3309:1984 specifies proposed modifications to allow the use of HDLC in asynchronous environments as well.

ISO 9000 Set of international quality-management standards defined by ISO. The standards, which are not specific to any country, industry, or product, allow companies to demonstrate that they have specific processes in place to maintain an efficient quality system.

ISOC Internet Society. International nonprofit organization, founded in 1992, that coordinates the evolution and use of the Internet. In addition, ISOC delegates authority to other groups related to the Internet, such as the IAB. ISOC is headquartered in Reston, Virginia, U.S.A. *See also* IAB.

isochronous transmission Asynchronous transmission over a synchronous data link. Isochronous signals require a constant bit rate for reliable transport. Compare with asynchronous transmission, plesiochronous transmission, and synchronous transmission.

ISODE ISO development environment. Large set of libraries and utilities used to develop upper-layer OSI protocols and applications.

ISP Internet service provider. A company that provides Internet access to other companies and individuals.

ISR Intermediate Session Routing. Initial routing algorithm used in APPN. ISR provides node-to-node connection-oriented routing. Network outages cause sessions to fail because ISR cannot provide nondisruptive rerouting around a failure. ISR has been replaced by HPR. Compare with HPR. *See also* APPN.

ISSI Inter-Switching System Interface. Standard interface between SMDS switches.

ITU-T International Telecommunication Union Telecommunication Standardization Sector. International body that develops worldwide standards for telecommunications technologies. The ITU-T carries out the functions of the former CCITT. *See also* CCITT.

IXC   inter-exchange carrier. A common carrier providing long distance connectivity between LATAs. The three major IXCs are AT&T, MCI, and Sprint, but several hundred IXCs offer long distance service in the US market.

jabber   1. Error condition in which a network device continually transmits random, meaningless data onto the network. 2. In IEEE 802.3, a data packet whose length exceeds that prescribed in the standard.

JANET   Joint Academic Network. X.25 WAN connecting university and research institutions in the United Kingdom.

jitter   Analog communication line distortion caused by the variation of a signal from its reference timing positions. Jitter can cause data loss, particularly at high speeds.

JPEG   Joint Photographics Expert Group. A graphic file format that has standard adopted as a standard by the ITU-T and the ISO. JPEG is most often used to compress still images using discrete cosine transform (DCT) analysis.

jumper   Electrical switch consisting of a number of pins and a connector that can be attached to the pins in a variety of different ways. Different circuits are created by attaching the connector to different pins.

JUNET   Japan UNIX Network. Nationwide, noncommercial network in Japan, designed to promote communication between Japanese and other researchers.

JvNCnet   John von Neumann Computer Network. Regional network, owned and operated by Global Enterprise Services, Inc., composed of T1 and slower serial links providing midlevel networking services to sites in the Northeastern United States.

Karn's algorithm   Algorithm that improves round-trip time estimations by helping Transport layer protocols distinguish between good and bad round-trip time samples.

KB   kilobyte.

Kb   kilobit.

KBps   kilobytes per second.

Kbps   kilobits per second.

keepalive interval   Period of time between each keepalive message sent by a network device.

keepalive message   Message sent by one network device to inform another network device that the virtual circuit between the two is still active.

Kerberos   A developing standard for authenticating network users. Kerberos offers two key benefits: it functions in a multivendor network and it does not transmit passwords over the network.

Kermit   Popular file-transfer and terminal-emulation program.

kilobit   Abbreviated Kb.

kilobits per second   Abbreviated Kbps.

kilobyte   Abbreviated KB.

kilobytes per second   Abbreviated KBps.

L2F Protocol   Layer 2 Forwarding Protocol. A protocol that supports the creation of secure virtual private dial-up networks over the Internet.

label swapping   Routing algorithm used by APPN in which each router that a message passes through on its way to its destination independently determines the best path to the next router.

LAN   local-area network. High-speed, low-error data network covering a relatively small geographic area (up to a few thousand meters). LANs connect workstations, peripherals, terminals, and other devices in a single building or other geographically limited area. LAN standards specify cabling and signaling at the physical and Data Link layers of the OSI model. Ethernet, FDDI, and Token Ring are widely used LAN technologies. Compare with MAN and WAN.

LANE   LAN emulation. Technology that allows an ATM network to function as a LAN backbone. The ATM network must provide multicast and broadcast support, address mapping (MAC-to-ATM), SVC management, and a usable packet format. LANE also defines Ethernet and Token Ring ELANs. *See also* ELAN.

LAN Manager   Distributed NOS, developed by Microsoft, that supports a variety of protocols and platforms. *See also* NOS.

LAN Server   Server-based NOS developed by IBM and derived from LNM. *See also* LNM.

LAN switch   High-speed switch that forwards packets between data-link segments. Most LAN switches forward traffic based on MAC addresses. This variety of LAN switch is sometimes called a frame switch. LAN switches are often categorized according to the method they use to forward traffic: cut-through packet switching or store-and-forward packet switching. Multilayer switches are an intelligent subset of LAN switches. Compare with multilayer switch. *See also* cut-through packet switching and store and forward packet switching.

LAPB   Link Access Procedure, Balanced. Data link layer protocol in the X.25 protocol stack. LAPB is a bit-oriented protocol derived from HDLC. *See also* HDLC and X.25.

LAPD   Link Access Procedure on the D channel. ISDN Data Link layer protocol for the D channel. LAPD was derived from the LAPB protocol and is designed primarily to satisfy the signaling requirements of ISDN basic access. Defined by ITU-T Recommendations Q.920 and Q.921.

LAPM   Link Access Procedure for Modems. ARQ used by modems implementing the V.42 protocol for error correction. *See also* ARQ and V.42.

laser   light amplification by stimulated emission of radiation. Analog transmission device in which a suitable active material is excited by an external stimulus to produce a narrow beam of coherent light that can be modulated into pulses to carry data. Networks based on laser technology are sometimes run over SONET.

LAT local-area transport. A network virtual terminal protocol developed by Digital Equipment Corporation.

LATA local access and transport area. Geographic telephone dialing area serviced by a single local telephone company. Calls within LATAs are called "local calls." There are well over 100 LATAs in the United States.

latency 1. Delay between the time a device requests access to a network and the time it is granted permission to transmit. 2. Delay between the time when a device receives a frame and the time that frame is forwarded out the destination port.

LCI logical channel identifier. See VCN.

LCN logical channel number. See VCN.

LCP Link Control Protocol. A protocol that establishes, configures, and tests data-link connections for use by PPP. *See also* PPP.

LCV line code violation. The occurrence of a bipolar violation (BPV) or excessive zeros (EXZ) error event.

leaf internetwork In a star topology, an internetwork whose sole access to other internetworks in the star is through a core router.

leaky bucket In ATM, a metaphor for the generic cell rate algorithm (GCRA), which is used for conformance checking of cell flows from a user or network. The hole in the bucket represents the sustained rate at which cells can be accommodated and the bucket depth represents the tolerance for cell bursts over a period of time. *See also* GCRA.

learning bridge Bridge that performs MAC address learning to reduce traffic on the network. Learning bridges manage a database of MAC addresses and the interfaces associated with each address. *See also* MAC address learning.

leased line Transmission line reserved by a communications carrier for the private use of a customer. A leased line is a type of dedicated line. *See also* dedicated line.

LE_ARP LAN Emulation Address Resolution Protocol. A protocol that provides the ATM address that corresponds to a MAC address.

LEC 1. LAN Emulation Client. Entity in an end system that performs data forwarding, address resolution, and other control functions for a single ES within a single ELAN. A LEC also provides a standard LAN service interface to any higher-layer entity that interfaces to the LEC. Each LEC is identified by a unique ATM address, and is associated with one or more MAC addresses reachable through that ATM address. *See also* ELAN and LES. 2. local exchange carrier. Local or regional telephone company that owns and operates a telephone network and the customer lines that connect to it.

LECS LAN Emulation Configuration Server. Entity that assigns individual LANE clients to particular ELANs by directing them to the LES that corresponds to the ELAN. There is logically one LECS per administrative domain, and this serves all ELANs within that domain. *See also* ELAN.

LED   light emitting diode. Semiconductor device that emits light produced by converting electrical energy. Status lights on hardware devices are typically LEDs.

LEN node   low-entry networking node. In SNA, a PU 2.1 that supports LU protocols, but chose CP cannot communicate with other nodes. Because there is no CP-to-CP session between a LEN node and its NN, the LEN node must have a statically defined image of the APPN network.

LES   LAN Emulation Server. Entity that implements the control function for a particular ELAN. There is only one logical LES per ELAN, and it is identified by a unique ATM address. *See also* ELAN.

Level 1 router   Device that routes traffic within a single DECnet or OSI area.

Level 2 router   Device that routes traffic between DECnet or OSI areas. All Level 2 routers must form a contiguous network.

LGN   logical group node. The node that represents its peer group in the peer group's higher-level peer group. *See also* peer group.

limited resource link   Resource defined by a device operator to remain active only when being used.

line   1. In SNA, a connection to the network. 2. See link.

line card   Any I/O card that can be inserted in a modular chassis.

line code type   One of a number of coding schemes used on serial lines to maintain data integrity and reliability. The line code type used is determined by the carrier service provider. *See also* AMI, B8ZS, and HBD3.

line conditioning   Use of equipment on leased voice-grade channels to improve analog characteristics, thereby allowing higher transmission rates.

line driver   Inexpensive amplifier and signal converter that conditions digital signals to ensure reliable transmissions over extended distances.

line of sight   Characteristic of certain transmission systems such as laser, microwave, and infrared systems in which no obstructions in a direct path between transmitter and receiver can exist.

line turnaround   Time required to change data transmission direction on a telephone line.

link   Network communications channel consisting of a circuit or transmission path and all related equipment between a sender and a receiver. Most often used to refer to a WAN connection. Sometimes referred to as a line or a transmission link.

link-state routing algorithm   Routing algorithm in which each router broadcasts or multicasts information regarding the cost of reaching each of its neighbors to all nodes in the internetwork. Link state algorithms create a consistent view of the network and are therefore not prone to routing loops, but they achieve this at the cost of relatively greater computational difficulty and more widespread traffic (compared with distance vector routing algorithms). Compare with distance vector routing algorithm. *See also* Dijkstra's algorithm.

LIS   Logical IP Subnet. A group of IP nodes (such as hosts and routers) that connect to a single ATM network and belong to the same IP subnet.

little-endian   Method of storing or transmitting data in which the least significant bit or byte is presented first. Compare with big-endian.

LLAP   LocalTalk Link Access Protocol. The link-level protocol that manages node-to-node delivery of data a LocalTalk environment. LLAP manages bus access, provides a node-addressing mechanism, and controls data transmission and reception, ensuring packet length and integrity.

LLC   Logical Link Control. Higher of the two Data Link layer sublayers defined by the IEEE. The LLC sublayer handles error control, flow control, framing, and MAC-sublayer addressing. The most prevalent LLC protocol is IEEE 802.2, which includes both connectionless and connection-oriented variants. *See also* Data Link layer and MAC.

LLC2   Logical Link Control, type 2. Connection-oriented OSI LLC-sublayer protocol. *See also* LLC.

LMI   Local Management Interface. Set of enhancements to the basic Frame Relay specification. LMI includes support for a keepalive mechanism, which verifies that data is flowing; a multicast mechanism, which provides the network server with its local DLCI and the multicast DLCI; global addressing, which gives DLCIs global rather than local significance in Frame Relay networks; and a status mechanism, which provides an on-going status report on the DLCIs known to the switch. Known as LMT in ANSI terminology.

LM/X   LAN Manager for UNIX. Monitors LAN devices in UNIX environments.

LNNI   LAN Emulation Network-to-Network Interface. Supports communication between the server components within a single ELAN. Phase 1 LANE protocols do not allow for the standard support of multiple LESs or BUSs within an ELAN. Phase 2 addresses these limitations.

LNM   LAN Network Manager. SRB and Token Ring management package provided by IBM. Typically running on a PC, it monitors SRB and Token Ring devices, and can pass alerts up to NetView.

load balancing   In routing, the ability of a router to distribute traffic over all its network ports that are the same distance from the destination address. Good load-balancing algorithms use both line speed and reliability information. Load balancing increases the utilization of network segments, thus increasing effective network bandwidth.

local acknowledgment   Method whereby an intermediate network node, such as a router, responds to acknowledgments for a remote end host. Use of local acknowledgments reduces network overhead and, therefore, the risk of time-outs. Also known as local termination.

local bridge   Bridge that directly interconnects networks in the same geographic area.

local explorer packet   Generated by an end system in an SRB network to find a host connected to the local ring. If the local explorer packet fails to find a local host, the end system produces either a spanning explorer packet or an all-routes explorer packet. *See also* all-routes explorer packet, explorer packet, and spanning explorer packet.

local loop   Line from the premises of a telephone subscriber to the telephone company CO.

LocalTalk   Apple Computer's proprietary baseband protocol that operates at the data link and Physical layers of the OSI reference model. LocalTalk uses CSMA/CD and supports transmissions at speeds of 230.4Kbps.

local traffic filtering   Process by which a bridge filters out (drops) frames whose source and destination MAC addresses are located on the same interface on the bridge, thus preventing unnecessary traffic from being forwarded across the bridge. Defined in the IEEE 802.1 standard. *See also* IEEE 802.1.

logical channel   Nondedicated, packet-switched communications path between two or more network nodes. Packet switching allows many logical channels to exist simultaneously on a single physical channel.

loop   Route where packets never reach their destination, but simply cycle repeatedly through a constant series of network nodes.

loopback test   Test in which signals are sent and then directed back toward their source from some point along the communications path. Loopback tests are often used to test network interface usability.

lossy   Characteristic of a network that is prone to lose packets when it becomes highly loaded.

LPD   line printer daemon. Protocol used to send print jobs between UNIX systems.

LSA   link-state advertisement. Broadcast packet used by link-state protocols that contains information about neighbors and path costs. LSAs are used by the receiving routers to maintain their routing tables. Sometimes called a link-state packet (LSP).

LSP   link-state packet. See LSA.

LU   logical unit. Primary component of SNA, an LU is an NAU that enables end users to communicate with each other and gain access to SNA network resources.

LU 6.2   Logical Unit 6.2. IN SNA, an LU that provides peer-to-peer communication between programs in a distributed computing environment. APPC runs on LU 6.2 devices. *See also* APPC.

LUNI   LAN Emulation User-to-Network Interface. The ATM Forum standard for LAN emulation on ATM networks. LUNI defines the interface between the LAN Emulation Client (LEC) and the LAN Emulation Server components. *See also* BUS, LES, and LECS.

MAC   Media Access Control. Lower of the two sublayers of the Data Link layer defined by the IEEE. The MAC sublayer handles access to shared media, such as whether token passing or contention will be used. *See also* Data Link layer and LLC.

MAC address   Standardized Data Link layer address that is required for every port or device that connects to a LAN. Other devices in the network use these addresses to locate specific ports in the network and to create and update routing tables and data structures. MAC addresses are 6 bytes long and are controlled by the IEEE. Also known as a hardware address, a MAC-layer address, or a physical address. Compare with network address.

MAC address learning   Service that characterizes a learning bridge, in which the source MAC address of each received packet is stored so that future packets destined for that address can be forwarded only to the bridge interface on which that address is located. Packets destined for unrecognized addresses are forwarded out every bridge interface. This scheme helps minimize traffic on the attached LANs. MAC address learning is defined in the IEEE 802.1 standard. *See also* learning bridge and MAC address.

MacIP   Network layer protocol that encapsulates IP packets in Datagram Delivery Protocol (DDP) packets for transmission over AppleTalk. MacIP also provides proxy ARP services.

MAN   metropolitan-area network. Network that spans a metropolitan area. Generally, a MAN spans a larger geographic area than a LAN, but a smaller geographic area than a WAN. Compare with LAN and WAN.

managed object   In network management, a network device that can be managed by a network management protocol.

management services   SNA functions distributed among network components to manage and control an SNA network.

Manchester encoding   Digital coding scheme, used by IEEE 802.3 and Ethernet, in which a mid-bit-time transition is used for clocking, and a 1is denoted by a high level during the first half of the bit time.

MAP   Manufacturing Automation Protocol. Network architecture created by General Motors to satisfy the specific needs of the factory floor. MAP specifies a token-passing LAN similar to IEEE 802.4. *See also* IEEE 802.4.

MARS   Multicast Address Resolution Server. A mechanism for supporting IP multicast. A MARS serves a group of nodes (known as a cluster); each node in the cluster is configured with the ATM address of the MARS. The MARS supports multicast through multicast messages of overlaid point-to-multipoint connections or through multicast servers.

MAU   media attachment unit. Device used in Ethernet and IEEE 802.3 networks that provides the interface between the AUI port of a station and the common medium of the Ethernet. The MAU, which can be built into a station or can be a separate device, performs Physical layer functions including the conversion of digital data from the Ethernet interface, collision detection, and injection of bits onto the network. Sometimes referred to as a media access unit, also abbreviated MAU, or as a transceiver. In Token Ring, a MAU is known as a multistation access unit and is usually abbreviated MSAU to avoid confusion. *See also* AUI and MSAU.

maximum burst   Specifies the largest burst of data above the insured rate that will be allowed temporarily on an ATM PVC, but will not be dropped at the edge by the traffic policing function, even if it exceeds the maximum rate. This amount of traffic will be allowed only temporarily; on average, the traffic source needs to be within the maximum rate. Specified in bytes or cells. Compare with insured burst. *See also* maximum rate.

maximum rate   Maximum total data throughput allowed on a given virtual circuit, equal to the sum of the insured and uninsured traffic from the traffic source. The uninsured data might be dropped if the network becomes congested. The maximum rate, which cannot exceed the media rate, represents the highest data throughput the virtual circuit will ever deliver, measured in bits or cells per second. Compare with excess rate and insured rate. *See also* maximum burst.

MB   megabyte. 1,000,000 bytes.

Mb   megabit. 1,000,000 bits.

MBS   maximum burst size. In an ATM signaling message, burst tolerance is conveyed through the MBS, which is coded as a number of cells. The burst tolerance together with the SCR and the GCRA determine the MBS that may be transmitted at the peak rate and still be in conformance with the GCRA.

MBONE   multicast backbone. The multicast backbone of the Internet. MBONE is a virtual multicast network composed of multicast LANs and the point-to-point tunnels that interconnect them.

Mbps   megabits per second.

MCA   micro channel architecture. Bus interface commonly used in PCs and some UNIX workstations and servers.

MCDV   maximum cell delay variation. In an ATM network, the maximum two-point CDV objective across a link or node for the specified service category. One of four link metrics exchanged using PTSPs to determine the available resources of an ATM network. There is one MCDV value of each traffic class.

MCLR   maximum cell loss ratio. In an ATM network, the maximum ratio of cells that do not successfully transit a link or node compared with the total number of cells that arrive at the link or node. One of four link metrics exchanged using PTSPs to determine the available resources of an ATM network. The MCLR applies to cells in the CBR and VBR traffic classes whose CLP bit is set to zero. *See also* CBR, CLP, PTSP, and VBR.

MCR   minimum cell rate. Parameter defined by the ATM Forum for ATM traffic management. MCR is defined only for ABR transmissions, and specifies the minimum value for the ACR. *See also* ABR (available bit rate), ACR, and PCR.

MCTD   maximum cell transfer delay. In an ATM network, the sum of the MCDV and the fixed delay component across the link or node. One of four link metrics exchanged using PTSPs to determine the available resources of an ATM network. There is one MCTD value for each traffic class. *See also* MCDV and PTSP.

MD   Mediation Device. A device that provides protocol translation and concentration of telemetry information originating from multiple network elements and transport to an OSS. *See also* OSS.

MD5   Message Digest 5. Algorithm used for message authentication in SNMP v.2. MD5 verifies the integrity of the communication, authenticates the origin, and checks for timeliness. *See also* SNMP2.

media   Plural of medium. The various physical environments through which transmission signals pass. Common network media include twisted-pair, coaxial and fiber-optic cable, and the atmosphere (through which microwave, laser, and infrared transmission occurs). Sometimes called physical media.

media rate   Maximum traffic throughput for a particular media type.

megabit   Abbreviated Mb. Approximately 1,000,000 bits.

megabits per second   Abbreviated Mbps.

megabyte   Abbreviated MB. Approximately 1,000,000 bytes.

mesh   Network topology in which devices are organized in a manageable, segmented manner with many, often redundant, interconnections strategically placed between network nodes. *See also* full mesh and partial mesh.

message   Application layer (Layer 7) logical grouping of information, often composed of a number of lower-layer logical groupings such as packets. The terms datagram, frame, packet, and segment are also used to describe logical information groupings at various layers of the OSI reference model and in various technology circles.

message switching   Switching technique involving transmission of messages from node to node through a network. The message is stored at each node until such time as a forwarding path is available. Contrast with circuit switching and packet switching.

message unit   Unit of data processed by any Network layer.

metasignaling   Process running at the ATM layer that manages signaling types and virtual circuits.

MHS   message handling system. ITU-T X.400 recommendations that provide message handling services for communications between distributed applications. NetWare MHS is a different (though similar) entity that also provides message-handling services. *See also* IFIP.

MIB   Management Information Base. Database of network management information that is used and maintained by a network management protocol such as SNMP or CMIP. The value of a MIB object can be changed or retrieved using SNMP or

CMIP commands, usually through a GUI network management system. MIB objects are organized in a tree structure that includes public (standard) and private (proprietary) branches.

MIC   media interface connector. FDDI de facto standard connector.

MID   message identifier. In ATM, used to identify ATM cells that carry segments from the same higher-layer packet.

microcode   Translation layer between machine instructions and the elementary operations of a computer. Microcode is stored in ROM and allows the addition of new machine instructions without requiring that they be designed into electronic circuits when new instructions are needed.

microsegmentation   Division of a network into smaller segments, usually with the intention of increasing aggregate bandwidth to network devices.

microwave   Electromagnetic waves in the range 1 to 30 GHz. Microwave-based networks are an evolving technology gaining favor due to high bandwidth and relatively low cost.

midsplit   Broadband cable system in which the available frequencies are split into two groups: one for transmission and one for reception.

MII   Media Independent Interface. A standard specification for the interface between network controller chips and their associated media interface chip(s). The MII automatically senses 10 and 100 MHz Ethernet speeds.

MILNET   Military Network. Unclassified portion of the DDN. Operated and maintained by the DISA. *See also* DDN and DISA.

MIME   Multipurpose Internet Mail Extensions. An Internet messages, as defined by RFC 822, consists of two parts: a header and a body. MIME defines a set of five extensions to RFC 822: a content type header field, a content transfer encoding header field, a MIME version header field, an optional content ID header field, and and optional content descriptions header field. MIME has become the standard for attaching non-text files to e-mail messages in a way that allows the attachment to be received intact over a network.

MIP   MultiChannel Interface Processor. Interface processor on the Cisco 7000 series routers that provides up to two channelized T1 or E1 connections via serial cables to a CSU. The two controllers on the MIP can each provide up to 24 1 or 30 E1 channel-groups, with each channel-group presented to the system as a serial interface that can be configured individually.

mips   millions of instructions per second. Number of instructions executed by a processor per second.

MLP   Multilink PPP. A method of splitting, recombining, and sequencing datagrams across multiple logical data links.

MMP   Multichassis Multilink PPP. Extends MLP support across multiple routers and access servers. MMP enables multiple routers and access servers to operate as a single, large dial-up pool, with a single network address and ISDN access number. MMP correctly handles packet fragmenting and reassembly when a user connection is split between two physical access devices.

modem   modulator-demodulator. Device that converts digital and analog signals. At the source, a modem converts digital signals to a form suitable for transmission over analog communication facilities. At the destination, the analog signals are returned to their digital form. Modems allow data to be transmitted over voice-grade telephone lines.

modem eliminator   Device allowing connection of two DTE devices without modems.

modulation   Process by which the characteristics of electrical signals are transformed to represent information. Types of modulation include AM, FM, and PAM. *See also* AM, FM, and PAM.

MOP   Maintenance Operation Protocol. Digital Equipment Corporation protocol that provides a way to perform primitive maintenance operations on DECnet systems. For example, MOP can be used to download a system image to a diskless station.

Mosaic   Public-domain WWW browser, developed at the National Center for Supercomputing Applications (NCSA). *See also* browser.

MOSPF   Multicast OSPF. Intradomain multicast routing protocol used in OSPF networks. Extensions are applied to the base OSPF unicast protocol to support IP multicast routing.

MPEG   Motion Picture Experts Group. A standard for compressing video. MPEG1 is a bit stream standard for compressed video and audio optimized to fit into a bandwidth of 1.5Mbps. MPEG2 is intended for higher quality video-on-demand applications and runs at data rates between 4 and 9Mbps. MPEG4 is a low-bit-rate compression algorithm intended for 64Kbps connections.

MPOA   Multiprotocol over ATM. An ATM Forum standardization effort specifying how existing and future network-layer protocols such as IP, IPv6, Appletalk, and IPX run over an ATM network with directly attached hosts, routers, and multilayer LAN switches.

MQI   Message Queuing Interface. International standard API that provides functionality similar to that of the RPC interface. In contrast to RPC, MQI is implemented strictly at the Application layer. *See also* RPC.

MSAU   multistation access unit. Wiring concentrator to which all end stations in a Token Ring network connect. The MSAU provides an interface between these devices and the Token Ring interface of a router. Sometimes abbreviated MAU.

MTU   maximum transmission unit. Maximum packet size, in bytes, that a particular interface can handle.

mu-law   North American companding standard used in conversion between analog and digital signals in PCM systems. Similar to the European alaw. *See also* a-law and companding.

multiaccess network   Network that allows multiple devices to connect and communicate simultaneously.

multicast   Single packets copied by the network and sent to a specific subset of network addresses. These addresses are specified in the destination address field. Compare with broadcast and unicast.

multicast address   Single address that refers to multiple network devices. Synonymous with group address. Compare with broadcast address and unicast address. *See also* multicast.

multicast forward VCC   A VCC set up by the BUS to the LEC as a leaf in a point-to-multipoint connection.

multicast group   Dynamically determined group of IP hosts identified by a single IP multicast address.

multicast router   Router used to send IGMP query messages on their attached local networks. Host members of a multicast group respond to a query by sending IGMP reports noting the multicast groups to which they belong. The multicast router takes responsibility for forwarding multicast datagrams from one multicast group to all other networks that have members in the group. *See also* IGMP.

multicast send VCC   In an ATM network, a bi-directional point-to-point VCC set up by a LEC to a BUS. One of three data connections defined by Phase 1 LANE. Compare with control distribute VCC and control direct VCC.

multicast server   Establishes a one-to-many connection to each device in a VLAN, thus establishing a broadcast domain for each VLAN segment. The multicast server forwards incoming broadcasts only to the multicast address that maps to the broadcast address.

multidrop line   Communications line having multiple cable access points. Sometimes called a multipoint line.

multihomed host   Host attached to multiple physical network segments in an OSI CLNS network.

multihoming   Addressing scheme in IS-IS routing that supports assignment of multiple area addresses.

multilayer switch   Switch that filters and forwards packets based on MAC addresses and network addresses. A subset of LAN switch. Compare with LAN switch.

multimode fiber   Optical fiber supporting propagation of multiple frequencies of light. *See also* single-mode fiber.

multiple domain network   SNA network with multiple SSCPs. *See also* SSCP.

multiplexing   Scheme that allows multiple logical signals to be transmitted simultaneously across a single physical channel. Compare with demultiplexing.

multivendor network   Network using equipment from more than one vendor. Multivendor networks pose many more compatibility problems than single-vendor networks. Compare with single-vendor network.

mux   A multiplexing device. A mux combines multiple signals for transmission over a single line. The signals are demultiplexed, or separated, at the receiving end.

NACS   NetWare Asynchronous Communication Services. Novell software that supports Novell's Asynchronous I/O (AIO) and NetWare Asynchronous Support Interface (NASI) programming interfaces. NACS promotes the sharing of communications resources such as modems, asynchronous hosts, and X.25 network services.

NADN   nearest active downstream neighbor. In Token Ring or IEEE 802.5 networks, the closest downstream network device from any given device that is still active.

Nagle's algorithm   Actually two separate congestion control algorithms that can be used in TCP-based networks. One algorithm reduces the sending window; the other limits small datagrams.

NAK   Negative acknowledgment. Response sent from a receiving device to a sending device indicating that the information received contained errors. Compare to acknowledgment.

name caching   Method by which remotely discovered host names are stored by a router for use in future packet-forwarding decisions to allow quick access.

name resolution   Generally, the process of associating a name with a network location.

name server   Server connected to a network that resolves network names into network addresses.

NAP   network access point. Location for interconnection of Internet service providers in the United States for the exchange of packets.

NARP   NBMA Address Resolution Protocol. A functional subset of NHRP that returns only the address mappings of nodes that are directly connection the NBMA network. Compare with NHRP.

NAT   Network Address Translation. A mechanism for reducing the need for globally unique IP addresses. NAT allows an organization with addresses that are not globally unique to connect to the Internet by translating those addresses into globally routable address space. Also known as Network Address Translator.

NAU   network addressable unit. SNA term for an addressable entity. Examples include LUs, PUs, and SSCPs. NAUs generally provide upper-level network services. Compare with path control network.

NAUN   nearest active upstream neighbor. In Token Ring or IEEE 802.5 networks, the closest upstream network device from any given device that is still active.

NBFCP   NetBIOS Frames Control Protocol.

NBMA nonbroadcast multiaccess. Term describing a multiaccess network that either does not support broadcasting (such as X.25) or in which broadcasting is not feasible (for example, an SMDS broadcast group or an extended Ethernet that is too large). *See also* multiaccess network.

NBP Name Binding Protocol. AppleTalk transport-level protocol that translates a character string name into the DDP address of the corresponding socket client. NBP enables AppleTalk protocols to understand user-defined zones and device names by providing and maintaining translation tables that map names to their corresponding socket addresses.

NBS National Bureau of Standards. Organization that was part of the U.S. Department of Commerce. Now known as NIST. *See also* NIST.

NCIA native client interface architecture. SNA applications-access architecture, developed by Cisco, that combines the full functionality of native SNA interfaces at both the host and client with the flexibility of leveraging TCP/IP backbones. NCIA encapsulates SNA traffic on a client PC or workstation, thereby providing direct TCP/IP access while preserving the native SNA interface at the end-user level. In many networks, this capability obviates the need for a standalone gateway and can provide flexible TCP/IP access while preserving the native SNA interface to the host.

NCP 1. Network Control Program. In SNA, a program that routes and controls the flow of data between a communications controller (in which it resides) and other network resources. 2. Network Control Protocol. A series of protocols for establishing and configuring different Network layer protocols, such as for AppleTalk over PPP. *See also* PPP.

NDIS network driver interface specification. Microsoft's specification for a generic, hardware- and protocol-independent device driver for NICs.

NE network element. In OSS, a single piece of telecommunications equipment used to perform a function or service integral to the underlying network.

NEBS Network Equipment Building Systems. In OSS, the Bellcore requirement for equipment deployed in a central office environment. Covers spatial, hardware and crafts person interface, thermal, fire resistance, handling and transportation, earthquake and vibration, airborne contaminants, grounding, acoustical noise, illumination, EMC and ESD requirements.

NEARNET Regional network in New England (United States) that links Boston University, Harvard University, and MIT. Now part of BBN Planet. *See also* BBN Planet.

neighboring routers In OSPF, two routers that have interfaces to a common network. On multiaccess networks, neighbors are dynamically discovered by the OSPF Hello protocol.

NET network entity title. Network addresses, defined by the ISO network architecture, and used in CLNS-based networks.

NetBEUI   NetBIOS Extended User Interface. An enhanced version of the NetBIOS protocol used by network operating systems such as LAN Manager, LAN Server, Windows for Workgroups and Windows NT. It formalizes the transport frame that was never standardized in NetBIOS and adds additional functions. NetBEUI implements the OSI LLC2 protocol. *See also* LLC2 and OSI.

NetBIOS   Network Basic Input/Output System. API used by applications on an IBM LAN to request services from lower-level network processes. These services might include session establishment and termination, and information transfer.

NETscout   Cisco network management application that provides an easy-to-use GUI for monitoring RMON statistics and protocol analysis information. NETscout also provides extensive tools that simplify data collection, analysis, and reporting. These tools allow system administrators to monitor traffic, set thresholds, and capture data on any set of network traffic for any segment.

NetView   IBM network management architecture and related applications. NetView is a VTAM application used for managing mainframes in SNA networks. *See also* VTAM.

NetWare   Popular distributed NOS developed by Novell. Provides transparent remote file access and numerous other distributed network services.

network   Collection of computers, printers, routers, switches, and other devices that are able to communicate with each other over some transmission medium.

network address   Network layer address referring to a logical, rather than a physical, network device. Also called a protocol address. Compare with MAC address.

network administrator   Person responsible for the operation, maintenance, and management of a network. *See also* network operator.

network analyzer   Hardware or software device offering various network troubleshooting features, including protocol-specific packet decodes, specific preprogrammed troubleshooting tests, packet filtering, and packet transmission.

network interface   Boundary between a carrier network and a privately-owned installation.

Network layer   Layer 3 of the OSI reference model. This layer provides connectivity and path selection between two end systems. The Network layer is the layer at which routing occurs. Corresponds roughly with the path control layer of the SNA model. *See also* Application layer, Data Link layer, Physical layer, Presentation layer, Session layer, and Transport layer.

network management   Generic term used to describe systems or actions that help maintain, characterize, or troubleshoot a network.

Network Node Server   SNA NN that provides resource location and route selection services for ENs, LEN nodes, and LUs that are in its domain.

network number   Part of an IP address that specifies the network to which the host belongs.

network operator   Person who routinely monitors and controls a network, performing such tasks as reviewing and responding to traps, monitoring throughput, configuring new circuits, and resolving problems. *See also* network administrator.

NFS   Network File System. As commonly used, a distributed file system protocol suite developed by Sun Microsystems that allows remote file access across a network. In actuality, NFS is simply one protocol in the suite. NFS protocols include NFS, RPC, XDR (External Data Representation), and others. These protocols are part of a larger architecture that Sun refers to as ONC. *See also* ONC.

NHRP   Next Hop Resolution Protocol. Protocol used by routers to dynamically discover the MAC address of other routers and hosts connected to a NBMA network. These systems can then directly communicate without requiring traffic to use an intermediate hop, increasing performance in ATM, Frame Relay, SMDS, and X.25 environments.

NHS   Next Hop Server. A server defined by the NHRP protocol that maintains next-hop resolution cache tables containing the IP-to-ATM address mappings of associated nodes and nodes that are reachable through routers served by the NHS.

NIC   network interface card. Board that provides network communication capabilities to and from a computer system. Also called an adapter. *See also* AUI.

NIS   Network Information Service. Protocol developed by Sun Microsystems for the administration of network-wide databases. The service essentially uses two programs: one for finding a NIS server and one for accessing the NIS databases.

N-ISDN   Narrowband ISDN. Communication standards developed by the ITU-T for baseband networks. Based on 64Kbps B channels and 16 or 64Kbps D channels. Contrast with BISDN. *See also* BRI, ISDN, and PRI.

NIST   National Institute of Standards and Technology. Formerly the NBS, this U.S. government organization supports and catalogs a variety of standards. *See also* NBS.

NLM   NetWare Loadable Module. Individual program that can be loaded into memory and function as part of the NetWare NOS.

NLSP   NetWare Link Services Protocol. Link-state routing protocol based on IS-IS. *See also* IS-IS.

NMA   Network Management and Analysis. A Bellcore OSS providing alarm surveillance and performance monitoring of intelligent network elements.

NMP   Network Management Processor. Processor module on the Catalyst 5000 switch used to control and monitor the switch.

NMS   network management system. System responsible for managing at least part of a network. An NMS is generally a reasonably powerful and well-equipped computer such as an engineering workstation. NMSs communicate with agents to help keep track of network statistics and resources.

NMVT   network management vector transport. SNA message consisting of a series of vectors conveying network management specific information.

NN   network node. SNA intermediate node that provides connectivity, directory services, route selection, intermediate session routing, data transport, and network management services to LEN nodes and ENs. The NN contains a CP that manages the resources of both the NN itself and those of the ENs and LEN nodes in its domain. NNs provideintermediate routing services by implementing the APPN PU 2.1 extensions. Compare with EN. *See also* CP.

NNI   Network-to-Network Interface. ATM Forum standard that defines the interface between two ATM switches that are both located in a private network or are both located in a public network. The interface between a public switch and private one is defined by the UNI standard. Also, the standard interface between two Frame Relay switches meeting the same criteria. Compare with UNI.

NOC   Network Operations Center. Organization responsible for maintaining a network.

node   1. Endpoint of a network connection or a junction common to two or more lines in a network. Nodes can be processors, controllers, or workstations. Nodes, which vary in routing and other functional capabilities, can be interconnected by links, and serve as control points in the network. Node is sometimes used generically to refer to any entity that can access a network, and is frequently used interchangeably with device. *See also* host. 2. In SNA, the basic component of a network, and the point at which one or more functional units connect channels or data circuits.

noise   Undesirable communications channel signals.

nonextended network   An AppleTalk Phase 2 network that supports addressing of up to 253 nodes and only one zone.

nonseed router   In AppleTalk, a router that must first obtain, and then verify, its configuration with a seed router before it can begin operation. *See also* seed router.

non-stub area   Resource-intensive OSPF area that carries a default route, static routes, intra-area routes, interarea routes, and external routes. Nonstub areas are the only OSPF areas that can have virtual links configured across them, and are the only areas that can contain an ASBR. Compare with stub area. *See also* ASBR and OSPF.

Northwest Net   NSF-funded regional network serving the Northwestern United States, Alaska, Montana, and North Dakota. Northwest Net connects all major universities in the region as well as many leading industrial concerns.

NOS   network operating system. Generic term used to refer to what are really distributed file systems. Examples of NOSs include LAN Manager, NetWare, NFS, and VINES.

NREN   National Research and Education Network. Component of the HPCC program designed to ensure U.S. technical leadership in computer communications through research and development efforts in state-of-the-art telecommunications and networking technologies. *See also* HPCC.

NRM   normal response mode. HDLC mode for use on links with one primary station and one or more secondary stations. In this mode, secondary stations can transmit only if they first receive a poll from the primary station.

NRZ   nonreturn to zero. NRZ signals maintain constant voltage levels with no signal transitions (no return to a zero-voltage level) during a bit interval. Compare with NRZI.

NRZI   nonreturn to zero inverted. NRZI signals maintain constant voltage levels with no signal transitions (no return to a zero-voltage level), but interpret the presence of data at the beginning of a bit interval as a signal transition and the absence of data as no transition. Compare with NRZ.

NSAP   network service access point. Network addresses, as specified by ISO. An NSAP is the point at which OSI Network Service is made available to a Transport layer (Layer 4) entity.

NSF   National Science Foundation. U.S. government agency that funds scientific research in the United States. The now-defunct NSFNET was funded by the NSF. *See also* NSFNET.

NSFNET   National Science Foundation Network. Large network that was controlled by the NSF and provided networking services in support of education and research in the United States, from 1986 to 1995. NSFNET is no longer in service.

NTRI   NCP/Token Ring Interconnection. Function used by ACF/NCP to support Token Ring-attached SNA devices. NTRI also provides translation from Token Ring-attached SNA devices (PUs) to switched (dial-up) devices.

null modem   Small box or cable used to join computing devices directly, rather than over a network.

NVE   network-visible entity. A resource that is addressable through a network. Typically, an NVE is a socket client for a service available in a node.

NVRAM   nonvolatile RAM. RAM that retains its contents when a unit is powered off.

NYSERNet   Network in New York (United States) with a T1 backbone connecting NSF, many universities, and several commercial concerns.

OAM cell   Operation, Administration, and Maintenance cell. ATM Forum specification for cells used to monitor virtual circuits. OAM cells provide a virtual circuit-level loopback in which a router responds to the cells, demonstrating that the circuit is up, and the router is operational.

OAM&P   Operations Administration Maintenance and Provisioning.

OARnet   Ohio Academic Resources Network. Internet service provider that connects a number of U.S. sites, including the Ohio supercomputer center in Columbus, Ohio.

object instance   Network management term referring to an instance of an object type that has been bound to a value.

OC   Optical Carrier. Series of physical protocols (OC-1, OC-2, OC-3, and so on), defined for SONET optical signal transmissions. OC signal levels put STS frames onto multimode fiber-optic line at a variety of speeds. The base rate is 51.84Mbps (OC-1); each signal level thereafter operates at a speed divisible by that number (thus, OC-3 runs at 155.52Mbps). *See also* SONET, STS-1, and STS-3c.

ODA   Open Document Architecture. ISO standard that specifies how documents are represented and transmitted electronically. Formerly called Office Document Architecture.

ODI   Open Data-Link Interface. Novell specification providing a standardized interface for NICs (network interface cards) that allows multiple protocols to use a single NIC. *See also* NIC.

OIM   OSI Internet Management. Group tasked with specifying ways in which OSI network management protocols can be used to manage TCP/IP networks.

OIR   online insertion and removal. Feature that permits the addition, replacement, or removal of cards without interrupting the system power, entering console commands, or causing other software or interfaces to shut down. Sometimes called hot swapping or power-on servicing.

ONA   Open Network Architecture. SNA/IBM.

ONC   Open Network Computing. Distributed applications architecture designed by Sun Microsystems, currently controlled by a consortium led by Sun. The NFS protocols are part of ONC. *See also* NFS.

ones density   Scheme that allows a CSU/DSU to recover the data clock reliably. The CSU/DSU derives the data clock from the data that passes through it. In order to recover the clock, the CSU/DSU hardware must receive at least one 1 bit value for every 8 bits of data that pass through it. Also called pulse density.

open architecture   Architecture with which third-party developers can legally develop products and for which public domain specifications exist.

open circuit   Broken path along a transmission medium. Open circuits will usually prevent network communication.

OPS/INE   Operations Provisioning System/Intelligent Network Element. A Bellcore OSS that provides provisioning services for intelligent network elements. *See also* OSS.

OSI   Open System Interconnection. International standardization program created by ISO and ITU-T to develop standards for data networking that facilitate multivendor equipment interoperability.

OSINET   International association designed to promote OSI in vendor architectures.

OSI reference model   Open System Interconnection reference model. Network architectural model developed by ISO and ITU-T. The model consists of seven layers, each of which specifies particular network functions such as addressing, flow control, error control, encapsulation, and reliable message transfer. The lowest layer (the Physical layer) is closest to the media technology. The lower two layers are implemented in hardware and software, while the upper five layers are implemented only in software. The highest layer (the Application layer) is closest to the user. The OSI reference model is used universally as a method for teaching and understanding network functionality. Similar in some respects to SNA. See Application layer, Data Link layer, Network layer, Physical layer, Presentation layer, Session layer, and Transport layer.

OSPF Open Shortest Path First. Link-state, hierarchical IGP routing algorithm proposed as a successor to RIP in the Internet community. OSPF features include least-cost routing, multipath routing, and load balancing. OSPF was derived from an early version of the ISIS protocol. *See also* Enhanced IGRP, IGP, IGRP, IS-IS, and IP.

OSS Operations Support System. A network management system supporting a specific management function, such as alarm surveillance and provisioning, in a carrier network. Many of these systems are large centralized systems running on mainframes or minicomputers. Common OSSs used within an RBOC include NMA, OPS/INE, and TIRKS.

OUI Organizational Unique Identifier. The 3 octets assigned by the IEEE in a block of 48-bit LAN addresses.

outframe Maximum number of outstanding frames allowed in an SNA PU 2 server at any time.

out-of-band signaling Transmission using frequencies or channels outside the frequencies or channels normally used for information transfer. Out-of-band signaling is often used for error reporting in situations in which in-band signaling can be affected by whatever problems the network might be experiencing. Contrast with in-band signaling.

packet Logical grouping of information that includes a header containing control information and (usually) user data. Packets are most often used to refer to Network layer units of data. The terms datagram, frame, message, and segment are also used to describe logical information groupings at various layers of the OSI reference model and in various technology circles. *See also* PDU.

packet switch WAN device that routes packets along the most efficient path and allows a communications channel to be shared by multiple connections. Formerly called an IMP. *See also* IMP.

packet switching Networking method in which nodes share bandwidth with each other by sending packets. Compare with circuit switching and message switching. *See also* PSN.

PAD packet assembler/disassembler. Device used to connect simple devices (like character-mode terminals) that do not support the full functionality of a particular protocol to a network. PADs buffer data and assemble and disassemble packets sent to such end devices.

PAM pulse amplitude modulation. Modulation scheme where the modulating wave is caused to modulate the amplitude of a pulse stream. Compare with AM and FM. *See also* modulation.

PAP   Password Authentication Protocol. Authentication protocol that allows PPP peers to authenticate one another. The remote router attempting to connect to the local router is required to send an authentication request. Unlike CHAP, PAP passes the password and host name or username in the clear (unencrypted). PAP does not itself prevent unauthorized access, but merely identifies the remote end. The router or access server then determines if that user is allowed access. PAP is supported only on PPP lines. Compare with CHAP.

parallel channel   Channel that uses bus and tag cables as a transmission medium. Compare with ESCON channel. *See also* bus and tag channel.

parallelism   Indicates that multiple paths exist between two points in a network. These paths might be of equal or unequal cost. Parallelism is often a network design goal: if one path fails, there is redundancy in the network to ensure that an alternate path to the same point exists.

parallel transmission   Method of data transmission in which the bits of a data character are transmitted simultaneously over a number of channels. Compare with serial transmission.

PARC   Palo Alto Research Center. Research and development center operated by XEROX. A number of widely-used technologies were originally conceived at PARC, including the first personal computers and LANs.

parity check   Process for checking the integrity of a character. A parity check involves appending a bit that makes the total number of binary 1 digits in a character or word (excluding the parity bit) either odd (for odd parity) or even (for even parity).

partial mesh   Term describing a network in which devices are organized in a mesh topology, with some network nodes organized in a full mesh, but with others that are only connected to one or two other nodes in the network. A partial mesh does not provide the level of redundancy of a full mesh topology, but is less expensive to implement. Partial mesh topologies are generally used in the peripheral networks that connect to a fully meshed backbone. *See also* full mesh and mesh.

Password Authentication Protocol   See PAP.

path control layer   Layer 3 in the SNA architectural model. This layer performs sequencing services related to proper data reassembly. The path control layer is also responsible for routing. Corresponds roughly with the Network layer of the OSI model. *See also* data flow control layer, data link control layer, physical control layer, presentation services layer, transaction services layer, and transmission control layer.

path control network   SNA concept that consists of lower-level components that control the routing and data flow through an SNA network and handle physical data transmission between SNA nodes. Compare with NAU.

path name   Full name of a DOS, Mac OS, or UNIX file or directory, including all directory and subdirectory names. Consecutive names in a path name are typically separated by a backslash (\) for DOS, a colon (for the Mac OS), or a forward slash (/) for the UNIX operating system.

payload   Portion of a cell, frame, or packet that contains upper-layer information (data).

PBX   private branch exchange. Digital or analog telephone switchboard located on the subscriber premises and used to connect private and public telephone networks.

PCI   protocol control information. Control information added to user data to comprise an OSI packet. The OSI equivalent of the term header. *See also* header.

PCM   pulse code modulation. Transmission of analog information in digital form through sampling and encoding the samples with a fixed number of bits.

PCR   peak cell rate. Parameter defined by the ATM Forum for ATM traffic management. In CBR transmissions, PCR determines how often data samples are sent. In ABR transmissions, PCR determines the maximum value of the ACR. *See also* ABR (available bit rate), ACR, and CBR.

PDN   public data network. Network operated either by a government (as in Europe) or by a private concern to provide computer communications to the public, usually for a fee. PDNs enable small organizations to create a WAN without all the equipment costs of long-distance circuits.

PDU   protocol data unit. OSI term for packet. *See also* BPDU and packet.

peak rate   Maximum rate, in kilobits per second, at which a virtual circuit can transmit.

peer-to-peer computing   Peer-to-peer computing calls for each network device to run both client and server portions of an application. Also describes communication between implementations of the same OSI reference model layer in two different network devices. Compare with client/server computing.

peer group   A collection of ATM nodes that share identical topological databases and exchange full link state information with each other. Peer groups are arranged hierarchically to prevent excessive PTSP traffic, so each peer group has a parent peer group.

performance management   One of five categories of network management defined by ISO for management of OSI networks. Performance management subsystems are responsible for analyzing and controlling network performance including network throughput and error rates. *See also* accounting management, configuration management, fault management, and security management.

peripheral node   In SNA, a node that uses local addresses and is therefore not affected by changes to network addresses. Peripheral nodes require boundary function assistance from an adjacent subarea node.

P/F   poll/final bit. Bit in bit-synchronous Data Link layer protocols that indicates the function of a frame. If the frame is a command, a 1 in this bit indicates a poll. If the frame is a response, a 1 in this bit indicates that the current frame is the last frame in the response.

PGL   Peer Group Leader. In ATM, a node in a peer group that performs the functions of the LGN. Peer group leaders exchange PTSPs with peer nodes in the parent peer group to inform those nodes of the peer group's attributes and reachability and to progagate information about the parent group and the parent group's parents to the nodes in the peer group.

PGP   Pretty Good Privacy. Public-key encryption application that allows secure file and message exchanges. There is some controversy over the development and use of this application, in part due to U.S. national security concerns.

phase   Location of a position on an alternating wave form.

phase shift   Situation in which the relative position in time between the clock and data signals of a transmission becomes unsynchronized. In systems using long cables at higher transmission speeds, slight variances in cable construction, temperature, and other factors can cause a phase shift, resulting in high error rates.

PHY   1. physical sublayer. One of two sublayers of the FDDI Physical layer. *See also* PMD. 2. Physical layer. In ATM, the Physical layer provides for the transmission of cells over a physical medium that connects two ATM devices. The PHY is comprised of two sublayers: PMD and TC.

physical control layer   Layer 1 in the SNA architectural model. This layer is responsible for the physical specifications for the physical links between end systems. Corresponds to the Physical layer of the OSI model. *See also* data flow control layer, data link control layer, path control layer, presentation services layer, transaction services layer, and transmission control layer.

Physical layer   Layer 1 of the OSI reference model. The Physical layer defines the electrical, mechanical, procedural and functional specifications for activating, maintaining, and deactivating the physical link between end systems. Corresponds with the physical control layer in the SNA model. *See also* Application layer, Data Link layer, Network layer, Presentation layer, Session layer, and Transport layer.

PHYSNET   Physics Network. Group of many DECnet-based physics research networks, including HEPnet. *See also* HEPnet.

piggybacking   Process of carrying acknowledgments within a data packet to save network bandwidth.

PIM   Protocol Independent Multicast. Multicast routing architecture that allows the addition of IP multicast routing on existing IP networks. PIM is unicast routing protocol independent and can be operated in two modes: dense mode and sparse mode. *See also* PIM dense mode and PIM sparse mode.

PIM dense mode   One of the two PIM operational modes. PIM dense mode is data-driven and resembles typical multicast routing protocols. Packets are forwarded on all outgoing interfaces until pruning and truncation occurs. In dense mode, receivers are densely populated, and it is assumed that the downstream networks want to receive and will probably use the datagrams that are forwarded to them. The cost of using dense mode is its default flooding behavior. Sometimes called dense mode PIM or PIM DM. Contrast with PIM sparse mode. *See also* PIM.

PIM sparse mode   One of the two PIM operational modes. PIM sparse mode tries to constrain data distribution so that a minimal number of routers in the network receive it. Packets are sent only if they are explicitly requested at the RP (rendezvous point). In sparse mode, receivers are widely distributed, and the assumption is that downstream networks will not necessarily use the datagrams that are sent to them. The cost of using sparse mode is its reliance on the periodic refreshing of explicit join messages and its need for RPs. Sometimes called sparse mode PIM or PIM SM. Contrast with PIM dense mode. *See also* PIM and rendezvous point .

ping   packet internet groper. ICMP echo message and its reply. Often used in IP networks to test the reachability of a network device.

ping-ponging   Phrase used to describe the actions of a packet in a two-node routing loop.

PLCP   Physical layer convergence procedure. Specification that maps ATM cells into physical media, such as T3 or E3, and defines certain management information.

PLSP   PNNI Link State Packet.

plesiochronous transmission   Term describing digital signals that are sourced from different clocks of comparable accuracy and stability. Compare with asynchronous transmission, isochronous transmission, and synchronous transmission.

PLIM   Physical layer interface module.

PLP   packet level protocol. Network layer protocol in the X.25 protocol stack. Sometimes called X.25 Level 3 or X.25 Protocol. *See also* X.25.

PLU   Primary LU. The LU that is initiating a session with another LU. *See also* LU.

PMD   physical medium dependent. Sublayer of the FDDI Physical layer that interfaces directly with the physical medium and performs the most basic bit transmission functions of the network. *See also* PHY.

PNNI   1. Private Network-Network Interface. ATM Forum specification for distributing topology information between switches and clusters of switches that is used to compute paths through the network. The specification is based on well-known link-state routing techniques and includes a mechanism for automatic configuration in networks in which the address structure reflects the topology. 2. Private Network Node Interface. ATM Forum specification for signaling to establish point-to-point and point-to-multipoint connections across an ATM network. The protocol is based on the ATM Forum's UNI specification with additional mechanisms for source routing, crankback, and alternate routing of call setup requests.

point-to-multipoint connection   One of two fundamental connection types. In ATM, a point-to-multipoint connection is a unidirectional connection in which a single source end-system (known as a root node) connects to multiple destination end-systems (known as leaves). Compare with point-to-point connection.

point-to-point connection   One of two fundamental connection types. In ATM, a point-to-point connection can be a unidirectional or bidirectional connection between two ATM end-systems. Compare withpoint-to-multipoint connection.

poison reverse updates   Routing updates that explicitly indicate that a network or subnet is unreachable, rather than implying that a network is unreachable by not including it in updates. Poison reverse updates are sent to defeat large routing loops.

policy routing   Routing scheme that forwards packets to specific interfaces based on user-configured policies. Such policies might specify that traffic sent from a particular network should be forwarded out one interface, while all other traffic should be forwarded out another interface.

polling   Access method in which a primary network device inquires, in an orderly fashion, whether secondaries have data to transmit. The inquiry occurs in the form of a message to each secondary that gives the secondary the right to transmit.

POP   1. point of presence. In OSS, a physical location where an interexchange carrier has installed equipment to interconnect with an LEC (local exchange carrier). 2. Post Office Protocol. Protocol that client e-mail applications use to retrieve mail from a mail server.

port   1. Interface on an internetworking device (such as a router). 2. In IP terminology, an upper-layer process that receives information from lower layers. Ports are numbered, and each numbered port is associated with a specific process. For example, SMTP is associated with port 25. A port number is also known as a well-known address. 3. To rewrite software or microcode so that it will run on a different hardware platform or in a different software environment than that for which it was originally designed.

POST   power-on self test. Set of hardware diagnostics that runs on a hardware device when that device is powered up.

POTS   plain old telephone service. See PSTN.

power-on servicing   Feature that allows faulty components to be diagnosed, removed, and replaced while the rest of the device continues to operate normally. Sometimes abbreviated POS. Sometimes called hot swapping. *See also* OIR.

PPP   Point-to-Point Protocol. A successor to SLIP, PPP provides router-to-router and host-to-network connections over synchronous and asynchronous circuits. Whereas SLIP was designed to work with IP, PPP was designed to work with several Network layer protocols, such as IP, IPX, and ARA. PPP also has builtin security mechanisms, such as CHAP and PAP. PPP relies on two protocols: LCP and NCP *See also* CHAP, PAP, and SLIP.

Presentation layer   Layer 6 of the OSI reference model. This layer ensures that information sent by the Application layer of one system will be readable by the Application layer of another. The Presentation layer is also concerned with the data structures used by programs and therefore negotiates data transfer syntax for the Application layer. Corresponds roughly with the presentation services layer of the

SNA model. *See also* Application layer, Data Link layer, Network layer, Physical layer, Session layer, and Transport layer.

presentation services layer   Layer 6 of the SNA architectural model. This layer provides network resource management, session presentation services, and some application management. Corresponds roughly with the Presentation layer of the OSI model. *See also* data flow control layer, data link control layer, path control layer, physical control layer, transaction services layer, and transmission control layer.

PRI   Primary Rate Interface. ISDN interface to primary rate access. Primary rate access consists of a single 64Kbps D channel plus 23 (T1) or 30 (E1) B channels for voice or data. Compare to BRI. *See also* BISDN, ISDN, and N-ISDN.

primary ring   One of the two rings that make up an FDDI or CDDI ring. The primary ring is the default path for data transmissions. Compare with secondary ring.

primary station   In bit-synchronous Data Link layer protocols such as HDLC and SDLC, a station that controls the transmission activity of secondary stations and performs other management functions such as error control through polling or other means. Primary stations send commands to secondary stations and receive responses. Also called, simply, a primary. *See also* secondary station.

print server   Networked computer system that fields, manages, and executes (or sends for execution) print requests from other network devices.

priority queuing   Routing feature in which frames in an interface output queue are prioritized based on various characteristics such as packet size and interface type.

process switching   1. Operation that provides full route evaluation and per-packet load balancing across parallel WAN links. Involves the transmission of entire frames to the router CPU where they are repackaged for delivery to or from a WAN interface, with the router making a route selection for each packet. Process switching is the most resource-intensive switching operation that the CPU can perform. 2. Packet processing performed at process level speeds, without the use of a route cache. Contrast with fast switching.

PROM   programmable read-only memory. ROM that can be programmed using special equipment. PROMs can be programmed only once. Compare with EPROM.

propagation delay   Time required for data to travel over a network, from its source to its ultimate destination.

protocol   Formal description of a set of rules and conventions that govern how devices on a network exchange information.

protocol converter   Enables equipment with different data formats to communicate by translating the data transmission code of one device to the data transmission code of another device.

protocol stack   Set of related communications protocols that operate together and, as a group, address communication at some or all of the seven layers of the OSI reference model. Not every protocol stack covers each layer of the model, and often a single protocol in the stack will address a number of layers at once. TCP/IP is a typical protocol stack.

protocol translator   Network device or software that converts one protocol into another, similar, protocol.

proxy   Entity that, in the interest of efficiency, essentially stands in for another entity.

proxy ARP   proxy Address Resolution Protocol. Variation of the ARP protocol in which an intermediate device (for example, a router) sends an ARP response on behalf of an end node to the requesting host. Proxy ARP can lessen bandwidth use on slow-speed WAN links. *See also* ARP.

proxy explorer   Technique that minimizes exploding explorer packet traffic propagating through an SRB network by creating an explorer packet reply cache, the entries of which are reused when subsequent explorer packets need to find the same host.

proxy polling   Technique that alleviates the load across an SDLC network by allowing routers to act as proxies for primary and secondary nodes, thus keeping polling traffic off of the shared links. Proxy polling has been replaced by SDLC Transport. See SDLC Transport.

PSDN   packet-switched data network. See PSN.

PSE   packet switch exchange. Essentially, a switch. The term PSE is generally used in reference to a switch in an X.25 packet-switch. *See also* switch.

PSN   packet-switched network. Network that utilizes packet-switching technology for data transfer. Sometimes called a packet-switched data network (PSDN). See packet switching.

PSTN   Public Switched Telephone Network. General term referring to the variety of telephone networks and services in place worldwide. Sometimes called plain old telephone service (POTS).

PTI   payload type identifier. A 3-bit descriptor in the ATM cell header indicating the type of payload that the cell contains. Payload types include user and management cells; one combination indicates that the cell is the last cell of an AAL5 frame.

PTSE   PNNI topology state element. A collection of PINNI information that is flooded among all logical notes within a peer group. *See also* peer group and PNNI.

PTSP   PNNI topology state packet. A type of PNNI routing packet used to exchange reachability and resource information among ATM switches to ensure that a connection request is routed to the destination along a path that has a high probability of meeting the requested QOS. Typically, PTSPs include bidirectional information about the transit behavior of particular nodes (based on entry and exit ports) and current internal state.

PTT   Post, Telephone, and Telegraph. Government agency that provides telephone services. PTTs exist in most areas outside North America and provide both local and long-distance telephone services.

PU   physical unit. SNA component that manages and monitors the resources of a node, as requested by an SSCP. There is one PU per node.

PU 2   Physical Unit 2. SNA peripheral node that can support only DLUs that require services from a VTAM host and that are only capable of performing the secondary LU role in SNA sessions.

PU 2.1   Physical Unit type 2.1. SNA network node used for connecting peer nodes in a peer-oriented network. PU 2.1 sessions do not require that one node reside on VTAM. APPN is based upon PU 2.1 nodes, which can also be connected to a traditional hierarchical SNA network.

PU 4   Physical Unit 4. Component of an IBM FEP capable of full-duplex data transfer. Each such SNA device employs a separate data and control path into the transmit and receive buffers of the control program.

PU 5   Physical Unit 5. Component of an IBM mainframe or host computer that manages an SNA network. PU 5 nodes are involved in routing within the SNA path control layer.

PUP   PARC Universal Protocol. Protocol similar to IP developed at PARC.

PVC   permanent virtual circuit. Virtual circuit that is permanently established. PVCs save bandwidth associated with circuit establishment and tear down in situations where certain virtual circuits must exist all the time. Called a permanent virtual connection in ATM terminology. Compare with SVC. *See also* virtual circuit.

PVP   permanent virtual path. Virtual path that consists of PVCs. *See also* PVC and virtual path.

PVP tunneling   permanent virtual path tunneling. A method of linking two private ATM networks across the public network using a virtual path. The public network transparently trunks the entire collection of virtual channels in the virtual path between the two private networks.

Q.2931   ITU-T specification, based on Q.931, for establishing, maintaining, and clearing network connections at the B-ISDN user-network interface. The UNI 3.1 specification is based on Q.2931. *See also* Q.931 and UNI.

Q.920/Q.921   ITU-T specifications for the ISDN UNI Data Link layer. *See also* UNI.

Q.922A   ITU-T specification for Frame Relay encapsulation.

Q.931   ITU-T specification for signaling to establish, maintain, and clear ISDN network connections. *See also* Q.93B.

Q.93B   ITU-T specification signaling to establish, maintain, and clear BISDN network connections. An evolution of ITU-T recommendation Q.931. *See also* Q.931.

QLLC   Qualified Logical Link Control. Data link layer protocol defined by IBM that allows SNA data to be transported across X.25 networks.

QOS   quality of service. Measure of performance for a transmission system that reflects its transmission quality and service availability.

QOS parameters   quality of service parameters. Parameters that control the amount of traffic the source in an ATM network sends over an SVC. If any switch along the path cannot accommodate the requested QOS parameters, the request is rejected, and a rejection message is forwarded back to the originator of the request.

quartet signaling   Signaling technique used in 100VG-AnyLAN networks that allows data transmission at 100Mbps over four pairs of UTP cabling at the same frequencies used in 10BaseT networks. *See also* 100VG-AnyLAN.

query   Message used to inquire about the value of some variable or set of variables.

queue   1. Generally, an ordered list of elements waiting to be processed. 2. In routing, a backlog of packets waiting to be forwarded over a router interface.

queuing delay   Amount of time that data must wait before it can be transmitted onto a statistically multiplexed physical circuit.

queuing theory   Scientific principles governing the formation or lack of formation of congestion on a network or at an interface.

RACE   Research on Advanced Communications in Europe. Project sponsored by the European Community (EC) for the development of broadband networking capabilities.

RDI   remote defect identication. In ATM, when the Physical layer detects loss of signal or cell synchronization, RDI cells are used to report a VPC/VCC failure. RDI cells are sent upstream by a VPC/VCC endpoint to notify the source VPC/VCC endpoint of the downstream failure.

RADIUS   A database for authenticating modem and ISDN connections and for tracking connection time.

RAM   random-access memory. Volatile memory that can be read and written by a microprocessor.

RARE   Réseaux Associés pour la Recherche Européenne. Association of European universities and research centers designed to promote an advanced telecommunications infrastructure in the European scientific community. RARE merged with EARN to form TERENA. *See also* EARN and TERENA.

RARP   Reverse Address Resolution Protocol. Protocol in the TCP/IP stack that provides a method for finding IP addresses based on MAC addresses. Compare with ARP.

rate queue   Value that is associated with one or more virtual circuits, and that defines the speed at which an individual virtual circuit will transmit data to the remote end. Each rate queue represents a portion of the overall bandwidth available on an ATM link. The combined bandwidth of all configured rate queues should not exceed the total bandwidth available.

RBHC   regional Bell holding company. One of seven regional telephone companies formed by the breakup of AT&T. RBHCs differ from RBOCs in that RBHCs cross state boundaries.

RBOC   regional Bell operating company. Seven regional telephone companies fromed by the breakup of AT&T. RBOCs differ from RBHCs in that RBOCs do not cross state boundaries.

rcp   remote copy protocol. Protocol that allows users to copy files to and from a file system residing on a remote host or server on the network. The rcp protocol uses TCP to ensure the reliable delivery of data.

rcp server   Router or other device that acts as a server for rcp. *See also* rcp.

reassembly   The putting back together of an IP datagram at the destination after it has been fragmented either at the source or at an intermediate node. *See also* fragmentation.

redirect   Part of the ICMP and ES-IS protocols that allows a router to tell a host that using another router would be more effective.

redirector   Software that intercepts requests for resources within a computer and analyzes them for remote access requirements. If remote access is required to satisfy the request, the redirector forms an RPC and sends the RPC to lower-layer protocol software for transmission through the network to the node that can satisfy the request.

redistribution   Allowing routing information discovered through one routing protocol to be distributed in the update messages of another routing protocol. Sometimes called route redistribution.

redundancy   1. In internetworking, the duplication of devices, services, or connections so that, in the event of a failure, the redundant devices, services, or connections can perform the work of those that failed. *See also* redundant system. 2. In telephony, the portion of the total information contained in a message that can be eliminated without loss of essential information or meaning.

redundant system   Computer, router, switch, or other computer system that contains two or more of each of the most important subsystems, such as two disk drives, two CPUs, or two power supplies.

relay   OSI terminology for a device that connects two or more networks or network systems. A Data Link layer (Layer 2) relay is a bridge; a Network layer (Layer 3) relay is a router. *See also* bridge and router.

reliability   Ratio of expected to received keepalives from a link. If the ratio is high, the line is reliable. Used as a routing metric.

reload   The event of a Cisco router rebooting, or the command that causes the router to reboot.

remote bridge   Bridge that connects physically disparate network segments via WAN links.

rendezvous point   Router specified in PIM sparse mode implementations to track membership in multicast groups and to forward messages to known multicast group addresses. *See also* PIM sparse mode.

repeater   Device that regenerates and propagates electrical signals between two network segments. *See also* segment.

RF radio frequency. Generic term referring to frequencies that correspond to radio transmissions. Cable TV and broadband networks use RF technology.

RFC Request For Comments. Document series used as the primary means for communicating information about the Internet. Some RFCs are designated by the IAB as Internet standards. Most RFCs document protocol specifications such as Telnet and FTP, but some are humorous or historical. RFCs are available online from numerous sources.

RFI radio frequency interference. Radio frequencies that create noise that interferes with information being transmitted across unshielded copper cabling.

RHC regional holding company.

RIF Routing Information Field. Field in the IEEE 802.5 header that is used by a source-route bridge to determine through which Token Ring network segments a packet must transit. A RIF is made up of ring and bridge numbers as well as other information.

RII Routing Information Identifier. Bit used by SRT bridges to distinguish between frames that should be transparently bridged and frames that should be passed to the SRB module for handling.

ring Connection of two or more stations in a logically circular topology. Information is passed sequentially between active stations. Token Ring, FDDI, and CDDI are based on this topology.

ring group Collection of Token Ring interfaces on one or more routers that is part of a one-bridge Token Ring network.

ring latency Time required for a signal to propagate once around a ring in a Token Ring or IEEE 802.5 network.

ring monitor Centralized management tool for Token Ring networks based on the IEEE 802.5 specification. *See also* active monitor and standby monitor.

ring topology Network topology that consists of a series of repeaters connected to one another by unidirectional transmission links to form a single closed loop. Each station on the network connects to the network at a repeater. While logically a ring, ring topologies are most often organized in a closed-loop star. Compare with bus topology, star topology, and tree topology.

RIP Routing Information Protocol. IGP supplied with UNIX BSD systems. The most common IGP in the Internet. RIP uses hop count as a routing metric. *See also* Enhanced IGRP, hop count, IGP, IGRP, and OSPF.

RJ connector registered jack connector. Standard connectors originally used to connect telephone lines. RJ connectors are now used for telephone connections and for 10BaseT and other types of network connections. RJ-11, RJ-12, and RJ-45 are popular types of RJ connectors.

RJE remote job entry. Application that is batch-oriented, as opposed to interactive. In RJE environments, jobs are submitted to a computing facility, and output is received later.

rlogin   remote login. Terminal emulation program, similar to Telnet, offered in most UNIX implementations.

RM   Resource Management. The management of critical resources in an ATM network. Two critical resources are buffer space and trunk bandwidth. Provisioning may be used to allocate network resources in order to separate traffic flows according to service characteristics.

RMON   Remote Monitoring. MIB agent specification described in RFC 1271 that defines functions for the remote monitoring of networked devices. The RMON specification provides numerous monitoring, problem detection, and reporting capabilities.

ROLC   Routing over Large Clouds. A working group in IETF created to analyse and propose solutions to problems that arise when performing IP routing over large, shared media networks such as SMDS, Frame Relay, X.25, and ATM.

ROM   read-only memory. Nonvolatile memory that can be read, but not written, by the microprocessor.

root account   Privileged account on UNIX systems used exclusively by network or system administrators.

root bridge   Exchanges topology information with designated bridges in a spanning-tree implementation in order to notify all other bridges in the network when topology changes are required. This prevents loops and provides a measure of defense against link failure.

ROSE   Remote Operations Service Element. OSI RPC mechanism used by various OSI network application protocols.

route   Path through an internetwork.

routed protocol   Protocol that can be routed by a router. A router must be able to interpret the logical internetwork as specified by that routed protocol. Examples of routed protocols include AppleTalk, DECnet, and IP.

route extension   In SNA, a path from the destination subarea node through peripheral equipment to a NAU.

route map   Method of controlling the redistribution of routes between routing domains.

route summarization   Consolidation of advertised addresses in OSPF and IS-IS. In OSPF, this causes a single summary route to be advertised to other areas by an area border router.

router   Network layer device that uses one or more metrics to determine the optimal path along which network traffic should be forwarded. Routers forward packets from one network to another based on Network layer information. Occasionally called a gateway (although this definition of gateway is becoming increasingly outdated). Compare with gateway. *See also* relay.

routing   Process of finding a path to a destination host. Routing is very complex in large networks because of the many potential intermediate destinations a packet might traverse before reaching its destination host.

routing domain   Group of end systems and intermediate systems operating under the same set of administrative rules. Within each routing domain is one or more areas, each uniquely identified by an area address.

routing metric   Method by which a routing algorithm determines that one route is better than another. This information is stored in routing tables. Metrics include bandwidth, communication cost, delay, hop count, load, MTU, path cost, and reliability. Sometimes referred to simply as a metric. *See also* cost.

routing protocol   Protocol that accomplishes routing through the implementation of a specific routing algorithm. Examples of routing protocols include IGRP, OSPF, and RIP.

routing table   Table stored in a router or some other internetworking device that keeps track of routes to particular network destinations and, in some cases, metrics associated with those routes.

routing update   Message sent from a router to indicate network reachability and associated cost information. Routing updates are typically sent at regular intervals and after a change in network topology. Compare with flash update.

RPC   remote-procedure call. Technological foundation of client-server computing. RPCs are procedure calls that are built or specified by clients and executed on servers, with the results returned over the network to the clients. *See also* client/server computing.

RPF   Reverse Path Forwarding. Multicasting technique in which a multicast datagram is forwarded out of all but the receiving interface if the receiving interface is one used to forward unicast datagrams to the source of the multicast datagram.

RR   relative rate. In ATM, one of the congestion feedback modes provided by ABR service. In RR mode, switches set a bit in forward and backward RM cells to indicate congestion. *See also* ABR.

RS-232   Popular Physical layer interface. Now known as EIA/TIA-232. See EIA/TIA-232.

RS-422   Balanced electrical implementation of EIA/TIA-449 for high-speed data transmission. Now referred to collectively with RS-423 as EIA-530. *See also* EIA-530 and RS-423.

RS-423   Unbalanced electrical implementation of EIA/TIA-449 for EIA/TIA-232 compatibility. Now referred to collectively with RS-422 as EIA-530. *See also* EIA-530 and RS-422.

RS-449   Popular Physical layer interface. Now known as EIA/TIA-449. See EIA/TIA-449.

rsh   remote shell protocol. Protocol that allows a user to execute commands on a remote system without having to log in to the system. For example, rsh can be used to remotely examine the status of a number of access servers without connecting to each communication server, executing the command, and then disconnecting from the communication server.

RP   Route Processor. Processor module on the Cisco 7000 series routers that contains the CPU, system software, and most of the memory components that are used in the router. Sometimes called a supervisory processor.

RSP   Route/Switch Processor. Processor module used in the Cisco 7500 series routers that integrates the functions of the RP and the SP. *See also* RP and SP.

RSRB   remote source-route bridging. SRB over WAN links. *See also* SRB.

RSUP   Reliable SAP Update Protocol. Bandwidth-saving protocol developed by Cisco for propagating services information. RSUP allows routers to reliably send standard Novell SAP packets only when the routers detect a change in advertised services. RSUP can transport network information either in conjunction with or independently of the Enhanced IGRP routing function for IPX.

RSVP   Resource Reservation Protocol. A protocol that supports the reservation of resources across an IP network. Applications running on IP end systems can use RSVP to indicate to other nodes the nature (bandwidth, jitter, maximum burst, and so on) of the packet streams they wish to receive. RSVP depends on IPv6. *See also* IPv6.

RTCP   RTP Control Protocol. A protocol that monitors the QOS of an IPv6 RTP connection and conveys information about the on-going session. *See also* RTP (Real-Time Transport Protocol).

RTMP   Routing Table Maintenance Protocol. Apple Computer's proprietary routing protocol. RTMP establishes and maintains the routing information that is required to route datagrams from any source socket to any destination socket in an AppleTalk network. Using RTMP, routers dynamically maintain routing tables to reflect changes in topology. RTMP was derived from RIP. *See also* RIP (Routing Table Protocol).

RTP   1. Routing Table Protocol. VINES routing protocol based on RIP. Distributes network topology information and aids VINES servers in finding neighboring clients, servers, and routers. Uses delay as a routing metric. *See also* SRTP. 2. Rapid Transport Protocol. Provides pacing and error recovery for APPN data as it crosses the APPN network. With RTP, error recovery and flow control are done end-to-end rather than at every node. RTP prevents congestion rather than reacts to it. 3. Real-Time Transport Protocol. One of the IPv6 protocols. RTP is designed to provide end-to-end network transport functions for applications transmitting real-time data, such as audio, video, or simulation data, over multicast or unicast network services. RTP provides services such as payload type identification, sequence numbering, timestamping, and delivery monitoring to real-time applications.

RTS   Request To Send. EIA/TIA-232 control signal that requests a data transmission on a communications line.

RTSP   Real Time Streaming Protocol. Enables the controlled delivery of real-time data, such as audio and video. Sources of data can include both live data feeds, such live audio and video, and stored content, such as pre-recorded events. It is designed to work with established protocols, such as RTP and HTTP, to provide a complete solution for streaming media over the Internet.

RTT   round-trip time. Time required for a network communication to travel from the source to the destination and back. RTT includes the time required for the destination to process the message from the source and generate a reply. RTT is used by some routing algorithms to aid in calculating optimal routes.

RU   request/response unit. Request and response messages exchanged between NAUs in an SNA network.

run-time memory   Memory accessed while a program runs.

SAC   single-attached concentrator. FDDI or CDDI concentrator that connects to the network by being cascaded from the master port of another FDDI or CDDI concentrator.

sampling rate   Rate at which samples of a particular waveform amplitude are taken.

SAP   1. service access point. Field defined by the IEEE 802.2 specification that is part of an address specification. Thus, the destination plus the DSAP define the recipient of a packet. The same applies to the SSAP. *See also* DSAP and SSAP. 2. Service Advertisement Protocol. IPX protocol that provides a means of informing network clients, via routers and servers, of available network resources and services. *See also* IPX.

SAR   segmentation and reassembly. One of the two sublayers of the AAL CPCS, responsible for dividing (at the source) and reassembling (at the destination) the PDUs passed from the CS. The SAR sublayer takes the PDUs processed by the CS and, after dividing them into 48-byte pieces of payload data, passes them to the ATM layer for further processing. *See also* AAL, ATM layer, CPCS, CS, and SSCS.

SAS   1. single attachment station. Device attached only to the primary ring of an FDDI ring. Also known as a Class B station. Compare with DAS. *See also* FDDI. 2. statically assigned socket. A socket that is permanently reserved for use by a designated process. In an AppleTalk network, SASs are numbered 1 to 127; they are reserved for use by specific socket clients and for low-level built-in network services.

satellite communication   Use of orbiting satellites to relay data between multiple earth-based stations. Satellite communications offer high bandwidth and a cost that is not related to distance between earth stations, long propagation delays, or broadcast capability.

SBus   Bus technology used in Sun SPARC-based workstations and servers. The SBus specification has been adopted by the IEEE as a new bus standard.

SCR   sustainable cell rate. Parameter defined by the ATM Forum for ATM traffic management. For VBR connections, SCR determines the long-term average cell rate that can be transmitted. *See also* VBR.

SCTE   serial clock transmit external. Timing signal that DTE echoes to DCE to maintain clocking. SCTE is designed to compensate for clock phase shift on long cables. When the DCE device uses SCTE instead of its internal clock to sample data from the DTE, it is better able to sample the data without error even if there is a phase shift in the cable. *See also* phase shift.

SDH   Synchronous Digital Hierarchy. European standard that defines a set of rate and format standards that are transmitted using optical signals over fiber. SDH is similar to SONET, with a basic SDH rate of 155.52Mbps, designated at STM-1. *See also* SONET and STM-1.

SDLC   Synchronous Data Link Control. SNA Data Link layer communications protocol. SDLC is a bit-oriented, full-duplex serial protocol that has spawned numerous similar protocols, including HDLC and LAPB. *See also* HDLC and LAPB.

SDLC broadcast   Feature that allows a Cisco router that receives an all-stations broadcast on a virtual multidrop line to propagate the broadcast to each SDLC line that is a member of the virtual multidrop line.

SDLC Transport   Cisco router feature with which disparate environments can be integrated into a single, high-speed, enterprise-wide network. Native SDLC traffic can be passed through point-to-point serial links with other protocol traffic multiplexed over the same links. Cisco routers can also encapsulate SDLC frames inside IP datagrams for transport over arbitrary (non-SDLC) networks. Replaces proxy polling. *See also* proxy polling.

SDLLC   SDLC Logical Link Control. Cisco IOS feature that performs translation between SDLC and IEEE 802.2 type 2.

SDSL   single-line digital subscriber line. One of four DSL technologies. SDSL delivers1.544Mbps both downstream and upstream over a single copper twisted pair. The use of a single twisted pair limits the operating range of SDSL to 10,000 feet. Compare with ADSL, HDSL, and VDSL.

SDSU   SMDS DSU. DSU for access to SMDS via HSSIs and other serial interfaces.

SDU   service data unit. Unit of information from an upper-layer protocol that defines a service request to a lower-layer protocol.

SEAL   simple and efficient AAL. Scheme used by AAL5 in which the SAR sublayer segments CS PDUs without adding additional fields. *See also* AAL, AAL5, CS, and SAR.

Secondary   See secondary station.

secondary ring   One of the two rings making up an FDDI or CDDI ring. The secondary ring is usually reserved for use in the event of a failure of the primary ring. Compare to primary ring.

secondary station   In bit-synchronous Data Link layer protocols such as HDLC, a station that responds to commands from a primary station. Sometimes referred to simply as a secondary. *See also* primary station.

Section DCC   Section Data Communications Channel. In OSS, a 192Kbps data communications channel embedded in the section overhead for OAM&P traffic between two SONET network elements. *See also* OAM&P and SONET.

security management   One of five categories of network management defined by ISO for management of OSI networks. Security management subsystems are responsible for controlling access to network resources. *See also* accounting management, configuration management, fault management, and performance management.

seed router   A router in an AppleTalk network that has the network number or cable range built in to its port descriptor. The seed router defines the network number or cable range for other routers in that network segment and responds to configuration queries from nonseed routers on its connected AppleTalk network, allowing those routers to confirm or modify their configurations accordingly. Each AppleTalk network must have at least one seed router. *See also* nonseed router.

segment   1. Section of a network that is bounded by bridges, routers, or switches. 2. In a LAN using a bus topology, a segment is a continuous electrical circuit that is often connected to other such segments with repeaters. 3. Term used in the TCP specification to describe a single Transport layer unit of information. The terms datagram, frame, message, and packet are also used to describe logical information groupings at various layers of the OSI reference model and in various technology circles.

serial transmission   Method of data transmission in which the bits of a data character are transmitted sequentially over a single channel. Compare with parallel transmission.

server   Node or software program that provides services to clients. *See also* back end, client, and front end.

service point   Interface between non-SNA devices and NetView that sends alerts from equipment unknown to the SNA environment.

session   1. Related set of communications transactions between two or more network devices. 2. In SNA, a logical connection enabling two NAUs to communicate.

Session layer   Layer 5 of the OSI reference model. This layer establishes, manages, and terminates sessions between applications and manages data exchange between Presentation layer entities. Corresponds to the data flow control layer of the SNA model. *See also* Application layer, Data Link layer, Network layer, Physical layer, Presentation layer, and Transport layer.

SF   Super Frame. Common framing type used on T1 circuits. SF consists of 12 frames of 192 bits each, with the 193rd bit providing error checking and other functions. SF has been superseded by ESF, but is still widely used. Also called D4 framing. *See also* ESF.

S-frame   Supervisory frame. One of three SDLC frame formats. *See also* I-frame and U-frame.

SGMP   Simple Gateway Monitoring Protocol. Network management protocol that was considered for Internet standardization and later evolved into SNMP. Documented in RFC 1028. *See also* SNMP.

shielded cable   Cable that has a layer of shielded insulation to reduce EMI.

shortest-path routing   Routing that minimizes distance or path cost through application of an algorithm.

signaling   Process of sending a transmission signal over a physical medium for purposes of communication.

signaling packet   Generated by an ATM-connected device that wants to establish a connection with another such device. The signaling packet contains the ATM NSAP address of the desired ATM endpoint, as well as any QOS parameters required for the connection. If the endpoint can support the desired QOS, it responds with an accept message, and the connection is opened. *See also* QOS.

silicon switching   Switching based on the SSE, which allows the processing of packets independent of the SSP (Silicon Switch Processor) system processor. Silicon switching provides high-speed, dedicated packet switching. *See also* SSE and SSP (Silicon Switch Processor).

simplex   Capability for transmission in only one direction between a sending station and a receiving station. Broadcast television is an example of a simplex technology. Compare with full duplex and half duplex.

single-mode fiber   Fiber-optic cabling with a narrow core that allows light to enter only at a single angle. Such cabling has higher bandwidth than multimode fiber, but requires a light source with a narrow spectral width (for example, a laser). Also called monomode fiber. *See also* multimode fiber.

single-vendor network   Network using equipment from only one vendor. Single-vendor networks rarely suffer compatibility problems. *See also* multivendor network.

SIP   SMDS Interface Protocol. Used in communications between CPE and SMDS network equipment. Allows the CPE to use SMDS service for high-speed WAN internetworking. Based on the IEEE 802.6 DQDB standard. *See also* DQDB.

sliding window flow control   Method of flow control in which a receiver gives transmitter permission to transmit data until a window is full. When the window is full, the transmitter must stop transmitting until the receiver advertises a larger window. TCP, other transport protocols, and several Data Link layer protocols use this method of flow control.

SLIP   Serial Line Internet Protocol. Standard protocol for point-to-point serial connections using a variation of TCP/IP. Predecessor of PPP. *See also* CSLIP and PPP.

slotted ring   LAN architecture based on a ring topology in which the ring is divided into slots that circulate continuously. Slots can be either empty or full, and transmissions must start at the beginning of a slot.

SMAC   source MAC. MAC address specified in the Source Address field of a packet. Compare with DMAC. *See also* MAC address.

SMB   Server Message Block. File-system protocol used in LAN Manager and similar NOSs to package data and exchange information with other systems.

SMDS   Switched Multimegabit Data Service. High-speed, packet-switched, datagram-based WAN networking technology offered by the telephone companies. *See also* CBDS.

SMI   Structure of Management Information. Document (RFC 1155) specifying rules used to define managed objects in the MIB. *See also* MIB.

SMRP   Simple Multicast Routing Protocol. Specialized multicast network protocol for routing multimedia data streams on enterprise networks. SMRP works in conjunction with multicast extensions to the AppleTalk protocol.

SMT   Station Management. ANSI FDDI specification that defines how ring stations are managed.

SMTP   Simple Mail Transfer Protocol. Internet protocol providing electronic mail services.

SNA   Systems Network Architecture. Large, complex, feature-rich network architecture developed in the 1970s by IBM. Similar in some respects to the OSI reference model, but with a number of differences. SNA is essentially composed of seven layers. See data flow control layer, data link control layer, path control layer, physical control layer, presentation services layer, transaction services layer, and transmission control layer.

SNADS   SNA Distribution Services. Consists of a set of SNA transaction programs that interconnect and cooperate to provide asynchronous distribution of information between end users. One of three SNA transaction services. *See also* DDM and DIA.

SNAP   Subnetwork Access Protocol. Internet protocol that operates between a network entity in the subnetwork and a network entity in the end system. SNAP specifies a standard method of encapsulating IP datagrams and ARP messages on IEEE networks. The SNAP entity in the end system makes use of the services of the subnetwork and performs three key functions: data transfer, connection management, and QOS selection.

SNI   1. Subscriber Network Interface. Interface for SMDS-based networks that connects CPE and an SMDS switch. *See also* UNI. 2. SNA Network Interconnection. IBM gateway connecting multiple SNA networks.

SNMP   Simple Network Management Protocol. Network management protocol used almost exclusively in TCP/IP networks. SNMP provides a means to monitor and control network devices, and to manage configurations, statistics collection, performance, and security. *See also* SGMP and SNMP2.

SNMP communities   Authentication scheme that enables an intelligent network device to validate SNMP requests.

SNMP2   SNMP Version 2. Version 2 of the popular network management protocol. SNMP2 supports centralized as well as distributed network management strategies, and includes improvements in the SMI, protocol operations, management architecture, and security. *See also* SNMP.

SNP   sequence number protection.

SNPA   subnetwork point of attachment. A Data Link layer address (such as an Ethernet address, X.25 address, or Frame Relay DLCI address). SNPA addresses are used to configure a CLNS route for an interface.

socket   1. Software structure operating as a communications end point within a network device. 2. An addressable entity within a node connected to an AppleTalk network; sockets are owned by software processes known as socket clients. AppleTalk sockets are divided into two groups: SASs, which are reserved for clients such as AppleTalk core protocols, and DASs, which are assigned dynamically by DDP upon request from clients in the node. An AppleTalk socket is similar in concept to a TCP/IP port.

socket client   A software process or function implemented in an AppleTalk network node.

socket listener   Software provided by a socket client to receive datagrams addressed to the socket.

socket number   An 8-bit number that identifies a socket. A maximum of 254 different socket numbers can be assigned in an AppleTalk node.

SONET   Synchronous Optical Network. High-speed (up to 2.5 Gbps) synchronous network specification developed by Bellcore and designed to run on optical fiber. STS-1 is the basic building block of SONET. Approved as an international standard in 1988. *See also* SDH, STS-1, and STS-3c.

source address   Address of a network device that is sending data. *See also* destination address.

SP   Switch Processor. Cisco 7000-series processor module that acts as the administrator for all CxBus activities. Sometimes called ciscoBus controller. *See also* CxBus.

span   1. Full-duplex digital transmission line between two digital facilities.
2. Switched Port Analyzer. Feature of the Catalyst 5000 switch that extends the monitoring abilities of existing network analyzers into a switched Ethernet environment. SPAN mirrors the traffic at one switched segment onto a predefined SPAN port. A network analyzer attached to the SPAN port can monitor traffic from any of the other Catalyst switched ports.

spanning explorer packet   Follows a statically configured spanning tree when looking for paths in an SRB network. Also known as a limited-route explorer packet or a single-route explorer packet. *See also* all-routes explorer packet, explorer packet, and local explorer packet.

spanning tree   Loop-free subset of a network topology. *See also* spanning-tree algorithm and Spanning-Tree Protocol.

spanning-tree algorithm   Algorithm used by the Spanning-Tree Protocol to create a spanning tree. Sometimes abbreviated STA. *See also* spanning tree and Spanning-Tree Protocol.

Spanning-Tree Protocol   Bridge protocol that utilizes the spanning-tree algorithm, enabling a learning bridge to dynamically work around loops in a network topology by creating a spanning tree. Bridges exchange BPDU messages with other bridges to detect loops, and then remove the loops by shutting down selected bridge interfaces. Refers to both the IEEE 802.1 Spanning-Tree Protocol standard and the earlier Digital Equipment Corporation Spanning-Tree Protocol upon which it is based. The IEEE version supports bridge domains and allows the bridge to construct a loop-free topology across an extended LAN. The IEEE version is generally preferred over the Digital version. Sometimes abbreviated STP. *See also* BPDU, learning bridge, MAC address learning, spanning tree, and spanning-tree algorithm.

speed matching   Feature that provides sufficient buffering capability in a destination device to allow a high-speed source to transmit data at its maximum rate, even if the destination device is a lower-speed device.

SPF   shortest path first algorithm. Routing algorithm that iterates on length of path to determine a shortest-path spanning tree. Commonly used in link-state routing algorithms. Sometimes called Dijkstra's algorithm. *See also* link-state routing algorithm.

SPID   service profile identifier. Number that some service providers use to define the services to which an ISDN device subscribes. The ISDN device uses the SPID when accessing the switch that initializes the connection to a service provider.

split-horizon updates   Routing technique in which information about routes is prevented from exiting the router interface through which that information was received. Split-horizon updates are useful in preventing routing loops.

spoofing   1. Scheme used by routers to cause a host to treat an interface as if it were up and supporting a session. The router spoofs replies to keepalive messages from the host in order to convince that host that the session still exists. Spoofing is useful in routing environments such as DDR, in which a circuit-switched link is taken down when there is no traffic to be sent across it in order to save toll charges. *See also* DDR. 2. The act of a packet illegally claiming to be from an address from which it was not actually sent. Spoofing is designed to foil network security mechanisms such as filters and access lists.

spooler   Application that manages requests or jobs submitted to it for execution. Spoolers process the submitted requests in an orderly fashion from a queue. A print spooler is a common example of a spooler.

SPP   Sequenced Packet Protocol. Provides reliable, connection-based, flow-controlled packet transmission on behalf of client processes. Part of the XNS protocol suite.

SPX   Sequenced Packet Exchange. Reliable, connection-oriented protocol that supplements the datagram service provided by Network layer (Layer 3) protocols.

Novell derived this commonly used NetWare transport protocol from the SPP of the XNS protocol suite.

SQE   signal quality error. Transmission sent by a transceiver back to the controller to let the controller know whether the collision circuitry is functional. Also called heartbeat.

SRAM   Type of RAM that retains its contents for as long as power is supplied. SRAM does not require constant refreshing, like DRAM. Compare with DRAM.

SRB   source-route bridging. Method of bridging originated by IBM and popular in Token Ring networks. In a SRB network, the entire route to a destination is prede-termined, in real time, prior to the sending of data to the destination. Contrast with transparent bridging.

SRT   source-route transparent bridging. IBM bridging scheme that merges the two most prevalent bridging strategies, SRB and transparent bridging. SRT employs both technologies in one device to satisfy the needs of all ENs. No translation between bridging protocols is necessary. Compare with SR/TLB.

SR/TLB   source-route translational bridging. Method of bridging where source-route stations can communicate with transparent bridge stations with the help of an intermediate bridge that translates between the two bridge protocols. Compare with SRT.

SRTP   Sequenced Routing Update Protocol. Protocol that assists VINES servers in finding neighboring clients, servers, and routers. *See also* RTP (Routing Table Protocol).

SS7   Signaling System 7. Standard CCS system used with BISDN and ISDN. Devel-oped by Bellcore. *See also* CCS.

SSAP   source service access point. The SAP of the network node designated in the Source field of a packet. Compare to DSAP. *See also* SAP (service access point).

SSCP   system services control points. Focal points within an SNA network for managing network configuration, coordinating network operator and problem deter-mination requests, and providing directory services and other session services for net-work end users.

SSCP-PU session   Session used by SNA to allow an SSCP to manage the resources of a node through the PU. SSCPs can send requests to, and receive replies from, indi-vidual nodes in order to control the network configuration.

SSCOP   Service Specific Connection Oriented Protocol. A data link protocol that guarantees delivery of ATM signaling packets.

SSCS   service specific convergence sublayer. One of the two sublayers of any AAL. SSCS, which is service dependent, offers assured data transmission. The SSCS can be null as well, in classical IP over ATM or LAN emulation implementations. *See also* AAL, ATM layer, CPCS, CS, and SAR.

SSE silicon switching engine. Routing and switching mechanism that compares the data link or Network layer header of an incoming packet to a silicon-switching cache, determines the appropriate action (routing or bridging), and forwards the packet to the proper interface. The SSE is directly encoded in the hardware of the SSP (Silicon Switch Processor) of a Cisco 7000 series router. It can therefore perform switching independently of the system processor, making the execution of routing decisions much quicker than if they were encoded in software. *See also* silicon switching and SSP.

SSP 1. Switch-to-Switch Protocol. Protocol specified in the DLSw standard that routers use to establish DLSw connections, locate resources, forward data, and handle flow control and error recovery. *See also* DLSw. *See also* SSP in the Cisco Systems section. 2. Silicon Switch Processor. High-performance silicon switch for Cisco 7000 series routers that provides distributed processing and control for interface processors. The SSP leverages the high-speed switching and routing capabilities of the SSE to dramatically increase aggregate router performance, minimizing performance bottlenecks at the interface points between the router and a high-speed backbone. *See also* silicon switching and SSE.

standard Set of rules or procedures that are either widely used or officially specified. *See also* de facto standard and de jure standard.

standby monitor Device placed in standby mode on a Token Ring network in case an active monitor fails. *See also* active monitor and ring monitor.

StarLAN CSMA/CD LAN, based on IEEE 802.3, developed by AT&T.

star topology LAN topology in which end points on a network are connected to a common central switch by point-to-point links. A ring topology that is organized as a star implements a unidirectional closed-loop star, instead of point-to-point links. Compare with bus topology, ring topology, and tree topology.

startup range A range of values (from 65280-65534) from which an AppleTalk node selects the network number part of its provisional address if it has no other number saved.

static route Route that is explicitly configured and entered into the routing table. Static routes take precedence over routes chosen by dynamic routing protocols.

statistical multiplexing Technique whereby information from multiple logical channels can be transmitted across a single physical channel. Statistical multiplexing dynamically allocates bandwidth only to active input channels, making better use of available bandwidth and allowing more devices to be connected than with other multiplexing techniques. Also referred to as statistical time-division multiplexing or stat mux. Compare with ATDM, FDM, and TDM.

STM-1 Synchronous Transport Module level 1. One of a number of SDH formats that specifies the frame structure for the 155.52Mbps lines used to carry ATM cells. *See also* SDH.

store and forward packet switching   Packet-switching technique in which frames are completely processed before being forwarded out the appropriate port. This processing includes calculating the CRC and checking the destination address. In addition, frames must be temporarily stored until network resources (such as an unused link) are available to forward the message. Contrast with cut-through packet switching.

STP   1. shielded twisted-pair. Two-pair wiring medium used in a variety of network implementations. STP cabling has a layer of shielded insulation to reduce EMI. Compare with UTP. *See also* twisted pair. 2. See Spanning-Tree Protocol.

STS-1   Synchronous Transport Signal level 1. Basic building block signal of SONET, operating at 51.84Mbps. Faster SONET rates are defined as STS-n, where n is a multiple of 51.84Mbps. *See also* SONET.

STS-3c   Synchronous Transport Signal level 3, concatenated. SONET format that specifies the frame structure for the 155.52Mbps lines used to carry ATM cells. *See also* SONET.

stub area   OSPF area that carries a default route, intra-area routes, and interarea routes, but does not carry external routes. Virtual links cannot be configured across a stub area, and they cannot contain an ASBR. Compare to non-stub area. *See also* ASBR and OSPF.

stub network   Network that has only a single connection to a router.

STUN   serial tunnel. Router feature allowing two SDLC- or HDLC-compliant devices to connect to one another through an arbitrary multiprotocol topology (using Cisco routers) rather than through a direct serial link.

subarea   Portion of an SNA network that consists of a subarea node and any attached links and peripheral nodes.

subarea node   SNA communication controller or host that handles complete network addresses.

subchannel   In broadband terminology, a frequency-based subdivision creating a separate communications channel.

subinterface   One of a number of virtual interfaces on a single physical interface.

subnet address   Portion of an IP address that is specified as the subnetwork by the subnet mask. *See also* IP address, subnet mask, and subnetwork.

subnet mask   32-bit address mask used in IP to indicate the bits of an IP address that are being used for the subnet address. Sometimes referred to simply as mask. *See also* address mask and IP address.

subnetwork   1. In IP networks, a network sharing a particular subnet address. Subnetworks are networks arbitrarily segmented by a network administrator in order to provide a multilevel, hierarchical routing structure while shielding the subnetwork from the addressing complexity of attached networks. Sometimes called a subnet. *See also* IP address, subnet address, and subnet mask. 2. In OSI networks, a collection of

ESs and ISs under the control of a single administrative domain and using a single network access protocol.

subvector   A data segment of a vector in an SNA message. A subvector consists of a length field, a key that describes the subvector type, and subvector specific data.

SURAnet   Southeastern Universities Research Association Network. Network connecting universities and other organizations in the Southeastern United States. SURAnet, originally funded by the NSF and a part of the NSFNET, is now part of BBN Planet. *See also* BBN Planet, NSF, and NSFNET.

SVC   switched virtual circuit. Virtual circuit that is dynamically established on demand and is torn down when transmission is complete. SVCs are used in situations where data transmission is sporadic. Called a switched virtual connection in ATM terminology. Compare with PVC.

switch   1. Network device that filters, forwards, and floods frames based on the destination address of each frame. The switch operates at the Data Link layer of the OSI model. 2. General term applied to an electronic or mechanical device that allows a connection to be established as necessary and terminated when there is no longer a session to support.

switched LAN   LAN implemented with LAN switches. See LAN switch.

synchronization   Establishment of common timing between sender and receiver.

synchronous transmission   Term describing digital signals that are transmitted with precise clocking. Such signals have the same frequency, with individual characters encapsulated in control bits (called start bits and stop bits) that designate the beginning and end of each character. Compare with asynchronous transmission, isochronous transmission, and plesiochronous transmission.

sysgen   system generation. Process of defining network resources in a network.

T1   Digital WAN carrier facility. T1 transmits DS-1-formatted data at 1.544Mbps through the telephone-switching network, using AMI or B8ZS coding. Compare with E1. *See also* AMI, B8ZS, and DS-1.

T3   Digital WAN carrier facility. T3 transmits DS-3-formatted data at 44.736Mbps through the telephone switching network. Compare with E3. *See also* DS-3.

TABS   Telemetry Asynchronous Block Serial. An AT&T polled point-to-point or multi-point communication protocol that supports moderate data transfer rates over intra-office wire pairs.

TAC   Terminal Access Controller. Internet host that accepts terminal connections from dial-up lines.

TACACS   Terminal Access Controller Access Control System. Authentication protocol, developed by the DDN community, that provides remote access authentication and related services, such as event logging. User passwords are administered in a central database rather than in individual routers, providing an easily scalable network security solution. *See also* TACACS+ in the Cisco Systems section.

TACACS+ Proprietary Cisco enhancement to TACACS. Provides additional support for authentication, authorization, and accounting. *See also* TACACS.

tag switching A high-performance, packet-forwarding technology that integrates Network layer (Layer 3) routing and Data Link layer (Layer 2) switching and provides scalable, high-speed switching in the network core. Tag switching is based on the concept of label swapping, in which packets or cells are assigned short, fixed-length labels that tell switching nodes how data should be forwarded.

tagged traffic ATM cells that have their CLP bit set to 1. If the network is congested, tagged traffic can be dropped to ensure delivery of higher-priority traffic. Sometimes called DE (discard eligible) traffic. *See also* CLP.

TARP TID Address Resolution Protocol. In OSS, a protocol that resolves a TL-1 Terminal Identifier (TID) to a CLNP address (NSAP).

TAXI 4B/5B Transparent Asynchronous Transmitter/Receiver Interface 4-byte/5-byte. Encoding scheme used for FDDI LANs as well as for ATM. Supports speeds of up to 100Mbps over multimode fiber. TAXI is the chipset that generates 4B/5B encoding on multimode fiber. *See also* 4B/5B local fiber.

TBOS protocol Telemetry Byte Oriented Serial protocol. A protocol that transmits alarm, status, and control points between NE and OSS. TBOS defines one physical interface for direct connection between the telemetry equipment and the monitored equipment.

TC transmission convergence. A sublayer of the ATM Physical layer (PHY) that transforms the flow of cells into a steady flow of bits for transmission over the physical medium. When transmitting, the TC sublayer maps the cells into the frame format, generates the header error check (HEC), and sends idle cells when there is nothing to send. When receiving, the TC sublayer delineates individual cells in the received bit stream and uses HEC to detect and correct errors. *See also* HEC and PHY.

T-carrier TDM transmission method usually referring to a line or cable carrying a DS-1 signal.

TCP Transmission Control Protocol. Connection-oriented Transport layer protocol that provides reliable full-duplex data transmission. TCP is part of the TCP/IP protocol stack. *See also* TCP/IP.

TCP/IP Transmission Control Protocol/Internet Protocol. Common name for the suite of protocols developed by the U.S. DoD in the 1970s to support the construction of worldwide internetworks. TCP and IP are the two best-known protocols in the suite. *See also* IP and TCP.

TCU trunk coupling unit. In Token Ring networks, a physical device that enables a station to connect to the trunk cable.

TDM time-division multiplexing. Technique in which information from multiple channels can be allocated bandwidth on a single wire based on preassigned time slots. Bandwidth is allocated to each channel regardless of whether the station has data to transmit. Compare with ATDM, FDM, and statistical multiplexing.

TDR   time domain reflectometer. Device capable of sending signals through a network medium to check cable continuity and other attributes. TDRs are used to find Physical layer network problems.

TEI   terminal endpoint identifier. A subfield in the LAPD address field that identifies a given TE device on an ISDN interface.

TE   terminal equipment. Any ISDN-compatible device that may be attached to the network, such as a telephone, fax, or a computer.

telco   Abbreviation for telephone company.

telecommunications   Term referring to communications (usually involving computer systems) over the telephone network.

telephony   Science of converting sound to electrical signals and transmitting it between widely removed points.

telex   Teletypewriter service allowing subscribers to send messages over the PSTN.

Telnet   Standard terminal emulation protocol in the TCP/IP protocol stack. Telnet is used for remote terminal connection, enabling users to log in to remote systems and use resources as if they were connected to a local system. Telnet is defined in RFC 854.

Tempest   U.S. military standard. Electronic products adhering to the Tempest specification are designed to withstand EMP. *See also* EMP.

TERENA   Trans-European Research and Education Networking Association. Organization that promotes information and telecommunications technologies development in Europe. Formed by the merging of EARN and RARE. *See also* EARN and RARE.

termid   SNA cluster controller identification. Termid is meaningful only for switched lines. Also called Xid.

terminal   Simple device at which data can be entered or retrieved from a network. Generally, terminals have a monitor and a keyboard, but no processor or local disk drive.

terminal adapter   Device used to connect ISDN BRI connections to existing interfaces such as EIA/TIA-232. Essentially, an ISDN modem.

terminal emulation   Network application in which a computer runs software that makes it appear to a remote host as a directly attached terminal.

terminal server   Communications processor that connects asynchronous devices such as terminals, printers, hosts, and modems to any LAN or WAN that uses TCP/IP, X.25, or LAT protocols. Terminal servers provide the internetwork intelligence that is not available in the connected devices.

terminator   Device that provides electrical resistance at the end of a transmission line to absorb signals on the line, thereby keeping them from bouncing back and being received again by network stations.

TFTP   Trivial File Transfer Protocol. Simplified version of FTP that allows files to be transferred from one computer to another over a network.

TH   transmission header. SNA header that is appended to the SNA basic information unit (BIU). The TH uses one of a number of available SNA header formats. *See also* FID0, FID1, FID2, FID3, and FID4.

THC over X.25   Feature providing TCP/IP header compression over X.25 links, for purposes of link efficiency.

THEnet   Texas Higher Education Network. Regional network comprising over 60 academic and research institutions in the Texas (United States) area.

Thinnet   Term used to define a thinner, less expensive version of the cable specified in the IEEE 802.3 10Base2 standard. Compare with Cheapernet. *See also* 10Base2, Ethernet, and IEEE 802.3.

throughput   Rate of information arriving at, and possibly passing through, a particular point in a network system.

TIA   Telecommunications Industry Association. Organization that develops standards relating to telecommunications technologies. Together, the TIA and the EIA have formalized standards, such as EIA/TIA-232, for the electrical characteristics of data transmission. *See also* EIA.

TIC   Token Ring interface coupler. Controller through which an FEP connects to a Token Ring.

TIRKS   Trunk Information Record Keeping System. A Bellcore OSS that provides record keeping for interoffice trunk facilities. *See also* OSS.

time-out   Event that occurs when one network device expects to hear from another network device within a specified period of time, but does not. The resulting time-out usually results in a retransmission of information or the dissolving of the session between the two devices.

TL-1   Transaction Language One. The Bellcore term for intelligent network elements.

TLAP   TokenTalk Link Access Protocol. The link-access protocol used in a Token-Talk network. TLAP is built on top of the standard Token Ring Data Link layer.

TMN   Telecommunication Management Network. The ITU-T generic model for transporting and processing OAM&P information for a telecommunications network. *See also* OAM&P.

TN3270   Terminal emulation software that allows a terminal to appear to an IBM host as a 3278 Model 2 terminal.

TNotify   Time Notify. Specifies how often SMT initiates neighbor notification broadcasts. *See also* SMT.

token   Frame that contains control information. Possession of the token allows a network device to transmit data onto the network. *See also* token passing.

token bus   LAN architecture using token passing access over a bus topology. This LAN architecture is the basis for the IEEE 802.4 LAN specification. *See also* IEEE 802.4.

token passing   Access method by which network devices access the physical medium in an orderly fashion based on possession of a small frame called a token. Contrast with circuit switching and contention. *See also* token.

Token Ring   Token-passing LAN developed and supported by IBM. Token Ring runs at 4 or 16Mbps over a ring topology. Similar to IEEE 802.5. *See also* IEEE 802.5, ring topology, and token passing.

TokenTalk   Apple Computer's data-link product that allows an AppleTalk network to be connected by Token Ring cables.

TOP   Technical Office Protocol. OSI-based architecture developed for office communications.

topology   Physical arrangement of network nodes and media within an enterprise networking structure.

TOS   type of service. See COS (class of service).

TP0   Transport Protocol Class 0. OSI connectionless transport protocol for use over reliable subnetworks. Defined by ISO 8073.

TP4   Transport Protocol Class 4. OSI connection-based transport protocol. Defined by ISO 8073.

TPD   A mechanism used by some ATM switches that allows the remaining cells supporting an AAL5 frame to be discarded when one or more cells of that AAL5 frame have been dropped. This avoids sending partial AAL5 frames through the ATM network when they will have to be retransmitted by the sender. Compare with EPD.

traffic management   Techniques for avoiding congestion and shaping and policing traffic, Allows links to operate at high levels of utilization by scaling back lower-priority, delay-tolerant traffic at the edge of the network when congestion begins to occur.

traffic policing   Process used to measure the actual traffic flow across a given connection and compare it to the total admissable traffic flow for that connection. Traffic outside of the agreed upon flow can be tagged (where the CLP bit is set to 1) and can be discarded en route if congestion develops. Traffic policing is used in ATM, Frame Relay, and other types of networks. Also know as admission control, permit processing, rate enforcement, and UPC (usage parameter control). *See also* tagged traffic.

traffic profile   Set of COS attribute values assigned to a given port on an ATM switch. The profile affects numerous parameters for data transmitted from the port including rate, cell drop eligibility, transmit priority, and inactivity timer. *See also* COS.

traffic shaping   Use of queues to limit surges that can congest a network. Data is buffered and then sent into the network in regulated amounts to ensure that the traffic will fit within the promised traffic envelope for the particular connection. Traffic shaping is used in ATM, Frame Relay, and other types of networks. Also known as metering, shaping, and smoothing.

trailer   Control information appended to data when encapsulating the data for network transmission. Compare with header.

transaction   Result-oriented unit of communication processing.

transaction services layer   Layer 7 in the SNA architectural model. Represents user application functions, such as spreadsheets, word-processing, or electronic mail, by which users interact with the network. Corresponds roughly with the Application layer of the OSI reference model. *See also* data flow control layer, data link control layer, path control layer, physical control layer, presentation services layer, and transaction services layer.

transit bridging   Bridging that uses encapsulation to send a frame between two similar networks over a dissimilar network.

translational bridging   Bridging between networks with dissimilar MAC sublayer protocols. MAC information is translated into the format of the destination network at the bridge. Contrast with encapsulation bridging.

transmission control layer   Layer 4 in the SNA architectural model. This layer is responsible for establishing, maintaining, and terminating SNA sessions, sequencing data messages, and controlling session level flow. Corresponds to the Transport layer of the OSI model. *See also* data flow control layer, data link control layer, path control layer, physical control layer, presentation services layer, and transaction services layer.

transmission group   In SNA routing, one or more parallel communications links treated as one communications facility.

TRANSPAC   Major packet data network run by France Telecom.

transparent bridging   Bridging scheme often used in Ethernet and IEEE 802.3 networks in which bridges pass frames along one hop at a time based on tables associating end nodes with bridge ports. Transparent bridging is so named because the presence of bridges is transparent to network end nodes. Contrast with SRB.

Transport layer   Layer 4 of the OSI reference model. This layer is responsible for reliable network communication between end nodes. The Transport layer provides mechanisms for the establishment, maintenance, and termination of virtual circuits, transport fault detection and recovery, and information flow control. Corresponds to the transmission control layer of the SNA model. *See also* Application layer, Data Link layer, Network layer, Physical layer, Presentation layer, and Session layer.

trap   Message sent by an SNMP agent to an NMS, console, or terminal to indicate the occurrence of a significant event, such as a specifically defined condition or a threshold that has been reached. *See also* alarm and event.

tree topology   LAN topology similar to a bus topology, except that tree networks can contain branches with multiple nodes. Transmissions from a station propagate the length of the medium and are received by all other stations. Compare with bus topology, ring topology, and star topology.

TRIP   Token Ring Interface Processor. High-speed interface processor on the Cisco 7000 series routers. The TRIP provides two or four Token Ring ports for interconnection with IEEE 802.5 and IBM Token Ring media with ports independently set to speeds of either 4 or 16Mbps.

trunk   Physical and logical connection between two switches across which network traffic travels. A backbone is composed of a number of trunks.

TTL   Time To Live. Field in an IP header that indicates how long a packet is considered valid.

tunneling   Architecture that is designed to provide the services necessary to implement any standard point-to-point encapsulation scheme. *See also* encapsulation.

TUD   trunk up-down. Protocol used in ATM networks that monitors trunks and detects when one goes down or comes up. ATM switches send regular test messages from each trunk port to test trunk line quality. If a trunk misses a given number of these messages, TUD declares the trunk down. When a trunk comes back up, TUD recognizes that the trunk is up, declares the trunk up, and returns it to service. *See also* trunk.

TULIP   TCP and UDP over Lightweight IP. A proposed protocol for running TCP and UDP applications over ATM.

TUNIP   TCP and UDP over Nonexistent IP. A proposed protocol for running TCP and UPD applications over ATM.

TUV   German test agency that certifies products to European safety standards.

twisted pair   Relatively low-speed transmission medium consisting of two insulated wires arranged in a regular spiral pattern. The wires can be shielded or unshielded. Twisted pair is common in telephony applications and is increasingly common in data networks. *See also* STP and UTP.

TWS   two-way simultaneous. Mode that allows a router configured as a primary SDLC station to achieve better utilization of a full-duplex serial line. When TWS is enabled in a multidrop environment, the router can poll a secondary station and receive data from that station while it sends data to or receives data from a different secondary station on the same serialline.

Type 1 operation   IEEE 802.2 (LLC) connectionless operation.

Type 2 operation   IEEE 802.2 (LLC) connection-oriented operation.

UART   Universal Asynchronous Receiver/Transmitter. Integrated circuit, attached to the parallel bus of a computer, used for serial communications. The UART translates between serial and parallel signals, provides transmission clocking, and buffers data sent to or from the computer.

UB Net/One   Ungermann-Bass Net/One. Routing protocol, developed by UB Networks, that uses hello packets and a path-delay metric, with end nodes communicating using the XNS protocol. There are a number of differences between the manner in which Net/One uses the XNS protocol and the usage common among other XNS nodes.

UBR   unspecified bit rate. QOS class defined by the ATM Forum for ATM networks. UBR allows any amount of data up to a specified maximum to be sent across the network, but there are no guarantees in terms of cell loss rate and delay. Compare with ABR (available bit rate), CBR, and VBR.

UBR+   unspecified bit rate plus. A UBR service complemented by ATM switches that use intelligent packet discard mechanisms such as EPD or TPD. *See also* EPD and TPD.

UDP   User Datagram Protocol. Connectionless Transport layer protocol in the TCP/IP protocol stack. UDP is a simple protocol that exchanges datagrams without acknowledgments or guaranteed delivery, requiring that error processing and retransmission be handled by other protocols. UDP is defined in RFC 768.

U-frame   Unnumbered frame. One of three SDLC frame formats. *See also* I-frame and S-frame.

UL   Underwriters Laboratories. Independent agency within the United States that tests product safety.

ULP   upper-layer protocol. Protocol that operates at a higher layer in the OSI reference model, relative to other layers. ULP is sometimes used to refer to the next-highest protocol (relative to a particular protocol) in a protocol stack.

unbalanced configuration   HDLC configuration with one primary station and multiple secondary stations.

UNI   User-Network Interface. ATM Forum specification that defines an interoperability standard for the interface between ATM-based products (a router or an ATM switch) located in a private network and the ATM switches located within the public carrier networks. Also used to describe similar connections in Frame Relay networks. *See also* NNI, Q.920/Q.921 and SNI (Subscriber Network Interface).

unicast   Message sent to a single network destination. Compare with broadcast and multicast.

unicast address   Address specifying a single network device. Compare with broadcast address and multicast address. *See also* unicast.

uninsured traffic   Traffic within the excess rate (the difference between the insured rate and maximum rate) for an ATM VCC. This traffic can be dropped by the network if congestion occurs. *See also* CLP, insured rate, and maximum rate.

unipolar   Literally meaning one polarity, the fundamental electrical characteristic of internal signals in digital communications equipment. Contrast with bipolar.

unity gain   In broadband networks, the balance between signal loss and signal gain through amplifiers.

UNIX   Operating system developed in 1969 at Bell Laboratories. UNIX has gone through several iterations since its inception. These include UNIX 4.3 BSD (Berkeley Standard Distribution), developed at the University of California at Berkeley, and UNIX System V, Release 4.0, developed by AT&T.

unnumbered frames   HDLC frames used for various control and management purposes, including link startup and shutdown, and mode specification.

UPC   usage parameter control. See traffic policing.

URL   Universal Resource Locator. Standardized addressing scheme for accessing hypertext documents and other services using a WWW browser. *See also* browser.

USENET   Initiated in 1979, one of the oldest and largest cooperative networks, with over 10,000 hosts and a quarter of a million users. Its primary service is a distributed conferencing service called news.

UTC   Coordinated Universal Time. Time zone at zero degrees longitude. Formerly known as Greenwich Mean Time (GMT) and zulu time.

UTP   unshielded twisted-pair. Four-pair wire medium used in a variety of networks. UTP does not require the fixed spacing between connections that is necessary with coaxial-type connections. There are five types of UTP cabling commonly used: Category 1 cabling, Category 2 cabling, Category 3 cabling, Category 4 cabling, and Category 5 cabling. Compare with STP. *See also* EIA/TIA-586 and twisted pair.

UUCP   UNIX-to-UNIX Copy Program. Protocol stack used for point-to-point communication between UNIX systems.

uuencode   UNIX-to-UNIX encoding. A method of converting binary files to ASCII so that they can be sent over the Internet via e-mail. The name comes from its use by the UNIX operating system's uuencode command. *See also* uudecode.

uudecode   UNIX-to-UNIX decode. A method of decoding ASCII files that were encoded using uuencode. See uuencode.

V.24   ITU-T standard for a Physical layer interface between DTE and DCE. V.24 is essentially the same as the EIA/TIA-232 standard. *See also* EIA/TIA-232.

V.25bis   ITU-T specification describing procedures for call setup and tear down over the DTE-DCE interface in a PSDN.

V.32   ITU-T standard serial line protocol for bidirectional data transmissions at speeds of 4.8 or 9.6Kbps. *See also* V.32bis.

V.32bis   ITU-T standard that extends V.32 to speeds up to 14.4Kbps. *See also* V.32.

V.34   ITU-T standard that specifies a serial line protocol. V.34 offers improvements to the V.32 standard, including higher transmission rates (28.8Kbps) and enhanced data compression. Compare with V.32.

V.35 ITU-T standard describing a synchronous, Physical layer protocol used for communications between a network access device and a packet network. V.35 is most commonly used in the United States and in Europe, and is recommended for speeds up to 48Kbps.

V.42 ITU-T standard protocol for error correction using LAPM. *See also* LAPM.

VBR variable bit rate. QOS class defined by the ATM Forum for ATM networks. VBR is subdivided into a real time (RT) class and non-real time (NRT) class. VBR (RT) is used for connections in which there is a fixed timing relationship between samples. VBR (NRT) is used for connections in which there is no fixed timing relationship between samples, but that still need a guaranteed QOS. Compare with ABR (available bit rate), CBR, and UBR.

VCC virtual channel connection. Logical circuit, made up of VCLs, that carries data between two end points in an ATM network. Sometimes called a virtual circuit connection. *See also* VCI, VCL, and VPI.

VCI virtual channel identifier. 16-bit field in the header of an ATM cell. The VCI, together with the VPI, is used to identify the next destination of a cell as it passes through a series of ATM switches on its way to its destination. ATM switches use the VPI/VCI fields to identify the next network VCL that a cell needs to transit on its way to its final destination. The function of the VCI is similar to that of the DLCI in Frame Relay. Compare to DLCI. *See also* VCL and VPI.

VCL virtual channel link. Connection between two ATM devices. A VCC is made up of one or more VCLs. *See also* VCC.

VCN virtual circuit number. 12-bit field in an X.25 PLP header that identifies an X.25 virtual circuit. Allows DCE to determine how to route a packet through the X.25 network. Sometimes called LCI (logical channel identifier) or LCN (logical channel number).

VDSL very-high-data-rate digital subscriber line. One of four DSL technologies. VDSL delivers 13Mbps to 52Mbps downstream and 1.5Mbps to 2.3Mbps upstream over a single twisted copper pair. The operating range if VDSL is limited to 1,000 to 4,500 feet. Compare with ADSL, HDSL, and SDSL.

vector Data segment of an SNA message. A vector consists of a length field, a key that describes the vector type, and vector-specific data.

VF variance factor. One of three link attributes exchanged using PTSPs to determine the available resources of an ATM network. VF is a relative measure CRM normalized by the variance of the aggregate cell rate on the link.

VINES Virtual Integrated Network Service. NOS developed and marketed by Banyan Systems.

VIP 1. Versatile Interface Processor. Interface card used in Cisco 7000 and Cisco 7500 series routers. The VIP provides multilayer switching and runs the Cisco IOS software. The most recent version of the VIP is VIP2. 2. virtual IP. Function that enables the creation of logically separated switched IP workgroups across the switch ports of a Catalyst 5000 running Virtual Networking Services software. *See also* Virtual Networking Services.

virtual circuit   Logical circuit created to ensure reliable communication between two network devices. A virtual circuit is defined by a VPI/VCI pair, and can be either permanent (a PVC) or switched (an SVC). Virtual circuits are used in Frame Relay and X.25. In ATM, a virtual circuit is called a virtual channel. Sometimes abbreviated VC. *See also* PVC, SVC, VCI, virtual route, and VPI.

virtual connection   In ATM, a connection between end users that has a defined route and endpoints. *See also* PVC and SVC.

virtualization   Process of implementing a network based on virtual network segments. Devices are connected to virtual segments independent of their physical location and their physical connection to the network.

Virtual Networking Services   Software on some Catalyst 5000 switches that enables multiple workgroups to be defined across switches and offers traffic segmentation and access control

virtual path   Logical grouping of virtual circuits that connect two sites. *See also* virtual circuit.

virtual ring   Entity in an SRB network that logically connects two or more physical rings together either locally or remotely. The concept of virtual rings can be expanded across router boundaries.

virtual route   In SNA, a logical connection between subarea nodes that is physically realized as a particular explicit route. SNA terminology for virtual circuit. *See also* virtual circuit.

virtual subnet   A logical grouping of devices that share a common layer 3 subnet.

VLAN   virtual LAN. Group of devices on one or more LANs that are configured (using management software) so that they can communicate as if they were attached to the same wire, when in fact they are located on a number of different LAN segments. Because VLANs are based on logical instead of physical connections, they are extremely flexible.

VLI   virtual LAN internetwork. Internetwork composed of VLANs. See VLAN.

VLSM   variable-length subnet mask. Ability to specify a different subnet mask for the same network number on different subnets. VLSM can help optimize available address space.

VP   virtual path. One of two types of ATM circuits identified by a VPI. A virtual path is a bundle of virtual channels, all of which are switched transparently across an ATM network based on a common VPI. *See also* VPI.

VPC   virtual path connection. Grouping of VCCs that share one or more contiguous VPLs. *See also* VCC and VPL.

VPI virtual path identifier. 8-bit field in the header of an ATM cell. The VPI, together with the VCI, is used to identify the next destination of a cell as it passes through a series of ATM switches on its way to its destination. ATM switches use the VPI/VCI fields to identify the next VCL that a cell needs to transit on its way to its final destination. The function of the VPI is similar to that of the DLCI in Frame Relay. Compare with DLCI. *See also* VCI and VCL.

VPL virtual path link. Within a virtual path, a group of unidirectional VCLs with the same end points. Grouping VCLs into VPLs reduces the number of connections to be managed, thereby decreasing network control overhead and cost. A VPC is made up of one or more VPLs.

VT-n Virtual Tributary level n. The SONET format for mapping a lower-rate signal into a SONET payload. For example, VT-1.5 is used to transport a DS-1 signal. *See also* DS-1 and SONET.

VTAM virtual telecommunications access method. Set of programs that control communication between LUs. VTAM controls data transmission between channel-attached devices and performs routing functions. *See also* LU.

VTP Virtual Terminal Protocol. ISO application for establishing a virtual terminal connection across a network.

WAIS Wide Area Information Server. A distributed database protocol developed by Thinking Machines Corporation to search for information over a network. WAIS supports full-text databases, which allows an entire document to be searched for a match (as opposed to other technologies that only allow an index of key words to be searched).

WAN wide-area network. Data communications network that serves users across a broad geographic area and often uses transmission devices provided by common carriers. Frame Relay, SMDS, and X.25 are examples of WANs. Compare with LAN and MAN.

watchdog packet Used to ensure that a client is still connected to a NetWare server. If the server has not received a packet from a client for a certain period of time, it sends that client a series of watchdog packets. If the station fails to respond to a predefined number of watchdog packets, the server concludes that the station is no longer connected and clears the connection for that station.

watchdog spoofing Subset of spoofing that refers specifically to a router acting for a NetWare client by sending watchdog packets to a NetWare server to keep the session between client and server active. *See also* spoofing.

watchdog timer 1. Hardware or software mechanism that is used to trigger an event or an escape from a process unless the timer is periodically reset. 2. In NetWare, a timer that indicates the maximum period of time that a server will wait for a client to respond to a watchdog packet. If the timer expires, the server sends another watchdog packet (up to a set maximum). *See also* watchdog packet.

waveform coding Electrical techniques used to convey binary signals.

W-DCS   Wideband Digital Cross-connect System. A SONET DCS capable of cross-connecting DS-1 and VT1.5 signals. *See also* DCS, DS-1, SONET, and VT-n.

wildcard mask   32-bit quantity used in conjunction with an IP address to determine which bits in an IP address should be ignored when comparing that address with another IP address. A wildcard mask is specified when setting up access lists.

WinSock   Windows Socket Interface . A software interface that allows a wide variety of applications to use and share an Internet connection. WinSock is implemented as dynamic link library (DLL) with some supporting programs, such as a dialer program that initiates the connection.

wiring closet   Specially designed room used for wiring a data or voice network. Wiring closets serve as a central junction point for the wiring and wiring equipment that is used for interconnecting devices.

WISCNET   TCP/IP network in Wisconsin (United States) connecting University of Wisconsin campuses and a number of private colleges. Links are 56Kbps and T1.

workgroup   Collection of workstations and servers on a LAN that are designed to communicate and exchange data with one another.

WorkGroup Director   Cisco SNMP-based network-management software tool. Workgroup Director runs on UNIX workstations either as a standalone application or integrated with another SNMP-based network management platform, providing a seamless, powerful management system for Cisco workgroup products. *See also* SNMP

workgroup switching   Method of switching that provides high-speed (100Mbps) transparent bridging between Ethernet networks and high-speed translational bridging between Ethernet and CDDI or FDDI.

wrap   Action taken by an FDDI or CDDI network to recover in the event of a failure. The stations on each side of the failure reconfigure themselves, creating a single logical ring out of the primary and secondary rings.

WWW   World Wide Web. Large network of Internet servers providing hypertext and other services to terminals running client applications such as a browser. *See also* browser.

X.121   ITU-T standard describing an addressing scheme used in X.25 networks. X.121 addresses are sometimes called IDNs (International Data Numbers).

X.21   ITU-T standard for serial communications over synchronous digital lines. The X.21 protocol is used primarily in Europe and Japan.

X.21bis   ITU-T standard that defines the Physical layer protocol for communication between DCE and DTE in an X.25 network. Virtually equivalent to EIA/TIA-232. *See also* EIA/TIA-232 and X.25.

X.25   ITU-T standard that defines how connections between DTE and DCE are maintained for remote terminal access and computer communications in PDNs. X.25 specifies LAPB, a Data Link layer protocol, and PLP, a Network layer protocol. Frame Relay has to some degree superseded X.25. *See also* Frame Relay, LAPB, and PLP.

X.28 ITU-T recommendation that defines the terminal-to-PAD interface in X.25 networks. *See also* PAD and X.25.

X.29 ITU-T recommendation that defines the form for control information in the terminal-to-PAD interface used in X.25 networks. *See also* PAD and X.25.

X.3 ITU-T recommendation that defines various PAD parameters used in X.25 networks. *See also* PAD and X.25.

X3T9.5 Number assigned to the ANSI Task Group of Accredited Standards Committee for their internal, working document describing FDDI.

X.400 ITU-T recommendation specifying a standard for electronic mail transfer.

X.500 ITU-T recommendation specifying a standard for distributed maintenance of files and directories.

X.75 ITU-T specification that defines the signalling system between two PDNs. X.75 is essentially an NNI. *See also* NNI.

XDMCP X Display Manager Control Protocol. Protocol used to communicate between X terminals and workstations running the UNIX operating system.

XID exchange identification. Request and response packets exchanged prior to a session between a router and a Token Ring host. If the parameters of the serial device contained in the XID packet do not match the configuration of the host, the session is dropped.

XNS Xerox Network Systems. Protocol suite originally designed by PARC. Many PC networking companies, such as 3Com, Banyan, Novell, and UB Networks used or currently use a variation of XNS as their primary transport protocol. *See also* X Window System.

XRemote Protocol developed specifically to optimize support for the X Window System over a serial communications link.

XStream Major public PSN in the United States operated by MCI. Formerly called TYMNET.

X terminal Terminal that allows a user simultaneous access to several different applications and resources in a multivendor environment through implementation of X Windows. *See also* X Window System.

X Window System Distributed, network-transparent, device-independent, multi-tasking windowing and graphics system originally developed by MIT for communication between X terminals and UNIX workstations. *See also* X terminal.

zero code suppression Line coding scheme used for transmission clocking. Zero line suppression substitutes a one in the seventh bit of a string of eight consecutive zeros. *See also* ones density.

ZIP Zone Information Protocol. AppleTalk Session layer protocol that maps network numbers to zone names. ZIP is used by NBP to determine which networks contain nodes which belong to a zone. *See also* ZIP storm and zone.

ZIP storm   Broadcast storm that occurs when a router running AppleTalk propagates a route for which it currently has no corresponding zone name. The route is then forwarded by downstream routers, and a ZIP storm ensues. *See also* ZIP.

zone   In AppleTalk, a logical group of network devices. *See also* ZIP.

zone multicast address   A data-link-dependent multicast address at which a node receives the NBP broadcasts directed to its zone. *See also* NBP.

Index

Note to the Reader: Page numbers in **bold** indicate the principal discussion of a topic or the definition of a term. Page numbers in *italic* indicate illustrations.

MCSE CORE REQUIREMENT STUDY GUIDES FROM NETWORK PRESS

Sybex's Network Press presents updated and expanded second editions
of the definitive study guides for MCSE candidates.

ISBN: 0-7821-2220-5
704pp; 7¹/₂" x 9"; Hardcover
$49.99

ISBN: 0-7821-2223-X
784pp; 7¹/₂" x 9"; Hardcover
$49.99

ISBN: 0-7821-2222-1
832pp; 7¹/₂" x 9"; Hardcover
$49.99

ISBN: 0-7821-2221-3
704pp; 7¹/₂" x 9"; Hardcover
$49.99

ISBN: 0-7821-2256-6
800pp; 7¹/₂" x 9"; Hardcover
$49.99

A $50.00 SAVINGS!

MCSE Core Requirements
Box Set
ISBN: 0-7821-2245-0
4 hardcover books;
3,024pp total; $149.96

STUDY GUIDES FOR THE MICROSOFT CERTIFIED SYSTEMS ENGINEER EXAMS

NT® IN THE REAL WORLD

E INFORMATION YOU NEED TO BUILD, SECURE, AND OPTIMIZE NT® NETWORKS

ISBN: 0-7821-2163-2
1,664 pp; 7^1/$_2$" x 9"; Hardcover
$59.99

ISBN: 0-7821-2123-3
544 pp; 7^1/$_2$" x 9"; Softcover
$44.99

ISBN: 0-7821-2006-7
929 pp; 7^1/$_2$" x 9"; Hardcover
$59.99

ISBN: 0-7821-2156-X
624 pp; 7^1/$_2$" x 9"; Hardcover
$54.99

SYBEX BOOKS ON THE WEB

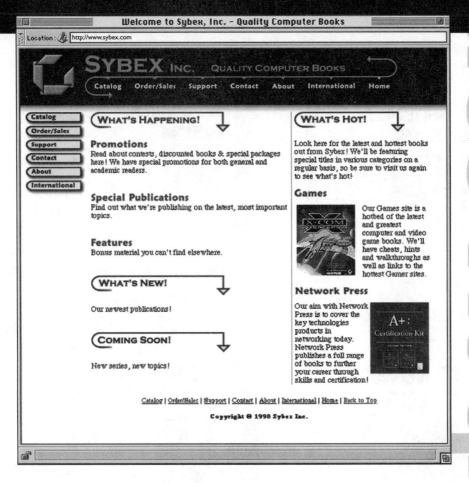

A t the dynamic and informative Sybex Web site, you can:

- view our complete online catalog
- preview a book you're interested in
- access special book content
- order books online at special discount prices
- learn about Sybex

www.sybex.com

SYBEX Inc. • 1151 Marina Village Parkway, Alameda, CA 94501 • 510-523-8233

SYBEX

In the dark? Shed light on your network with EtherPeek!

G Group's award-winning EtherPeek is an intuitive and powerful protocol analyzer and packet debugger for Ethernet tworks. Available for Windows 95/98, Windows NT 4.0 and Macintosh computers, EtherPeek is designed to make the mplex task of troubleshooting mixed-platform, multi-protocol networks simple and straightforward. EtherPeek sets e industry standard for ease-of-use while offering all of the expert debugging capabilities expected of a full-featured alyzer. Well known for its friendly graphical interface, EtherPeek provides a wide variety of detailed information on twork utilization, node conversations and packet contents in a colorful and easy-to-read manner.

npoint problem sources with protocol decoders, which allow you to view packet contents from protocol layers to closed data. Save time by limiting captures to data of interest with filters and triggers. Plan and test configurations d devices by using EtherPeek to generate substantial traffic loads.

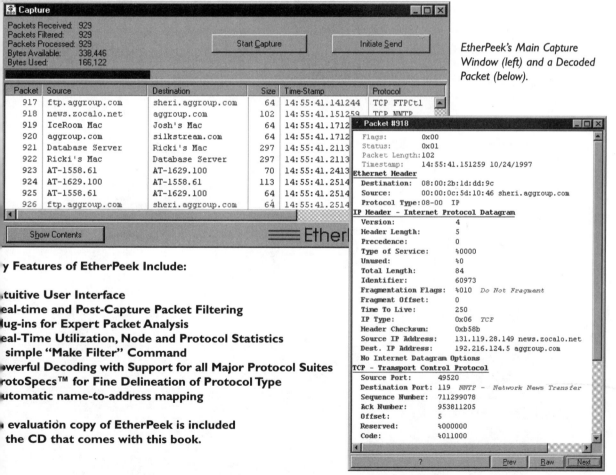

EtherPeek's Main Capture Window (left) and a Decoded Packet (below).

y Features of EtherPeek Include:

tuitive User Interface
eal-time and Post-Capture Packet Filtering
lug-ins for Expert Packet Analysis
eal-Time Utilization, Node and Protocol Statistics
simple "Make Filter" Command
werful Decoding with Support for all Major Protocol Suites
rotoSpecs™ for Fine Delineation of Protocol Type
utomatic name-to-address mapping

evaluation copy of EtherPeek is included the CD that comes with this book.

For more information contact AG Group, Inc.
2540 Camino Diablo, Suite 200 • Walnut Creek, CA 94596
(925)937-7900 • (800)466-2447 • Fax (925)937-2479
http://www.aggroup.com

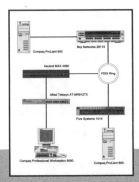

Here's What You Get on the CD:

The CD included with the *CCNA: Cisco Certified Network Associated Study Guide* contains invaluable programs and information to help you prepare for the CCNA exam. You can access and install the files through a user-friendly graphical interface by running the CLICKME.EXE file located in the root directory of the CD.

NOTE The Sybex CD Interface is supported only by Windows 95/98 and Windows NT 4.

Edge Test ACRC Exam Prep Program

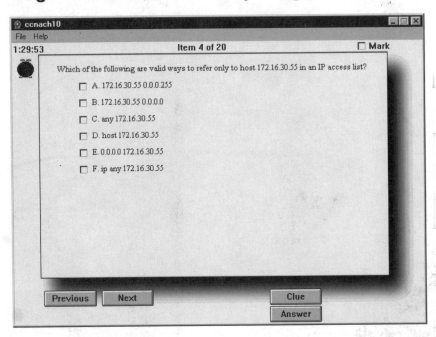

Test your knowledge with the Edge Test ACRC Exam Preparation program. The version included on the CD was produced exclusively for Sybex by EdgeTek. Click on the Instructions button on the opening screen for a detailed explanation of how to navigate this advanced testing program.

Visio Network Professional 5 & Network Equipment

Visio® Professional and Visio Network Equipment allow you to tap into a library of more than 13,000 exact-replica, vendor-specific network device shapes. Create proposals, design and document LANs, WANs, wiring closets, whatever you need. Link diagrams with databases to keep your graphics and data in synch.